THE SUSTAINABLE SITES

SITES

HANDBOOK

THE SUSTAINABLE SITES

HANDBOOK

A Complete Guide to the Principles, Strategies, and Practices for Sustainable Landscapes

Meg Calkins

John Wiley & Sons, Inc.

Published by John Wiley & Sons, Inc., Hoboken, New Jersey

Published simultaneously in Canada

For general information about our other products and services, please contact our Customer Care Department within the United States at (800) 762-2974, outside the United States at (317) 572-3993 or fax (317) 572-4002.

Wiley publishes in a variety of print and electronic formats and by print-on-demand. Some material included with standard print versions of this book may not be included in e-books or in print-on-demand. If this book refers to media such as a CD or DVD that is not included in the version you purchased, you may download this material at http://booksupport.wiley.com. For more information about Wiley products, visit www.wiley.com.

Library of Congress Cataloging-in-Publication Data:

Calkins, Meg, 1965-
  The sustainable sites handbook: A complete guide to the principles, strategies, and best practices for sustainable landscapes / Meg Calkins.
     p. cm. — (Wiley desktop editions)
  Includes index.
   ISBN 978-0-470-64355-6 (hardback); 978-1-118-10003-5 (ebk.); 978-1-118-10004-2 (ebk.); 978-1-118-10608-2 (ebk.); 978-1-118-10609-9 (ebk.); 978-1-118-10611-2 (ebk.)
 1. Landscape ecology—Handbooks, manuals, etc. 2. Sustainable development—Evaluation—Handbooks, manuals, etc. 3. Environmental management—Evaluation--Handbooks, manuals, etc. 4. Sustainable Sites Initiative. I. Title.
  QH541.15.L35C35 2011
  577.5'5—dc22
                                        2011013754

Printed in the United States of America

10 9 8 7 6 5 4 3 2 1

CONTENTS AT A GLANCE

Foreword ▷ **ix**

Letter from SITES™ Partners ▷ **xi**

Chapter 1 ▷ Introduction **1**

Chapter 2 ▷ Predesign: Site Selection, Assessment, and Planning **33**

Chapter 3 ▷ Site Design: Water **65**

Chapter 4 ▷ Site Design: Vegetation **197**

Chapter 5 ▷ Site Design: Soils **247**

Chapter 6 ▷ Site Design: Materials and Resources **323**

Chapter 7 ▷ Human Health and Well-Being for Sustainable Sites **429**

Chapter 8 ▷ Operations, Maintenance, Monitoring, and Stewardship **479**

Resources ▷ **521**

Index ▷ **535**

CONTENTS

Foreword ix
MICHAEL VAN VALKENBURGH

Letter from SITES™ Partners xi

Chapter 1 ▶ **Introduction** 1
MEG CALKINS
Sustainable Site Design Defined 2
The Contents and Structure of This Book 27

Chapter 2 ▶ **Predesign: Site Selection, Assessment, and Planning** 33
HEATHER VENHAUS
Site Selection 33
Understanding the Site 41
Team Development and Planning Strategies 54
Developing Project Direction: Principles, Goals,
and Performance Targets 58

Chapter 3 ▶ **Site Design: Water** 65
**ALFRED VICK, JOHN CALABRIA, STUART ECHOLS,
MICHAEL OGDEN, and DAVID YOCCA**
Sustainable Stormwater Management .72
Stormwater Design Approaches 104
Water Conservation 148
Onsite Wastewater Treatment, Disposal, and Reuse 166

Chapter 4 ▶ **Site Design: Vegetation** 197
STEVE WINDHAGER, MARK SIMMONS, and JACOB BLUE
Vegetation and Ecosystem Services 202
Vegetation Protection Techniques 213
Sustainable Planting Design and Management 216

Chapter 5 ▶ **Site Design: Soils** 247
NINA BASSUK and SUSAN DAY
Integrating Soil into the Design Process 249
Soils in the Site Assessment 251
Soil Characteristics and Associated Tests 265
Managing Soils for a Sustainable Site .295
Soil Replacement and Specialized Soils 310
The Soil Management Plan 316

Chapter 6 ▶ **Site Design: Materials and Resources**   **323**

MEG CALKINS

The Lifecycle of Construction Materials and Products. 327
Environmental Impacts of Materials and Products. 331
Human Health Impacts of Materials 344
Evaluating Environmental and Human Health
Impacts of Materials 348
Inventory and Analysis for Materials 358
Resource Efficiency. 360
Low-VOC Materials and Products 390
Materials to Minimize Heat Island Impacts 390
Concrete 396
Aggregates and Stone 398
Asphalt 401
Brick Masonry 403
Earthen Materials 404
Plastics 407
Metals 409
Bio-Based Materials 413
Wood 416
Site Lighting 421

Chapter 7 ▶ **Human Health and Well-Being for Sustainable Sites**   **429**

ROBERT RYAN

Assessing the Site's Social Setting 432
Sustainability Awareness and Education .436
Social Equality in Site Development, Construction,
and Use 440
Site Accessibility 445
Site Wayfinding. 449
Site Safety 454
Design for Physical Activity 458
Restorative Settings 462
Design for Social Interaction and Community Building 466
Preserving Historic and Cultural Features 470

Chapter 8 ▶ **Operations, Maintenance, Monitoring, and Stewardship**   **479**

AMY BELAIRE and DAVID YOCCA

Environmental and Human Health Impacts of Sustainable
Site Operations, Maintenance, and Monitoring 480
Incorporating Operations, Maintenance, and Monitoring
Considerations into Site Design. 482
Monitoring to Inform Active and Adaptive Stewardship 519

Resources 521

Index. 535

FOREWORD

THE EMERGENCE OF THE SUSTAINABLE SITES Initiative Program (SITES) and what it says about the ecological awakening that has taken place over the last twenty-five years are quite encouraging. SITES addresses the urgent need for a coordinated response among landscape design professionals to take on the environmental imperatives of the twenty-first century. The information, methods, and approaches contained in *The Sustainable Sites Handbook*, an essential companion to realizing the goals of SITES, offer guidance for beginning and established practitioners alike. It has the potential to have a profound effect on how the built landscapes of our time are designed, constructed, and managed, and how they perform within their larger environmental and ecological context.

Ecology and landscape architecture are inseparable, as is demonstrated by the broad range of specialists consulted in the development of SITES and the *Handbook*. In fact, these were precisely the types of concerned and far-sighted professionals who laid the philosophical groundwork for sustainable site design in the last century. In the 1930s, for instance, naturalist Aldo Leopold stirred the Western world's consciousness of nature's complex and interrelated systems. Two decades later, Rachel Carson, an ecologist and scientist, warned us about the dangers of destabilizing natural systems, pointing to both environmental havoc and the potential for associated human tragedy. By the late 1960s, thanks in large part to both Ian McHarg and Carl Steinitz, landscape architects were awakened to a methodology for regional and local planning that firmly placed ecology at its center.

The urgency of environmental stewardship is not in question, and the fact that landscape architects can and will play a leadership role in the drive to create a more sustainable exchange between humans and our environment is clear. Our profession knows that nature will not simply reestablish or mend itself in many of the critically disturbed systems on which we all now work. Up until now, the question of how landscape architects might intelligently and effectively transform our practice to meet current challenges has been loosely defined on an individual basis. The *Handbook* has the potential to help a great deal: It consolidates a body of knowledge about environmentally positive design approaches and frames it as a response to the challenges of contemporary practice, where ideals and on-the-ground performance must be reconciled.

With the SITES standards, landscape architects—and indeed all site designers—have a framework for sustainable site design defined by acknowledged experts in their respective specialties and a means of bringing recognition to clients who dedicate themselves to building sustainably. *The Sustainable Sites Handbook* is an important first step in trying to define what sustainability means with respect to the multitude of social, environmental, economic, and experiential concerns that impact everything we design and build. The future is very much about taking on the promise these guidelines offer and raising them to a higher and more defensible level, in terms of both the science and the economics of how these endeavors improve public health. I look forward to future editions of this book that demonstrate that our field is growing based on new research, postoccupancy monitoring, and further innovation.

MICHAEL VAN VALKENBURGH

LETTER FROM SITES™ PARTNERS

WHILE THE GREENING OF THE BUILT ENVIRONMENT has been widely embraced, a key element has largely been missing: robust standards to guide the creation of sustainable landscapes, with and without buildings. Traditionally, designed landscapes have been major consumers of scarce resources, but—unlike buildings—when done correctly, can improve and regenerate natural systems. Yet until now, no "green" design and construction standards existed for large campuses, public parks, conservation areas, private resorts, recreation areas, or transportation and utility corridors.

This significant challenge spurred the formation of the Sustainable Sites Initiative™ (SITES™), an interdisciplinary partnership of the American Society of Landscape Architects, the Lady Bird Johnson Wildflower Center at the University of Texas at Austin, and the United States Botanic Garden, which has developed voluntary guidelines and a rating system for landscape sustainability. In developing the guidelines, SITES tapped the expertise of a diverse group of stakeholder organizations and more than 70 nationally respected authorities on soil, hydrology, materials, vegetation, and the impact of the environment on human health and well-being. Their collective expertise guided a rigorous science- and research-based process to produce the *Sustainable Sites Initiative: Guidelines and Performance Benchmarks 2009*.

In the *Sustainable Sites Handbook*, editor Meg Calkins, ASLA, and John Wiley & Sons, Inc., have created a comprehensive resource for all those who seek to create sustainable landscapes and especially those who hope to attain certification under the SITES Rating System™. Incorporating the work of many of the SITES experts, *The Sustainable Sites Handbook* is a valuable companion document to the SITES Guidelines and Performance Benchmarks and has been carefully reviewed for technical accuracy and adherence to SITES prerequisites and credits.

Use of these design approaches will provide tangible benefits to our cities and communities, including cleaner air and water, climate regulation, conservation of energy and other natural resources, and protection of biodiversity. We hope SITES and the *Sustainable Sites Handbook* will encourage all those who teach and practice landscape design, construction, and maintenance to adopt sustainable best practices and create sustainable landscapes.

NANCY C. SOMERVILLE, HON. ASLA, EXECUTIVE VICE PRESIDENT/CEO
AMERICAN SOCIETY OF LANDSCAPE ARCHITECTS

SUSAN RIEFF, EXECUTIVE DIRECTOR
LADY BIRD JOHNSON WILDFLOWER CENTER AT THE UNIVERSITY OF TEXAS AT AUSTIN

HOLLY SHIMIZU, EXECUTIVE DIRECTOR
UNITED STATES BOTANIC GARDEN

ACKNOWLEDGMENTS

JUST LIKE A SUSTAINABLE PROJECT requires collaboration among many disciplines to create complex, living systems, the richness of this book results from the efforts of many dedicated professionals who each bring an important perspective to the work.

Chapter Authors, most of whom were technical advisors to development of the SITES Guidelines and Performance Benchmarks, generously shared their expertise by creating rich content for each chapter. Each chapter was thoughtfully reviewed by the experts listed below who gave freely of their time and expertise with many insightful comments. Heather Venhaus, in particular, offered invaluable input over the many phases of book development.

Perhaps the largest group I must acknowledge are the varied professionals listed below who originally developed the SITES Guidelines and Performance Benchmarks. They contributed immeasurably to this book by identifying the broad reach of design and management considerations for sustainable sites and by creating the SITES Guidelines—an extremely important tool for twenty-first century site development.

I would also like to thank the SITES partners: The Ladybird Johnson Wildflower Center, The American Society of Landscape Architects and the US Botanic Garden for their support of this book. Thank you to Margaret Cummins, Senior Editor at Wiley for supporting this project from the initial idea to its completion.

Many professional design firms generously contributed images of their work to this book. I thank them for this and more importantly, for the wonderful work they are doing to design, build and manage sustainable sites that will serve as fine examples and offer many lessons for sustainable site projects to come. Many of the projects depicted in the photos are SITES case studies or pilot projects.

Jody Rosenblatt Naderi, John Motloch, and Martha Hunt, my colleagues at Ball State University, offered me support and guidance during the process of developing and editing this book. I would also like to thank graduate student Ryan Smith for his research assistance (and persistence) with obtaining images and permissions, and the many students in my Sustainable Site Design seminar who contributed insight and in a few cases, research to the book.

Lastly, I owe a huge thank you to my family and friends for their support over the duration of this book's development. My husband, George Elvin, was immeasurably helpful with encouragement and feedback on book ideas AND he also willingly took up the parenting slack over and over during the many long deadlines. My parents, sister, and friends provided a supportive structure for my children as well, allowing me time and space to devote to the creation of this book.

Chapter reviewers:

Heather Venhaus
Nina Bassuk
Steve Benz
Larry Costello
George Elvin
Martha Hunt
Alison Kinn Bennett
John Motloch
Jerry Smith
Laura Solano
Alfred Vick
Ken Willis
David Yocca

SITES Technical Experts:

José Almiñana
Michael Barrett
Nina Bassuk
Amy Belaire
Jacob Blue
Meg Calkins

Michael Clar
Kimberly Cochran
Scott Cloutier
Fred Cowett
Susan D. Day
Richard J. Dolesh
Deon Glaser
Nora Goldstein
Robert Goo
Deb Guenther
Liz Guthrie
Len Hopper
William Hunt
Karen C. Kabbes
Alison Kinn Bennett
Nick Kuhn
Frances (Ming) Kuo
Tom Liptan
Ed MacMullan
Chris Martin
David McDonald
Ray Mims
Karen R. Nikolai

James Patchett
Danielle Pieranunzi
Kristin Raab
Robert Ryan
Jean Schwab
Melanie Sifton
Mark Simmons
Jerry Smith
Laura Solano
Fritz Steiner
Eric Strecker
John C. Swallow
Rodney Swink
Janice E. Thies
John Peter Thompson
Megan Turnock
Valerie Vartanian
Heather Venhaus
Lynne M. Westphal
Julie Wilbert
Steve Windhager
Kathleen L. Wolf
David J. Yocca

CHAPTER 1

INTRODUCTION

► Meg Calkins

THE NATURAL ENVIRONMENT IS COMPRISED OF COMPLEX, interrelated systems of water, soil, air, atmosphere, flora, and fauna that are constantly evolving, balancing, changing, and rebalancing. These ecosystems offer services such as air and water cleansing, water supply and regulation, and productive soil that sustain and enhance human systems—services that are critical to survival of all species. Designed sites can protect, sustain, and even provide these critical ecosystem services. Offering potential to serve multiple functions, sites can be productive, provide ecosystem services, *and* offer rich aesthetic experiences to the site occupants.

This idea of ecosystem services as a basis for design is a profound shift in the way that we think about the role of designed sites. If we are to design and manage sites that support and engage natural processes, we need to shift our focus from creating and maintaining static, isolated landscapes to that of designing and managing complex, interrelated living systems of the built environment. And as a model for designing site systems that can ensure sustainable development, we need look no further than the principles inherent in our planet's ecosystems, principles that include zero waste, adaptation, and resiliency.

If we are to protect the world's ecosystems for future generations, the human-made environment must foster the health of both ecological and human systems. Design of the built environment, including site design, plays a critical role in this. In 2000, the United Nations commissioned the Millennium Ecosystem Assessment, a global study by 1,360 scientists from an international consortium of governments, universities, nonprofits, and businesses. The 2005 concluding report stated that "human activity is having a significant and escalating impact on the biodiversity of world ecosystems, reducing both their resilience and biocapacity" (MEA 2005). The report, referring to natural systems as humanity's "life support system," established that "ecosystems are critical to human well-being—to our health, our prosperity, our security, and to our social and cultural identity" and unless we change the way that we develop land, use resources, and produce food, these services will be seriously compromised for future generations. The report warns: "At the heart of this assessment is a stark warning. Human activity is putting such a strain on the natural functions of Earth that the ability of the planet's ecosystems to sustain future generations can no longer be taken for granted" (MEA 2005).

In response to this imperative, the Sustainable Sites Initiative™ (SITES™), a partnership of the American Society of Landscape Architects, the Lady Bird Johnson Wildflower Center at the University of Texas at Austin, and the United States Botanic Garden, have released *Guidelines and Performance Benchmarks* to guide development of sustainable sites through a voluntary credit rating system. These guidelines and benchmarks encourage the protection, restoration, and provision of ecosystem services as a basis for sustainable site design. They address the design and management of systems of vegetation, soils, water, materials, energy, and culture.

This book has been created to offer comprehensive and detailed information on strategies, technologies, tools, and best practices for sustainable site design. This book, like the SITES *Guidelines and Performance Benchmarks*, is based on the premise that any site in any location can be designed and managed to foster healthy ecosystems, and promote ecosystem services and sustainable human systems. It is intended to assist practitioners with successful implementation of the SITES rating tool, and it will also stand as a resource guide for the design and management of sustainable sites. This publication, developed with the cooperation of the Sustainable Sites Initiative, will complement the *Guidelines and Performance Benchmarks*, the prerequisites and credits, and future SITES publications. It will be a companion resource that practitioners can turn to for deeper guidance on the topics of hydrology, vegetation, soils, materials, human health and well-being, and site selection.

SUSTAINABLE SITE DESIGN DEFINED

Sustainable design as defined by SITES is "design, construction, operations and maintenance practices that meet the needs of the present without compromising the ability of future generations to meet their own needs" (SITES 2009a). This is based on the definition of sustainable development from the United Nations World Commission on Environment and Development's Bruntland Report, *Our Common Future* (UNWCED, 1987). For site design, this translates to fostering both human and natural ecosystem health, closing material and resource loops, and designing with respect for nutrient and water cycles. Sustainable site design emphasizes design of whole, complex functioning systems; a widened scale of analysis and design consideration; highly site-specific (as opposed to universal) design responses; and continued monitoring, management, and adaption to ensure healthy, functioning systems for the life of the landscape.

Design of sustainable sites involves a fundamental shift in the way that we think about the Earth and its resources. We must shift from the extractive mind-set of viewing the Earth's resources as abundantly available for human consumption to the understanding that Earth's resources and ecosystems are the sustainers of life on this planet and must be protected. New development must work toward fostering the health of ecosystems and the services they provide through their protection and restoration. We must forge a new and respectful relationship with natural systems, acknowledging their critical role in our health and the health of the planet.

Triple Bottom Line

Sustainability encompasses not only environmental conservation, but also the ideals of social equity and economic feasibility. This "triple bottom line" is the key to truly sustainable development (Figure 1-1). While this book primarily focuses on environmental sustainability, it addresses areas of social and economic sustainability as they relate to environmental issues and sustainable site design. Design of the built environment also has a direct impact on human and cultural systems. Therefore, a chapter is devoted to human health and well-being considerations of site development.

Ecosystem Services

Ecosystem services are defined in the Millennium Ecosystem Assessment as "the benefits humans obtain from ecosystems" (MEA 2007). Living elements of ecosystems, such as vegetation and soil organisms, interact with the nonliving elements such as water, air, and bedrock in ecosystem processes to produce goods and services that offer direct or indirect benefits to humans. The MEA groups ecosystem services into four broad categories (MEA 2005):

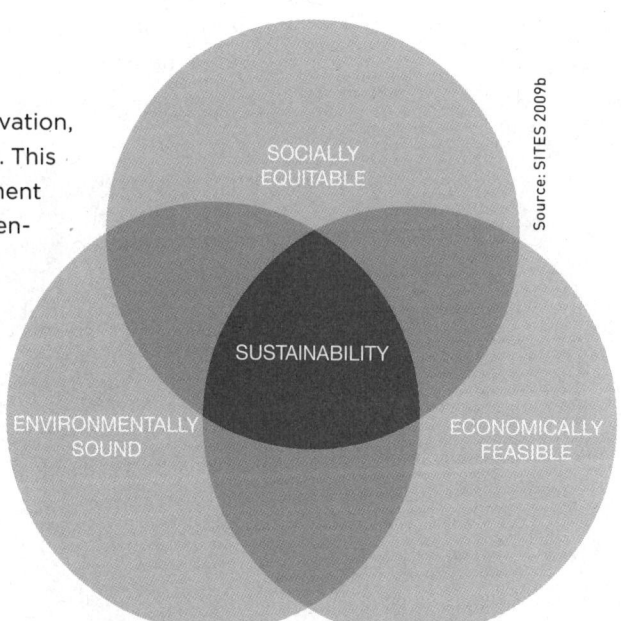

Source: SITES 2009b

FIGURE 1-1: Sustainable design addresses overlapping aspects of environmentally sound, socially equitable, and economically feasible development.

- ▶ *Provisioning,* such as the production of water, clean air, food, and medicines;
- ▶ *Supporting,* such as pollination, waste decomposition, and nutrient cycling;
- ▶ *Regulating,* such as global and local climate regulation, erosion control, disease control; and
- ▶ *Cultural,* such as health, spiritual, recreation, and relaxation benefits.

There are many ecosystem services that can be provided by sites (Figure 1-2) (Table 1-1). Some examples are:

▶ Trees regulate local climate through evapotranspiration, shade, and wind control.

▶ Vegetation mitigates local air quality.

▶ Soils and vegetation infiltrate and purify stormwater protecting adjacent waterways and the water table.

▶ Vegetation and construction materials mitigate heat island impacts in urban areas.

▶ Vegetation, water, and materials are combined to make parks, gardens, and open spaces for human health and well-being and cultural benefits.

▶ Water and soil organisms break down waste and cycle nutrients.

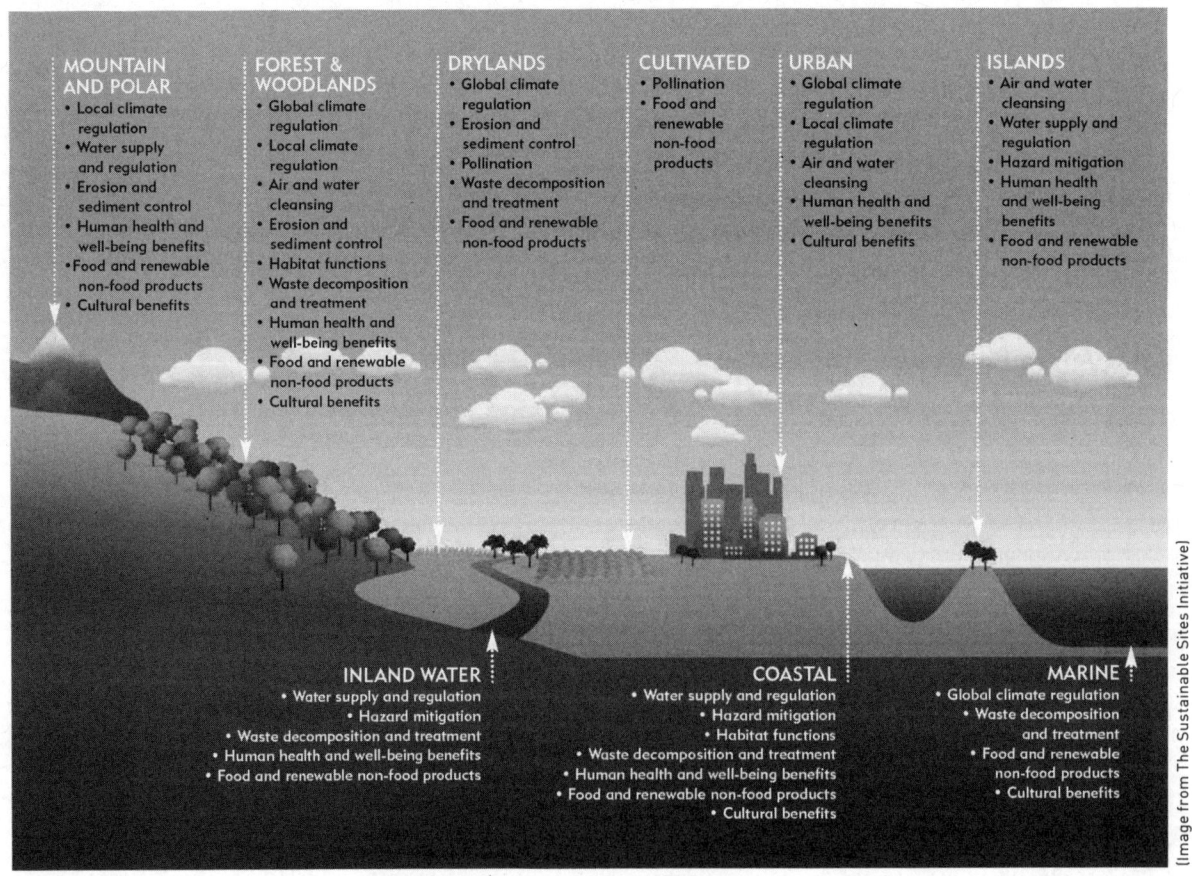

(Image from The Sustainable Sites Initiative)

FIGURE 1-2: Ecosystem services by landscape type.

It is important to note that site development decisions can impact ecosystem services far away from a site as well—and these impacts are not often easily seen or understood. Decisions about stormwater management and vegetation inputs (e.g., fertilizers and herbicides) can impact waterways hundreds of miles downstream. Resource extraction and material manufacturing can impact ecosystems halfway around the world. And air currents can carry airborne pollutants far away from the manufacturing plant that released them.

TABLE 1-1: Ecosystem Services

ECOSYSTEM SERVICE	FUNCTION
Global climate regulation	Maintaining balance of atmospheric gases at historic levels, creating breathable air, and sequestering greenhouse gases
Local climate regulation	Regulating local temperature, precipitation, and humidity through shading, evapotranspiration, and windbreaks
Air and water cleansing	Removing and reducing pollutants in air and water
Water supply and regulation	Storing and providing water within watersheds and aquifers
Erosion and sediment control	Retaining soil within an ecosystem, preventing damage from erosion and siltation
Hazard mitigation	Reducing vulnerability to damage from flooding, storm surge, wildfire, and drought
Pollination	Providing pollinator species for reproduction of crops or other plants
Habitat functions	Providing refuge and reproduction habitat to plants and animals, thereby contributing to conservation of biological and genetic diversity and evolutionary processes
Waste decomposition and treatment	Breaking down waste and cycling nutrients
Human health and well-being benefits	Enhancing physical, mental, and social well-being as a result of interaction with nature
Food and renewable nonfood products	Producing food, fuel, energy, medicine, or other products for human use
Cultural benefits	Enhancing cultural, educational, aesthetic, and spiritual experiences as a result of interaction with nature

Source: SITES 2009a

THE ECONOMIC VALUE OF ECOSYSTEM SERVICES

The services that healthy ecosystems provide have economic value. And while these services are often viewed as "free" or "public" and are left off the balance sheets of manufacturing and development costs, the value of these services is substantial. One of the few comprehensive studies placed the value of ecosystem services at $33 trillion per year in 1997—nearly twice the global gross national product at that time of $18 trillion (Costanza, d'Arge, deGroot et al., 1997). The Millennium Ecosystem Assessment estimates the value of the services that wetlands alone provide to humanity at $15 trillion annually, including the water supply on which an estimated 1.5 to 3 billion people depend. Yet human practices are destroying and degrading wetlands at a faster rate than any other type of ecosystem (Nature Conservancy 2005). The price of resources is often based on the cost of extraction and fails to reflect the true cost of environmental degradation and depletion for future generations. Such an economic system can undervalue these services and encourage wasteful use of resources.

While a 2002 study estimated the economic value of the approximately 3.8 billion urban trees in the United States at $2.4 trillion (Nowak, Crane, and Dwyer 2002b), their actual value goes far beyond this in terms of the ecosystem services that urban trees provide. Benefits of urban forests include: sequestering carbon, moderating climate and energy use, cleaning the air, improving water quality and slowing stormwater runoff, reducing noise, providing habitat for urban wildlife, remediating contaminated soils, enhancing real estate values, and generally providing economic and social well-being to communities. Following are some results from studies identified in a report by Nowak et al. for the U.S. Department of Agriculture, Forest Service that have quantified values of some individual urban forest ecosystem services (Nowak et al. 2010). The studies found:

- ▶ Urban trees in the conterminous United States remove an estimated 784,000 tons of air pollution annually, with a value of $3.8 billion (Nowak, Crane, and Stevens 2006).

- ▶ The establishment of 100 million mature trees around residences in the United States is estimated to save about $2 billion per year in reduced energy costs (Akbari et al. 1992; Donovan and Butry 2009).

- ▶ Urban trees in the conterminous United States currently store 770 million tons of carbon, valued at $14.3 billion (Nowak and Crane 2002).

- ▶ During an intense storm in Dayton, OH, the tree canopy was estimated to reduce potential runoff by 7 percent (Sanders 1986).

- ▶ A stronger sense of community and empowerment to improve neighborhood conditions in inner cities has been attributed to involvement in urban forestry efforts (Kuo and Sullivan 2001a, 2001b; Sommer et al. 1994a, 1994b; Westphal 1999, 2003).

In addition to global economic benefits of ecosystems services, economic returns can be realized from the provision of healthy ecosystems at both the site scale and regional scale. Therefore the key to widespread adoption of sustainable site design strategies may lie in the economic value of the ecosystem services they provide. The economic benefits of sustainable development strategies are being increasingly quantified, and this is having a direct impact on their adoption. For example, research has shown savings in infrastructure and development costs with sustainable stormwater management (Wise 2008); reduced air-conditioning costs with shading of buildings and cooling of adjacent pavements (Akbari, Pomerantz, and Taha 2001); increased worker productivity and patient healing with views to vegetation and natural elements (S. Kaplan 1995; R. Kaplan 2007; Ulrich 1984); and cost savings in reuse of onsite structures (U.S. EPA 2000). At the regional scale, savings from sustainable site development can include reduced loads on wastewater treatment plants as a result of sustainable stormwater strategies (Wise 2008); reduced healthcare costs related to poor air quality (Romley, Hackbarth, and Goldman 2010); and reduced material costs for roadway projects with use of recycled materials (PCA 2005). These cost savings are either directly or indirectly related to services that are provided by healthy ecosystems. And they hold the potential to be a strong selling point for use of sustainable development strategies, hastening their widespread adoption.

ECOSYSTEM SERVICES AS A BASIS FOR DESIGN

Providing new ecosystem services, or protecting existing ones, creates a firm basis for sustainable site design project goals. This is a way to make environmental, economic, and even social goals clear and sometimes measureable (SITES 2009b). For example, construction of a green roof can reduce rainwater runoff through retention and evapotranspiration of plants. These same plants can offer other ecosystem services, such as heat-island reduction, air quality improvements, and contributions to human well-being through views of plants from adjacent buildings (Figure 1-3).

Measuring the contribution of a site strategy to one or more ecosystem services offers a way to assess the performance of the strategy and its contribution to the goals of a sustainable site. It also may provide some measure of the economic benefit of the strategy (Windhager et al. 2010). Using the green roof example, it is possible to quantify the reduced air-conditioning loads on the building with the green roof, yet it would be very challenging to measure the improved air quality from just one green roof. We know there will be some improvement, but we are not sure just how much, and it is difficult to assign a dollar value to the benefit.

FIGURE 1-3: Office workers at the Washington Mutual roof garden lunch adjacent to meadow grasses and native trees in downtown Vancouver. The roof garden offers ecosystem services including human health and well-being benefits, wildlife habitat, stormwater management, and others. *(Design by: Phillips Farevaag Smallenberg, Vancouver BC; Photo by Lara Swimmer)*

The accurate assessment of the economic value of ecosystem services is at the heart of challenges to use of ecosystem services as a basis for design. Windhager and colleagues identify the following major challenges to use of ecosystem services as a basis for design (Windhager et al. 2010):

1. Not every ecosystem service can be evaluated economically with accuracy—and this often results in undervaluation of the services.

2. The economic value of an ecosystem service is a snapshot of a point in time and the value will change, sometimes significantly, as supply diminishes.

3. If a design objective focuses on a single ecosystem service, opportunities may be missed for use of a design strategy that supports multiple ecosystem services.

4. Direct measurement of services that sustainable design strategies provide can be challenging and likely outside the scope of most design projects. Strategy performance may be modeled during the design process for some strategies, such as stormwater infiltration, but minimal monitoring of strategies during the operation phase is performed due to associated costs, potential liabilities, and disconnections between the design phase of a project and the operations of the built project.

Sustainable Sites and the Urban Realm

Nearly 83 percent of the U.S. population (250 million people) lives in urban areas (U.S. Census Bureau 2011). This statistic underscores the imperative for healthy urban ecosystems and the provision of natural settings in the urban environment. In addition, the resource needs and negative environmental impacts of urban areas are often greater than those of nonurban areas so it is practical to address these issues with design and planning for the provision of ecosystems services in urban areas to the extent possible.

The urban setting offers a vast opportunity to be a productive place, particularly in the public realm. Rather than an underutilized vastness of hardscape, pavement, and a car-dominated urban fabric, what if every square foot beyond roads, buildings, and sidewalks is used to produce food, provide wildlife habitat, produce and manage energy, infiltrate and cleanse stormwater, and offer places for human interaction with nature? The role of sustainable sites in cities is therefore threefold: to provide ecosystem services and habitat, to be productive places, and to sustain cultural connections to nature (Figure 1-4).

(Photo from Darrin Nordhal)

FIGURE 1-4: In Seattle, a forgotten strip of land that once attracted only those engaged in illicit behavior is now a source of fresh food and community pride. Residents of the Queen Anne neighborhood worked with the Department of Transportation to transform a neglected street median, rampant with invasive plants and pricked with hypodermic syringes, into a community garden and gathering space. They cleared the median of its debris and weeds and constructed raised vegetable beds and planted fruit trees.

FIGURE 1-5: Michael Van Valkenburgh Associates designed Teardrop Park to offer natural environments in a highly urban setting, Battery Park City in New York. Natural stone, interactive water fountains, and native plantings are combined to offer "nature play" spaces for adventure and sanctuary to urban children.

Proximity to nature in urban settings can lead to long-term cultural and environmental sustainability by increasing human respect for and care of the environment. Contact with nature can improve conservation behavior by raising awareness and increasing knowledge of and respect for natural processes. The closer that people are to processes of rainwater cycles, vegetation growth, and food production, the more aware they will be of what happens to the rainwater, what kind of vegetables are in season and where they are grown, and what kind of wildlife depend on our urban forests. It is well documented that the people who care most about the natural environment are those who have had many experiences in it (Figure 1-5). In some locations, a native plant garden on an office building roof may be the only green space around, but if people can eat lunch next to flowering plants with birds and bees, they will be connected to natural processes in addition to receiving the benefits of relaxation, stress reduction, and healing that are well documented through exposure to vegetated places (S. Kaplan 1995, Kellert 2005).

When we recognize that ecosystems can and sometimes do function in cities, we recognize their enormous potential for providing ecosystem services and resources. Instead of a place of consumption and waste, sites can be a place of production. Instead of collecting stormwater and sending it as quickly as possible to receiving streams and then bringing in potable water for irrigation, sprinkler systems, and toilet flushing, why not capture the rainwater and reuse it onsite or close to the place that the rain falls?

Cities do not have to be consumers. They can be producers of resources for their consumption, closing the loops of resource flows. Additionally, a city with food production, habitat, and wildlife in the public realm holds the potential to draw people outside to care for these systems, increasing a sense of community and common purpose—important components of cultural sustainability. It also makes them more desirable places to live and work, contributing to economic sustainability (Figure 1-6).

[Design by Hoerr Schaudt Landscape Architects; Photo by Scott Shigley]

FIGURE 1-6: The roof garden at the Gary Comer Youth Center in Chicago's Grand Crossing Neighborhood is an after-school learning space for youth and seniors in a neighborhood with little access to safe outdoor environments. The garden is used for horticultural learning, environmental awareness, and food production.

Learning from Natural Systems

Natural systems can offer many lessons for sustainable site systems. The concept of biomimicry argues that the best and most efficient responses to environmental challenges are those that mimic natural processes that have maintained and self-regulated over millennia. Biomimicry draws lessons from nature and views "the conscious emulation of life's genius as a survival strategy for the human race and a path to a sustainable future" (Benyus 2002). Construction ecology, an idea coined by Charles Kibert and co-editors of *Construction Ecology,* is "a view of the construction industry based on natural ecology and industrial ecology for the purpose of shifting the construction industry. . . onto a path closer to the ideals of sustainability" (Kibert, Sendzimir, and Guy 2002). They add: "Construction ecology embraces a wide range of symbiotic, synergistic, built environment–natural environment relationships to include large-scale, bioregional, 'green infrastructure' in which natural systems provide energy and material flows for cities and towns and the human occupants provide nutrients for the supporting ecological systems."

The shared concept of these ideologies is that nature has already solved many of the problems that humans are struggling with and that we can learn the solutions to our environmental problems from natural templates. This idea can offer direct applications of ecological concepts to sustainable site design. For example, bioretention strategies mimic the natural processes of stormwater infiltration and pollutant removal in natural landscapes. Onsite wastewater treatment components emulate natural processes with a trickling filter acting as a waterfall or river rapids, and a sand filter as a riparian edge. Constructed wetlands mimic the processes of natural wetlands, and a rain garden can reflect a depression found in a natural landscape.

CHARACTERISTICS OF ECOSYSTEMS IN NATURE

An ecosystem is defined as "a dynamic complex of plant, animal, and microorganism communities and the nonliving environment interacting as a functional unit" (MEA 2005). The complexity of relationships within an ecosystem makes them nearly impossible to replicate exactly, even in ecological restoration projects. Therefore, that should not be the aim of sustainable site design. Instead, ecosystem functions can offer a model for the complex, functional, adaptive systems of sustainable sites. We can learn from the way that ecosystems work to design living site systems that can interface in a positive way with ecosystems and provide ecosystems services.

Some characteristics of ecosystems that can offer lessons for sustainable site design are (Lowe 2002):

▶ Efficiency and productivity are in dynamic balance with resiliency.

▶ Ecosystems remain resilient in the face of change through a high biodiversity of species organized in a complex web of relationships.

▶ The web of relationships is maintained through self-organizing processes.

▶ Each individual in a species acts independently yet its activity patterns cooperatively mesh with the patterns of other species. Cooperation and competition are interlinked and held in balance.

▶ Waste from one process is food for another. There is no waste in nature.

▶ The sole source of power for ecosystems is solar energy.

▶ Feedback loops can move systems toward balance.

Attributes of a Sustainable Site

Landscapes are the place where human and natural systems come together; thus they are uniquely positioned to foster both ecosystem and cultural health and well-being if they are designed and operated with sustainability aims in mind. Sustainable sites possess many unique qualities that can be quite different from conventionally designed sites. Sustainable sites are comprised of complex, interrelated, living dynamic systems that are often wholly unique to a particular place. Cultural and natural systems are well integrated, and closed-loop, balanced systems are constantly managed and adapted either by natural processes or by human intervention to ensure positive flows of resources. The following describes in more detail the unique attributes of sustainable sites and the processes that will create and sustain their function (Figure 1-7).

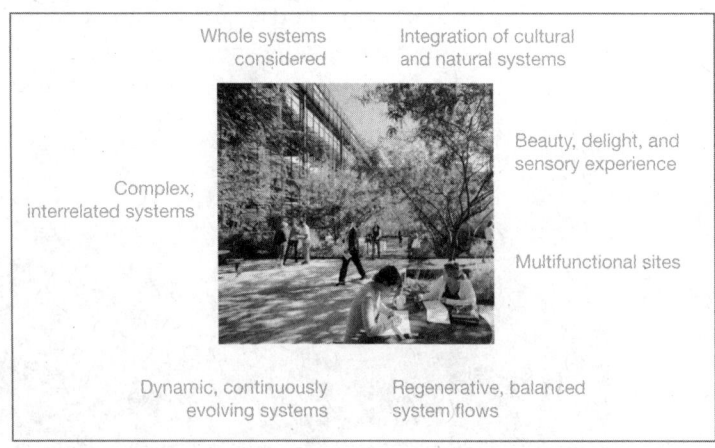

Whole systems considered

Integration of cultural and natural systems

Beauty, delight, and sensory experience

Complex, interrelated systems

Multifunctional sites

Dynamic, continuously evolving systems

Regenerative, balanced system flows

(Project design by Ten Eyck Landscape Architects; Photo by Bill Timmerman)

FIGURE 1-7: Sustainable sites are comprised of complex, interrelated, living dynamic systems that are often wholly unique to a particular place. Cultural and natural systems are well integrated, and closed-loop, balanced systems are constantly managed and adapted either by natural processes or by human intervention to ensure positive flows of resources.

COMPLEX INTERRELATED SYSTEMS

Sustainable sites are comprised of complex interrelated systems of water, vegetation, fauna, soil, materials, and culture. Healthy relationships among these systems are critical to achievement of a sustainable site as they are all tightly woven together, both impacting and supporting each other. For example, stormwater quality can be improved through pollutant removal by plants and soil, yet stormwater flow across sparsely vegetated soil can carry valuable topsoil into receiving waters, causing sedimentation and loss of soil fertility. Decisions about paving materials directly impact water quality, air quality, and soil and vegetation health both on and off the site. Planting design impacts habitat value, water use, and building energy use. Cultural systems are uniquely intertwined with these natural systems—both in negative and positive ways.

WHOLE SYSTEMS DESIGN

Whole systems design engages complex systems across their entire spectrum—from building to site to region. Design of whole systems can maximize positive relationships both within a system and with other systems (Figure 1-8). For example, it's not enough to just infiltrate stormwater on a site without considering its potential to contribute to the water supply for a project or its potential role for treatment of wastewater from the building onsite.

Consideration of whole, interrelated systems will likely give rise to design synergies. For instance, installation of a green roof can benefit water, faunal, energy, material, and atmospheric systems. And if a project is engaging in a voluntary rating system, like SITES or LEED (Leadership in Energy and Environmental Design), these synergies resulting from whole systems design can result in achievement of multiple credits.

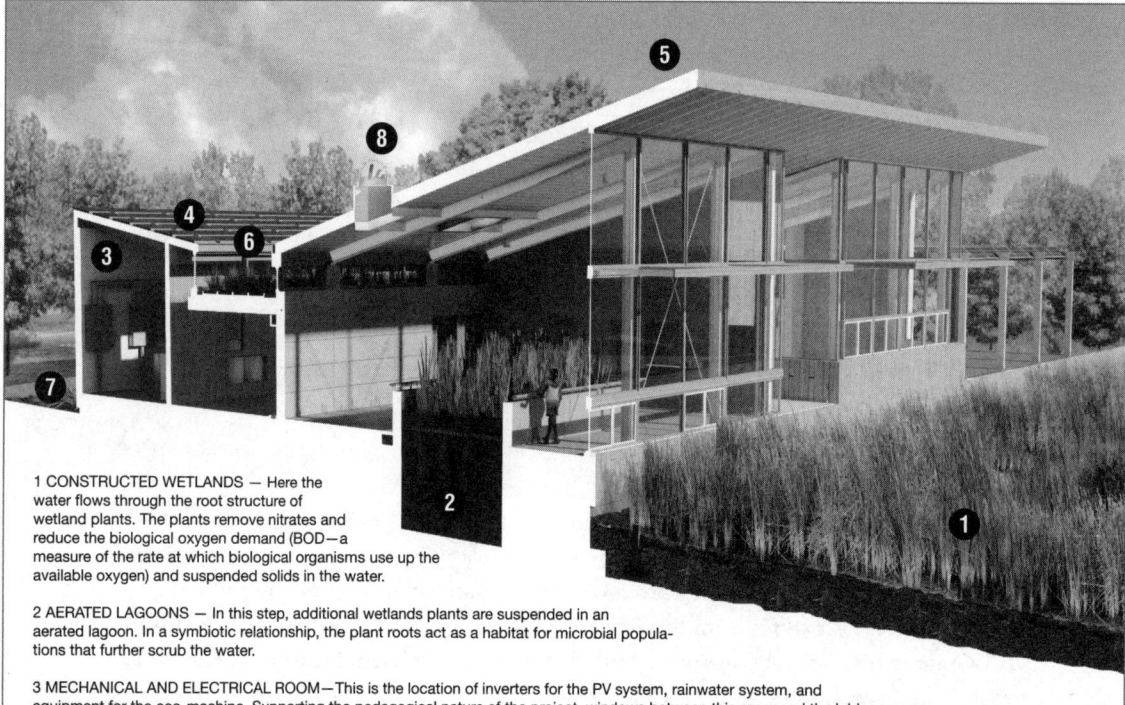

1 CONSTRUCTED WETLANDS — Here the water flows through the root structure of wetland plants. The plants remove nitrates and reduce the biological oxygen demand (BOD—a measure of the rate at which biological organisms use up the available oxygen) and suspended solids in the water.

2 AERATED LAGOONS — In this step, additional wetlands plants are suspended in an aerated lagoon. In a symbiotic relationship, the plant roots act as a habitat for microbial populations that further scrub the water.

3 MECHANICAL AND ELECTRICAL ROOM—This is the location of inverters for the PV system, rainwater system, and equipment for the eco-machine. Supporting the pedagogical nature of the project, windows between this room and the lobby expose the inner workings of the building systems.

4 PHOTOVOLTAIC COLLECTORS — While being strategically located to provide shade for a portion of the roof, the photovoltaic collectors provide all of the buildings electricity.

5 METAL ROOF — Made from recycled metal, the reflective properties keep the interior spaces cooler and mitigate the "heat island" effect.

6 GREEN ROOF — This living roof system provides additional thermal insulation for the building, while protecting the waterproofing material from the elements.

7 RAIN GARDENS — Water shed from the building roof is temporarily detained here during a rain shower while plants work to cleanse the water of contaminants before it enters the Rainwater Cistern or is absorbed into the soil.

8 SOLAR TRACKING SKYLIGHT — These maximize the sunlight available for the plants and people working in the greenhouse.

(Design by BNIM; photo by Assassi)

FIGURE 1-8: The water systems of the Omega Center for Sustainable Living buildings and landscape were conceived holistically. All water is used and purified in a closed hydrological loop. The project draws water from deep wells that tap the aquifer below the campus for building uses. Wastewater is treated in the EcoMachine then released into the onsite subsurface flow wetland where it is allowed to infiltrate the ground, eventually replenishing the groundwater supply.

INTEGRATION OF CULTURAL AND NATURAL SYSTEMS

The health of cultural and natural systems is inextricably linked (Wilson 1984). Cultural and natural systems can impact each other in both positive and negative ways. Development of the built environment has, more often than not, negatively impacted natural systems of a site, but it is possible for cultural and natural systems to coexist and even enrich each other. In addition to life-sustaining ecosystem services, the psychological benefits of interaction with natural systems are increasingly important as a growing percentage of the population resides in urban areas. Visual access to natural areas can increase worker productivity, student learning, and healing of hospital patients. Opportunities to occupy landscapes can reduce feelings of stress, anxiety, and aggression and restore calm in our increasingly fast-paced world; and recreational opportunities in built landscapes can contribute to physical fitness and improved human health.

BEAUTY, DELIGHT, AND SENSORY EXPERIENCE

The aesthetic potential of sustainable landscapes is a crucial aspect of sustainable cultural systems. Beauty, delight, and the sensory qualities of a designed landscape are important for human health and human connection to natural systems and processes. Elizabeth Meyer, in "Sustaining Beauty: The Performance of Appearance," contends that landscape architects and designers have the unique responsibility to make "places that are constructed performing ecosystems and constructed aesthetic experiences." She emphasizes the "performance" of a landscape's appearance and argues that "the experience of beauty should have as much currency in debates about what a sustainable landscape might, and should, be as the performance of its ecological systems" (Meyer 2008).

Meyer maintains that "it will take more than ecologically regenerative design for culture to be sustainable, that what is needed are designed landscapes that provoke those who experience them to become more aware of how their actions affect the environment, and to care enough to make changes." Aesthetically engaging environmental experiences, including beauty, can "re-center human consciousness from an egocentric to a more bio-centric perspective" (Meyer 2008).

The eco-revelatory potential of sustainable site design, revealing natural processes to site occupants, holds potential to foster an enduring bond between humans and nature, increasing the likelihood of their healthy coexistence (Figures 1-9 and 1-10).

[Design by Miller Company Landscape Architects]

FIGURE 1-9: This stormwater feature at the Pacific Cannery lofts in Oakland, CA, brings roof rainwater down past a bench next to the front door of a unit, connecting residents to the natural processes of rainfall.

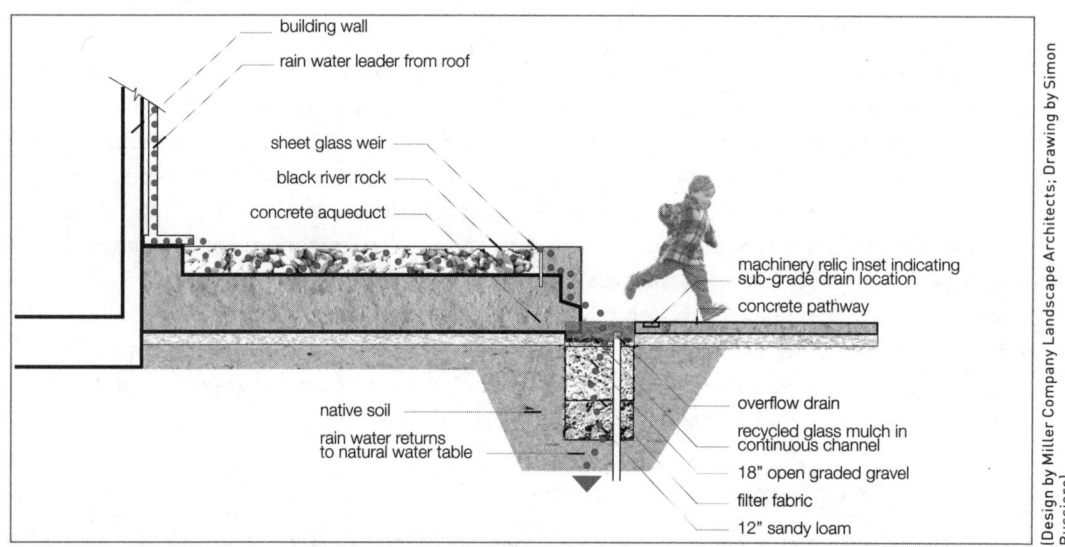

[Design by Miller Company Landscape Architects; Drawing by Simon Bussiere]

FIGURE 1-10: This section through the Pacific Cannery Lofts stormwater feature illustrates water flow through a concrete seatwall aqueduct into a recycled glass infiltration trench "river" where it infiltrates the garden soil.

MULTIFUNCTIONAL SITES

Sustainable sites are designed for multiple functions and must simultaneously create environmental, economic, social, and aesthetic value. For example, tree planting in urban areas must consider heat island issues, habitat provision, carbon sequestration, stormwater mitigation, and aesthetics. And site systems can be productive as well as decorative. A corporate landscape can produce food as well as offer places for worker relaxation. Water can be harvested, spilling into an open cistern water feature, and then be used for irrigation or toilet flushing. A bicycle trail right-of-way can be planted with berry bushes and other plants that produce food, offer a connectivity corridor for wildlife between patches of woodland and a recreational opportunity for exercise. An integrated approach to the design of sites will promote these values and demonstrate that functional sites can complement, not displace, aesthetic value (Figure 1-11).

FIGURE 1-11: A multifunctional space, this accessible, sunken outdoor classroom of permeable stabilized granite at the Underwood Family Sonoran Landscape Laboratory at the University of Arizona provides a place for student study, building projects, and gathering. It serves an alternative function of water detention during desert storm events.

REGENERATIVE BALANCED SYSTEMS

An important aspect of the Bruntland definition of sustainability is provision for intergen-erational equity—in other words, preserving the ability of future generations to meet their needs. This idea necessitates the design of regenerative systems as opposed to systems that consume and degrade resources, compromising the possibility of their use for future gen-erations. A regenerative site system will balance or achieve positive resource flows and cre-ate closed-loop systems where "waste" from one process is "food" for another. For example, a regenerative water system might capture rainwater from an impermeable surface, use it to irrigate food crops, then allow the excess water in the soil to evaporate or feed the water table, returning it to the natural water cycle.

DYNAMIC, CONTINUOUSLY EVOLVING SYSTEMS

Like natural ecosystems, sustainable sites are comprised of dynamic, living systems that will grow, change, and require adaptation over their life. Resilience is the ability of an ecosystem to withstand or recover from disturbance or stress (Walker and Salt 2006). Disturbances such as drought, floods, disease, and urbanization will all impact an ecosystem's ability to perform specific functions and provide ecosystem services. Resilience science argues that complex ecological systems possess multiple protective mechanisms to help buffer these stresses and return to a stable state. And change, even drastic change, offers new opportu-nities for positive developments, change, and adaptation.

Sustainable site design can foster the natural processes of resilience by integrating with natural systems and planning for change, adaptation, and resilience over time. And like the concept of resilience in ecosystems science, which argues that change, even dras-tic change, offers new opportunities for positive developments, change and adaptation in sites, if guided well, can offer many positive opportunities. Additionally, if sites are designed with the possibility of eventual change and adaptation in mind, the life of the site will likely be longer than that of a more constrained site form. Recognition of this attribute is critical to the function of sustainable sites as postoccupancy management activities must support and guide the change that will occur both naturally and intentionally. The traditional idea of maintenance ("to maintain") implies a static landscape where change is halted and brought back to the original design concept. These current maintenance practices do not support the living, changing, and evolving ecosystems and human systems of sustainable sites.

Uncertainty, change, and uniqueness must be the design approach as we design dynamic living systems. Natural conditions are not static, nor should our site design solutions be. Site systems must perform over the life of the landscape—and there should be room for change, and opportunities for adaption must be built into our places (Figure 1-12).

[Design by Hargreaves Associates; Photo by John Gollings]

FIGURE 1-12: Louisville's Waterfront Park by Hargreaves Associates is in the 100-year flood zone and parts of the park flood regularly. The park spaces were designed to accommodate these flood events, and the riparian edges along part of the park edge are designed to change and adapt as a natural riparian edge would.

Design and Management Processes for Sustainable Sites

The characteristics of sustainable sites discussed above previously can be supported by design and management processes, such as: interdisciplinary collaboration on complex systems, engagement of a wide variety of project stakeholders during both design and operation of the site, measurement and verification of site system performance, and postoccupancy management and monitoring (Figure 1-13). These processes are discussed in greater detail in Chapter 2.

MEASUREMENT AND ECOLOGICAL ACCOUNTING FOR BALANCED SYSTEMS

In order to achieve a balance or positive flow of resources for truly regenerative design, one must quantify the inputs and outputs through ecological accounting and lifecycle analysis activities both during site design and on an ongoing basis during site operation. Results of ecological accounting and ecosystem services measurement can inform initial design decisions over many points in the design process, and can continue to inform management and adaptation decisions over the life of the landscape. Performance benchmarks of some

SITES credits, such as those related to stormwater management, water efficiency, and organic waste, require ecological accounting activities and strive for a zero or positive balance flow of resources and closed loops.

The activities of ecological accounting and life-cycle accounting can be complex and time consuming. And it is extremely complicated to quantify all input and output flows for multiple processes; however, if measurement begins in the design process, activities can proceed more easily into systems during site operation. For instance, if irrigation efficiency metrics are established during design, efficiency during operation will be easily measured against the established metrics.

Temporal fluctuations must be considered during accounting activities as well, adding an additional challenge to quantification. Human and natural systems will vary with changing seasons, variations in weather patterns, and unexpected human interventions. For example, a cistern for captured rainwater storage in California may stand empty from June to October just when one would

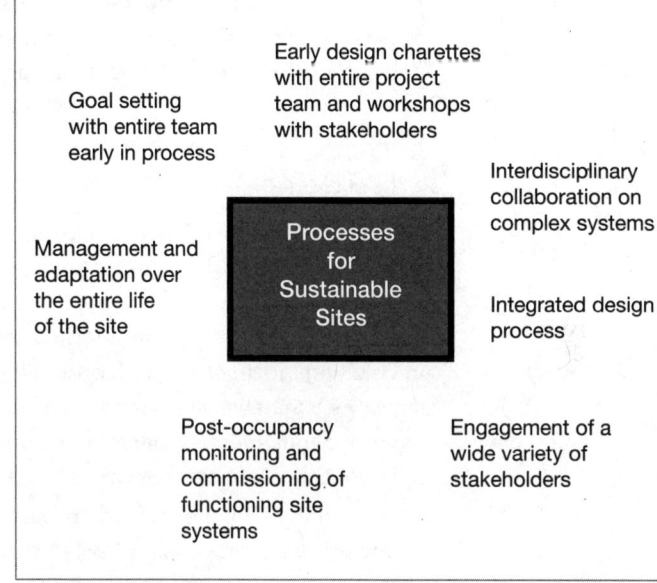

FIGURE 1-13: Sustainable sites require design and management processes that may vary from conventional practices, such as: integrated design, interdisciplinary collaboration on complex systems, engagement of a wide variety of project stakeholders during both design and operation of the site, measurement and verification of site systems performance, and postoccupancy management and monitoring.

like to have the irrigation water, then it may fill and overflow during the four-month rainy season when irrigation water is not needed. Or solar lights at an office complex might provide lighting in the evening after the sun goes down, but be "out of juice" at 7 a.m. when it is still dark as office workers arrive for work.

Given the challenging nature of ecological accounting activities, the results and methods of quantification should be shared with other professionals to assist in their activities. There are a growing number of databases and venues including and beyond peer-reviewed journals where this type of information can be shared.

INTERDISCIPLINARY COLLABORATION ON COMPLEX SYSTEMS

Design of whole, sustainable systems necessitates a broader design approach with expertise and input from multiple disciplines. The environmental and social issues that must be addressed in sustainable design are too complex for just landscape architects or just civil engineers. By necessity, the sustainable site design process must include multiple disciplines that will collaborate on the complex, interrelated systems. For example, decisions about water systems for a project may be addressed by landscape architects, civil engineers, architects, mechanical engineers, and hydrologists in collaboration. They may even collaborate with city planners and code officials on innovative approaches to water capture, conservation, and reuse.

ENGAGE A WIDE RANGE OF STAKEHOLDERS IN BOTH DESIGN AND MANAGEMENT OF THE SITE

A highly collaborative, multidisciplinary process can support the design and operation of complex and interrelated systems. An inclusive and integrated design team will vary by project, but is typically comprised of a variety of consultants, owners, contractors, and stakeholders (including users, citizens, regulators, and site managers). Early engagement of the entire team in visioning, goal-setting, and budgeting can ensure ethical and equitable decision making and socially sustainable sites. In addition, inclusion of a wide variety of stakeholders, such as future users and management personnel, during design phases will increase the chances of continuity of design intent and maximize the potential for good management decisions in the future.

Inclusion of a wide range of project stakeholders can necessitate intensive education, advocacy, and persuasion efforts by designers, other consultants, and/or proponents of sustainable site design. These efforts must often be tailored to the individual concerns of the stakeholders, and information provided can take the form of cost-benefit analysis, performance and maintenance information, and case study research. Some forums for stakeholder inclusion are charettes, workshops, or public meetings. It is important to note that broad stakeholder involvement can increase the likelihood of some participants having a continued role in the operation of the site.

POSTOCCUPANCY MANAGEMENT AND MONITORING

A crucial activity to ensure positive function for the dynamic systems of sustainable sites are feedback loops of postoccupancy monitoring, management, and adaptation. Continued involvement of the design team postconstruction can be a challenge, as many owners do not understand the importance of ongoing management with input from the professional consultants. Development of monitoring protocols and management plans can guide these activities over the life of the landscape and can connect design intentions with ongoing management activities. This book, like the Sustainable Sites Initiative, takes an unprecedented approach to the design and management of sustainable sites in that it thoroughly addresses postconstruction management activities.

Goals of Sustainable Sites

Sustainable design holds the potential to heal unhealthy sites and regenerate many of the services of damaged ecosystems. Therefore, projects should avoid development of healthy sites where an intervention might actually degrade the existing systems, and focus new development on damaged sites where design can heal degraded ecosystems. A major facet of this idea is to "do no harm" with design. The impacts, both onsite and away from the site, should be considered for every design decision. Sensitive sites should be avoided, and sensitive areas on the development site should be protected and untouched.

USE CAUTION IN DEVELOPMENT, DON'T WAIT FOR PROOF OF HARM

Development intervention in complex systems, both cultural and ecological, can have unintended and unexpected consequences for both on- and offsite systems. The Precautionary Principle, as summarized in 1998 by the Wingspread Conference by the Science and Environment Health Network, states, "When an activity raises threats of harm to human health or the environment, precautionary measures should be taken even if some cause and effect relationships are not fully established scientifically." In site development, the precautionary principle can be applied to decisions made about site interventions. Caution should be exercised, and where impacts of the decisions are unknown or unproven, the measure should likely be avoided.

STRIVE FOR THE HIGHEST BENEFIT FIRST

The highest priority of any development should be to preserve healthy ecosystems, to conserve natural resources, and to regenerate damaged ecosystems. For various reasons, the best strategy or approach will not always be possible; therefore, the next best approach should be considered with every attempt made to maximize the most sustainable outcome. It is important to note that priorities will vary depending on region, owner goals, cultural needs, and local ecosystem issues. Establishment of priorities and goals early in the design process will assist the design team in evaluating various approaches to site development.

The depth to which a design strategy will meet the definition of sustainable design will vary. Many strategies may reduce harm by "conserving," "reducing," or "recycling" resources. They may not achieve the "balancing," "producing," or "regenerating" that is necessary to meet the true definition of sustainability—meeting the needs of the present without compromising the ability of future generations to meet their needs. Table 1-2 provides a few examples illustrating a range of approaches to water, vegetation, soils, materials, and energy systems.

Regenerative design, or truly sustainable design, is the ultimate goal; however, any progress toward this and away from wasteful, destructive site design is a positive thing. This book acknowledges that any effort toward sustainability is not too small, even though larger steps are preferable. The ultimate goal is a shift in the way we think about the Earth, our place in it, and its resources. But many small steps can add up to large impacts, and small steps taken over and over can result in significant change to site development and management practices. Radical change, if it can be accomplished, is a great thing, but the reality is that incremental changes may be a much more realistic approach within the mainstream design and construction industry.

TABLE 1-2: Range of Approaches to Sustainable Site Design and Operation

WATER SYSTEMS

Conserve	Reuse	Balance	Regenerate
Use efficient irrigation, specify low-water-use plants, employ low-impact development.	Harvest rainwater, capture graywater, reuse for irrigation, toilet flushing, sprinklers. Infiltrate small storms' rainwater onsite.	Net zero use. Capture rain and all wastewater (both black water and graywater); purify, store, reuse onsite for *all* water needs, and provide some to other sites. Infiltrate and cleanse rainwater.	Capture rain and all wastewater; purify, store, reuse onsite for *all* water needs, and provide some to other sites. Match predevelopment hydrologic conditions.

VEGETATION

Preserve	Protect	Restore	Regenerate
Minimize removal of existing native vegetation. Identify critical vegetation areas and protect during the development process.	Do not introduce exotic species that could naturalize in the local environment. Do not use chemical treatments that pose a threat to the ecosystem.	Remove invasive plant species. Specify plants to create a native plant community. Restore appropriate plant biomass.	Maximize ecosystem services of vegetation. Use vegetation to reduce heating and cooling loads on buildings, cleanse stormwater, minimize urban heat island effect, and provide habitat.

SOILS

Preserve	Reuse	Restore	Regenerate
Protect healthy soils from damage due to construction and development. Prevent access to healthy soil areas during the construction process.	Reuse healthy soils that cannot be protected onsite. Take care to reduce damage during the removal and replacement process.	Use appropriate techniques to remediate damaged soils that will restore desired physical, chemical, or biological properties lost during the development process or due to previous site activity.	Use soil restoration and soil and vegetation management that will create opportunities for soil to regenerate over time, maintaining healthy soils and rebuilding damaged soils.

MATERIALS AND RESOURCES

Reduce and Recycle
Use recycled content products and reprocessed materials. Recycle construction and demolition debris.

Reuse
Salvage and reuse construction and demolition materials. Design for disassembly and deconstruction.

Balance
Do not rebuild. Reuse structures in place. Use durable materials and detail durable structures.

Regenerate and Renew
Design sites and structures for adaptation and reuse.

Use living materials for structures.

Use renewable materials.

ENERGY SYSTEMS

Reduce
Design to reduce heating and cooling loads on buildings and maximize the benefits of solar and wind energy. Design to reduce heat island energy impacts.

Offset
Purchase green energy credits and carbon offsets for building and site energy needs. Use solar-powered pumps, lighting, and site fixtures.

Renew
Use passive and active energy production methods that rely on natural systems such as sun, wind, and water for all the energy needs of the site and building.

Produce
Use passive and active energy production methods that rely on natural systems such as sun, wind, and water. Produce more energy than is needed for the site and building, and sell back to the local energy provider.

CULTURAL SYSTEMS

Preservation
Identify the social and economic needs of the community and engage the community and other stakeholders in the design process.

Rehabilitation
Consider how the site will educate, build community, and create a sense of place.

Create a program that will increase mental health, physical health, and social equity.

Restoration
Use the project to encourage the development of job skills and create economic opportunities during and after development.

Reconstruction
Design for human comfort and accessibility.

Design for physical activity and mental restoration.

Design for social interaction and community building.

The Sustainable Sites Initiative

The Sustainable Sites Initiative (SITES) is an interdisciplinary endeavor by the American Society of Landscape Architects, the Lady Bird Johnson Wildflower Center at the University of Texas at Austin, the United States Botanical Garden, and allied stakeholder organizations to promote sustainable site planning and design, construction, and maintenance practices. The Initiative developed and administers voluntary national guidelines and performance benchmarks to promote sustainable land development and management practices for the maintenance and regeneration of ecosystem services (Table 1-3).

The Initiative's central message is that any landscape has potential to contribute to ecosystem services and can address urgent environmental issues, such as global climate change, loss of biodiversity, and resource consumption, if properly designed and managed. The guidelines and performance benchmarks can be applied to a range of sites, with or without buildings; rural, suburban, and urban; large or small. Like this book, the guidelines are intended to be used by those who design, construct, operate, and maintain landscapes including landscape architects, engineers, developers, architects, planners, maintenance crews, restoration ecologists, horticulturalists, governments, and land stewards.

The *Guidelines and Performance Benchmarks* for soils, hydrology, vegetation, human health and well-being, and materials selection were developed by a multidisciplinary group of technical experts and a steering committee representing 11 stakeholder groups. Providing benchmarks based on sustainable outcomes, the guidelines are performance based rather than prescriptive instructions to encourage flexible use of technologies and strategies appropriate to each project, site condition, and region.

The *Guidelines and Performance Benchmarks* are organized as a series of prerequisites and credits for creating sustainable sites. The prerequisites are required and must be achieved for a site to participate in this voluntary program. Achievement of credits is optional, but a number of them must be attained in order for a project to be recognized as a sustainable site by SITES. Many credits offer a range of points depending on the level of achievement of the credit. For instance, a site may be awarded one credit for reducing irrigation use by 50 percent below the standard baseline and may receive an additional point for a 100 percent reduction. Some credits are worth more points than others based on carefully considered prioritization by the technical and steering committees.

SITES prerequisites and credits can be downloaded from the Sustainable Sites website. As they are periodically updated and revised, they are not listed in this book, although each chapter contains a summary of SITES credit content related to each chapter topic. SITES prerequisites and credits are organized into sections reflecting a typical site development project process. The sections are:

- ▶ Site Selection
- ▶ Predesign Assessment and Planning
- ▶ Site Design: Water
- ▶ Site Design: Soil and Vegetation
- ▶ Site Design: Materials Selection
- ▶ Site Design: Human Health and Well-Being
- ▶ Construction
- ▶ Operations and Maintenance
- ▶ Monitoring and Innovation

TABLE 1-3: SITES Guiding Principles of a Sustainable Site

Do no harm.

Make no changes to the site that will degrade the surrounding environment. Promote projects on sites where previous disturbance or development presents an opportunity to regenerate ecosystem services through sustainable design.

Precautionary principle

Be cautious in making decisions that could create risk to human and environmental health. Some actions can cause irreversible damage. Examine a full range of alternatives—including no action—and be open to contributions from all affected parties.

Design with nature and culture

Create and implement designs that are responsive to economic, environmental, and cultural conditions with respect to the local, regional, and global context.

Use a decision-making hierarchy of preservation, conservation, and regeneration.

Maximize and mimic the benefits of ecosystem services by preserving existing environmental features, conserving resources in a sustainable manner, and regenerating lost or damaged ecosystem services.

Provide regenerative systems as intergenerational equity.

Provide future generations with a sustainable environment supported by regenerative systems and endowed with regenerative resources.

Support a living process.

Continuously reevaluate assumptions and values and adapt to demographic and environmental change.

Use a systems thinking approach.

Understand and value the relationships in an ecosystem and use an approach that reflects and sustains ecosystem services; reestablish the integral and essential relationship between natural processes and human activity.

Use a collaborative and ethical approach.

Encourage direct and open communication among colleagues, clients, manufacturers, and users to link long-term sustainability with ethical responsibility.

Maintain integrity in leadership and research.

Implement transparent and participatory leadership, develop research with technical rigor, and communicate new findings in a clear, consistent, and timely manner.

Foster environmental stewardship.

In all aspects of land development and management, foster an ethic of environmental stewardship—an understanding that responsible management of healthy ecosystems improves the quality of life for present and future generations.

Source: The Sustainable Sites Initiative *Guidlelines and Performance Benchmarks*, 2009

Leadership in Energy and Environmental Design (LEED)

The LEED Green Building Rating Systems™ are voluntary national standards for developing sustainable and high-performance buildings and sites. LEED provides third-party verification that a building or community was designed and built using strategies aimed at improving performance across metrics such as: energy savings, water efficiency, Carbon dioxide emissions reduction, improved indoor environmental quality, and stewardship of resources and sensitivity to their impacts (USGBC 2009).

LEED is a product of the U.S. Green Building Council (USGBC), a national coalition of building industry professionals, contractors, policy makers, owners, and manufacturers. Their stated mission is "to transform the way buildings and communities are designed, built, and operated, enabling an environmentally and socially responsible, healthy, and prosperous environment that improves the quality of life." Council members work in a committee-based, consensus-focused way to develop LEED products and resources, policy guidance, and educational and marketing tools to facilitate the adoption of green building. The council develops alliances with industry and research organizations and with federal, state, and local governments.

The USGBC states that "LEED™ was created to provide the people who design, build, and operate buildings with an organized consensus benchmark for defining and evaluating green buildings." USGBC members developed and continue to refine the system through a membership consensus process.

Registered projects can choose from a variety of sustainable strategies and earn points toward a certified project in the following key areas:

- ► Sustainable Sites
- ► Water Efficiency
- ► Energy & Atmosphere
- ► Materials & Resources
- ► Indoor Environmental Quality
- ► Locations & Linkages
- ► Awareness & Education
- ► Innovation in Design
- ► Regional Priority

The USGBC offers a wide range of LEED Rating Systems that differ by project type. By meeting enough credits, a project can gain certification under one of the following:

- ▸ LEED for New Construction and Major Renovations
- ▸ LEED for Existing Buildings: Operations & Maintenance
- ▸ LEED for Commercial Interiors
- ▸ LEED for Core & Shell
- ▸ LEED for Schools
- ▸ LEED for Retail
- ▸ LEED for Healthcare
- ▸ LEED for Homes
- ▸ LEED for Neighborhood Development

THE RELATIONSHIP BETWEEN LEED AND SITES

SITES was designed to complement LEED® (Leadership in Energy and Environmental Design) Green Building Rating System™ and other rating systems that focus on sustainability in buildings. While LEED does contain credits for sites, it addresses sustainable site issues in a limited way. The US Green Building Council and the Sustainable Sites ® Initiative are partnering to align and integrate credits in future editions of the rating systems.

THE CONTENTS AND STRUCTURE OF THIS BOOK

The *Sustainable Sites Handbook* is offered as a comprehensive resource for design professionals engaging in sustainable site planning, design, construction, maintenance, and monitoring activities. It offers current and detailed information on principles, strategies, technologies, tools, and references for sustainable sites. Diagrams, charts and tables, construction details, photos, calculations, and specification considerations are provided for a broad range of technologies and strategies.

While this book is intended to be a resource for designers who are either formally or informally using the SITES guidelines and performance benchmarks, it will not discuss specific SITES prerequisites and credits as they are continually being altered and refined. In addition, SITES credits are performance based, not prescriptive. There are a wide variety of strategies and technologies that can be employed to achieve a given credit, and this book offers technical information on these strategies and technologies. It is important to note also that use of one technology can achieve multiple credits or sustainable goals. For example, a green roof can reduce stormwater quantities, provide habitat, reduce energy use for building air-conditioning, and contribute to reductions in the heat island effect.

Chapter authors are some of the same experts who carefully shaped the SITES rating tool, ensuring thorough coverage of the broad range of topics related to sustainable site systems.

This book is structured along the environmental and human systems of sustainable sites and is organized into the following chapters:

- ▶ Chapter 1, Introduction
- ▶ Chapter 2, Predesign: Assessment, Planning, and Site Selection
- ▶ Chapter 3, Site Design: Water Systems
- ▶ Chapter 4, Site Design: Vegetation Systems
- ▶ Chapter 5, Site Design: Soil Systems
- ▶ Chapter 6, Site Design: Materials and Resources
- ▶ Chapter 7, Site Design: Human Health and Well-Being Strategies
- ▶ Chapter 8, Site Occupancy: Operations, Maintenance, and Monitoring

Chapter 1, Introduction, lays out the ideological basis on which the book rests and introduced the Sustainable Sites Initiative. Following are summaries for the additional seven book chapters.

Chapter 2, Predesign: Assessment, Planning and Site Selection, discusses activities that should happen prior to the design phase of a sustainable site project. Discussion of site selection focuses on avoidance of inappropriate sites, such as those on prime farmland, adjacent to wetlands, floodplains and sensitive ecosystems, habitat of endangered species, and fireprone areas. Site types (e.g., greenfield, brownfield, grayfield, etc.) are defined and opportunities and design considerations for each are identified. Site assessment, inventory, and analysis techniques to better understand the regional context, climate, and energy issues, microclimates, hydrology, soils, vegetation, materials and resources, and cultural contexts are summarized. Techniques of integrated design, project design team formation, and engagement of stakeholders in design are discussed relative to goal-setting, performance target establishment, and programming.

Chapter 3, Site Design: Water Systems, leads the site design chapters with detailed information on the integrated strategies of sustainable water systems for stormwater, wastewater, and conservation of water. Discussion of stormwater technologies and strategies is guided by the following objectives: to control downstream flow rates, to reduce nonpoint source pollution, to infiltrate water at predevelopment levels, and to protect groundwater. Practices discussed are those that: reduce runoff, mitigate runoff by emulating evapotranspiration and infiltration, convey runoff from larger events, protect or restore receiving water bodies, and maintain sediment and control erosion. Water conservation strategies are offered for rainwater and graywater capture, efficient irrigation, and water features using captured rainwater as the makeup water supply.

Chapter 3 also discusses onsite wastewater treatment techniques for primary, secondary, and tertiary treatment and disinfection. And systems such as solar aquatic systems and surface and subsurface constructed wetlands are explained. Last, options for reuse of treated water are offered.

Chapter 4, Site Design: Vegetation Systems, emphasizes the wide variety of ecosystem services provided by vegetation and provides information on fostering healthy plant communities in a variety of settings. It discusses criteria for appropriate plant and plant community selection, use of salvaged plants, and sustainable nursery and plant production practices. Use of plants in urban settings is addressed along with considerations for use of vegetation in stormwater structures, green roofs, and living walls. Vegetation protection techniques, ecological restoration, and firewise landscape principles are also discussed.

Chapter 5, Site Design: Soil Systems, emphasizes healthy soil as the foundation of a sustainable site. It presents detailed techniques for soil assessment, preservation, and management based on soil texture, organic matter, structure, compaction, volume, drainage, chemical status and nutrient availability, soil pH, biological activity, cation exchange capacity, soluble salts, and contamination. Soil replacement strategies, specialized soils, and soil management plans are also discussed.

Chapter 6, Site Design: Materials and Resources, addresses techniques to minimize environmental and human health impacts of construction materials across their entire lifecycle. It provides methods to evaluate impacts of materials and techniques of site and regional assessment for materials and resources. The chapter offers strategies for resource efficiency of materials such as deconstruction, material reuse, design for durability, and use of recycled content and reprocessed materials. Strategies to reduce the environmental and human health impacts are provided for the following basic site construction materials: concrete, stone and aggregates, brick, earthen materials, asphalt pavement, plastics, metals, biobased materials, and wood.

Chapter 7, Site Design: Human Health and Well-Being, offers techniques for the design of culturally sustainable sites beginning with techniques for assessing a site's social setting. It offers design strategies for sustainability awareness and education, equity in site development, construction and use, site accessibility, wayfinding, and safety. Design considerations for physical activity, restorative settings, and social interaction and community building are provided; and techniques for preserving historic and cultural features and patterns are offered.

Chapter 8, Site Occupancy: Operations, Maintenance, and Monitoring, offers detailed information for ongoing function of sustainable site systems during the site operations phase. Techniques for incorporating operations, maintenance, and monitoring considerations into site design are offered as well as a detailed discussion of the development of maintenance and management plans. Operations and maintenance strategies are provided for: recycling site waste from operations and maintenance, nourishing soil with sustainable soil amendments, integrated pest management, controlling and managing invasive plants, maintaining landscapes to reduce risk of catastrophic wildfire, reducing environmental and human health impacts from maintenance equipment, maintaining bioretention features, green roofs, and green walls, conserving potable water and treating makeup water in created water features, and maintaining pavements. The chapter discusses techniques of monitoring sites to inform active and adaptive stewardship.

References

Akbari, H., M. Pomerantz, and H. Taha. 2001. "Cool Surfaces and Shade Trees to Reduce Energy Use and Improve air Quality in Urban Areas." *Solar Energy*, 70(3):295–310.

Akbari, H., S. Davis, S. Dorsano, J. Huang, and S. Winnett. 1992. *Cooling Our Communities: A Guidebook on Tree Planting and Light-Colored Surfacing*. Washington, DC: U.S. Environmental Protection Agency.

Benyus, J. M. 2002. *Biomimicry*. New York: Harper Collins.

Costanza, R., R. d'Arge, R. de Groot, S. Farber, M. Grasso, B. Hannon, K. Limburg, R.V. O'Neill, J. Paruelo, R.G. Raskin, P. Sutton, and M. van den Belt. 1997. "The Value of the World's Ecosystem Services and Natural Capital." *Nature*, 387:253–260.

Donovan, G.H., and D. Butry. 2009. "The Value of Shade: Estimating the Effect of Urban Trees on Summertime Electricity Use." *Energy and Buildings*, 41(6): 662–668.

Kaplan, R. 2007. "Employees' Reactions to Nearby Nature at Their Workplace: The Wild and the Tame." *Landscape and Urban Planning*, 82:17–24.

Kaplan, R., and S. Kaplan. 1989. *The Experience of Nature: A Psychological Perspective*. Cambridge, MA: Cambridge University Press.

Kaplan, S. 1995. "The Restorative Benefits of Nature: Toward an Integrative Framework." *Journal of Environmental Psychology*, 15: 169–182.

Kellert, S. 2005. *Building for Life: Designing and Understanding the Human Nature Connection*. Washington, DC: Island Press.

Kibert, C.J., J. Sendzimir, and B. Guy, eds. 2002. *Construction Ecology: Nature as the Basis for Green Buildings*. London: Spon Press.

Kuo, F.E., and W. C. Sullivan 2001a. "Environment and Crime in the Inner City: Does Vegetation Reduce Crime?" *Environment and Behavior* 33(3): 343–365.

_____. 2001b. Aggression and Violence in the Inner City: Impacts of Environment via Mental Fatigue. *Environment and Behavior*, 33(4): 543–571.

Lowe, Ernest. 2002. "Foreword." In *Construction Ecology: Nature as the Basis for Green Buildings*, C.J. Kibert, J. Sendzimir, and B. Guy, eds. London: Spon Press.

Meyer, Elizabeth K. 2010. "Sustaining Beauty: The Performance of Appearance. A Manifesto in Three Parts." *Journal of Landscape Architecture* (Spring 2008): 6–23.

Millennium Ecosystem Assessment (MEA). 2005. *Ecosystems and Human Well-being: Synthesis*. Washington, DC: Island Press.

———. 2007. *A Toolkit for Understanding and Action*. Washington, DC: Island Press.

Nature Conservancy press release. 2005. "The Time to Choose." Available at www.nature.org/pressroom/press/press1838.html.

Nowak, D.J., S. Civerolo, R. Trivikrama, G. Sistla, C.J. Luley, and D.E. Crane. 2000. "A Modeling Study of the Impact of Urban Trees on Ozone." *Atmospheric Environment*, 34:1601–1613.

Nowak, D.J., and D.E. Crane. 2002. "Carbon Storage and Sequestration by Urban Trees in the USA." *Environmental Pollution*, 116(3):381–389.

Nowak, D.J., D.E. Crane, and J.F. Dwyer. 2002. "Compensatory Value of Urban Trees in the United States." *Journal of Arboriculture*, 28(4):194–199.

Nowak, D.J., D.E. Crane, and J.C. Stevens. 2006. "Air Pollution Removal by Urban Trees and Shrubs in the United States." *Urban Forestry & Urban Greening*, 4:5–123.

Nowak, D.J., S.M. Stein, P.B. Randler, E.J. Greenfield, S.J. Comas, M.A. Carr, and R.J. Alig. 2010. "Sustaining America's Urban Trees and Forests: A Forests on the Edge Report." Gen. Tech. Rep. NRS-62. Newtown Square, PA: U.S. Department of Agriculture, Forest Service, Northern Research Station.

Portland Cement Association (PCA). 2005. "Full-Depth Reclamation (FDR): Recycling Roads Saves Money and Natural Resources." Skokie, IL: Portland Cement Association.

Romley, J.A., A. Hackbarth, and D.P. Goldman. 2010. *The Impact of Air Quality on Hospital Spending*. Santa Monica, CA: RAND Corporation.

Rosenfeld A.H., J.J. Romm, H. Akbari, and M. Pomerantz. 1998. "Cool Communities: Strategies for Heat Islands Mitigation and Smog Reduction." *Energy and Building*, 28:51–62.

Sanders, R.A. 1986. "Urban Vegetation Impacts on the Urban Hydrology of Dayton, Ohio." *Urban Ecology*, 9: 361-376.

SITES. 2009a. "Sustainable Sites Initiative: Guidelines and Performance Benchmarks 2009." Available at www.sustainablesites.org/report.

———. 2009b. "Sustainable Sites Initiative: The Case for Sustainable Landscapes." Available at www.sustainablesites.org/report.

Sommer, R., F. Learey, J. Summit, and Tirell, M. 1994a. Social Benefits of Resident Involvement in Tree Planting: Compressions with Developer Planted Trees. *Journal of Arboriculture*, 20(6): 323–328.

———. 1994b. "Social Benefits of Residential Involvement in Tree Planting." *Journal of Arboriculture* 20(3): 170-175.

Ulrich, R.S. 1984. "View through a Window May Influence Recovery from Surgery." *Science*, 224:420–421.

———. 1986. "Human Responses to Vegetation and Landscapes." *Landscape and Urban Planning*, 13:29–44.

United Nations World Commission on Environment and Development. 1987. *Our Common Future*, Report of the World Commission on Environment and Development. Published as Annex to General Assembly document A/42/427, Development and International Co-operation: Environment, August 2.

U.S. Department of Commerce, Census Bureau. 2011. *Statistical Abstract of the United States, 2011*. Table 1046. Available at www.census.gov//compendia/statab/cats/population.html.

U.S. Green Building Council. 2009. "Foundations of LEED." July 17.

U.S. Environmental Protection Agency (U.S. EPA). 2000. "Building Savings: Strategies for Waste Reduction of Construction and Demolition Debris from Buildings." Available at www.Epa.Gov/Wastes/Nonhaz/Municipal/Pubs/Combined.pdf.

Walker, B, and D. Salt. 2006. *Resilience Thinking: Sustaining Ecosystems and People in a Changing World*. Washington, DC: Island Press.

Westphal, L.M. 1999. "Empowering People through Urban Greening Projects: Does It Happen?" In: Kollin, C., Ed. Proceedings: 1999 National Urban Forest Conference. Washington, Dc: American Forests, 60–63.

_____. 2003. "Urban Greening and Social Benefits: A Study of Empowerment Outcomes." *Journal of Arboriculture*, 29(3): 137–147.

Wilson, E.O. 1984. *Biophilia: The Human Bond with Other Species.* Cambridge, MA: Harvard University Press.

Windhager, S., F. Steiner, M.T. Simmons, and D. Heymann. 2010. "Towards Ecosystem Services as a Basis for Design." *Landscape Journal*, 29(2):107–123.

Wise, Steve. 2008. "Green Infrastructure Rising: Best Practices in Stormwater Management." *Planning*, 74(8):14–19.

CHAPTER 2

PREDESIGN: SITE SELECTION, ASSESSMENT, AND PLANNING

▶ Heather Venhaus

PLANNING FOR SUSTAINABILITY STARTS IN THE PREDESIGN PHASE of the project. A holistic approach that considers the larger context of the site is required. Each project decision, starting with the selection of the site, should be viewed as an opportunity to reduce consumption, eliminate waste, nurture healthy ecosystems, and connect people with nature.

Sustainable outcomes are not inherent to site development and should not be assumed just because landscapes are made up of vegetation, soil, and other natural components. Like all successful aspects of a project, it should be intentional and nurtured throughout all development phases. Beneficial impacts are limited when sustainable design is considered separate from the overall design process and reduced to intermittent "green" components such as native plants or recycled materials that are inserted into a project.

Traditional design processes and team interactions do not always support the development of sustainable sites. To help overcome this issue, a commitment to sustainability should be acknowledged at the onset of a project and the design process should be adjusted to allow time for reflection, reinvestigation, and research of new ideas. This adjustment need not result in an increase in project time or costs, as the additional time spent in the predesign phase can provide clear project focus and encourage collaboration between team members, allowing design solutions to evolve more quickly and allowing for design synergies.

SITE SELECTION

Location is one of the most important factors when developing a sustainable site. It determines options to access existing infrastructure, utilize public transportation, restore degraded ecosystems, and employ many other sustainable design practices.

Site design and planning consultants can encourage sustainable outcomes by prioritizing the selection of previously developed properties and avoiding environmentally sensitive areas. Redevelopment of grayfield and brownfield sites provides an opportunity to not only protect greenfields but also restore and regenerate landscapes and the ecosystem services they provide. In addition to finding a site that is suitable for the proposed program, consultants should also guide the client in understanding the larger environmental, social, and economic impacts of the development.

Obtaining the best-suited property for a project can require the coordination of numerous organizations and many different financial and political factors. The process can easily become onerous and overly complicated without a systematic approach. To address this issue, LaGro (2008) has identified seven discrete steps to guide site selection.

1   Clarify the project purpose, goals, and requirements.

2. Determine the site selection criteria and factors such as access, utilities, and size.

3. Identify potential sites.

4. Evaluate the suitability of each site. Weigh the environmental, economic, and social opportunities and constraints.

5. Rank and prioritize the selected sites.

6. Select the most suitable site and develop a site selection report to document the results of the evaluation. The report is useful when project teams need to revisit decisions or select alternative properties.

7. Conduct feasibility studies to determine items such as market analysis, design concepts, and project costs.

Working through this methodical process will help ensure the selected site is a good match for the proposed project. The importance of each step and the anticipated timeline should be discussed with all team members and project stakeholders. Open communication throughout the process will be helpful when managing expectations and building support of the outcome.

Site Selection Criteria

A project's commitment to sustainability begins with site selection. Site characteristics such as previous use, location, ecological condition, and connection to the surrounding community determine the extent to which sustainable outcomes can be achieved. Poor site selection can have negative implications that in many cases cannot be resolved or overcome through the design process. The following criteria for site selection can assist the design team in achieving sustainable outcomes.

- ▶ Include all appropriate consultants and stakeholders in the site selection process.
- ▶ Locate development on grayfield and brownfield sites. Use development to heal damaged sites and restore ecosystem services. Look for opportunities to reuse existing structures or hardscape.
- ▶ Select sites within existing communities.
- ▶ Locate development near public transportation access (e.g., ¼ mile walk from bus stop or ½ mile from rapid transit).
- ▶ Locate development near existing pedestrian and bicycle networks.
- ▶ Avoid sites that are prime farmland, unique farmland, or farmland of local or state-wide importance.
- ▶ Avoid sites that are habitat for threatened or endangered species.
- ▶ Avoid development of sensitive ecological areas, such as wetlands, and provide ample buffers to protect the site features.
- ▶ Avoid development of greenfield sites within the 100-year floodplain for waterways of all sizes.
- ▶ Avoid development of greenfield sites whose topography and other natural characteristics are not well suited to the proposed development and will require significant site disturbance and resource use.

Following are opportunities and design considerations associated with various site types and major landscape characteristics that should be carefully considered prior to selecting a site for development.

Table 2-1: Site Types and Characteristics That Impact Sustainable Outcomes

- ▶ Brownfields

   Brownfields are properties where the expansion, redevelopment, or reuse may be complicated by the presence or potential presence of hazardous substances, pollutants, or contaminants. Brownfields include properties contaminated with petroleum, mine-scarred land, and former sites of methamphetamine laboratories (EPA 2010a).

   - ▷ Authority and regulations

      State environmental agencies in cooperation with the Environmental Protection Agency (EPA) regulate the investigation and cleanup of brownfield sites. Requirements can differ significantly between states. The Small Business Liability Relief and Brownfields Revitalization Act (Pub. L. No. 107-118, 115 Stat. 2356, "the

Brownfields Law") promotes the cleanup and reuse of brownfields, provides financial assistance for revitalization, clarifies liability, and enhances state and tribal response programs.

▷ Opportunities and design considerations

Developing on brownfield properties has numerous environmental and economic benefits for the community and surrounding area. Reinvesting in brownfield sites has been shown to increase local tax bases, facilitate job growth, ameliorate public health risks, create community assets, and regenerate previously lost or disturbed ecosystem services. Brownfield redevelopments have varying remediation requirements depending on the location, proposed reuse, contamination type, and extent of hazardous substances or pollutants. Federal and state grants are often available to aid in environmental assessment, clean-up, job training, technical assistance, and other related activities. It is estimated that there are over 450,000 brownfields in the United States (EPA 2010a).

▷ Resources

U.S. EPA Brownfields and Land Revitalizaton, `www.epa.gov/brownfields/index.html`.

▶ Urban Infill

Urban infill is the practice of developing vacant or underutilized properties within an existing community. Infill sites are surrounded by older urban growth and are usually already serviced by utilities.

▷ Authority and regulations

Urban infill, grayfield, and greenfield developments are primarily regulated by local governments or government entities. Communities can utilize comprehensive plans, tax benefits, and other incentives to promote development in desirable locations.

▷ Opportunities and design considerations

Infill projects can play an important role in revitalizing neighborhoods, removing safety hazards, and preserving greenfields. Urban redevelopment reduces sprawl and vehicle miles traveled, resulting in energy conservation and air quality benefits. Substantial energy and cost savings are also gained by the community and developer when infill projects utilize existing infrastructure and municipal services. Infill development can assist communities in obtaining the thresholds necessary for amenities such as park space, community services, retail establishments, and affordable housing (Sustainable Cities Institute 2010).

▷ Resources

Urban Land Institute, `www.uli.org/`; Municipal Research and Service Center of Washington, "Infill Development: Completing the Community Fabric," www.mrsc.org/Subjects/Planning/infilldev.aspx; Atlanta Regional Commision: Community Choices Toolkit, www.atlantaregional.com/local-government/ local-planning/best-practices.

► Grayfields

Grayfields are underutilized or abandoned retail and commercial sites located in urban and suburban areas. The sites are often characterized by large commercial buildings surrounded by parking lots and little or no vegetation.

▷ Authority and regulations

Urban infill, grayfield, and greenfield developments are primarily regulated by local governments or government entities. Communities can utilize comprehensive plans, tax benefits, and other incentives to promote development in desirable locations.

▷ Opportunities and design considerations

Grayfield sites offer the opportunity to sustainably redevelop large tracts of land within existing communities. They are commonly available in many established areas, typically near public transit, and have the potential to be used for a variety of retail and residential uses. Reinvesting in grayfield sites can provide avenues to increase economic diversity, build the local tax base, and restore numerous ecosystem services. Redevelopment makes better use of existing infrastructure and public services such as schools, public safety, water, and sewer. Reuse of underutilized or abandoned sites reduces urban sprawl and the time, money, and energy associated with commuting, resulting in improved air quality and other benefits.

▷ Resources

Urban Land Institute, www.uli.org/

► Greenfield

Greenfields are sites that have not been previously developed or extensively graded. Examples include agricultural fields, pastureland, park lands, and conservation areas.

▷ Authority and regulations

Urban infill, grayfield, and greenfield developments are primarily regulated by local governments or government entities. Communities can utilize comprehensive plans, tax benefits, and other incentives to promote development in desirable locations.

▷ Opportunities and design considerations

Greenfield sites provide a variety of ecosystem services that are critical to the health, security, and prosperity of humans and other organisms. Services such as air and water cleansing, climate regulation, food production, habitat, and enhanced cultural identity are all provided by greenfields in various capacities in both urban and rural locations. Development of this limited resource all too often results in the degradation or complete loss of ecosystem services.

▷ Resources

Urban Land Institute, www.uli.org/

► Prime farmland, unique farmland, and farmland of statewide or local importance

Prime farmland is undeveloped farmland that has the best combination of physical and chemical characteristics for producing food, feed, fiber, and oilseed crops. Prime farmland has the combination of soil properties, growing season, and moisture supply needed to produce sustained high yields of crops in an economic manner if treated and managed according to acceptable farming methods (NRCS 2010a).

Unique farmland is undeveloped farmland other than prime farmland that is used for the production of specific high-value food and fiber crops. It has the special combination of soil quality, location, growing season, and moisture supply needed to economically produce sustained high quality and/or high yields of a specific crop when treated and managed according to acceptable farming methods. Examples of such crops are citrus, tree nuts, olives, cranberries, fruit, and vegetables (NRCS 2010a).

Farmland of statewide or local importance is farmland defined by state agencies to be "important" for the production of food, feed, fiber, forage, and oilseed crops. Farmlands of statewide importance include those that are similar to prime farmland and that economically produce high yields of crops when treated and managed according to acceptable farming methods. Some may produce yields as high as prime farmlands if conditions are favorable (NRCS 2010a).

▷ Authority and regulations

The National Resource Conservation Service (NRCS) identifies and inventories prime, unique, and farmland of statewide importance to inform the nation of the extent and location of the best land for producing food, feed, fiber, forage, and oilseed crops. The Farmland Protection Policy Act (FPPA) Subtitle I of Title XV, Section 1539-1549, is intended to "minimize the impact Federal programs have on the unnecessary and irreversible conversion of farmland to nonagricultural uses." Projects are subject to FPPA requirements if they are completed by a federal agency or with assistance from a federal agency and have the potential to irreversibly convert farmland, directly or indirectly, to nonagricultural use.

▷ Opportunities and design considerations

Prime, unique, and farmlands of statewide importance produce crops more efficiently than other soils, requiring fewer inputs such as fuel, water, and fertilizers.

Development of these soils reduces the availability of food sources and forces marginal lands into food production. Loss of agricultural land due to urban development is an unnecessary and essentially irreversible loss of a critical resource. Over 10 million acres of prime farmland have been lost in the United States since 1982 (NRCS 2010b).

▷ Resources

Natural Resource Conservation Service: Prime Farmland, www.nrcs.usda.gov/technical/NRI/maps/prime.html.

► Floodplains

Floodplains are the lowlands and relatively flat areas adjoining inland and coastal waters and other flood-prone areas, such as offshore islands. At a minimum, areas defined as floodplains are subject to a 1 percent or greater chance of flooding in any given year.

▷ Authority and regulations

Through the Flood Plain Management Services Program, the U.S. Army Corps of Engineers uses its floodplain management technical expertise to help those outside of the Corps deal with floods and floodplain-related matters. Section 206 of the 1960 Flood Control Act (PL 86-645) directs the program to "foster public understanding of the options for dealing with flood hazards and to promote prudent use and management of the Nation's floodplains." The Corps provides technical assistance with regard to land subject to flooding from streams, lakes, and oceans. A range of "Special Services" is provided that involve all aspects of floodplain management including studies investigating the potential impacts of land use changes on the physical, socioeconomic, and environmental conditions of the floodplain.

▷ Opportunities and design considerations

Healthy, functioning floodplains provide valuable ecosystem services, such as reduced severity of floods, groundwater recharge, wildlife habitat, and pollutant filtration. The development and alteration of floodplains has resulted in an increase in the incidence of flooding, danger to humans, and loss of ecosystem services.

▷ Resources

U.S. Army Corps of Engineers, www.usace.army.mil/Pages/default.aspx.

▶ Wetlands

The Clean Water Act defines wetlands as "areas that are inundated or saturated by surface or ground water at a frequency and duration sufficient to support, and that under normal circumstances do support, a prevalence of vegetation typically adapted for life in saturated conditions." Wetlands found in the United States fall into four general categories—marshes, swamps, bogs, and fens.

▷ Authority and regulations

Wetlands are protected under the Clean Water Act (CWA), which is jointly administered by the U.S. Army Corp of Engineers and the EPA. The CWA is the foundation of surface water quality protection in the United States and strives to restore and maintain the chemical, physical, and biological integrity of the nation's waters in order that they may support "the protection and propagation of fish, shellfish, wildlife and recreation in and on the water." Groundwater or water quantity issues are not dealt with directly through the CWA. Program administration is handled by the Corps and the EPA provides program oversight. The agencies work under a "No-Net-Loss" policy that strives to maintain or increase the acreage of wetlands currently existing in the United States. The sequence process for permit review and issuance is described in the guidelines found in Section 404(b)(1) of the Clean Water Act.

▷ Opportunities and design considerations

Wetland ecosystems provide a range of valuable ecosystem services that contribute to human well-being, such as water cleansing, flood control, wildlife habitat, biological productivity, and recreation. Worldwide, wetlands are estimated to provide $14.9 trillion of ecosystem services each year (Costanza et al. 1997). Land use changes to support population growth and economic development have been the primary reasons for degradation and loss of wetlands. Over half of the wetlands in the United States have been drained or filled. Both urban and rural sites have the opportunity to protect and restore wetlands (EPA 2010b).

▷ Resources

U.S. Environmental Protection Agency: Wetlands, www.epa.gov/owow/wetlands/.

▶ Sites with endangered or threatened species habitat

An *endangered species* is an animal or plant in danger of extinction within the foreseeable future throughout all or a significant portion of its range.

A *threatened species* is an animal or plant likely to become endangered within the foreseeable future throughout all or a significant portion of its range.

▷   Authority and regulations

The Endangered Species Act (ESA) was established to protect and recover imperiled plant and animal species and the ecosystems upon which they depend. The Act recognizes that endangered and threatened species of wildlife and plants "are of aesthetic, ecological, educational, historical, recreational and scientific value to the Nation and its people." The ESA is administered by the U.S. Fish and Wildlife Service and the National Oceanic and Atmospheric Administration. State agencies also have programs for the management of threatened or endangered species and lists specific to their area. Many incentive-based strategies, such as candidate conservation agreements and "safe harbor" agreements, are available to landowners. ESA Section 9 describes the activities which are prohibited in order to protect species and their habitat.

▷   Opportunities and design considerations

Ecosystems with a variety of life forms are better able to recover from natural and human-induced stresses. Destruction of habitat due to sprawling urban development, agriculture and invasive species are common drivers of species extinctions.

▷   Resources

U.S. Fish and Wildlife Service: Endangered Species Program, `www.fws.gov/endangered/`.

UNDERSTANDING THE SITE

Site Assessment: Inventory and Analysis

A broad knowledge and thorough understanding of the local ecology and culture is essential to the design and development of a sustainable site. Each site has a unique set of physical, biological, and cultural attributes that define the overall character of the landscape and determine the suitability for specific uses (LaGro 2008). When the context of a site is not well understood, design decisions can unnecessarily and unknowingly lead to damaging environmental, social, and economic outcomes. Design teams should work with a full understanding of the living systems and communities that they are impacting.

Site inventories communicate and map the physical, biological, and cultural components of a site and surrounding area. The initial reconnaissance provides the information required to begin the design process, and as the project develops, additional information is gathered to inform design solutions. This inventory should not be an open-ended process of information gathering but rather a focused compilation of site conditions that is prompted by the requirements of the program plan and questions or concepts that arise in the design process.

Understanding the full context of a site may require multiple visits from a variety of specialists. Expertise from ecologists, hydrologists, soil scientists, or building experts may be necessary to collect, map, and analyze the information needed to fully and accurately understand the opportunities and limitations of the site. Including specialists in the assessment aids the design team in understanding the current and potential function of the site's systems and provides opportunities to optimize design solutions within the existing parameters of the site.

SITE INVENTORY

REGIONAL CONTEXT

Site Inventory and Analysis

- ▸ Identify the EPA Level III Ecoregion and major native plant communities and environmental conditions of the region.

- ▸ Research existing comprehensive community plans and zoning codes that may influence the site.

- ▸ Study the surrounding area and identify adjacent site conditions and current uses. Determine whether the surrounding conditions will be beneficial to the site or have a negative impact. Note any aesthetically pleasing visual qualities and stressful factors, such as excessive noise, odor, or pollution.

- ▸ Determine the importance of the site to the wildlife of the region. Identify areas of habitat, migratory routes, and wildlife corridors in the areas surrounding the site.

- ▸ Identify potential for damage to the site from natural disasters such as hurricanes, wildfire, and floods.

- ▸ Identify existing and planned public transit, bicycle, or pedestrian systems located within 0.25 miles of the site.

Information Gathering

- ▸ Locate the site's region on the EPA Level III Ecoregion maps. Field check and compare descriptions to the actual site conditions

- ▸ Contact local planning agencies and authorities.

▶ Spend time exploring the area surrounding the site to become familiar with the local culture, amenities, and community resources. Interview neighbors, community leaders, and other project stakeholders.

▶ Contact local wildlife authorities. Conduct a regional habitat inventory. Interview neighbors, community leaders, and other project stakeholders.

▶ Research the natural disasters history of the area. Interview community residents and local authorities.

▶ Contact local and state transportation authorities.

Design Considerations

▶ Sites are part of a larger ecological and social community. It is important to understand the surrounding conditions and explore design options that mutually benefit the site and surrounding area. Developing connections to the community and supporting the local character of a region enhances feelings of stewardship and sense of place. Understanding the local context also allows the project team to identify and mitigate any negative impacts from surrounding sites.

▶ Thoughtful site selection, design, and management can reduce the risk and impact of natural disasters. Special attention should be given to building location, materials, and construction methods.

▶ Mass transit and other alternative transportation options such as bicycles reduce the generation of greenhouse gases and improve air and water quality. Understanding the local transportation systems provides opportunities for the site to connect with and encourage the use of public transit and nonmotorized transportation.

Resources

▶ U.S. EPA Western Ecology Division, Level III Ecoregions: www.epa.gov/wed/pages/ecoregions/level_iii.htm

▶ USGS EarthExplorer: http://edcsns17.cr.usgs.gov/EarthExplorer/

▶ Google Earth: http://earth.google.com/.

▶ USGS EarthExplorer: http://edcsns17.cr.usgs.gov/EarthExplorer/

▶ Google Earth: http://earth.google.com/

▶ U.S. Fish and Wildlife Service management offices: www.fws.gov/offices/statelinks.html

▶ Firewise communities: www.firewise.org

▶ USGS Geologic Hazards Science Center: http://geohazards.cr.usgs.gov/

▶ Public Transportation Takes Us There: www.publictransportation.org/systems/

CLIMATE AND ENERGY

Site Inventory and Analysis

▸ Determine the average annual and monthly precipitation, humidity, and temperature of the site.

▸ Identify onsite conditions that provide opportunities for renewable energy strategies, such as wind, solar, and geothermal.

Information Gathering

▸ Research historical weather data from local meteorologists, weather stations, and universities.

Design Considerations

▸ Sites that are designed to thrive within their natural climatic conditions require less resources to sustain. Rainfall and temperatures affect design issues such as vegetation and material selection, stormwater management, and site layout.

▸ Renewable energy sources reduce greenhouse gas emissions and air pollution from fossil fuels. Consider the effects of existing vegetation, topography, and structures that may cast shadows or act as wind breaks or deflectors.

Resources

▸ National Oceanic and Atmospheric Administration local climatological data: www7.ncdc.noaa.gov/IPS/lcd/lcd.html

▸ USDA Plant hardiness zones: www.usna.usda.gov/Hardzone/ushzmap.html

▸ National Renewable Energy Laboratory Energy Analysis: www.nrel.gov/analysis/analysis_tools.html

MICROCLIMATE

Site Inventory and Analysis

▸ Study the path of the sun. Determine shadow configurations from trees, topography, and structures.

▶ Research ground-level prevailing wind direction in various seasons. Consider the effects of site features such as topography, vegetation, and buildings.

▶ Identify surfaces that heat or cool the site, such as bodies of water, dark pavements, or roofs.

Information Gathering

▶ Create a solar path diagram for the site to map the path of the sun through the day and year.

▶ Create or study existing wind rose diagrams. Research historical weather data from local meteorologists, weather stations, and universities.

▶ Field check locations and surface materials. Cross-reference findings with wind direction and shadow patterns to determine the effects on the microclimate.

Design Considerations

▶ Sites often have unique microclimatic conditions that differ from regional weather patterns. Understanding the microclimate allows the design team to utilize and create site conditions that increase user comfort and reduce building energy use. Special attention should be given to building orientation and the location of seating, outdoor gathering spaces, and plant selection.

Resources

▶ *Architectural Graphic Standards*, 10th edition.

▶ University of Oregon Solar Radiation Monitoring Laboratory: `http://solardat.uoregon.edu/SunChartProgram.html`

▶ Natural Resource Conservation Service, Wind Rose data: `www.wcc.nrcs.usda.gov/climate/windrose.html`

▶ National Oceanic and Atmospheric Administration, local climatological data: www7.ncdc.noaa.gov/IPS/lcd/lcd.html

▶ USGS EarthExplorer; `http://edcsns17.cr.usgs.gov/EarthExplorer/`

HYDROLOGY

Site Inventory and Analysis

▶ Study the site topography. Map the natural overland water flow and areas of ponding.

- ► Estimate the volume of rainwater or other nonpotable water sources, such as stormwater, graywater, and wastewater, available onsite for reuse.

- ► Map the 100-year floodplain.

- ► Map existing water bodies (e.g., lakes and streams) and their associated shorelines or vegetated buffer zones. Describe existing conditions, such as habitat quality, bank stability, and artificial modifications. Note ecological restoration opportunities.

- ► Locate and delineate existing wetlands and their associated buffers.

- ► Identify water bodies onsite or downstream from the site that are listed as impaired by the state water-quality agency. Determine the specific pollutants of concern for the impaired water bodies.

- ► Identify sources or potential sources of water pollution and health hazards existing onsite.

- ► Determine seasonal groundwater elevations.

Information Gathering

- ► Gather topographic maps derived from satellite imagery or physical surveys. The topographic detail required will depend on the size of the site and specific design objectives.

- ► Work with building architects and engineers to understand the water use and wastewater flow of the building. Utility bills and records can be useful in establishing baseline data. Check local codes for model requirements—often TR-55 and other.

- ► Consult Federal Emergency Management Agency (FEMA) flood maps, state environmental agencies, or local studies to determine the 100-year floodplain.

- ► Use aerial photos or site maps to locate existing water bodies. Ground truth the location and extent of vegetated buffer. Insert guidance on how to map, determine habitat quality, bank stability, or reference resource.

- ► Check with local and regional governments on accepted methods to delineate wetlands and buffer zones

- ► Wetland delineations are regulated by many jurisdictions depending on the state or county. Research the delineation requirements associated with the state of the project to determine if special state or county conditions preside.

- ► Research the Clean Water Act Section 303(d) list provided by the state water-quality agency.

- ► Research existing drainage infrastructure. Identify the water source, treatment location, and strategy. Field check and identify building, hardscape, and landscape materials, such as treated lumber or galvanized metal, that can be sources of pollutants. Interview the maintenance contractor or other individuals responsible for the site's care to identify potential pollution sources.

▶ Landscape cues such as springs, seeps, and water-loving vegetation can indicate areas of shallow groundwater. Use groundwater monitoring wells or similar technology to accurately determine the groundwater depth across the site.

Design Considerations

▶ Topography influences many aspects of the site, such as the microclimate, distribution of plant and animal species, water movement, and stormwater management practices. Consider options for minimizing disturbance and artfully incorporating the existing topography into the design solution.

▶ Sustainable sites treat all water as a resource and strive to promote water quality and support healthy hydrologic processes. Potable water requirements can be reduced or eliminated through design strategies such as rainwater harvesting, graywater reuse, or stormwater treatment trains.

▶ Development of floodplains or alterations in floodplain topography can increase the risk of flooding and property damage.

▶ Changes to water bodies and their associated buffers are often regulated by state and federal authorities. Project teams should consider the impact of site design, construction, and maintenance decisions on the quality, habitat, aesthetics, and recreational value of the water bodies.

▶ Wetlands are protected by state and federal authorities. Altering the site's drainage patterns, soil conditions, and groundwater levels can impact the health of wetlands. Existing natural wetlands should not be used for stormwater management or wastewater practices.

▶ Through careful design and maintenance, sites can reduce pollutant sources and the volume of stormwater runoff. Special attention should be given to the selection of materials, onsite treatment of stormwater, and maintenance practices.

▶ Building materials and maintenance practices can be pollution sources. Water-quality impacts should be considered when selecting materials and construction and maintenance strategies.

▶ Groundwater elevations can impact the site's hydrology and suitability for excavation, storm- and wastewater management, and other site features. Special consideration should be given to site development and maintenance strategies to avoid the contamination of groundwater.

Resources

▶ USGS EarthExplorer: http://edcsns17.cr.usgs.gov/EarthExplorer/

▶ Texas Water Development Board: The Texas Manual on Rainwater Harvesting: www.twdb
.state.tx.us/publications/reports/rainwaterharvestingmanual_3rdedition.pdf.

▶ FEMA Map Service Center: www.msc.fema.gov.

▶ USGS EarthExplorer: http://edcsns17.cr.usgs.gov/EarthExplorer/

▶ U.S. Fish and Wildlife Service: National Wetlands Inventory: www.fws.gov/wetlands/

▶ Clean Water Act Section 303(d) impairment lists compiled by state water-quality
agencies.

SOILS

Site Inventory and Analysis

▶ Research the site geology and subsoil conditions.

▶ Determine soil type and document characteristics, such as texture, bulk density,
pH, infiltration, drainage, erosion potential, and depth. Field check and map healthy
and degraded soils. Determine the areas to be protected and those best suited for
development.

▶ Investigate the site to determine if any soils are categorized as prime farmland,
unique farmland, or farmland of statewide importance by the NRCS.

Information Gathering

▶ Obtain Natural Resource Conservation Service soil maps of the site. In areas where
maps are not available, contact the local NRCS office for more information. Graded
areas will likely have missing or altered soil layers, typically A horizons. In areas where
significant grading/cut and and fill has occurred, subsoil horizons may also be absent
or severely disrupted. Field testing of site characteristics will be required.

▶ In greenfield areas where maps are not available, contact the local NRCS office for
more information. In areas described as "Urban Land Complex" or known to have
been graded, visit the site and determine areas of cut and fill by visual inspection.
These general assessments should be followed by on site soil testing. Refer to "Soils
in the Site Assessment" in Chapter 5 for more detailed guidance.

Design Considerations

► Geology influences a site's suitability for excavation, grading, wastewater disposal, stormwater management, pond construction, and other common landscape amenities.

► Healthy soils provide a variety of ecosystem services, such as water cleansing and storage, carbon sequestration, and habitat. Protecting healthy soils reduces restoration costs and improves plant performance. Areas of degraded soils should be considered first for design elements that require significant soil and vegetation disturbance.

► Prime farmland, unique farmland, and farmland with soils of statewide importance produce crops more efficiently than other soils requiring fewer inputs such as fuel, water, and fertilizers. The development of these unique and high-quality soils should be avoided.

Resources

► Natural Resource Conservation Service web soil survey: `http://websoilsurvey.nrcs.usda.gov/app/HomePage.htm`

► Natural Resource Conservation Service: Prime Farmland: `www.nrcs.usda.gov/technical/NRI/maps/prime.html`

VEGETATION

Site Inventory and Analysis

► Identify and map vegetative communities (i.e., woodland, tall grass prairie, riparian). Conduct a qualitative inventory to determine the health and quality of the community. Note wildlife species associated with the community. Record current maintenance and management practices. Identify areas to be protected or those suitable for development.

► Investigate the site for habitat that may support plant or animal threatened and endangered species.

► Survey existing site vegetation. Create a vegetative cover map that identifies (1) trees over 6" dbh or as required by local ordinance, (2) heritage or special status trees, (3) invasive species, and (4) other significant vegetation.

▶ Identify areas to be protected and those suitable for development. In addition, generate a general species list of dominant vegetation in the canopy, subcanopy, and herbaceous level. Include common and Latin names.

▶ Estimate the frequency or percent cover.

▶ Note any unusual or unique vegetation. Determine whether the vegetation is native to the region.

Information Gathering

▶ Conduct vegetative and wildlife surveys. Review aerial photos and satellite imagery. Local habitat mapping can often be found through the state system of higher education or regional "friends" groups that have collected and mapped habitat assemblies. Local state resources departments may also provide habitat feature information.

▶ Research federal and state threatened or endangered species lists. Contact local state agencies for guidelines on conducting species surveys and development requirements.

▶ Conduct vegetative surveys. Review aerial photos and satellite imagery.

▶ Map existing vegetation by parcels en masse, where possible by community. Note particular anomalies such as invasive species or prevalent old-growth species.

▶ General species lists for the site or parcel can be developed using the time meander approach. An evaluation of species composition can be developed using random quadrats.

▶ Woody and herbaceous species are typically measured separately.

Design Considerations

▶ Both urban and rural sites can provide a variety of plant and animal habitats. Look for opportunities to improve or restore habitat onsite or connect and extend surrounding areas of habitat. Avoid the development of threatened or endangered species habitat. Areas of low quality habitat should be considered first for design elements that require significant soil and vegetation disturbance

▶ Incorporating existing vegetation into the site design provides a variety of environmental and economic benefits. Look for opportunities to minimize disturbance and artfully incorporate existing vegetation into the design solution. Areas of degraded vegetation or invasive species should be considered first for design elements that require significant soil and vegetation disturbance.

Resources

▶ U.S. Geological Survey, Land Cover Institute: http://landcover.usgs.gov/

▶ U.S. Fish and Wildlife Service Endangered Species Program: www.fws.gov/endangered/

▶ USGS EarthExplorer: http://edcsns17.cr.usgs.gov/EarthExplorer/

MATERIALS

Site Inventory and Analysis

▶ Identify and map existing buildings and landscape materials, such as outdoor structures, roads, and pathways. Note the materials size, condition, and potential for reuse or recycling.

▶ Identify sources of locally extracted, manufactured, and/or processed and distributed construction materials

Information Gathering

▶ See site surveys and aerial and satellite imagery. Field check all surfaces and materials to determine conditions.

▶ A site and building deconstruction inventory will include: a list of the structures or components to be removed; material types, quantities, and dimensions; removal notes; existing finish and refurbishing actions required.

▶ Information on location of raw material extraction, manufacture, and processing is important to obtain. Many materials or products that are locally distributed may actually be produced far from a project site.

Design Considerations

▶ Reusing and recycling materials reduces the use of virgin natural resources, which in turn minimizes habitat destruction, waste generation, and air and water pollution. Throughout the design and construction processes, explore opportunities to reuse or recycle onsite materials.

▶ Use of locally extracted and manufactured materials can reduce transportation resource use and the associated pollution impacts.

Resources

▶ *Materials for Sustainable Sites*, Meg Calkins

▶ *Sustainable Landscape Construction*, Thompson and Sorvig

▶ Local building supply facilities

▶ Material and product manufacturers can identify locations of raw material extraction and manufacturing of their products.

CULTURAL INVENTORY

Site Inventory and Analysis

▶ Research the site's history and prior uses.

▶ Determine the locations of existing public infrastructure such as roads and utility networks.

▶ Identify project stakeholders.

▶ Document existing site uses and their associated user groups.

▶ Identify and map historical or cultural landscape features.

▶ Map characteristic site features that are unique or memorable such as rock outcroppings or view corridors.

▶ Identify potential or existing odors, noise pollution, or unsightly features that may be considered an annoyance

Information Gathering

▶ Interview property owners and neighbors. Research city and county records and historic aerial photos. Survey the site for indicators of previous use. Test soils for possible contamination.

▶ Contact local utility and transportation agencies and authorities.

▶ Work with neighborhood leaders and other local "experts" to identify individuals and groups that need to be involved in the design process.

▶ Observe the site during various times of the day.

▶ Interview neighbors, community leaders, and other project stakeholders. Contact historical commissions and associations.

► Determine the source of any odor and direction of prevailing winds. Use a sound level meter to measure the level of noises. Follow ASTM E1014-08, Standard Guide for Measurement of Outdoor A-Weighted Sound Levels, or similar standard noise measurements.

Design Considerations

► Understanding the site history and prior use is helpful in identifying conditions that may not be obvious or are unforeseen.

► Existing public infrastructure can influence the placement of items such as buildings and site entrance and egress locations.

► Site users and other stakeholders can provide unique insight and become active stewards of the site.

► Locations with a unique sense of place connect the community to the site and encourage stewardship. Look for opportunities to get project stakeholders involved in the design process and provide feedback on the site conditions and amenities they value.

► Existing landscape features that are loud or unsightly can have negative impacts on the site user's experience. Special attention should be given to the location of existing and planned equipment, such as HVAC systems. Locate design components, such as buildings or vegetation, to screen or block unwanted views and sounds.

Resources

► National Register of Historic Places: www.nps.gov/nr/

► National Trust for Historic Preservationwww.preservationnation.org/

► *With People in Mind*, Kaplan, Kaplan, and Ryan 1998

► *People Place*, Claire Cooper Marcus

SITE ANALYSIS

Site analyses interpret inventory information to identify areas best suited for specific uses, test the feasibility of the program plan, and provide a framework for design. The analysis is developed through a diagnostic process that cross-references the program plan with information generated in the site inventories. Optimal areas for programmatic elements are identified along with locations that may be too costly—environmentally, culturally, or economically—to develop.

A common site analysis method for synthesizing inventory data is to develop a series of informational maps—soil conditions, habitat type, zoning restrictions, or groundwater levels—that can be superimposed on top of one another and holistically examined. The overlays allow the design team to analyze the data in ways that reveal relationships and patterns between site conditions and opportunities and constraints. The maps can be generated on a transparent media and manually compiled or a more advanced and efficient geographic information system (GIS) can be used.

GIS is a powerful land planning and analysis tool that captures, manages, stores, integrates, analyzes, and displays data linked to a specific location. It can generate new information from existing data sources by revealing hidden trends that are not easily recognized in spreadsheets or statistical format. GIS enables the user to easily incorporate new information, evaluate design overlays, and run a variety of analytical operations. Information generated in GIS can be visually communicated with maps, charts, reports, and other features. GIS is compatible with programs such as AutoCAD and can utilize databases in a variety of formats.

TEAM DEVELOPMENT AND PLANNING STRATEGIES

Multidisciplinary Team

Design decisions create a cascade of outcomes that influence the site and surrounding area. This interrelationship of materials, systems, and spatial elements requires holistic thinking and a broad spectrum of expertise and skills that are best obtained through a multidisciplinary and integrated effort.

In order to create high-quality, sustainable landscapes, the design team should—at a minimum—include the client and professionals proficient in the local ecology and sustainable landscape design, construction, and maintenance practices. Depending on the unique criteria of the site and design program, additional expertise may be required. In some circumstances, one person may play multiple roles, such as a homeowner who is also the client and has the experience and interest in maintaining their landscape. Situations where one person serving multiple roles may impact quality control measures or generate conflicts of interest should be avoided.

ASSEMBLING THE DESIGN TEAM

The success of a project is largely dependent on the ability and commitment of the design team. Ideally, the team would be made up of professionals who specialize in sustainable solutions and have valuable project experience. In situations where this is not the case, sustainable outcomes can still be successfully achieved if the project team is carefully assembled and the expectations are clear (Mendler, Odell, and Lazarus 2006).

At a minimum, all team members should be competent professionals who meet the following criteria:

▶ Willingness to learn from others

▶ Positive attitude toward achieving an innovative project

▶ Comfortable with an integrative design process that questions conventional assumptions and tests new ideas

▶ Committed to going beyond minimum code performance and achieving sustainable outcomes

▶ Willingness to work collaboratively, navigate obstacles, and test new ideas (Kwok and Grondzik 2007; Mendler, Odell, and Lazarus 2006)

Team members who do not sincerely meet these criteria may stifle progress, prevent innovation, and increase time and overall project costs. Design teams with centrally aligned goals and expectations are more likely to create an enjoyable and beneficial professional experiences for all those involved, and may be better suited to create a successful project within budget parameters.

PROJECT STAKEHOLDERS AND COMMUNITY INVOLVEMENT

A stakeholder is a person or group that has an investment, share, or interest in a site or project. Common stakeholders include the client, site users, personnel, neighbors, and investment partners. They can provide unique insights into the current site conditions and opportunities for sustaining the health and productivity of the project over time. Neighborhood leaders and other local "experts" can help identify individuals and groups that need to be involved in the design process. Project teams should engage stakeholders in meaningful activities that consider the diverse range of values and opinions and look for design solutions that offer mutual benefits.

The Integrated Design Process

Integrated design is an iterative process of research and analysis, communication, and design exploration that collectively occurs between all team members throughout all phases of the project (7 Group and Reed 2009). Whereas the conventional design process is typically a linear approach comprised of a collection of discrete tasks often proceeding from owner to landscape architect to subconsultants to general contractor to subcontractor to site user, the integrated process encourages the multidisciplinary team to be collectively involved throughout the design process and utilizes the varying perspectives of team members to develop design solutions holistically. The process provides the necessary input and interaction required to recognize the relationship between the physical, biological, and cultural components of the site and to be more aware of the impacts of design decisions (Keeler and Burke 2009).

To establish a culture of integrated design, projects often begin with a charrette or other collaborative setting that creatively explores design options, uncovers areas of conflict, and establishes the project concept. Team members are expected to provide input and discuss areas beyond their conventional areas of expertise to help reveal how their work interacts with and affects other portions of the project. Bringing the multidisciplinary team together to explore the site's environmental and social systems can encourage synergy and the optimization of design solutions early in the process, thus limiting environmental impacts and saving time and money over the life of the project (Mendler, Odell, and Lazarus 2006).

Throughout the project, the design team should assemble often to share research and analysis findings, discuss options, discover new opportunities, and make design decisions. The team then separates to design and analyze in more detail with the intent of reassembling at the next juncture (7 Group and Reed 2009). This open dialogue can build trust and mutually supportive working relationships between team members.

In circumstances where the integrated design process requires higher design fees, the diverse problem-solving approach often leads to lower construction and reduced maintenance costs (Keeler and Burke 2009). For example, including the land care professional in the design process provides opportunities to discuss the maintenance requirements of proposed design solutions and adjust accordingly to eliminate unnecessary damage and long-term project costs. Input from the contractor may result in creative opportunities to reuse existing site structures and materials to reduce waste and speed up the construction process. Guidance from the ecologist can provide strategies for protecting healthy soil and vegetation during construction, resulting in improved site performance and avoided restoration and replacement costs.

The key to achieving an integrated design is to maintain coordination and collaboration between team members in all project phases. Even though the integrated design process actively seeks input of all team members, it is not design by committee (Yudelson 2009). A project manager who is involved in all aspects of the project is still necessary. However, it is important that the project manager act as more of a team leader and genuinely welcome input from all team members rather than as a sole decision maker. Giving all members of the team an opportunity to engage in the design process and vet concerns results in a significantly higher level of project ownership and commitment to achieving the project's goals and performance targets within budget (7 Group and Reed 2009).

Strategies for encouraging integrated design and multidisciplinary collaboration include:

▸ Develop consensus on the strategies and tools that will be used to share information and foster collaboration.

▸ Structure a project schedule to allow time for integrated design, reflection, and multi-disciplinary collaboration.

▸ Clarify and communicate the roles and responsibilities of each team member.

▸ Diagram the design process and create feedback loops at each design phase. Note where professionals will be collaborating and why.

▸ Develop consensus on the project goals and performance targets.

▸ Focus research, charrettes, and other collaborative design activities at the beginning of the design process. Encourage team members to explore design solutions from multiple perspectives and utilize team knowledge to create innovative solutions.

▸ Conduct regular team meetings scheduled around project milestones. Mandate active participation from all team members even in areas where they do not have a particular expertise. Look for overlapping benefits and opportunities across disciplines.

▸ Encourage interim meetings between team members to continue information sharing and collaboration.

▸ Sincerely solicit and integrate the input of other team members. View the diversity of opinions as an asset and use it to thoroughly analyze and explore design solutions.

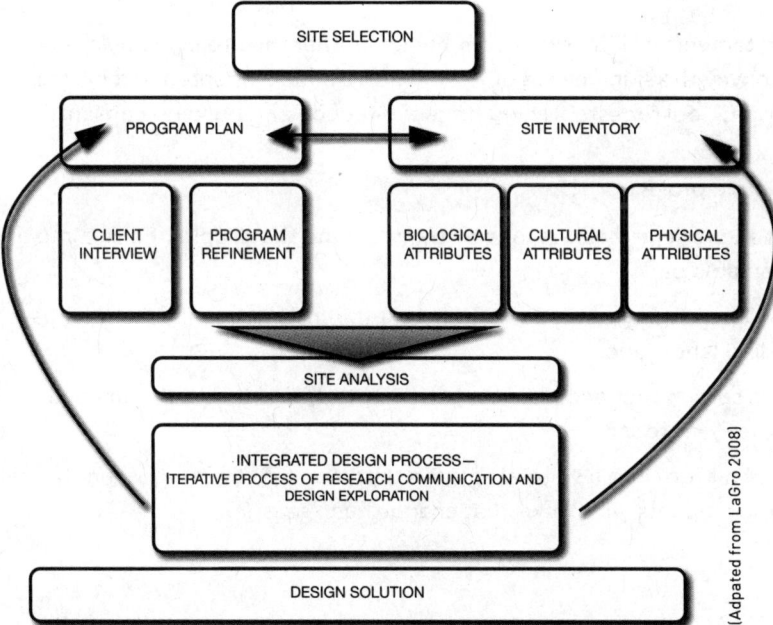

(Adpated from LaGro 2008)

FIGURE 2.1: The integrated design process is an iterative process of research, communication, and design exploration. Integrated design brings the project team together at important junctures to share research and analysis findings, discuss options, discover new opportunities, and make design decisions. Throughout the process, additional site inventory and analysis is often required, and the program plan may need to be revisited to accommodate new challenges or criteria that are revealed.

DEVELOPING PROJECT DIRECTION: PRINCIPLES, GOALS, AND PERFORMANCE TARGETS

Lack of alignment around a common purpose may create competing goals and priorities that impede the overall success of a project (7 Group and Reed 2009). Prior to starting the design process, it is important for all members of the project team to work together to define and support the values, goals, and performance targets that will guide a project. Providing clear direction can keep the project team focused and encourage collaboration, allowing design solutions to evolve more quickly.

Guiding Principles of a Sustainable Site

Guiding principles are commonly held values or fundamental beliefs that steer an organization, team, or individual's actions and decisions. They are applicable in all circumstances irrespective of leadership, constraints, or resources. Guiding principles establish broad expectations and can be used in a variety of circumstances ranging from the selection of a site or project team to directing individual design decisions. The principles can also be used as a tool to measure success. Principles established by the Sustainable Site Initiative to inform its work and all aspects of sustainable site development are listed in Chapter 1 of this book.

Project Goals

Goals are meaningful statements of intent that communicate what the project should realistically achieve. They convey the significance of a project, are action-oriented and measurable. Goal-setting is a useful tool for establishing project direction and building consensus among team members.

Below are some example project goals:

▶ Increase tourism and reduce maintenance by transforming the dilapidated site into a vibrant and sustainable park.

▶ Design a safe and challenging outdoor environment for children to play that blends into the surrounding landscape.

▶ Create a backyard setting that encourages the family to spend time outdoors and connect with nature year round.

▶ Transform the asphalt roof into a vegetated oasis that reduces stormwater runoff and provides building occupants with views that change each season.

Performance Targets

In addition to the project goals, the team should establish performance targets to fully define and clarify desired outcomes and project success. The targets are specific performance goals related to site sustainability that are developed at the onset of a project and agreed upon by the entire team. Performance targets should challenge the team to go beyond standard design criteria and reach a higher level of site performance and sustainable outcomes. Once the performance targets are established, oversight of specific targets can be assigned to team members to track progress and champion attainment. The targets serve as common starting points for the design team and may need to be adjusted as the project progresses.

Below are some example performance targets:

▶ Reuse or recycle 100 percent of the existing materials and vegetation on site.

▶ Reduce potable water use by 75 percent of the established baseline.

▶ Preserve and protect 90 percent of the trees over 6˝ dbh.

▶ Limit disturbance to 15 percent of the project area.

▶ Reduce stormwater runoff by 90 percent

Green rating certification programs such as SITES or LEED have established targets and specific documentation requirements to demonstrate criteria have been met. Whether or not a project is pursuing certification, review of these targets can be helpful in establishing realistic and challenging goals.

Projects hoping to achieve certification should be familiar with the necessary parameters from the onset of the project and clarify the roles and responsibilities of team members for documentation and certification. Deciding to pursue certification later in the design process generally leads to increased time and costs. Design teams should avoid selecting performance targets based solely on their point value and the short-term goal of certification. Instead, they should focus on design of sustainable site systems.

Program Plan

A design solution that does not address the needs of the client is just as ill-suited as one that does not properly fit the conditions of the site (Booth 1990). Clear communication and a thorough understanding of the desires and concerns of the client are key to a successful project. The program plan is a written description of the characteristics and requirements the design solution must satisfy. The program clearly articulates the expectations of the client and guides the design team. It is important to recognize sustainability as a necessary and integral component of the program plan. If a program does not directly address the desire to meet sustainable outcomes, it is unlikely the project will fulfill the requirements (Williams 2007).

The plan should be revisited throughout design and construction to ensure the project is progressing as envisioned. It is often necessary to revise the program to accommodate new challenges or criteria revealed by the design process. Any revisions should be discussed and agreed upon by the design team. It is important to remember that the client is part of the design team and important to the overall buy-in and long-term success of the project.

Client Interview

The client interview is the first step in developing the program plan and includes feedback from the client, site users, and additional project stakeholders.

The following items should be discussed with the client and clearly documented:

- ▶ Project purpose—Identify why the project is being built. What is it the clients would like to accomplish?

- ▶ Key decision makers—Identify the individuals who will make the final decisions. Discuss how they will be involved in the design process.

- ▶ Site users—Identify the site users, their ages, and any special requirements.

- ▶ Design elements and activities—Make a list of the elements and activities site users need or desire. Outline the minimum and maximum requirements of each element and prioritize the list. It is important to stay focused on the desired function of the site and not get sidetracked with design options.

- ▶ Health benefits—Identify the health benefits—physical, mental, and social—the design solution should offer.

- ▶ Environmental concerns—Identify any regional or site-specific environmental concerns the design solution needs to address.

- ▶ Aesthetic preferences—Discuss the design style and aesthetic preferences of the client. To help clients communicate their preferences, it can be helpful to provide visual examples. The intent is not to find a design solution but to gain an understanding of the client's definition of beauty.

- ▶ Maintenance—Outline the maintenance expectations. How much time and money would the client like to spend maintaining the site? Is the client interested in physical activity benefits of doing the maintenance? Will the client or someone else carry out the maintenance? How much maintenance is considered reasonable in a given month? Identify any maintenance activities the client would like to avoid, such as pesticide use or lawn mowing.

▶ Budget—Identify the overall budget for the project separating the initial investment, future phases, operations, and ongoing maintenance. The budget should be realistically taken into account, however, should not limit creativity. Ongoing dialogue with the client about the design solutions and their associated costs and benefits will be needed throughout the design process.

Information gathered during the client interview should be checked by the client for accuracy and shared with the design team. Collaboratively, the team should review and discuss the interview and initial site inventory. During this meeting the team should also identify additional tasks or research necessary to support program refinement and assign items to appropriate team members. Because no new information is being generated, it is probably not necessary for the client to be part of this discussion.

Program Refinement

During program refinement, the project team should work with the client to define the project direction and potential in greater detail. The opportunities and constraints of the site should be discussed as well as project goals and performance targets. Development of this final portion of the program plan typically includes the client, all members of the integrated design team, and any additional site users or stakeholders. A workshop is often a good setting for this activity.

The following items should be thoroughly discussed and documented:

▶ Site issues—Discuss the findings of the initial site inventory and analysis. Identify any existing site issues that require careful evaluation and assign appropriate team members with gathering the information. If needed, discuss portions of the program that are not a good match or suitable for the site without major site changes or extensive resource use or maintenance.

▶ Project goals—Establish project goals. Goals are broad statements of intent describing what the project should realistically achieve.

▶ Performance targets—List the performance targets the team is striving to achieve. Discuss which team members will champion the successful attainment of the performance targets.

▶ Client interview—Review the information gathered in the client interview and determine whether any revisions need to be made due to recent discussions.

The finalized program plan can provide clear direction and vision to keep the project focused as it evolves. Because the entire team has discussed key issues and developed clear direction, the project can unfold more rapidly, saving both time and money.

Inspiring the Client

Clients and citizens are becoming increasingly aware of the benefits of green building and as a result are incorporating sustainability into their definition of project success. According to a survey of 381 firms conducted by the American Society of Landscape Architects, 96 percent of clients were knowledgeable or interested in sustainable design. The driving factors for wanting to incorporate sustainability into projects were reduced utility and maintenance costs; government regulation, code, or construction standards; marketing cachet; and reducing environmental harm (American Society of Landscape Architects 2009).

Design teams and their attitude toward sustainable design can strongly influence the desires and expectations of the client. Teams should provide the information necessary to help clients feel comfortable with green building practices and inspire clients to go beyond regulated standards. Initial client meetings are an opportunity to gain an understanding of the client's sustainable design knowledge and interest as well as beginning an ongoing dialogue about the environmental and health benefits landscapes can provide to site users and the surrounding region. Clients should be engaged in the design process and brainstorming of sustainable design solutions. In many instances, it can be helpful to visit or provide examples of other sustainable projects.

References

7 Group and B. Reed. 2009. *The Integrative Design Guide to Green Building*. Hoboken, NJ: John Wiley and Sons.

American Society of Landscape Architects. 2009. *Positive Economic News Continues for Landscape Architecture Firms*. Press release, October 21, 2009.

Booth, N. 1990. *Basic Elements of Landscape Architecture Design*. Prospect Heights, IL: Waveland Press.

Costanza, Robert, Ralph d'Arge, Rudolf de Groot, Stephen Farberk, Monica Grasso, Bruce Hannon, Karin Limburg, Shahid Naeem, Robert V. O'Neill, Jose Paruelo, Robert G. Raskin, Paul Sutton, and Marjan van den Belt. 1997. "The Value of the World's Ecosystem Services and Natural Capital." *Nature*, 387 (May 15): 253–260.

Keeler, M., and B. Burke. 2009. *Fundamentals of Integrated Design for Sustainable Building*. Hoboken, NJ: John Wiley and Sons.

Kwok, A.W., and W. Grondzik. 2007. *The Green Studio Handbook: Environmental Strategies for Schematic Design*. New York: Architectural Press.

LaGro, J.A. 2008. *Site Analysis: A Contextual Approach to Sustainable Land Planning and Site Design*. Hoboken, NJ: John Wiley and Sons.

Mendler, S., W. Odell, and M.A. Lazarus. 2006. *The HOK Guidebook to Sustainable Design*. Hoboken, NJ: John Wiley & Sons.

National Resources Conservation Service (NRCS). 2010a. "National Soil Survey Handbook." Available at `http://soils.usda.gov/technical/handbook/contents/part622.html` (accessed December 19, 2010).

_____. 2010b. "Prime Farmland." Available at www.nrcs.usda.gov/technical/NRI/maps/prime.html (accessed October 12, 2010).

Sustainable Cities Institute. 2010. "Urban Infill: Overview." Available at www.sustainablecitiesinstitute.org/view/page.basic/class/feature.class/Lesson_Urban_Infill_Overview (accessed December 19, 2010).

U.S. Environmental Protection Agency. 2010a. "Brownfields and Land Revitalization." Available at www.epa.gov/brownfields/index.html (accessed December 12, 2010).

_____. 2010b. "Wetlands Research." Available at www.epa.gov/ecology/quick-finder/wetlands-research.htm (accessed December 12, 2010).

Williams, D.E. 2007. *Sustainable Design: Ecology, Architecture, and Planning.* Hoboken, NJ: John Wiley and Sons.

Yudelson, J. 2009. *Green Building through Integrated Design.* New York: McGraw-Hill Companies, Inc.

CHAPTER 3

SITE DESIGN: WATER

▶ Alfred Vick, John Calabria, Stuart Echols, Michael Ogden, and David Yocca

UNDISTURBED NATURAL LANDSCAPES PROVIDE clean freshwater, infiltrate rainfall, and prevent excessive erosion. Sustainable site development must protect, restore, or replicate processes of *natural* water systems including the infiltration, evaporation, transpiration, and runoff that occur in undisturbed landscapes. It must also protect natural water resources and aquatic habitats. Constructed landscapes, and the buildings and surfaces within them, should be functional participants in the hydrologic cycle by integrating hydrologic function and appropriate site water balance with other design goals.

The central aim of water design for sustainable sites is to integrate water, vegetation, and soil systems to manage, protect, and restore this critical natural resource. We are both dependent on and subject to water, hydrologic processes, and the ecosystem services that they provide. When water resources are valued, protected, and well managed, human communities benefit. Ignorance or mismanagement of water resources can contribute to many serious problems, such as flooding, aquifer depletion, water pollution, ecosystem degradation, and many other impacts.

Water systems are complex, and when we change one thing in a complex system there will always be changes that occur somewhere else in the system. Impacts or modifications from human intervention made in one part of a water system (e.g., consumption, development, or modifications to water bodies) can have impacts "downstream" in another part of the system. These impacts are not always easily predicted or well understood and have resulted in some negative outcomes. Table 3-1 lists some impacts that water consumption and site development can have on water systems and it highlights solutions discussed in this chapter that can be employed to reduce and even reverse these impacts.

TABLE 3-1: Human Impacts on Water Systems and Approaches to Mitigate Them

IMPACTS	CAUSES	SOLUTIONS (DESCRIBED LATER IN THIS CHAPTER)
Water Quality Degradation Increased pollutant load, including: sediment, nutrients, heavy metals, pathogens, temperature, anthropogenic constituents Degraded aquatic habitat Degraded human use potential, including: recreation, food supply, visual and other sensory enjoyment	Nonpoint source pollution: chemicals, pollutants, heavy metals that gather on impervious surfaces such as roofs and pavement, heated impervious surfaces that warm rainwater, polluted runoff, agriculture, golf courses, lawns, and feed lots Point source pollution: discharges from industrial, municipal, or other point sources	*Practices that reduce runoff* will reduce pollutant load mobilized by stormwater. *Practices that mitigate runoff by mimicking evapotranspiration and infiltration* will remove pollutants from runoff by creating contact between water, soil, and vegetation. *Practices that convey runoff from large events* may provide additional treatment through conveyance stormwater control measures. *Practices that protect or restore receiving water bodies* help to provide resilience, stability, and multiple-use opportunities (such as recreation) associated with water resources.
Stream Channel Degradation Geomorphic instability resulting in excessive erosion or deposition Disconnection of stream and active floodplain Potential threat to life, limb, and property Degraded aquatic habitat	Increased stormwater discharge rate, volume, frequency, and duration from higher-density impervious development and traditional detention systems Mechanical alteration of stream channels, riparian areas, and floodplains through: straightening, filling, moving, removing vegetation, etc.	*Practices that reduce runoff* will help to maintain or restore predevelopment runoff volume. *Practices that mitigate runoff by mimicking evapotranspiration and infiltration* will help to maintain or restore predevelopment runoff volume. *Practices that convey runoff from large events* will help to maintain or restore predevelopment runoff rate. *Practices that protect or restore receiving water bodies* may help preserve natural drainage patterns and connectivity.
Reduced Water Supply Reduced groundwater supply Limited surface water supply Increasing demand for potable water Increasing cost for water treatment, infrastructure, and supply Loss of soil moisture which affects temperature, local climate, and habitat	Population growth and sprawling development patterns drive increasing demand Impervious surface associated with development: • Reduce groundwater recharge • Reduce baseflow of streams • Degrade water quality forcing higher levels of treatment • May overwhelm stormwater infrastructure and exacerbate ecological and human impacts	*Practices that reduce runoff* reduce pressure on stormwater infrastructure and may recharge groundwater. *Practices that mitigate runoff by mimicking evapotranspiration and infiltration* reduce pressure on stormwater infrastructure and recharge groundwater. *Practices that convey runoff from large events* can be more cost-effective than conventional infrastructure. *Practices that protect or restore receiving water bodies* will help protect water quality and water supply. *Practices that maximize the use of vegetated systems* balance soil moisture, moderate local climate, and support healthy habitat.

ACCELERATING DEVELOPMENT AND DETERIORATING STORMWATER

According to the U.S. Department of Agriculture, over 2 million acres of rural land are being lost to development each year (U.S. Department of Agriculture 2000). Likewise, according to a study by the Chesapeake Bay Foundation, in the greater Washington, DC, region alone, 800,000 more acres will be developed in the next 30 years resulting in detrimental effects on the Chesapeake Bay's ecosystems (Chesapeake Bay Foundation n.d.). Development can increase runoff as much as 5 to 10 times over predevelopment conditions (Coffman 2001). This runoff includes pollutants from a variety of nonpoint sources including sediment, heavy metals, toxic chemicals, nutrients, grease, and oils. Parking lots generate almost 16 times more nonpoint source runoff than a meadow of comparable land area (U.S. Department of Housing and Urban Development 2000). Numerous studies have identified alarming levels of stream degradation as a direct result of such pollution. With renewal of the Clean Water Act and the subsequent National Pollutant Elimination System, thousands of municipal governments are required to develop, adopt, and implement strategies to reduce nonpoint source pollution.

It is clear that ecology, water quality, and runoff volume, agricultural productivity, and quality of life are linked by our land-use practices. Future development should be channeled to previously developed or infill sites in order to maintain the benefits of greenfield land and to minimize resource consumption. Good land-use planning is an important component of a comprehensive approach to stormwater management.

(Source: Stuart Echols)

FIGURE 3-1: Typical "old-school" single-goal detention design that does not address environmental concerns, community impacts, or property values.

Given that all outcomes cannot be predicted in complex systems, human intervention must work within natural water systems to modify them as little as possible or to restore them. Changes to natural water systems should be limited, and changes that are unavoidable should be mitigated. Sustainable stormwater management needs to reinitiate the long-term environmental processes that occurred before the land was developed and the processes were disturbed. It should:

▶ Preserve and restore the interaction of rainfall, vegetation, and soil

▶ Promote onsite infiltration of rainfall and runoff

▶ Protect or improve surface water quality

▶ Promote groundwater recharge

▶ Maintain predevelopment streambank baseflow

▶ Cleanse wastewater onsite

▶ Reuse or infiltrate wastewater onsite

▶ Minimize use of potable water

▶ Capture and reuse rainwater, graywater, and treated blackwater onsite

Sustainable water systems are an important part of ensuring responsible water management and protecting the quality of our natural and built environments. Decisions about sustainable water systems—be it stormwater management, wastewater management, or water use for buildings and landscape—must be considered holistically. When viewed as a connected system of water supply and demand, rather than discrete and independent uses, many opportunities may be identified to eliminate waste, reuse or recycle byproducts, assign the appropriate type of water for a particular use, and integrate natural processes.

Holistic consideration of water systems demands integrated design and should involve multiple experts, such as: landscape architects, architects, civil engineers, mechanical engineers, geotechnical engineers, hydrologists, ecologists, and many others. It will also involve owners, users, operators, and other project stakeholders who will be connected to and responsible for the site and buildings on a daily basis.

This chapter addresses water systems for sustainable site design. It provides principles, strategies, and technologies for sustainable stormwater management approaches, onsite treatment of wastewater, and water resource conservation. While these aspects of a water system are linked, for the purposes of this chapter they have been organized into three discrete sections.

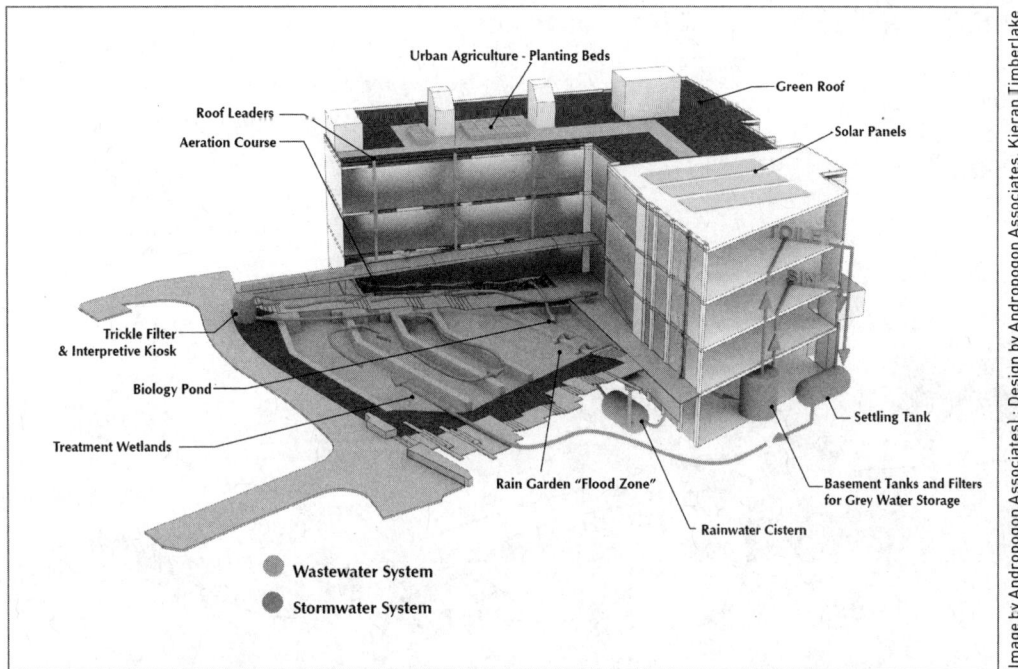

(Image by Andropogon Associates); Design by Andropogon Associates, Kieran Timberlake Associates and Living Systems International

FIGURE 3-2: The water system at the Sidwell Friends School is an example of a holistically designed water system incorporating rainwater retention, harvesting, reuse, and onsite wastewater treatment.

A PRIMER ON THE WATER CYCLE

The water cycle is the continuous recycling of water, evaporating from the oceans, circulating through the atmosphere, precipitating on the landscape, and flowing back to the oceans. The cycle remains in balance on a global scale but is often altered on a site and regional scale as precipitation is diverted from its natural flow paths of infiltration, evapotranspiration, and surface runoff. Developed landscapes interrupt the water cycle and alter specific components such as filtration, infiltration, evapotranspiration, surface storage, recharge, and stream flow. Some of the greatest impacts from development occur during small storms, the 95th percentile storm event and below. It is these small storms which carry the majority of nonpoint source pollution from impervious surfaces and account for the majority of lost groundwater recharge due to the roofs, pavements and pipes of the built environment.

continues

A PRIMER ON THE WATER CYCLE (CONTINUED)

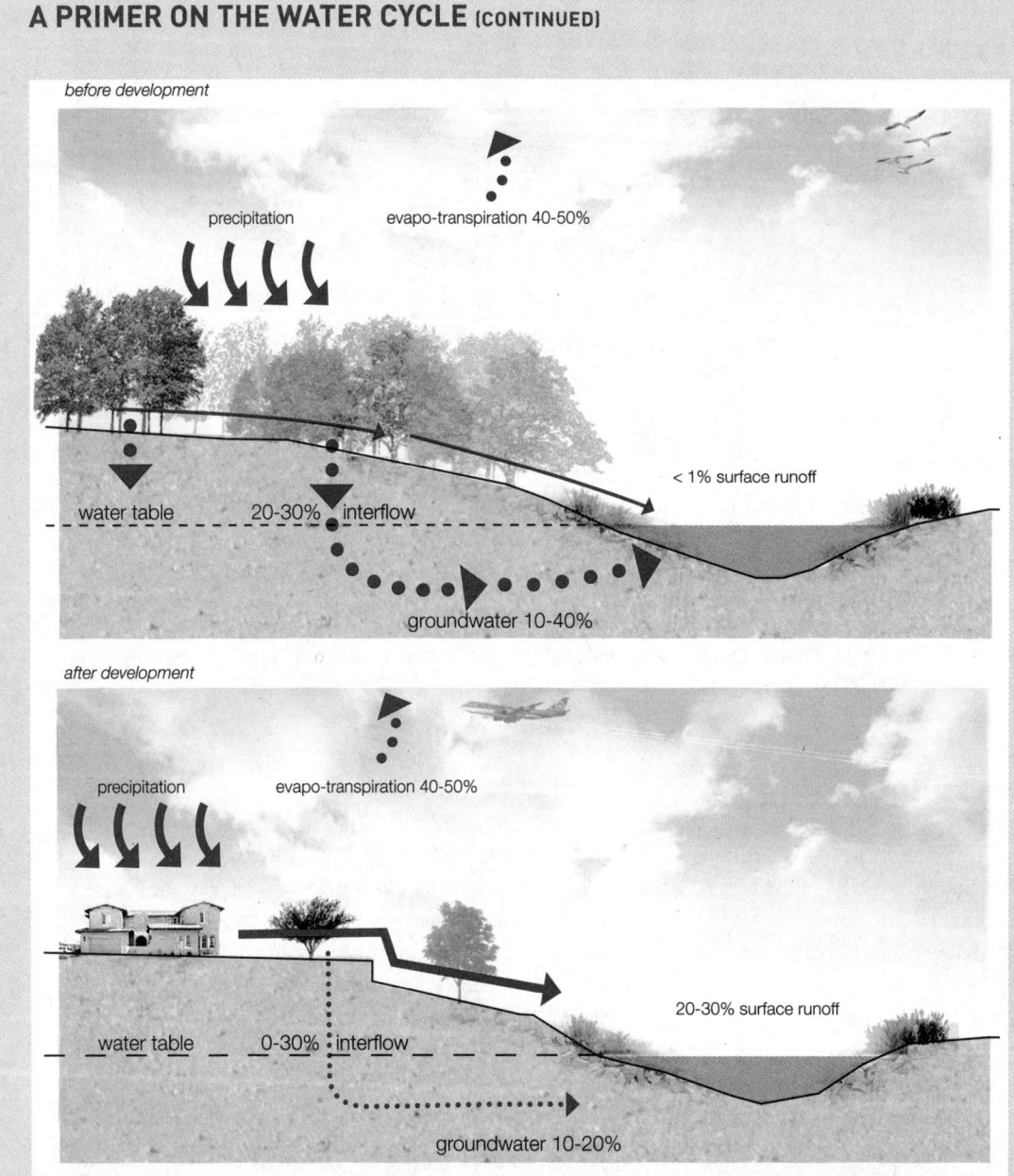

before development

precipitation

evapo-transpiration 40-50%

water table

20-30% interflow

< 1% surface runoff

groundwater 10-40%

after development

precipitation

evapo-transpiration 40-50%

water table

0-30% interflow

20-30% surface runoff

groundwater 10-20%

Source: Stuart Echols; Drawn by Simon Bussiere

FIGURE 3-3: Before development almost all rainfall is taken up by plants (transpiration), evaporates, or infiltrates through the ground. After conventional development, surface runoff increases significantly while evapotranspiration and infiltration decrease.

Precipitation is water released from clouds in the form of rain, freezing rain, sleet, snow, or hail. It is the primary connection in the water cycle that provides for the delivery of atmospheric water to Earth.

Stream flow is water discharge that occurs in a natural channel. A more general term than runoff, stream flow may be applied to discharge whether or not it is affected by diversion or regulation.

Evaporation is the process of liquid water becoming water vapor, including vaporization from water surfaces, land surfaces, and snow fields but not from leaf surfaces.

Transpiration is the process of liquid water becoming water vapor through movement through and off of vegetation, including vaporization from leaf surfaces.

Evapotranspiration is the sum of evaporation and transpiration from soil, plants, and water bodies.

Groundwater is water that flows or seeps downward and saturates soil or rock, supplying springs and wells. The upper surface of the saturate zone is called the water table.

Groundwater recharge is inflow of water to a groundwater reservoir from the surface. Infiltration of precipitation and its movement to the water table is one form of natural recharge.

Base flow is sustained flow of a stream in the absence of direct runoff. It includes natural and human-induced stream flows. Natural base flow is sustained largely by groundwater discharges.

First flush is the initial surface runoff from impervious surfaces with high proportions of concentrated pollution compared to the remainder of the storm.

Interflow is the lateral movement of water through soil in the upper part of the unsaturated zone. It directly enters a stream channel without having occurred first as surface runoff.

Nonpoint source pollution is contamination that occurs when rainwater, snowmelt, or irrigation washes off plowed fields, city streets, rooftops, or suburban backyards.

Infiltration is the process by which rainwater on the ground surface enters the soil. **Recharge** is the process where rainwater moves downward from surface water to groundwater.

Excess runoff is the water flow that occurs when land is sealed or saturated and water from rainfall or snowmelt drains away.

SUSTAINABLE STORMWATER MANAGEMENT

Stormwater and the Natural Water Cycle

Natural landscapes gather, absorb, hold, and release rainwater much like a sponge, effectively controlling floods, recharging groundwater, and sustaining diverse ecosystems. Natural landscapes manage rainfall through processes of evapotranspiration, infiltration, and runoff. While the role each of these systems plays differs greatly with varying rainfall levels and different regions, these three processes occur in some form everywhere rain falls and are fundamental to the health of all ecosystems. In the eastern deciduous forests of the United States, evapotranspiration dissipates nearly half of all annual rainfall under natural conditions, and adequate infiltration levels are critical resources to groundwater recharge and stream base flow, as shown in Figure 3-4.

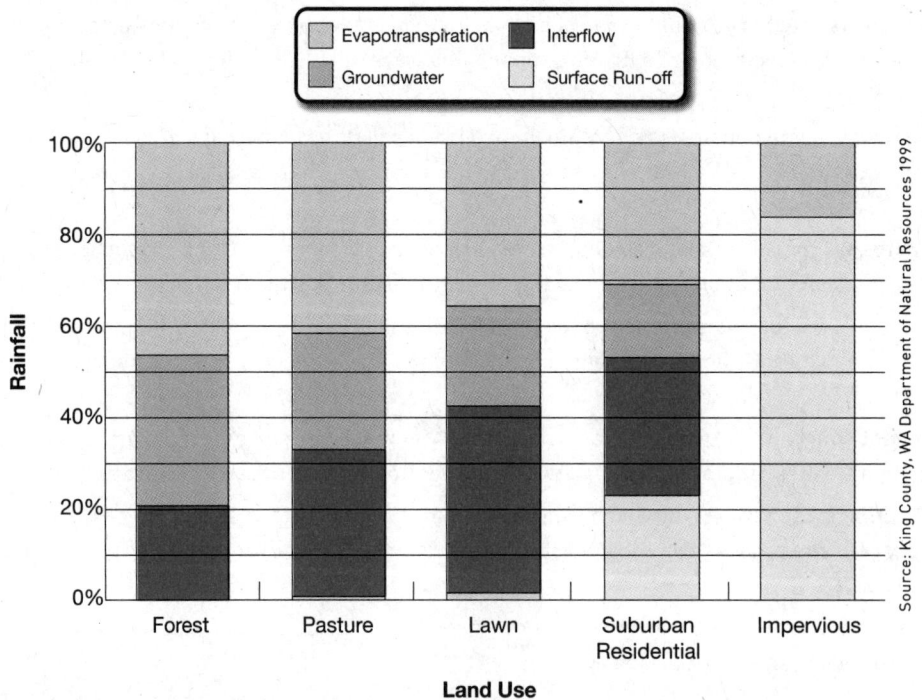

FIGURE 3-4: Comparison of annual levels of evapotranspiration, groundwater recharge, surface runoff, and interflow under different development conditions. As land uses are intensified, surface water runoff increases and evapotranspiration is diminished.

In all regions of the country, the most frequent rainfall events are small. For example, 95 percent of the storm events in Portland, OR, are less than 1.0 in. of rainfall; in Atlanta, GA, 95 percent are less than 1.8 in.; in Phoenix, AZ, 95 percent are less than 1.0 in. In most regions, small storms account for the majority of annual rainfall volume and carry the vast majority of nonpoint source pollution, as shown in Figure 3-5.

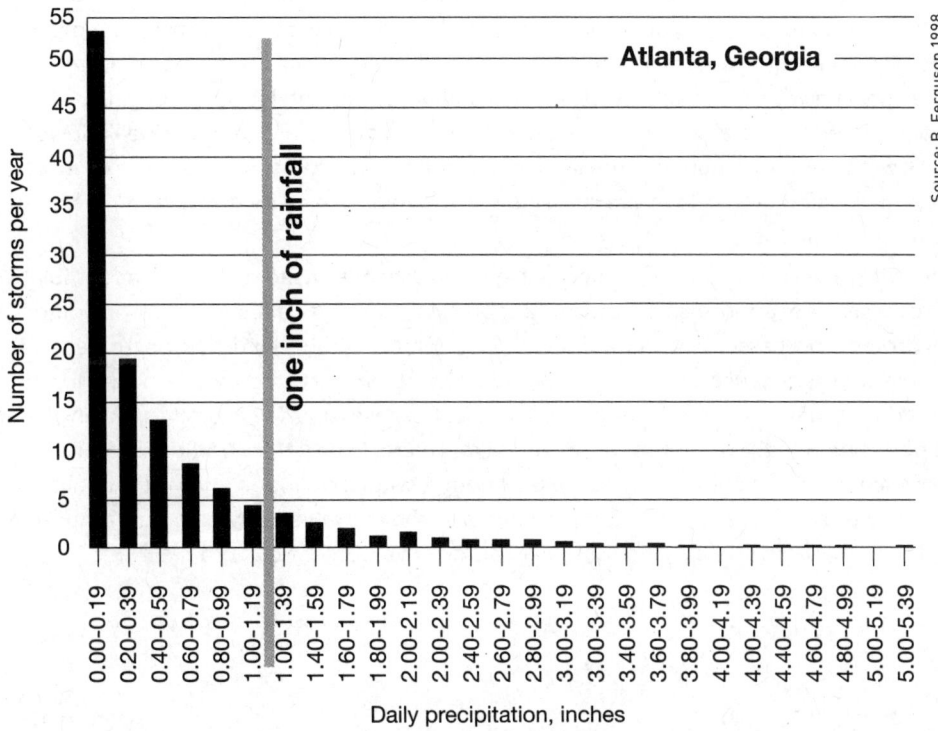

FIGURE 3-5: Daily precipitation for Atlanta grouped according to intensity shows that the vast majority of annual rainfall occurs in small storm events.

Traditional Stormwater Management Practices

Traditional stormwater management practices have historically been designed around a drainage system's ability to quickly convey a storm's peak flow. The goals of this approach were not to simply calculate the maximum expected runoff rate and design infrastructure accordingly. Instead, the problems created downstream by conveyance systems, such as flash flooding, forced stormwater professionals to begin using detention structures to detain and release urban runoff at rates that did not exceed predevelopment peak flow rates.

Stormwater detention is based on the idea that downstream property can be protected from flooding by controlling the rate of runoff discharged to streams so that increased stormwater runoff caused by urban development does not exceed the existing flow rates before development. These systems only control flow rates and are not intended to address runoff quality or additional runoff volume. Rather, they are intended to satisfy the anthropocentric needs of human development without addressing larger ecological issues. Although the term "zero runoff" may imply that there is no runoff or that there is no net change in the stormwater system, this management system actually allows unlimited increases in total runoff *volumes* while extending the duration of flows as long as necessary to control the peak flow *rates*. This detention-based method is widely accepted in this country as standard practice for dealing with increased runoff from urban development. However, because such systems do not address total water volume, flooding often occurs as extended peak flows combine downstream. Alternatively, the landscape is generally dewatered as the volume of water that was traditionally held in the landscape is allowed to migrate downstream, resulting in drought conditions.

These traditional stormwater management systems are not based on and do not emulate natural processes of evapotranspiration, infiltration, and runoff. As a result, far from aiding natural hydrologic processes, these traditional management methods further destroyed healthy ecosystems, because the true environmental problems created by urban development are reduced infiltration and evaporation, not just excess runoff. Generally speaking, excess runoff is merely the symptom of the actual problem. In addition, traditional stormwater management practices did not address nonpoint source pollution and water quality issues because they did not try to limit the changes to the stormwater system but rather to solve the problem of downstream flooding caused by development (Figure 3-6).

FIGURE 3-6: Contrast between rainfall converted from evapotranspiration, infiltration, and runoff to all surface runoff by impervious surface.

Sustainable Stormwater Design Practices

The objective of sustainable stormwater management is to create a system that manages stormwater by emulating the predevelopment water cycle through retaining, evaporating, and infiltrating the excess runoff created by impervious surfaces in small distributed systems. Examples of these collection mechanisms include, but are not limited to, green roofs, bioretention facilities, rainwater harvesting systems, or any other features that allow water to infiltrate and evaporate. These holding systems can be sized and engineered to slow, cool, cleanse, and infiltrate/evapotranspire runoff volume equal to the predevelopment level of the natural landscape (Table 3-2).

TABLE 3-2: Benefits of Sustainable Stormwater Management

Reduce onsite and downstream flooding—Runoff can be collected, held onsite, and then released slowly by a variety of detention methods including conventional dry basins, wet ponds, extended detention basins, extended detention ponds, and multiple pond systems.

Reduce flooding caused by combining detained runoff—Distributing stormwater into small retention and infiltration systems will help lower the amount is water released downstream and reduces combined detention runoff.

Lower site and regional stormwater systems cost—Stormwater management systems can be designed to allow for smaller detention systems and systems that are easier to maintain because of reduced mowing, potentially reducing infrastructure and lowering cost.

Lower peak storm flow frequency and duration—Bioretention, infiltration, and water harvesting systems can reduce the duration of elevated stream flows by capturing water onsite, which will also reduce the frequency of local nuisance flooding.

Reduce soil erosion, stream siltation, and downstream scouring—Reducing the duration, frequency, and volume of peak flows with retention and infiltration will also reduce soil erosion, stream siltation, and stream-bank scouring.

Reduce nonpoint source and thermal pollution—Rainwater diverted into bioretention, infiltration, and water harvesting systems also diverts nonpoint source pollution away from streams, wetlands, ponds, and lakes, as well as lowing thermal pollution during summer months.

Replenish groundwater—Distributed stormwater infiltration systems can recharge groundwater in most all soil conditions with proper preventive precautions taken to prevent groundwater contamination.

Supplement domestic water supply—Rainwater can be directed from impervious surfaces directly into planted areas to maximize use of water for irrigating plants. It can also be harvested from impervious surfaces and stored in cisterns or harvesting ponds for domestic uses such as irrigation, toilet flushing, and building sprinkler systems.

continues

TABLE 3-2: Benefits of Sustainable Stormwater Management *(continued)*

Restore low stream base flow—Rainwater that is frequently collected and allowed to infiltrate will replenish groundwater storage, which will then in turn restore nearby stream base flows and wetlands water levels during times of drought.

Improve aesthetics—Stormwater design can provide enhanced public experience of beauty and pleasure through effective compositional treatment of the water trail and even the sound of moving water.

Enhance recreational opportunities—Designs can be created that allow people to interact with the stormwater system in different ways from using a dry detention area for play between storms, or design systems in ways that are relaxing, amusing, or simply allow people to follow an enticing water trail.

Provide wildlife habitat—Open space and wildlife habitat can be created by designing stormwater systems with wet detention ponds and wetlands rich with riparian plants.

Improve safety—Danger associated with stormwater can be mitigated by dispersing water into small shallow systems or providing barriers to access if needed.

Maintain appropriate soil moisture—Soil moisture and habitat can be maintained within the rhyzosphere by maximizing vegetated surfaces and root mass both on roof surfaces and at ground level, resulting in generally cooler ambient temperatures in warmer weather.

Evapotranspiration and infiltration are important ecological processes widely recognized in evolving stormwater design, and as a result these methods are gaining popular acceptance as practical design solutions. This is partly due to the shortcomings of past stormwater management methods but more commonly an overriding acceptance that retention and infiltration can be realistic methods for managing stormwater. Most of these gains have come about by new understandings that traditional systems addressed excess stormwater runoff as a hazard that should be collected, treated, and removed rather than as a valuable resource that could potentially benefit ecosystems, reduce costs, and enhance communities. It is critical that stormwater management professionals continue to implement sustainable stormwater management practices to eliminate excess surface water runoff and restore natural hydrologic function to our landscapes.

Because small rain events are most common and contain the most pollutants, designers can emphasize capturing and treating the first flush of runoff from frequent small rain events when managing runoff for water quality. Furthermore, if first-flush runoff volume is diverted and retained through the integration of green roofs, porous pavement, and bioretention facilities, downstream flooding and ecological degradation can be reduced. The first flush is typically defined as the runoff from small storms between 0.5 and 1.5 in. that are responsible for about 75 percent of the pollutant discharge in stormwater (Pitt 1999).

Figures 3-7 through 3-9 suggest how precipitation changes to runoff and interacts with the site and the receiving waters. The natural flow path (Figure 3-7) represents the presettlement condition and serves as the baseline for interventions shown in the other flow paths. The conventional flow path (Figure 3-8) illustrates how conventional development practices divert precipitation from infiltrating into the ground, but rather collect and release it in a rate- or quantity-controlled detention system. This conventional flow path minimizes hydrologic function critical to sustaining the environment. The SITES flow path (Figure 3-9) illustrates that functions such as interception, infiltration, and increased time of concentration can be accomplished by site design and techniques that emulate predevelopment hydrology and reduce constituents and pollutants.

FIGURES 3-7 AND 3-8: Comparison of natural stormwater flow paths with conventional stormwater management flow paths.

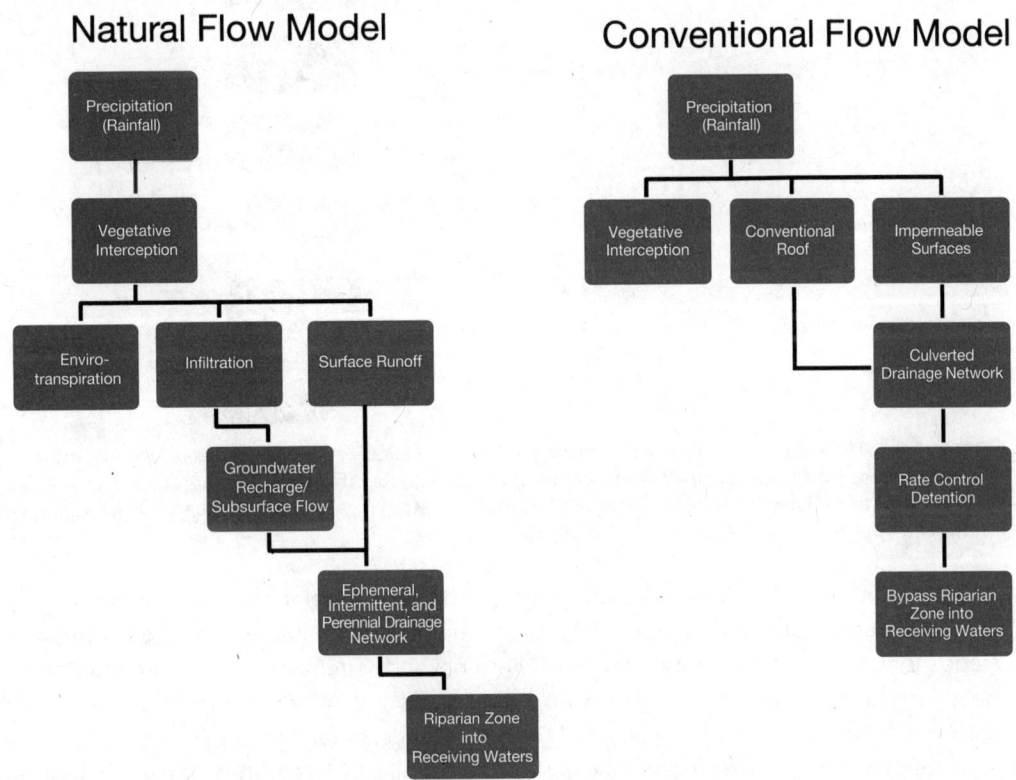

FIGURE 3-7: The natural flow path represents the presettlement condition and serves as the baseline for interventions shown in the other flow paths.

FIGURE 3-8: The conventional flow path illustrates how conventional development practices divert precipitation from infiltrating into the ground, but rather collect and release it in a rate- or quantity-controlled detention system.

SITES Flow Model

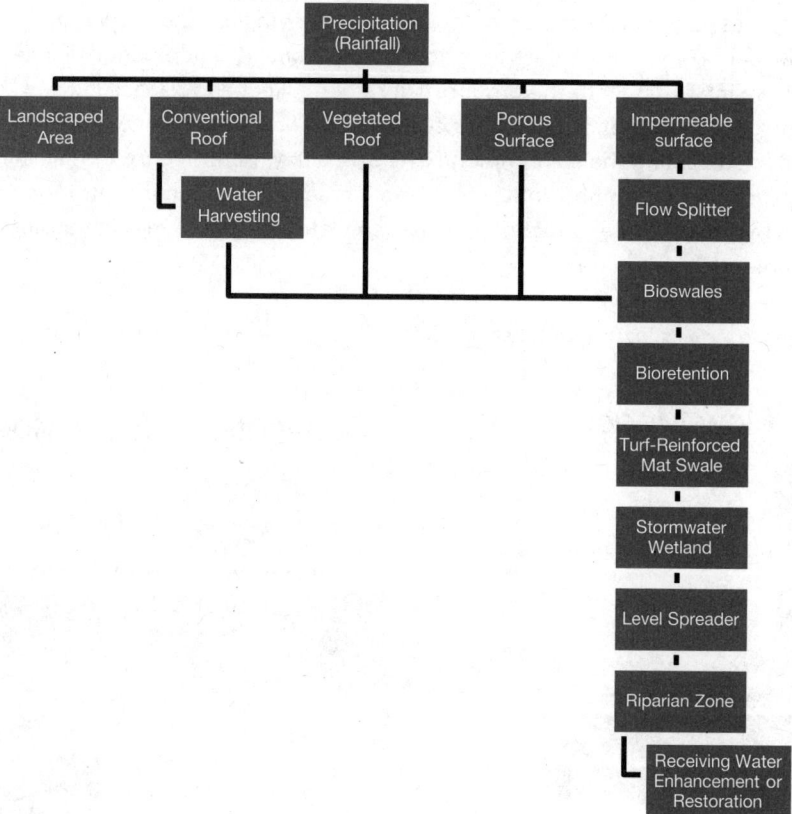

FIGURE 3-9: SITES sustainable stormwater management flow path. Depending on site constraints and landscape connectivity, landscaped areas, conventional roofs, vegetated roofs, and porous surfaces can all interconnect or be directed through a flow splitter into a variety of treatment techniques that are represented in the column below the flow splitter.

Nonpoint source pollution regulations have prompted development of stormwater systems that contain and filter polluted first-flush runoff onsite by managing runoff from small, frequent rain events. Fortunately, many of these new management systems are modeled on natural landscape processes to absorb, retain, filter, and infiltrate runoff. Sustainable stormwater design combine elements of the conveyance, detention, and retention to create management systems that more effectively and ecologically integrate stormwater applications with landscape design. In theory, stormwater management based on the combination of detention, retention, and infiltration strategies can also better duplicate a site's predevelopment runoff rate, volume, frequency, duration, and quality. The following four sections discuss basic principles of sustainable stormwater management address broad ecological, social, and economic goals applicable to stormwater.

PRESERVE FUNCTIONAL NATURAL AREAS

The stormwater benefits of an undisturbed site cannot be understated. Presettlement conditions serve as a baseline for performance and water balance that a combination of sustainable stormwater strategies strive to emulate. It follows that preservation (and restoration/long-term stewardship as appropriate) of intact natural landscapes should be a primary goal of sustainable site design. New development deployed with sustainable strategies should be directed toward previously developed sites in order to minimize the disturbance of intact natural systems, preserve functional natural hydrology, and restore stable, natural hydrology to previously disturbed sites. On previously developed sites, restoration of vegetation that mimics the structural and botanical diversity of the native plant community can be an important component of a comprehensive stormwater management strategy. Public or political perception of the need to shift development away from hydrologically valuable or sensitive areas may be challenging as the value of these areas may not be recognized by these stakeholders. Accurate accounting of ecosystem service benefits and efforts to educate stakeholders may help to secure support.

PRESERVE, RESTORE, OR REPLICATE NATURAL HYDROLOGY

To successfully apply the concept of replicating a site's predevelopment runoff rate, volume, frequency, duration, and quality to urban development projects, numerous small stormwater treatment systems can be distributed throughout a site to keep individual treatment volumes low. The distribution of runoff into small facilities across the site more suitably emulates a site's natural landscape hydrological processes. They are less likely to overwhelm the infiltration capacity of the site's soil, they are more easily integrated into the site design or existing conditions, and they offer greater aesthetic and connectivity opportunities. Dispersal of rainwater to smaller areas is illustrated in Figure 3-10.

FIGURE 3-10: Contrast between concentrated flow design that collects water in one location and dispersed flow design that distributes water around the site.

Major objectives of sustainable stormwater management are to promote evaporation and infiltration of rainwater. To meet these objectives, the majority of runoff from small-frequency rainstorms can be captured in retention facilities and allowed to evaporate, addressing first-flush pollution. Systems can be designed so that runoff in excess of the evapotranspiration volume can overflow from the small, distributed retention facilities into infiltration facilities. Runoff from moderate-sized storm events can be distributed more evenly between evapotranspiration, infiltration, and discharge, reducing peak flows to pre-development levels, thus preventing flooding of downstream properties. Majority runoff from rare large storms is discharged downstream.

Stormwater infiltration can play a major role in maintaining a balance between groundwater recharge and withdrawal (Ferguson 1990). As a result, some regions of the country accept and actively advocate the concept of maintaining the groundwater "balance" through planned onsite stormwater infiltration and bioretention. As might be expected, stormwater recharge has been more commonly accepted in regions dependent on groundwater reserves. In addition to balancing water resources, infiltration-based hydrology is also essential to provide base flow throughout the year for aquatic landscapes—streams, ponds, wetlands, and fens. The protection or reestablishment of infiltration-based hydrology and base flow is essential to create the habitat native landscape systems rely upon.

Groundwater recharge through stormwater infiltration can:

- Prevent lowering of groundwater levels
- Supplement domestic water supplies
- Restore stream base flow
- Help maintain wetlands and riparian areas
- Prevent wells and springs from going dry
- Reduce land subsidence
- Prevent saline water intrusion
- Provide treatment and storage for reclaimed surface water for possible reuse
- Provide additional uses for land otherwise used for detention basins
- Reduce the cost of typical regional stormwater management systems
- Maintain a watershed's existing drainage patterns
- Help increase recharge of underlying aquifers
- Restore the annual water budget

PROTECT HUMAN HEALTH, SAFETY, AND WELFARE

The previous two principles, preserving functional natural areas and preserving, restoring, or replicating natural hydrology, contribute to the protection of human health, safety, and welfare

Flash flooding and channel instability are increased in developed watersheds. High peak flow rates result when urban development increases surface imperviousness and accelerates runoff. Existing detention design can control the peak flow rates at the predevelopment levels. However, these detention systems are designed to limit the rate of peak flow only to predevelopment levels and coincidentally prolong the time of peak flow. They do not consider water quality, soil erosion, stream siltation, and downstream scouring—all of which play an important role in overall stream vitality.

Reducing peak flows can help control:

- Soil erosion

- Stream siltation

- Downstream scouring

- Magnitude and frequency of severe floods

- Frequency of erosive bankfull floods

- Channel widening, down-cutting, and relocation

- Stream-bank erosion

- Shifting bars of coarse-grained sediments

- Imbedding of stream sediments

While it may be convenient to create larger regional detention systems that can reduce some of these problems immediately below their outfall, these larger systems fail to protect smaller streams upstream from the facility from degradation and stream-bank erosion. Also, they often create costly, unattractive, and potentially dangerous facilities. In addition, the extension of peak flows that these larger systems can create prolongs many of the adverse environmental effects listed above.

FLOW RATES

Infiltration and bioretention methods can help to shorten the time of peak flow by reducing the volume of water released downstream. The primary method used to control peak flow rate using infiltration or bioretention is to retain sufficient runoff volume to maintain the predevelopment peak flow rate. This is commonly referred to as the truncated hydrograph method, due to the fact that it captures and retains a portion of the rising line of the hydrograph, in other words, the first flush (Coffman 2000).

Some limitations of this expanded retention method are:

▶ The onsite storage volume necessary to maintain the predevelopment runoff volume using retention may not adequately maintain both the predevelopment volume and peak runoff rate (Coffman 2000).

▶ There may be too much water for all but the least intense development to retain.

▶ Onsite facilities may lose their effectiveness over time.

▶ Not all homeowners will maintain the facilities as needed.

▶ The method may not be able to be implemented under current zoning, subdivision, and stormwater regulations (Strecker 2001).

▶ There may be difficulties inherent in retaining or infiltrating the volume of stormwater in the truncated hydrograph. The greatest of these difficulties is that the truncated hydrograph method is based on a specific design storm. The ability of infiltration of bioretention to reduce peak flows, however, is most effective for small storms and directly related volume of stormwater retained onsite. As long as the truncated hydrograph is less than the total volume retained onsite, the peak flow rate will be reduced.

▶ If rainfall exceeds the design storm, the peak flow rate will not be controlled at the predevelopment level, while rainfalls less than the design storm's natural stream storm flows are eliminated. However, if the truncated hydrograph is more than the total volume retained onsite, the peak flow rate will not be controlled.

▶ Some stream flows from small rainfall events may be eliminated.

Using the truncated hydrograph method to control peak flow rates has limitations; however, using retention and infiltration, it is still a good method for reducing excess runoff and emulating the natural water process. The main advantage of using retention and infiltration is that the first flush is captured onsite. This will reduce stormwater pollution, reduce the frequency of nuisance flooding, lower the amount of rainwater discharged downstream, and increase groundwater recharge and stream base flow (Figure 3-11).

(Photo from Jon Calabria)

FIGURE 3-11: Typical stream erosion and bank destruction caused by not adequately controlling downstream flow rates.

UTILIZE WATER RESOURCES EFFICIENTLY AND WITHOUT DIMINISHING THEM

Integrated water balance planning and site design focuses on creating holistic strategies that integrate with natural hydrological processes. The primary purpose of water balance design is to support and protect water resources by integrating water supply, water storage, water use, and water disposal, via site design, into one process that joins land and water planning together as a single design and problem-solving technique.

The goal of a water balance for a sustainable site is to limit the water input to only site-derived precipitation and condensation, eliminating the use of municipal potable water and groundwater-sourced water. Reusing graywater and reclaimed wastewater on the site is an important strategy to accommodate water needs using only the water resources that are provided to the site naturally. This lofty goal is quite achievable on many landscape projects. With accommodations made for establishment-period watering, many appropriately selected native plantings will be able to survive quite well on local rainfall. Rainwater harvesting can serve the dual purpose of keeping rainfall onsite when it lands on impervious surfaces and providing a source of water during unusually dry periods.

Taking the water balance concept further, a site may actually replicate the natural "partitioning" of precipitation that occurred prior to development. Precipitation falling on a predevelopment site would naturally be partitioned into volumes of evapotranspiration, infiltration, and runoff based on site characteristics of slope, vegetation, soils, and rainfall distribution. The appropriate application of stormwater strategies can successfully replicate this natural partitioning by directing small storms (e.g., the 95th percentile storm event for the site's location) into onsite retention and infiltration practices. The infrequent large events, which would have generated surface runoff in the predevelopment condition, should be allowed to safely bypass infiltration practices.

Interconnected water supply systems include captured rainwater supply, municipal or well water supply, and graywater reuse. Each of these supplies is most appropriate for different purposes. Without treatment, rainwater should not be used for drinking or cooking. However, it can be used for washing, human waste disposal, irrigation, heating and cooling, and other nonpotable uses. Graywater can easily be used for irrigation, especially underground or drip systems, as discussed later in this chapter. All water uses on a project can be accounted for in the water balance, including building use and other uses. It is a greater challenge to meet all site and building water needs with site-derived water and continue to replicate the natural hydrological outputs. It is possible that projects will find creative ways to recycle water onsite for multiple uses before releasing it from the site with infiltration or evapotranspiration. Site size, building size, building occupancy, precipitation, and many other factors will determine whether a sustainable water balance is possible for a particular site.

Protecting water quality is essential to sustaining water resources. Half of all nonpoint source pollutants entering rivers, lakes, bays, and streams are from stormwater runoff from developed land covered with buildings, parking lots, and streets. This runoff contains chemicals, nutrients, sediments, bacteria, and heavy metals. According to the EPA's National Water Quality Inventory, polluted runoff affects about 40 percent of our estuaries, rivers, and lakes. While there are many proprietary underground products to filter runoff, such as catch basin filters, vortex separators, and oil grit collectors, there are also landscape-based systems using the filtering qualities of plants and soils that can be easily integrated into site design.

NONPOINT SOURCE POLLUTION

Onsite infiltration and bioretention allows the soil and plants to naturally filter stormwater as it percolates into and through the ground, thus controlling surface nonpoint pollution. The key water quality advantage of infiltration and bioretention compared to a standard detention basin is that the pollutants in the first-flush flows are separated out and not released downstream at all. Water quality is achieved through the absorption of phosphorus and nitrogen by plant roots and filtering action of the soil, accumulating metals, phosphorus, and other constituents in the upper few inches of the soil. An additional advantage of these systems is that as these pollutants are filtered out, they are easily contained onsite where contaminants can later be removed for disposal if needed.

As development increases, new designs have also been developed to improve a detention system's reduction of nonpoint source water pollution by adding small bioretention and infiltration facilities to treat the first flush of runoff. This can often also be achieved in existing systems by simply retrofitting detention systems to hold and infiltrate small amounts of runoff. The most common way to retrofit an existing detention basin is to excavate the floor down 6 inches and rip-plow the basin to restore some level of infiltration. With each of these options, the goal is to direct the runoff to a location where it can be filtered or allowed to infiltrate into the soil.

THERMAL POLLUTION

Increasing stream temperatures through thermal pollution is another type of urban nonpoint source pollution. As warm water flows off of hot roads and parking lots, it increases the water temperature in streams and lowers the amount of dissolved oxygen available in the water. Water temperatures can be reduced by shading impervious surfaces, using light-colored, high-albedo surfaces, and using permeable pavements. Additionally, many innovative stormwater management structures developed in the 1980s, such as extended detention basins, which detained small volumes of runoff for a day or more, can actually cause stream warming through increased absorption of solar radiation. Infiltration reduces thermal pollution by diverting, retaining, and infiltrating the first flush, which is the warmer runoff, and reducing reliance on detention basins. Onsite infiltration and bioretention methods further reduce adverse effects of nonpoint source pollution on aquatic habitat by preserving groundwater levels that maintain base flows (Figure 3-12).

(Designers Olin Partnership and Judith Nitsch Engineering, Inc.; Photo source Stuart Echols)

FIGURE 3-12: The Outwash Basin at MIT is an excellent example of a sustainable stormwater management design that reduces nonpoint source pollution.

NONPOINT SOURCE PROGRAMS

Under the requirements of the 1987 Water Quality Act, the following stormwater discharges required NPDES permits:

▶ Discharges associated with industrial activity

▶ Discharges from separate sewers serving populations greater than 250,000 persons ("large" municipal discharges)

▶ Discharges from separate sewers serving populations of between 100,000 and 250,000 persons ("medium" municipal discharges)

▶ Discharges contributing to violations of water quality standards or constituting significant contributors of pollutants to U.S. waters (EPA 1987 Water Quality Act)

In 1999, phase II of the NPDES set minimum control measures, including: public education and outreach, public participation and involvement, illicit discharge detection and elimination, construction site runoff control, postconstruction runoff control, and pollution prevention and good housekeeping. The postconstruction runoff control recommended practices including:

(1) infiltration practices to facilitate the percolation of runoff through the soil to groundwater and, thereby, result in reduced stormwater quantity and reduced mobilization of pollutants;

(2) vegetative practices to enhance pollutant removal, maintain/improve natural site hydrology, promote healthier habitats, and increase aesthetic appeal.

(Designer KPFF Consulting Engineers and Atlas Landscape Architecture; Photo source Stuart Echols)

FIGURE 3-13: The bioretention at Epler Hall at Portland State University is an excellent example of a simple design that enhances pollutant removal and increases aesthetic appeal.

GROUNDWATER CONTAMINATION

While recharging groundwater is a central principle of sustainable stormwater design, infiltrating polluted runoff can pose risks to groundwater quality. Therefore, sustainable stormwater design must prevent groundwater contamination from pollution in surface runoff. Because of the great volume of groundwater, it is often thought of as an unlimited resource. It has also been thought of as protected from human actions because it is concealed under deposits of rock and soil. However, contamination of groundwater can occur when contaminants such as gasoline, oil, road salts, and chemicals infiltrate through sandy soils and soils underlain with fracture bedrock. Common sources include: gas stations, storage areas, manufacturing sites, and widespread applications of fertilizers, pesticides, and road salts. Once groundwater is contaminated, it is extremely costly to clean up. As a result, the best way to protect this valuable resource is to prevent contamination in the first place.

Preventing aquifer contamination is critically important because we draw so much of our drinking water from the ground, and cleaning aquifers once they are contaminated is very difficult. According to Robert Pitt, "Few pollutants ever disappear from the urban landscape. They are merely transferred from one medium to another—from air to land, from land to surface water, or from soil to groundwater"(Pitt et al. 1996). So, the cost and effect of groundwater contamination must be carefully weighed against the benefits of preserving surface water, and steps must be taken to remove pollutants from rainwater prior to it recharging groundwater.

The U.S. EPA has identified the following sources of groundwater pollution:

► Septic infiltration

► Direct injection

► Inter-aquifer exchange

► Recharge from contaminated surface water

Not all contaminants pollute groundwater equally. Soil profiles have a large influence on the actions of contaminants. Soil characteristics such as permeability, organic matter, and texture, influence the probability of a pollutant reaching an aquifer, as well as its likely concentrations. A contaminant's main traits in determining its potential to pollute the groundwater are the extent to which it binds to soil and how quickly it degrades (EPA 1987b). Risk of potential groundwater contamination is dependent on site conditions and the type of contaminant (Table 3-3).

TABLE 3-3: Groundwater Contaminants from Stormwater

CONTAMINANT AND SOURCE	RISKS
Nutrients: lawns, crops, feed lots, golf courses	Nitrate has a low to moderate groundwater contamination potential for both surface percolation and subsurface infiltration/injection practices because of its relatively low concentrations found in most stormwater. If the stormwater nitrate concentration were high, then the groundwater contamination potential would likely also be high.
Pesticides: lawns, crops, golf courses	Lindane and chlordane have moderate groundwater contamination potentials for surface percolation practices and for subsurface injection. The groundwater contamination potentials for both of these compounds would likely be substantially reduced with adequate sedimentation pretreatment.
Volatile organics: gas stations, wood preservatives, coal storage, fuel storage	Carbon-based pollution such as dichlorobenzene may have high groundwater contamination potential for subsurface infiltration/injection. However, it would likely have a lower groundwater contamination potential for most surface percolation practices because of its relatively strong sorption to vadose zone soils. Both pyrene and fluorantene would also likely have high groundwater contamination potential for subsurface infiltration/injection practices, but lower contamination potential for surface percolation practices because of their more limited mobility through the unsaturated zone. Others may also have moderate contamination potential, if surface percolation with no pretreatment or subsurface infiltration/injection is used. These compounds would have low contamination potential if surface infiltration were used with sedimentation pretreatment. Volatile organic compounds may also have high groundwater contamination potential if present in the stormwater (likely for some industrial and commercial facilities such as vehicle service establishments).
Pathogens: septic systems, feed lots, pet waste	Enteroviruses likely have a high groundwater contamination potential for all percolation practices and subsurface infiltration/injection practices, depending on their presence in stormwater (likely if contaminated with sanitary sewage). Other pathogens, including *Shigella*, *Pseudomonas aeruginosa*, and various protoza, will also have high groundwater contamination potentials if subsurface infiltration/injection practices are used without disinfection. If disinfection is used, then disinfection byproducts would have high groundwater contamination potentials.

CONTAMINANT AND SOURCE	RISKS
Metals: metal roofs, brake linings, metal processing facilities	Nickel and zinc would likely have high groundwater contamination potentials if subsurface infiltration/injection were used. Chromium and lead would have moderate groundwater contamination potentials for subsurface infiltration/injection practices. All metals would likely have low groundwater contamination potentials if surface infiltration were used with sedimentation pretreatment.
Salts: road salts from ice melting applications	Chloride would likely have a high groundwater contamination potential in northern areas where road salts are used for traffic safety, irrespective of the pretreatment, infiltration, or percolation practice used (Pitt et al. 1996).

Of the potential contaminants,, "chlorides appear to be a chronic risk for groundwater contamination, particularly in northern areas where they are applied on roads and highways. No method of pretreatment of percolation appears capable of reducing this potential" (Pitt 2000). Elevated salt levels in groundwater cause a variety of problems, including:

▶ Human health risk for people on low-sodium diets

▶ Corrosion of pipes and equipment

▶ Reduction of plants' ability to extract water from the soil

▶ Toxicity to plants

▶ Elevated soil pH levels

If stormwater is properly retained onsite pretreated with sedimentation or filtering, most contaminants can be controlled before they have a chance to enter the groundwater. Concerns about site selection and facilities maintenance, however, are especially important when considering the possibility of groundwater contamination. Special care must be taken when infiltration practices are used near:

▶ Water wells

▶ Gasoline stations

▶ Vehicle maintenance operations

▶ Chemical storage areas

▶ Industrial manufacturing

▶ Contaminating commercial activities

▶ Fertilizer storage and retailing

▶ Feed lots

▶ Karst geology

▶ Coarse, sandy soils

Proper site and stormwater management system design can prevent most groundwater contamination because most contaminants adhere to fine soil particles as long as runoff infiltrates slowly. In sandy conditions, an "aquatard" (a layer of fine textured soil) should be added to the infiltration and bioretention facility to prevent groundwater contamination. In residential areas and commercial designs with proper design and filtration, however, the risk of groundwater pollution from runoff is low (Pitt et al. 1996). Pretreatment in the form of filtering, such as bioretention, is needed for all land uses other than residential. These recharge strategies should not be used for gas stations without proper filtration before discharge into infiltration facilities.

Site and Regional Assessment for Stormwater Systems

Because the objectives of sustainable stormwater management seek to preserve and restore a site's natural water cycle, site inventory and assessment activities must focus on the site's natural vegetation, soils, drainage, and topography. Inventory and assessment activities and site design for sustainable rainwater systems are shown in Table 3-4 and in Chapter 2.

TABLE 3-4: Site and Regional Assessment for Stormwater Systems

NATURAL SYSTEM FOR INVENTORY AND ASSESSMENT	SITE ASSESSMENT ACTIVITIES	SITE DESIGN FOR SUSTAINABLE RAINWATER SYSTEMS
Soils: Conserving and restoring soils is critical to successfully implementing sustainable stormwater management because healthy soils store water and cultivate healthier plants, increasing infiltration and evapotranspiration.	**Inventory and map:** Soils based on infiltration rates Soils based on water-holding capacity Disturbed soils Compacted soils Contaminated soils Groundwater recharge areas **Evaluate:** Existing infiltration capacity	Preserve and protect high-infiltration soils Build on low-infiltration soils Preserve and protect healthy native soils Build on compacted soils Build on urban or disturbed soils Restore compacted topsoil by tilling and adding the appropriate compost

NATURAL SYSTEM FOR IN-VENTORY AND ASSESSMENT	SITE ASSESSMENT ACTIVITIES	SITE DESIGN FOR SUSTAIN-ABLE RAINWATER SYSTEMS
Drainage: Conserving and restoring natural drainage systems is critical to successfully implementing sustainable stormwater management because these systems collect, hold, infiltrate, evaporate, and distribute water in ways that preserve existing ecosystems.	**Inventory and map:** Closed depressions and sinkholes Fractures in bedrock Existing streams, ponds, and wetlands **Evaluate:** Needed buffers to protect sensitive drainage areas Drainage coming onto site from uphill development or clearing Different drainage points discharging from the site	Avoid changing drainage volume to closed depressions and sinkholes Avoid infiltration over fractures bedrock without aquatard Protect and incorporate natural drainage features and patterns Avoid draining directly into existing streams, ponds, and wetlands Maintain channel shapes and patterns Maintain existing drainage divides Maintain dispersed flow paths
Topography: Conserving and restoring topography is critical to successfully implementing sustainable stormwater management because existing topographic features can be used to slow and store water onsite.	**Inventory and map:** All slopes All drainage subbasins	Locate development in most suitable areas Maintain existing topography to the greatest extent possible Slope ground surface to hold water on the surface Maintain surface roughness Maximize overland sheet flow
Vegetation: Conserving and restoring vegetation is critical to successfully implementing sustainable stormwater management because plants protect soils, slow runoff, adsorb nitrogen and phosphors, and restore evapotranspiration.	**Inventory and map:** Native vegetation groups Nonnative vegetation Soils based on their ability to support vegetation	Preserve native vegetation Replant and restore native vegetation Evaluate the ability of existing nonnative vegetation to hold water Install plants that develop deep root systems Limit use of turf to recreation requirements

Calculations

There are many design strategies to lower the volume of excess runoff from development, including site design strategies to reduce runoff and stormwater design strategies to mitigate it. Likewise, there are also different stormwater runoff prediction models, such as the Rational Method, TR-55, and Small Storm Hydrology, to help estimate the impacts of these design strategies. Designs to capture, hold, filter, infiltrate, or reuse rainwater generally focus on small storms of less than 1.5 in. This is because rainfall between 0.5 and 1.5 in. normally accounts for about 75 percent of all stormwater pollutants. So, capturing and treating runoff from these small storms is the key to addressing pollutant discharge (Pitt 1999 and 2003). As a result, many regulations require that sustainable stormwater designs capture and treat 0.5 to 1.5 in. of rainfall onsite. Sustainable stormwater design strategies that capture these small storms will reduce runoff and as a result can also lower a site's overall runoff curve number, or runoff coefficient, for small rainfall events.

WATER QUALITY VOLUMES

While design storms for traditional detention systems are large, infrequent storms, the design storms for water quality control are small, frequent storms for the reasons discussed above. Different regulations will set varying targets for water quality volumes depending on local conditions and policies—always refer to local requirements when available. These water quality volumes generally will vary from 0.5 to 1.5 in. of runoff depth from impervious surfaces.

A simple method of estimating water quality volumes is as follows:

1. Use the site plan to individually outline existing and new impervious areas.

2. Calculate the area of each impervious area.

3. Multiply each impervious area by allowed depth (note 1 in. = 0.083 ft) to derive the water quality volume in cubic feet for each impervious area.

For example, a 1,000 ft² parking lot would have a 1 in. water quality volume of 83 ft³.

1,000 ft² × .083 runoff depth = 83 ft³ water quality volume

It is also good practice to create a spreadsheet to document each individual impervious area, the site's total individual impervious areas, as well as the water quality volumes for both.

SIZING BIORETENTION SYSTEMS

Bioretention systems are commonly sized for the water quality volume but can also be sized to hold larger volumes if needed. These systems should be designed as shallow systems to reduce standing water with water depths. They are often designed with no more than 6 to 12 in. water depths depending on local regulations and site conditions.

To size each bioretention system designers need to:

1. Determine the desired bioretention water volume (often the water quality volume—see above).

2. Determine the bioretention system depth, width, and length by either:

Dividing the available area for the bioretention system by the desired volume to determine the storage depth

(Length × Width) / Volume = Depth

or dividing the storage volume by the desired volume to determine the bioretention system area:

Volume / Depth = Bioretention System Area

For example, a 100 ft² (20 ft × 5 ft) bioretention system sized for 83 ft³ would need to be .83 ft deep (about 10 in.). So, a 1,000 ft² parking lot, as discussed above, would need a 2 ft × 50 ft bioretention system that is .83 ft deep to capture 1 in. of runoff depth.

SIZING INFILTRATION SYSTEMS

Infiltration systems are also commonly sized for the water quality volume but can also be sized to hold larger volumes, especially when groundwater recharge is one of the intended goals. Calculations for infiltration systems are very similar to retention systems except that the infiltration facilities are underground and need to consider soil infiltration rates.

To size each infiltration system, designers need to:

1. Determine the desired water volume to be Infiltrated (Vinf) (often the water quality volume, but can be more dependent on the design goals).

2. Determine the infiltration basin volume (Vb) based on the void space in the infiltration facility. The Vb is equal to the Vinf divided by the reservoir void space (Vd). (Above-ground facilities will not need this step.)

Basin volume (Vb) = Vinf / Vd

3. Determine the maximum infiltration basin depth (d) based on drying time days (Td) multiplied by the limiting soil infiltration rate feet/day (K) and the safety factor (Sf).

Max depth (d) = (Td × K × Sf) / Vd

4. Determine the Minimum Floor Area (Fa) by dividing the Vb by the maximum basin depth (d).

Legend

(Vinf)	Infiltration volume—this is determined by the designer as the water quality volume or some other standard.
(Vb)	Infiltration basin volume—this is based on the void space in the infiltration facility.
(Td)	Drying time days—this is normally about 3 days but can be changed according to local regulations or site conditions.
(K)	Limiting soil infiltration rate feet/day—this is a function of infiltration rates, which are normally measured in inches per hour and multiplied by 2 to the rate converted into feet per day.
(SF)	Infiltration rate safety factor—this is a simple safety/risk factor. Lower risk conditions can use lower numbers 1 to 2, and high-risk conditions should use higher numbers 2 to 5.
(Vd)	Reservoir void space—this is normally about 30 percent when using crushed gravel but can be increased using structural methods such as pipes, culverts, or other systems.

WATER HARVESTING AND REUSE VOLUMES

Rainwater is available for collection onsite and can be divided into water from roofs and water from surface pavements such as parking lots and walkways. This separation is suggested because runoff from parking often contains harsh chemicals, such as deicing salts and other contaminants from automobiles, that could be problematic for many applications within a building, such as washing or toilets. Average rainwater supply can easily be determined as a direct relationship between depth of monthly rainfall and the catchment area.

Monthly Rainfall × Catchment Area = Monthly Rainwater Supply

The monthly water demand is determined based on the number of building occupants and their nonpotable water use. However, nonpotable water use can also change throughout the year with required landscape irrigation or changes in demand. For example, there is variation in the number of students for school and the respective water used for toilets and urinals, as shown in Figure 3-14.

The storage needed is a function of both monthly rainfall supply and variation in monthly water demand. The monthly difference in the supply and demand is subtracted from or added to the previous month's surplus or shortage and repeated for the full 12-month yearly cycle. The storage size can be optimized based on the volume of rainwater supply and nonpotable demand such that there will be sufficient stored water to meet demand for each month as shown in the figure.

(Monthly Supply – Monthly Demand) +/– (Surplus or Shortage) = Monthly Storage

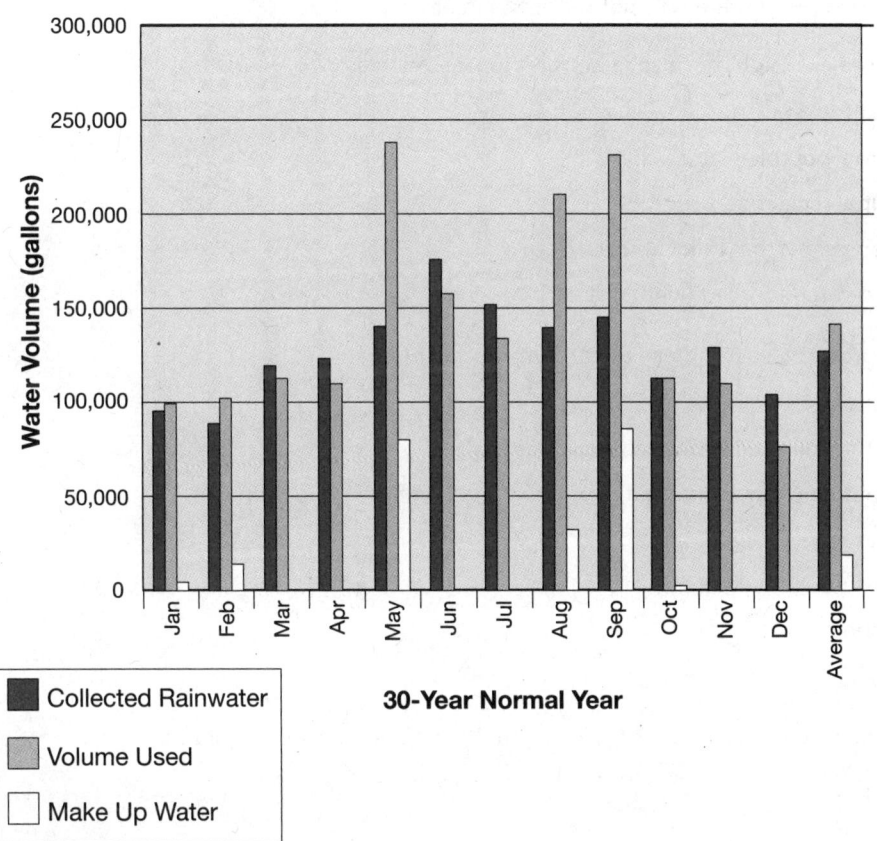

FIGURE 3-14: Example monthly water budget as a function of variation in collected rainwater, water demand for nonpotable uses, and extra water needed to make up the difference between supply and demand.

To achieve a cost-effective design under most conditions, storage systems should be sized for 75 to 90 percent of the nonpotable demand to be supplied by rainwater. Wastewater disposal quantities are simply determined directly from the number of building occupants and other uses, such as manufacturing processes. Disposal quantities are not related to monthly water supply or storage. As a result, designers can connect water and site planning and design practices to create integrated site–water systems that are economically viable and ecologically beneficial.

SIZING WATER BALANCE SYSTEMS

The goal of a water balance design is to limit the water sources to onsite precipitation and reduce the use of municipal and groundwater-sourced water resources.

At its most basic level, a site-based water balance is very simple:

Water Input = Water Output + Change in Storage

A typical project might have several water inputs, such as:

- ► Rainfall
- ► Municipal potable water supply
- ► Municipal reclaimed water
- ► Condensation from mechanical systems
- ► Groundwater-sourced (well) water

A typical project also has many water outputs, including:

- ► Infiltration
- ► Evapotranspiration from the landscape
- ► Evaporation (from water features, building conditioning equipment)
- ► Runoff
- ► Wastewater conveyed offsite
- ► Irrigation
- ► Other

The change in storage accounts for water that is retained onsite, including:

- ► Cisterns
- ► Wet ponds
- ► Water features

Amenity Opportunities of Stormwater Design

The concept of designing rainwater/stormwater features to provide a landscape amenity is based on the premise that new stormwater management techniques focusing on non-point source pollution, water balance, and small storm hydrology can also be used to create new site amenities. Unlike pipe conveyance systems that hide water beneath the surface and work independently of surface topography, an open drainage system for sustainable stormwater design can work with natural landforms and land uses to become a major design element of a site plan.

Peter Stahre has documented the array of "positive values of open storm drainage," which he classifies as aesthetic, biological, cultural, ecological, economic, technical, educational, environmental, historical, recreational, and public relations (the last value being a result of the others) (Stahre 2006).

These designs can result in greater user satisfaction and perceived value—design that not only addresses stormwater management in better ways, but also transforms these management systems into site design assets. Sustainable stormwater approaches present significant amenity design opportunities that deserve to be recognized and exploited to transform stormwater management into experientially rich landscape amenity. This section presents examples of how stormwater treatment can provide landscape amenity in the following categories of amenity types: education, recreation, safety, public relations, and aesthetic richness (Echols and Pennypacker 2006).

Originally the amenity designation focused on creating wildlife habitat and open space; however, the Sustainable Urban Drainage Systems regulations revised the definition to include "community value, resource management (e.g., rainwater use), multi-use of space, education, water features, habitat creation, biodiversity action plans" (National SUDS Working Group 2003).

EDUCATION

In the context of stormwater treatment as landscape amenity, education is understood as creating favorable conditions for learning about rainwater and/or related issues. Examples include presenting opportunities to learn about sustainable stormwater design, the site's historical water condition, riparian plant associations, and so forth. These ideas may be gleaned directly from the design as specific "lessons learned" or, less didactically, as enriched experience of place. Stormwater treatment as landscape amenity may also entail providing programmed educational opportunities through tours, games, and the like (Figure 3-15). Strategies include:

- ▶ Make the stormwater treatment system visible and legible.
- ▶ Create a narrative of stormwater and the hydrologic cycle.
- ▶ Make stormwater-related artifacts integral to design.
- ▶ Create symbols of past watershed conditions.
- ▶ Make the stormwater treatment system playful, intriguing, or puzzling.
- ▶ Include a variety of stormwater treatment systems in the design.
- ▶ Create systems that visibly collect and store trash and pollution.
- ▶ Provide a variety of visible riparian plant types and communities.

- ▸ Provide a variety of interesting wildlife habitat by using plants that provide wildlife food and, different water depths, and create shelter for wildlife, such as bird and bat houses.

- ▸ Provide simple signage or exhibits with brief text and clear graphics.

- ▸ Design the stormwater treatment systems to invite educational games or activities.

- ▸ Create visual interest by varying the appearance of different parts of the stormwater treatment system.

- ▸ Create a variety of spaces for groups to explore, gather, or sit near the stormwater treatment system.

- ▸ Create treatment systems that are touchable.

Design by The Miller|Hull Partnership, LLP, Bruce Dees & Associates, LLC; Photo from Stuart Echols

FIGURE 3-15: The small yellow signs at Pierce County Environmental Services, Tacoma, are an excellent example of creating fun education opportunities that lead visitors through the design from one treatment system to another.

RECREATION

As a design category, recreation means providing conditions that are favorable for interacting with the stormwater treatment system in ways that are relaxing, amusing, and/or refreshing. In contrast to the education category, the focus here is on playful interaction with enjoyment as the intent. The distinction between "education" and "recreation" is admittedly nuanced, with considerable overlap; but they are presented here as distinct categories to help designers who wish to emphasize one over the other (Figure 3-16). Strategies include:

- ▶ Create overlooks with views of the stormwater system.

- ▶ Create destination points related to stormwater treatment systems.

- ▶ Provide seating using walls, benches, and/or tables and chairs with views of the stormwater system.

- ▶ Provide paths in strategic locations that ensure encounters with the stormwater treatment system.

- ▶ Connect onsite trails to offsite trail systems and destinations that ensure encounters with the stormwater treatment system.

- ▶ Provide clear points of entry into the stormwater system that are visually inviting, mysterious, and easily accessible.

- ▶ Provide a variety of small and large places to play in or explore the stormwater treatment system.

- ▶ Make areas that invite climbing and physical exploration that balance perceptions of safety with adventure.

- ▶ Create systems that can be safely modified by the user, such as small movable river rocks and weirs.

Design by Mayer/Reed; photo from Stuart Echols

FIGURE 3-16: The scale and accessibility of the stormwater design at the Oregon Convention Center, Portland, OR, is an excellent example of recreation opportunities.

SAFETY

Danger associated with stormwater cannot be overlooked. In the litigious context of the United States, the goal of addressing safety concerns effectively is central to making possible stormwater treatment as landscape amenity. Standing and/or running water often forms a central part of the experience, but it must be designed to avoid a potential drowning hazard or even perception of danger (Figure 3-17). Strategies include:

- ► Be aware of what the water quality is likely to be. Most rainwater and runoff is generally safe to touch, but not to drink, soak, or swim in.

- ► Provide walls, screens, or railings that allow views but prevent access to stormwater, if deemed necessary.

- ► Provide upland, riparian, or wetland plant massing that allows views but prevents access to stormwater.

- ► Use bridges, boardwalks, or platforms to allow users to view stormwater safely from above.

- ► Use water-themed aboveground water storage facilities such as rain barrels, water towers, or cisterns.

- ► Disperse stormwater into shallow storage facilities using flow splitters or tiered basins.

- ► Limit stormwater depth by creating horizontal space for water to spread out or by adding large river stone to basins where people can have access.

- ► Do not collect or move stormwater in large centralized conveyance facilities.

- ► Create "water brakes" to slow stormwater by abruptly changing flow direction or by creating small waterfalls that dissipate energy.

(Designer Greenworks, PC and Atelier Dreiseitl; Photo source Stuart Echols.)

FIGURE 3-17: The recirculating rain water system at Tanner Springs Park in Portland, OR, is an excellent example of water that is safe and touchable because of the small shallow design.

PUBLIC RELATIONS

As a category, public relations can be a specific aim, but even when not intended, the overall design character makes a semiotic statement about the values of those who created and/or own the site. Any such design message is inherently a public relations gesture, whether overt or implicit. Once again, the reader may find considerable overlap between this category and others mentioned in this text; we present it as a distinct category so that readers may understand different public relations message types and design techniques used to achieve them (Figure 3-18). Strategies include:

- Locate stormwater treatment systems near entries, courtyards, or windows for high visibility.
- Use signage explaining stormwater treatment strategies to make the stormwater trail easy to find and follow.
- Create opportunities for programming educational activities.
- Use commonly available materials.
- Create small-scale replicable interventions.
- Use common settings such as sidewalks and parking lots.
- Use new forms and materials.
- Use traditional stormwater treatment methods in new ways.
- Be opportunistic by using small, leftover, and unexpected spaces.
- Achieve additional functions such as traffic calming and beautification.
- Make the stormwater trail mysteriously disappear and reappear.
- Make the stormwater or water treatment system touchable.
- Make the stormwater audible: Include plunge pools and downspouts.
- Make the stormwater move in different ways: tumble, run, and splash.
- Create elegantly simple composition.
- Use refined/expensive materials.
- Use refined/expensive construction methods.
- Use restraint in diversity of materials and forms.
- Design for a manicured look: clipped, trimmed, and clean.
- Use unusual water presentation forms and themes.

(Designer Mithun; Photo source Stuart Echols)

FIGURE 3-18: The signage that accompanies the porous paving and bioretention at High Point Housing, Seattle, WA, is an excellent example of public relations opportunities.

AESTHETIC RICHNESS

An aesthetically rich design can be composed to create an experience of beauty and pleasure focused on stormwater. Many sustainable stormwater practices provide opportunities to achieve this, while conventional stormwater management practices can be limited in aesthetic opportunities and often turn into eyesores. One could argue that aesthetic richness is embedded in all the categories presented here; but sometimes richness of experience is created simply through the arresting combinations of forms, colors, and sounds of the composition itself. Articulation of strategies that encourage attention to stormwater strictly through compositional means is worth calling out. In the broadest terms, the composition may address visual, auditory, tactile, and/or olfactory experience but are often limited to the visual, auditory, and tactile (see Figure 3-19). Strategies include:

- ▶ Create water collection basins as features/focal points.
- ▶ Create visual emphasis on water direction change using scuppers, basins, cisterns, and splash-blocks.
- ▶ Use downspouts, runnels, flumes, bioswales, and the like to draw attention to the line of the stormwater trail, enhancing legibility as well as interest and curiosity.
- ▶ Stack horizontal and vertical planes such as pools and falls to exploit the visual interest of stormwater flowing over surfaces, plunging down planes, through weirs or over edges.
- ▶ Create visual interest or themes with basins that hold plants and water: sunken, raised, orthogonal, curved, organic, geometric, small, or large.
- ▶ Contrast natural elements with man-made elements, such as clipped lawn, steel, or concrete.
- ▶ Juxtapose river rock and riparian grasses for compositional contrast.
- ▶ Dramatize an implied axis by aligning treatment systems, basins, and runnels connected by the water trail.
- ▶ Create unified design themes by repeating systems of bioswales, basins, weirs, ponds, raingardens, and the like.
- ▶ Create a variety of sounds and volumes by allowing stormwater to fall from various heights onto different materials, such as stone or steel.
- ▶ Create changes in sound pitch by allowing stormwater to fall on different forms, such as flat block, metal tubes, drums, and ponds.
- ▶ Create different sound rhythms by varying the amount and rate of stormwater falling and flowing through the treatment system.
- ▶ Use a variety of water-related plants within visitors' reach, such as rushes and grasses.

▶ Use various water-related hardscape, such as river pebbles and driftwood, to provide interesting surfaces.

▶ Allow people to touch stormwater in different forms, such as flowing, falling, splashing, standing, sheeting, or damp surfaces where water can soak in or evaporate.

(Designer Koch Landscape Architecture; Photo source Stuart Echols)

FIGURE 3-19: The Courtyard in 10th@Hoyt, Portland, OR, is an excellent example of aesthetic richness opportunities as the rain trail is captivating and easy to follow.

STORMWATER DESIGN APPROACHES

Stormwater design should seek to maximize the functional contributions of the built environment to site ecology. The following stormwater design approaches are organized into sections and presented sequentially, as:

- ▸ Practices that reduce runoff
- ▸ Practices that mitigate runoff by emulating evapotranspiration and infiltration
- ▸ Practices that convey runoff from larger events
- ▸ Practices that protect or restore receiving water bodies

All four of these outcomes are critical to balance ecological health and public health, safety, and welfare in an economical and durable manner.

GENERAL INSTALLATION GUIDANCE FOR STORMWATER PRACTICES

- ▸ Always conduct a preconstruction meeting between the landscape architect, contractor, owner, and other involved consultants (such as engineers) to ensure proper installation.
- ▸ Use an experienced contractor who can demonstrate previous successful installations.
- ▸ Construction sequence is important—for instance, stormwater practices should be installed after the site is stabilized.
- ▸ Protect stormwater practice and infiltration locations from compaction or sedimentation during construction, unless these impacts will be corrected prior to acceptance.
- ▸ Restrict construction traffic or other uses that may introduce sediment.
- ▸ Do not compact engineered soil during or after installation.
- ▸ Ensure that the site has been permanently stabilized with vegetation or mulch.
- ▸ Excavation and fine grading operations should avoid glazing the *in situ* soils and preferably rake the surface with the teeth of the bucket.
- ▸ Verify submittals of all materials including soil mixes, aggregates, mulches, and pavements.
- ▸ Follow all manufacturers' recommendations for proprietary products.
- ▸ Topsoil, amendments, and mulch should be composted and weed free.
- ▸ Ensure that final grades meet plans and specifications.
- ▸ Do not compact soil or alter final grades during planting.
- ▸ Ensure vegetative coverage occurs within time span as specified on plans.
- ▸ Temporary irrigation may be required during vegetation establishment.

Practices That Reduce Runoff

The first step in a sustainable stormwater strategy is to avoid creating additional runoff. Built structures are a necessary component of almost any site design; however, there are many strategies to create built surfaces that also have beneficial hydrologic functions. Rooftops, parking lots, roads, sidewalks, playgrounds—all have the potential to be multifunctional surfaces that meet programming requirements for type of use and traffic loads as well as evapotranspiring or infiltrating stormwater.

A familiar refrain of low-impact development is to "start at the source." Minimizing impervious surfaces reduces the source of site runoff. In addition to impervious surfaces, there are many semi-pervious surfaces in the built environment that are in poor condition. Most landscaped areas on urban and suburban sites have been graded and compacted to a degree that reduces their capacity to infiltrate rainfall. Improving the permeability of these landscaped areas will also reduce site runoff. The following practices all minimize the creation of additional runoff from the built environment.

SITE DESIGN TO REDUCE IMPERVIOUS SURFACE

Reducing the development patterns that create excess runoff in the first place should be a primary aim of sustainable site design. Many proven techniques that focus on preserving existing site attributes are often ignored or perceived as added cost when development focuses simply on minimizing construction cost and complying with existing development codes. In order for any particular strategy to be effective and provide long-term value, it should be wholly integrated with the total site design and be supportive of clearly identified project objectives, site context, and other factors. The starting point for any sustainable stormwater design is to limit the amount of impervious surface that contributes to increased runoff generated by the site. Common strategies are:

- ▶ Reduce roof area—Where practical, reduce roof areas by using multistory buildings instead of single-story buildings.
- ▶ Use green roofs—Establish extensive vegetated roofs and intensive garden roofs. Design green roof systems to hold a minimum of 0.5 in. of rainfall to reduce runoff volumes and filter pollutants.
- ▶ Reduce road lengths and widths—Reduce the area of imperviousness by using alternative street designs that minimize the length and width of streets; reduce building setbacks to shorten driveways and make sidewalk widths narrower.
- ▶ Reduce parking areas—Reduce pavement with efficient parking lot designs, downsizing parking stalls, reducing parking aisle widths, and using shared parking for adjoining uses.

▶ Use pervious pavement—Use permeable paving for low-traffic areas, overflow parking, sidewalks, emergency access, and driveways with materials that allow water to infiltrate.

▶ Reduce use of curbs and gutters—Remove curbs and gutters from streets, alleys, parking lots, and loading areas so that runoff can flow directly into adjacent vegetated areas.

▶ Reduce connected impervious surfaces—Minimize impervious surfaces that quickly convey runoff offsite. Disconnect or break up flow paths of excess runoff over impervious areas. Disconnect downspouts and direct stormwater into vegetation or collection systems.

▶ Reduce drainage directly to storm sewers or surface waters—Locate parking and buildings away from discharge points, and send runoff away from the storm drain using flow splitters and retention systems.

▶ Use existing open or proposed open areas—Direct runoff across vegetated areas to help filter runoff and encourage groundwater recharge by utilizing wildflowers, prairie grasses, and riparian plants.

▶ Reduce turf—Use open vegetated areas planted with native landscaping as an alternative to traditional turf grass to reduce excess runoff and lower the maintenance requirements of traditional turf grass.

▶ Direct runoff to soils that infiltrate—Reduce discharge to hard surfaces such as curbs, gutters, storm sewers, concrete channels, or compacted clay soils and protect areas that provide groundwater infiltration benefits.

▶ Reduce clearing and grading—Designate limits of work onsite to protect existing vegetation, including understory vegetation and ground cover.

▶ Reduce development areas—Increase development densities on previously developed land and preserve undeveloped land as common space amenities to reduce imperviousness. See Figure 3-20.

COMPOST BLANKETS

Compost blankets are a 1- to 3-in. layer of approved compost loosely applied to disturbed soil in order to prevent erosion, reduce runoff, and increase infiltration, and facilitate plant growth. They are a flexible stormwater strategy that can be used successfully in almost any situation producing sheet flow runoff, including steep slopes, rocky soils, frozen ground, and around existing vegetation.

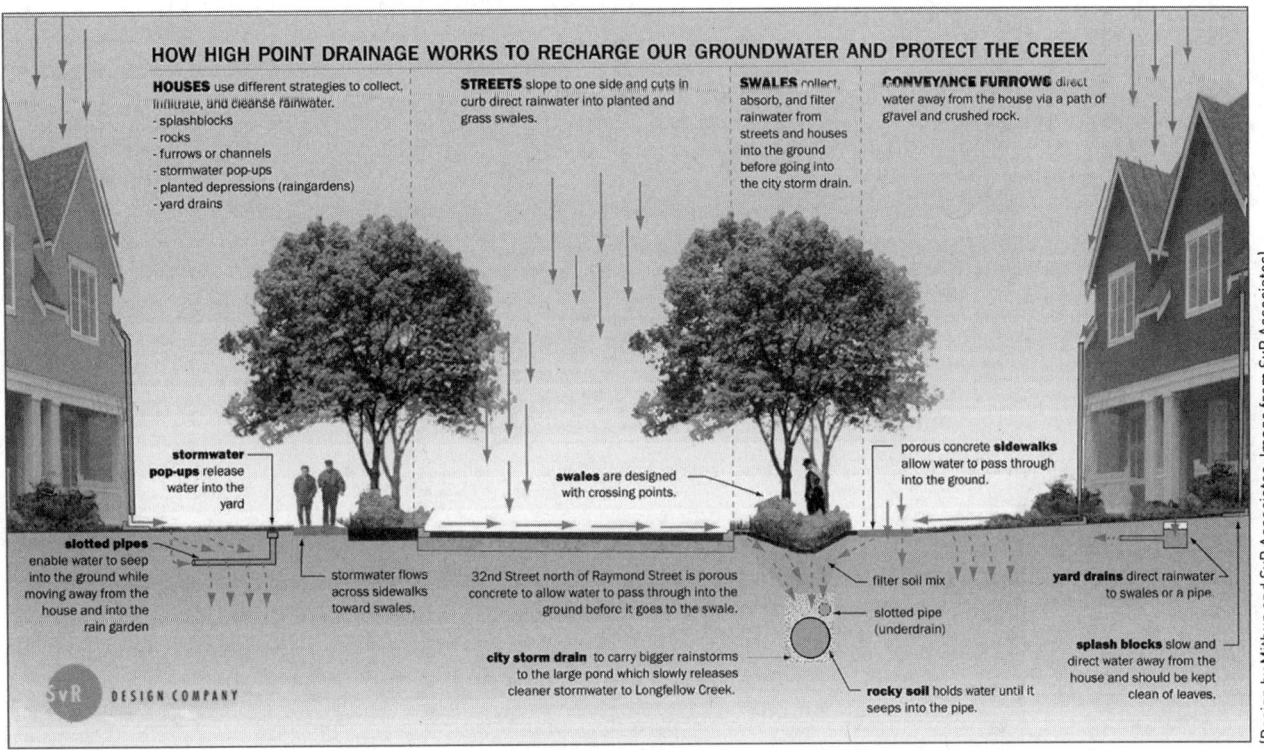

FIGURE 3-20: The street cross section at High Point is an excellent example of a integrated site design that prevents excess runoff.

According to the U.S. EPA, compost blankets reduce erosion in three primary ways: They increase the surface permeability of the site which delays, and reduces runoff; they fill in small rills and voids, which helps to prevent concentrated flow; and they promote the growth of temporary or permanent vegetation, which enhances site stability.

Compost blankets can be applied by hand, mechanical spreader, or by a pneumatic blower. Research has shown that properly applied compost blankets provide better surface coverage than typical straw or mulch applications and that compost blankets can significantly reduce runoff volumes from disturbed soils (U.S. EPA 2010). The benefits of using compost blankets are maximized when a seed mix of noninvasive temporary stabilization species and permanent native species is incorporated into the mix prior to application. In this manner, the erosion control strategy becomes a part of the permanent landscaping of the site (see Figure 3-21).

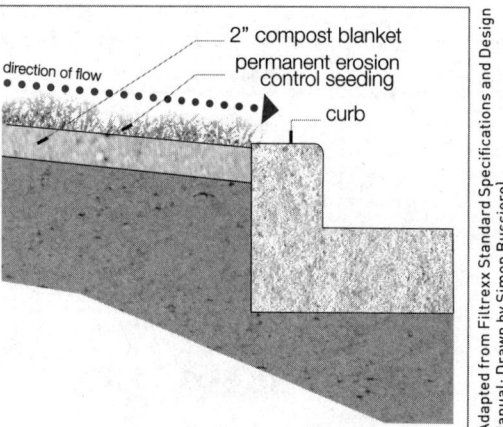

FIGURE 3-21: Typical compost blanket section.

DESIGN CRITERIA

▶ Apply to slopes between 4:1 and 1:1.

▶ Incorporate seed mixes into the compost prior to application for best results establishing vegetation.

▶ Completely cover the slope from top to bottom to discourage concentration of runoff.

▶ Use high-quality compost that complies with local, state, and federal requirements (many state Departments of Transportation or environmental departments have approved compost blanket specifications).

▶ Biosolids must comply with the Standards for Class A Biosolids outlined in 40 Code of Federal Regulations (CFR) Part 503.

▶ The U.S. Composting Council certifies compost products under its Seal of Testing Assurance (STA) Program.

POTENTIAL LIMITATIONS

▶ Do not use in area of concentrated or high-velocity runoff.

▶ Some compost may contain high levels of nutrients and metals. Select mature, stable compost with nutrient and pH levels compatible with the requirements of the permanent vegetation incorporated into the application.

UNDEVELOPED AND RESTORED NATURAL AREAS

The stormwater benefits of an undisturbed site cannot be overstated. Presettlement conditions serve as baseline for performance and water balance that a combination of other strategies strive to emulate. It follows that preservation of intact natural landscape should be a primary goal of sustainable site design. New development should be directed toward previously developed sites in order to minimize the disturbance of intact natural systems and preserve functional natural hydrology. On previously developed sites, restoration of vegetation that mimics the structural and botanical diversity of the native plant community can be an important component of a comprehensive stormwater management strategy.

Areas conserved should be managed or restored to approach the ecological trajectory of a plant community appropriate for the environmental context of the site. Although the presettlement plant communities are an important reference condition, contemporary land use and disturbance regime may require a different equilibrium condition. Look for stable reference sites that have a similar environmental context (ecoregion, watershed characteristics, land-use context), which can provide guidance for the ecological goals of the restoration. This may be different than the historic plant communities of the site. This is discussed in greater detail in chapter 4.

FIGURE 3-22: Undeveloped and restored natural areas such as this provide many important ecological and cultural benefits.

(Photo from Jon Calabria)

Undeveloped and restored areas should be multifuntional areas and may integrate wildlife habitat, human recreation, stormwater management, and a variety of other ecosystem services. It is important that these areas are valued by the people who manage or live near the site, because ongoing management and protection are likely necessary for long-term success. It is unrealistic that natural areas in most developed areas will remain healthy—in light of continued pressure from invading exotic plants, air and water pollution, and human abuse—if ongoing management is not provided. See Figures 3-22 through 3-24.

(Design by Jake McLean and Jon Calabria; photo by Jon Calabria)

FIGURE 3-23: Restored natural area in urban context provides many important ecological and cultural benefits.

Design by Ball State Landscape Architecture Students and Faculty, Les Smith; Photo by Meg Calkins

FIGURE 3-24: Children and local wildlife enjoy the wetland and pond at the Minnetrista Center in Muncie, Indiana. The pond receives surrounding runoff through bioswales. The boardwalk and other structures were designed and built by Ball State University landscape architecture students and faculty.

DESIGN CRITERIA

▶ Select areas to be conserved based on a site inventory and analysis, and give priority to the following critical environmental features:

    ▷ Large tracts of native vegetation that connect and create contiguous riparian protection areas

    ▷ Natural drainage patterns, including ephemeral, intermittent, and perennial streams, terraces, active floodplains and wetlands

    ▷ Groundwater recharge areas

> ▷ Good soils—those with high infiltration rates or high fertility
>
> ▷ Steep or erodible slopes
>
> ▷ High-quality or rare ecosystems or habitat
>
> ▷ Large tracts of critical habitat and wildlife habitat area that create or connect contiguous protection areas

- ► Identify reference conditions for the site or an appropriate reference site that guides restoration goals and strategies. Vegetation density and diversity should strive to emulate the site's reference condition (presettlement) or another appropriate reference condition.

- ► Design the site to accommodate and complement the conserved or restored areas.

  - ▷ Manage the conserved or restored area.

  - ▷ Manage aggressive exotic vegetation.

  - ▷ Manage human use/abuse.

  - ▷ Manage wildlife conflicts.

  - ▷ Manage aesthetics and perceived value.

POTENTIAL LIMITATIONS

- ► May be in conflict with density goals in urban or urbanizing areas.

- ► Management may be required to sustain a healthy natural area in a developed context.

- ► Public or political perception of value may not lead to support of protecting natural areas in urban settings. Accurate accounting of ecosystem service benefits and efforts to educate stakeholders may help to secure support.

RAINWATER HARVESTING AND REUSE FOR STORMWATER MANAGEMENT

Rainwater harvesting is the collection, storage, and reuse of runoff from impervious surfaces. Runoff from rooftops or other surfaces is screened and possibly filtered into a collection system, such as a rain barrel, cistern, dry well, harvesting pond, or other containment system (bladder). Captured water is suitable for irrigation or other nonpotable uses, such as providing water for cooling condensers or toilet flushing. If filtered and treated correctly, captured water may be used for potable uses.

Key components of a water harvesting system are the catchment area, filter, cistern, and distribution system. While many technological advances have been made over the last few decades, the basic concept is simple and thousands of years old. The challenge before landscape architects and other designers today is to find ways to maximize the environmental benefits of this age-old technology.

In addition to helping meet the water use needs of a project, which is discussed in more detail in the "Water Conservation" section of this chapter, water harvesting can function as a stormwater management strategy. Water quantity benefits can be maximized by releasing captured water in advance of the next storm event by applying it to landscaped areas through irrigation systems. Can we begin to think of irrigation as a stormwater infiltration and groundwater recharge strategy rather than as the consumptive use that it has been for the last half century? When water harvesting is the source, this is certainly possible.

Runoff from different catchment surfaces should be managed differently. Coated steel, slate, terra cotta, and other clean roof surfaces are better suited for water harvesting. This runoff is generally free from dangerous contaminants, other than what may have been deposited on the surface between rain events, and with simple first-flush diversion and filtering can be stored and reused for nonpotable uses. Runoff from asphalt shingle roofs, parking lots, and other surfaces that may be conveying higher levels of pollutants is better managed through a practice that will naturally filter and infiltrate the runoff, such as bioretention. Also, the runoff that comes off vegetated roofs may contain nutrients and organic constituents, and it should be directed to other treatment practices. (See Figures 3-25 , 3-26, and 3-27).

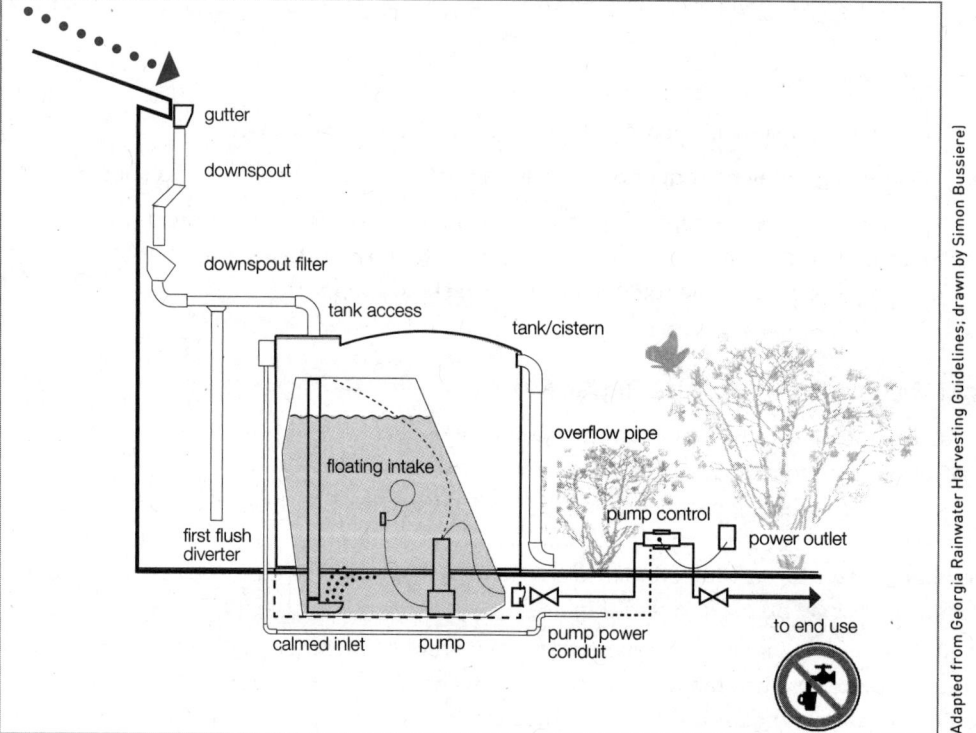

(Adapted from Georgia Rainwater Harvesting Guidelines; drawn by Simon Bussiere)

FIGURE 3-25: This diagram illustrates the typical components and configuration of aboveground cisterns.

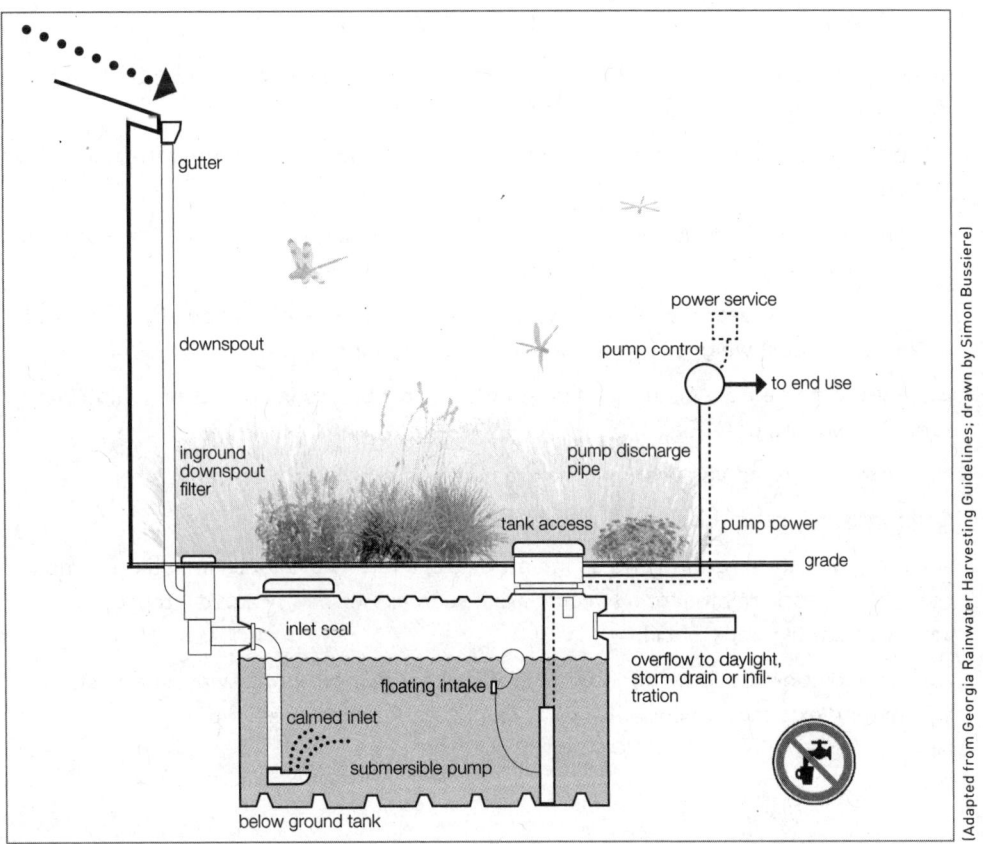

(Adapted from Georgia Rainwater Harvesting Guidelines; drawn by Simon Bussiere)

FIGURE 3-26: This diagram illustrates the typical components and configuration of belowground cisterns.

Photo by Sebastian Sommer.

FIGURE 3-27: An aboveground cistern system collects roof runoff for irrigation and water for dyeing fabrics at the North Carolina Arboretum.

DESIGN CRITERIA

► Water harvesting system should be sized based on supply area and intended uses and/or infiltration capability of the site.

► Runoff should be screened, or even filtered, prior to the water entering the harvesting system.

► Supply valve should be mounted on side of tank to avoid draining fines that settle to bottom of tank.

► Locate water harvesting system down gradient of supply area and on adequate foundation to support weight of water and its containment system.

► Buoyancy of an empty cistern can be problematic if buried in an area with high water table or flooding potential.

► Underground pump vaults should be drained to prevent submersion.

► Often requires separate nonpotable distribution system.

► A variety of cistern routing and usage models are widely available, including some based on historic rainfall for a specific area, such as `www.bae.ncsu.edu/topic/ waterharvesting/model.html`.

► Design and construct appropriate foundation based on weight of water harvesting system and existing site conditions, for example, bearing capacity of soil.

POTENTIAL LIMITATIONS

► Local regulations may prohibit water harvesting and reuse.

► A separate nonpotable system has to be labeled and marked.

► The primary goal may be to accumulate water for use in case of drought and not to release it for infiltration prior to the next storm.

GREEN AND VEGETATED ROOF SYSTEMS

A green roof or vegetated roof is a system that incorporates lightweight growing media and plants to provide vegetative cover on rooftops. Green roofs are typically categorized as either intensive or extensive, based on the depth of growing media (the "soil" of the green roof). Intensive green roofs have deeper growing media (over 6 in.) and tend to be heavy and more expensive, although the deeper soil allows for greater diversity in plant selection and more attractive spaces for human enjoyment. Extensive green roofs (approximately 1 to 6 in. of growing media) are most easily used on nearly flat roofs, although they can be installed on sloped roofs with some modifications to prevent soil migration and to slow run-off movement. Green roofs have many benefits; however, stormwater reduction and heat island mitigation are perhaps the two most significant (see Figures 3-28 and 3-29).

Green roof vegetation intercepts rainfall and, together with the growing media and the drainage layer of the green roof system, can contribute to significant reductions in stormwater runoff and increases in time of concentration. Most green roof media is extremely porous and permeable; however, green roof drainage layers capture and hold rainfall to make it available to the roots of green roof vegetation. Research has shown that extensive green roofs can reduce annual runoff volume by 50 to 90 percent and can double the time of concentration for roof runoff (Scholz-Barth 2001; VanWoert et al. 2005).

Green roofs can provide cover for ground-nesting birds and insects. Sedums are a nectar source for pollinators. Wildlife habitat can be enhanced significantly by providing a diverse planting and including native perennials as well as sedums. The greater soil depth provided on intensive green roofs affords a larger palette of vegetation to choose from and may result in better habitat.

In dense urban settings, green roofs may provide some of the only vegetation in sight. They can have a tremendous positive impact on people by providing more green vegetation in hard urban environments and by softening building architecture. They provide significant environmental benefits without compromising development density. With attention to safety (pavers, guardrails, and accessibility), green roofs can accommodate human access and enjoyment. In many situations, green roofs may be the most accessible greenspace available to building occupants. Consider including opportunities for rooftop gardening or food production, where appropriate. Vegetation for green roofs is addressed in greater detail in Chapter 4, Site Design: Vegetation.

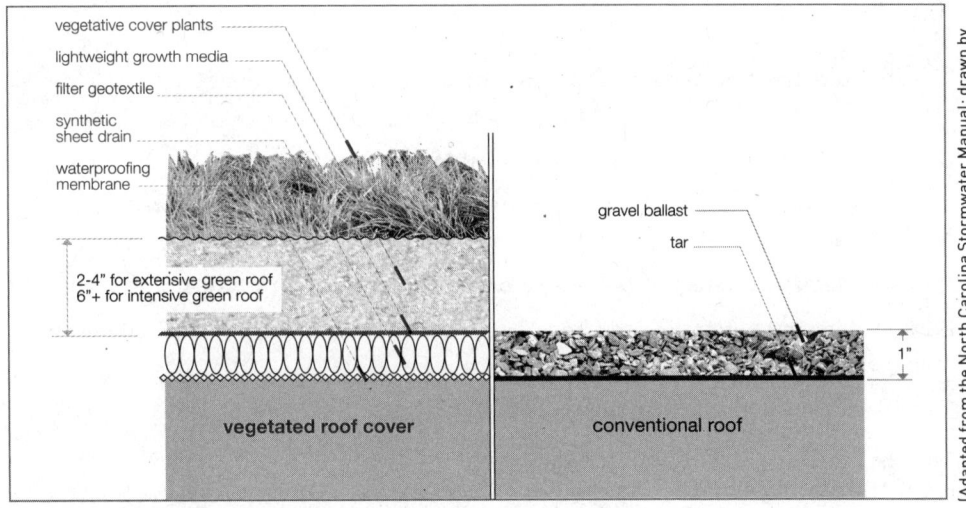

FIGURE 3-28: Components of a typical extensive green roof.

(Designed by Melissa Acker and Carter Cone; photo by Jon Calabria)

FIGURE 3-29: Extensive vegetated roof at University of North Carolina, Asheville, with species representative of the rich, forested herb layer.

DESIGN CRITERIA

▶ The structure must be capable of supporting the saturated weight of the green roof system.

▶ Determine whether the roof will be visible and/or accessible.

▶ Plant selection must carefully consider growing media depth and rooftop microclimate.

▶ Provide adequate drainage from green roof to accommodate larger rainfall events.

▶ Edge system and perimeter area free of plants (ballast) to minimize wind (sheer) from rolling up roof during high-wind events.

▶ Identify local incentives for green roofs that may benefit the project.

▶ A good waterproof membrane is key to a successful green roof. Be sure all manufacturers' recommendations are followed to ensure compliance with warranty requirements.

POTENTIAL LIMITATIONS

▶ Even with a lightweight growing media, leachate occurs, and should be directed into the other stormwater control measures.

▶ It is undesirable to direct leachate into water harvesting, particularly if water is reused for nonpotable uses such as toilet flushing.

▶ Structural assessment and design is required to determine if the structure can support the weight of a green roof.

▶ Growing media installation may be accomplished via crane/hopper, blower truck, helicopter, or freight elevator.

▶ Green roof plantings should be irrigated with a drip system until plants are established.

▶ Frequent monitoring should focus on leaks, plant survivability, and managing aggressive exotic vegetation removal as needed.

POROUS PAVEMENTS

A porous pavement is a load-bearing surface with sufficient porosity or permeability to allow rainfall to pass through to the pavement base course, typically a well-graded aggregate, several inches to a few feet deep, that provides reservoir capacity for infiltrated water. Porous pavements are an excellent stormwater management strategy on nearly any site, project type, or land use. Many different styles, materials, and costs make this strategy more appealing than ever. Runoff can be detained for slower release or retained for infiltration (Ferguson 2005).

Porous pavements overcome a major impact created by impervious surfaces by allowing rainfall to permeate the pavement surface and interact with the soil below it. Because they encourage infiltration, porous pavements can be an important strategy to replicate natural hydrology on developed sites that must accommodate pedestrian and vehicular traffic loads. Porous pavements can be used on most sites.

Porous pavements can also be educational—their function is visible; precipitation disappears through the pavement instead of running off, surface puddles are absent, and glare and tire spray are minimized. The strategic use of porous pavements may reinforce a perception or understanding of natural processes. The variety of porous pavements that are available today makes it easier to maintain aesthetic appeal.

Porous pavements should not be designed to filter sediment or pollutants because of the potential for clogging. However, because porous pavements reduce runoff volume, they are a very effective component of an overall water quality protection strategy. See Figures 3-30 and 3-31.

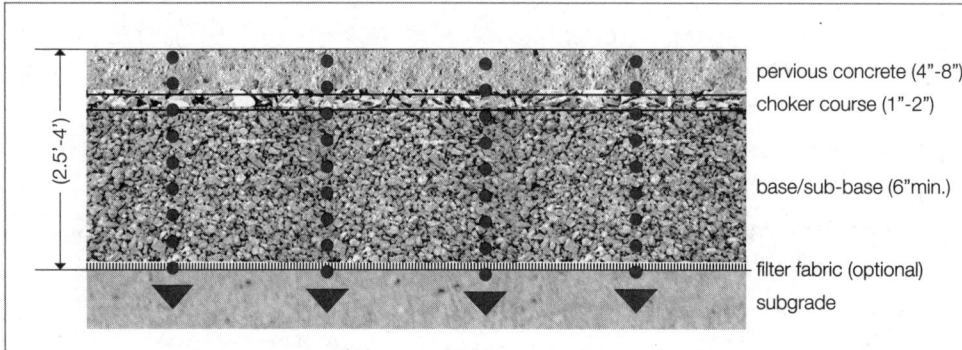

FIGURE 3-30: Typical pervious concrete pavement section.

FIGURE 3-31: Permeable unit paving installed over a washed gravel dry well capable of retaining the 10-year storm event at the North Carolina Arboretum.

DESIGN CRITERIA

► Locate where existing soils have an infiltration rate of 0.5 in. per hour or more, to allow for adequate infiltration

► The porous pavement subgrade should be flat to encourage infiltration and minimize conveyance/downgradient migration.

► Adjacent sediment sources (e.g., landscaped areas) should drain away from the porous pavement.

► Pavement type, thickness, and base course profile are dependent on anticipated traffic load and desired water storage capacity of the base course.

POTENTIAL LIMITATIONS

► Do not use in the following site conditions:

  ▷ Rolling to steep slope gradients

  ▷ Excessive sediment load to the pavement surface

  ▷ Traffic load or anticipated use that exceeds the pavement's capacity

  ▷ Pollution hot spots where groundwater contamination is a concern

► Clogging potential if not swept and vacuumed, particularly on porous concrete and asphalt where binding may occur several inches below the surface

Practices that Mitigate Runoff by Encouraging Evapotranspiration and Infiltration

Additional runoff generated by the built environment should be retained and infiltrated onsite to match the site's undisturbed hydrologic conditions. This can be calculated directly if sufficient knowledge of the site's undisturbed condition can be ascertained. Alternatively, there are several other methods of determining a volume of water to retain onsite. Many municipalities require that a first-flush volume (or water quality volume) is captured and treated onsite; depending on the region, this volume is typically based on a rainfall depth of 0.5 to 1.5 in. (Pitt 1999). The EPA and other organizations require the onsite retention of the 95th percentile storm event, which ranges from 0.7 to 1.8 in., depending on the region (U.S. EPA 2009a). Some general guidance for planning successful mitigation practices is: Slow it down, spread it out, soak it in. Create designs that slow down excess runoff, spread out runoff into shallow holding areas, and lengthen the time water sits on the site to mimic natural landscape processes by using design that slows runoff, such as vegetated swales, extended detention basins, green roof , cisterns, bioretention, infiltration basins, or porous pavements (see Figure 3-32). Strategies include:

► Combine different management systems—Combine practices such as bioretention, permeable pavement, and vegetated roofs. For example, parking lots can drain to retention systems that overflow to infiltration systems that filter water into cisterns that store clean excess runoff for irrigation or nonpotable use.

► Build redundant stormwater systems—Increase safety and reliability by providing multiple, redundant, and distributed facilities that reduce the chance of system failure. Many small facilities will be more effective than one big facility because if any of the small facilities fail, the other facilities will still work and can function while the failed facility is repaired.

▶ Minimize reliance on pipes, inlets, gutters, curbs, paved channels, and other below-surface hard infrastructure elements to the degree possible. Keeping stormwater systems on the surface increases opportunity for evaporation, filtration, and infiltration; creates systems that are easier to monitor and maintain; and has more opportunities to integrate stormwater management into landscape design.

▶ Recycle runoff—Install rain barrels, cisterns, or subsurface retention facilities to capture runoff from roofs, parking, and plazas for use as irrigation and nonpotable purposes. Use small solar pumps to reticulate captured runoff to landscape areas in a looped system that increases plant health, refilters runoff, and reduces municipal water use.

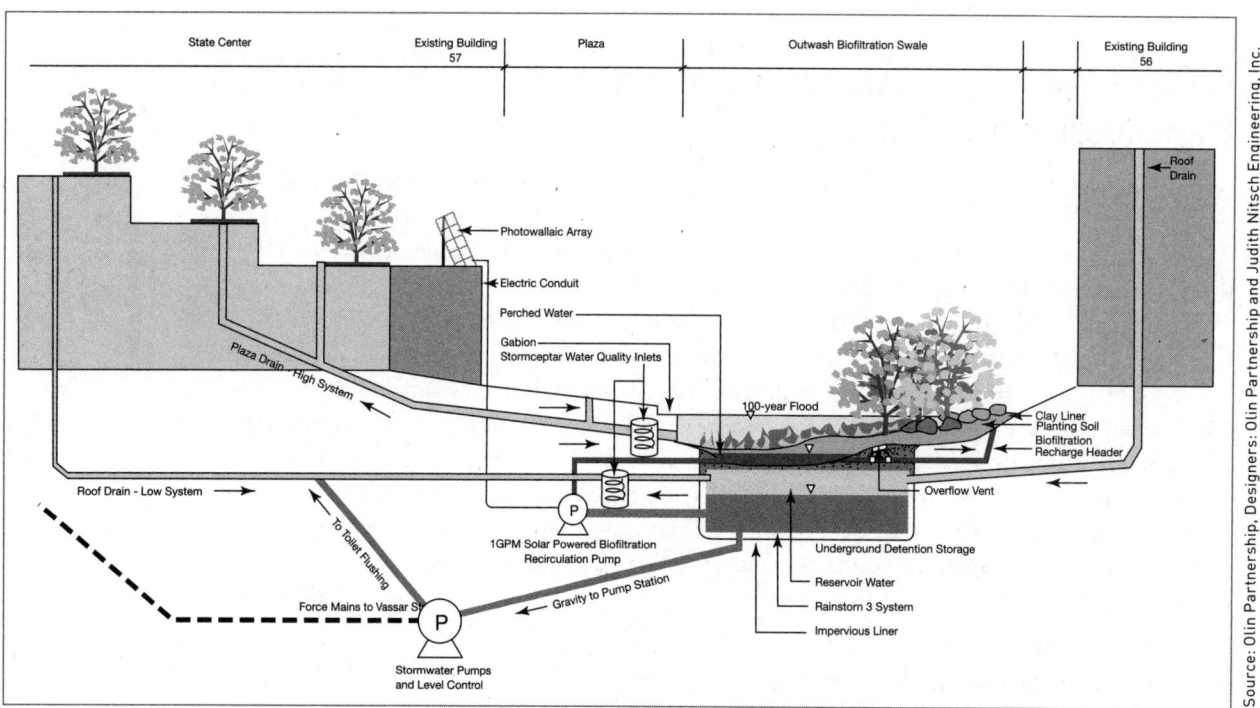

(Source: Olin Partnership, Designers: Olin Partnership and Judith Nitsch Engineering, Inc.

FIGURE 3-32: The Plaza cross section at MIT is an excellent example of an integrated site design that mitigates excess runoff.

The following specific strategies are based on the beneficial relationship between precipitation, vegetation, and soil found in the natural environment. By filtering and infiltrating runoff, they can significantly improve water quality and decrease runoff volume. They are flexible in form and easily constructed on new sites or retrofitted into existing sites. While they typically require substantial surface area, there are options for high-density sites that are challenged for landscape space. Many proprietary systems are available for below-grade infiltration, allowing water to collect and infiltrate below parking lots, fields, or other site uses. There are also many proprietary oil/water/grit separators that provide some water quality benefits and can be installed at catch basin locations on the site.

The strategies described in this section are most successful when distributed throughout the site, collecting water from small drainage areas (less than one acre). This is in direct contrast to the conventional approach of collecting runoff from the site in pipes and delivering it to one location for temporary detention.

RAIN GARDENS AND RAIN POCKETS

A rain garden/rain pocket is usually a small, shallow (6 to 8 in. deep) depressed area that encourages water to briefly pond and infiltrate within a day. From a conceptual standpoint, rain gardens may be seen as a strategy to mimic the depressed features and irregularities that are common throughout many natural landscapes. Occurrences such as depressions from the roots of toppled trees, sinkholes, and wildlife burrows create microcatchments that store and infiltrate surface runoff in a natural landscape. In developed areas, small, frequently occurring rain gardens distributed throughout a site can be linked to other stormwater control measures (SCMs) to begin emulating natural conditions.

Rain gardens are best suited to landscaped areas with soils that infiltrate greater than 0.5 in. per hour. They are most effective when many small rain gardens are distributed throughout a site to infiltrate runoff as close to the source of the runoff or impervious surface as possible. These features usually do not include an underdrain, unlike bioretention areas. Rain gardens should be landscaped with appropriate species and designed to enhance the plant species diversity and aesthetic appeal of the site.

Indigenous plant species could be selected to emulate plant communities capable of withstanding temporary inundation and also periods of drought. Many floodplain species are adapted to these conditions and offer habitat that may have been displaced by development or land-use change, such as ephemeral pools that support amphibians. Because of the small area, herbaceous species may be better suited than woody species and may offer enhanced constituent adsorption and sequestration abilities (Figures 3-33 to 3-35).

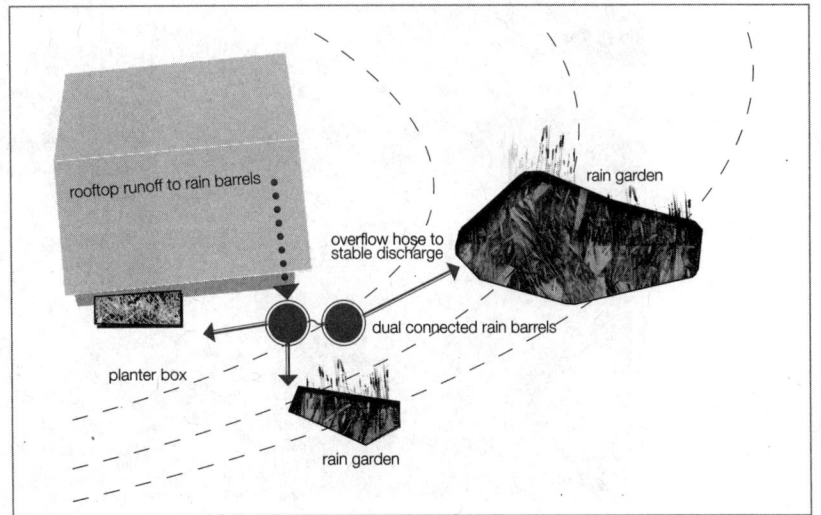

[Adapted from *Maryland Stormwater Design Manual*; drawn by Simon Bussiere]

FIGURE 3-33: Typical rain garden in a residential application.

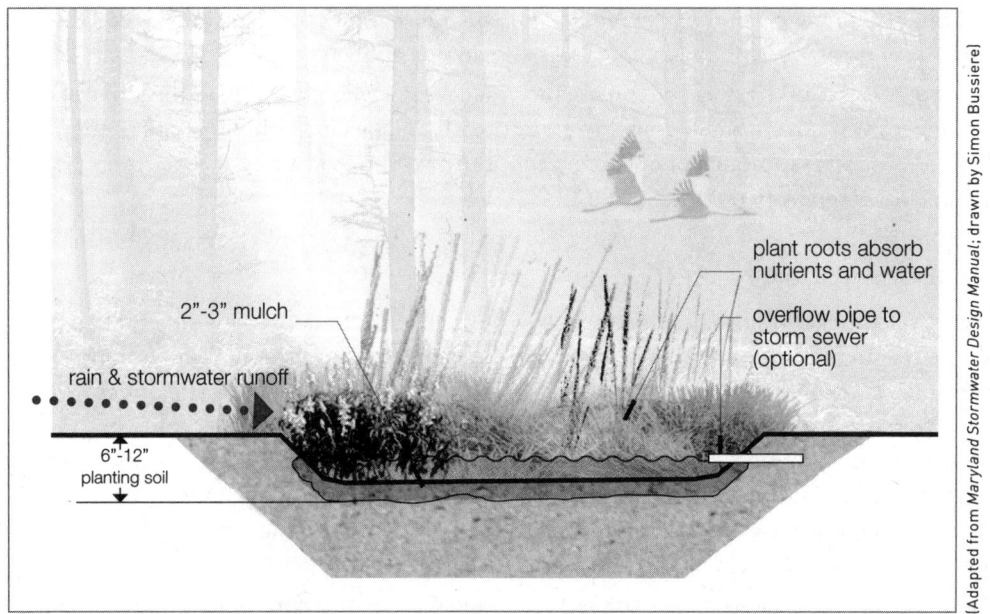

2"-3" mulch

plant roots absorb
nutrients and water

overflow pipe to
storm sewer
(optional)

rain & stormwater runoff

6"-12"
planting soil

(Adapted from *Maryland Stormwater Design Manual*; drawn by Simon Bussiere)

FIGURE 3-34: Typical rain pocket in a residential application.

(Design by Mac Franklin; photo by Jon Calabria)

FIGURE 3-35: The "pocket rain garden," a name coined by Glenn Palmer, is generally smaller than a bioretention area and consists of amended, indigenous soils and plants.

DESIGN CRITERIA

▶ Rain gardens can receive runoff from a variety of surfaces, vegetated roof systems, and cistern overflow.

▶ Most suitable sites have (undisturbed) soils with higher percolation rates and preferably full sun. Sandy soils with high infiltration rates should be amended to reduce the infiltration rate. Avoid siting in areas with a high water table.

▶ Determine soil percolation rate by excavating soil to the proposed elevation of the rain garden, filling with water, and measuring infiltration. Sites with less than 0.5 in. per hour should be avoided or designed as a bioretention area with an underdrain. (See Chapter 5 for more discussion of soil testing for infiltration rates.)

▶ Locate in headwater of catchment but downgradient of structures (with crawlspace).

▶ Holding capacity is based on catchment runoff and the infiltration rate of the soils and subsoils, which should percolate capture volume of design storm within 24 hours.

POTENTIAL LIMITATIONS

▶ Generally drains a very small impervious area and is usually considered an in-line practice that should be sited downgradient of structures.

▶ Excessive runoff velocities can erode the bottom and sides of the basin and contribute sediment and other constituents downstream, reversing the benefits of the rain garden.

▶ Occasionally, frequent rain events that exceed infiltration rates will result in extended saturated conditions and might result in standing water that could breed mosquitoes.

▶ It is common for the rain garden to require supplemental irrigation to sustain some of the plant species acclimated to mesic conditions.

BIORETENTION AREAS

Bioretention areas are shallow, upland stormwater basins that use vegetation and highly permeable soils to filter and infiltrate runoff. First conceived of in the early 1990s, bioretention areas have become perhaps the most widely used low-impact stormwater practice in use today. They are functional, flexible, attractive, and cost effective. Bioretention areas generally consume between 5 and 10 percent of the surface area for the catchment they are treating, so they may be challenging to implement on sites with extremely limited space.

As previously stated, a major objective of sustainable stormwater management is to emulate the predevelopment hydrology of a site, replicating the interception, evapotranspiration, infiltration, and runoff that occurred under natural conditions. Bioretention contributes to this goal by providing vegetation to intercept and evapotranspire precipitation, porous soils to infiltrate rainfall and runoff, and a flow splitter or an overflow to allow the safe conveyance of larger storm events.

Bioretention is most effective when small bioretention areas are distributed throughout the site and utilized to capture and treat contaminated runoff from impervious sites, such as hardscapes, close to the source. Clean runoff from roofs and nonvehicular hardscapes should be considered for rainwater harvesting before bioretention.

Bioretention areas can incorporate native vegetation and the ephemeral presence of water to create attractive, revelatory designs that can contribute to the project's sense of place. They can provide rich opportunities to interpret the hydrologic cycle, urban stormwater management, and water resource stewardship. Vegetation used in bioretention areas can also create habitat for wildlife.

Bioretention delays the flow of runoff by capturing small runoff events and filtering stormwater through vegetation and soil before releasing a portion of it to subsoils or through underdrains to downstream SCMs or infrastructure. A portion of runoff absorbed by bioretention areas may be returned to the atmosphere through evapotranspiration by vegetation. In smaller storms, a lag in the peak discharge may occur due to this interception.

Bioretention can contribute to stormwater infiltration; however, this is limited by the infiltration rate of *in situ* soils, depth to water table, depth to bedrock, confining soil layer, and the potential for groundwater contamination. Bioretention design that includes an underdrain will limit the volume of water that infiltrates into the *in situ* soil. Bioretention should be designed to infiltrate all captured water within 48 hours in order to avoid mosquito breeding. Bioretention areas should never be located in poorly drained soils or wetland areas. Soils should have a minimum drawdown rate of 9 in. in 12 hours.

Bioretention areas can remove some pollutants, such as sediments, nutrients, metals, and solids. Unless a submerged aquatic zone is created within the plant rooting area, nutrient uptake and transformation may be limited.

Recent research has helped to identify many variations on the "standard" bioretention design, specifically adapting the practice to: street rights-of-way, sloped sites, designs that target specific pollutants, filtration-only designs for pollution hot spots and low-permeability soils, and other site-specific situations. The designer must understand what specific functions are expected from the bioretention area and tailor a design that meets those objectives (Figures 3-36 , 3-37, 3-38, and 3-39).

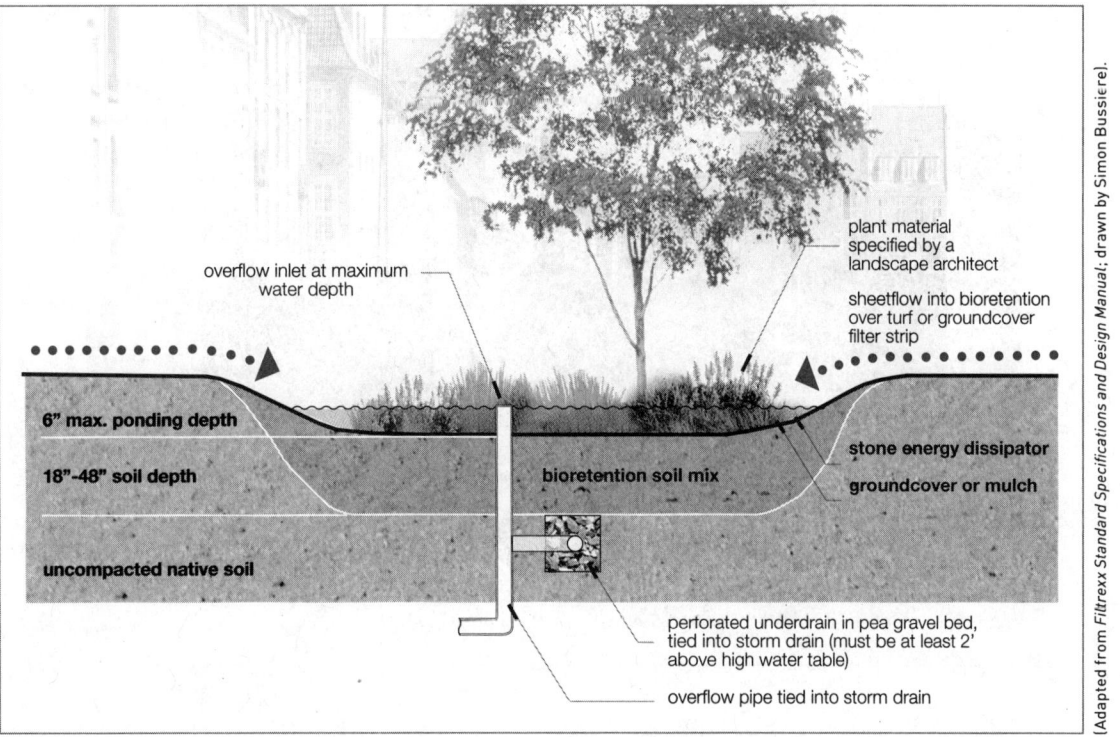

overflow inlet at maximum water depth

plant material specified by a landscape architect

sheetflow into bioretention over turf or groundcover filter strip

6" max. ponding depth

18"–48" soil depth

bioretention soil mix

stone energy dissipator

groundcover or mulch

uncompacted native soil

perforated underdrain in pea gravel bed, tied into storm drain (must be at least 2' above high water table)

overflow pipe tied into storm drain

(Adapted from *Filtrexx Standard Specifications and Design Manual*; drawn by Simon Bussiere).

FIGURE 3-36: Typical bioretention section.

(Photo from Jon Calabria)

FIGURE 3-37: Bioretention area at the North Carolina Arboretum.

(Photo from Stuart Echols)

FIGURE 3-38: This bioretention area in the parking lot at the Oregon Museum of Science and Industry receives runoff from adjacent pavement.

(Design by Jon Calabria and Bill Skelton; photo by Jon Calabria)

FIGURE 3-39: Bioretention area at an elementary school that features indigenous species to treat roof runoff.

DESIGN CRITERIA

▶ Size to capture design storm (first flush/small storms/95th percentile event) from a maximum contributing drainage area of 1 acre.

▶ Locate bioretention areas as close to the source of runoff as possible to minimize necessary conveyance velocity and cost, yet downgradient of structures to avoid infiltration into soil adjacent to crawlspace/basements.

▶ Distribute numerous small bioretention areas throughout a site, each collecting runoff from a drainage area of 1 acre or less.

▶ Bioretention soil depth should be sufficient to meet vegetation requirements and meet pollutant removal targets. Depths of 4 ft have been shown to reduce thermal loading in the southeastern United States.

▶ Bioretention soil should consist of mostly inert media (approximately 85 percent), coarse sand, and weed-free compost (carefully consider using biosolids).

▶ Internal water storage zone can promote nutrient treatment/transformation.

▶ Plant selections must be tolerant of periodic inundation and dry periods typical of the local climate.

▶ Allow larger storms to safely bypass bioretention area by using a flowsplitter.

▶ Sites with compacted or low-permeability soils (less than 2 in. per hour) will likely require an underdrain to ensure drawdown within 48 hours.

▶ Surface ponding is temporary and usually less than 1 day.

POTENTIAL LIMITATIONS

▶ Do not locate in poorly drained, low-infiltration, or wetland soils.

▶ Do not locate where depth to water table or bedrock is less than 2 ft below the invert elevation of the bioretention facility.

▶ Existing native vegetation should not be disturbed to install bioretention.

▶ Do not locate near wells, septic system drain fields, building foundations, and basements.

▶ Do not locate in sandy, quick-draining soil where treatment may not occur before reaching and potentially contaminateing groundwater.

▶ Construction should occur late in the construction sequence and when the site is stabilized to prevent clogging.

ENHANCED INFILTRATION BASINS OR TRENCHES

A good infiltration basin is an excavated trench or cell filled with washed, well-graded, coarse aggregate to maximize voids for water storage and designed to exfiltrate collected water into the surrounding soil. Infiltration basins are best suited for areas where uncontaminated, sediment-free runoff can be collected and infiltrated, and their primary benefits are groundwater recharge and runoff-volume reduction.

Infiltration basins/trenches do not have underdrains; therefore the *in situ* soil must have an adequate infiltration rate (0.5 in. per hour or more) in order to ensure timely drawdown of collected water. It is also important that water entering the basin or trench is sediment-free to minimize clogging. This can be achieved by minimizing erosion from the drainage basin, providing pretreatment of runoff to remove sediment. See Figure 3-40.

FIGURE 3-40: Enhanced infiltration trenches help to infiltrate small storm events and mitigate the impact of impervious surfaces; however, they are not always compatible with aesthetic goals. This trench at the Oregon Convention Center is planted at the edges and filled with attractive stone.

DESIGN CRITERIA

▶   Locate close to the source of runoff in order to minimize conveyance infrastructure, cost, and velocity.

▶   Keep drainage area less than 1 acre, and distribute infiltration areas throughout the site as necessary.

- ► Provide a forebay, or other means of pretreatment, in order to prevent clogging from fine suspended particles in runoff.

- ► Locate where *in situ* soils have an infiltration rate of at least 0.5 in. per hour.

- ► Size the infiltration area (surface area and aggregate depth) to ensure complete infiltration of storage volume within 48 hours.

- ► Washed, well-graded aggregate has approximately 40 percent void space.

- ► A variety of proprietary infiltration chambers are available to substitute for washed, well-graded aggregate. Many of these systems provide a much higher void space than aggregate.

- ► Incorporate observation wells to monitor infiltration basin performance.

POTENTIAL LIMITATIONS

- ► Do not use in pollution hot spots as it may cause groundwater contamination.

- ► Typically does not incorporate plants, and may be aesthetically unappealing.

- ► Limited to areas with infiltration rates of 0.5 in. per hour or more.

- ► Use may be restricted in areas with Karst geology.

Practices That Convey Runoff from Larger Storm Events

Large, infrequent storm events can exceed the capacity of infiltration and bioretention practices, which are sized specifically to address small storms. It is imperative that large storms can be safely conveyed through the site and routed to an appropriate discharge point or receiving water body. Flow splitters can direct excessive velocities or quantities to an overflow system, yet direct the first flush into the appropriate practices. There are opportunities to create conveyances that provide additional benefits, including filtration, infiltration, wildlife habitat, aesthetics, and education.

The following practices are beneficial alternatives to conventional pipes and armored channels. They emulate natural conveyance by allowing vegetation, soil, rock, and water to interact.

VEGETATED SWALES AND STEP POOLS

A vegetated swale is an open channel conveyance lined with vegetation, preferably a dense planting of native species with fibrous roots, although turf grass is functional as well. Vegetated swales are typically less expensive than conventional concrete gutters and culverts, but they require additional maintenance and consume more surface area. The environmental benefits of using vegetated swales include limited filtration of sediment and , increased roughness and visibility of stormwater runoff. Swales serve as an effective pretreatment for runoff before entering other practices that may be compromised by sediment (e.g., infiltration basins). Vegetated swales are designed to safely convey larger storm events, typically the 25-year storm event. (Figure 3-41)

Several variations of the vegetated swale include the turf-reinforced matted swale (TRM) and the step pool conveyance. The first variation of the vegetated swale includes the TRM. If velocities exceed design conditions of vegetated swales, then matting can be applied to reinforce the vegetation and resist velocities that would otherwise erode. The temporary or permanent matting is applied directly to the seeded, finish grade of the swale. Vegetation sprouts through the firmly anchored material. TRM is useful for constrained conditions where slope or channel dimensions are limiting factors. If the slope is excessively steep, a step pool conveyance may be appropriate.

A second variation includes a step pool conveyance similar to a swale. The step pools should be constructed of material that conveys runoff over a nonerosive material, which splashes into pools where it dissipates energy into the bottom of the pool. Erosive energies may dislodge material in the pool but should not destabilize the conveyance. The step pool may be a preferred alternative to aesthetically convey runoff in steeply sloping areas. Expense and construction sequencing may be limiting factors for step pool conveyances. See Figure 3-42.

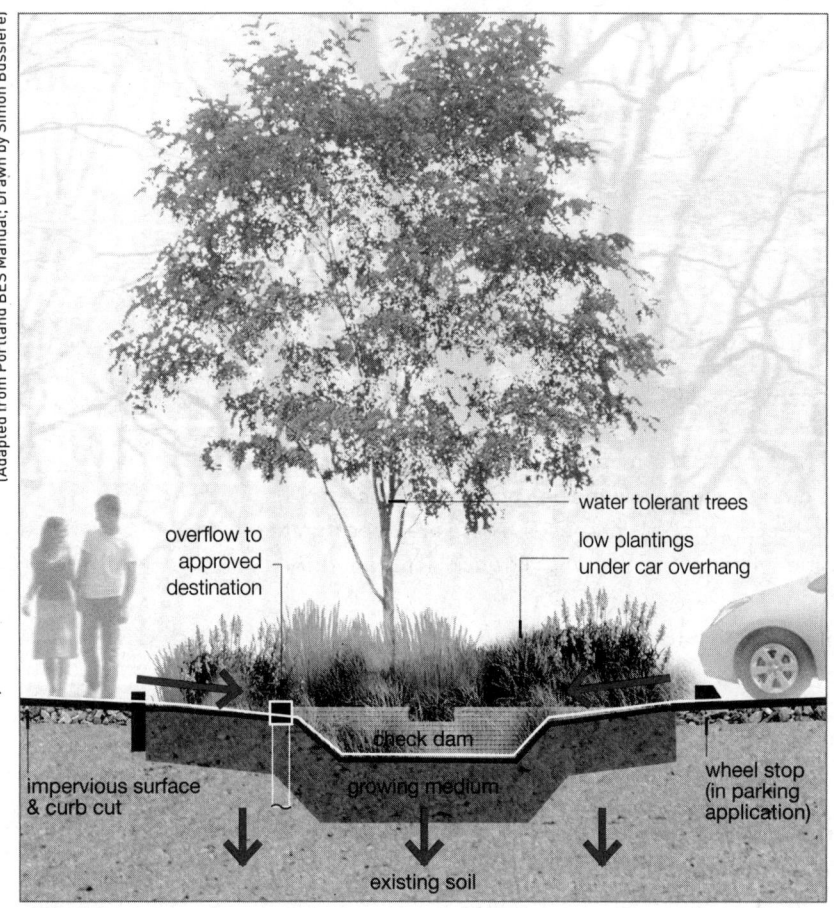

(Adapted from Portland BES Manual; Drawn by Simon Bussiere)

water tolerant trees

overflow to approved destination

low plantings under car overhang

check dam

impervious surface & curb cut

growing medium

wheel stop (in parking application)

existing soil

FIGURE 3-41: Typical vegetated swale.

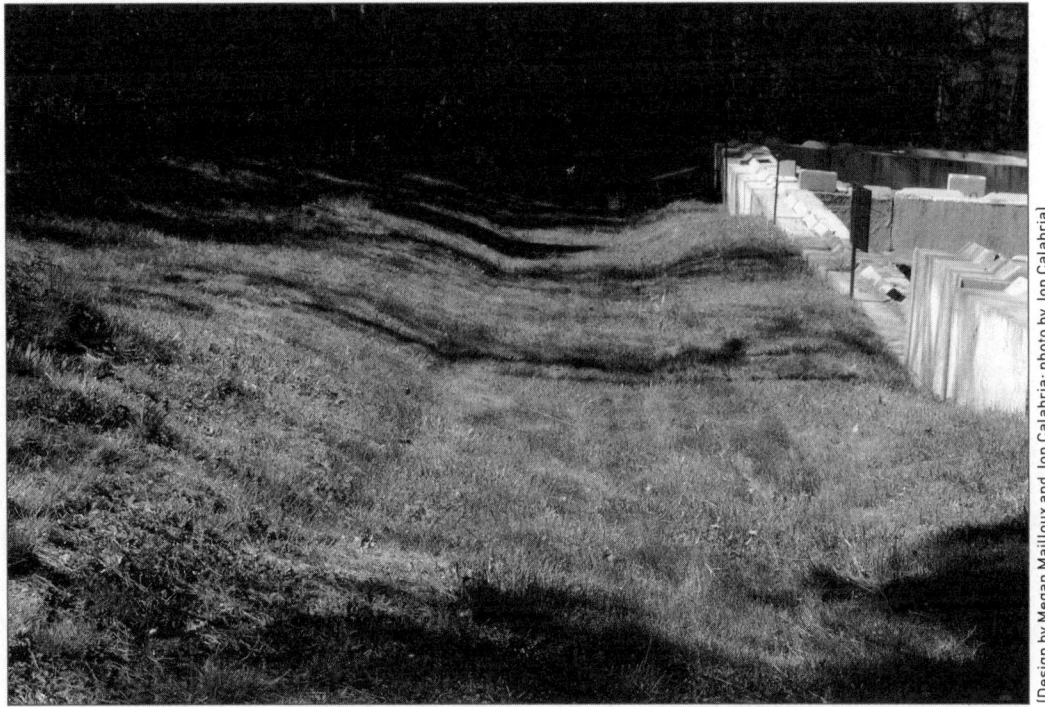

(Design by Megan Mailloux and Jon Calabria; photo by Jon Calabria)

FIGURE 3-42: TRM channels can tolerate greater velocities and steeper slopes than vegetated swales. Grasses and forbs are seeded and matting is stapled overtop to allow vegetation to sprout through matting.

DESIGN CRITERIA

► Flatter slopes are preferred; switch to TRM or step pools if design storm velocities may cause scour.

► Size the width and channel dimensions to minimize velocity and safely convey the design storm.

► Do not exceed 2:1 side slopes.

► Ensure 100 percent vegetative cover to prevent erosion, except in pool bottoms of step pool systems.

POTENTIAL LIMITATIONS

► Requires more surface area than conventional gutters and pipes.

► Cannot be used on erodible soils.

► Requires maintenance.

BIOSWALES WITH MICROPOOLS

Bioswales are essentially linear bioretention areas designed to convey runoff, as well as filter and infiltrate it. They are subject to the same slope and sizing design criteria as vegetated swales, and incorporate the engineered soil media, underdrains, and vegetation of bioretention. The infiltration function of bioswales can be enhanced by installing check dams that create micropools behind them, which then infiltrates into the engineered soil.

Bioswales can provide an excellent opportunity to make stormwater conveyance an attractive site feature. Vegetation, conveyance, micropools, and infiltration are all important components of natural hydrological processes and exposing and interpreting them may increase public awareness. (See Figures 3-43 , 3-44, 3-45, 3-46, 3-47, and 3-48).

[Photo from Jon Calabria]

FIGURE 3-43: Significant grade changes require energy dissipation in order to prevent scouring—the natural model of a step pool swale/cascade provides an attractive and functional solution.

[Design and photo by Andrew Bick, Confluence Engineering]

FIGURE 3-44: Step pools focus erosive energy to the bottoms of pools and away from the banks to minimize erosion.

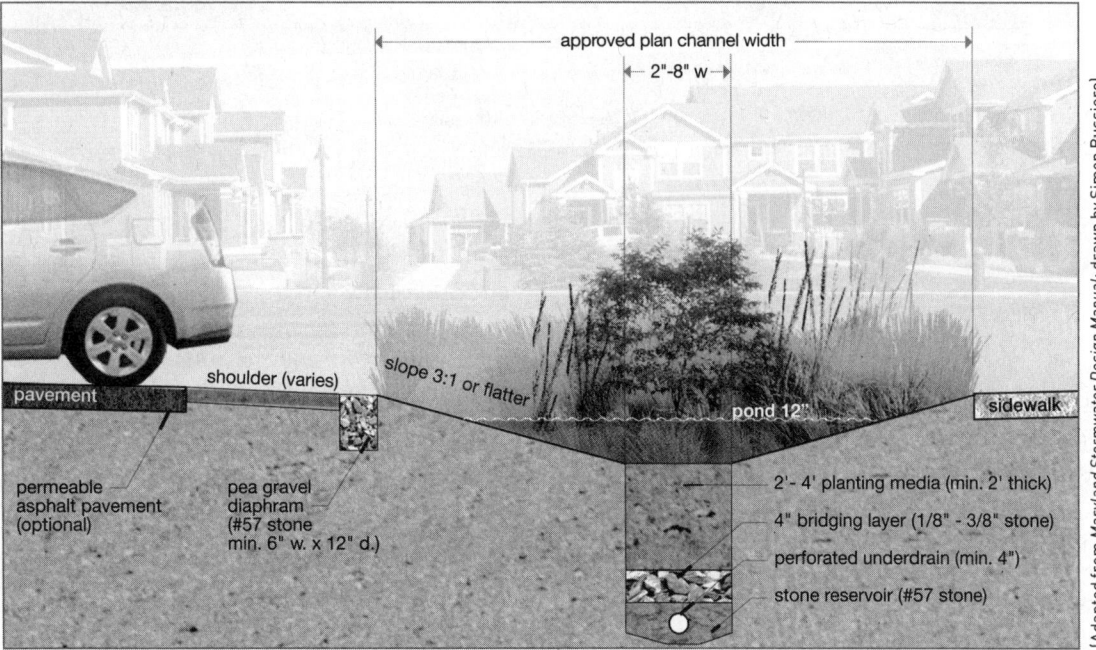

[Adapted from *Maryland Stormwater Design Manual*; drawn by Simon Bussiere]

FIGURE 3-45: Typical bioswale with micropools section.

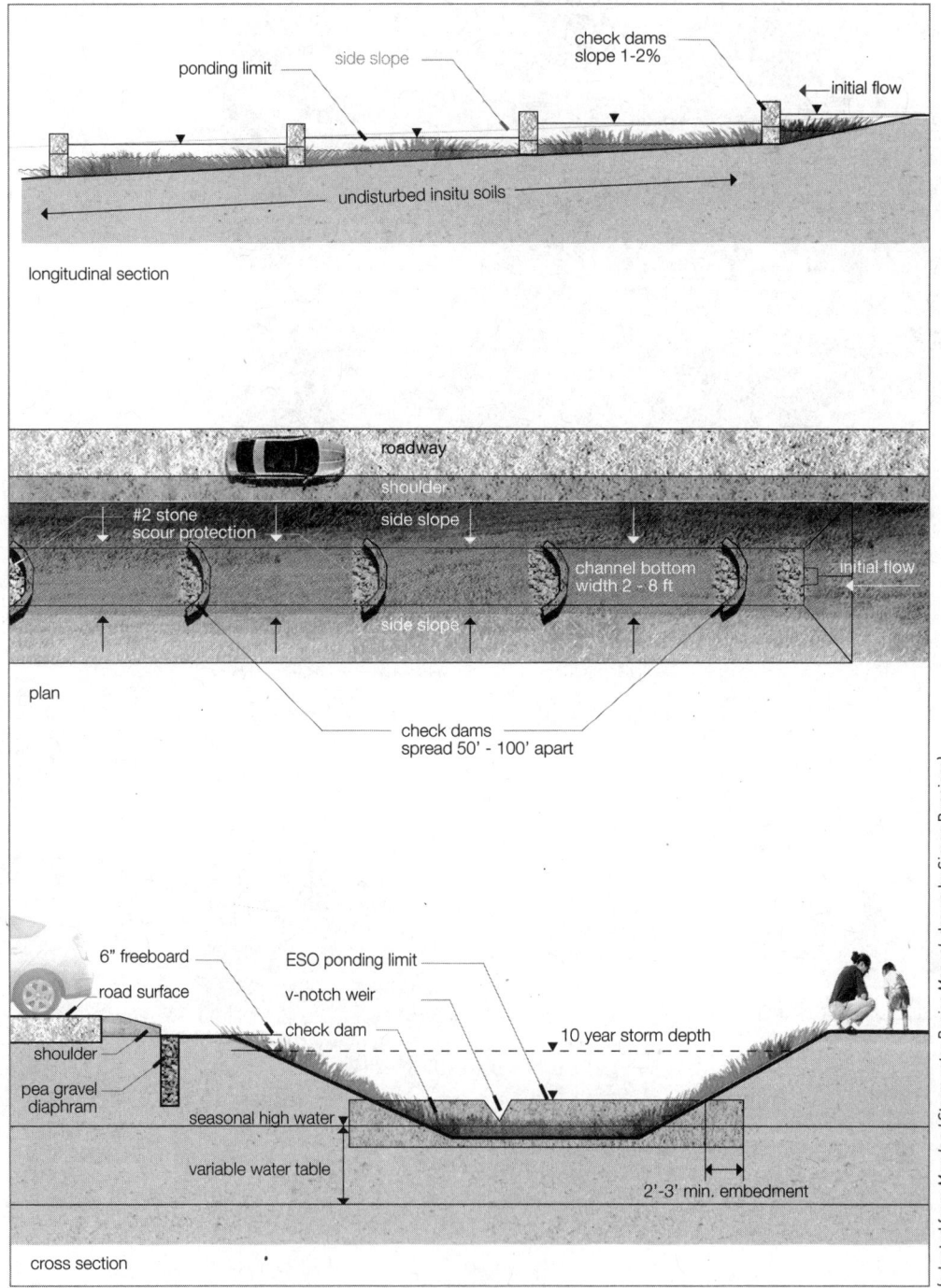

FIGURE 3-46: Typical bioswale with micropools section.

(Design by Mac Franklin and Jon Calabria; photo by Jon Calabria)

FIGURE 3-47: Bioswale with micropools. Roof and parking lot runoff is treated by flowing through swales and pools.

(Design by Mac Franklin; photo by Jon Calabria)

FIGURE 3-48: Bioswale planted with American wisteria, blue flag iris, and soft rush to treat parking lot runoff before draining to stormwater wetland.

DESIGN CRITERIA

▶ See the sections on "Bioretention Areas" and "Vegetated Swales and Step Pools." vegetated swales and bioretention areas.

POTENTIAL LIMITATIONS

▶ Flow splitter or restriction may be needed to limit erosion or scour from excessive velocities.

▶ May re-suspend sediment and other pollutants collected from previous storm events.

▶ See the sections "Bioretention Areas" and "Vegetated Swales and Step Pools" for more information.

Practices That Protect or Restore Receiving Water Bodies

All water flows down gradient until ultimately discharging into a surface water body. Surface runoff moves faster than subsurface flow or groundwater flow. Conventional development tends to increase surface runoff and diminish subsurface and groundwater flow, thereby degrading the receiving water bodies. The stormwater management strategies described in this book strive to maintain runoff levels equal to the undisturbed site hydrology. Runoff will still occur during large storm events, and adjacent development or watershed conditions will impact receiving streams.

The following practices can be used to protect receiving water bodies from site runoff, as well as to restore and protect riparian water resources.

LEVEL SPREADERS

Level spreaders are used to convert concentrated stormwater flow into low-velocity sheet flow. As flow is discharged from a pipe, headwall, swale, or other conveyance, it is detained and spread horizontally along a contour by a low, level, nonerodible barrier such as concrete wall. When the flow fills the storage volume behind the level spreader, it will spill over the spreader as low-velocity sheetflow (Hathaway and Hunt 2006).

Level spreaders are important when concentrated flow is discharged into vegetated areas, natural areas, riparian buffers, or other stormwater management practices. See Figures 3-49 and 3-51.

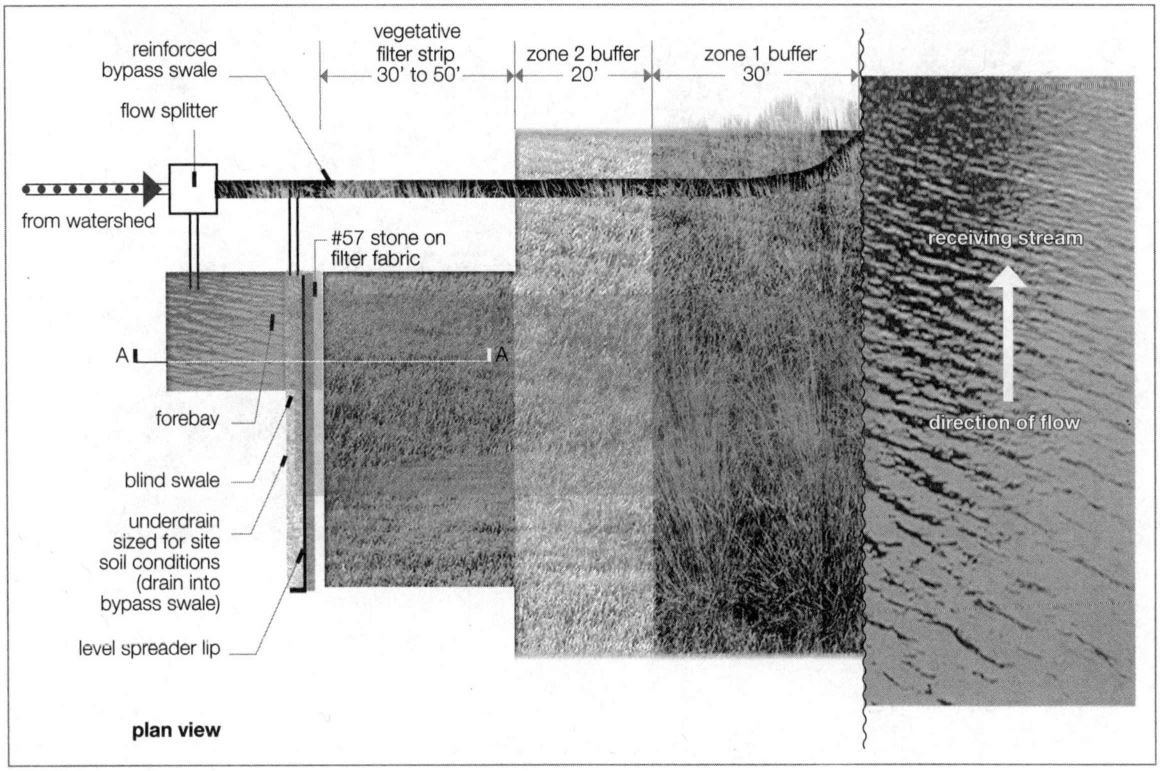

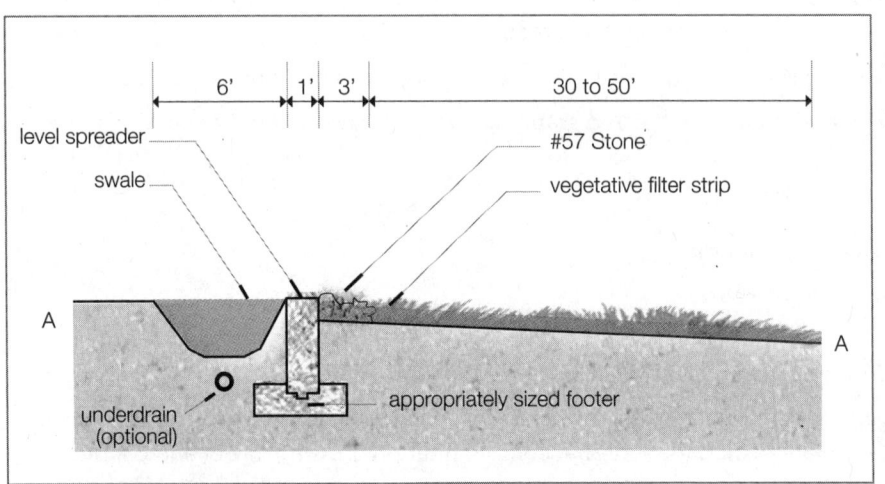

reinforced
bypass swale

flow splitter

from watershed

vegetative
filter strip
30' to 50'

zone 2 buffer
20'

zone 1 buffer
30'

#57 stone on
filter fabric

A

A

receiving stream

direction of flow

forebay

blind swale

underdrain
sized for site
soil conditions
(drain into
bypass swale)

level spreader lip

plan view

[Adapted from *North Carolina Stormwater Manual*; drawn by Simon Bussiere]

FIGURE 3-49: Typical level spreader plan and section.

6'   1'   3'   30 to 50'

level spreader

swale

A

#57 Stone

vegetative filter strip

A

underdrain
(optional)

appropriately sized footer

[Adapted from *North Carolina Stormwater Manual*; drawn by Simon Bussiere]

FIGURE 3-50: Typical level spreader plan and section.

(Design by Lappas+Havener; photo by Jon Calabria)

FIGURE 3-51: Runoff is diverted into a series of drop boxes that convey into a level spreader, bioretention area, and littoral shelf at the North Carolina Museum of Art.

DESIGN CRITERIA

▶ Required level spreader lengths depend on the flow rate and the characteristics of the receiving area. Some recommendations include a minimum length of 13 ft to pass 1 ft³ per second onto a grassed area while 100 linear feet of level spreader may be needed to pass 1 ft³ into a mulched area. In both scenarios, runoff may recollect and scour receiving areas. Refer to local requirements.

▶ The level spreader must be perfectly level and nonerodible or failure will occur.

▶ Receiving area should be flat and stabilized with permanent vegetation.

POTENTIAL LIMITATIONS

▶ Requires nearly flat area

▶ Requires a large area

STORMWATER WETLANDS WITH EMERGENT AQUATIC VEGETATION

Stormwater wetlands are similar to a slowly leaking pond . They collect runoff and treats it with intentionally planted, abundant herbaceous vegetation growing in wetland conditions. Well-designed stormwater wetlands can be attractive, provide habitat, and treat nutrients and other constituents found in the stormwater runoff. Undulations in the bottom of the stormwater wetland and the accompanying plants could be designed to interpret the subtleties of the microhabitat and corresponding plant species. It is important to state that existing natural wetlands should not be used for this purpose because of the potential damage to the system.

The planting regime should mimic early stages of wetland succession and only allow for open water in limited areas, such as the permanent pools. Runoff from the catchment, which is preferably pretreated by other SCMs, can be diverted into the stormwater wetland based on the volume of runoff from the design storm. Runoff from the design storm fills the shallow depression and is slowly released over a several-day period. More specifically, the stormwater wetland consists of undulating microtopography with saturated soils and a few permanent pools. These conditions enable emergent aquatic vegetation whose roots foster conditions necessary for treating some nutrients and other constituents. The flatter topography and surface area required for the stormwater wetland may not be conducive for constrained sites, but the stormwater wetland is generally considered the most cost-effective solution for treating runoff.

Stormwater wetlands share many of the same characteristics with constructed wetlands described later in this chapter. However, stormwater wetlands usually rely on inflow from precipitation events and the resulting fluctuation in water surface over several days. Constructed wetlands usually have constant flows and often have a structural soil contained within a liner. The water depth in the stormwater wetland should fill the wetland to no more than 9 in. above the permanent pool elevation. Water control structures should consist of spillways sufficient to allow for a 72-hour drawdown, or other regulated drawdown period, and pass flows greater than the design storm as well as large storm events. The volume from the design storm should be passed prior to the next rain event, but also drain slowly enough to maximize treatment potential. See Figures 3-52 , 3-53, and 3-54.

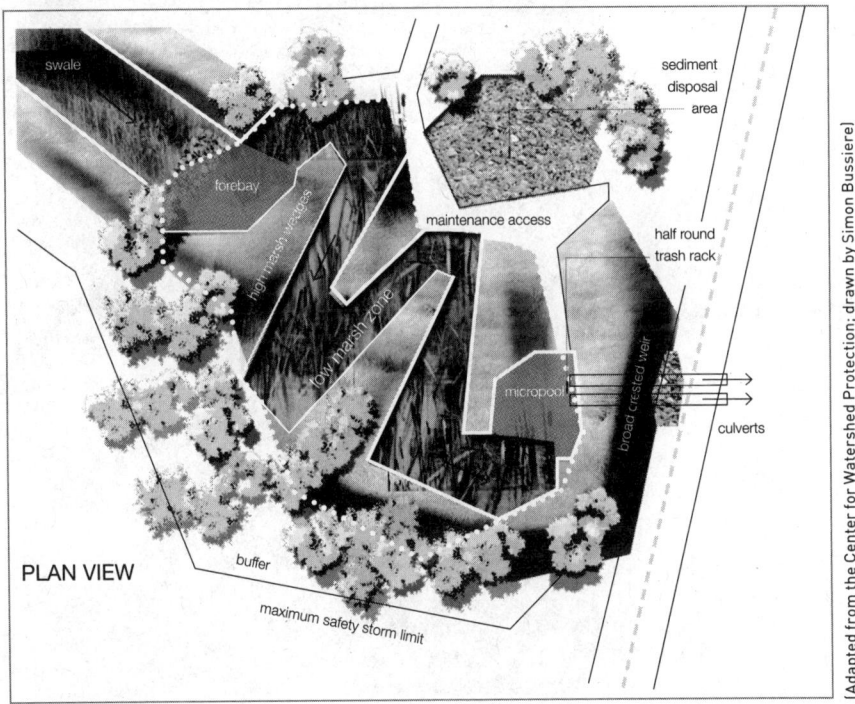

PLAN VIEW

swale

forebay

high marsh wedges

low marsh zone

micropool

broad crested weir

buffer

maximum safety storm limit

sediment disposal area

maintenance access

half round trash rack

culverts

[Adapted from the Center for Watershed Protection; drawn by Simon Bussiere]

FIGURE 3-52: Typical stormwater wetland plan and section. Note the forebay for settling solids and slowing flow into the sinuous low marsh zone with permanent pools..

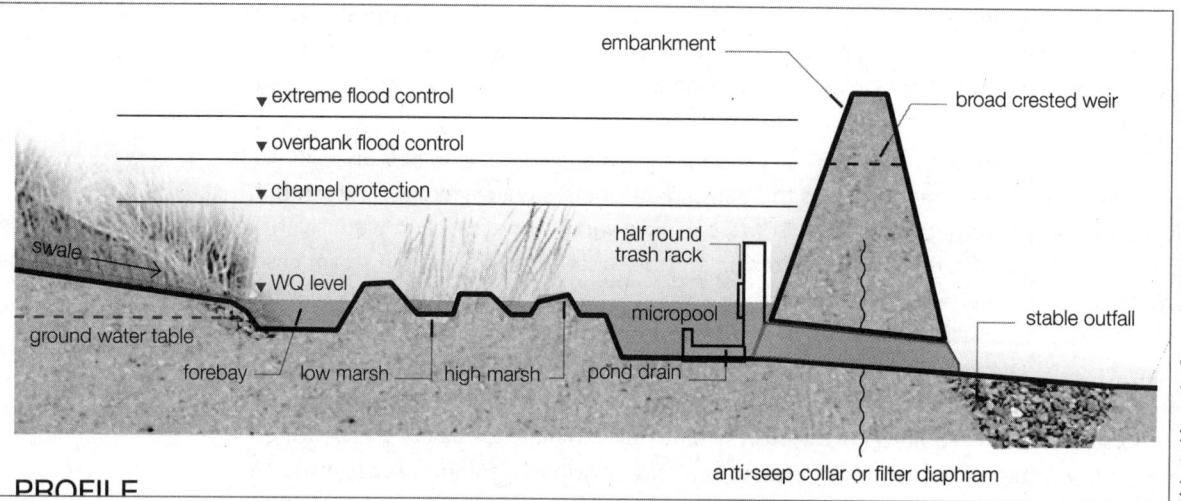

FIGURE 3-53: Typical stormwater wetland plan and profile. Note undulations in the bottom of the wetland to create some permanent pools for a variety of plant habitats that respond to the variety of inundation depths..

FIGURE 3-54: Stormwater wetland that treats parking lot runoff and is planted with indigenous, emergent aquatic vegetation.

DESIGN CRITERIA

Although diffuse flow is preferred, most runoff will be conveyed into the stormwater wetland through a flow splitter, then into a small pool called a forebay. This area collects sediment and other trash and can be periodically accessed for dredging or removal. After runoff flows through the forebay, it should be directed through a sinuous flow path complete with permanent pools and diverse microtopography that fosters a variety of plant species responding to different inundation depths.

▶ Surface area of the stormwater wetland is often 5 to 10 percent of the catchment area depending on land cover.

▶ Siting of the stormwater wetland should be downgradient of other SCMs and structures and release into level spreaders or riparian areas.

▶ Construction sequence should include constructing the stormwater wetland after the site has been stabilized.

▶ A perched water table condition groundwater interception can be created to sustain emergent aquatic vegetation.

▶ Runoff should flow through flowsplitter, then forebay, then sinuous flow path with permanent pools.

▶ Extended drawdown device is usually through a small orifice. A reducer on a larger-diameter pipe should be considered to allow for flexibility of regulating flow and also for ease of maintenance.

▶ Design for approximately 9 in. of freeboard with 72-hour drawdown.

▶ Strongly consider adding an emergency drawdown device or incorporate it into the extended drawdown device, such as a flashboard riser with an inverted orifice.

POTENTIAL LIMITATIONS

Although a variety of factors contribute to the design volume, the catchment should be less than five acres. Often, areas in the floodplain that lie farthest from the streams are the most suitable because they mimic the valley toe wetland system. Site conditions, such as a low water table or infiltrating soils, may require perching a water table to create saturated soils to sustain emergent aquatic vegetation. Often clayey soils are used to create a confining layer to reduce infiltration in lieu of a fabricated liner. Either treatment may be necessary to prevent groundwater contamination if treatment efficiencies are exceeded.

The several-day drawdown of the design volume often requires the use of a small orifice to slowly drain the volume. The orifice may clog with floatables, other solids, or plant growth. Most weekly inspection visits should monitor and remedy clogging conditions. A screened, inverted orifice may alleviate clogging, but compressed air or other mechanical methods can clear obstructions.

Less frequent monitoring should investigate the volume of settled materials in the forebay and dredge and properly dispose of those materials if the forebay partially fills in or looses its ability to settle materials. If the forebay fills in with material, it can migrate and fill in the permanent pools, which may compromise their function. Aggressive exotic vegetation and unchecked woody plant growth should also be monitored. Corrective action will be needed to prevent the site from going through later successional stages complete with woody vegetation, which may foster undesirable organisms (e.g., mosquitos).

STREAM, RIPARIAN, AND FLOODPLAIN ENHANCEMENT OR RESTORATION

Many streams destabilize as a result of land-use change, which influences hydrologic, sediment, and nutrient loads. Even minor increases in catchment imperviousness, such as converting as little as 3 percent of the area to impervious surfaces, can destabilize a stream system and threaten its biological integrity. Stream enhancement and restoration interventions generally seek to create an equipoised stream capable of conveying water and sediment supplied by the current watershed conditions.

When a stream system becomes destabilized, its riparian area and floodplain function diminish. An unstable stream might incise and become disconnected from the floodplain. Intensified stream flows then scour vegetation and destabilize the stream bank, which releases excessive sediment into the stream system. The stream is likely to re-create a floodplain at a lower elevation by eroding the old floodplain (terrace) until it forms a new floodplain. Successful stream enhancement and restoration interventions should reconnect the streams with an active floodplain and restore riparian areas and associated floodplain function.

Riparian vegetation is the stream-side, vegetated buffer that supplies organic material to support organisms in the stream, holds the stream banks, filters pollutants, and creates habitat. These functions are diminished when vegetation is altered or removed. Floodplains also provide storage of overbank flows and flooding, which contains sediment that is deposited onto the floodplain and sustains the riparian vegetation (see Figure 3-55).

[Design by David Bidelspach and Dan Clinton; photo by Jon Calabria]

FIGURE 3-55: Stream, riparian, and floodplain enhancement and restoration is a multifunctional strategy to protect the stability and health of receiving water bodies. An excessively eroding outside meander was enhanced with in-stream structures to reduce erosion, and provide habitat and public access as part of the Town of Fletcher greenway system.

DESIGN CRITERIA

▶ Reference conditions should guide stream channel and floodplain interventions.

▶ Design should strive to convey water and sediment supplied by the watershed.

▶ Planting design should incorporate succession phases to reach restoration trajectory.

POTENTIAL LIMITATIONS

▶ Stream enhancement and restoration may be most successful when the catchment hydrologically emulates a reference watershed and stable stream system. If the catchment is not stable, stream enhancement or restoration activities may not improve the biological diversity and richness.

- ► Areas with impervious cover of more than 3 to 5 percent may not be stable enough to support stream restoration, so stream enhancement should be considered.

- ► Continued changes in watershed conditions may compromise stream restoration efforts if they are not anticipated accurately.

- ► Property constraints may limit the options that are available for consideration.

- ► Extensive permitting may be required before construction may begin.

- ► Experienced contractors are critical, but may be difficult to find in some regions.

- ► Reference reaches may not be available or reference conditions preclude restoration and the objective is enhancement.

- ► Biological restoration or enhancement may be compromised by watershed inputs and may never exceed existing condition.

- ► Aggressive exotic species may compromise restoration or enhancement if left unchecked or unmonitored.

- ► Successional vegetation stages may not be congruent with romantic/pastoral aesthetic expectations and may be maintained contrary to restoration trajectory.

- ► Streams convey sediment and water so any pollution attached or dissolved will be conveyed downstream.

OVERSIZED CULVERT TO ACCOMMODATE BANK-FULL FLOW AND LARGER FLOWS

Stream crossings should be limited to as few as possible, although they are necessary to provide access to many sites and communities. If possible, they should be located at stable reaches of stream with a narrow bank-full and flood-prone width. Conventional practice was to simply install a box or pipe culvert sized to convey a design storm (typically 25- or 100-year storm, depending on the circumstances). The problem with many conventional culverts is that they constrict the flow, which causes increased velocity and downstream scouring, and they disrupt the channel bed, which degrades habitat and may completely disconnect upstream and downstream habitat.

Oversized culverts should be designed to span the entire bank-full width of the stream. They should be bridges, bottomless culverts, or pipe/box culverts large enough to embed the culvert bottom below the stream channel. This allows continuous channel bed features and habitat.

Flood events larger than bank-full should not be constricted through a culvert sized for the bank-full flow. Additional culverts should be installed in the floodplain and at the floodplain elevation to allow flood flow to pass without constriction. See Figure 3-56.

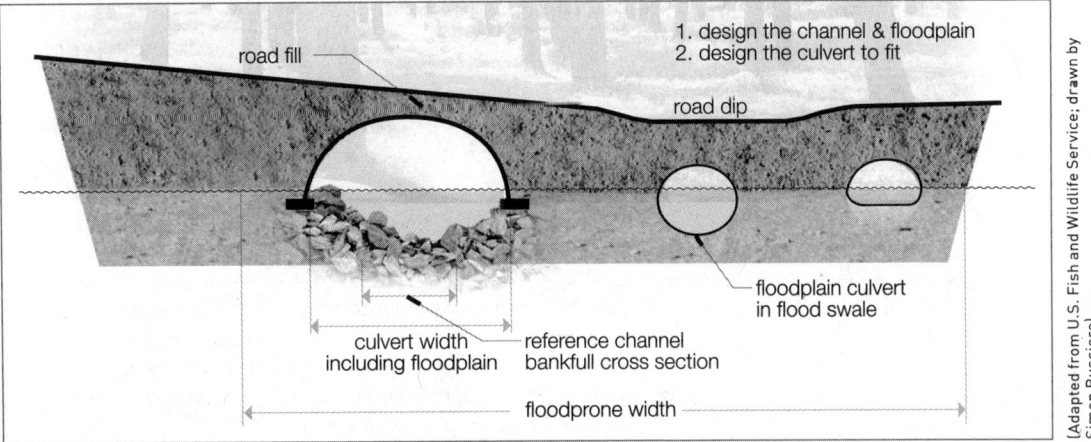

road fill

1. design the channel & floodplain
2. design the culvert to fit

road dip

floodplain culvert
in flood swale

culvert width
including floodplain

reference channel
bankfull cross section

floodprone width

(Adapted from U.S. Fish and Wildlife Service; drawn by Simon Bussiere)

FIGURE 3-56: Typical section of an oversized culvert to accommodate bank-full flow and larger flows.

DESIGN CRITERIA

▸ Size culvert to accommodate bank-full channel width and channel banks.

▸ Size bank-full culvert and floodplain culverts to safely convey the design flood.

▸ Ensure continuous channel bed features through the culvert.

▸ Consider the use of natural channel design practices such as v-weirs or J-hooks in concert with the crossing in order to protect banks and provide channel grade control, as appropriate.

POTENTIAL LIMITATION

▸ Larger culverts may cost more than conventionally sized culverts.

Sediment and Erosion Control

Without properly planned and functioning sediment and erosion control techniques and practices, many land disturbance activities or restoration activities may have an adverse impact upon receiving aquatic resources. Sediment becomes detached by erosive energy from precipitation, wind, or freeze/thaw cycling, and then mobilizes. Because of the risks to the health, safety, and welfare of the public, many regulations suggest minimum performance guidelines to retain sediment onsite and prevent it from entering riparian areas. In early 2010, EPA proposed an average maximum turbidity limit. As states possibly impose these requirements, strategies to minimize detachment of sediment particles and filter discharge become increasingly important.

Most grading activities are regulated and must follow approved plans that indicate techniques and practices to control erosion and sediment. Some activities are listed in Table 3-5 and may vary depending on the regulating entity.

TABLE 3-5: Sediment and Erosion Control Methods*

Erosion Control	Stabilization	Carefully plan and sequence grading activities to minimize exposed areas. In these areas, stockpile and reapply top-soil, then cover with mulching or temporary or permanent vegetation, which may be reinforced with matting to assist vegetation establishment and reduce erosion.
Sediment Control	Runoff Control and Conveyance	Diverting and conveying runoff based on a design storm into a variety of sediment treatment practices can improve their performance. Diversion practices define watershed areas and can control velocities. Conveyances include open channels protected with vegetation and slope drains to minimize sedimentation.
Sediment Control	Inlet and Outlet Protection	Outlet protection techniques minimize scour by reducing velocities or resisting erosion. A level spreader is useful in this situation if flatter land is available. Inlet protection techniques include various protection methods such as filter strips and various configurations of gravel to ensure structural integrity.
Sediment Control	Sediment Collection	Sediment basins and traps efficiency can be enhanced with porous baffles, topwater release devices, and flocculants.
Sediment Control	Maintenance	Maintenance of these practices includes frequent inspections to correct failures and remove accumulated materials to ensure proper function.

*Table follows the *North Carolina Erosion and Sediment Control Planning and Design Manual* (North Carolina Sedimentation Control Commission 2009).

The highest priority is to prevent erosion by minimizing areas of disturbance, limiting clearing, and protecting existing vegetation. Disturbed areas should be stabilized by quickly establishing ground cover and protecting conveyances, which minimizes detachment of soil particles in areas with sheet flow. Although regulations may govern maximum land disturbance areas and establishment time periods, careful planning of construction sequencing can further minimize destabilized areas. In areas of active construction, ground cover is the best way to control erosion. Ground cover usually consists of establishing temporary or permanent vegetation that may be reinforced by suitable matting. Ground cover may also consist of a mulch or compost blanket sometimes planted with permanent vegetation representative of early stages of plant community succession.

Unfortunately, once sheet flow accumulates, erosive energy can scour the landscape. Protecting these conveyances with vegetation, matting, or other methods can minimize sedimentation and protect riparian areas. Conveyances should direct flow to standard sediment control practices prescribed by the regulatory authority. These temporary sediment control practices are less effective than erosion control because they are intended to filter sediment from the runoff. Recent refinements to standard practices, such as placing porous baffles perpendicular to the flow paths, are helpful for reducing sedimentation. However, the discharge concentrations may exceed regulatory limits, and should likely be routed through several practices prior to release into receiving aquatic systems.

An effective sediment and erosion control plan considers siting many practices throughout the site and avoiding centralized treatment with fewer, larger practices. One primary benefit of this strategy includes retrofitting sediment control practices into stormwater management practices (described previously) after the site is stabilized. Therefore, sediment and erosion control plans should be designed in concert with the permanent stormwater management strategies to be installed on the site. An integrated design can achieve temporary and permanent strategies that mitigate short-term construction impacts and provide long-term benefit by protecting and emulating natural site hydrology (see Figure 3-57).

[NC DOT Highway widening project; photo by Jon Calabria]. Cite Section 6.64.1 of Erosion and Sediment Control Planning and Design Manual. A cooperative effort between the North Carolina Sedimentation Control Commission, the North Carolina Department of Environment and Natural Resources, and the North Carolina Agricultural Extension Service. Research by Rich McLaughlin, NCSU.

FIGURE 3-57: Skimmer sediment basin with porous baffles. Porous baffles promote laminar flow, and topwater drawdown devices help minimize turbidity and sediment discharge into receiving waters.

WATER CONSERVATION

One of the primary considerations in a sustainable or restorative site design is to evolve a healthy, beautiful, living landscape primarily with the water available to the site as a renewable resource, and without depletion of precious drinking water or impact to ground and surface water systems and associated habitat. While many naturalized or native landscapes and vegetated systems like certain green roof applications are designed and maintained to thrive with only the water that falls on them as rainwater, there are certain cultural landscapes that will need supplemental water in order to thrive. Also, many sites will generate surplus stormwater from impervious or semipervious surfaces (roofs, hardened surfaces), or from other sources associated with site and building operations.

In order to minimize water need for irrigation, a number of interrelated sustainable site strategies should be employed and managed over time. Building and maintaining healthy soil with appropriate nutrients and organic material is essential for plant vigor and soil moisture retention. Selecting and nurturing climate-appropriate native and/or adapted plant species suitable for the habitat being created or nurtured will minimize or eliminate supplemental water requirements once established. Sustainable maintenance practices such as holistic, integrated pest management, and natural, toxin-free landscape care will minimize plant stress and provide a stable, suitable plant habitat. Turf areas can be managed with natural lawn-care practices such as fewer mowing events, leaving grass taller; aeration; and overseeding with grass suitable for microclimate conditions. When watering is done, slow, deep, less frequent watering will produce healthier conditions with less water use. These strategies are closely linked to other sustainable site strategies, including the use of locally adapted native plants as appropriate for the context and maintenance regime and the re-creation of natural, infiltration-based hydrology.

The ideal sustainable water conservation approach is to match renewable (reused, recycled, or reclaimed) and/or surplus water available onsite with potential water demand or need in the landscape, creating a water balance. By taking water from otherwise impervious surfaces and conditions, holding it, and making it available during dry periods, a net water balance can be achieved, allowing supplemental water for a potentially wider range of cultural landscapes and promoting natural hydrology at the same time. In addition to strategies covered in other sections, two additional water conservation design strategies are necessary in order to integrate this approach into sustainable sites—the water supply, through water reuse and recycling, and the water delivery and distribution, with efficient irrigation. In addition to landscapes, open water features or elements can also consume water in the landscape.

Water Reuse and Recycling

A natural landscape thrives with only the rainwater, groundwater, and condensation (dew) available onsite. A sustainable site with created or modified landscape elements also should thrive with only the water available to the site as a renewable resource—primarily rainwater, but also potentially building process water, stormwater runoff from impervious or semipervious surfaces, and treated wastewater. In order to make surplus water usable in the landscape, it must approximate natural water—chemistry/quality, low sediment content, close to ground temperature, and so forth. Sustainable stormwater strategies discussed previously in this chapter can help accomplish this as part of an integrated design solution. Green roofs, bioretention, porous pavement systems, and constructed wetlands can all be designed and engineered to slow, cool, and cleanse water from various sources to make it suitable for use in landscape irrigation, created water features, and other potential applications in a sustainable site.

The Water Reuse Association defines reused, recycled, or reclaimed water as water that is used more than one time before it passes back into the natural water cycle. Water recycling is generally the reuse of harvested rainwater or treated wastewater for a variety of beneficial purposes, including landscape irrigation, created water features, and groundwater recharge. It can also be used for building processes that do not require potable water quality—toilet flushing, wash-down water, industrial process water, and the like.

A water reuse strategy entails the identification of potential sources of surplus water available onsite or from a building, targeting potential uses for that water, and then designing the appropriate methods to collect, treat (if necessary), store, and redistribute and deliver that water to the appropriate site and/or building elements. See Figure 3-58.

(Photo from Conservation Design Forum)

FIGURE 3-58: Mill Creek golf course in Kane County, IL, is designed with nonirrigated native and natural landscape for the portions not in play to minimize water need, and the tees, greens, and fairways are irrigated with reclaimed wastewater from nearby homes, businesses, schools, and churches treated onsite with an aerated lagoon system.

DESIGN INTEGRATION

A major way to optimize water resources for a sustainable site is through an integrated design process involving appropriately trained professionals. Water recycling and reuse is a simple concept but has many aspects which must be carefully and thoughtfully addressed. They include:

- ► What is the source or sources of water to be collected, recycled, and reused?
- ► What is the potential use or uses for the reclaimed water?
- ► What are the daily water demands for each use of reclaimed water?
- ► What local codes and ordinances will apply?
- ► Will the water be used indoors?
- ► Will there be human contact with the reclaimed water, and is it in a public setting?
- ► Will the water be applied or used to support plant life?

Depending upon the answer to these and other questions, the design team will need to include water resource engineers or other professionals trained in these areas to integrate with the landscape architect and other relevant professionals—mechanical engineer, architect, living systems/ecological engineer, horticulturalist, soil scientist, and others.

WATER COLLECTION AND CONVEYANCE

The water intended for recycling and reuse will need to be collected in order to make it available for treatment (if necessary) and reuse. Sources of water that might be captured are:

- ► Stormwater from roofs
- ► Stormwater from paved site surfaces
- ► Graywater from buildings (e.g., sink water, laundry water)
- ► Process water from buildings (e.g., condensate from air-conditioning units or ventilation units)
- ► Treated wastewater

Rainwater collection and conveyance elements can be an artful, interesting site design features. Runnels, channels, aqueducts, rain chains, scuppers, and other water conveyance elements are excellent alternatives to below-ground pipes and help reinforce the perception of water as a sustainable priority. These elements must be designed and maintained to accommodate the local climate. For example, in a cold-weather climate, freezing conditions must not allow for blockage of a rainwater conveyance element that is part of the stormwater management system and must function throughout the year (Figures 3-59, 3-60, 3-61).

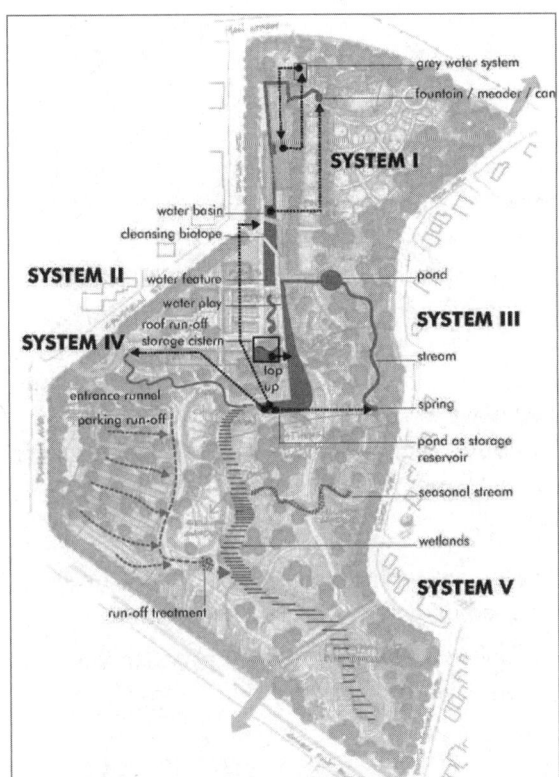

Design by Conservation Design Forum, Atelier Dreiseitl, and BKSK Architects; (Photos from Conservation Design Forum)

FIGURE 3-59: An integrated rainwater system illustrated in the master plan for the Queens Botanical Garden in Flushing, NY, is designed so that rainwater is treated as a resource with each phase of improvements.

FIGURE 3-60: Harvested rainwater is celebrated in visible, accessible water elements that also clean the water and provide for nonpotable uses.

FIGURE 3-61: A roof scupper becomes a visual focal point as it carries rainwater from the roof into the stormwater water feature for holding and eventual reuse.

WATER STORAGE

If the quantity of the reclaimed water matches the re-use needs, it is possible to simply direct the flow to where it is needed, as would be the case with a rain garden receiving water from a downspout. This is an example of a passive water harvesting and reuse system. However, it is more likely that water needs will not be perfectly timed with available reclaimed water supply. Instead, the surplus water will need to be stored for later use in the site.

Water storage involves the creation of a water holding facility suitable to temporarily detain an *adequate* volume of water to provide supplemental water for landscape irrigation and other nonpotable water needs throughout the year, without spending resources on surplus storage beyond what is needed. In order to determine the size, or capacity, of the water storage device, calculations are made based upon water supply and water demand. Typically, as part of the water system design process, an algorithm is used to model water supply and water demand throughout the year (typically by month):

- ▶ Water Supply
  - ▷ Net precipitation (by month) × area of rainwater harvesting surface (roof, pavement, lawn, etc.); net amount = rainfall amount - ET (evapotranspiration)
  - ▷ Other sources of nonpotable water available (by month), such as air-conditioning condensate, reclaimed gray- and/or black water, and so forth
- ▶ Water Demand
  - ▷ Estimated water need for landscape (by month; see "Water Demand/Watering Zones" later in the chapter)
  - ▷ Estimated need for water features and other landscape elements (by month)
  - ▷ Estimated need for other nonpotable water uses on site or in the building (by month)

If the water supply is greater than the demand, then the surplus is diverted to other rainwater management elements, such as bioretention/infiltration features. If the water demand is greater than the supply, then the site design is modified to reduce the demand further, or other sources of water considered, until a balance is reached. The water storage size is generally a percentage of the largest monthly water demand as available from the water supply. A percentage (less than 100 percent, usually 75 to 90 percent) of the maximum is used, as to provide assurance of the last 10 to 25 percent may require considerably more storage size, and can be much less cost-efficient in most applications. Since rainfall patterns (and to some degree water demand) fluctuate, the volume of the water storage needed is only an estimate, even with fairly sophisticated modeling. Therefore, provisions are usually made to top off the water storage device in long periods of drought.

Following are the primary types of devices typically used to provide active rainwater storage for nonpotable uses:

Surface Storage: Surface storage is simply creating a depression within the landscape to store water for irrigation and other uses. Typically a pond or basin is lined to hold water, with appropriate water quality measures included. Usually gravity fed, this method allows for greater evaporation off the surface, but is generally fairly simple if it can be integrated into the site, especially as an amenity.

Cisterns: A cistern is a tank or vessel constructed to store water for reuse. It can be installed above grade or below—water stored below grade is kept at ground temperature (generally cooler), which can be an advantage for water quality. A cistern can be designed to be filled with gravity-fed or pumped water, directed from roof or other surfaces. There are numerous manufactured cisterns of various sizes—above-ground are typically metal, concrete, or masonry; below-ground are typically fiberglass or metal (see Figures 3-62 and 3-63).

(Photo from Conservation Design Forum)

(Photo from Marcus de la Fleur)

FIGURE 3-62: This 30,000-gallon fiberglass cistern stores harvested rainwater, which is then used for toilet flushing and irrigation water for a largely drought-tolerant ornamental landscape at a corporate headquarters office complex in Wisconsin. It was sized using a site water budget that determined the best balance between generally available rainfall and potential demand for nonpotable water onsite.

FIGURE 3-63: Rain barrels are part of a simple rainwater harvesting technique to direct rainwater from existing downspouts and store it for use in a garden; typically done more on individual home landscapes. These rain barrels are repurposed storage containers artfully decorated as garden features. They are part of a remarkable sustainable home landscape designed and installed by Marcus de la Fleur in Elmhurst, Illinois.

Modified Cisterns: Water storage can be created simply underneath paved surfaces in combination with a porous pavement/infiltration system by adding depth to the open-graded gravel or a proprietary structural reservoir system with liners. Cisterns can also be artfully integrated into the building or site architecture (see Figure 3-64).

Other Design Considerations: In addition to size and water quality, design considerations include the pumping systems and energy use. Simpler systems that use gravity or renewable energy will generally be easier and less costly to operate and maintain over time. Water storage devices can also be a great way to make the sustainable site water conservation approach more visible and didactic (see Figure 3-65).

(Image from Quinn Evans Architects)

FIGURE 3-64: The water system at the new Ann Arbor, MI, municipal complex includes a below-grade cistern that is a portion of the open-graded gravel below the public "rain terrace." Stored rainwater is circulated through the water sculpture and used for supplemental irrigation for the drought-tolerant plantings.

(Photo from David Yocca)

FIGURE 3-65: Visitors are greeted and drawn to the main entrance of the Ladybird Johnson Wildflower Center in Austin, TX, with a stone aqueduct and created wetland pool at this botanical gardens—one of the more extensive applications of artful, visible rainwater harvesting and reuse as part of a sustainable site design.

WATER FILTRATION AND TREATMENT

In order to be used in the landscape, building, or in accessible, touchable water features, reclaimed or recycled water must be made safe and appropriate. Ideally, this is done with living systems as part of the overall integrated site strategy. Green roofs and walls, rain gardens, and porous pavement systems can all work to cool rainwater (or keep it cool), and filter out sediment. Living systems with vegetation can also use nutrients. Other living systems such as constructed wetlands and biological wastewater treatment systems can be used depending upon the constituency of the water.

Initial filtration removes catchment debris, sediment, and particulates. Methods of initial filtration include green roofs, rain gardens, bioswales, and constructed wetlands (see Figure 3-66).

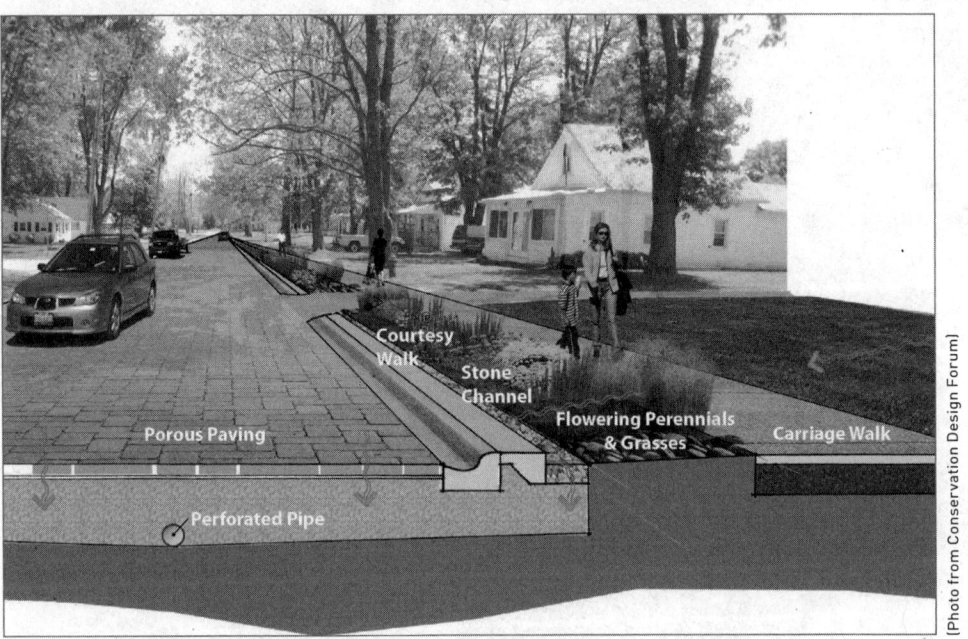

(Photo from Conservation Design Forum)

FIGURE 3-66: This green street retrofit in Charles City, IA, includes a porous pavement system, made of interlocking concrete unit pavers, in combination with parkway bioswales, that effectively treats and infiltrates the vast majority of the rainwater that falls in this 16-block neighborhood.

When water will be reused for flushing of toilets, sprinkler systems, or irrigation of food crops, it must be of a suitable quality and temperature. *Water treatment* is a necessary step in the process of storage for reuse. Purification methods include treatment in living systems, UV disinfection, and membrane filters. These methods are discussed in greater detail in the "Onsite Wastewater Treatment, Disposal, and Reuse" section of this chapter (see Figure 3-67).

FIGURE 3-67: A living system at the Omega Center for Sustainable Living in Rhinebeck, NY, treats all of the wastewater generated on this 500-acre learning center campus; clean water is then infiltrated through a series of chambers below the parking lot.

WATER REDISTRIBUTION AND DELIVERY

The reclaimed or recycled water needs to be distributed back to where it is required onsite. Ideally, this is done with gravity or pumps powered by renewable energy sources, and with minimal capital and long-term operations costs, although this will vary widely depending upon the use. For distributing the water into the landscape, an efficient irrigation system is used.

Efficient Irrigation

An efficient irrigation system is one designed and maintained to keep the landscape it is serving healthy without wasting water, by using water from renewable or surplus sources, and minimal or no nonrenewable energy. The overall landscape approach on a site is to program as much of the site with low-input, nonirrigated vegetation as fits with the intended use, and then to plan the other portions of the landscape with available renewable or surplus water sources in mind. Once the landscape elements of the site have been generally programmed and the portions of landscapes that may need or benefit from supplemental water have been determined, then a way to deliver that water to the landscape can be considered.

As with any of the site elements, the irrigation system should be designed by an appropriate professional trained and experienced in irrigation system design and water-conserving methods, and in close collaboration with the other design professionals through an integrated design process. The system should be installed, operated, and maintained by properly trained professionals to ensure that it performs as intended.

The primary objective of an efficient irrigation system is to minimize the use of potable water for landscape maintenance, while providing other benefits and value at the same time. Considerations include:

- ► Size the portion of the landscape needing supplemental water to supplemental rainwater or other water surpluses available onsite.

- ► Harvesting and reusing rainwater can be part of managing water onsite, and a planting approach with native or locally adapted species can be part of a biodiversity improvement approach.

- ► Employ a properly designed and operated irrigation system to distribute water appropriate for the application, such as a drip system with smart controls supplied with collected rainwater for an ornamental garden landscape.

- ► Rainwater and other surplus water available to the site should influence the landscape design approach.

- ► Rainwater harvesting and pumping equipment should be coordinated with other necessary mechanical systems.

TYPES OF IRRIGATION SYSTEMS

Many conventional landscape irrigation systems use considerably more water than is necessary, even for water-consumptive turf, vegetable gardens, or ornamental beds planted with exotic species. Some of this water waste comes from systems that are simply not maintained properly—there are leaks, or too much water gravity-flows to certain portions of the landscape leaving other areas too dry, or portions of the system get damaged or broken. The regular maintenance of an irrigation system is an essential aspect of the maintenance and monitoring plan for a site that includes one (see Figure 3-68).

(Photo from David Yocca)

FIGURE 3-68: Conventional above-ground lawn irrigation systems can use considerably more water than is necessary due to overspray, excessive overlap of head ranges, leaks, evaporation, or poor maintenance of the system.

Most traditional irrigation systems use a series of above-ground jets, sprays, or rotating heads to spread water over a portion of the landscape. Heads are laid out to provide coverage for each portion of the landscape with minimal overlap. While above-ground systems are relatively low cost, they provide a significant opportunity for water evaporation and surface water runoff.

High-efficiency irrigation systems use a combination of water distribution and delivery techniques to target supplemental water to vegetation zones based upon actual need, thus minimizing water use and maximizing plant health. One alternative is to use a below-ground or at-ground drip irrigation system. This consists of a series of small-diameter hoses that are distributed through the portion of landscape that will need supplemental water by watering zone (see the following section), which are typically operated as needed and determined with water sensors. Plants need water in their root zone, and this method delivers a very controlled amount of water directly to the root zone, thus using a small fraction of the water that would be used by a conventional above-ground system. Drip irrigation systems also have to be maintained properly in order to remain functioning. Due to the smaller openings, and being buried, they are more prone to clogging, and can be cut or damaged if dug into. Therefore, a close connection between the drip irrigation system and landscape/site maintenance operations is critical.

Alternative methods of providing irrigation water include flood or furrow irrigation or surface ponding of water for irrigation use. These methods capture rainwater onsite and direct it to channels to spread into the landscape. This type of approach can work well to avoid surface water runoff, provide supplemental moisture to the landscape, and function without energy for pumping. It is a method generally better suited for larger landscapes with a fair degree of tolerance for moisture variation.

In smaller areas, hand-watering is an option. It is generally less expensive to install hose bibs with quick-connectors for hoses, and if supplemental watering needs are very infrequent, it may be practical to utilize hand-watering for both initial establishment of plants and long-term supplemental water. It is critical that the watering be done at the appropriate times to maintain plant health and vigor. If portions of the landscape are to be watered by hand, they must be identified in the landscape maintenance plan, and appropriate human and financial resources allocated to ensure the watering is done properly.

WATER DEMAND/WATERING ZONES

Different plantings have different needs for water, and the irrigation system should be tuned to their requirements. The portion of the landscape that is intended to be irrigated should be further broken down into zones according to water needs and the system designed, installed, and operated accordingly. An irrigation calculator or model is used to determine water need by zone. The calculator takes into account water needs by landscape typology, estimated evapotranspiration, and rainfall. The following sidebar is a typical approach to estimating water demand by landscape hydrozone.

SITES-DESIGNED LANDSCAPE WATER REQUIREMENTS

In order to calculate the amount of water needed to irrigate a designed landscape, SITES offers the following methods of calculation. Determine the design landscape water requirements (DLWR) for the actual site by entering the average monthly precipitation (inches/month) for the site's peak watering month; the area of each hydrozone (in square feet); and the plant type, landscape coefficient, and distribution uniformity for each hydrozone in of the Irrigation Calculator (sample data shown here). Note that the sum of the hydrozone areas must equal the total area of the irrigated landscape. These calculations for DLWR were adapted by SITES from the U.S. Environmental Protection Agency WaterSense Water Budget Tool's equation for Landscape Water Requirement (U.S. EPA 2009c).

continues

SITES DESIGNED LANDSCAPE WATER REQUIREMENTS *(CONTINUED)*

$DLWR = RTM \times [(ET_0 \times K_L) - R_a] \times A \times C_u$

Where:

RTM = Run time multiplier, equal to 1/lower quarter distribution uniformity*
(dimensionless)

ET_0 = average reference evapotranpiration for the site's peak watering month, provided locally (inches/month)

K_L = Landscape coefficient for type of plant in that hydrozone

R_a = Allowable rainfall (25% of average monthly rainfall for the site's peak watering month, provided locally (inches/month))

A = Area of hydrozone (square feet)

C_u = Conversion factor (0.6233 for results in gallons/month)

The sum of all DLWRs for each hydrozone equals the site DLWR (Table 3-6).

► Information for the landscape coefficient (K_L) is provided in Table 3-7.

► Information on the distribution uniformity is provided in Table 3-8.

► Area of the hydrozone is the area (in square feet) to be watered.

TABLE 3-6: Designed Landscape Water Requirement

ET_0 = AVERAGE MONTHLY REFERENCE EVAPOTRANSPIRATION FOR THE SITE'S PEAK WATERING MONTH (INCHES/MONTH)			R_A = ALLOWABLE RAINFALL = 25% OF AVERAGE MONTHLY RAINFALL FOR THE SITE'S PEAK WATERING MONTH (INCHES/MONTH)	
4			2	
AREA OF HYDROZONE (SQUARE FEET)*	PLANT TYPE WITHIN HYDROZONE	K_L = LANDSCAPE COEFFICIENT**	DISTRIBUTION UNIFORMITY*** (ENTER FRACTION %, I.E., 80% = 0.80)	LANDSCAPE WATER REQUIREMENT (GALLONS/MONTH)
5,000	Trees	0.5	0.75	6,233
5,000	Turfgrass	0.7	0.75	9,557
Designed Landscape Water Requirement (gallons/month)				15,790

*The sum of the areas of all hydrozones should match the total area of the landscape designed with permanent irrigation systems.

**See Table 3-7.   ***See Table 3-8.

TABLE 3-7: Plant Type and Estimated Landscape Coefficient (K_L)

PLANT TYPE	K_L WATER REQUIREMENTS		
	LOW	MEDIUM	HIGH
Ground cover	0.2	0.5	0.7
Shrubs	0.2	0.5	0.7
Trees	0.2	0.5	0.7
Turfgrass	0.6	0.7	0.8

Note: The estimated K_L values in table are taken from the U.S. EPA WaterSense Water Budget Tool (May 2009 revision).

TABLE 3-8: Distribution Uniformity

IRRIGATION TYPE	$DU_{(LQ)}$ OR EU*
Drip—Standard	70%
Drip—Press Comp	90%
Fixed Spray	65%
Micro Spray	70%
Rotor	70%

Note: The lower quarter distribution uniformity values in Table 3-8 are taken from the U.S. EPA WaterSense Water Budget Tool (May 2009 rev.).

Original source: The Irrigation Association, "Landscape Irrigation Scheduling and Water Management," IA 2005.

*Lower quarter distribution uniformity $DU_{(LQ)}$ applies to sprinker zones and emission uniformity (EU) applies to drip/microirrigation zones.

Source: SITES 2009.

IRRIGATION CONTROLS

Irrigation systems are typically operated by controls that turn the water on and off according to need. Very simple systems have manual controls, which have to be carefully attended to in order to provide the right amount of water without watering excessively. Some systems use automatic timers, which turn the system on for a certain amount of time each day. Timers can be set to vary by week or season, and can have manual overrides to turn off if there is recent precipitation. Some timer systems are connected to weather stations that predict precipitation and will only irrigate when it is not raining.

The most efficient irrigation systems use more sophisticated climate-based control systems that turn watering zones on and off based upon water need as determined by weather (or soil moisture) sensors. Weather sensors monitor weather and precipitation conditions and communicate the need for supplemental irrigation water only when natural precipitation is inadequate for the season. The weather sensors are connected to a central control, which then signals the switch for each zone to turn on and off. This type of control system, sometimes referred to as "smart controls," can provide suitable irrigation water with minimal waste. When coupled with a drip irrigation system customized for each zone, the ideal amount of supplemental moisture needed for a particular landscape will be provided with a fraction of the water of a conventional system.

An alternative method to determine water need is through moisture sensors that monitor the amount of moisture in the root zone of vegetation. Plants need supplemental water only when rainfall hasn't kept the ground moist enough for their needs. Therefore, the irrigation system should only provide water when the ground goes below a certain moisture content. Moisture sensors can be placed in the soil within each plant zone to detect the soil moisture level. The system can be designed and operated to only turn on when the moisture sensor signals the need for supplemental water, and then turn off again. This prevents water from being applied excessively.

Water Feature Efficiency

One of the most satisfying and beautiful landscape elements is healthy open water. Natural ponds, lakes, streams, and rivers draw people to their movement and beauty. Water provides habitat for birds, animals, and a myriad of aquatic organisms. We are attracted to water more than perhaps any other single component of the landscape. Created or man-made water features can also provide a valuable, beautiful, beneficial aspect of a sustainable site. Access to water onsite is beneficial to people—it provides a more calming visual and audio environment, changes with the seasons, and attracts wildlife. Open water features can also be integrated with a site's stormwater management and water quality approach to provide multiple benefits. Created water features offer an artful, ecological element to integrate into a sustainable site for multiple benefits when properly adapted to the unique characteristics and conditions of a particular site.

Created water features can range in size from a small courtyard fountain to a large created pond covering many acres. Created water features include ponds, streams, pools, fountains, water gardens, created wetlands (ornamental, functional for water cleansing, or ecological enhancements), and any other water element in the landscape with permanent or intermittent open water. Water features have become increasingly popular as landscape amenities. The traditional approach to creating an open water feature is to create a lined basin of some sort and then use a combination of pumped recirculation, mechanical aeration, and/or water treatment, including the addition of chemicals, to maintain water clarity. A lined basin will evaporate water and will therefore need makeup water added periodically to keep the water level at the normal or designed elevation. Sometimes basins are excavated into groundwater, which can result in suitable water movement and therefore quality, and relatively constant elevation, with seasonal fluctuations.

A sustainable created water feature is one that is created and maintained with only a positive impact to the site's ecology and hydrology, and can be maintained with surplus water available onsite. Typical created water features draw or receive makeup water from potable sources, diverted natural streams or water courses, or water mined from a groundwater aquifer, all of which can deplete nonrenewable sources or impact local ecology in some way. A sustainable water feature, on the other hand, is kept healthy and vital with minimal or no makeup water from potable sources or depletion of water from other natural surface or subsurface water resources. The best way to do this is to use harvested or redirected stormwater from less permeable portions of a site as part of an integrated sustainable site water strategy.

The primary objective of water-efficient water features is to minimize the use of potable water for created amenity water in the landscape, while providing other benefits and value at the same time. Considerations include:

- Maintain water quality with minimal use of potable water for created water features.
- Avoid impact to surface or subsurface water resources in the creation and ongoing maintenance of created water features.
- Size created water features based upon the surplus water available onsite. Rainwater and other surplus water available to the site should influence the water feature design approach.
- Harvesting and reusing rainwater can be part of managing water onsite; planting with native or locally adapted species can be part of a biodiversity improvement approach.
- Water design and water budget should be coordinated with overall site water approach.
- Rainwater harvesting and pumping equipment should be coordinated with other necessary mechanical systems.

Figures 3-69 and 3-70 show two examples of efficient water feature design.

FIGURE 3-69: Part of a sustainable site is to make healthy water visually and physically accessible to site users. This water feature creates an artful display of water at the main entrance to the Queens Botanical Garden in Flushing, NY. Designed by Herbert Dreiseitl of Atelier Dreiseitl based in Uberlingen, Germany, the fountain is run with harvested rainwater cleaned for human contact with cleansing biotopes and UV disinfection.

FIGURE 3-70: This water expression is part of a sustainable water-based landscape at the Coffee Creek Center Conservancy, a large community park in Chesterton, IN. Surplus rainwater from roads and roofs is infiltrated and re-creates base-flow subsurface discharge for a restored wetland pond; water is drawn from the pond and run through ornamental pools and waterfalls created with natural stone and planting pockets, which provides aeration for the water and a visible, touchable water experience.

MIMIC NATURE

A sustainable water feature will vary with different ecological, climatic, and geological conditions. The best clue to learn how to adapt a created water feature into the local ecological context is to study and analyze how water is deployed in the natural landscape locally and attempt to mimic those conditions and characteristics in the site landscape, including created water features. For example, the Peggy Notebaert Nature Museum in Chicago, IL, has an isolated open water element of relatively small size as part of its sustainable landscape. In nature, a water feature like this could have been a prairie depression created by a clay lens close to the ground surface. The water would have come from adjacent seeps in the upland prairie landscape. This condition is mimicked in the created landscape by directing vegetated surfaces on green roofs over the adjacent museum building toward an open water element created with a liner to hold the water. The water level is kept constant to maintain a stable habitat that supports various aquatic species. Surplus water overflows to a below-ground cistern, where it is stored for makeup water for the wetland/pond feature and for irrigation of the adjacent "living wall" plantings. When the water level drops below a certain point, a float switch activates a pump (powered with energy derived from a photovoltaic array on a portion of the roof), and fills the pond back up to normal water level. The amount of water moving through the pond from the green roof overflow is enough to maintain water quality (see Figure 3-71).

(Photo from Conservation Design Forum)

FIGURE 3-71: The facade of the Peggy Notebaert Nature Museum building includes a "water wall" made of natural limestone veneer over a CMU block wall that allows surplus rainwater from the green roof to cascade down to provide water to small planting pockets; overflow water is stored in a cistern and recirculated with solar energy to irrigate the wall and provide makeup water for the created wetland in an outdoor classroom space.

WATER BUDGETING

The water needed to maintain a created water feature is part of the same water budget that is used to establish a water balance onsite along with other potential water uses, including landscape irrigation. As part of the integrated design process, a water budget is created for the site, which takes into account all inputs (rainwater, offsite surface water runoff, surplus building process water, and the like), outputs, including infiltration and evapotranspiration, and potential uses for any surplus water not essential to maintain natural hydrology and vegetation onsite. By definition, this approach will help determine the size and scale of open water features. Open water will evaporate a certain amount of water throughout the year, which can be calculated. This volume of water by month is then used to determine how much surplus site water needs to be directed to maintain the open water. It is also used to help calculate the size of water storage devices.

ONSITE WASTEWATER TREATMENT, DISPOSAL, AND REUSE

Onsite treatment, disposal, and reuse of wastewater can have many environmental and economic benefits. Onsite treatment can conserve water resources by providing a source of water for irrigation and as a supply for toilets or other non-potable building uses. Natural treatment systems, such as wetlands, can create habitat, and the effluent water quality can be superior to that of the nearby municipal wastewater treatment plant. Onsite treatment will reduce the hydraulic and pollutant load on the local wastewater treatment system, and if land application systems are incorporated into the design, the onsite treatment system can recharge the underlying aquifer. In regions of the United States where storm drains and sewers are combined in common pipes, every gallon of wastewater treated onsite is one less gallon that ends up untreated in a stream, river, or lake during a combined sewer overflow (CSO) event. Operational and maintenance costs can also be less (see Figures 3-72 , 3-73, 3-74, 3-75, and 3-76).

There are some drawbacks to onsite wastewater treatment. The owner of the system is responsible for maintaining and operating it, meeting permit requirements, covering costs of testing, and ensuring that users do not abuse the system with toxic chemicals. Onsite systems require land which might otherwise be used for development purposes.

There are many cases when new construction or even remodels of existing buildings cannot connect to existing municipal wastewater treatment plants. The treatment plant may not exist, it may be too far away, or it has no additional capacity. This situation is becoming more common in the urban environment because of two factors:

▶ Funding to expand the municipal treatment plant may not be available. Generally this requires issuance of a bond and a public vote, which may not be politically possible.

▶ Environmental constraints on the discharge limitation of pollutants. The total daily mass of regulated pollutants has been reached in the discharge stream. In many regions, these limits have already been reached, and there are no additional allocations available.

Onsite treatment systems are usually small systems, generally less than a million gallons per day (gpd), and for most projects the total wastewater flow will be less than 100,000 gpd. Sources of wastewater should be relatively simple to deal with and will usually be from homes, offices, stores, and restaurants. One of the most important design issues is to understand the amount of wastewater that is generated by different types of buildings. Residential, commercial, schools, restaurants, and retail buildings all generate different amounts of wastewater. Restaurants, and especially fast-food restaurants, generate fats, oils, and grease that can present major treatment challenges.

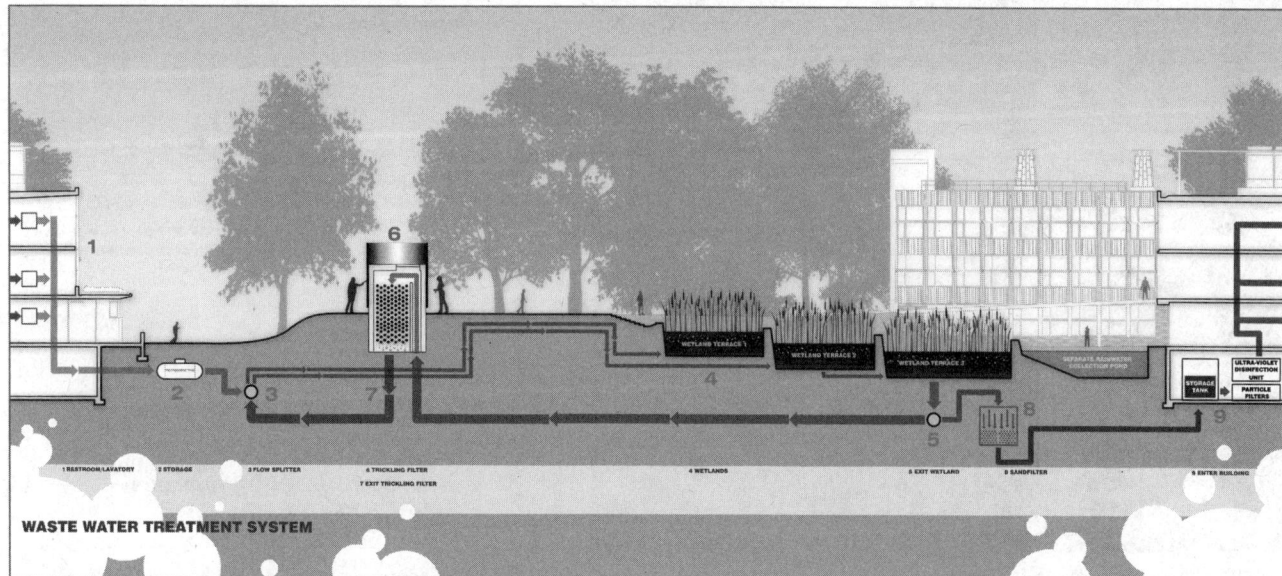

FIGURE 3-72: The Sidwell Friends Middle School incorporates a constructed wetland that is part of a closed system that recycles the water back to the building and lavatories. (Design by Natural Systems International, Kieran Timberlake Associates and Andropogon Associates; image by Kieran Timberlake Associates)

The generation of wastewater also differs by time of day and day of the week. Peak flow is different from average flow. For example, schools' peak wastewater flow occurs after lunch, while in homes there are two peaks—one in the morning and one in the evening. Offices typically have almost no wastewater flow on the weekend. These patterns will affect the size of the treatment system.

FIGURE 3-73: A constructed wetland uses biological processes to clean water, providing students with a vivid example of how such systems work in nature. (Design by Natural Systems International, Kieran Timberlake Associates and Andropogon Associates; Image from Andropogon Associates)

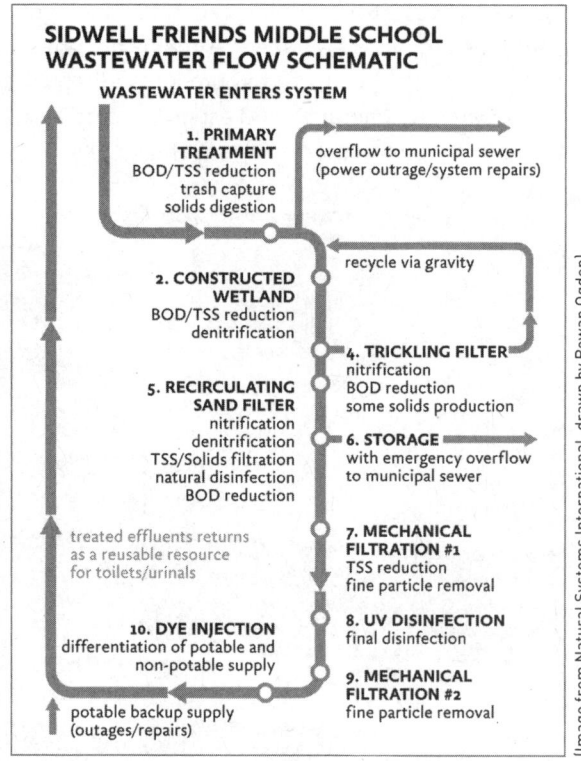

FIGURE 3-74: The design flow of 3,000 gpd is treated with a series of terraced constructed wetland cells, a recirculating sand filter, and trickling filter, which are all tightly integrated into the site.

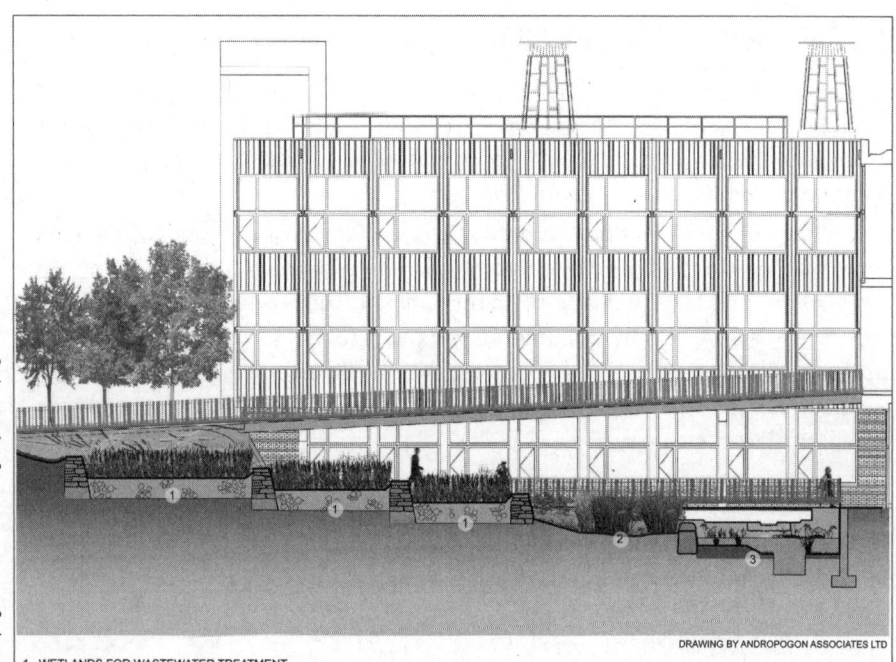

(Design by Natural Systems International, Kieran Timberlake Associates and Andropogon Associates; image by Andropogon Associates)

1. WETLANDS FOR WASTEWATER TREATMENT
2. RAIN GARDEN
3. POND

DRAWING BY ANDROPOGON ASSOCIATES LTD

FIGURE 3-75: Constructed wastewater treatment wetland terraces, a rain garden for stormwater and wet pond for holding water form an integrated water system for this LEED Platinum project.

(Sources: Kiernan Timberlake, Andropogon Associates and Natural Systems International; Figure 3-74 drawing by Rowan Ogden)

FIGURE 3-76: The Sidwell Friends Middle School incorporates a constructed wetland, the first in Washington, DC, that treats building wastewater onsite. Other wetlands and rain gardens treat onsite stormwater.

Water Quality Parameters of Wastewater

The earliest measures of wastewater, which originated in the Victorian era in England, were biological oxygen demand, settleable solids, and total solids. As the science of bacteriology developed, human pathogens were added with fecal matter as a water quality parameter and coliform bacteria becoming the indicator organism.

More recently it has been recognized that nitrate levels in drinking water have adverse effects on pregnant women, infants, and the elderly. The role of phosphorus in creating algal blooms in streams, rivers, and lakes has also been recognized. There are many other regulated compounds (such as EPA priority pollutants), and more recently the impact of common compounds such as antibiotics, estrogen, antidepressants, and personal care pharmaceutical products has been recognized. Table 3-9 summarizes the most common regulated compounds and measures of water quality in wastewater.

TABLE 3-9: **Common Regulated Compounds and Measures of Water Quality in Wastewater**

REGULATED COMPOUND	DEFINITION AND ENVIRONMENTAL AND HUMAN HEALTH IMPACTS	TYPICAL RANGE (MG/L)
Carbonaceous Biological Oxygen Demand (CBOD)	Measure oxygen required to stabilize carbon compounds in the wastewater. Large concentrations of carbon compounds create anaerobic conditions in the receiving stream or river. This leads to die-off of fish, odors, and conditions that support human pathogens.	200–250
Total Suspended Solids (TSS)	TSS are those solids that can be filtered from the wastewater sample on a 5 micron filter and then dried (at 103° C) and weighed. Solids affect clarity, and taste, and may harbor human pathogens.	200
Settleable Solids (SS)	This is the volume of solids that will settle out from a water sample in 1 hour.	
Ammonium Nitrogen—(NH4+)	This is the primary form of nitrogen leaving septic tanks. In fresh water, depending on the pH, a certain amount, typically <1.0 mg/L, will be in a disassociated form, NH3, which is toxic to freshwater fish.	25–45
Nitrate Nitrogen—(NO3)	Grows algae; toxic in concentrations greater than 10 mg/L for infants, elderly, and fetuses.	20–40
Phosphate (PO4)	Supports algal growth in streams, rivers, and ocean.	8–10
Fecal Coliform Bacteria	This is an indicator organism although some strains may be fatal; usual effects are diarrhea.	1,000,000+

REGULATED COMPOUND	DEFINITION AND ENVIRONMENTAL AND HUMAN HEALTH IMPACTS	TYPICAL RANGE (MG/L)
Dissolved Solids (TDS)	Typically these are calcium compounds, but may include sodium compounds, carbonates, and sulfates. Deposits on pipes; concentrations over 1,000 mg/L may lead to diarrhea and hardening of the arteries.	50–1,200+
Alkalinity	Reported as CaCO3, buffers acidic water; will create deposits on pipes and in hotwater heaters.	Varies
pH	A measure of the hydrogen ion concentration. A pure acid will have a pH of 1 while a pure base will have a pH of 14.	6.5–8
Heavy Metals	Cadmium, chromium, mercury, lead, arsenic, and antimony are toxic to humans and most forms of life. Toxicity will depend on the metal and concentration.	Varies
Priority Organic Pollutants	There are 126 priority pollutants which may be carcinogens, mutagens, endocrine disrupters, haemo-toxic, nervous system disruptors, reproductive disruptors, and brain, liver, lung, and kidney disruptors.	<10 µg/L

Wastewater Treatment

Wastewater treatment processes are categorized as primary, secondary, or tertiary levels of treatment. Wastewater treatment is organized as a sequence of events, each stage producing improved water quality. (see tables 3-10, 3-11, and 3-12)

PRIMARY TREATMENT

Primary treatment reduces settleable solids and in some cases includes anaerobic digestion (e.g., septic tanks). All primary treatment systems rely on gravity. CBOD is generally reduced by 40 percent and TSS by 50 percent. Typical water quality concentrations after primary treatment are CBOD 140–160 mg/L and TSS 100 mg/L. TSS levels can be reduced even further with the installation of effluent filters. Table 3-10 summarizes common primary wastewater treatment options.

TABLE 3-10: Primary Treatment Options

TYPE OF PRIMARY TREATMENT	PROS AND CONS
Screens: The primary function of screens is to remove inorganic trash from the raw wastewater. This can be a particularly noisome task hence larger systems are typically automated and enclosed. Screens can be very simple bar screens placed in an open concrete box and inclined in the direction of flow or mechanical screens of various configurations.	**Pros:** Bar screens are simple, easy to construct Protects subsequent treatment steps from fouling Effective removal of inorganic solids **Cons:** Produces odors Breeding area for flies Manual bar screens require daily maintenance Mechanical screens are expensive and require regular maintenance
Primary Clarifier: Primary clarifiers are rectangular or circular tanks that use gravity to settle solids in wastewater. Unlike anaerobic digesters or septic tanks, there is no biological treatment. The design is based on the principle that organic solids whose specific gravity is about 1.02 to 1.03 will take a certain amount of time to settle to the bottom of a tank. As particles become smaller and smaller, Brownian motion will begin to affect settling time, so typically clarifiers will only remove about 50 percent of the solids. The volume of the tank is typically about 1/6 of the average daily flow. In addition, to ensure maximum effectiveness, an overflow rate (the rate at which water leaves the clarifier) of 400 to 600 gal/ft²/day is usually specified. Settled solids are removed daily for further dewatering or composting. Clarifiers are very cost effective for larger systems (>25,000 gpd), but since they require daily removal of solids to a holding tank, this makes anaerobic primary treatment more cost effective.	**Pros:** Simple, easy to construct Works by gravity Passive system Relatively inexpensive **Cons:** Requires daily removal of solids Produces odors Not appropriate for small systems Concrete construction (usual)

TYPE OF PRIMARY TREATMENT	PROS AND CONS
Concrete Tanks: The most commonly used material to build primary treatment tanks is concrete. Whether the tank is a residential septic tank or a primary treatment tank for a small community of 5,000, the versatility and ease of site construction make reinforced concrete primary treatment tanks a logical choice. Concrete tanks serve a dual function—settling solids and anaerobic digestion. Residential primary treatment tanks, also known as septic tanks, are generally sized by state Department of Health codes, which specify a volume based on the number of bedrooms. Typically, these tanks vary in size from 1,000 to 2,000 gallons. The solids and scum layer must be periodically pumped out and the liquid transported to an appropriate facility for further treatment.	**Pros:** Moderately inexpensive Good structural properties Readily available Durable Easy to maintain Works by gravity; relies on naturally occurring bacteria for additional treatment Passive system—no energy required Underground, out of site **Cons:** Concrete contains cement—very high CO_2 emissions to produce Heavy, requires crane for installation Requires periodic pump-out of accumulated solids Subject to corrosion if not properly protected Excavation required
Fiberglass Tanks: Fiberglass tanks can be the ideal construction for primary treatment of wastewater. They are lightweight and essentially corrosion proof. Fiberglass tanks are typically made from woven glass fibers coated with resins in large 6- to 10-ft diameter cylinders. Typically they are available from 1,000 to 50,000 gallons. They can be installed in series or parallel. Since they were developed for the underground storage tank business, they can support heavy vehicle traffic. Buried tanks are out of the way—they can be placed under parking lots, landscapes, or buildings. Although fiberglass tanks are used for residential units, they are more commonly used in larger installations (e.g., multiple units of housing, offices, and retail complexes, and other applications where the wastewater flow is 5 to 50,000 gpd or larger). The solids, and scum layer, must be periodically pumped out and the liquid transported to an appropriate facility for further treatment.	**Pros:** Strong Lightweight Corrosion resistant Easy to install Works by gravity; relies on naturally occurring bacteria Passive system Installed underground—out of sight **Cons:** Expensive Toxic resins during curing process Inefficient storage volume to excavation volume ratio Excavation required Transportation costs Tank must be periodically pumped out

SECONDARY TREATMENT

In secondary treatment, CBOD and TSS levels are further reduced to 30 mg/L CBOD and 30 mg/L TSS. With the exception of constructed wetlands, some additional energy is required to recirculate and/or aerate the wastewater. Usually some form of disinfection is required.

CONSTRUCTED WETLANDS—SUBSURFACE FLOW

Constructed wetlands are used to reduce CBOD and SS after some form of primary treatment. They are the most energy efficient of all secondary treatment processes. In addition, they are excellent at removing nitrates and human pathogens. Subsurface flow (SSF) constructed wetlands are more cost effective when the wastewater flow is less than 100,000 gpd. SSF systems are lined gravel beds approximately 24 to 30 in. deep that are planted with native wetlands plants. The plant roots and gravel provide a substrate for the microbial community that provides treatment. Wastewater is introduced in one end and flows horizontally through the gravel bed, coming in contact with the microbial community that is attached to the roots and gravel. In order to survive in saturated soils, wetlands have developed the ability to pump oxygen through the fine root hairs. This keeps the roots from rotting while providing needed oxygen for the microbial community feeding on the nutrients in the wastewater (see Figure 3-17).

Potential benefits of SSF constructed wetlands:

▶ Wetlands are easy to construct.

▶ They can be used as a landscape amenity.

▶ They provide habitat.

▶ Materials are generally locally available.

▶ They are very effective in reducing CBOD and TSS to secondary levels.

▶ They do not require any energy.

▶ They are excellent for removal of nitrates.

Potential challenges of SSF constructed wetlands:

▶ They require more land than other treatment systems.

▶ They require annual cutting of plants and removal of weeds.

Wetlands are temperature-dependent systems, and January temperatures will be one of the key factors in determining the area required. The average daily flow and the influent CBOD, are also relevant factors. Although many European regulations do not require primary treatment for wetland systems, it is standard practice in the United States.

Besides the passive nature of wetlands, one of their advantages is that they can be used as landscape features. The gravel beds are ideal for growing many different varieties of flowering or otherwise attractive plants. There are three species of plants that are excellent for the wastewater treatment process that are appropriate to many regions. They are *Typha* spp., *Scirpus* spp., and *Carex* spp. *Phragmites* spp. are effective in wastewater treatment but are invasive species so they should be avoided.

For the primary treatment area, (the area needed to treat the wastewater), the three species identified here are usually most often specified. As a general rule it is good practice to use locally available native species as these will adapt more readily than exotics; however, there are some excellent choices of nonnative plants that can be planted around the edges. There are approximately 7,000 species of plants in the U.S. Department of Agriculture (USDA) wetlands database as well as other plants, such as daffodils and tulips, that will do quite well when planted in the gravel bed.

Gravel is an ideal media for growing many plants, and most plants, including nonwetlands species, will grow in the gravel bed. Weeds will also take advantage of the gravel bed, so maintenance will be required.

Rectangular shapes are often specified for the treatment volume, but the edges can be made irregular, or geometric shapes such as ovals can enclose the rectangle. The areas outside the boundaries of the rectangle are ideal for a wetlands garden.

[Drawn by Simon Bussiere from drawing by Natural Systems International]

FIGURE 3-77: Constructed wetlands subsurface flow.

CONSTRUCTED WETLANDS—SURFACE FLOW

Surface flow constructed wetlands can also be used to reduce CBOD and settleable solids (SS) after some form of primary treatment. Like subsurface flow wetlands they are the most energy efficient of all secondary treatment processes, and in addition, they are excellent at removing nitrates and human pathogens. Surface flow (SF) systems are also lined beds like SSF wetlands, but in place of gravel, a layer of soil 12 to 18 in. deep is placed on the liner in which wetlands plants are grown. Water level is usually kept below 18 in. but occasionally is set at 24 in., especially in warmer climates. SF wetlands can be designed as a landscape amenity and also provide excellent habitat. Instead of relying on the gravel and fine root hairs in subsurface flow wetlands, the stems of wetland plants growing in the water column provides the necessary substrate for the microbial community. The same factors used to size subsurface flow wetlands are used to size surface flow wetlands.

Typically, surface flow wetlands are used as part of treatment elements in larger systems. As a rule of thumb, SF wetlands are probably more cost effective over 100,000 gpd.

Surface flow wetlands may be more challenging as landscape features because the number of plant species is more limited, primarily because of the operating depth of the wetlands (usually 18 in.). Most of the more colorful and interesting plants found in the USDA plant database will be confined to the edges of the wetlands because of the depth of water. These larger wetlands are more suited to wildfowl than as landscapes, primarily because of scale. When looking at these larger wetlands, it is like looking over a meadow from a distance; the apparent diversity can be lost. For functional reasons, the larger wetlands tend to be masses of plants, reaching up to 12 ft (depending on the species), and can serve as a backdrop for more ornamental plants in beds in front of the wetlands (Figure 3-78).

Potential benefits of both surface and subsurface flow constructed wetlands include:

- ▶ Wetlands are easy to construct.
- ▶ They can provide a landscape amenity.
- ▶ They provide habitat.
- ▶ Materials are generally locally available.
- ▶ They are very effective in reducing CBOD and TSS to secondary levels.
- ▶ They do not require any energy.
- ▶ They are excellent for removal of nitrates.

Potential challenges of surface and subsurface flow constructed wetlands include:

- ▶ They require more land than other treatment systems.
- ▶ They require annual cutting of plants and removal of weeds.
- ▶ They contain nonpotable water. Human contact with the water through touching, wading, swimming, or drinking should be avoided.

[Drawn by Simon Bussiere from a drawing by Natural Systems International]

SURFACE WETLAND

FIGURE 3-78: Constructed wetlands surface flow.

CONSTRUCTED WETLANDS—VERTICAL FLOW

Vertical flow wetlands are essentially sand filters that have been planted with wetland plants. Wastewater is introduced onto the top and then flows vertically to be collected in underdrains. These types of systems are very effective in removing CBOD, suspended solids, and nitrates. The ecology is very similar to subsurface flow wetlands; however, they rely on more fine-grained materials. Their use is more common in Europe.

Because of the importance of the root mass, vertical flow wetlands tend to rely primarily on deep-rooting plants, such as *Carex* spp. and *Scirpus* spp. However, the edges are ideal for planting a great variety of plants.

Potential benefits of vertical flow constructed wetlands include:

▶ Excellent removal of CBOD, TSS, and nitrates.

▶ Materials are generally available locally.

▶ They are a passive treatment system.

Potential challenges of vertical flow constructed wetlands include:

▶ Prone to clogging

▶ Require more land than other energy-intensive treatment technologies

▶ Require annual maintenance

INTERMITTENT SAND FILTER

Intermittent sand filters (ISF), sometimes referred to as single-pass sand filters, are excellent for the removal of CBOD and SS. They can be used after most types of primary treatment or secondary treatment. ISFs are essentially lined beds of graded sand 24 in. deep with gravel underdrains and a system of piping on top which provides an intermittent dose of wastewater. The sand grains support a highly diverse microbial community consisting of attached growth microorganisms, which are responsible for reducing CBOD and SS. Although ISFs can remove suspended solids, it is important that the primary treatment reduce suspended solids to 30 mg/L or less in order to prolong the life of the filter.

Potential benefits of intermittent sand filters include:

▶ Easy to construct

▶ Very effective in reducing CBOD and TSS to secondary levels

▶ Do not require any energy

▶ Simple to operate and maintain

Potential challenges of intermittent sand filters include:

▶ Produce nitrates

▶ Subject to clogging and have a limited life

▶ Depend on properly graded, washed sand

PRESSURE-DOSED SAND MOUNDS

Pressure-dosed sand mounds are essentially unlined intermittent sand filters that are sized to also allow treated effluent to percolate into the underlying soil. They serve two functions—treatment and disposal. The sand grains support a highly diverse microbial community consisting of attached growth microorganisms, which are responsible for reducing CBOD and SS. The disposal area, also referred to as the basal area, depends on the permeability of the underlying soil. Determining soil permeability and preparation of the soil prior to placing the sand are two crucial tasks that will affect performance. Soil permeability will affect the size and therefore the cost. The slower the percolation rate, the larger will be the sand mound. A sand mound is an excellent choice for small onsite systems when there are appropriate soils. When covered with a clay cap, grasses, and wildflowers, sand mounds can be inconspicuous parts of the landscape. The life of a sand mound can be extended by reducing suspended solids to as low a level as possible in the primary treatment step.

Potential benefits of pressure-dosed sand mounds include:

▸ Materials are generally locally available

▸ Very effective in reducing CBOD and TSS to secondary levels

▸ Sand mounds require minimal energy

▸ Simple to operate and maintain

Potential challenges of pressure-dosed sand mounds include:

▸ Produce nitrates

▸ Subject to clogging and have a limited life

▸ Require comprehensive soil investigation

▸ Preparation of soil surface can be challenging

PRESSURE-DOSED SOIL ABSORPTION FIELDS

Pressure-dosed soil absorption fields are an improvement over the gravity-fed soil absorption fields discussed in the following section. The addition of a dosing tank after the septic tank, and the installation of a 1- to 2-in. line that has 1/8 in. holes drilled every 2 ft ensures the uniform distribution of the primary effluent in the gravity trench or half-chambers. The life of the field is prolonged, and the soil column directly under the trench is also more uniformly loaded so concentrations of pollutants are decreased and the aerobic quality of the soil retained. The soil microbial community develops a slime layer at the bottom of the trench which acts like a membrane. This biological membrane filters organic compound, and removes some ammonia and nitrate. The soil microbial community under the bottom of the trench also provides additional filtration and treatment. Gravel trenches are sometimes replaced with half-chambers that form tunnels 11 to 16 in. high. The half-chambers provide for air movement. Because air can move more freely through the chambers, they are less likely to clog and fail. Soil investigations that provide information on soil permeability, depth to groundwater, and depth to limiting layer are essential for designing soil absorption fields.

Potential benefits of pressure-dosed soil absorption fields include:

- ▶ Easy to construct
- ▶ Inexpensive
- ▶ Recharges groundwater
- ▶ Uniform distribution of effluent
- ▶ Longer life of the field
- ▶ Better water quality than leach field

Potential challenges of pressure-dosed soil absorption fields include:

- ▶ Produce nitrates
- ▶ Soil interface subject to clogging
- ▶ Require comprehensive soil investigation
- ▶ Can contaminate groundwater
- ▶ Distribution of effluent is below the root zone
- ▶ Require significantly more excavation than drip irrigation

SOIL ABSORPTION FIELDS

Soil absorption fields, sometimes called leach fields, are gravel-filled trenches containing perforated pipes that are set into the soil. The soil microbial community develops a slime layer at the bottom of the trench which acts like a membrane. This biological membrane filters organic compounds and removes some ammonia and nitrate. The soil microbial community under the bottom of the trench also provides additional filtration and treatment. Soil absorption fields are the simplest of all secondary treatment systems and, when combined with septic systems, form the most basic of all onsite treatment systems. They rely on gravity for distribution of effluent in the trench, which results in most of the water percolating at the front of the trench. This usually leads to progressive field failure. Gravel trenches are some-times replaced with half-chambers that form half-tunnels 11 to 16 in. high. The half-chambers provide for air movement, and they are less likely to clog and fail. Soil investigations that provide information on soil permeability, depth to groundwater, and depth to limiting layer are essential for designing soil absorption fields.

Potential benefits of soil absorption fields include

▶ Easy to construct

▶ Inexpensive

▶ Recharges groundwater

▶ No moving parts

▶ No electricity required

Potential challenges of soil absorption fields include:

▶ Produce nitrates

▶ Soil interface subject to clogging

▶ Require comprehensive soil investigation

▶ Can contaminate groundwater

TRICKLING FILTER

Trickling filters are used to reduce CBOD from primary treatment levels (140 to 150 mg/L) to secondary levels (<30 mg/L) after some form of primary treatment. They are the most energy efficient means of introducing oxygen into the wastewater and developing the aerobic microbial community essential for reducing CBOD to secondary levels. Trickling filters were originally constructed using 2- to 3-in. rocks placed in a circular concrete tank with a rotating arm that trickled the water over the rocks. More recent advances in this technology have replaced rocks with random pack and sheet media made of polypropylene or high-density polyethylene. The advantage of the new materials is to increase the surface to volume ratio, providing more substrate for the microbial community. For small onsite wastewater treatment systems, trickling filters as small as 3 ft in diameter can become very effective additions. Typical applications will include 4- to 10-ft-diameter concrete pipe or manhole sections filled with random pack media upon which wastewater is sprayed intermittently. Larger systems up 120 ft (or more) in diameter, or rectangular filters, rely on rotating arms or distribution troughs to deliver the water to the top of the media.

Potential benefits of trickling filters include:

▶ Simple, easy to construct

▶ Very effective in reducing CBOD to secondary levels

▶ Most efficient of aerobic processes

▶ Very low maintenance requirements

Potential challenges of trickling filters are:

▶ Require pump(s) and rotating distribution arm or spray nozzles

▶ Must be followed by a secondary clarifier

▶ Spray nozzles and rotating distributor arms require periodic cleaning

▶ Occasional sloughing of solids from media leads to high TSS numbers

TERTIARY TREATMENT

In tertiary treatment (Table 3-11), CBOD and TSS levels are reduced to 10 mg/L or less. Additionally, total nitrogen must be reduced to less than 10 mg/L. Disinfection is required. Often phosphorus levels are regulated for stream discharges.

TABLE 3-11: Tertiary Treatment

TERTIARY TREATMENT TYPE	PROS	CONS
Nitrification Trickling Filter: Once the CBOD in wastewater has been reduced to 30 mg/L or less, trickling filters can be used to oxidize ammonia to nitrate. This is a naturally occurring process mediated by nitrifying bacteria. These bacteria are the most energy efficient means of converting ammonia to nitrate. This treatment step is essential to reach tertiary treatment levels since total nitrogen (all forms of nitrogen) must be less than 10 mg/L. The trickling filter effluent must be sent to an anaerobic environment where denitrification can take place ($NO_3 \rightarrow N_2$). Typically this is accomplished by returning the trickling filter effluent to an anaerobic primary treatment tank. For small onsite wastewater treatment systems, nitrifying trickling filters as small as 3 ft in diameter can become very effective additions. Typical applications will include 4- to 10-ft-diameter concrete pipe or manhole sections filled with random pack media upon which wastewater is sprayed intermittently. Larger systems up 120 ft in diameter, or rectangular filters, rely on rotating arms or distribution troughs to deliver the water to the top of the media.	Trickling filters are simple, and easy to construct. Very effective in converting ammonia to nitrate Most efficient of aerobic processes Very low maintenance requirements	Require pump(s) and rotating distribution arm or spray nozzles Must be followed by a secondary clarifier. Rotating arms or spray nozzles require periodic cleaning. Occasional sloughing of solids from media leads to high TSS numbers. Nitrifying bacteria are very sensitive to pH ranges, temperature, and toxic compounds.

TERTIARY TREATMENT TYPE	PROS	CONS
Recirculating Sand Filters: Recirculating sand filters (RSFs) are lined beds of graded sand 24 in. deep with gravel underdrains and a pressure-dosed distribution system placed on top. Pumps recirculate wastewater a minimum of three times through the sand to improve water quality. Multiple passes through the sand filter will reduce CBOD and TSS to levels less than 10 mg/L. Like all tertiary and secondary systems, RSFs must have adequate pretreatment of the wastewater before they can be effective. Ideally they would be combined with some form of primary and secondary treatment. Because RSFs are aerobic systems, they will convert ammonia to nitrate. RSFs will reduce total nitrogen but not to tertiary levels without some additional recirculation to anoxic or anaerobic pretreatment elements. When combined with a denitrification step, total nitrogen will be less than 2 mg/L. If suspended solids are reduced to levels below 30 mg/L before wastewater is introduced into the RSF, an extended life of the system can be expected.	Materials are generally locally available. Very effective in reducing CBOD and TSS to tertiary levels Almost complete nitrification is possible. Simple to operate and maintain	Produces nitrates Requires pumps and control system Requires graded and washed sand that must meet particular specifications Requires energy
Bag Filters: The primary function of bag filters (5 to 10 microns) is to further remove very fine suspended solids that have escaped the fine-mesh screen. Bag filters are made of nonwoven polypropylene that are inserted in a stainless steel or plastic container. Any solids larger than the specified size are removed. This additional filtration makes UV and ozone disinfection systems more effective than just using a fine-mesh filter. By adding a screen filter in front of the bag filter, the bag does not have to be changed as frequently. Pressure gauges installed on the influent and effluent side of the bag housing indicate when the bag must be removed and replaced. Bag filters affect only suspended solids. No other water quality parameter is affected.	Removes fine particles in the specified range or larger Improves subsequent disinfection processes Improves performance of additional downstream filtration	Requires periodic maintenance; bags must be removed periodically Needs hydraulic pressure to operate; creates line losses

continues

TABLE 3-11: Tertiary Treatment *(continued)*

TERTIARY TREATMENT TYPE	PROS	CONS
Cartridge Filter: The primary function of cartridge filters (0.25 to 5.0 microns) is to further remove very fine suspended solids (e.g., colloidal clay particles), most bacteria, and some viruses that have escaped the previous screens and filters, and other treatment processes. Cartridge filters are made of nonwoven polypropylene that is inserted in a stainless steel or plastic housing. Any solids larger than the specified size are removed. This additional filtration makes UV and ozone disinfection systems more effective than just using a fine-mesh filter. By adding a screen filter and a bag filter in front of the cartridge filter, the cartridge does not have to be changed as frequently. Pressure gauges installed on the influent and effluent side of the filter housing indicate when the cartridge must be removed and replaced. Cartridge filters remove suspended solids and many bacteria and some viruses. These filters are essential when considering reuse in buildings to supply toilets and urinals. Some states will require this level of filtration prior to discharge into rivers or streams.	Remove fine particles in specified range or larger Improve subsequent disinfection processes Improve turbidity especially when clay particles are present Remove bacteria and some viruses	Require periodic maintenance; cartridges must be removed periodically. Need hydraulic pressure to operate; creates line losses
Fine-Mesh Screens: The primary function of fine-mesh screens (80 to 100 microns) is to remove very fine suspended solids and any remaining sand and grit from previous treatment steps prior to additional filtration and disinfection. Alternatively, fine-mesh screens can be installed in front of drip irrigation systems to protect the emitters. Water required for reuse in buildings or for spray irrigation systems will require disinfection. This additional filtration makes UV and ozone disinfection systems more effective. These filters can be ordered with an automatic backwash system that cleans the screen using the hydraulic pressure generated by pumps. Fine-mesh screens' effect is solely on suspended solids. No other water quality parameter is affected.	Remove fine particles in the specified range or larger Improve subsequent disinfection processes Improve performance of additional downstream filtration	Require periodic maintenance Need hydraulic pressure to operate; creates line losses.

TERTIARY TREATMENT TYPE	PROS	CONS
Ozone Disinfection: Ozone (O_3) is a naturally occurring molecule found in Earth's atmosphere that is created in the lightning discharge. It is a highly reactive molecule that breaks down cellular walls of bacteria and destroys the DNA. It is extremely effective on viruses, destroying the RNA. Ozone will also react with any other unoxidized compounds in the wastewater such as ammonia and hydrogen sulfide as well as dissolved iron. Usually the resulting discharge has elevated levels of oxygen, eliminating the need for re-aeration. Ozone is created by running a high-voltage electric discharge through a stream of pure oxygen (or air). The resulting ozone is introduced into the treated wastewater via a venturi, which meters an appropriate amount of ozone into the discharge piping. The importance of prior filtration before subjecting the water to ozone disinfection cannot be overstressed. The better the water quality, the better the disinfection. Ozone is also very good at removing iron as well as colorants such as tannin.	Does not require any toxic chemicals No downstream side effects Very effective on human pathogens Short residence time Will remove iron and colorants	Requires periodic maintenance including annual changing of air filters Ozone will oxidize compounds such as ammonia, hydrogen sulfide, and iron before acting on bacteria and viruses. Uses energy Leaks in enclosed spaces are hazardous to humans.
Sodium Hypochlorite: Sodium hypochlorite is a chlorine salt that reacts with organic matter such as bacteria and viruses. The reactive chlorine is highly destructive of DNA and RNA and is thus a good disinfectant. When dissolved in water, it is commonly known as bleach. In small wastewater treatment operations, the solid sodium hypochlorite is formed into hockey-puck-sized tablets which are held in a column that is inserted into the wastewater discharge stream. The pellets dissolve in the flowing water, which then discharges into a mixing chamber. The size of the mixing chamber allows sufficient residence time to complete the disinfection process. Although extremely effective and one of the compounds that is thought to have the most positive effect on human health because of its ability to destroy human pathogens, sodium hypochlorite has some undesirable side effects. The reactive chlorine combines with amino acids to create chloramines and with other organic compounds to create trihalomethanes. Both sets of compounds are considered carcinogens. To eliminate further production of these compounds, the U.S. EPA generally requires the introduction of sodium sulfite, which reacts with the remaining chlorine to produce salt and sulfate.	Inexpensive Easy to use Very effective on human pathogens	Toxic Dangerous; must be handled carefully Produces potentially hazardous byproducts

TABLE 3-12: Treatment Type Summary

TYPE OF TREATMENT	LEVEL OF TREATMENT	ESTIMATED COST $/GPD	ENVIRONMENTAL IMPACT	OPERATING ENERGY	POTENTIAL FOR SITE AMENITY	CONSTRUCTABILITY	MAINTENANCE
Constructed Wetlands, Subsurface Flow	Secondary	$3.60	Low	Zero	High	Easy	Low
Constructed Wetlands, Surface Flow	Secondary	$2.10	Low	Zero	High	Easy	Low
Constructed Wetlands, Vertical Flow	Secondary	$4.10	Low	Zero to very low	Medium	Easy	Low
Intermittent Sand Filter	Secondary	$2–$4	Low	Low	Medium	Easy	Low
Pressure-Dosed Sand Mounds	Secondary	$5–$10	Low	Low	Medium	Difficult	Low
Pressure-Dosed Soil Absorption Fields	Secondary	$2–$10	Low	Low	High	Easy	Low
Soils Absorption Fields	Secondary	$1.50–$8.00	Low	Low	High	Easy	Low
Trickling Filters	Secondary	$5–$8	Medium	Low	Medium	Easy	Low
Nitrification Trickling Filter	Tertiary	$5–$8	Medium	Low	Medium	Easy	Low
Recirculating Sand Filters	Tertiary	$3.90	Low	Low	High	Difficult	Low
Bag Filters	Tertiary	$0.001	Low	Minor—pressure loss across filter	None	Easy	Low

TYPE OF TREATMENT	LEVEL OF TREATMENT	ESTIMATED COST $/GPD	ENVIRONMENTAL IMPACT	OPERATING ENERGY	POTENTIAL FOR SITE AMENITY	CONSTRUCTABILITY	MAINTENANCE
Cartridge Filters	Tertiary	$0.01	Low	Minor — pressure loss across filter	None	Easy	Low
Fine-Mesh Screens	Tertiary	n/a	Low	Low	None	Easy	Medium
Ozone Disinfection	Disinfection	$0.06	Low	Low to medium	None	Intermediate	High
Sodium Hypochlorite	Disinfection	$0.001	High	Zero	None	Easy	Low
Ultraviolet Disinfection	Disinfection	$0.04	Low	Low	None	Easy	Medium

Water Reuse Options

The sequence of treatment options will depend on the water quality requirements for the discharge or land application permit. If the treated effluent will be used for irrigation, then the water quality standard will be lower than if the wastewater is discharged to a stream, river, or lake. It is almost always better to land-apply the treated effluent than to discharge it into surface water.

What to do with the treated effluent from onsite wastewater can be a bigger challenge than the treatment of the wastewater itself. Land application or irrigation requires suitable soils and enough land to irrigate every day of the year (or provide for winter storage). Reuse in buildings or cooling towers will reduce the total amount of water that must be discharged to the ground or to a stream. A pipe to a nearby stream or drainage ditch may seem easier, but the water quality standards are often more strict and will require lower levels of nitrogen and phosphorus in the water.

Decisions regarding discharge and reuse are subject to local, state, and federal mandates. Meeting with the regulatory agency prior to making any design decisions is a crucial step after determining the design flow. The discharge and/or reuse of wastewater is one of the most highly regulated industries in the United States, and addressing the permit issues from the very beginning of the project should be a priority (see Table 3-13).

IRRIGATION

One of the most important potential reuse options is irrigation. This use is considered beneficial because when land-applied, the remaining nitrogen and phosphorus compounds assist plant growth. Crops, trees, hayfields, and landscapes all benefit from the nitrogen and phosphorus in the wastewater. This option also eliminates nitrogen and phosphorus pollution of streams, lakes, and rivers. Reuse for irrigation is a very important practice and is an element of the SITES and LEED systems. Perhaps more important, land application/irrigation provides additional treatment of the more recalcitrant compounds in wastewater, such as antibiotics, personal care products, estrogen, herbicides, pesticides, antidepressants, and so forth.

The least expensive option is to use impact sprinklers. Reclaimed water is applied to the appropriate vegetated area based on needs. Because of the potential for downwind drift of microdroplets, buffer strips and control access are usual requirements. Drip irrigation does not have the same setbacks or control issues. Reclaimed water in drip systems is a common practice in commercial office landscapes, public parks, and residential landscapes.

REUSE IN BUILDINGS

Most water used in buildings is potable water, yet there are uses such as toilet flushing, sprinkler systems and air conditioning cooling towers that don't require potable water for operation. Reclaimed wastewater that has achieved tertiary levels of water quality and has been ultra-filtered and disinfected is very suitable for these purposes. Besides saving potable water, one of the major potential advantages for reuse in buildings is that the amount of water that must be discharged is reduced.

As potable supplies become more and more limited, reuse makes a great deal of economic and environmental sense. Both the Uniform Plumbing Code and the International Plumbing Code have provisions for this reuse option, which essentially requires that the bathrooms be plumbed with purple pipe to indicate that the supply is nonpotable.

Many buildings rely on chilled water for air-conditioning. The chilled water is produced in cooling towers by evaporating water. Potable water is the typical source, and the amount of water required often exceeds all other water demands, yet this is a good use for reclaimed and treated wastewater.

TABLE 3-13: Reuse Options

TYPE OF TREATMENT	LEVEL OF TREATMENT	COST $/ GPD	ENVIRON- MENTAL IMPACT	EMBODIED ENERGY	POTENTIAL FOR SITE AMENITY	CONSTRUC- TABILITY	MAINTE- NANCE
Irrigation— Impact Sprinklers	Secondary	$0.50–$2	Low	Medium	High	Easy	Low
Irrigation— Drip	Tertiary	$1.50–$5	Low	Low	High	Medium	Low
Cooling Towers	Tertiary	Minor	Low	Low	Low	Easy	Low
Supply for Toilets and Urinals	Tertiary	Minor	Low	Medium	None	Medium	High

Permit Requirements for Onsite Wastewater Treatment

Every onsite treatment project will be required to meet discharge water quality parameters established by state and local agencies. Permit review can be a time-consuming process and may involve multiple agencies, and will depend on the state regulations, environmental sensitivity of the site, and the concerns of neighboring landowners. The entire permit process can take months or years. Therefore, it is extremely important to engage an experienced wastewater engineer and the environmental regulatory agencies at the very beginning of the project so that all of the permit requirements are understood, and the options are clear to all participants. Design decisions can be made at or after this initial meeting. Because of the potentially complex nature of the wastewater treatment process and public health and safety issues, the regulatory agencies will require that all plans and specifications be designed by a registered professional engineer.

Energy Content of Treated Effluent and Energy Efficiency of Treatment Processes

It is possible to attach an energy value to each gallon of treated effluent based on the treatment processes used. Some treatment processes used for onsite treatment systems use much more energy than others. For example, a passive treatment system using septic tanks and constructed wetlands typically uses about 0.5 kW of energy per 1,000 gallons of wastewater treated, while an extended aeration mechanical package treatment system might use 4 to 5 kW per 1,000 gallons treated. There is also a direct relationship between water quality and energy required to treat the wastewater. A higher standard of water quality will often require more energy (refer to Table 3-12). Since there are many options, including proprietary mechanical systems not discussed in this book, it is worthwhile to analyze the water-energy nexus and attempt to minimize both.

Types of Onsite Wastewater Treatment Systems

The nonproprietary technologies that make up the bulk of the onsite treatment technologies are essentially applied ecologies. Table 3-14 is a summary of the treatment elements and their associated ecologies.

TABLE 3-14: Treatment Elements and Associated Ecologies

TREATMENT ELEMENT	ECOLOGY
Septic Tank	Bottom of the pond—the microbial community found in the anaerobic sediment of ponds is essentially the same as found in a septic tank.
Leach Field	Soil—a highly diverse microbial ecosystem with a mineral and humic substrate enables the almost total remediation of the remaining compounds in the applied wastewater.
Sand Filter	Riparian—the sand and gravel adjacent to and in the riparian corridor are host to an amazing ecosystem consisting of a microbial community, micro- and macro-invertebrates, as well as the roots of macrophytes and trees.
Irrigation System and Vegetated Area	Meadow, savannah, woodland—the complex ecosystem of the grasslands or woodlands provide a wonderfully diverse substrate for the microbial community working in a symbiotic relationship with the plants. The root matrix, in combination with the fungal community, provides the means to almost entirely remove all applied compounds in the wastewater as well as utilize the nutrients for plant growth and increased carbon sequestration.
Trickling Filter	River rapids or waterfall—the falling water aerates the water while the rocks, sand, and gravel provide substrate for the microbial community—bacteria, bryophytes, algae, and invertebrates that recycle the organic compounds, which are a food source.
Constructed Wetlands	Wetlands—although the constructed wetlands are not as diverse an ecosystem as natural wetlands, it is possible to establish very productive ecosystems that rely primarily on *Typha* spp., *Scirpus* spp., *Carex* spp., which are able to remove organic compounds, nitrate, metals, most pathogens and viruses, as well as many of the priority pollutants. There are over 5,000 wetlands plants in the North American database that, along with many other species, allow the wetlands to be used as part of a very colorful landscape feature.

By combining these various different ecologies, the designer can obtain the desired effluent water quality. The wastewater treatment system is the aggregate of two or more treatment elements. For example, this might be a septic tank and a leach field, as shown in the first line in Figure 3-79. Or it might be a septic tank followed by a subsurface flow constructed wetlands and then a leach field. It is the designer's and engineer's task to select the appropriate treatment elements to meet the following design conditions. (see Figures 3-80 and 3-81):

► Flow volume and daily variations

► CBOD concentrations

► Nitrogen concentrations

► Reuse options—irrigation and/or reuse in buildings

► Discharge water quality standards for stream discharge (in lieu of land application)

► Site conditions

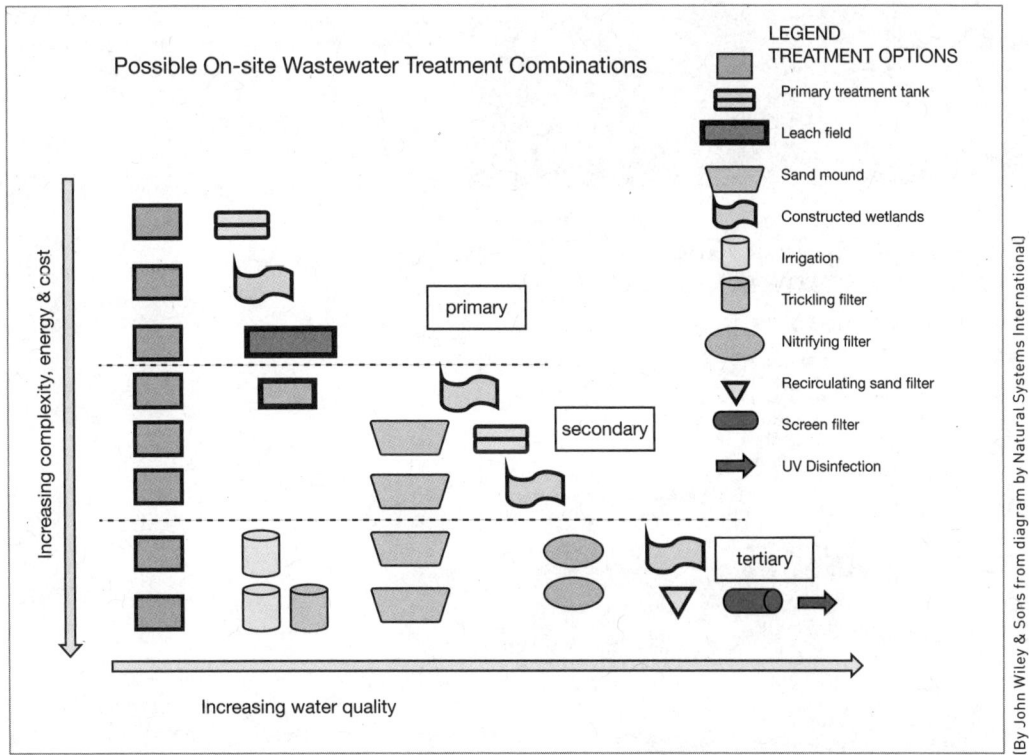

FIGURE 3-79: Possible onsite wastewater treatment combinations. The simplest system is the first system shown at the top of the figure and this is the most common. It is the least expensive option but has the lowest effluent water quality. The last system, which consists of primary treatment (which could include any of the options listed), CBOD-reducing trickling filters, nitrifying trickling filters, nitrogen reduction wetlands, CBOD and TSS sand filters, fine filtration and UV disinfection, produces a water quality suitable for reuse in buildings. As more complex combinations are selected (vertical downward movement in this graphic), capital and operating costs go up, but water quality improves (horizontal axis). The basic idea is that as more treatment ecologies are combined, water quality improves and costs increase. The other combinations produce effluent water quality that is not as good, but may be appropriate for the permit requirements and the intended reuse. Reuse for irrigation does not have to meet the same water quality standard as reuse in buildings.

[Photo from Luke Gascho]

FIGURE 3-80: The Merry Lea Environmental Learning Center was created to house Goshen College's expanding environmental science program and to enable students to live near the ecosystems they study. At Merry Lea, this cycle is achieved in Phase 1 by passing effluent through the constructed wetland and the recirculating sand filter. Including a trickling filter and an aerated lagoon in the treatment process for Phase 2 enhances the nitrogen cycle. The trickling filter and lagoon nitrify the effluent, which is subsequently denitrified as it passes through the wetlands. A similar process occurs within the sand filter, which provides final nitrogen reductions prior to disposal or reuse.

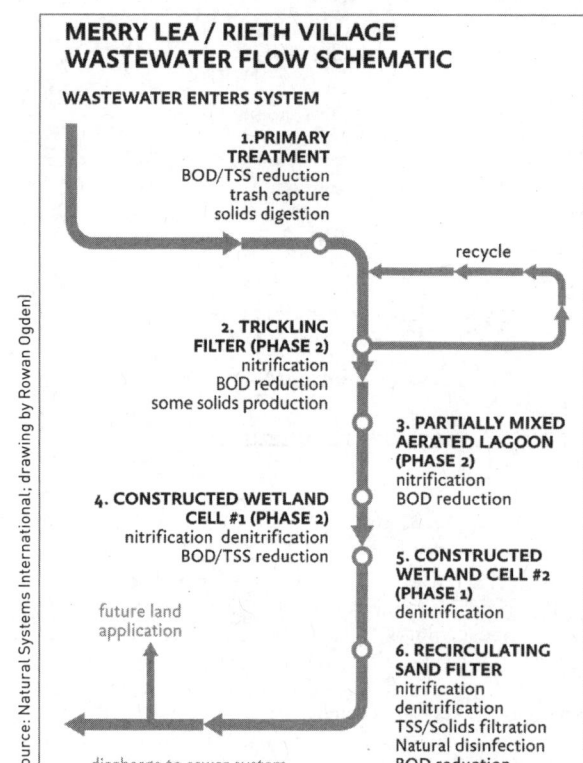

[Source: Natural Systems International; drawing by Rowan Ogden]

FIGURE 3-81: The onsite treatment system for the Merry Lea Environmental Learning Center consists of a primary treatment tank (septic tank), constructed wetlands, a sand filter, and a trickling filter. Water from the septic tank flows to a trickling filter (CBOD/TSS reduction), then to a constructed wetlands (nitrification, denitrification, CBOD reduction), and finally to a recirculating sand filter (nitrification, denitrification, TSS/solids filtration, natural disinfection, CBOD reduction). The cycle of nitrification and denitrification is crucial to the wastewater treatment process.

PROPRIETARY SYSTEMS

The options described previously are all nonproprietary. They are public domain technology. However, there are many additional systems that are proprietary and rely on the ecology of the pond, or are "package" treatment systems that can be purchased and installed by the manufacturer or its agent. The package treatment systems typically use mechanical aeration systems (air bubbles are injected into the wastewater using blowers and air diffusion manifolds) that treat septic tank effluent. One of the exceptions relies on the use of a trickling filter in lieu of an aeration system. These types of systems, also called "tank and treat" systems, have the virtue of being delivered by a truck and quickly installed. Their disadvantage is that they require maintenance from the installer or manufacturer. The owner is thus tied to the success of the manufacturer and the ability of the manufacturer to provide adequate maintenance.

SOLAR AQUATIC AND LIVING MACHINE SYSTEMS

The "solar aquatic system" (SAS) and the "living machine" (LM) wastewater treatment systems are patented or copyrighted systems originally developed by John Todd, Ph.D., and are based on the ecology of the pond. These are quite attractive aerated systems relying on masses of plants floating in aerated tanks that are enclosed in greenhouses. Because of the greenhouse requirement and the energy required to aerate the tanks, these types of systems are usually expensive to build and operate. The primary virtue of these systems is the great mass of plants growing in a tropical greenhouse environment. This makes the wastewater treatment process an attraction as well as an opportunity for the architect and landscape architect specializing in interior plant palettes to design something unique and visually interesting as well as educational (see Figures 3-82 to 3-84).

(Source BNIM Architects and Natural Systems International)

FIGURE 3-82: The Solar Aquatic System at the Omega Center for Sustainable Living in Rhinebeck, New York, designed by John Todd Ecological Engineering and Natural Systems International, is part of an integrated water system for the building and site.

SAS and LM systems require some form of primary treatment, and some additional treatment is required if the reclaimed effluent is to be used in buildings as a supply for water closets or urinals. Primary treatment may be in the form of a septic tank, followed by SAS/LM tanks which are designed to settle additional solids. This first set of tanks has a fine bubble diffuser which supplies the additional oxygen to the root zones of the plants floating on the surface of these tanks. Solids accumulate on the roots and are periodically sloughed off to be captured and returned to the primary treatment tank. Subsequent tanks, also with floating plants, require diminishing amounts of aeration. The final tank in the series is usually nitrifying so the SAS or LM systems are often followed by subsurface flow constructed wetlands (denitrifying) and recirculating sand filters (final polishing).

(Source BNIM Architects and Natural Systems International)

FIGURE 3-83: Constructed wetlands outside the Omega Institute Solar Aquatic System greenhouse treat wastewater and stormwater onsite.

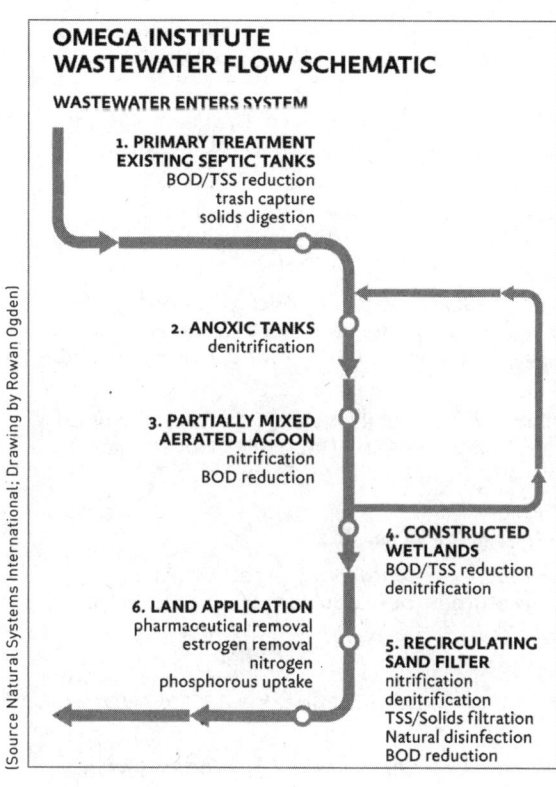

[Source Natural Systems International; Drawing by Rowan Ogden]

FIGURE 3-84: The Omega Institute treatment system elements include primary treatment tanks, an anoxic tank (for denitrification, subsurface flow constructed wetlands, and a recirculating sand filter in addition to the Solar Aquatic System (in the greenhouse). The order of treatment elements is not rigid except that all the elements follow some form of primary treatment.

References

Calabria, J., and D. Nadenicek. 2007. *Restoration of Urban Riparian Area: Case Study*. NOVATECH: 6th International Conference on Sustainable Techniques and Strategies in Urban Water Management (June 25–28, 2007). Lyon, France.

Chesapeake Bay Foundation. (n.d.) *Future Growth in the Washington, D.C. Metropolitan Area*. Available at www.savethebay.org/land/landuse/maps/future_growth.html.

Coffman, L. 2000. *Low-Impact Development Manual*. Prince Georges County, Maryland Department of Environmental Resources.

_____. 2001. "Low Impact Development Creating a Storm of Controversy." *IMPACT*, Vol. 3 No. 6 (November).

Echols, S., and E. Pennypacker. 2006. "Stormwater Special: RainArt—Art for Rain's Sake (Stormwater Management)." *Landscape Architecture,* 96(9):24*ff.*

Ferguson, B., 1998. *Introduction to Stormwater*. New York: John Wiley and Sons.

_____. 2005. *Porous Pavements*. Boca Raton, FL: CRC Press.

Ferguson, B. and T. Debo. 1990. *On-Site Stormwater Management* (2nd ed.). New York: Van Nostrand Reinhold.

Hathaway, J.H., and W.F. Hunt. 2006. *Level Spreaders: Overview, Design and Maintenance* (AGW-588-09). Available at www.bae.ncsu.edu/stormwater/PublicationFiles/LevelSpreaders2006.pdf.

King County, WA, Department of Natural Resources. 1999. *The Relationship Between Soil and Water How Soil Amendments and Compost Can Aid in Salmon Recovery.* Available at http://depts.washington.edu/cuwrm/publictn/s4s.pdf.

National SUDS Working Group. 2003. Framework for Sustainable Urban Drainage Systems (SUDS) in England and Wales, www.environmentgency.gov.uk/commondata/105385/suds_book_902564.pdf.

North Carolina Sedimentation Control Commission. 2009. *Erosion and Sediment Control Planning and Design Manual.* Available at www.dlr.enr.state.nc.us/pages/publications.html#eslinks (accessed 12/2010).

Pitt, Robert. 1999. "Small Storm Hydrology and Why It Is Important for the Design of Stormwater Control Practices." In *Advances in Modeling the Management of Stormwater Impacts,* Vol. 7. (W. James, ed.). Guelph, ON: Computational Hydraulics International, and Lewis Publishers/CRC Press.

_____. 2000. "The Risk of Groundwater Contamination from Infiltration of Stormwater Runoff," in *The Practice of Watershed Protection* (Thomas R. Schueler and Heather K. Holland, eds.). Ellicott City, MD; also available as Technical Note #34 from *Wat. Prot. Techniques.* 1(3): 126–128.

Pitt, Robert, Shirley Clark, Keith Parmer, and Richard Field. 1996. *Groundwater Contamination from Stormwater Infiltration.* Chelsea, MI: Ann Arbor Press, Inc.

Scholz-Barth, K. 2001. *Green Roofs, Stormwater Management from the Top Down. Environmental Design and Construction.* Available at www.greenroofs.com/pdfs/archives-katrin.pdf.

Stahre, Peter. 2006. *Sustainability in Urban Storm Drainage: Planning and Examples.* Stockholm, Sweden: Svenskt Vatten.

Strecker, E. W. 2001. "Low Impact Development (LID): How Low Impact Is It?" *IMPACT,* Vol. 3, No. 6 (November), 10–15.

U.S. Department of Agriculture. 2000. *Summary Report: 1997 National Resources Inventory* (revised December 2000). Natural Resources Conservation Service, Washington, DC, and Statistical Laboratory, Iowa State University, Ames, IA. Available at www.nrcs.usda.gov/technical/NRI/1997/summary_report/report.pdf (accessed May 19, 2011).

U.S. Department of Housing and Urban Development. 2000. *The State of the Cities.* Available at: http://archives.hud.gov/reports/socrpt.pdf.

U.S. Environmental Protection Agency (EPA). 1987. *Agricultural Chemicals in Ground Water—Proposed Pesticide Strategy.* Washington, DC: Office of Pesticides and Toxic Substances.

_____. 2009a. *Technical Guidance on Implementing the Stormwater Runoff Requirements for Federal Projects under Section 438 of the Energy Independence and Security Act.* Washington, DC.

_____. 2009b. *Pervious Concrete Pavement.* Available at: http://cfpub.epa.gov/npdes/stormwater/menuofbmps/index.cfm?action=factsheet_results&view=specific&bmp=137&minmeasure=5

_____. 2009c. *WaterSense Landscape Water Budget Tool.* Available at: http://water.epa.gov/action/waterefficiency/watersense/spaces/water_budget_tool.cfm

_____. 2010. *Compost Blankets.* Available at: http://cfpub.epa.gov/npdes/stormwater/menuofbmps/index.cfm?action=factsheet_results&view=specific&bmp=118

VanWoert, N. D., D. B. Rowe, J. A. Andresen, C. L. Rugh, R. T. Fernandez, and L. Xiao. 2005. "Green Roof Stormwater Retention: Effects of Roof Surface, Slope, and Media Depth." *Journal of Environmental Quality,* Vol. 34, No. 3, 1036–1044.

CHAPTER 4

SITE DESIGN: VEGETATION

▶ Steve Windhager, Mark Simmons, and Jacob Blue

OF ALL THE MATERIAL AVAILABLE TO THE DESIGNER, vegetation may be the most versatile and the most powerful. When vegetation is selected to fit the conditions on the site, it can maintain as well as rebuild a landscape's capacity to provide a wide range of ecosystem services.

Recent studies have documented a number of direct human benefits that come from our interaction with vegetation. Those benefits include inspiration (Chenowith and Gobster 1990), reduction of mental fatigue (R. Kaplan and Kaplan 1989; S. Kaplan 1995), reduction of sick days and patient recovery time (Ulrich 1986; Ulrich et al. 1991), and reduction of the crime rate (Kuo 2001). Vegetation has even been suggested to have a spiritual connection with us (de Groot, Wilson, and Boumans 2002). A lack of interaction with vegetation and the out-of-doors in general has been linked to increased obesity, as well as a wide range of behavioral problems, particularly in children (Louv 2005) (Figure 4-1).

(Design by Andropogon Associates)

FIGURE 4-1: The wetland plantings at the Sidwell Friends' School in Washington, DC, provide recreational and educational opportunities for students.

While any vegetation will likely provide some type of service, sites that are explicitly designed to harness the beneficial services of vegetation often provide a larger range of benefits (SITES 2009b). Appropriately selected vegetation can meet site-specific resources, habitat, pollution control, and energy performance needs such as:

- ► Reduction of the local heat island effect
- ► Reduction of stormwater runoff and improvement of water quality
- ► Improved air quality, particularly related to reductions in surface ozone
- ► Improved visual and physical access to greenspace, an increasingly recognized component of a livable city, which positively affects property values and human health

OVERVIEW OF SITES VEGETATION-RELATED CREDITS

Ensuring that the built environment, even as it expands into undeveloped greenfield lands, is able to continue to provide the same or greater levels of ecosystem services that it provided before development is the hallmark of a sustainable site. *The Sustainable Sites Initiative: Guidelines and Performance Benchmarks* prerequisites and credits associated with vegetation are intended to help ensure that the design, construction, and maintenance of vegetation onsite not only minimizes resource inputs, but also serves to ensure that the site will provide those ecosystem services that are critical for the region.

SITES prerequisites and credits associated with vegetation can be grouped into three primary categories:

1. Preserving existing healthy vegetative communities to the extent possible
2. Selection of vegetation that is well adapted to site conditions and unlikely to cause adverse consequences
3. Utilizing vegetation to provide a range of ecosystem services

The importance of preservation of healthy functioning systems is made clear through prerequisites that limit soil impacts in prime or unique farmland, wetlands, and other highly productive landscapes.

Prerequisites and credits emphasize that critical areas of the site should be protected from damage during the development and construction process. In addition, plants that remain or are brought onto the site should fit the conditions of the site and the needs of the site post-construction. Critical issues here are the control of invasive species and appropriate plant selection. The project team can further earn credits by utilizing a greater proportion of native plants and restoring entire vegetative communities native to the ecoregion of the site.

The final category of vegetation-related prerequisites and credits are those associated with ensuring the provisioning of ecosystem services on the site. Performance associated with a range of these optional credits help to move a landscape from merely causing no harm to actually improving the conditions at a site or within a region. The credits are intended to:

▶ Improve or maintain receiving water quality

▶ Preserve and restore appropriate plant biomass

▶ Minimize building heating or cooling requirements .

▶ Reduce the heat island effect

▶ Reduce the risk of catastrophic wildfire

▶ Encourage use of plant material produced with sustainable plant production practices

▶ Ensure visual and physical interaction between humans and plants to provide for mental restoration

These prerequisites and credits contribute to vegetation use that can lower consumption of critical resources (such as petrochemicals—i.e., fuel, chemical derived fertilizers, pesticides), water, and time, as well as contribute to the provisioning of the ecosystem services critical for humans and their well-being and that of other plants and wildlife (SITES 2009a).

Understanding the Site

Sustainable site design requires significant knowledge and understanding of the site conditions both pre- and postconstruction in order to be successful. Successful planting design within the context of SITES can be summarized as: right plant, right place.

SITES has an explicit bias toward the preservation of healthy ecosystems because these systems are likely to be the most effective at producing the broadest range of ecosystem services with fewer additional inputs. For this reason, SITES has also prioritized the redevelopment of existing brownfields and grayfields. Brownfields and grayfields represent sites where ecosystem services have been severely impacted. Redevelopment of these sites with sustainability in mind will allow for a net increase in ecosystem services produced at the site. SITES is designed such that it is easier to accumulate credits on brownfields and grayfields where most ecosystem services have been lost.

Ensuring that plants are chosen to match site needs does not always equate to using species that may have historically occurred onsite. Built environments—whether urban or rural—will alter the existing ecological conditions of a site. Soils and hydrology are frequently altered, and local climate and reflectance or other light patterns can be impacted as well.

Not all plants can or should go everywhere; while some accommodations can be made, selection of plants should be driven by the site and regional conditions. The designer must consider the ecosystem services a species or plant community can provide for the site.

Selecting species based on information gathered about a site's conditions before construction and comparing this data against predictions about a site's conditions postconstruction often require a designer to identify a series of environmental conditions found on the site or perhaps a reference site, where these conditions occur naturally. The reference site can allow the designer to view a local suite of plant communities in action to evaluate if the species will fit the needs of the site. For example, in spite of its name, a rain garden is typically dry (Beuttell 2008) and therefore needs to be designed to be able to handle the extremes of hydraulic conditions. In natural systems, first-order streams in the same ecoregion of the site will experience the same ranges in hydrological conditions, and therefore are appropriate communities to use as models for species selection in a rain garden. Table 4-1 offers common data-gathering questions for plant selection.

TABLE 4-1: Sample Site Data-Gathering Questions for Plant Selection

Soil and hydrology conditions	Is the site (or portions of the site) wet, mesic, or dry? Does the soil drain? Is the soil compacted? What about soil depth and overall usable soil volume? What is the soil pH? Are there any unusual chemical conditions in the soil? Are salts used seasonally? Is there evidence of biological activity in the soil? Where is the site located relative to flood waters and tidal influences?
Vegetation and existing plant communities	What is the predominant habitat of the region? What are the existing vegetative communities on the site? Are there naturally occurring vegetative communities that occupy habitats with conditions similar to those of the site? What are the primary invasive species in the region, on the site, or on neighboring properties?
Context/geography	Where is the site located? How are habitats connected at or near the site? What is the site exposure? Hours of sun or shade? At what elevation is the site located? What is the precipitation, hardiness zone, or heat zone levels?
Cultural conditions and built context	How will users interact with the vegetation? From where will vegetation be seen by users? What services is the vegetation expected to provide?

Selecting the Right Plant for the Right Place

The most important factor in selecting vegetation is the appropriateness of a plant to the site and programmatic requirements. Both native and nonnative vegetation can have unsustainable outcomes if it is not suited to the conditions of the site. It is important to consider the living, changing qualities of a plant, its role in a larger plant community, its role on the site, and its specific horticultural needs when selecting plants for a sustainable site design. Sites will also change over time, and selecting appropriate species includes anticipating the changes of a site. Selecting plants, based on their individual characteristics or culled from a community, requires that the designer anticipate how the selected species will perform within the context of the new site.

Ensuring species will meet the ecosystem needs of the site means species should be evaluated based on the role an individual plant plays in its natural vegetative community to confirm its compatibility with the new site. It also means vegetative communities should be paired with expected, desired, or needed ecosystem services of a site.

▶ Plants should be selected based on the role a particular species provided in their natural plant community that matches an expected or needed plant community for the ecosystem services of the site. For example, species from predominantly wet natural plant communities should be used where excess water or moisture is expected on the site.

▶ Species should be selected to address specific ecosystem goals and constraints of the site, such as phytoremediation or shade.

▶ Species should be selected to fill structural needs of a desired habitat, providing appropriate cover, shelter, and food resources or other needed ecosystem services.

Appropriate plant selection does not require a native-only principle in order to be sustainable, but designers must understand the ecological conditions in which the desired plant would naturally occur.

In order to anticipate a particular plant's behavior, it is often helpful to examine the following questions:

▶ What are the types of plant communities where this plant is typically found?

▶ What role does the selected plant play in its natural vegetative community?

▶ Where does the selected plant occur in the structure of its natural vegetative community?

▶ How prominent is the plant in its natural vegetative community and why?

Appropriate selection and placement requires an understanding of the soil conditions, water regime, potential interactions between species, and an estimation of future maintenance needs. The designer must also consider longevity of the plant or community in the postconstruction site. Disturbance, natural or manmade, is often part of the built environment, and the designer must consider the plant or vegetative community's ability to withstand physical disturbances that are likely to occur onsite, such as compaction, physical impact or bumping, browsing, or unusually high winds (Table 4-2).

TABLE 4-2: Criteria for Evaluating Appropriate Plants

Adaptability and environmental tolerance	Species selected provides expected and desired growth to thrive within the built conditions of the site in the space provided (both above ground and below ground), sun/shade, wet/dry, salt, heat/cold, nutrient, management, pest conditions
Function	Species selected provides the desired ecosystem services and programmatic functions as intended
Plant management	Selected species is derived from appropriate sources and nursery grown, is suitable for expected maintenance techniques of the site management plan Selected species is not expected to become invasive or aggressive to the site or surrounding region
Design intent	Selected species meets the desired design goal, such as screening, color, form, or spatial definition

VEGETATION AND ECOSYSTEM SERVICES

Any time a plant is used in the landscape, there are ecosystem services produced. Most plant ecosystem services can be attributed to physical architecture (e.g., shade, wind brake) or processes associated with plant physiology (e.g., transpirational cooling, biomass production, nutrient cycling). The critical element in the design, operation, and maintenance of a truly sustainable site is ensuring that the site is able to continue to produce as much (or more) of the regionally critical ecosystem services than it did before development (or redevelopment). This effort is a significant expansion of the explicit design goals within landscape architecture in the past and represents a new way of thinking about the landscape: where landscape ecological performance is as critical as other design constraints such as safety, aesthetics, and occupancy (Windhager et al. 2010).

Combining multiple ecosystem services within one planting is the fastest way to ensure that the postconstruction conditions meet or exceed preconstruction ecosystem service function. Vegetative communities in nature provide many ecosystem services in concert; this should be the goal of the sustainable designer (Table 4-3).

TABLE 4-3: Ecosystem Services Provided by Plants

Oxygen production	Plants produce oxygen through photosynthesis where water and carbon dioxide are pulled apart and recombined to form sugar and oxygen.
Carbon sequestration	CO_2 fixed by the plant can be locked in plant tissue (up to hundreds of years) or into the soil via the sloughing of roots and leaves for thousands of years (Lal 2003).
Air pollutant removal	Pollutants such as ozone, NO_2, SO_2 volatile organic compounds (VOCs), and particulate matter all can be absorbed and broken down by plants (Nowak, Crane, and Stevens 2006).
Soil/water pollutant removal	Plants can be effective vectors to uptake pollutants in solution, particularly heavy metals from saturated or unsaturated soils (Weis and Weis 2004).
Transpiration	Removal of groundwater can be essential to environmental health, for example, lowering water table to reduce soil salinization (Schofield 1992), or removal of stormwater from green roofs (Dunnett et al. 2008).
Cooling	Plants not only provide direct shade over surfaces, thereby decreasing radiant heating on those surfaces; they also reduce air temperature transpiration of water from their stomata (Hunhammar 1999).
Wildlife habitat	Plants provide food and cover for many species of organisms.
Food and pharmaceuticals	Plants provide the majority of the food consumed by humans. In addition, most of the pharmaceuticals used today are derived from or based on physical and chemical properties of plants.

Plant Physiology and Ecosystem Services

The ecosystem services provided by plants are a result of the plant's physiological functions. The most basic of these functions—photosynthesis and water uptake—account for oxygen production, carbon sequestration, flood control, water quality improvement, phytoremediation, and cooling of the surrounding environment and ambient air temperatures. Understanding the basics of plant physiology is key to understanding the services vegetation can provide.

BIOMASS DENSITY INDEX

The number and quality of ecosystem services provided by vegetation is often directly correlated with the amount of vegetation present, or living biomass. Living biomass density can provide some indication of many of the ecosystem services a site could produce.

The Biomass Density Index (BDI) is used by SITES guidelines as a surrogate for some ecosystem services. This approach was taken to simplify the quantification of ecosystem services provided by a site. In SITES, BDI is calculated from information gathered in the pre-design site analysis, by first totaling the percent of the total area of the site covered by various vegetation types (trees with understory, trees without understory, shrubs, desert plants, annual plantings, grasslands, ground cover and turf grass, and emergent wetlands) as well as amount of impervious cover.

The SITES guidelines provide a "biomass density" estimate for each vegetation cover category based on a literature review of research associated with the leaf area index of the various cover classes. By combining the percent cover of each vegetation class with the appropriate biomass density value supplied in the guidelines, an existing site BDI can be determined. The appropriate BDI will vary by location and is determined by the historic ecosystem within the region, taking into account climate and other geographically significant variables.

PHOTOSYNTHESIS

The fundamental process of plant physiology is photosynthesis—the process through which carbohydrates (e.g., sugar, $C_6H_{12}O_6$) necessary for growth and metabolism are manufactured using light energy, gaseous carbon from air (CO_2) (carbon sequestration), and water (H_2O) (flood control, water quality improvement), primarily from the ground, resulting in the release of oxygen (O_2) (oxygen production, air quality improvement) through the process of photosynthesis.

FORMULA $6CO_2 + 6H_2O \rightarrow$ (light) $\rightarrow C_6H_{12}O_6 + 6O_2$

WATER

Water is essential for many plant physiological processes including the manufacture of other essential physiological products as well as the transport of organic nutrients and cooling. These functions require the movement of water from the ground throughout the living plant tissue network.

Internal water flow can be regulated by a plant several ways, but water flow is dependent on and affected by the soil at the soil-root interface, by air, and by the water availability of the soil.

In the soil, water availability is dependent on a number of factors including soil texture, soil density, presence of organic matter, symbiotic relationships with soil biota, and other chemical factors. The finer the soil texture, the lower the porosity (less air and water volume) can be held in the soil; finer-grained soils can hold water, through molecular forces, at much lower volume compared to coarser soil. Together these components determine how much water is available to the plant.

Plant roots also need air in order to function; when soils are saturated for several days, needed air is not available, which can lead to root death. Under most circumstances, excess water drains from saturated soil through gravity, while the force of capillary action holds on to a proportion of that water based on the soil texture. Alternatively, too much air and a plant's internal water pressure will decrease. Air passing over the stomata of a plant's leaf strips the moisture from the plant in a process called desiccation. This, in turn, triggers the plant's water flow regulation system to draw moisture from the soil at the root-soil interface. As the soil dries further (through evaporation or plant uptake), soil water pressure reaches a point whereby the plant can no longer extract water from the soil. The plant can reduce the water pressure so severely that it reaches a wilting point from which it cannot recover. (See Figure 4-2.)

For most species of plants, plant-available water is greatest on medium-textured soils (e.g., loams). Fortunately, the diversity of plants means that plants can survive and even prefer different soil textures. Understanding soil texture allows the designer to optimize water storage and availability within the soil in order to reduce water use. Where existing site soil is used, this understanding helps to clarify when irrigation will be needed. Modifying the plant species composition, the soil texture, or both will ensure that plant selection will be matched with soil conditions to ensure optimal water usage across the range of plant conditions on the site.

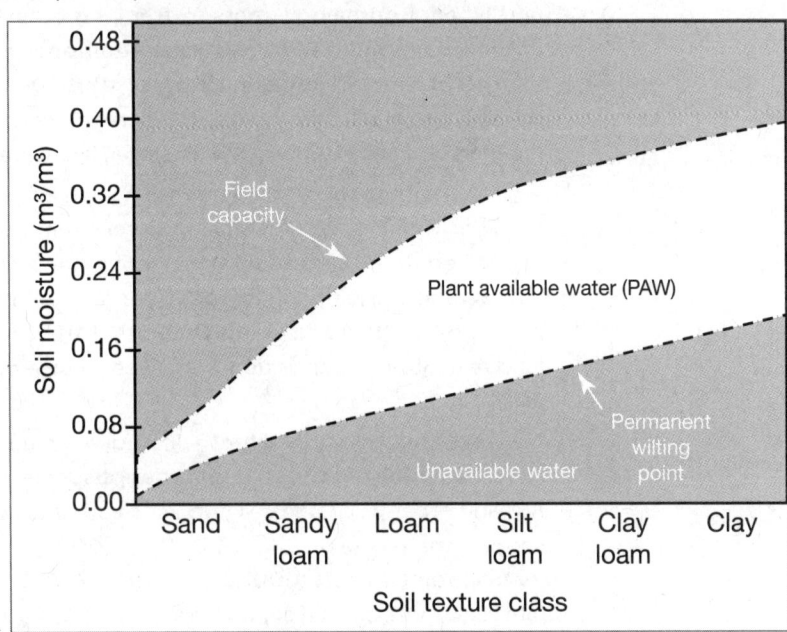

FIGURE 4-2: The relationship between soil texture and plant-available water, wilting point, and field capacity based on soil texture class. As water becomes unavailable, plants experience wilting and death; as water exceeds needs, plants approach suffocation and death.

OXYGEN PRODUCTION, COOLING, AND CARBON SEQUESTRATION

Plant respiration is essential for photosynthesis and is the primary process by which carbon dioxide is exchanged for oxygen. The process of photosynthesis includes gas exchange, such as the capture of carbon dioxide (CO_2) and the manufacturing and release of dioxygen (O_2), the stable form of oxygen. However, during respiration, it is common for unbound water (H_2O) to escape as well. This is no different than our own respiration. The gases themselves not only convert to moisture easily, but the release of gases also results in the release of moisture.

AIR QUALITY

Stripping carbon from the air in the form of CO_2 for photosynthesis is just one way plants can improve air quality. Plants also release moisture in the air through respiration, as described above. The release of moisture can help reduce pollen content, dust particles, and other airborne pollutants by trapping them with heavy water molecules that drop out of the air or condense on surfaces. Additionally, plants are literally screens, mechanical filters that as particle-laden air passes through the plant, it is slowed down by the friction of the limbs and leaves acting as a screen (Bernatzky 1983; Bolund and Hunhammar 1999; McPherson et al. 1997). As the air slows, like water, it drops out heavier particles.

Trees with greater foliage density, such as evergreens, strip more airborne pollutants than deciduous species (Beckett, Freer-Smith, and Taylor 2000). Modeling studies have suggested that trees in sufficient populations can reduce airborne smog through evapotranspiration resulting in temperature reductions of 0.5 to 3°F (Taha, Konopacki, and Gabersek 1996). Others have suggested that trees improve air quality by splitting smog and acid rain into dry deposition NO_x, O_3, and other particulates (Akbari, Pomerantz, and Taha 2001).

Trees are best studied for their air quality impacts but an increasing body of knowledge is exploring the effects of other types of species, such as the reduction of carbon by prairies and other grasslands. Whittaker's estimates of net potential productivity (NPP) (1975) suggest that some grasslands (100 to 2,000 g/m²/yr) may have higher potential productivity than some forests (600 to 2,500 g/m²/yr). The increased potential productivity translates into more carbon capture per year. These estimates are consistent with those of Odum (1959) who estimated the NPP of grasslands near 440 g/m²/yr and forests near 1,500 g/m²/yr. (C_4 species of grasses are known to increase growth and production in the presence of elevated CO_2 [Owensby et al. 1993]).

Vegetation for Heat Island Reduction

There are three vegetative strategies to reduce the heat island effect and improve energy conservation: replace, cover, and remove. Determining which strategy will be employed to impact the site will determine which type of vegetation should be used (Table 4-14).

TABLE 4-4: Vegetative Strategies to Reduce the Urban Heat Island Effect

	JUSTIFICATION	STRATEGIES
Replace hardscape and reflective surfaces with vegetation	The reflective albedo of vegetation is much higher than on most paved or roofing surfaces, resulting in lower insolation absorption (Akbari, Pomerantz, and Taha 2001). Increased atmospheric moisture combined with shading reduces temperature (Huang, Akbari, and Taha 1990; Kurn et al. 1994).	Reduce the area of solar-reflective hardscape surfaces and replace with solar-absorptive vegetative surfaces. Increase the areas of evapotranspiration, which increases gaseous water in the atmosphere (Bell et al., unpublished).
Cover hardscape and reflective surfaces with vegetation	Use of species that provide shade is another way to reduce the heat island effect. However, cover strategies often place vegetation in areas where impacts from the heat island negatively affect the vegetation. Impacts can include: ▶ Excessive heat ▶ Air pollution ▶ Reflected light ▶ Increased evaporation ▶ Increased exposure to wind	Species that tend to perform are those that occur in habitats with direct daily sunlight, exposure to reflected heat from bedrock, or are fire resistant, such as savanna and woodland edge species. Plants with smaller leaves may also perform better because the leaves have smaller surfaces and are less susceptible to solar- or wind-generated desiccation. Vines can also be used to provide cover or shading in areas where soil depth is expected to be insufficient to support healthy trees. Place vegetation to provide shade for: ▶ Parking lots and other paved surfaces (walks, driveways, etc.) ▶ Western or eastern faces of buildings and structures (trees should be placed no closer than 5 ft and no less than 50 ft) ▶ Roofs ▶ Vehicles ▶ Outdoor gathering spaces ▶ Water bodies and streams

continues

TABLE 4-4: Vegetative Strategies to Reduce the Urban Heat Island Effect *(continued)*

	JUSTIFICATION	STRATEGIES
Removal of pollutants and CO_2	Plants remove existing smog through evapotranspiration. Trees and grasslands are particularly effective at removing smog and CO_2 from the atmosphere. Rosenfeld et al. (1998) found modeled estimates of smog in Los Angeles were significantly reduced when trees were planted in appropriate densities. Akbari et al. (2001) suggested this would reduce the maximum smog concentration by 5 percent, or 175 tons/day—25 times more effective than proposed power plant emission reductions.	Use vegetation to: ▶ Shade air-conditioners, reduce building heating/cooling needs with shade, green roofs, green walls, and buffers, cooling vehicular gas tanks. ▶ Screen or buffer the north side of building facades to reduce winter winds. ▶ Replace high-maintenance turf areas with perennial vegetation to minimize mowing.

(Design by Ten Eyck Landscape Architects, Inc.; Photo by Bill Timmerman)

FIGURE 4-3: Shaded pavement surfaces reduce potential heat island impacts at the Underwood Family Sonoran Landscape Laboratory designed by TenEyck Landscape Architects

Vegetation for Energy Conservation and Microclimate Modification

When placed appropriately, vegetation can offer shade to adjacent buildings or site spaces and it can act as a windbreak or a funnel to channel desirable breezes. Therefore, vegetation can be an effective passive energy conservation strategy for adjacent buildings and it can modify the microclimate of exterior site spaces to increase human comfort.

When placed as a screen in linear formation or a mass, vegetation can be extremely effective at reducing the impacts of wind. It can redirect prevailing wind up and, if tall enough, over a protected structure. In addition, vegetation breaks up the velocity of wind through frictional loss. In temperate climates evergreen species provide the most windbreak potential, because of the density of the branching, leaves, and year-round foliage. However, deciduous vegetation does also provide a mitigating effect.

Vegetation should be placed in the direct path of the prevailing wind, adjacent to but not directly beside the protected structure. Space should be reserved between the windbreak and the building to provide insulating, "dead air," or air that isn't moving. Vegetation should be placed at least half of the height at maturity away from the face of the structure to provide sufficient dead-air space.

In addition, vegetation is most effective when arranged in rows or en mass perpendicular to the prevailing wind. Some have proposed a 10:1 ratio for the length of windbreaks (10 times the length of the vegetation height at maturity) (Wilson and Josiah, 2010).

Vegetation can also be used to funnel desired air flow. Instead of placing vegetation perpendicular to the prevailing air flow, it is placed parallel, or nearly so, in a funnel pattern to capture the wind and redirect it where desired. Funneling desired air flow can not only direct air but increase the speed of the air (Figure 4-4).

Woody vegetation is best suited for windbreaks and air funneling. Taller herbaceous plantings such as prairies have some frictional effect on flow but not as much as taller, less flexible vegetation.

Vegetation has long been used for the shade it can produce. When placed on the southern and western sides of structures (in the northern hemisphere), vegetation can shade a structure from the sun during the hottest part of the day. Less screening is typically needed on northern or eastern faces. Shade is directly proportional to the amount of sun intercepted—larger, wider, and taller species produce more beneficial shade. Increasing the interception is a matter of species selection or providing

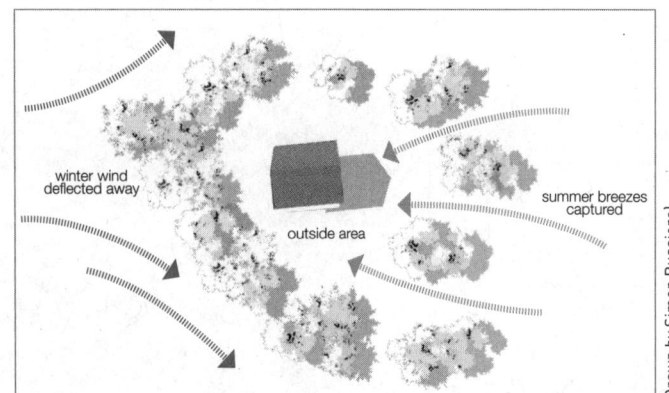

(Drawn by Simon Bussiere)

FIGURE 4-4: Vegetation can act as both a windbreak for buildings and a funnel to capture and direct breezes into buildings when desired. In temperate and cold climates, evergreen trees can offer protection on the north and northwest of the building from prevailing winter winds. Trees can also be arranged to channel prevailing summer winds toward the building for passive cooling.

suitable structure for species success. Shade structures such as arbors and green walls can be comprised of many individuals that collectively provide sufficient desired shade (Figures 4-5 and 4-6).

(Drawn by Simon Bussiere)

FIGURE 4-5: Deciduous trees placed around the south and southwestern faces of a building will shade the building in summer, reducing cooling loads and, without leaves in winter, will allow for penetration of the sun when it is needed. This can be a very effective passive energy conservation strategy for buildings.

Deciduous species are often used for shade because of the wider, larger leaf structures typically found on deciduous vegetation. In addition, appropriately placed deciduous vegetation can provide seasonal shade, screening in the summer when the sun is most intense, and dropping leaves and opening up during the winter when beneficial heating from the sun is desired (Table 4-5).

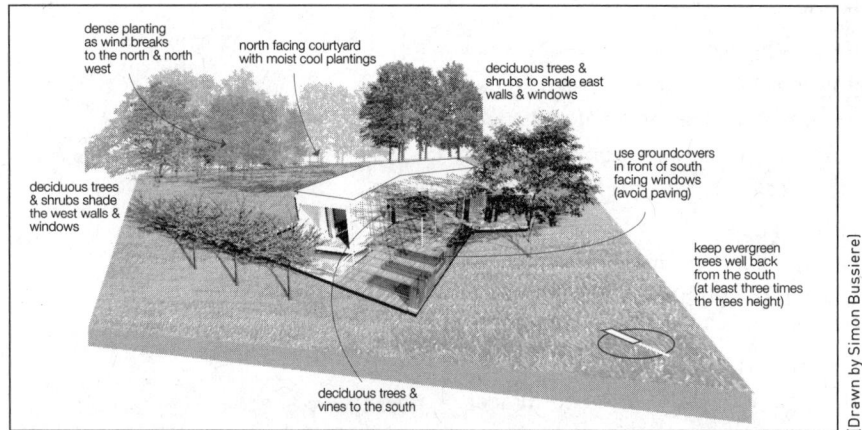

(Drawn by Simon Bussiere)

FIGURE 4-6: A carefully considered planting design around buildings can reduce energy consumption in the building and provide comfortable exterior spaces for occupation throughout the year. The strategies shown in this image are directed primarily for temperate and cold climates, but many having to do with shade apply to hot arid and hot humid climates as well.

TABLE 4-5: Summary of Regional Bioclimatic Strategies

CLIMATE ZONES

FACTORS MODIFIED BY LANDFORM, VEGETATION, AND STRUCTURES	HOT ARID	HOT HUMID	TEMPERATE	COLD
Sun	Avoid heat-absorbing materials. Use thick walls or earth shelters. Use trellis and trees for shade. Provide large overhangs on buildings.	Maximize shade through the use of plantings. Use pergola and trellis structures for shade. Screened terraces provide relief from direct heating of main structure. Provide large overhangs on buildings.	Site structures on southerly slopes for solar gain in winter. Plant deciduous trees for afternoon shade. Provide overhangs on buildings sized to block summer sun and invite winter sun.	Site structures on southerly slopes for solar gain in winter. Cold climate siting benefits from steeper slopes for better solar access. Plant deciduous trees for afternoon shade. Provide overhangs on buildings sized to block summer sun and invite winter sun.
Wind	Site structures at toe of slopes for exposure to cold air flows at night. Use plant material to block desiccating winds. Deflect hot winds with walls and screens.	Site structures at top of slope for exposure to breezes. Avoid excessive earth-mounding that may trap moist air. Maximize breezes through use of high-canopy trees and with a loose, open planting pattern.	Site structure on middle to upper slope for access to light winds, but protection from high winds. Landforms, plants, and structures can be used to divert northerly winter winds while allowing cooling summer breezes.	Site structure on middle to lower slope for wind protection. Plant coniferous shelter belts to block cold winds. Avoid topographic depressions that collect cold air.
Water	Use moisture-conserving plants—xeriscape. Limit impervious surface to minimize runoff; porous paving can be used.	Avoid siting next to stagnant bodies of water. Maximize infiltration of stormwater runoff.	Use of retention/detention ponds for stormwater provides for evaporative cooling of the site. Foundations for structures and pavement must drain well to prevent damage from frost/thaw action.	Use of retention/detention ponds for stormwater provides for evaporative cooling of the site. Foundations for structures and pavement must drain well to prevent damage from frost/thaw action.

(Adapted from Dines 1998)

Phytoremediation and Bioremediation

Bioremediation and *phytoremediation* are general terms for a suite of environmental techniques that rely on the physiology of plants to provide pollutant treatment or capture. Polluted soil, water, and air are treated by exposing the polluted medium to the growth, nutrient-capturing, and physiological processes of vegetation. Through phytoremediation vegetation can store, degrade, or break down harmful pollutants such as organic compounds, metals, fuels and petroleum, solvents, pesticides, and other chemical pollutants.

Evapotranspiration and nutrient sequestration are the two primary mechanisms for phytoremediation of pollutants. Pollutants are taken up at the root/soil interface as part of the maintaining of internal water flow and as part of the capture of desired nutrients. As plants strip desired nutrients off of soil particles or out of the water for growth and development, they capture pollutants by breaking down the chemical bonds of pollutants to sequester the desired nutrient molecules or incorporate a pollutant molecule in the sequestration of a desired nutrient or water.

Other forms of phytoremediation depend on symbiotic relationships between a particular species of plant and soil microorganisms that break down pollutants, chemical compounds in the plant that break down pollutants, or the relationship between plant material and solar radiation.

Capturing, or sequestering, the pollutant traps it in the vegetative structure of the plant until the plant is removed. Various phytoremediation techniques call for the removal or harvesting of the plant in order to stimulate continued growth and uptake. Depending on the pollutant captured, harvested vegetation is beneficially used or carefully disposed of (Table 4-6).

TABLE 4-6: Select Phytoremediation Techniques

Rhizosphere Biodegradation	Pollutant breakdown by microorganisms found on or in the plant
Rhizofiltration	Pollutant screening and trapping in the rooting structures of plants
Phytostabilization and Phytotransformation	Pollutant immobilization, reduction, or conversion to another substance through the chemical processes or metabolism of the plant
Phytoaccumulation (Phytoextraction)	Pollutant sequestration within the plant biomass
Phytovolatization	Pollutant capture and conversion to an inert gaseous form and release into the atmosphere
Phytodegredation	Pollutant destruction by the plant tissue

Often phytoremediation is paired with aerobic and anaerobic soil conditions that contribute to the treatment and breakdown of pollutants.

Phytoremediation requires the expertise of an ecotoxicologist, chemist, or chemical engineer to identify the chemicals to be treated and appropriate species of vegetation for treatment. The need for phytoremediation and mitigation techniques in general are expected to increase as federal and state guidelines decrease allowable pollutant limits and fewer and fewer chemical or mechanical treatment facilities are sized to meet the new regulations.

VEGETATION PROTECTION TECHNIQUES

Existing and new vegetation can be exposed to many impacts during construction of a site and in the postconstruction phase during maintenance activities. It is important to protect vegetation from the following types of impacts:

- ▶ Abrasion and blunt trauma
- ▶ Grading, trenching, boring, or drilling
- ▶ Material, equipment, and site facilities storage and stockpiling (including soil)
- ▶ Paving
- ▶ Compaction
- ▶ Changes in the existing water flow and storage patterns
- ▶ Impacts associated with planting new vegetation onsite, digging, spading, irrigation, and mulching work
- ▶ Pruning, trimming, or clearing work
- ▶ Pollutant runoff, such as washout from a concrete truck, or sediment-laden overland flow

Protection zones should be used to protect both existing and new vegetation, specimen plantings, and fragile habitat around aquatic systems such as wetlands, coastlines, or riparian areas. They can also be used to protect important soil types, special status vegetation, plant communities, or endangered species. Protected vegetation may be required because of a species status as threatened or endangered. Species should be protected because of their rarity, size, or association with other rare species (such as providing habitat to threatened or endangered species).

Protecting an individual species or clumps of specific species requires careful planning. Protection of species can be accomplished in one of two very general ways: protecting existing vegetation and protecting new, expected vegetation.

PROTECTING EXISTING VEGETATION

Protecting existing vegetation is typically done with fencing or barriers that restrict vehicles and other equipment from impacting the selected species. Barrier mechanisms should be placed to protect the above- and below-ground structures of the plant. Installation of barrier fencing is typically at the edge of a preserved plant community or the dripline of individual plants, the approximate limit of feeder roots, though fine roots may extend farther. However, additional space should be considered—the roots, including feeder roots, of many trees extend beyond the dripline (see Figure 5-34).

Some species will tolerate modest disturbance to the above- or below-ground structure—cutting, pruning, mowing, air pruning or filling—but many more species simply will not. The age of the vegetation can also impact its ability to survive; geriatric vegetation is especially susceptible to disease or insects following disturbance or impact.

Protected species may require additional maintenance following site work and protection. Required maintenance may include:

- ▶ Supplemental watering

- ▶ Mulching

- ▶ Pruning

- ▶ Fertilizing

- ▶ Wrapping or wind protection

Protecting existing vegetation from new plantings should also be considered. Large vegetation, particularly trees, can be adversely affected by new trees that in time crowd their roots or canopies. This can be avoided by spacing new plantings sufficiently far away to accommodate future maturity.

With the right equipment, clumps or communities of herbaceous vegetation can be moved en masse. Deep cutting, rolling, and placing existing sod of protected species has been accomplished on several project sites.

PROTECTING NEW VEGETATION

Protecting new vegetation requires no less planning than does protecting existing vegetation. Care should be taken to anticipate potential impacts on new vegetation. The following strategies should be considered:

- ▶ Appropriate species selection is the first step in protecting new vegetation. Species that are not appropriate for the site are deliberately removed, inappropriately managed to meet the site needs, or die.

- Siting vegetation appropriately is as important as finding the right plant for the project and site. Species should be selected and placed to avoid growth impediments due to hardscape surfaces, fencing, or other types of structures.

- Future impacts can include impacts from other vegetation onsite, such as shading or allelopathy, and competition for space, water, and other resources. Proper spacing, placement, and appropriate species selection can avoid these issues.

- Plan for potential pests or disease. Caution should be taken when planting a species susceptible to a known existing pest or disease. It is difficult to predict these types of events, but they can be ameliorated by avoiding homogenous planting schemes that require too much uniformity of species or age class.

- While planting a variety of species onsite is one way of reducing impacts from disease or pests, planting varied age classes allows for size and maturity distribution in a planting that will accommodate replacements if needed.

- Other techniques for protecting the expected vegetation include soil amendment and protection; providing suitable access to water; controlling invasive species; understanding the vegetation, the site, and the design program; and establishing an appropriate maintenance plan.

SITES GUIDELINES AND VEGETATION AND SOIL PROTECTION ZONES

The primary vehicle for the preservation of valuable habitat within the SITES framework is the establishment of the Vegetation Soil and Protection Zones (VSPZ). The VSPZ reduces the likelihood that desirable and sensitive areas will be adversely affected during the development process while still allowing acceptable levels of utilization after construction. The VSPZ are zones set aside and protected throughout the construction process. Vegetation and soil protection zones must meet the following requirements:

- Construction impacts from overall site development should not decrease the capacity of the VSPZ to support the desired vegetation. For example, construction activities outside of the VSPZ should not change drainage patterns and microclimate effects within the VSPZ.

- The VSPZ should be protected with a fence or other physical barrier that cannot be easily moved (wildlife-permeable barrier, if appropriate) that protects the zone during construction from equipment parking and traffic, storage of materials, and other construction activities.

- All construction and maintenance personnel should be educated about the locations and protective measures of the VSPZ. In construction documents, outline consequences to contractor if VSPZ boundaries are not respected.

- VSPZ can encompass one plant or can include several plants in a group.

- Only a very small part of the VSPZ can contain minimal impact development such as paths or picnic tables.

- Incorporate into the site maintenance plan ongoing management activities to protect the integrity of the VSPZ.

SUSTAINABLE PLANTING DESIGN AND MANAGEMENT

Using Native Plants

Use of native plants can satisfy the following goals:

▶ To select species most suited for the site or region and thereby reduce maintenance needs

▶ Provide beneficial habitat for native organisms

▶ Restore a sense of place to regional design

Despite the fact that predeveloped site conditions are often unlike the historic conditions of a site, regional analogs for developed conditions can be found in nature. With an understanding of plant biology, soil and climactic conditions, and an understanding of how these interact, it is quite possible to select regionally native species to fit urban environments. For example, a green roof—possibly the epitome of a manufactured, "unnatural" environment—has an analogue in a first-order ephemeral stream community—particularly those that are windswept and exposed, as is often encountered in mountainous or rocky soil communities.

Carefully selected native species perform well in a wide range of conditions. Studies in Texas have shown that a suite of native species—including several that are not yet in commercial production—can establish more rapidly (450 percent more rapidly) than can Bermuda grass—a commonly used invasive species (Tinsley, Simmons, and Windhager 2006). It is likely possible that carefully selected regionally native plants will be able to equal or exceed the performance of nonnative species. Native species should be known to be native within the region of the project site. Generally, a 250-mile radius from the project site is appropriate for the selection of native plant species. Specialized conditions may merit a wider radius.

Criterion for the selection of a native species is no different than that of any other plant: adaptability and environmental tolerance, intended function, plant management issues, and design intent (Figure 4-7).

(Design by Phillips Farevaag Smallenberg; Photo by Joe Fry)

FIGURE 4-7: Native vegetation on the green roof at the Washington Mutual Bank in Seattle, WA, emulates a Pacific Northwest habitat aesthetic.

Xeriscaping

The goal of xeriscaping is to design a landscape that is capable of surviving without supplemental water inputs. This concept of surviving without supplemental inputs is expanding, and the principle has been applied to the selection of plants that survive with reduced water as well as other supplemental resource inputs (e.g., nutrients, soil amelioration, disturbance). Historically many landscapes, including residential landscapes, were a form of xeriscaping. Most homes and commercial properties until the late 1970s to mid-1980s couldn't afford in-ground irrigation systems and consequently utilized plants that survived after planting establishment without significant irrigation.

Selecting species that will survive with only ambient water requires the designer to understand which vegetation has performed well on the site before project construction, evaluate if any of those species would still perform well after the project construction, consider additional habitats and species which are a good match for the conditions post-construction, and make an appropriate selection for the design.

The Denver Water Utility has defined seven key principles associated with xeriscaping:

- ▶ Plan and design the site with limited water use in mind, funnel rain-water, or other excess water to vegetation, and protect established mature vegetation, and so forth.

- ▶ Limit turf areas—because of the shallow roots and active growing exacerbated by mowing, turf requires tremendous amounts of water to stay alive; reducing turf minimizes water needs on a site.

- ▶ Select new plants that will tolerate the expected hydraulic regimes of the site.

- ▶ Improve the soil where needed to increase soil moisture-holding capacity.

- ▶ Use mulch to reduce desiccation of the soil.

- ▶ Irrigate efficiently, at the plant (such as through drip irrigation rather than spraying across the site) and at the right time when the sun and temperature are low.

- ▶ Maintain the landscape.

Regardless of the site or region, the overarching principle of the xeriscape approach is the same: to design a landscape and select a planting palette that does not require supplemental resource input following plant establishment. However, that doesn't mean site runoff couldn't be directed into a xeriscape area. Rain gardens are an excellent xeriscaping strategy in temperate climates. The runoff provides the necessary water for the vegetation without supplemental irrigation, and the plant palette selected is comprised of species adapted for drought punctuated with periodic flooding (rain events). Xeriscaping can be applied for control of stormwater, absorption of wastewater streams (such as air-conditioner condensate), and reduced maintenance (Figure 4-8).

(Design by Ten Eyck Landscape Architects, Inc.; Photo by Bill Timmerman)

FIGURE 4-8: Vegetation selected for the shade plaza at the Sonoran Landscape Laboratory relies on recycled water for 83 percent of the irrigation needs. Because species selected are drought tolerant, it is expected that after establishment, the plantings will rely only on recycled water, eliminating the need for potable water irrigation.

Invasive Species

Invasive species cost the United States millions of dollars to control and threaten the livelihood of most resource-based economic structures by supplanting the desired resource with the invasive species through competition, predation, or suppression. Therefore, invasive species management should begin prior to proposed planting installation, and specification of plants should not include known or suspected invasive species. The U.S. Federal Invasive Species Advisory Committee defines invasive species as species that "are not native to the ecosystem under consideration and that cause or are likely to cause economic or environmental harm or harm to human, animal or plant health" (Table 4-7).

Not all nonnative species are by default invasive. Only about 15 percent of nonnative species introduced in the United States are known to be invasive (Czarapata 2005). The majority of nonnative species are not known to cause any harm to humans or other species, and indeed, most of our commercially grown produce (Pimentel, Rodolfo, and Morrison 2005) are not native, and a number of ornamental species are benign nonnative species as well. "Known" invasive species are defined as those that are on regional invasive species lists developed through a "vetted, transparent process accepted by regional stakeholders" such as those used by Exotic Pest Plant Councils (EPPCs) around the nation, or those species identified by state or federal noxious weed laws (SITES 2009a). Many states or regions have EPPCs. Unfortunately, some lists are incomplete and identify species after they are a problem and not before. However, some general characteristics regarding invasive species will help the designer identify potential threats.

TABLE 4-7: Common Characteristics of Invasive Species

General Characteristics	Grow rapidly
	Respond quickly to opportunity or disturbance
	Often not susceptible to local competition pressures that control similar niche native species (fire, browsing, mowing)
	Often are successful in many habitats
Control Competition	Allelopathy, release of chemical toxins that prohibit or restrict growth of other species (Callway and Ashehoug 2000).
	Shade suppression, to inhibit light penetration to species that might compete with the invasive (Blue 2000, unpublished data)
	Fitness homeostasis permits many species to become successful with varying limited resources, such as reduced water, nutrients, sun, or other resources (Hoffman and Parsons 1991)
Spread Easily	Produce large quantities of seed or spread easily through rhizomatous stolons
	Many invasive species have been deliberately planted in extremely high populations for ornamental or agricultural purposes
Risks	Invasive species when used in professional designs, under controlled conditions, can be mistakenly used by the general public in uncontrolled conditions
	Invasive species that were once thought to be limited by climatic regions are now moving north due to global warming

The challenge is in determining, in advance, what species are likely to become invasive when introduced to new environments. Most invasive species follow an exponential growth curve that is initially a very gradual increase until reaching the inflection point where population density allows for much more rapid increases in population numbers (Radosevich 2006) (Figure 4-9). Some species simply take a long time to reach that inflection point, and unfortunately, once they have reached that point and populations are skyrocketing, they are both difficult and expensive to control (if control is even possible). Additionally, the probability of invasiveness increases with population size and introduction attempts (Williamson 1989). Finally, the longer a species has been introduced, the more likely it is to become invasive (Rejmánek 2000). For these reasons, avoiding introduction of potentially invasive species is the only reasonable course of action.

Species are considered invasive when spread of the species overcomes biological and physical barriers resulting in mass dispersal (Rejmánek 2000). This should be distinguished from naturalization of a species, which is considered to be stationary with little or no spread from an origin of introduction for at least 25 years (Tutin et al. 1964) (Figure 4-10).

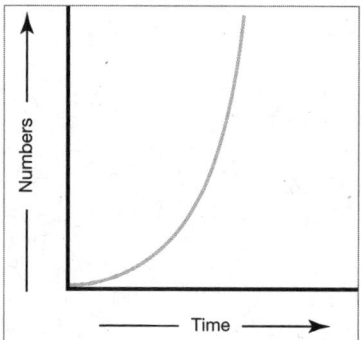

FIGURE 4-9: The spread of invasive species may be marginal initially, but after reaching a point of inflection, where numbers exceed existing controls, the spread becomes exponential.

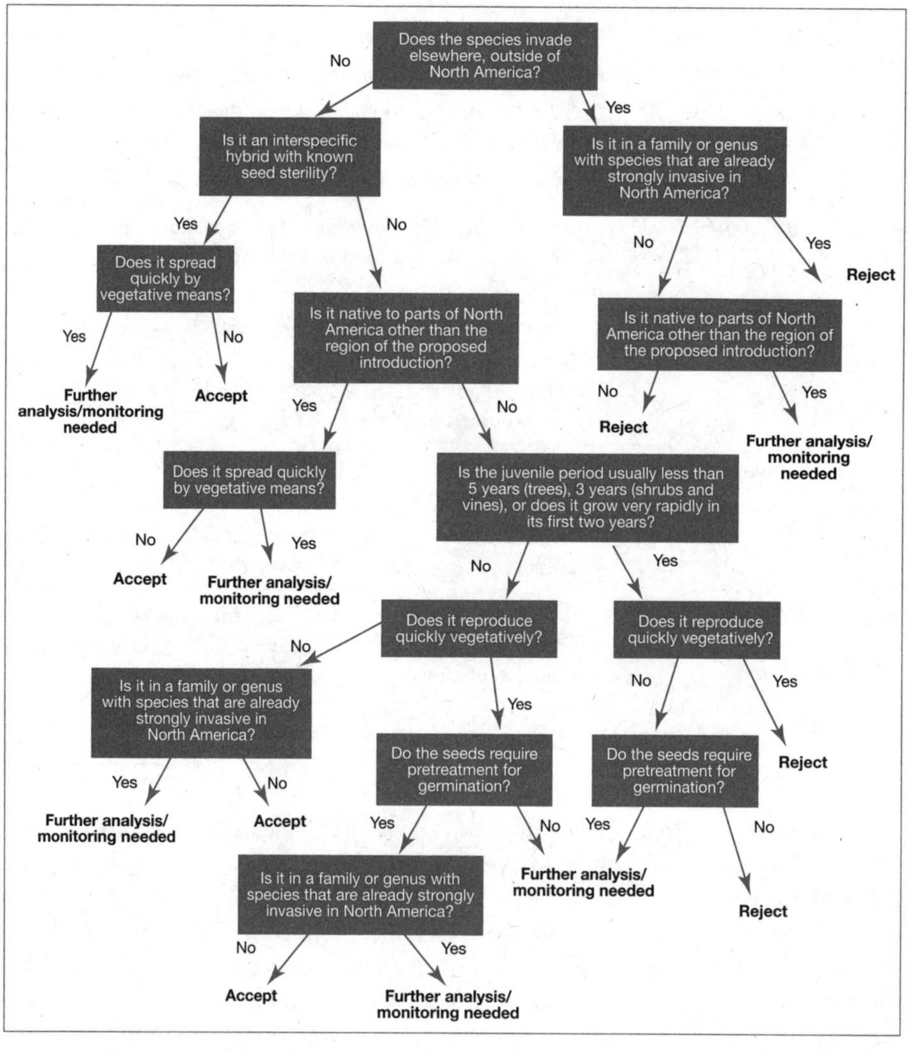

FIGURE 4-10: The Decision Tree, originally proposed by Reichard and Hamilton (1997), suggests questions designers can ask themselves before selecting an individual species. This proposed process can help reduce accidental introduction of invasive species.

AVOIDING INTRODUCTION OF INVASIVE SPECIES

Even with extensive analysis in advance, it is not always possible to predict which species are likely to become invasive. If the designer is unsure of the impact a particular species will have on surrounding ecosystems, don't use it, and instead select a different species.

Invasive species should not be specified or intentionally introduced at any point in the construction phase, even if only used as a "temporary" erosion control measure. Even without intentional introduction, there are still a number of ways that invasive species can become established during construction activities. Invasive or simply undesired species can arrive at the site from adjacent properties, from equipment brought onsite, or through organism or wind dispersal. Key control measures for these include limiting disturbance of healthy systems (intact healthy communities are more resistant to invasion) and limiting bare dirt through coverage with several species of desired plants which would fill different ecological niches. This could include several cool-season grasses, several warm-season grasses, and possibly forbs. This wide variety of species allows greater utilization of resources and leaves less available to undesired species.

DEALING WITH ESTABLISHED INVASIVE SPECIES ONSITE

Existing invasive species identified on the site should be controlled or managed to prevent further invasion and limit damage to local ecosystem services. Control measures for invasive plants vary based on plant characteristics (annual, biennial, perennial; herbaceous or woody, terrestrial or aquatic; flowering and dormant season; and so forth) and the species' primary dispersal pathway for invasive expansion. Control measures can include changes in general land management, targeted mechanical control, and targeted chemical control. All control measures should be integrated into a site's Integrated Pest Management plan, which is part of the site maintenance plan (Table 4-8).

TABLE 4-8: Invasive Species Control Measures

Avoidance	Invasive species should not be introduced to a site, and specification and contamination of the site during construction should be avoided. Weed-free soils should be specified, equipment should be cleaned prior to entering and exiting the site, clean mulch should be used, and bare soil exposure should be minimized.
General Land Management	Techniques that are not targeted at specific individual plants (in contrast, wick application of herbicides directly targets individual undesired species) but which impact all species, some to their detriment and others to their advantage. General land management techniques are applied over an entire property (such as burning) (Figure 4-11). General land management techniques include prescribed fire (variables: season, intensity, type), mowing (variables: frequency, height, season), grazing (variables: grazer species, intensity, duration), and in some instances flooding.

continues

TABLE 4-8: Invasive Species Control Measures *(continued)*

Targeted Mechanical Control	Selective cutting or shredding of undesired species. Most effective against nonherbaceous, non-resprouting species which will be killed or significantly damaged by mechanical removal. Persistent mechanical removal of some species will be sufficient to result in mortality; other species will persist aggressively.
Targeted Chemical Control	Selective herbicides applied broadly or general herbicides applied in a targeted manner. Small outbreaks or species not susceptible to the above measures are appropriate to target chemically. Some invasive species are known to be controlled only through chemical treatment. When applied correctly by licensed practitioners, chemical treatment is very safe (Figure 4-12).
Untargeted Biological Control	Other organisms can be used for the control of invasive species, though they rarely are capable of completely eliminating an invasive species once it is established. In some instances, biological control can reduce an invasive species population to a manageable size. Domestic goats have been found to be very successful at controlling and managing kudzu. Herds of goats can be rotated through portions of a site infested with kudzu. This type of management requires additional management of the goats but in some instances may be beneficial for the site desiring to control its kudzu population as well as the goat farmer. Unfortunately, goats, like other forms of biological control, are nondiscriminatory control measures; the goats don't just browse the kudzu, they browse everything. This is frequently the case with biological controls—they require additional management to place on and pull out of a site and, depending on the organism, might not be constrained.

(Photo from Matt C. Kocourek, Applied Ecological Services, Inc.)

FIGURE 4-11: A burn technician ignites a backfire with a drip torch to promote native prairie growth. The backfire will consume the fuel at the margins of the controlled burn and prevent accidental spread.

(Photo from Applied Ecological Services, Inc.)

FIGURE 4-12: Licensed herbicide applicators spot spray invasive species to control their spread at a prairie restoration in Minnesota.

Deciding which approach, or mixture of approaches, is the appropriate one to deal with the invasive species on a site can be difficult. Local expertise familiar with controlling the invasive species should be employed as part of the Integrated Design Team in order to define the correct control measures. Identifying invasive species threats will begin with the predesign site assessment, but this information will need to be incorporated into the design, construction, and long-term management of the site.

After initial control, care should be taken to ensure that the species is not allowed to set seed (such as through periodic mowing or harvesting) during the construction phase to ensure that seeds are not transported to other areas of the site. The above-ground biomass of some woody invasive species can be mulched and used for erosion control onsite as long as there is little to no seed present in the canopy and the species is not known to sprout from live stakes. If there is seed present, this material may still be mulched, but should be thoroughly composted before use. As design progresses, areas contaminated with invasive species should be identified in construction documents so that soils borrowed from this area are either composted to kill any invasive seeds or living plants or buried greater than 18 in. below finished grade.

Sustainable Plant Production

Selection of appropriate species includes selection of species from plant producers that promote sustainable practices. Plant production is a resource-intensive process requiring large amounts of energy, water, nutrients, and space. Selecting species from producers that have demonstrated resource protection sends a message to all producers that sustainable practices are desired.

Nurseries are often located in floodplains or near aquatic resources. A desirable nursery will have demonstrated protection of the aquatic resources including providing sufficient buffers between production and habitat corridors, capture and treatment of runoff, and reduced and targeted nutrient application to prevent eutrophication of aquatic resources.

Desirable production practices include:

▶ Reduced use of peat and other nonrenewable resources for planting media or pot manufacturing

▶ Reduced runoff from irrigation

▶ Minimized energy consumption, including reduced greenhouse gas emissions from onsite equipment, and use of renewable energy sources

▶ Use of an integrated pest management program

▶ Minimal use of potable water, reuse of gray- or blackwater or effluent

▶ Reduced waste

▶ Use of recycled organic matter

▶ Do not grow or sell invasive species in regions where they are known or suspected to be invasive.

▶ Appropriately sourced seed and parent material. Nurseries should be able to demonstrate the source of their plant material, including material purchased by other growers. Desired material will be appropriately sourced from legally collected parent material or seed sources (preferably as locally as possible).

Salvaged and Reused Vegetation

Protection of desired individual plants *in situ* isn't always possible. When appropriate, vegetation should be salvaged for use elsewhere on the site or at another location. This is particularly important for native vegetation that may not be commercially available. For example, the proposed design of a site may call for a new road that will impact a young, but healthy, tree. The tree can and should be moved elsewhere onsite instead of simply being destroyed.

Salvage and reuse material is frequently sourced from a location that will be destroyed or materially changed in such a way that the existing material would not survive or be desired.

▶ Salvage in a fashion that supports healthy plant growth and reuse. Older individual plants can be moved, but often the cost for effectively moving the plant increases and success is lower.

▶ Care should be taken to collect as much of the rooting material as possible. Deep-rooting species will require careful excavation to extract sufficient root material without damage.

- Feeder roots of trees and shrubs should be cut cleanly for removal; hacked or disjointed cuts can result in infection to the plant.
- Care should be taken when removing vegetation to minimize damage to the site during removal.
- After a specimen has been obtained, it should be healed into mulch or other protective medium and immediately watered.
- Species stored for longer periods may require wind or sun protection; extended storage requires temporary planting.
- All vegetation in storage will require routine watering until it is located in its final placement.
- Broken limbs or branches should be cut away cleanly.
- Plants that have been stressed by a move are particularly susceptible to damage caused by predation. Care should be taken to protect specimens in storage from predation by insects or other pests.
- Not all species can be salvaged or reused. For example, the root depth of butterfly milkweed (*Asclepias tuberosa*) makes this species especially difficult to move after it is established; moves are rarely successful.
- Cuttings, rather than whole plant removal or reuse, may be more advantageous for some species.

Vegetation in the Urban Setting

Plants can be effectively used in the urban environment to provide some of the most critical ecosystem services. Street trees have been reported to remove up to 70 percent of pollutants from the air (Bernatzky 1983); a 1997 study by McPherson and colleagues reported that urban trees in Chicago provided more than $9 million of air cleaning annually. Street trees act as primary interceptors of wet and dry particulates, literally screening the air (Bolund and Hunhammar 1999). It has been estimated that appropriately spaced street trees could reduce heating and cooling costs for some structures by as much as $50 to $90 annually (McPherson et al. 1997).

The selection of vegetation for urban sites can be more challenging than for rural sites due to the more highly manufactured and concentrated conditions in the urban environment. Runoff in urban systems can be more concentrated and contain hydrocarbons, plastics, and other manufactured particles or chemicals. Because of past land use, urban soils are frequently highly compacted, lack structure, and are altered with additional material and debris. Hardscape surfaces can serve as an impediment to growth, reflect additional heat and light, or in the case of vertical structures, completely obscure light. In addition, urban sites tend to have higher concentrations of traffic. Pedestrian, bike, and car volumes are higher in urban environments.

Light duration, type, and intensity in the built environment are different than in the natural environment. In the natural environment, the normal exposure to shade may be less dichotomous than in the built environment where vegetation can be exposed to deep shade for one part of the day and intense sun with reflective light at another part of the day. Temperatures are also markedly different in built environments than in natural environments; for example, the reflected light and heat found on the underside of vegetation adjacent to a parking lot is very different than the same light and heat found in a turf area of the same size.

Another issue that has plagued the urban use of vegetation has been the balance between diversity and homogeneity. Too much diversity and the planting can look weedy; too much homogeneity and the planting can be susceptible to a complete loss through disturbance or disease. This risk is especially pronounced in urban trees. Dutch elm disease (DED) serves as the textbook example of the problem with homogeneity. When DED struck the United States and Britain in the 1920s, the disease spread rapidly through urban cores dominated by elms. In the United States, the American elm (*Ulmus americana*) was devastated. The overuse of this species left little to replace the stately trees that once lined so many urban streets. A more contemporary example, though perhaps only slightly less devastating, has been the recent impact of emerald ash borer (*Agrilus planipennis*) on ash (*Fraxinus*) trees, again overused in places dominating the street tree canopy.

The qualities of many urban environments that plants must tolerate include:

- ▶ Nutrient-poor soils
- ▶ Compacted and poorly drained soils
- ▶ Disturbance (compaction, abrasion, bruising, and fractures)
- ▶ Poor water quality
- ▶ Excessive heat
- ▶ Air pollution
- ▶ Low soil-water availability
- ▶ Restricted growth

From a fecundity and longevity standpoint, many of the best-performing plant species in the urban environment are also frequently considered to be "weedy." This observation has led some to argue that specifically employing nonnative invasive species in the urban environment is the best strategy for plant success (e.g., see Del Tredici 2006). This strategy, while potentially effective for the specific site in question, also poses a threat to other adjacent or downstream habitats and ecosystems. Moreover, the assumptions that underlie the supposition that only nonnative invasive species can compete in urban environments is patently false (Simmons and Venhaus 2006; Simmons, Venhaus, and Windhager 2007). In situations where conditions are such that early successional weedy species are needed, there are appropriate native species that will not cause offsite problems.

TREES IN THE URBAN SETTING

Trees in urban environments require special consideration. Trees are typically the largest and most expensive individual vegetation unit used in an urban context. In addition to pest and disease concerns, the size of trees makes them more prone to other types of urban disturbances such as compaction, used for hanging signs, impacts from vehicles, and so forth. Vegetation with permanent woody growth is particularly susceptible to the stresses found in urban environments. Many herbaceous species have the advantage of replacing nearly all of their above-ground structure annually or seasonally. In addition, herbaceous material tends to have a smaller stature. Backing a car into a stand of ornamental grass will hardly have the same effect on the car or the vegetation as backing the same car into a tree.

Restricted space and root/soil compaction are two major concerns for trees in the urban environment. Research conducted at Cornell University demonstrated that reducing root/soil compaction by employing engineered soils, resistant to compaction and formulated to provide preferred nutrient and water storage without drowning a tree, significantly impacted a tree's longevity (Trowbridge and Bassuk 2004). Limited space for root growth is another major impact of urban vegetation (Urban 2008). Trees are large organisms requiring large space, both above- and below-ground. Too often trees are expected to grow in a compacted space that limits safe root growth or trunk expansion without impacting hardscape surfaces (concrete walks, pavers, and the like) or utilities. In the absence of suitable space, some trees adapt, sometimes to the detriment of the hardscape or utilities; others die. Providing suitable space means providing room for 360° of growth, as well as access to needed resources for survival. Providing sufficient space and access to needed resources is key to urban tree longevity.

Strategies for ensuring tree success in an urban condition include:

- ▶ Protect soil/roots from compaction protection with engineered soil, or other structural or mechanical protection
- ▶ Provide sufficient space for above- and below-ground structure growth and development; root space needed for a tree is nearly equivalent to the expected crown width at maturity
- ▶ Provide access to resources needed for growth
- ▶ Prevent resource pooling

- ▶ Place vegetation for full growth potential, providing adequate spacing between trees adjacent to hardscapes and buildings and vehicles

- ▶ Reduce impacts from other organisms. (Street tree pits in Chicago have been observed to provide cover for burrowing rats that impacted the root development.)

- ▶ Select species adapted for the lighting conditions (building shade, reflected light, and street lights).

- ▶ Reduce exposure to airborne and waterborne pollutants.

- ▶ Minimize impacts from concentrated wind flow.

- ▶ Identify species resistant to heat.

- ▶ Provide sufficient moisture for growth.

Furthermore, trees are expected to be well behaved while in an urban setting. Some species of trees by their nature or in response to stress exhibit characteristics that are not preferred in many urban settings, such as:

- ▶ Fruit or nut deposition

- ▶ Weak limbs

- ▶ Suckering and stoloniferous spreading

- ▶ Reduced leaf production

- ▶ Slow growth

- ▶ Vigorous root growth (Silver maples, *Acer saccharinum*, are especially problematic, collapsing and clogging storm sewers and septic lines.)

Vegetation for Stormwater Structures

Stormwater control methods have evolved in recent years toward reducing quantity and improving quality of stormwater prior to its release from the site. The once tried and true process of moving water off of a site as quickly and directly as possible is no longer germane. This radical shift in how we deal with water has required us to rethink the type of vegetation used in these types of features.

Until recently, most conventional stormwater structures (swales and retention basins) were nearly always planted with turf. Turf was preferred because of its ease of maintenance, establishment, and availability. In addition, this vegetation was compatible with the intent of the stormwater systems themselves, namely moving water as directly and efficiently as possible to appropriate discharge or collection facilities such as wetlands, streams, rivers, and lakes. Turf also behaved well near concrete structures, growing right up to the edge of the concrete without having dangerous root systems that threatened the structural integrity of the concrete.

Stormwater systems that are designed for retention, infiltration, filtration, and water quality improvement strive to slow water, allowing it to pond for short durations. Vegetation used in these structures must be appropriate to both wet and dry conditions. Vegetation for these systems requires a different suite of characteristics (Figure 4-13). They are detailed in Table 4-9.

(Design by Conservation Design Forum)

FIGURE 4-13: Stormwater and graywater collect in the treatment wetland at the Queens Botanical Garden in Flushing, NY. The wetland is comprised of native species that treat the water before being recycled into the building for specified use.

TABLE 4-9: Characteristics of Desired Stormwater Vegetation

Functional Characteristics	Resistant to flood/drought conditions
	Deep-rooting vegetation with perennial root die-back resulting in microchannel development
	Resistant to heavy flows and shear stress
	Resistant or recoverable from siltation events
	Vigorous growth without becoming aggressive
	Well-behaved, but capable of adapting to rapid change
	Resistant to pollutant loads
	Capable of stripping pollutants from the water or saturated soil
	Reliable
	Capable of holding soil and preventing erosion
	Resilient to wilt in flood or drought conditions
Aesthetic Characteristics	Uniform color and texture
	Managable
	Healthy vibrant growth with minimal maintenance
	Fits the design program

Typical planting constraints of a stormwater feature include:

▶ Volume, duration, depth, and frequency of water

▶ Rate at which water enters and leaves the feature, and how

▶ Water quality and source

▶ Type of feature (swale, wetland, rain garden, buffer, aerobic/anaerobic)

▶ Site location or geography

▶ Desired vegetative impact (slow water, infiltrate water, clean water, habitat)

▶ Placement of the stormwater feature in the site design program (site-user visual access, formal/informal)

▶ Expected site-user interface (interactive, visual, obscured. For example, will bikes, balls, or pets impact the feature? Will users get in to the feature?)

▶ Permanency of the feature

▶ Required maintenance to the feature, the vegetation, and other elements such as utilities that may share the space with the stormwater feature

▶ Soil conditions of the feature (anticipated soil amendments?)

▶ Other vegetation in the feature or surrounding the feature that may impact the planting (shade suppression, expected seeds from the runoff area or watershed, potentially aggressive species)

Vegetation for Green Roofs

Green roofs are an increasingly popular technology that provide many ecosystems services in urban settings including managing stormwater onsite, providing appropriate plant biomass, providing wildlife habitat, and reducing heat island impacts. In highly urban environments they may serve as the only greenscape within an occupant's immediate viewshed. Green roofs are highly engineered systems designed to provide for both a planting medium and typically some stormwater detention, while also ensuring that weight of the roof, when saturated, is not extreme. To achieve this, most green roofs are composed of multiple layers of growing media (often proprietary to the various manufacturers), root barrier, and an additional water retention component all overlying the waterproofing membrane for the roof.

Almost any plant can be grown on a green roof given adequate depth of growing media and appropriate water availability. The limits of the planting media impact the selection of appropriate species for green roofs. This section focuses on vegetation for extensive green roofs (less than 8 in. deep) rather than intensive (greater than 8 in. deep) ones. Deep-rooted species tend not to perform well, and large woody species are restricted not simply because of size, in most cases, but also root impacts to the membrane integrity.

Variables to consider when selecting vegetation for green roofs include:

▶ Water availability

▶ Available depth and type of growing media

▶ Wind velocities

- ▶ Soil temperatures
- ▶ Solar access
- ▶ Climate

Vegetation species for green roofs should be those that are ecological generalists—that is, they can tolerate both very dry *and* saturated conditions for extended periods. Potentially successful types of vegetation include:

- ▶ Succulents
- ▶ Bulbs and corms
- ▶ Biannual or annual self-seeders
- ▶ Bunch and stoloniferous gramnoids
- ▶ Many modal wetland species

Some perennial forbs and biannual shrubs also appear to be well suited to the conditions found in green roof plantings. Unfortunately, within these groups there are many species that will not tolerate the conditions on a green roof.

Succulents, and in particular the genus *Sedums,* have been the preferred plants for green roof design for decades based principally on their habitats of origin, which are normally low available water due to climate or soil conditions or both. This preference is not without merit; sedums are characterized by low maintenance, drought tolerance, and establish relatively easily in temperate climates. However, perceptions of green roofs are changing, and many designers are exploring with other species, particularly as this technology is applied outside of temperate environments (Figure 4-14).

In ecosystems that experience extreme cold, heat, or sustained heavy wet conditions, succulents may struggle to survive or outcompete other plant guilds, such as grasses, forbs, or even shrubs (Heinze 1985). The study of alternative species for North American green roofs is still in its infancy, but studies have demonstrated that where cooling or stormwater retention is a priority, grasses, forbs, and shrubs may have an advantage over succulents due to their physiology and higher transpiration rates. However, the need for reducing or carefully selecting grass species where dry biomass may constitute a fire hazard must be considered.

(Design by Conservation Design Forum)

FIGURE 4-14: The green roof courtyard at the Kresge Foundation in Troy, MI, accommodates large- and small-scale vegetation.

Green roofs are not easy growing conditions and consequently require hearty species. Some growing constraints include:

- Lack of irrigation (most green roofs are not irrigated)
- Desiccation
- Rapidly draining soils—the planting media is designed to store water only temporarily and not as long as soil in the ground
- Shallow soil depths (even green roofs of 12 to 18 in. are shallow for many species)
- Rapid soil saturation
- Deep shade and full sun periods
- Urban heat island effect and reflected radiation
- Low maintenance

Green roofs can provide wildlife habitat (Dvorak and Volderb 2010; Getter and Rowe 2006). In urban systems where green space is rare, promotion of urban biodiversity may be a priority. Natural plant communities with similar abiotic conditions to green roofs may serve as a useful template for selecting green roof vegetation with habitat value (Kadas 2006; Lundholm 2006). In Europe, researchers have attempted to optimize this characteristic by using high plant species richness and native soil (Brenneisen 2006) to attract both common and rare vertebrates and invertebrates.

Vegetation for Green Walls

Like green roofs, green walls exhibit unique growing conditions that require specialized selection of appropriate species. Green walls have specialized needs—they are expected to form nearly dense, living screens, avoid desiccation, grow up and out rapidly to fill in but stay where desired without spreading in undesired locations.

Heavily engineered green wall systems, hedgerows, and even seasonal hedges are all capable of providing similar ecosystems services:

- Shading
- Stormwater control or water quality improvement
- Screening
- Buffering
- Insulating
- Aesthetics

There are three types of green wall structures: panel, pocket, and trellis systems. In addition, woody and perennial hedges can act as green walls without support structures.

1. Panel walls are comprised of modular panels that contain growing medium and are arranged horizontal to the face of the support structure. Shallow-rooted species, succulants, mosses, and lichens, or other species common to cliff-face and extreme slope habitats perform best in these systems.

2. Pocket walls arrange growing medium–filled pocket planters along the face of a wall or support structure. Again, shallow-rooted, crawling species perform well, as do species suited for rocky soil–deprived communities, such as goat-prairie species.

3. Trellis walls provide a suitable structure, sufficiently offset from a building's face, for climbing vines. Above-ground or in-ground planters house the plants. If they are against a building, planters typically occur at every story.

Considerations for green walls are:

▶ These systems are typically not connected to groundwater; therefore, a high level of maintenance is often required to meet the water needs of the vegetation.

▶ Wall height can sometimes limit species success, where wind and lack of shade can become impediments to growth.

▶ Specialized soil is required.

▶ Where living walls are attached to buildings, protective measures should be taken to prevent moisture from penetrating building walls.

▶ Consideration should be given to maintenance access and activities.

Vegetation for Food Production

Gardening for food production has long been a staple of our relationship with vegetation. We are absolutely dependent on vegetation for our physical health, our nutrition and well-being. Community gardening and edible landscapes share one obvious feature: They are for our human benefit. However, in addition, gardening and edible landscapes can be strategies for reducing energy consumption, lowering one's carbon footprint, strengthening communities and reconnecting people with the landscape at a visceral level. To that end they should really be reserved for sites where the users of the site can and will benefit from these types of planting schemes. Edible landscapes benefit humans only where there is a population or individual monitoring the vegetation in order to harvest the goods at the appropriate time. Additionally, community gardening and edible landscapes may not always be appropriate in publicly used spaces, such as parks.

COMMUNITY GARDENING

Community gardening is the collective gardening of a single land parcel. Typically the parcel is subdivided into units; each unit is then the responsibility of an individual or smaller group of people (such as a family) to manage. Private and public models of these gardens can be found around the world. In the United States, the products of the smaller garden units are for the direct use or consumption of the individual who managed that unit and are not intended for resale or commercial enterprises. In other models, the individuals who manage the total of the garden units share the rewards of the gardens with each other. At a community garden, in addition to the rewards afforded the individual unit gardener, there is often the reward of shared passion with all those at the gardens. Everyone is "pulling in the same direction," namely, the success of their garden unit. This shared passion provides opportunities for social interaction that may not be afforded in other aspects of one's day-to-day life (Figure 4-15).

FIGURE 4-15: Community gardens at High Point in Seattle, WA, provide a mechanism for knitting the existing neighborhood with newer neighbors.

Community gardens can be public, where individuals sign up for garden units and are assigned the unit for their use for the season, as well as private, where individuals pay a fee to secure their gardening unit for a season or longer. Depending on the community garden, water, tools, even compost may be provided free of charge.

Appropriate vegetation for community gardening is no different than that used for ordinary private gardening. Species are:

▶ State or regionally legal

▶ Typically annual species (most of the plants used for produce gardening are, anyway)

▶ Most garden plants are arranged in clear patterns, such as straight lines, and species used in most annual gardens tend to follow the imposition of the pattern without a lot of deviation

▶ Suitable for the region and climate in which the garden is located

Because soil is often amended with compost and, if well gardened, provided with ample water, the opportunity to grow a variety of species that might not otherwise perform well in a region is presented. At the beginning of the next season, most community garden units are tilled over and ready for new planting.

EDIBLE LANDSCAPING

Edible landscaping is the incorporation of vegetation within the design program of a landscape that will produce some source of desired food. It should be noted that edible landscapes are primarily focused on food products for human consumption and are distinguishable from habitat for attracting wildlife, though often what we like, wildlife likes. Unlike community gardening, which is intensive plant management in a designated area, the garden, edible landscaping explores the use of vegetation that produces consumable goods within the fabric of the site's landscape program. Typically species are perennial, many times woody species.

Whereas in community gardening, plants are selected primarily for a single attribute (nutrition or aesthetic), in edible landscapes a single species is often expected to provide nutritional and aesthetic benefits. Fortunately, perennial food-bearing plants often have conspicuous flowers that become the food later in the season (Figure 4-16).

(Design by Hoerr Schaudt Landscape Architects; Photo from Scott Shigley)

FIGURE 4-16: The food garden at the Gary Comer Youth Center in Chicago is also a green roof. The combined green roof/garden makes for a unique edible landscape that encourages urban youth to take an active role in the development of sustainable food production.

These landscapes are not intended to be heavily managed; species are expected to conform to the landscape design of the desired program. Hedges are meant to be hedges, even if they bear fruit.

Appropriate species for edible landscapes:

- Require little daily/weekly maintenance other than that provided for the entire planting area in which a species is included. Because these species are meant to "blend" in with the rest of the planting scheme, they should also be more or less expected to adopt the same maintenance as the remainder of the planting in which they are found. Requiring overly burdensome maintenance often results in failure of the landscape design.
- Provide food as well as other desirable landscape design program benefits (shade, aesthetics, water control, etc.).
- Produce food that requires little refinement for consumption. Many species of vegetation produce edible goods but are edible only after some level of refinement. For example, acorns from some oaks can be refined into a usable flour but not without considerable processing including reducing some of the bitter tannins found in the acorns. The best species are those that can be picked and consumed right away, like blueberries, strawberries, pawpaws, and prickly pear.
- Are typically perennial rather than annual species. The intent of this planting is to have a permanent edible feature in the landscape; annual species can be used, but the annual soil preparation, planting, and establishment could easily become disruptive for the surrounding vegetation.
- Should be naturally pest and disease resistant.

Vegetation for Wildlife Habitat

Four vegetative characteristics must be considered when selecting vegetation to attract wildlife: cover, food, water, and space. Yet these characteristics are not the same for all types of wildlife. Most developed landscapes attract generalist, edge species of birds and mammals. The vegetative conditions found in most developed landscapes that favor these types of species are:

- Open canopy structure
- Abundant fruiting or flowering species
- Open-grown trees with multiple branches close to the ground
- Rich diversity of plant species
- Some disturbance

Attracting less generalized species requires careful consideration of the habitat needs of the desired organism. Desirable mosquito predators, such as dragon- and damselflies, are attracted to the nesting capabilities of native vegetation structure that are not found in other types of vegetated communities, such as cattails. Bats too are attracted to appropriate roosting structures, which vary with species of bat.

The U.S. Fish and Wildlife Services have published a number of Habitat Suitability Index (HSI) models for many species of organisms throughout the United States. Though the HSI models are intended for measuring an existing habitat's suitability for a given species, they can also serve to outline appropriate habitat characteristics to emulate in order to attract desired species. HSI models are available through a number of federal websites including the U.S. Fish and Wildlife Service, USGS, Army Corps of Engineers, and The National Wetland Research Center.

In addition, habitat needs may include access to live as well as dead vegetation. This may not be practical in all instances, but where appropriate dead vegetation such as snags, downed trees, and even leaf litter are essential for attracting and maintaining some types of wildlife.

Establishing habitat on a developed site may also serve a larger regional need of providing appropriate habitat corridors. Even paring back a habitat to the vegetative core constituents helps maintain and connect fractured regional habitat. The developed landscape is a patchwork of largely generalist, largely unaccommodating habitat for most species of organisms. Efforts to reduce that patchwork pattern and provide contiguous habitat patches, if only in part, help to maintain the larger organism hierarchy within an ecosystem.

Successful habitat design begins with identifying the desired as well as probable wildlife species for a site:

▶ Examine regional corridors and habitat patches adjacent to and perhaps crossing the site.

▶ Identify the wildlife species that occupy existing corridors and patches as well as those that might use the corridor if patches like the project site were enhanced.

▶ Explore the habitat conditions of these corridors and compare against the habitat potential.

▶ Evaluate the probability of improving the corridor and attracting desired wildlife species.

▶ Compare corridor and patch potential against the habitat needs (cover, food, water, and space) of the desired wildlife species.

▶ Select and arrange species to mimic the habitat characteristics of the desired wildlife species.

Regionally native vegetation can provide for the precise needs of native wildlife. Native vegetation can provide the right cover, the right nest-building materials, and even the right dietary nutrition native organisms need for survival. Some nonnative species of vegetation, such as honeysuckles and buckthorn, have been equated to sugary substitutes in a native organism's diet that contribute to poor nutrition. Pair these strategies with protection zone strategies as well as those targeted at improving or restoring plant communities and habitats.

Firewise Landscape Design

Many regions in North America are prone to wildfire in varying degrees. Many native plants and animals rely on a fire cycle for their survival, either directly or indirectly. Fire maintains the diversity of these systems by "resetting" the natural progression or succession of plant species over time. For example, in the southern Great Plains, wildfire in prairies removes dead biomass, allowing sunlight to penetrate to the base of perennial grasses so they can resprout and make use of recycled nutrients in the ash. This also promotes the germination and resprouting of wildflowers, thus maintaining the prairie. Removal of fire from this system for long periods (decades) allows trees and shrubs to encroach, turning the grassland into a savanna and eventually a woodland. Similarly, mountainous conifer forests of the western United States and the Pine Barrens of New Jersey are fire adapted. Species such as Douglas fir can resist fire because of thick bark, while other species, like lodge pole pine, perish in wildfire; however, lodge pole cones, which are sealed shut with resin, will open and release seeds due to the intense heat of the fire, thus perpetuating the species.

While wildfire has an ecological place in our landscapes, the threats posed to life and property are very real. The intense heat and speed which characterize a wildfire often prohibit extinguishing these types of fires before damage to property can be prevented. The best defense for structures in fire-prone areas therefore is to reduce the risks through effective building and landscape design.

The National Fire Protection Association's (NFPA) Firewise Communities program was established to provide information to homeowners, community leaders, planners, developers, firefighters, and others in the effort to protect people and property from the risk of wildfire. NFPA provides excellent information for both building and landscape design. Following is a summary of their landscape design principles.

The appropriate design for the prevention of fire depends on local fire history, the relative site location with respect to overall neighboring terrain, prevailing winds and seasonal weather, property elevations, characteristics of vegetation (flammability and fuel load), and irrigation requirements/availability. Management of available fuel loads for a wildfire is the primary defense against these events as the amount, concentration, and distribution of readily flammable plant material directly contributes to the severity of a wildfire event.

The Firewise program proposes segmenting the property around a structure, such as a home, into four zones (Figure 4-17):

▶ Zone 1: Within 30 ft of structure. A well irrigated or very low flammability buffer no less than 30 ft deep on all sides of the structure. Zone 1 provides structure protection and access for fire suppression equipment. Plants should be spaced apart and low flammability species used.

▶ Zone 2: 30 to 100 ft from structure. Low-flammability plant species, low growing, and if necessary irrigated with few trees.

▶ Zone 3: 100 to 200 ft from structure. Low-growing plants with well-spaced trees; pruning may be needed to manage fuel loads.

▶ Zone 4: Greater than 200 ft from structure. Potentially well-vegetated (natural) area but pruned and managed to remove highly flammable (dead) material.

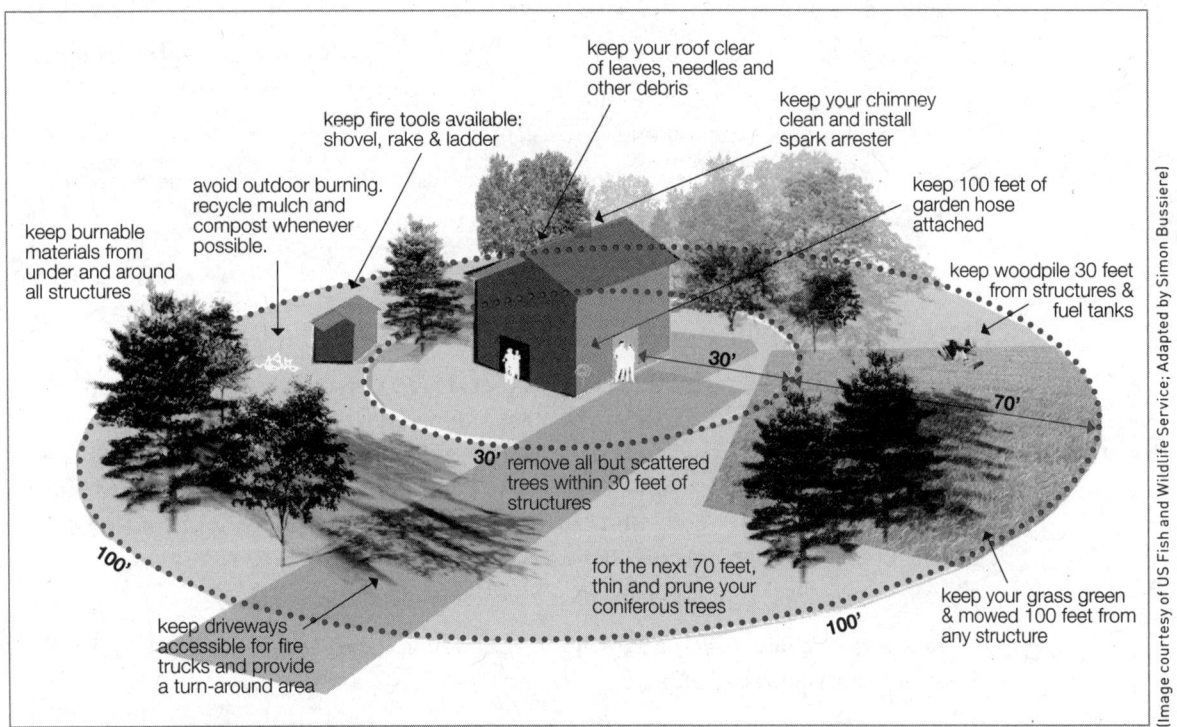

keep your roof clear of leaves, needles and other debris

keep your chimney clean and install spark arrester

keep fire tools available: shovel, rake & ladder

keep 100 feet of garden hose attached

avoid outdoor burning. recycle mulch and compost whenever possible.

keep burnable materials from under and around all structures

keep woodpile 30 feet from structures & fuel tanks

30'

70'

30' remove all but scattered trees within 30 feet of structures

for the next 70 feet, thin and prune your coniferous trees

100'

100'

keep your grass green & mowed 100 feet from any structure

keep driveways accessible for fire trucks and provide a turn-around area

(Image courtesy of US Fish and Wildlife Service; Adapted by Simon Bussiere)

FIGURE 4-17: Planting zones are designed to reduce risk of fire spread and destruction of homes. Zones 1 through 4 gradually increase the density, height, and diversity of species away from the home.

Other basic guidelines include:

▶   Manage plant material (by mowing, pruning, raking, fire wood storage, etc.) to keep potential fuel to a minimum.

▶   Add landscape structures for firebreaks, such as driveways and lawns, in all zones where appropriate.

▶   Widely space and carefully situate trees.

▶   Remove "ladder fuels"—vegetation that links the ground to tree tops, allowing fire to spread upward.

▶   Prune up all trees with limbs 6 to 10 ft from the ground.

▶   Consider using deciduous plants, as they are more fire resistant due to a higher moisture content in the leaves and carry less fuel when dormant.

▶   Choose plants that grow without accumulating large amounts of litter (fuel)—dead branches, needles, leaves—or have open branches with a low volume of total vegetation.

▶   Group plants in small, irregular clusters/islands; large masses concentrate sources of fuel.

▶   Use decorative rock and stone to break up masses of vegetation.

▶   Use mulch, as it conserves moisture and reduces weed growth but avoid pine bark/needles that can easily carry fire.

Ecological Restoration

The Society for Ecological Restoration International (SER) defines ecological restoration as "the process of assisting the recovery of an ecosystem that has been degraded, damaged or destroyed." While the term *ecological restoration* specifically refers to repairing a system which historically existed in that specific location, the process and skills used in restoration can be used for mitigation or creation of these systems where they historically did not exist, but, due to modified ecological conditions, are now appropriate.

There are five primary contexts in which ecological restoration occurs:

▶   **Recovery** of a degraded or damaged ecosystem to a previous condition (e.g., overgrazed grassland to healthy tall-grass prairie)

▶   **Replacement** of an ecosystem that was completely destroyed with one of the same kind (e.g., cultivated pasture to tall-grass prairie).

▶   **Transformation** of an ecological system from one type to another occurring within the same bioregion due to changes in the larger regional context which make the historical landscape no longer viable (e.g., overgrazed prairie to wetland).

▸ **Substitution of "novel" landscape**, which may have never previously existed in the bioregion when that system can no longer support a historic ecosystem. This system should be derived from species and community associations but assembled to suit new site conditions (e.g., invaded urban drainage channel to moisture-loving, tall-grass prairie species which can survive without adversely affecting flood control).

▸ **Substitution of a replacement ecosystem** where the site lacks any data as to historic condition. The replacement ecosystem may resemble a historic system, but there are no reference systems left for comparison (e.g., invaded urban drainage channel to riparian woodland composed of native species likely present historically).

For restoration to be successful, human interaction with the landscape must support or reestablish feedback loops whereby the processes within the ecosystem will move toward a self-perpetuating system. Feedback loops are processes within an ecosystem that direct change or maintain a system. For example, if the keystone species of a food chain becomes extinct, the food chain begins to crash. There are some conditions that self-correct in order to bring the ecosystems back into equilibrium. An example of this is vegetation providing nutrients and organic matter to soil, which creates healthier soil, which in turn allows more and different plant species to grow, thus increasing biodiversity. Allowing systems to self-correct can be termed passive restoration.

Restoration projects not only require appropriate species selection but also necessitate decisions about appropriate sources of those species—whether as direct transplants, wild harvested seed, or commercially grown seed. The genetic makeup of seed may affect estab-lishment success. Correct species selection using propagules with genetic traits adapted to different soils, climate, elevation, and so forth may not adapt to the environmental and eco-logical conditions of their transplant sites and likely will be unable to respond to long-term evolutionary demands.

GENOTYPE

Incorrect choice of seed could also contaminate the local gene pool of the restoration site and change the direction of ecological succession (Gustafson et al. 2004). Appropriate native plant stock is defined very differently among various federal and state agencies and is open to a wide range of interpretations. When genetic stock is even considered, this is often done solely with a distance parameter or hardiness zone limit as the guiding factor in seed selection. It is likely that there may be additional factors that may be more relevant to proj-ect success beyond distance from collection site and can serve as better guides in decision making.

The major controlling factor in genetic diversity of the species is the ecosystem in which it grows. For this reason many seed collection guides refer to "local genotype" material. This has typically been understood to limit the distance between the plant propagule source and the restoration site, but should also consider selecting donor sites with similar environmental conditions, particularly for those species with either restricted seed dispersal ability or breeding systems which could reduce genetic differentiation. When determining sites for collection, factors such as climate, soil types, elevation, plant community, and other biotic conditions should be matched as closely as possible between collection site and restoration site. For populations that are likely already exchanging genetic resources between populations (through wind dispersal or far-ranging pollination), propagules should be collected from areas having similar ecological conditions and from numerous individuals in that population in order to improve the probability of a successful long-term survival in the restoration project.

For ease of obtaining seed, commercially available cultivars of native species have been widely used in many restoration and revegetation projects. A cultivar is a variety of a species that has been bred for one or more unique physical characteristics, or in some cases, bred from a mixture of genetic stock from a subset of a species' range (such as a specific hardiness zone or soil type). Using cultivars of native species can result in the modification of the original genotypes of the species at a given site, particularly where the number of individuals introduced far outweighs the numbers of individuals of the original genetic stock in the area. Several studies have found that cultivars have ultimately altered the genetic population structure and, over time, the ecosystem structure and function of the community.

WHAT IS RESTORATION?

Ecological restoration is the process of repairing past damage (anthropogenic or otherwise) to a specific ecosystem or habitat. It involves the following activities:

- ▶ Describe the ecosystem to be restored
- ▶ Identify a reference ecosystem
- ▶ Identify historic ecological processes or drivers that are no longer present on the site which will need to be reestablished or simulated
- ▶ Identify those historical occurrences that have led to the need for restoration
- ▶ Perform a full ecological site assessment to understand the current ecological drivers on the site
- ▶ Identify site conditions that could inhibit restoration and recovery of the desired system
- ▶ Identify biota, particularly plant species and "keystone" animals without which the restoration will not be stable. The feasibility and methods of returning these species to the site should be assessed.

▶ Describe the landscape context of the restoration area and identify features in the landscape that could preclude, inhibit, or enhance needed ecological mechanisms (such as pressures against flooding or prescribed fire in an urban landscape).

▶ Identify ecological feedback loops that either will continue to degrade the system or could be converted to be used to restore the system.

▶ Identify propagule sources for the restoration project. Genetics and local provenance should be considered.

▶ Identify necessary management efforts (prescribed fire, invasive species control, stand thinning) which could be necessary, and identify those monitored variables which will trigger their application.

▶ Develop a schedule for the process of restoration that extends out at least 10 years after installation, with identification of specific information that should be monitored to assess restoration trajectory and allow for adaptive management.

▶ Identify the restoration "endpoints" that will signify the end of restoration and the beginning of ecosystem maintenance. What are the measures of success?

References

Akbari, H., M. Pomerantz, and H. Taha. 2001. "Cool Surfaces and Shade Trees to Reduce Energy Use and Improve Air Quality in Urban Areas." *Solar Energy*, 7(3):295–310.

Beckett, K.P., P. Freer-Smith, and G. Taylor. 2000. "Tree Species and Air Quality." *Journal of Arboriculture*, 26(1):12–19.

Bernatzky, A. 1983. *The Effects of Trees on the Urban Climate: Trees in the 21st Century.* New York: Academic Publishers, pp. 59–76. Based on the first International Arborcultural Conference.

Beuttell, K. 2008. "A Paradox of Nature: Designing Rain Gardens to Be Dry." *Stormwater* 9(7). Available at www.stormh2o.com/october-2008/dry-rain-gardens.aspx.

Boland, P., and S. Hunhammar. 1999. "Ecosystem Services in Urban Areas." *Ecological Economics* 29: 293–301.

Brenneisen, Stephan. 2006. *"Space for Urban Wildlife: Designing Green Roofs as Habitats in Switzerland." Urban Habitats*, 4.

Callaway, R.M., and E.T. Aschehoug. 2000. "Invasive Plants versus Their New and Old Neighbors: A Mechanism for Exotic Invasion." *Science,* 290: 521–523.

Chenowith, R.E., and P.H. Gobster. 1990. "The Nature and Ecology of Aesthetic Experience in the Landscape." *Landscape Journal*, 9(1):1–8.

Czarapata, E. 2005. *Invasive Plants of the Upper Midwest: An Illustrated Guide to Their Identification and Control.* Madison: University of Wisconsin Press.

de Groot, R.S., M.A. Wilson, and R.M.J. Boumans. 2002. "A Typology for the Classification, Description and Valuation of Ecosystem Function, Goods and Services." *Ecological Economics,* 41:393–408.

Del Tredici, P. 2006. "Brave New Ecology." *Landscape Architecture Magazine,* 96 (February): 46–52.

Dines, Nicholas T. 1998. "Section 220 Energy and Resource Conservation." In Charles W. Harris, Nicholas T. Dines, and Kyle D. Brown (eds.), *Timesaver Standards for Landscape Architecture* (2nd ed.), pp. 220.1–220.13. New York: McGraw-Hill.

Dunnett, N., A. Nagase, R. Booth, and P. Grime. 2008. "Influence of Vegetation Composition on Runoff in Two Simulated Green Roof Experiments." *Urban Ecosystems,* 11:385–398

Dvorak, B., and A. Volderb. 2010. "Green Roof Vegetation for North American Ecoregions: A Literature Review." *Landscape and Urban Planning,* (96):197–213.

Getter, K.L., and D.B. Rowe. 2006. "The Role of Green Roofs in Sustainable Development." *HortScience,* 42:1276–1285.

Gustafson, D.J., D.J. Gibson, et al. 2004. "Conservation Genetics of Two Co-dominant Grass Species in an Endangered Grassland Ecosystem." *Journal of Applied Ecology,* 41(2): 389–397.

Heinze, W. 1985. "Results of an Experiment on Extensive Growth of Vegetation on Roofs. " *Rasen Grünflachen Begrünungen* 16 (3):80–88.

Hoffman, A.A., and P.A. Parsons. 1991. *Evolutionary Genetics and Environmental Stress.* Oxford, England: Oxford University Press.

Huang, J., H. Akbari, and H. Taha. 1990. *The Wind-Shielding and Shading Effects of Trees on Residential Heating and Cooling Requirements.* ASHRAE Winter Meeting, American Society of Heating, Refrigerating, and Air-Conditioning Engineers. Atlanta, GA.

Hunhammar, S. 1999. "Ecosystem Services in Urban Areas." *Ecological Economics,* 29:293–301.

Kadas, G. 2006. "Rare Invertebrates Colonizing Green Roofs in London." *Urban Habitats,* 4.

Kaplan, R., and S. Kaplan. 1989. *The Experience of Nature: A Psychological Perspective.* Cambridge, MA: Cambridge University Press.

Kaplan, S. 1995. "The Restorative Benefits of Nature: Toward and Integrative Framework." *Journal of Environmental Psychology,* 15:169–182.

Kuo, F.E. 2001. "Coping with Poverty: Impacts of Environment and Attention in the Inner City." *Environment and Behavior,* 33(1):5–34.

Lal, R. 2003. "Global Potential of Soil Carbon Sequestration to Mitigate the Greenhouse Effect." *Critical Reviews in Plant Sciences,* 22:151–184.

Louv, R. 2005. *Last Child in the Woods: Saving Our Children from Nature-Deficit Disorder.* Chapel Hill, NC: Algonquin Books.

Lundholm, J.T. 2006. "Green Roofs and Facades: A Habitat Template Approach." *Urban Habitats,* 4:87–102.

McPherson, E.G., D. Nowak, G. Heisler, S. Grimmond, C. Souch, R. Grant, and R. Rowntree. 1997. "Quantifying Urban Forest Structure, Function, and Value: The Chicago Urban Forest Climate Project." *Urban Ecosystems,* 1:49–61.

Nowak, D.J., D.E. Crane, and J.C. Stevens. 2006. "Air Pollution Removal by Urban Trees and Shrubs in the United States." *Urban Forestry & Urban Greening,* 4:5–123.

Odum, Eugene Pleasants. 1959. *Fundamentals of Ecology* (2d ed.). Philadelphia: W.B. Saunders Company.

Owensby, C.E., P.I. Coyne, J.M. Ham, L.M. Auen, and A.K. Knapp. 1993. "Biomass Production in a Tallgrass Prairie Ecosystem Exposed to Ambient and Elevated CO_2." *Ecological Applications*, 3(4):644–653.

Pimentel, D., Z. Rodolfo, and D. Morrison. 2005. "Update on the Environmental and Economic Costs Associated with Alien-Invasive Species in the United States." *Ecological Economics*, 52:273–288.

Radosevich, S.R. 2006. Plant Population Biology and the Invasion Process. In *Center for Invasive Plant Management Online Textbook.* Available at www.weedcenter.org/textbook/2_radosevich_invasion_process.html#invasion_process.html.

Rejmánek, M. 2000. "Invasive Plants: Approaches and Predictions." *Austral Ecology*, 25:497–506.

Rosenfeld A.H., J.J. Romm, H. Akbari, and M. Pomerantz. 1998. "Cool Communities: Strategies for Heat Islands Mitigation and Smog Reduction." *Energy and Buildings*, 28:51–62.

Schofield, N.J. 1992. "Tree Planting for Dryland Salinity Control in Australia." *Agroforestry Systems* 20:1–23.

Simmons, M., and H. Venhaus. 2006. "Urban Design Without Ecological Risk." *Landscape Architecture Magazine*, May.

Simmons, M.T., H.C. Venhaus, and S. Windhager. 2007. "Exploiting the Attributes of Regional Ecosystems for Landscape Design: The Role of Ecological Restoration in Ecological Engineering." *Ecological Engineering*, 30:201–205.

SITES 2009a. *Sustainable Sites Initiative: Guidelines and Performance Benchmarks 2009.* Available at www.sustainablesites.org/report.

_____. 2009b. *Sustainable Sites Initiative: The Case for Sustainable Landscapes.* Available at www.sustainablesites.org/report.

Taha, H., S. Konopacki, and S. Gabersek. 1996. *Modeling the Meteorological and Energy Effects of Urban Heat Islands and their Mitigation: A 10-Region Study.* Lawrence Berkeley Laboratory Report LBL-38667, Berkeley, CA.

Tinsley, J., M.T. Simmons, and S. Windhager. 2006. "The Establishment Success of Native versus Non-Native Seed Mixes on a Revegetated Roadside in Central Texas." *Ecological Engineering*, 26(3):231–240.

Trowbridge, P.J., and N.L. Bassuk. 2004. *Trees in the Urban Landscape: Site Assessment, Design, and Installation.* Hoboken, NJ: John Wiley & Sons, Inc.

Tutin, T. G., V.H. Heywood, N.A. Burges, D.H. Valentine, S.M. Walters, and D.A. Webb. 1964–1980. *Flora Europaea.* Vols. 1 to 5. Cambridge, UK: Cambridge University Press.

Ulrich, R.S. 1986. "Human Responses to Vegetation and Landscapes." *Landscape and Urban Planning*, 13:29–44.

Ulrich, R.S., R.F. Simons, B.D. Losito, E. Fiorito, M. Miles, and M. Zelson. 1991. "Stress Recovery during Exposure to Natural and Urban Environments." *Journal of Environmental Psychology*, 11:201–230.

Urban, James. 2008. *Up by Roots: Healthy Soils and Trees in the Built Environment.* Champaign, IL: International Society of Arboriculture.

Weis, J.S., and P. Weis. 2004. "Metal Uptake, Transport and Release by Wetland Plants: Implications for Phytoremediation and Restoration." *Environment International*, 30:685–700.

Whittaker, R.H. 1975. *Communities and Ecosystems*. New York: Macmillan.

Wilson, Jon S., and S.J. Josiah. 2010. *Windbreak Design*. NebGuide. March 2004. Nebraska Forest Services. Web. 25. Available at http://nfs.unl.edu/documents/windbreakdesign.pdf.

Williamson, M.H. 1989. "Mathematical Models of Invasion." In *Biological Invasions: A Global Perspective* (J.A. Drake et al., eds.), pp.329–350. Chichester, UK: John Wiley and Sons.

_____. 1996. *Biological Invasions*. London: Chapman & Hall.

Windhager, S., F. Steiner, M.T. Simmons, and D. Heymann. 2010. "Toward Ecosystem Services as a Basis for Design." *Landscape Journal*, 29(2): 107–123.

CHAPTER 5

SITE DESIGN: SOILS

► Nina Bassuk and Susan Day

SOIL IS THE FOUNDATION OF LIFE ON EARTH. It is made up of mineral solids, water, air, and organic matter. It supports vegetation that we rely upon for the air we breathe and the food we eat. Sustaining soil itself is an important component of a sustainable site. However, soils play a much broader role in the health of ecosystems (Figure 5-2). Healthy soils:

► Protect water quality and supplies. They filter and retain water, helping to clean contaminated water and reduce runoff, erosion, sedimentation, and flooding.

► Store carbon and support a healthy population of microorganisms.

► Can reduce inputs (irrigation, pesticides, fertilizers) that might otherwise be needed to sustain plants and landscapes.

► Produce healthy plants.

► Help trees achieve desired size more quickly.

Soil, however, is slow to form and its many benefits can be easily lost during site development. Soil structure and quality can be damaged due to erosion, compaction, relocation, contamination, and overfertilization. In urban environments most soil has been modified or imported (Figure 5-1).

Thus the twin goals of soils management for a sustainable site are:

► Protect existing soil with desirable traits.

► Improve soils with undesirable traits.

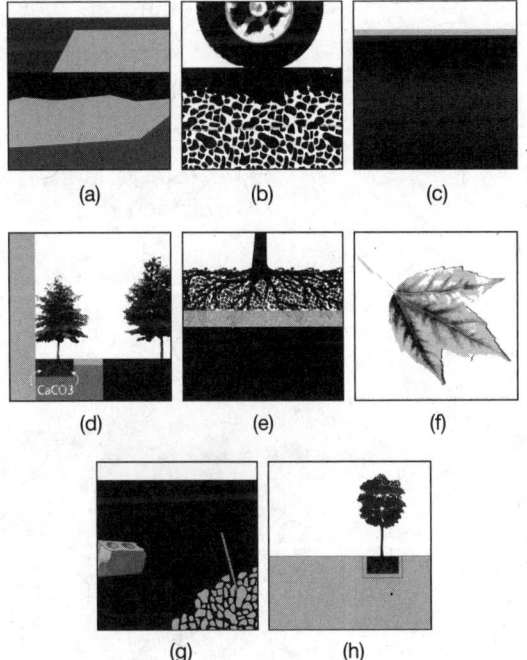

(Adapted by John Wiley & Sons from drawings by Hannah Carlson)

FIGURE 5-1: Common characteristics of urban soils include (a) grade changes caused by cut and fill, (b) compaction and loss of aggregate stability, (c) impervious crust, (d) altered soil pH, (e) poor drainage caused by compaction, (f) nutrient deficiencies, (g) anthropeic materials (buried rubble and debris), and (h) small soil volumes inadequate for plant growth (Craul 1985). These characteristics are detrimental not only to plant growth, but they reduce other natural soil values and benefits as well.

Achieving these goals requires identification of healthy soils, protection of these soils, and an understanding of the science of creating situations where soil can form again. Careful site assessment, design, and construction permits the greatest contributions to site sustainability from the soil. This chapter provides hands-on, practical approaches for understanding site soils and preserving and ameliorating soil conditions in the landscape.

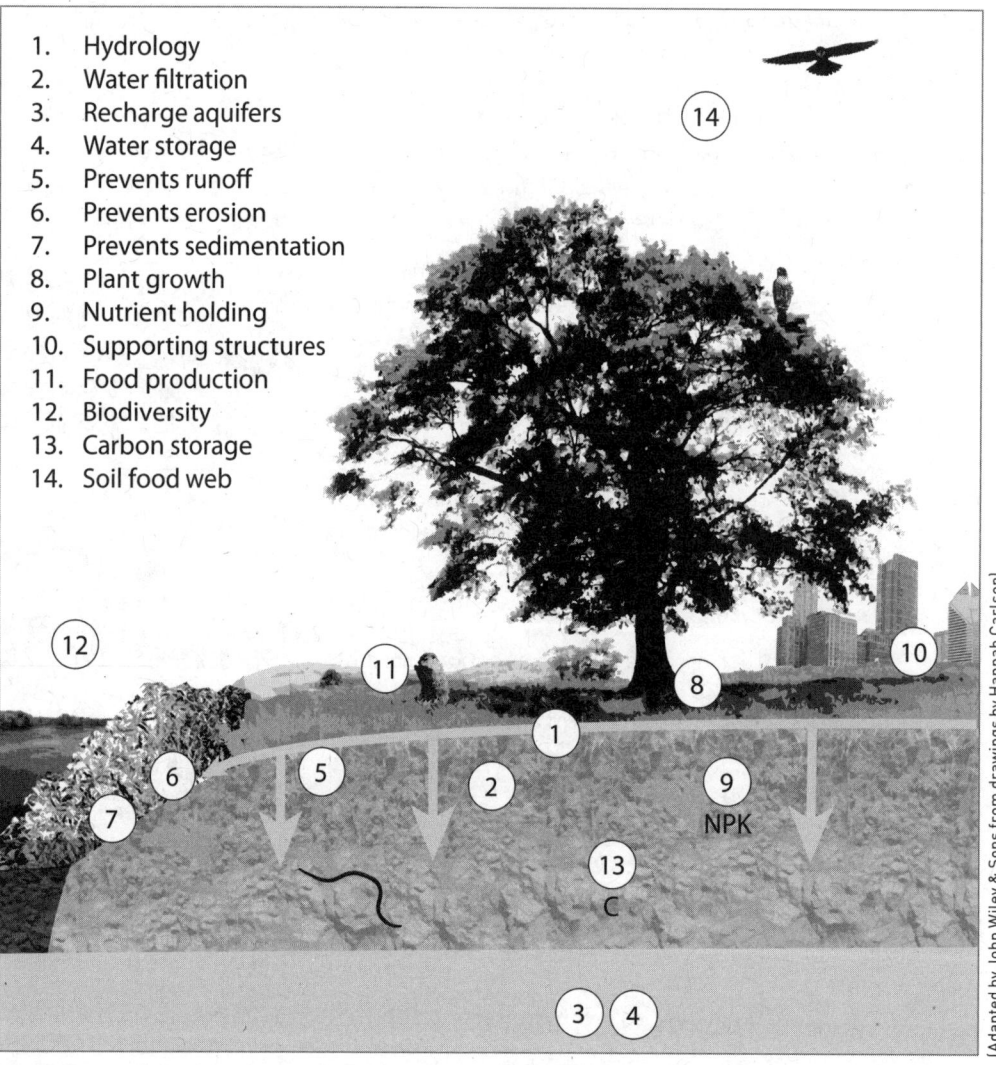

1. Hydrology
2. Water filtration
3. Recharge aquifers
4. Water storage
5. Prevents runoff
6. Prevents erosion
7. Prevents sedimentation
8. Plant growth
9. Nutrient holding
10. Supporting structures
11. Food production
12. Biodiversity
13. Carbon storage
14. Soil food web

(Adapted by John Wiley & Sons from drawings by Hannah Carlson)

FIGURE 5-2: Highlights of ecosystem functions performed by soils. The role of soil in a healthy ecosystem is complex, and these functions, both present and future, need to be considered in creating a sustainable landscape.

SITES AND SOILS

The *SITES Guidelines and Performance Benchmarks* for soils focus on soil protection and restoration, although sites where soil is absent or unusable are also addressed. Like other areas, SITES soils credits aim to maximize ecosystem service provision outcomes. Soil quality determines the type and health of vegetation that can be established and maintained sustainably. Soil characteristics in combination with vegetation influence site hydrology, including the potential for stormwater capture. Thus soil credits must be viewed in the context of related vegetation and water credits, rather than in isolation. Soil can be considered the infrastructure upon which a sustainable site is built, supporting vegetation, hydrologic cycles, and other ecosystem processes.

SITES credits place a high value on protecting healthy soils. Even simple trafficking or grading can destroy or damage soils that have developed over millennia, releasing carbon and reducing the soil's ability to serve as a support system for the site. Credits are available for restoring previously damaged soils while restoring soils damaged during current construction is a prerequisite.

Soils are the foundation of any site, supporting both plants and structures; they are complex, varied, and integral to other ecosystem functions. For these reasons, credits and prerequisites are found in all sections of the guidelines: site selection, predesign assessment, site design, construction, operations and maintenance, and monitoring and innovation. Site selection restricts allowable uses for valuable soils, such as those designated prime farmland, because they are part of our global environmental commons. Prerequisites include assessing the soil resources in the predesign site assessment and creating a soil management plan. Credits include protecting soils and vegetation in joint *vegetation and soil protection zones (VSZP)*. In construction, maintenance, and monitoring, additional credits focus on restoring soils and managing and monitoring them for continued health and function. The level of previous soil disturbance, including brownfield designation, is also considered in the SITES *Guidelines*.

INTEGRATING SOIL INTO THE DESIGN PROCESS

The sustainable site protects and utilizes the potential of the site and its ecosystem service values. There are many ways that a site can offer such benefits, and soil plays a key role. In many ways, soils form the foundation for a site. They support plants, walkways, and buildings. They determine the flow of water through the site and the potential for water capture and storage. Yet soils are highly varied and can be considerably altered by even slight disturbances. Soils also change over time, especially if they are supporting plant life and are biologically and physically active. Finally, project steps are not linear; they inform each other. Being flexible to changes based on assessment results, remediation, and maintenance requirements (and even future monitoring results) will help to create a more sustainable site design.

Guidelines for Integrating Soils into the Design Process

▶ **Include both protection and utilization of ecosystem benefits.** For example, a significant ecosystem benefit provided by soils is carbon storage. Grading can destroy soil structure and accelerate decomposition, resulting in carbon losses to the atmosphere. In addition, strategically capitalizing on the inherent water infiltration and storage capacity in a healthy undisturbed soil is an example of utilizing the potential ecosystem benefits provided by soils.

▶ **Realize the investment in soils will create opportunities for enhanced sustainability in other aspects of the site.** Protecting and restoring soils, especially those that are severely disturbed, will bring a whole host of indirect benefits, such as those provided by vegetation supported by the soil and reduction in irrigation needs as root systems are able to obtain adequate resources from a healthy soil that they cannot from an unhealthy soil.

▶ **Make site-specific soil analyses since soils can change over short distances and relevant characteristics depend on site plans.** Learning to read a site's soils and determine where soil variations are likely to occur takes practice (see "Big Picture Soil Assessment" later in the chapter). For example, using a composite soil sample for soil pH testing when there are roads, sidewalks, construction debris, or other items that will change pH over short distances is at best useless and, at worst, will create an unsustainable landscape if pH-sensitive plants are placed in soil with an inappropriate pH.

▶ **Allow time and flexibility for obtaining site assessments and making changes to the plan.** The site assessment must include several iterations to be successful. Some information is required to make design plans, but a complete and detailed site assessment at this point would be costly and wasteful. For example, assessing soil pH for plantings in great detail in an area where it is later decided to locate a building is pointless. Therefore, numerous visits are required to gather the level of information needed for the current stage of the design and decision-making process.

► **Create conditions for soil protection and soil formation for the long term.** Will site use compact restored or undisturbed soils? Possibly a change of design can reduce this impact. In addition, soils may meet restoration specifications but cannot be fully restored in a day—good restoration will set the conditions in place (organic matter inputs, root activity, and so forth) that will build a high-quality, well-structured soil over time.

SOILS IN THE SITE ASSESSMENT

The first step in creating a sustainable site is the site assessment—the evaluation of environmental limitations and opportunities in the context of the intended function of the site. What is learned about the soils on the site at this stage should inform the layout and design of the entire project. In short, the design needs to form *around* the soils and other site resources—capitalizing on the opportunities and working with the limitations they present. This is a novel approach for many, but the potential of the site to provide ecosystem services cannot be ignored if sustainability is going to be achieved. Thus, buildings and roads cannot be placed before the soils are understood. The design team needs to have a clear understanding of what can and should be learned from the site assessment about site soils and when it is necessary to go back for more detailed information.

The first activity is to identify the type and quality of soils existing on the site. Questions should include:

► Where has the soil been disturbed, and in what way?

► Where are the soils healthy? Healthy soils should have a high priority for protection and preservation.

► Where are there soils that can be restored, or at least set on their way for developing the characteristics of healthy soils down the road?

► Are there areas where soil is wholly absent, or where soils are contaminated?

Each of these areas presents different limitations and opportunities for ecosystem service provision. Thus, each of these areas must be identified in a preliminary site assessment before the design phase can proceed (Table 5-1).

TABLE 5-1: Defining General Soil Categories

Healthy Soils	Defining healthy soils for all sites is difficult to do succinctly because soils vary with climate and region. For example, physical, chemical, and biological characteristics that would be recognized as healthy for some soils in arid regions where native soils might be low in nutrients or very sandy would bear little resemblance to a healthy soil in the upper Midwest, where healthy soil is rich in organic matter and well structured. In defining a healthy soil for the site, consider both the characteristics of undisturbed native soils in the region (the *reference soil*) *and* the expectations for the soil on the site and the plant life, nutrient cycling, and hydrologic processes it will need to support. A healthy soil may be present, if: ▶ Soil horizons are similar to the reference soil ▶ Both topsoil and subsoils are uncompacted ▶ Organic matter content is equal to or exceeds that of the reference soil Soil pH, salinity, cation exchange capacity, and mineral contents are similar to the reference soil ▶ Soils do not contain compounds toxic to anticipated plants ▶ Existing vegetation is representative of native plant communities Soils that have not been significantly disturbed by previous human development activities are more likely to be healthy soils.
Minimal Soil Disturbance	"Minimal soil disturbance" describes soils that are very minimally graded or only somewhat compacted. SITES specifies Maximum Allowable Bulk Densities (MABDs) for a given soil texture (see Figure 5-19). Minimally disturbed soils may exceed this compaction level in the surface horizons, but are not covered with impervious surfaces and do not have significant subsoil compaction or disturbance. An example would be a soil that has been compacted by heavy foot traffic, but the subsoil has not been graded.
Moderate Soil Disturbance	Moderate soil disturbance is very common around existing buildings and previously developed sites. These include areas where topsoil is absent, and where subsoil has been graded (either contouring, cut and fill, or simply excessive construction traffic). Topsoil, if present, likely exceeds the MABD specified by SITES. Subsoils in areas of moderate soil disturbance will have been altered, compacted, or mixed. For example, topsoil horizons may be underneath subsoil layers. Cut-and-fill areas are likely to be moderately disturbed, as are soils within unpaved or temporary roads.
Severe Soil Disturbance	Severe soil disturbance combines the characteristics of moderately disturbed soils but are also paved over or contaminated. Examples include soil beneath existing asphalt or buildings, or brownfields.

SOIL HORIZONS AND LAYERS

Understanding the soil horizons that are normally present in relatively undisturbed sites will make it easier to discern and understand the origin of what is encountered in disturbed soils. Soils that have not been heavily disturbed have layers, or horizons, that may consist of a top layer of organic matter (termed the O horizon), a second layer of topsoil (typically the A horizon), subsoil layers, and lastly parent material and bedrock. Topsoil usually contains higher levels of nutrients, organic matter, and microorganisms than the other layers. On disturbed sites, topsoil is an elusive layer, often having been removed or tampered with, undermining its positive attributes. Disturbed soils may also have buried soil horizons, such as a layer of topsoil buried by construction fill, or layers that are not parallel to the surface (Figures 5-3 and 5-4).

(Photo from Susan Day)

FIGURE 5-3: Soil horizons, or layers, are readily visible in some soils but may be indistinct or discontinuous in others. The A and B horizons are easily distinguishable, partly because this soil has been in agricultural use and has developed a plow pan. Note the excavated soil that has been placed on top of the soil creating a buried A horizon. This is a common situation in disturbed sites.

(Photo from Rachel M. Layman)

FIGURE 5-4: A soil profile excavated with an auger and laid out in a tray. Note the typical color and structure progression from left to right (surface to subsoil) of this Shottower loam soil that has been under agricultural production for many years.

Soil maps and surveys paint soils with a broad brush. In land that is undisturbed except for agricultural or forest uses, soil survey maps can be very helpful. However, if there is any additional use—such as roads, outbuildings, excavations, dumps, or drainage—onsite assessments are needed at each place where land-use history indicates there might be a disruption. Thus, if the NRCS soil survey describes an area as "Groseclose Urban Land Complex," it is very likely that little remains of the character of the Groseclose soil series. This is not to say that original soil does not have an influence on the site. The influence of some aspects of soil chemistry and texture can persist even through long periods of urban land use. However, the characteristics such as drainage, pH content, soil structure, and soil horizons may be altered beyond recognition. Therefore, there is no substitute for getting out on the site and testing. The site assessment is not an activity carried out in the office with maps but a close inspection of the land itself. For each set of information gathered, maps should be created on top of a site plan, either manually or using GIS, so that the information can be overlaid and interpreted to help inform the other stages of the project.

Big Picture Soil Assessment

The first step of assessing the site soils should focus on the big picture questions. What occurred here in the past? What are the major soil areas and challenges within the site? What are the regulatory concerns, if any? Onsite observational assessments are a valuable tool for understanding the big picture in soil assessment, and they can also offer indications of underlying soil issues. Gathering the information discussed in the following sections is the first step in the iterative process described in the project steps flow chart shown in Figure 5-6.

LAND-USE HISTORY AND THE OBSERVATIONAL SOIL ASSESSMENT

The history of how the site has been used is extraordinarily useful in understanding what the existing conditions are. The soil, hydrology, and vegetation may have drastically changed over time, through land use or natural events affecting how the site can be used or modified today. By making observational assessments and researching the historical land use of the site, the ecological narrative of the site is revealed. Historical aerial photography and maps can help determine the history of the site. Knowing the historic uses of the site can help illuminate what potential opportunities or pitfalls there might be. It can also contribute to a better understanding of how the site can be modified to protect or enhance ecosystem services. Historic land uses can indicate potential contamination and the past natural state, indicating potential subsurface limitations. For example, the site may have once been wetlands and therefore may have compressible soils. Both of these situations—contamination and compressible soils—can greatly reduce site viability or increase the cost of development.

A site visit, especially in conjunction with conversations with owners, former owners, land managers, and neighbors, is a good first step in assessing soils. This can help quickly identify potential "hot spots" where soil conditions may not be what is expected. Bringing a shovel, penetrometer, and a push tube along on a site visit for informational "poking around" can reveal or confirm conditions such as hidden paving or compacted soils (Table 5-2).

TABLE 5-2: Strategies for Reading the Site and Site History

THINGS TO LOOK FOR	WHAT THIS MIGHT INDICATE
Development and construction	Soil is likely to be disturbed and compacted. Site hydrology and vegetation may also be altered in disturbed areas. Potential for soil contamination.
Grade changes, cut and fill	Grade changes are common around buildings, parking lots, playing fields, or any other flat area, especially if the natural topography is not flat. Cuts will reveal subsoil layers and may or may not have a restored topsoil layer. Fill can contain just about anything, including rubble and building debris. Grading can also cause eroded areas.
Areas of materials storage or construction debris	Soil likely to be compacted. If materials include limestone gravel, cement, or similar, soil pH may be elevated. May be buried "artifacts." May also have areas of instability since dumped and covered materials may not be properly compacted.
Vehicular and pedestrian routes	Even unofficial roads and pathways will result in soil compaction, sometimes severe, and possible contamination.
Evidence of soil contamination or dumping areas	If contamination or dumping may have introduced materials toxic to humans or plants, then further soil tests may be required for these areas.
Buildings both present and past	Soils are likely highly disturbed around building sites, depending upon the type of construction.
Land use adjacent to the site and within the same watershed	Can give insight into how water may move onto the site. May also have a zone of influence on contamination and erosion.

EXISTING VEGETATION AND THE OBSERVATIONAL SOIL ASSESSMENT

Existing vegetation can add to an understanding of land-use history, but also can help identify areas with special soil characteristics. A knowledgeable plants person can quickly identify areas where soils might be disturbed or have particular qualities during a site visit. This examination can also lay the foundation for the soil sampling plan. For example, interveinal chlorosis (leaf yellowing) on some trees and shrubs may indicate a change in soil pH, or other chemical imbalance. The presence of certain species, such as tree-of-heaven (*Ailanthus altissima*), is an indication of site disturbance. Large, healthy trees may indicate that a site has been undisturbed for some time, or has only been disturbed very recently.

TABLE 5-3: Strategies for Interpreting Soil Characteristics by Analysis of Existing Vegetation and Landscapes

THINGS TO LOOK FOR	WHAT THIS MIGHT INDICATE
Health of vegetation. Nutrient deficiencies can sometimes be detected by leaf color (Figure 5-5)	Nutrient deficiencies might indicate altered soil chemistry. Plants with leaf scorch, leaf drop, or poor vigor may indicate soil compaction, drought, or poor drainage.
Irrigation systems	If a functioning irrigation system is in place, this should be taken into consideration when interpreting soil information based on plant health.
Tree decline. Stag-heading (when large dead branches protrude through the live canopy of a tree) indicates serious decline in large trees.	Serious decline of large trees generally follows root disturbance. Disturbance may have occurred as much as 20 years earlier. Pests may be secondary causes of decline.
Poor vigor, especially on younger trees, can be observed by growth increment. Suckering may also indicate stress.	May indicate poor soil quality or compromised conditions (i.e., low soil volume, compaction) on developed sites or disturbance on mostly undeveloped sites. May help identify areas that need soil restoration.
Healthy and culturally or ecologically valuable specimens or plant groups	This may be an area that is likely to have healthy soils and may merit a soil and vegetation protection zone.
Invasive species	Often indicates disturbance.
Indicator species. Look for species that were not planted but have occurred naturally or self-sown.	Species can indicate disturbance, or wet soils, thin soils, or high-quality or low-quality soils. An accomplished plants person may be required to identify.
Witch's-broom, branch dieback, or leaf scorching	Can indicate salt exposure. Look for location patterns that might indicate a source of salt.

(Photo from Nina Bassuk)

FIGURE 5-5: Interveinal chlorosis in trees and shrubs can indicate micronutrient deficiencies brought on by elevated soil pH. These leaves are all from a pin oak (*Quercus palustris*) tree and show no chlorosis on the left, to moderate chlorosis on the right.

HYDROLOGY AND TOPOGRAPHY AND THE OBSERVATIONAL SOIL ASSESSMENT

The hydrology of a site is the movement and distribution of water across the site and through the soil. This is largely governed by the topography and soils of the site. However, understanding topographic and hydrologic patterns on a site can augment the interpretation of soils. There are numerous links between hydrology and the soil assessment. These links should help inform decisions to manage runoff, maximize the efficient use of water for plant use, recharge ground aquifers, and retain and filter water onsite. Signs of soil erosion, flooding, or sediment deposits can indicate where soils may be vulnerable or where improved infiltration would be desirable. A hydrologic assessment might include topographic maps, watershed delineation, location and area of impervious surfaces, and precipitation data. Observations of a working hydrological system can give important information about where to preserve existing conditions or, if development makes it necessary to disturb the existing functioning hydrological system, how the site design can compensate for the disturbance.

TABLE 5-4: Strategies for Interpreting Site Soils Through Observations of Hydrology and Topography

THINGS TO LOOK FOR	WHAT THIS MIGHT INDICATE
Signs of erosion: gullies, rills, sedimentation, sediment-laden stormwater or stream flow during rain events	Nutrient deficiencies might indicate altered soil chemistry. Plants with leaf scorch, leaf drop, or poor vigor may indicate soil compaction, drought, or poor drainage.
Original topography, floodplains	Original topography may indicate where soil characteristics will shift. Floodplains may have deep fertile soil.
Impervious surfaces and the path of runoff they generate	Where large amounts of water are delivered during rain events, soils are vulnerable to erosion. Adjacent soils may suggest opportunities for stormwater capture.
Ponding, slow drainage, wetland plants	In less disturbed sites, slow drainage may be associated with special soils and plant communities. In disturbed sites, ponding can indicate areas of compacted soil, poor internal drainage, or both.

In urban areas, sites are often cut off from natural water sources and rely on pipes to bring water to and from the site. When the site is separate from any watershed, it is important to understand the system by which water is transported onsite. It is important to have a recent topographic survey of the site for understanding and mapping the site hydrology and to understand necessary soil volume and conditions. Older topographic maps may not be up to date, but comparing older surveys to a new survey can show if and how the topography of the site has changed over time, providing valuable insight into soil disturbance patterns.

Mapping and Planning Soils Data Collection

After working through the previous sections, the "lay of the land" as far as soils are concerned should be apparent. The next step is to bring this information together by mapping it on a plan. The goal in this first level of the soil assessment is to classify distinct areas of the site and thus lay the foundation for preliminary design work and planning, and for formulating a soil sampling plan. Soils should be classified based on both current condition and eventual use. To help identify these groups, look for conditions that likely coincide with different soil conditions, such as:

▶ Historical change in management, development, or land use

▶ Differences in soil type including imported soil

▶ Differences in soil maintenance/management

▶ Areas of vehicular and pedestrian traffic

▶ Location of and differences in plant growth/plant type

▶ Areas near sidewalks, parking lots and buildings

▶ Areas treated with de-icing salts/not treated areas

▶ Eroded/noneroded areas

▶ Differences in slope

▶ Wet/dry areas

▶ Rock outcrops or ledges

▶ Watersheds

This is far from an exhaustive list, but it is a good starting place. The initial site investigation is like a bit of detective work, looking for clues about the land. Use this information to map both general soil categories on the site and areas within those categories where one might expect to find changes in soil characteristics. A good time to do preliminary site planning is after general soil areas and conditions are outlined, but before a detailed soil sampling plan is made. Maintaining flexibility in the design process makes achieving a sustainable site more likely. The process must be iterative, not linear, in order to be successful.

Step 1: Classify soils into general categories (refer to Table 5-1)

▶ Healthy soils—preservation is highly desirable

▶ Minimally disturbed soils—some restoration may be required

▶ Moderately disturbed soils—restoration may be required

▶ Severely disturbed soils—major restoration and/or consulting experts may be required

▸ No soils, or buried soils—major restoration or reintroduction of soils may be required, or may be suitable building sites

▸ Not applicable—existing building or other use that will remain

Step 2: Identify locations within those categories where soil characteristics may be expected to shift or special characteristics are likely

▸ Locations where pH may be elevated

▸ Where soils may be more compacted

▸ Where drainage may shift

▸ Where soils are vulnerable to erosion or compaction

▸ Where soils may be deeper or shallower from natural topography or grading

▸ Where soils may be contaminated

TYPES OF MAPS AND MAP OVERLAYS

Soil survey maps are just that, surveys. They can help to identify site conditions and shifts in soil series. However, on urban sites they may provide little information. Even on greenfield sites, localized disturbances will result in soils that have been compacted, modified, moved around, or taken offsite. Therefore, although these maps may be helpful in understanding past conditions of the site and characteristics of underlying soil, soil testing must be done to know what the existing conditions are.

For USDA soil maps go to:

▸ U.S. Department of Agriculture (USDA), National Resource Conservation Service (NRCS) Soils website

▸ U.S. Department of Agriculture (USDA), National Resource Conservation Service (NRCS) Web Soil Survey

NEXT STEPS

From the information gathered about soils during this first level of site assessment, choices can be made about where to take soil samples and what areas might require modification or protection. This is also the time to combine soils information with other components of the site assessment for preliminary design and planning.

Keep in mind, however, that this is just the first cut in the soils site assessment, much more detailed information will be required to progress in the planning and design of a sustainable site. The next section goes into detail about not only conducting soil tests but, just as importantly, deciding where to sample. A truly informative soils assessment depends not so much on the number of samples taken, but the logic of the sampling design. This assessment will be a reliable foundation for a sustainable soils management plan (Figure 5-6).

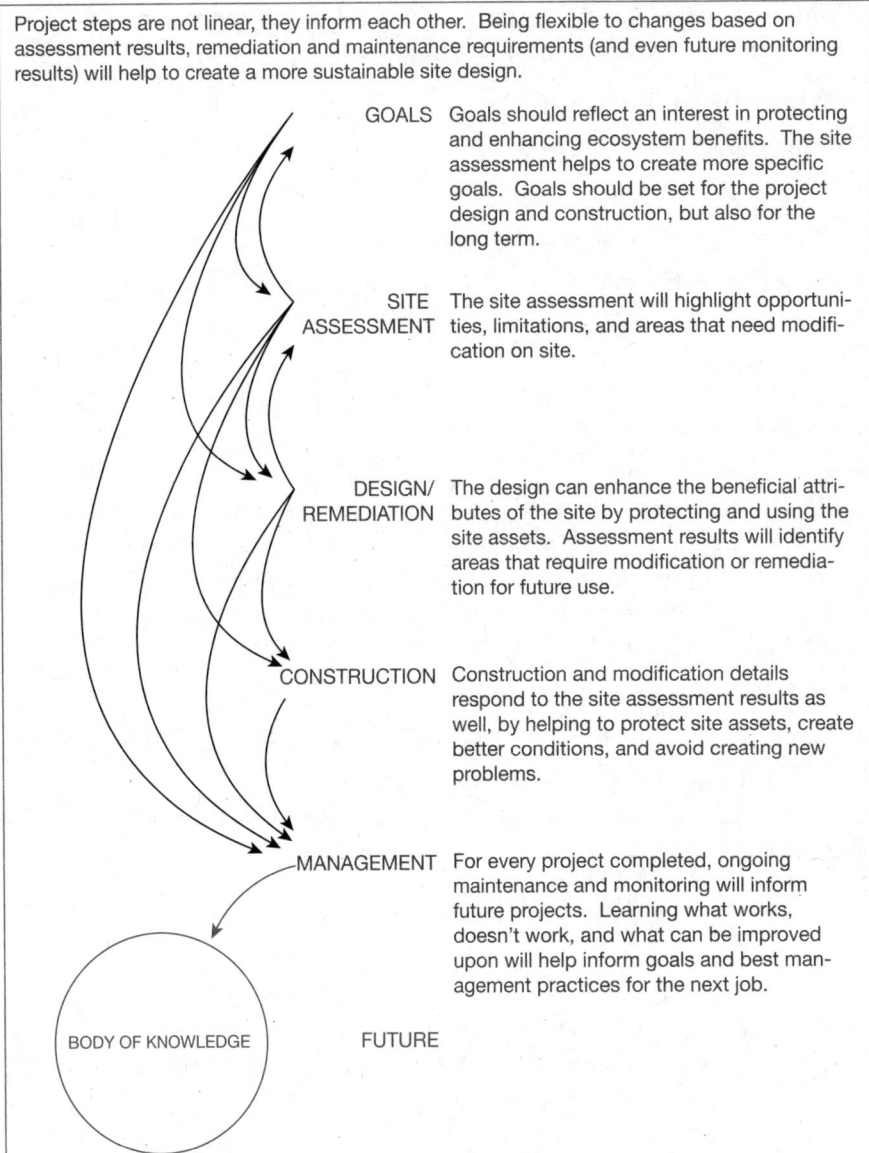

Project steps are not linear, they inform each other. Being flexible to changes based on assessment results, remediation and maintenance requirements (and even future monitoring results) will help to create a more sustainable site design.

GOALS   Goals should reflect an interest in protecting and enhancing ecosystem benefits. The site assessment helps to create more specific goals. Goals should be set for the project design and construction, but also for the long term.

SITE ASSESSMENT   The site assessment will highlight opportunities, limitations, and areas that need modification on site.

DESIGN/ REMEDIATION   The design can enhance the beneficial attributes of the site by protecting and using the site assets. Assessment results will identify areas that require modification or remediation for future use.

CONSTRUCTION   Construction and modification details respond to the site assessment results as well, by helping to protect site assets, create better conditions, and avoid creating new problems.

MANAGEMENT   For every project completed, ongoing maintenance and monitoring will inform future projects. Learning what works, doesn't work, and what can be improved upon will help inform goals and best management practices for the next job.

BODY OF KNOWLEDGE   FUTURE

(Adapted by John Wiley & Sons from drawings by Hannah Carlson)

FIGURE 5-6: A decision flow chart showing the iterative process where project goals are informed by soils information in the site assessment and vice versa.

Designing a Sampling and Data-Collection Scheme

The preliminary site assessment—based on topographic maps, soil surveys, historical information, conversations with landowners and visitors, and the essential site visit—should by now be translated into a plan or plan overlays as described in the previous section, "Mapping and Planning Soils Data Collection." Soil samples should be taken throughout the site where site analyses show potential differences in the soil. Preference of sample locations should be given to areas in need of remediation, preservation, or, if known, planting sites. Thus, at this point, depending on the complexity of the site and design, one of two situations will present themselves. They are detailed in Table 5-5.

TABLE 5-5: Potential Soil Sampling Sitautions

SITUATION A	SITUATION B
The site analysis has progressed sufficiently to allow preliminary design decisions concerning land use and placement of vegetative, hardscape, and building elements. This is typical only on a relatively small or uncomplicated site where there has been the opportunity to walk the entire property and take some preliminary measurements with a penetrometer, dig a few exploratory samples with a shovel snd observe telltale signs of former planting beds, changes in turf quality, or other signs of past activity. If the status is like Situation A, it is time to create a detailed soils sampling plan to complete the pre–site modification assessment.	Maps of where one *expects* to find the elements described in "Mapping and Planning Soils Data Collection" are complete, but the entire site has not been walked or observed in detail. This is typical of a large or complex site. Preliminary design decisions can be made at a coarse scale only, such as approximate building or trail placement. Even these will have to be revisited one or more times as site information emerges. If the status is like Situation B, make an intermediate sample plan to answer particular questions that will inform the design and bring the project to the level of Situation A.

This chapter focuses primarily on Situation A, where the assessment is already honing in on the site details. Each of the soil tests and investigations discussed in the following sections describes how to select sampling sites and perform these tests in this context. However, Situation B is worth considering in a little more detail. Following are some examples where additional information is necessary before a detailed sampling plan can be made. Most situations are likely to be more complex and involve information well beyond soils.

▶ The site is a forested greenfield and a visitors' center will be placed on the site. Additional information about tree condition, cover type, and the presence of significant or unusual trees and other plants is needed to make preliminary decisions about the visitors' center. If only one section of the property is to be disturbed or planted, the detailed site assessment will focus there. It is clearly inefficient to sample with equal intensity over the entire site.

▶ A possible wetland has been observed on the site. Delineate the wetland accurately before proceeding to detailed soils assessments. Keep in mind that a skilled professional is required to properly delineate wetlands, including the required setbacks. Every state defines wetlands differently, usually by soil type, the presence of water, and/or plant specifics.

▶ In walking the site, an area of struggling vegetation was observed. This might be a good location for a parking lot, or if the plants are of significance, this may be an area to remediate the soils to improve plant health. Either way, more information is needed. In this case, soils sampling and more digging (literally) for information should be undertaken related to this specific location before a detailed sampling plan can be devised.

▶ There is an old unpaved haul road in the forest, and the absence of plants on the road points to potentially compacted conditions. Consideration should be given as to whether this road could be used for circulation but more data is needed to determine if the soil is stable and suitable for supporting paving. Samples from several portions of the road can give a quick assessment of whether this is a worthy material for this use.

THE SAMPLING PLAN

The principles of soil sampling are quite simple. Sampling plans should meet these criteria, regardless of whether the areas are man-made, naturally occurring, or both:

▶ Samples should be representative of the location being characterized.

▶ Soil should not be combined across disparate areas to create a composite sample.

These criteria can seem contradictory. On the one hand, if a representative sample of a similarly characterized area is needed, many small soil samples should be taken then combined and mixed into a composite sample and a portion of that extracted for testing. This prevents error introduced by chance selection of a portion of soil that is different from the whole. The likelihood of error can be very high since some soil tests use very small amounts of soil and soil is heterogeneous. On the other hand, soil samples should not be combined if there may be location-related differences that should be mapped separately.

As an example, suppose that soil pH is to be documented for a courtyard surrounded by a concrete walkway. If the sampling plan designer is ignorant of the pH-raising properties of concrete walkways and their subgrades, he or she might reasonably take 10 soil samples ranged across the courtyard and create a composite sample. Then a sample is extracted and pH measured at 7.0. The resulting data very likely will not accurately depict the soil pH for the courtyard and may lead to plant choices or soil modifications that are inappropriate or unnecessary. This is because the areas within 2 to 3 meters of the walkway likely have a greatly elevated pH compared to the interior of the courtyard. Thus imagine that the pH within 2 meters of the walkway is 8.1 and the center of the courtyard is 6.4. Characterizing the entire courtyard as having a pH of 7.0 will lead to incorrect management decisions for the entire courtyard.

Identifying where such differences might lie is an essential component of creating a soil sampling plan. Learn to identify clues indicating where and how much soil characteristics might shift in the landscape. Good sampling plan design relies on an understanding of the variability of the characteristic being measured. Skill in identification of such nuances improves with experience. Fortunately, there are many quick, approximate, field tests that can assist the novice. In the above example, the novice can take quick field tests of pH (no sample mixing, just informal checks with a pH meter) to help gauge the location and degree of soil pH variation (Figure 5-7).

Sometimes soil sampling reveals unexpected conditions. In such cases, other soil samples should be taken in the area to confirm the findings and define the scope of the newfound conditions. This is part of the iterative process of the site assessment. The number of samples to be taken depends on the scale of the project site as well as the variety of conditions found during assessment. Increasing the number of samples can increase the confidence with which conclusions can be drawn. Guidelines on variability are provided with each characteristic in the following discussion.

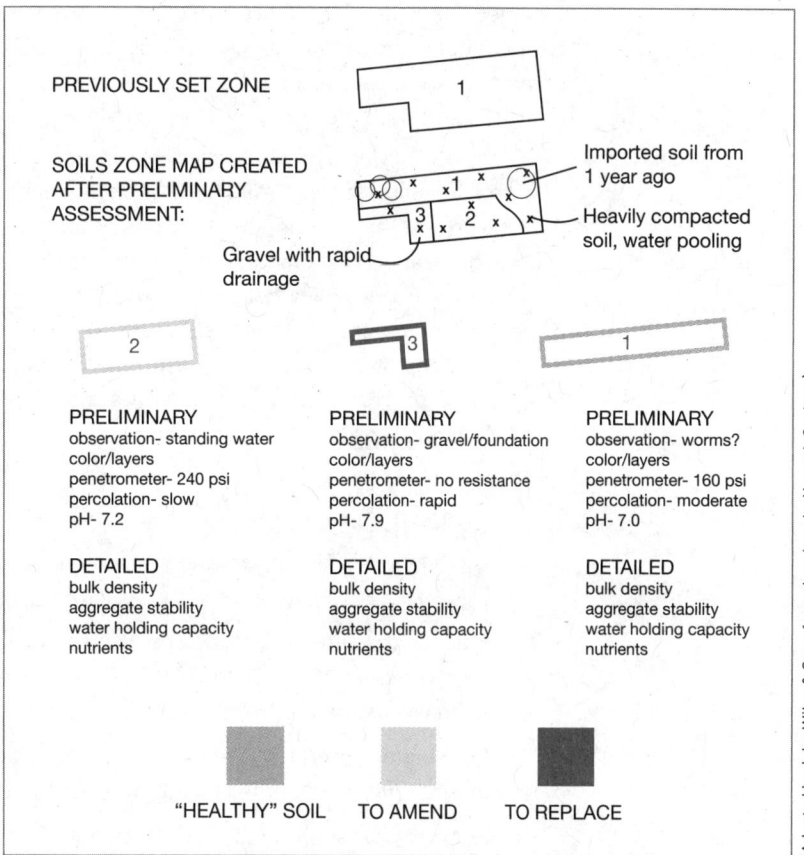

(Adapted by John Wiley & Sons from drawings by Hannah Carlson)

FIGURE 5-7: Schematic of a soil sampling plan for basic physical and chemical characteristics based on preliminary analysis and mapping. Three distinct areas were identified, and sampling is designed to characterize each zone.

THE SOIL SAMPLE

Many of the soil tests described in the following sections can be done in the field. Reliability depends on disciplined sample selection and accurate equipment and procedures, whether the test is conducted in the field or in the lab. When sending samples to a commercial lab, look for a reputable lab that will interpret the results. A lab should offer horticultural soil testing. Some labs test soils for engineering purposes and may not have the correct sieve cluster or perform all the required tests. Existing standardized tests are listed at the end of each test description.

These instructions are generally for taking a soil sample for the formal data collection, whether one completes the test in the field or sends it to a lab. Make sure to assign a number to and label samples with their exact location, and track soil sample locations and numbers on a plan. For example, samples taken from a courtyard might be labeled as C-1, C-2, and so forth. If using a lab, be sure that they use this same designation on the test results.

For tests completed in the field, perform at least one test in each soil sample zone. Record all results on a site map/data sheet for each test. When analysis will be performed by a lab, follow the handling instructions of that particular lab. Different tests may require slightly different soil sampling steps. At a minimum, take a composite sample in each soil sampling zone, but only where it is clear that soil conditions are relatively uniform. However, depending on the lab and the tests to be performed, multiple samples in each soil sampling zone may need to be collected and sent. In this case, keep the samples separate and do not mix them so that it is possible to compare the results of the different sites later on if desired. The following steps are adapted from the Cornell University Soil Health Manual (Gugino et al, 2009):

1. Scrape off the surface debris such as mulch or grass until soil layer is reached.

2. Dig a hole to desired depth of potential planting or other depth of interest.

3. Remove a slice of soil with a shovel or a spade about 2 cm thick from the side of the hole, so the sample includes the depth range of interest. This depth range should not be more than 20 cm (8 in.). Alternatively, use a metal push tube to extract a sample from the desired depth.

4. For single samples: Without handling the sample too much so that aggregates remain intact, gently place the soil into the sample container. Do not mix up soil.

5. For composite samples: Repeat sampling procedure in six to ten locations in the desired area and place in a bucket (only one depth range at a time). Thoroughly mix the samples while still being careful not to destroy soil aggregates. Extract sufficient

soil for a sample and place into the sample container (usually .25 L is enough, but follow instructions of the soil analysis laboratory).

6. Keep samples out of direct sunlight; store samples in refrigerator or cold room until analyzed. Never collect wet or frozen soil. The importance of storage and handling will depend on the test being performed.

SOIL CHARACTERISTICS AND ASSOCIATED TESTS

This section describes characteristics of soils and the tests that should be performed to define these characteristics. Each test description explains the importance of the test, the possible results, and what the results mean. The next section on design lists ways to modify the conditions of the soil based on the test results. When there is more than one option for a test, a choice should be made as to which test to conduct, or more than one type of test could be performed to double check the results. The tests are written as if one sample were being used and do not include sample collection unless it is an integral part of the test. Make sure to have enough materials and follow the instructions for each soil sample to be taken.

Soil Texture

Knowing a soil's texture is important to understand the results of most of the tests in this chapter. Particles of sand, silt, and clay give a soil its texture. The three types of particles are divided according to their size—sand being the largest particle and clay being the smallest. Convention uses this particle size analysis to place soils into textural classes based on the percentages of sand, silt, and clay in the soil. The texture of a soil influences its structural properties as well as the capacity of the soil to hold and drain water. For example, water drains more quickly in sand soil while clay soil holds water for longer. The textural classes were designed to describe the way a soil behaves—its predominant properties. Note, for example, the relative size of the area indicating clay and sand textural classes (Figure 5-8). The clay textural class is much larger, because a relatively smaller amount of clay has a larger effect on the way a soil behaves. Thus a soil with only 20 percent clay particles can still be classified as a clay soil, because the characteristics of the clay (high nutrient- and water-holding capacity, ability to form structure, compactability, ability to bind organic matter, and so forth) predominate (Figure 5-8). Soil samples can be sent to a lab for a detailed particle size analysis. Results typically report percentages of sand, silt, and clay. Labs may also further subdivide sand based on coarseness. For site assessment purposes and understanding existing soils, quick field tests are extremely useful (Table 5-6; Figures 5-9, 5-10, 5-11, 5-12).

Soil texture affects:

▶ Drainage

▶ Water-holding capacity

▶ Compactability/porosity

▶ Fertility

▶ Which plants will grow successfully

▶ Interpretation of compaction tests

▶ Calculations for modifying soil pH and remediating compacted soils

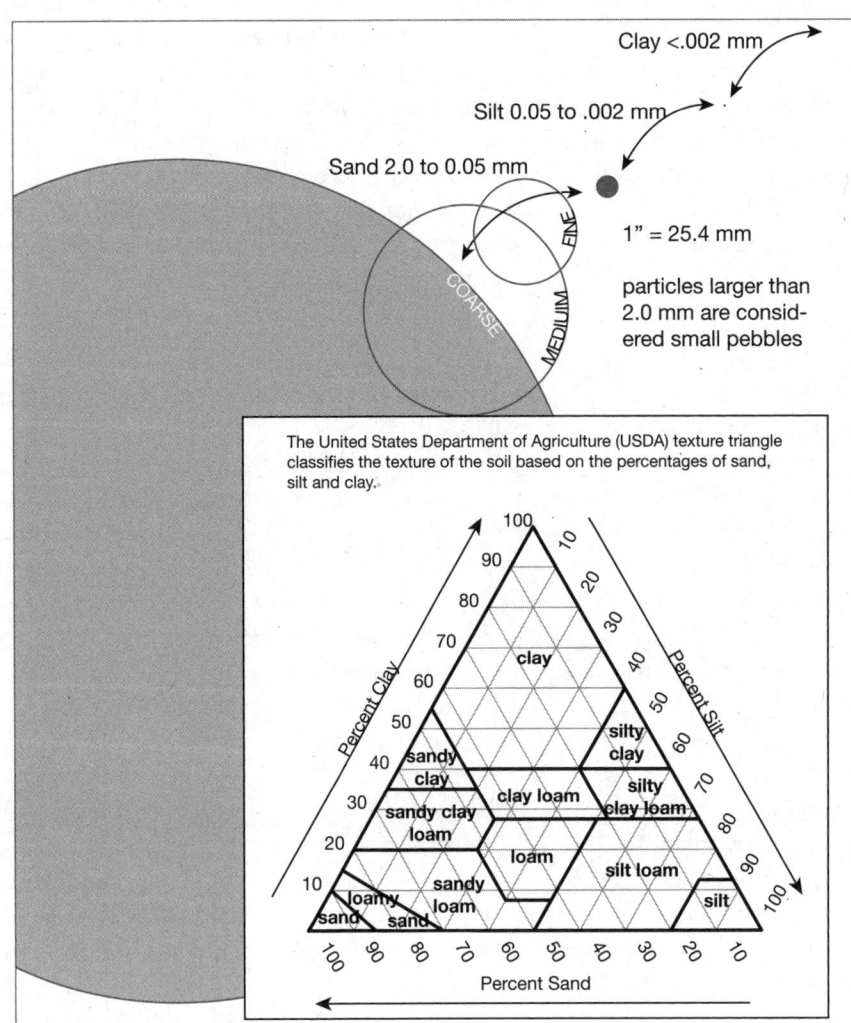

Clay <.002 mm

Silt 0.05 to .002 mm

Sand 2.0 to 0.05 mm

1" = 25.4 mm

particles larger than 2.0 mm are considered small pebbles

The United States Department of Agriculture (USDA) texture triangle classifies the texture of the soil based on the percentages of sand, silt and clay.

FIGURE 5-8: The USDA soil texture triangle represents the soil textural classes based on the percentages of sand, silt, and clay. For example, a soil with 40 percent sand, 35 percent clay, and 25 percent silt is classified as a "clay loam." Note that although there is a higher percentage of sand than of clay in this soil, the characteristics of clay predominate and the soil is therefore classified as a clay loam.

[Adapted by John Wiley & Sons from drawings by Hannah Carlson]

TABLE 5-6: Soil Texture: Texture-by-Feel Method

Materials Needed	Water
	Towel or a place to clean hands
Procedure	Knead a small handful of soil with just enough water so it sticks together (Figure 5-9).
	Form a ribbon (Figure 5-10) with the soil and record its length as described in the texture-by-feel flow chart (Figure 5-11).
	Discard the majority of the soil, retaining approximately a teaspoon or less in the palm of the hand. Wet it past saturation (Figure 5-12).
	Rub the soil in the palm, following the flow chart directives (Figure 5-11).
	The flow chart should indicate a soil textural class.
Pros	Accurately indicates textural class when performed by operator with minimal experience. Can be performed quickly in the field.
Cons	Only indicates the textural class, and is less reliable as an indication of position within the textural class. This may limit use for determining MABDs.
Use Recommendations	Recommended for preliminary site assessment and interpretation of past disturbance. Other methods exist for estimating texture, such as the mason jar method. For a precise analysis, however, soils should be sent to a lab.

(Photo from Nina Bassuk)

FIGURE 5-9: A kneaded clump of moistened soil ready for analysis by texture-by-feel.

(Photo from Nina Bassuk)

FIGURE 5-10: To form the "ribbon" for texture-by-feel, gently push the soil over the index finger with the thumb. A well-kneaded sample facilitates forming the ribbon.

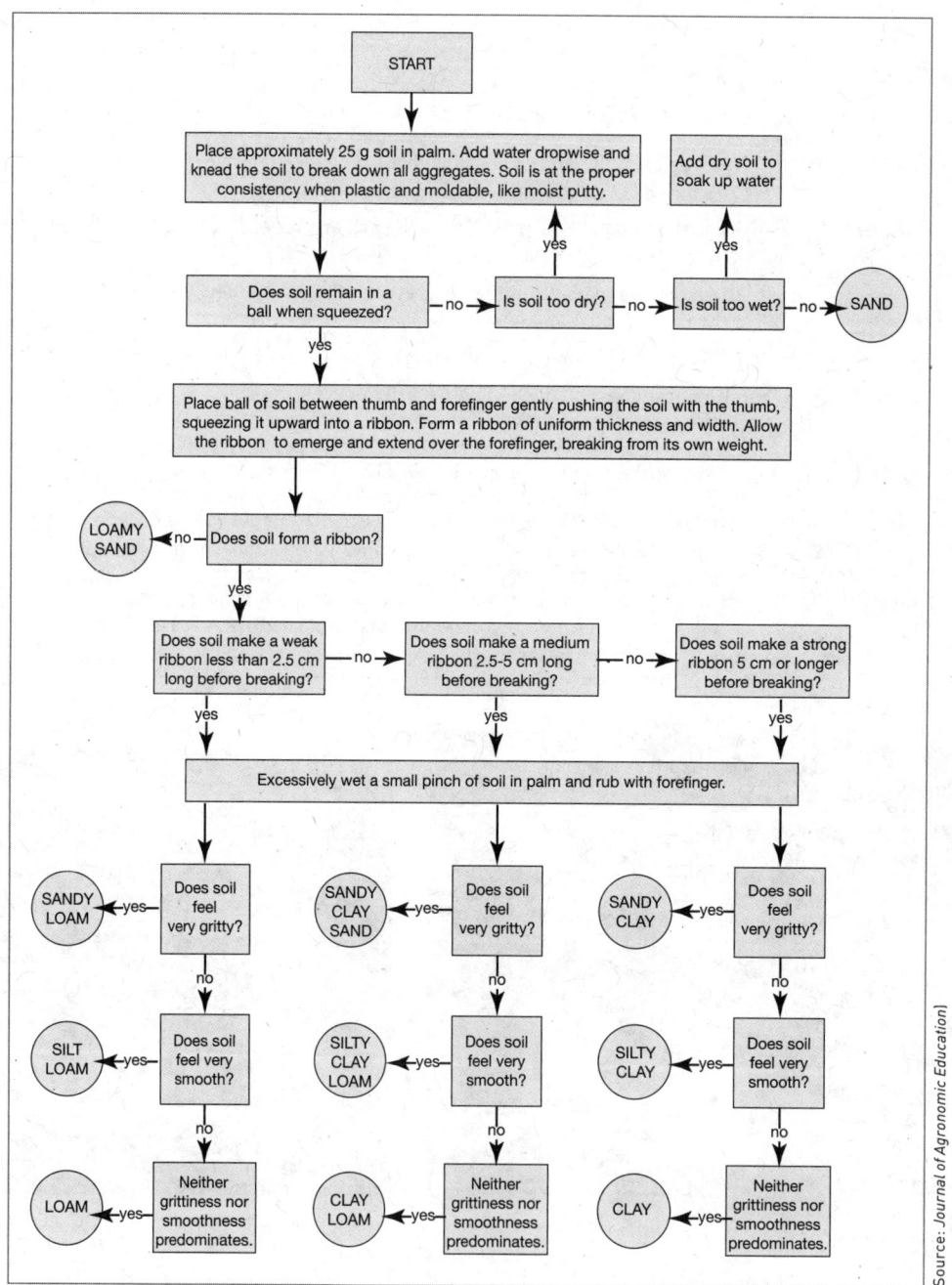

(Source: *Journal of Agronomic Education*)

FIGURE 5–11: The texture-by-feel decision flow chart. Following this chart produces a surprisingly accurate measure of soil textural class. Chart reproduced from the USDA and is modified from S.J. Thien, 1979. A flow diagram for teaching texture-by-feel analysis.

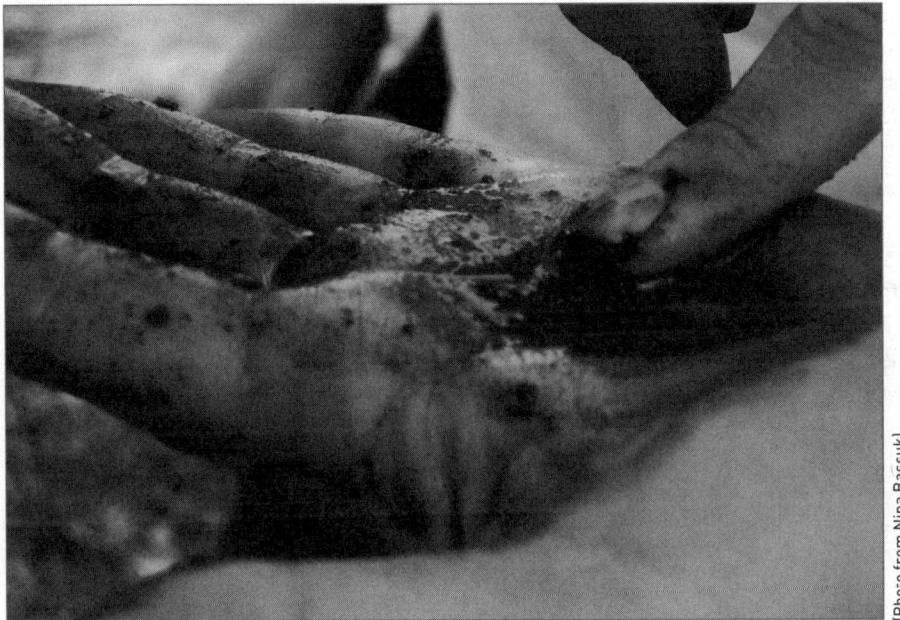

(Photo from Nina Bassuk)

FIGURE 5-12: Rubbing excessively wet soil in the palm of the hand is the final step of the texture-by-feel analysis.

STANDARDS RELATING TO SOIL TEXTURE

▶ ASTM D422–63(2007), Standard Test Method for Particle-Size Analysis of Soils

▶ ASTM D 2487, Unified Soil Classification System—The Texture by Sieve Test

INTERPRETING SOIL TEXTURE

The different mineral fractions of a soil (i.e., sand, silt, and clay) have very different properties. Sand particles are very large compared to the others, while clays can be microscopic. Thus clays will have vastly greater surface areas and retain more water. Clays also have special properties: They tend to be negatively charged (and thus hold nutrients, but also resist changes in soil pH), and they have binding properties that promote soil structure formation and carbon retention. The texture of the soil also relates to bulk density. Bulk density is the dry weight of soil in a given volume, a measure of soil compaction. Bulk density is typically expressed as $g\ cm^{-3}$, but also g cc or $Mg\ m^{-3}$. These units have a 1:1 conversion and can be used interchangeably. Finer-textured soils (i.e., more clays and silts and less sand) tend to have lower bulk densities in their healthy states. This is clearly illustrated by viewing the typical bulk density (gathered from a survey of thousands of agricultural and forested soils) of a particular soil texture, accessed by clicking on the soil textural triangle at this interactive website: www.pedosphere.com/resources/bulkdensity/triangle_us.cfm. Thus, soil texture is necessary for interpreting many of the other soil characteristics and for specifying soil modification and rehabilitation. Altering soil texture is generally not desirable for a sustainable site. Understanding the existing textural characteristics instead informs modifications intended to affect properties such as soil structure, drainage, pH, and more. Note that there is a large variation of particle sizes within the sand component of a soil. When replacement soils are required, the soil particle size analysis is typically more precisely specified to include particular grades of sand. (See "Specifying Replacement Soils" later in the chapter for more information.)

MAPPING SOIL TEXTURE

Creating a site map of the various soil textures will, when combined with other site and design information, help determine what areas should be protected or have potential for modification relevant to the design and suitability for planting. Modifying soil texture itself typically requires large inputs and rarely achieves desired results. The most productive soils cannot be "mixed" on demand, since their desirable characteristics usually depend on soil structure and biological activity, qualities that must be developed within the soil itself. Thus, if possible, the design should respond to the existing soil textures, instead of trying to replace or amend them.

Soil Organic Matter

Organic matter comes from living organisms and can be either living or dead material. Examples include compost, leaf litter, and manure. Organic matter is a food source for microorganisms that break down the compounds creating available nutrients, increased humus which stores nutrients, and sticky substances that help soil aggregation (Figure 5-13).

Essential to soil health, organic matter contributes to soil structure, water infiltration, water-holding capacity, available nutrients, nutrient retention, microbial activity, and the buildup of new soil. The top 30 cm (12 in.) of most healthy soils in temperate regions should contain 3 to 5 percent of organic matter. Some soils may naturally have very high organic matter contents (e.g., wetlands), while others may have very low levels. In such cases, identifying an appropriate healthy "reference" soil is especially helpful for making appropriate soil management decisions. A high percentage of organic matter in certain areas may make the soil more compressible and susceptible to compaction. This is not suitable for high-traffic areas.

Soil organic matter affects:

▶ Soil structure

▶ Compactability

▶ Nutrient-holding capacity

▶ Potential for rebuilding structure over time

▶ Soil biological activity

▶ Nutrient cycling

▶ Water-holding capacity

TESTING SOIL ORGANIC MATTER

Some information concerning organic matter can be derived simply by visual inspection, with darker coloring generally indicating more organic matter. A Munsell® Soil Color Chart can enhance the consistency of visual inspection. However, a laboratory test is required to accurately quantify soil organic matter content. In addition, soil samples will immediately begin to lose organic matter upon collection and should be stored in a refrigerator (at approximately 4° C) and tested within four weeks. Many options for testing soil organic matter are available, each with their strengths and limitations (Table 5-7).

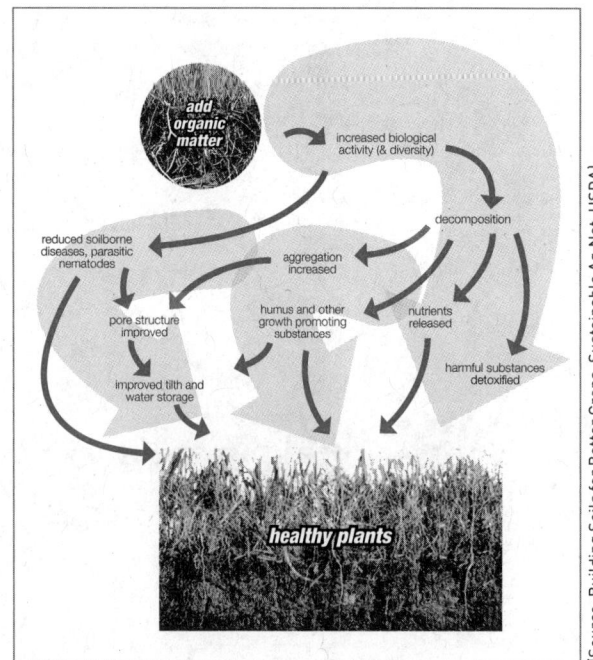

FIGURE 5-13: The fate of organic matter inputs into soils. Organic matter is key to soil health and requires ongoing inputs to sustain biological activity. In addition to intentional additions of organic materials such as compost, organic inputs can come from a variety of sources including fallen leaves, root turnover, root exudates, microbes, arthropods, and other creatures.

(Source: Building Soils for Better Crops. Sustainable Ag.Net. USDA)

TABLE 5-7: Comparison of Methods for Determining Soil Organic Matter Content

METHOD: LOSS ON IGNITION (LOI)	
How it works	LOI tests involve heating soils at a high temperature such that organic carbon is burned off but inorganic carbon is mostly not. Then, after application of a correction factor, the weight of the carbon lost is determined by subtraction.
Pros	A straightforward, inexpensive, and commonly available lab test. It is sufficiently accurate for site assessment.
Cons	May somewhat overestimate organic carbon in clay soils or soils with high carbonates. Reliability diminishes when soils have very low organic carbon.

continues

TABLE 5-7: Comparison of Methods for Determining Soil Organic Matter Content *(continued)*

METHOD: WALKLEY-BLACK PROCEDURE	
How it works	After inorganic carbonates are removed with an acid, organic carbon is removed via wet oxidation. Newer "modified" Walkley-Black procedures are generally more accurate and are commonly used.
Pros	More involved than LOI, but still a rapid, inexpensive, and commonly available lab test. More accurate than LOI.
Cons	Requires the use of potentially hazardous reagents. Incomplete oxidation of organic carbon may occur, and additional procedures and/or correction factors are needed to compensate for this.
METHOD: DRY COMBUSTION	
How it works	After complete removal of inorganic carbonates, soil is heated to extremely high temperatures to ensure combustion of all carbon. Carbon loss may be estimated by weighing, but, more typically, evolved gases are analyzed via spectrophotometry. There are numerous variations on this method, the most accurate being the automated approaches with pretreatment of samples to remove inorganic carbon.
Pros	Probably the most accurate method available.
Cons	Expensive. Requires specialized and extremely expensive equipment.

STANDARDS RELATING TO ORGANIC MATTER

▸ ASTM D2974, Test Methods for Moisture, Ash, and Organic Matter of Peat and Other Organic Soils

▸ TMECC 05.07A, Loss-on-Ignition Organic Matter Method

INTERPRETING SOIL ORGANIC MATTER

In many soils, less than 3 to 5 percent of organic matter suggests problems with soil structure and water-holding capacity. Without organic matter there can be poor aggregate stability, low water-holding capacity, poor drainage, and few available nutrients. Plants may be more reliant on fertilizer inputs for nitrogen sources. Organic soil amendments, such as compost, are thus frequently specified to address these problems initially. Building soil structure and stable organic matter requires time, however, and is also influenced by the type of organic amendment. If there is an overabundance of particular types of organic matter, such as manure or sludge, then excess nitrogen or phosphorus can harm plants and leach into water, becoming an environmental hazard. Another concern relating to manure or sludge is a potentially high salt content that can be toxic to plants. The results from the organic matter test should be compared with results from other physical assessment tests before final decisions can be made on remediation. The big picture should be considered for soil organic matter, such as where organic inputs will come from when the site is complete and if the inputs and decomposition rate will create a sustainable system.

MAINTAINING SOIL ORGANIC MATTER CONTENT

If soil organic matter is lower than optimal in comparison to reference soils or other healthy soil benchmarks, it is essential to reflect on the reasons for this. Otherwise, even if organic matter is provided initially, it may rapidly decompose and the situation revert to its former state. Soil organic matter content is simply a question of inputs, storage, and losses. Understanding these will help form a framework explaining how carbon cycles through the system (Figure 5-14) (see Table 5-8).

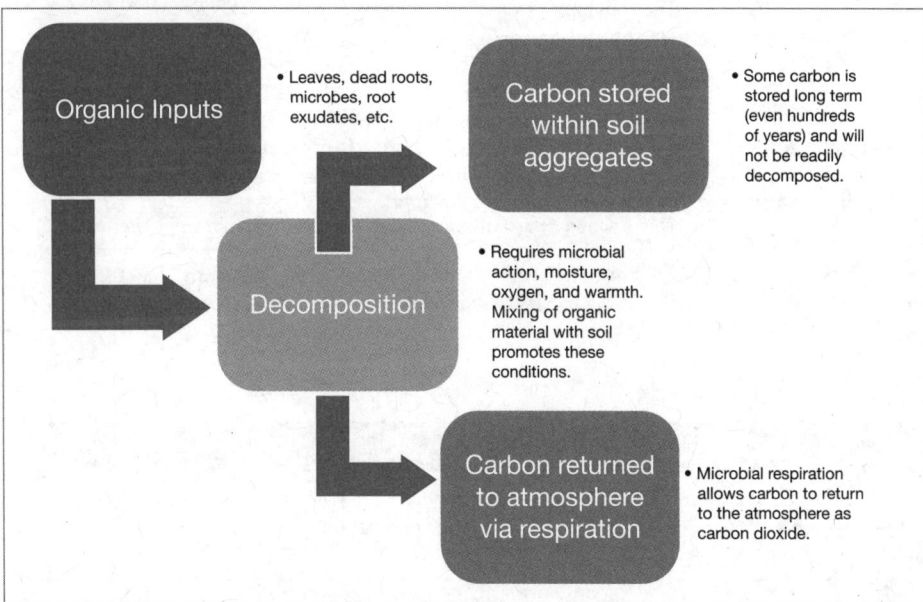

FIGURE 5-14: Understanding the carbon cycle in soil can assist in creating a balanced and sustainable soil organic matter. Note that carbon can have greatly varying residence times in the soil, from a few weeks to many hundreds of years.

TABLE 5-8: Sources and Characteristics of Inputs, Storage, and Losses of Organic Carbon in Soils

INPUTS TO ORGANIC CARBON IN SOILS

TYPES	COMMENTS
Leaves	Both evergreen and deciduous plants shed leaves each year.
Root turnover	Some fine roots live only a few weeks and then new roots take their place.
Microorganisms	Populations wax and wane, and secretions also contribute to organic matter.
Macro-invertebrates	Also affect soil structure through mechanical activity
Soil amendments	Compost, manure, biosolids, and so forth

Note: The physical action of many of these sources (roots, organisms) accelerates decomposition and incorporation of organic matter into the soil.

STORAGE OF ORGANIC CARBON IN SOILS

TYPES	COMMENTS
Free organic matter	The most active organic matter that may quickly decompose. May be recognizable as a nonmineral soil component. Residence time is affected by degree of incorporation into the soil and environmental conditions.
Protected within aggregates	Carbon stored within aggregates is protected from further decomposition and may have a residence time of decades.
Bound to soil minerals	This carbon may remain resident for many hundreds of years.

Note: The decomposition process is enhanced by greater surface area contact, warmth, moisture, and air. Thus shredded leaves mixed into the soil will decompose much more rapidly than whole leaves on the surface.

LOSSES OF ORGANIC CARBON IN SOILS

TYPES	COMMENTS
Release of CO_2 to the atmosphere from microbial respiration	Microbes decompose carbon, and when they use this for energy, they release CO_2 through respiration.

Note: Soil can store extremely large amounts of carbon, but carbon is also readily released to the atmosphere from decomposition. Grading, tilling, and other soil disturbance can bring elements in contact with each other in new ways, resulting in a large flux of CO_2 into the atmosphere.

Soil Structure

Soil structure is the arrangement of soil particles into aggregates (peds) or other formations and is closely associated with organic matter content. Small particles of clay and organic matter act as binding agents that form particles into aggregates in the soil. Larger spaces, such as those in between the aggregates, are macropores that allow air and water infiltration and drainage. Smaller micropores inside the aggregates help to retain water in the soil through the forces of adhesion and cohesion. When a soil is well structured, it can have the desirable drainage characteristics created by sufficient macropores as well as the water-holding capacity conferred by the micropores. Soil structure takes a long time to build and is very easily destroyed by grading, excavation, foot or vehicular traffic, or other disturbance.

Soils with more clays and more organic matter content have a greater potential to build structure. Promoting and protecting soil structure is critical to a sustainable site, especially in fine-textured soils. Soil structure is a qualitative measurement, but there are numerous quantitative measures that indirectly characterize soil structure. These include aggregate stability, drainage, and compaction.

Soil structure affects:

▶ Drainage

▶ Water-holding capacity

▶ Biological activity

▶ Aeration

▶ Organic matter retention

AGGREGATE STABILITY

Aggregate stability is a measure of the capacity of soil aggregates to resist falling apart when disrupted by water, wind, or other forces. Unstable aggregates can form a soil crust which blocks water infiltration, increasing the runoff and erodibility of the soil. Mulches can provide some protection to aggregates, but overall aggregate stability determines if the soil can retain its structure when exposed to flowing water—it will resist forming a crust or eroding. This structure provides air and water movement, biological activity, nutrient cycling, root growth, and the preservation of organic matter in the soil (Figure 5-15).

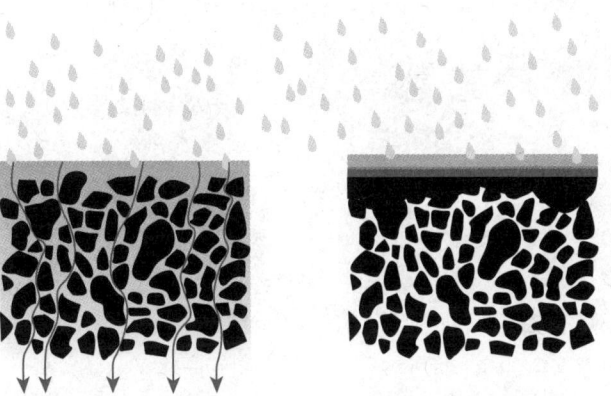

FIGURE 5-15: The aggregates at the surface of the soil on the right have broken apart, reducing pore space and thus blocking water movement into the soil.

(Adapted by John Wiley & Sons from drawings by Hannah Carlson)

SOIL COMPACTION

More than any other physical attribute, highly compacted soils will limit plant growth. In a nutshell, compacted soils have been compressed and their structure has been damaged, reducing macro- and micropore space necessary for water infiltration, air exchange, and biological activity. Plant selection alone cannot address the problems created by compacted soils—the soil structure must be rebuilt as far as is possible and conditions for building structure over time must be put in place. Compaction can occur when there is vehicular or pedestrian traffic, especially when the soil is wet. Mixing, grading, cutting the soil, and other construction techniques are also typical sources of compaction that will persist if not addressed.

(Photo from Nina Bassuk)

FIGURE 5-16: An inexpensive soil cone penetrometer. Wider cone tips are fitted on the rod for softer soils.

Soil compaction affects:

▸ Ability of roots to penetrate soil (mechanical impedance)

▸ Drainage (and thus aeration)

▸ Water-holding capacity

▸ Biological activity

▸ Organic matter retention

▸ Susceptibility of plants to drought

▸ What plants will grow and their ultimate size and health

TESTING SOIL COMPACTION

There are two basic approaches to measuring soil compaction. First is evaluating the density of dry soil for a given volume. This is soil bulk density or soil dry bulk density. This provides a static measure of soil compaction for a given soil. Soil texture information is essential for interpreting bulk density. The second approach is to measure soil strength, or resistance to penetration. This is determined by the amount of force required to insert a metal rod in the soil. This measure is dynamic, as the soil strength will change as soil moisture changes. Wetter soils are generally softer; drier soils are harder. Both measures have their advantages and disadvantages, and a combination of both is generally used to characterize a site (Table 5-9) (Figure 5-16).

TABLE 5-9: **Testing Soil Compaction via Soil Strength—Cone Penetrometer**

Materials Needed	A cone penetrometer
	A partner to record data if the penetrometer is not automated (optional)
	A soil moisture meter such as a TDR if absolute comparisons of soil compaction need to be made.
Procedure	Soil moisture: If comparing different parts of a site, penetrometer readings should be done when they are at the same moisture level. It is more difficult to push the penetrometer through the soil when it is dry. Ideally, it is best to take cone penetrometer readings a few days after rain saturates the soil. In such cases a relative measurement is achieved. This is sufficient for exploratory measurements and detecting soil layers. Otherwise, take a simultaneous soil moisture measurement.
	Apply slow, even pressure while pushing the penetrometer vertically into the soil (4 seconds per 6 in. or less). Read the gauge while pushing the penetrometer into the soil. The gauge will indicate the force required in pounds per square inch (psi) or mega- or kilopascals (MPa or kPa). Automated penetrometers will record readings at fixed depth increments.
	Note how far the penetrometer will go into the soil and if there are layers with different readings, for example, hardpans.
	If the penetrometer hits a stone, move the penetrometer to an adjacent area. In very stony soils, this method cannot be used, and the bulk density test should be used instead.
Pros	This method allows a quick measurement of soil compaction and soil depth throughout the site. Hundreds of measurements can be made with little effort, allowing detection of areas where soil compaction changes. Also useful post-soil remediation for quality control. Only an approximate soil texture is needed for interpreting soil strength measurements.
Cons	Must be made when soil is moist. For absolute comparisons to standards or across sites, moisture must be at field capacity or a series of measurements made at different soil moisture levels.
Use Recommendations	The cone penetrometer is ideal for quick measurements on a preliminary site visit and for detecting hardpans, buried pavement, and more. Considerably more information can be gleaned if these measurements are made when soil is neither dry nor wet. Not to be used in rocky or stony soils.

BULK DENSITY (DRY DENSITY)

Bulk density is the weight of dry soil divided by its wet volume, generally expressed as g/cm^3 or occasionally as Mg/m^3. Both units give the same value, so no conversion is necessary. All bulk density tests basically accomplish the same thing: A measurable or known volume of soil is extracted from the site, the soil is dried in an oven at 103 to 105° C until a constant weight is reached. The soil is weighed and the weight is divided by the volume. Rocks and large roots should be excluded from both the weight and volume measurements, so samples without these are preferable. Each site has different characteristics that can make the logistics of one method or another preferable.

Soils of different textures have more or less porosity; therefore, the texture of the soil should be identified to understand the results of the bulk density tests (Table 5-10).

TABLE 5-10: Testing Soil Compaction via Bulk Density—The Undisturbed Core Method

Materials Needed	Soil slide hammer
	At least two sample sleeves. Note: Do not use just one sample sleeve at a time, doing so will result in either an incomplete sample or a compacted sample.
	Aluminum foil
	Soil knife (an old steak knife is ideal)
	Spade or shovel
	Drying oven
	Scale (accurate to 1 g or less)
Procedure	Prepare the sampling site by removing any turf, mulch, or other surface layer with the spade. Excavate to slightly above the desired depth of the sample, keeping the surface close to level.
	Insert the sample sleeves into the core sampler and screw it onto the hammer. Note: The top sleeve must act as a spacer to avoid compaction of the sample.
	Hammer the sampler vertically into the soil until the top of the soil is about midway up the spacer sleeve.
	Remove the core sampler. Be careful rocking the sampler back and forth in hard soils, the joint is easily broken. If extraction is difficult, try digging around the sampler with a spade and/or backing it out of the hole by hammering upward with the slide hammer (Figures 5-17 and 5-18).
	Carefully slide the sample sleeves out and trim the soil flush with the middle or bottom sleeve. Wrap the sleeve and soil in foil to prevent soil loss. Label, and transport to drying oven.
	Dry sample at 105° C for at least 24 hours.
	Weigh the sample, subtracting the weight of the foil and clean sleeve to get a net weight of soil.
	Divide this by the volume of the interior of the sleeve ($\pi r^2 * h$).
Pros	Relatively rapid in surface soils and soils with few obstructions. Can be objectively compared across sites. Provides a single number to report.

Cons	No instantaneous information is available. To measure bulk density at depth, a fairly large hole must be dug to that depth. If there are a lot of rocks or large roots, undisturbed cores may be impossible to extract. Requires soil texture at the depth of interest in order to interpret. Sample size is relatively small, and sloppy trimming or extraction can decrease accuracy.
Use Recommendations	This approach is a standard method for those making regular measurements of soil bulk density but does require some up-front equipment costs. Because of the small sample measured, it is best used in combination with the cone penetrometer, and samples should be collected at multiple depths. Subsamples are also recommended to improve precision. Other methods are also available, such as the plastic wrap method (Lichter and Costello 1994).

(Photos from Rachel M. Layman)

FIGURE 5-17: A soil slide hammer showing three sample sleeves next to the core sampler.

FIGURE 5-18: Once the sample sleeves are fitted inside the core sampler, it is mounted on the hammer and positioned over the area to be sampled. After the soil core is extracted, the center sample sleeve is trimmed with a knife to create an undisturbed sample of a known volume. Some core samplers will only take two sleeves; in that case, the bottom sleeve may be used to prevent compaction by the hammer.

INTERPRETING SOIL COMPACTION

Maintaining uncompacted soils will often be the single most important measure of a highly functioning soil and landscape. From the point of view of growing plants, soil compaction cannot be too low. However, when soils have been disturbed, their stabilizing characteristics will likely be disrupted, and other site demands (supporting foot traffic, pathways, or stabilizing slopes) may call for a minimum level of compaction. In general, any such compaction efforts should be prevented in planting areas if at all possible. Here our discussion will focus on how to interpret soil compaction in terms of promoting plant growth and soil biological and hydrological processes.

Measures of soil compaction must be interpreted carefully. The most reliable measure for objectively comparing soil compaction across sites is the soil bulk density. However, interpreting this measure is impossible without soil texture. Different soil textures have different bulk densities in their uncompacted state. They also have different ranges of possible compaction. Sands, for example, have higher initial bulk densities but are more difficult to compact. They do not have the soil structure and degree of aggregation that clay soils have. The soil texture of the same soil for which bulk density was measured must be known to determine the effect of compaction on root growth. Sandier soils can have a higher bulk density (approximately 1.7 g/cm³) than clayey soils (about 1.3 g/cm³) without severely inhibiting root growth (Figures 5-19 and 5-20).

The Maximum Allowable Bulk Density (MABD) must also be interpreted carefully. Soil below the MABD is not necessarily uncompacted, and roots may still be restricted. In any soil, root growth is increasingly restricted as soil compaction increases. There is no "threshold" level below which roots grow normally. Instead there is a continuum of root restriction—any increase in soil compaction may reduce plant growth. The terms "growth-limiting" or "maximum allowable" bulk density usually describe the upper end of that continuum, where root growth is severely curtailed or even halts altogether.

The penetrometer test measures the depth of usable soil. The higher the psi, the more compacted the soil is. Compacted soils drain poorly, have limited infiltration and low water retention capabilities, and restrict plant growth.

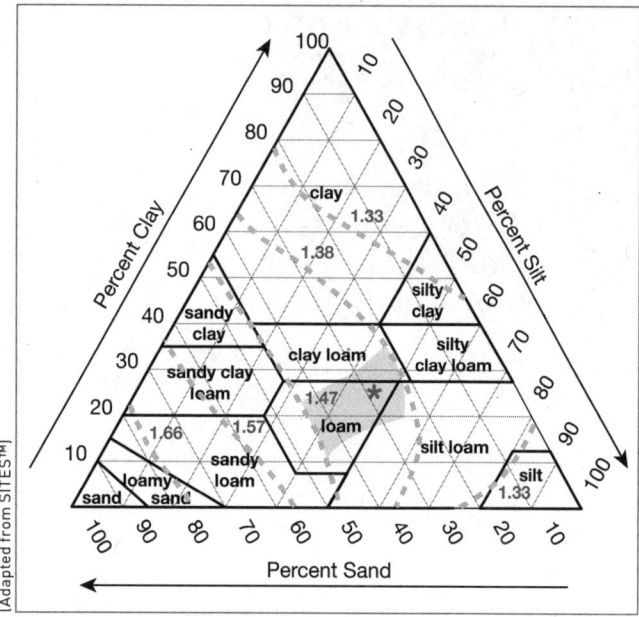

[Adapted from SITES™]

FIGURE 5-19: Soil textural triangle indicating maximum acceptable soil bulk density (MABD) for a given texture. The maximum acceptable bulk density can be interpolated by looking to the values associated with the adjacent dotted lines. In the example soil marked with an asterisk (*), the particle size analysis is 24 percent clay, 46 percent silt, and 30 percent sand. By interpolation across the gray screened area, the maximum allowable bulk density is around 1.42 g/cm³.

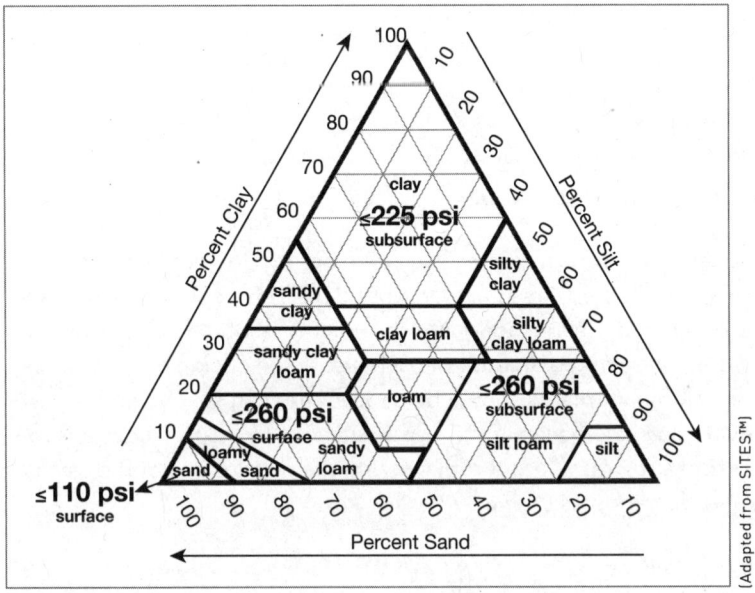

FIGURE 5-20: Soil textural triangle indicating maximum acceptable soil strength. Soil texture influences the compactability; therefore, the acceptable psi varies. For sand, the acceptable psi refers to the surface resistance. For silt and clay, it refers to the subsurface psi.

STANDARDS

- ► ASTM D4564, Standard Test Method for Density and Unit Weight of Soil in Place by the Sleeve Method
- ► ASTM D2167, Standard Test Method for Density and Unit Weight of Soil in Place by the Rubber Balloon Method
- ► ASTM D6938, Standard Test Method for In-Place Density and Water Content of Soil and Soil
- ► ASTM D3441–05, Standard Test Method for Mechanical Cone Penetration Tests of Soil

Soil Volume

Soil volume can be a concern where soils are confined, or bordered by pavements or buildings. Plants need adequate soil resources for roots to explore to acquire water and nutrients.

Soil volume affects:

► Ultimate plant size

► Plant longevity

► Plant health and vigor

► Need for irrigation or supplemental nutrients

Soil volume is most frequently a concern where trees are planted. However, shrubs and other plants can also be similarly affected. Trees are larger and many times longer lived, and thus the concern is most pronounced. Having adequate soil volume is integral to designing a sustainable landscape. If there is a limited amount of usable soil, site design or soils should be modified to increase soil volume, or plants should be chosen that can survive in the existing soil volume. An inadequate soil volume limits the water available to plants. A certain volume of soil is necessary for root growth. Without root growth, the mature size of the tree is limited and cannot support large canopies (Table 5-11).

TABLE 5-11: Estimating Existing Soil Volume

When to Measure Soil Volume	Soil volume should be measured in conditions where soil is circumscribed by pavement or buildings and the surface area of exposed soil is either: (1) < 80 m^2, or (2) < 5 m in any one dimension. Areas larger than this may merit measurement if more than two trees will be planted.
Materials Needed	Site measurements (intended or existing) Penetrometer or design details
Procedure	Calculate surface area of exposed soil. Estimate depth where soil is likely to severely impede root growth via 5 to 10 soil penetrometer measurements when soil is moist (where readings exceed 300 to 350 psi or 2 to 2.3 MPa) (see "Soil Compaction" section in this chapter). Discard measurements where a root or rock or other obstacle is encountered. Average these measurements to determine average soil depth. If depth is greater than 1 m, use 1 m for further calculations. Multiply area by average soil depth. Note: Specialized tree pits such as vaulted sidewalks or those with structural soils or other soil-volume-enhancing techniques will need calculations specific to their situation.
Pros	Relatively quick and easy
Cons	Penetrometer readings can vary considerably, especially if there are rocks or other underground obstacles.
Use Recommendation	Only use where roots of plants have access to a confined volume of soil that may be restrictive.

INTERPRETING SOIL VOLUME

Interpretations of soil volume must be made in the context of what plantings are intended for the soil in question. There are several ways to determine appropriate soil volume, but in all cases the *ultimate* size of the desired plants should be considered. Irrigation can affect the soil volume required, especially in arid climates. Water-holding capacity is also essential to tree health and relates to soil volume as well as texture. Calculations can be made for individual trees and soil types using the Leaf Area Index method. However, in general, the minimum required is at least 3 m³ of soil per 5 m² of ultimate canopy projection in the case of trees (or 2 ft³ of soil per 1 ft² of canopy projection). The maximum depth of usable soil is about 1 m or 3 to 4 ft, although in many cases much less soil depth will be available. When rooting volume is restricted, trees will not attain their full size. Trees can still be planted, but it must be recognized that ultimate size will be reduced, growth will slow more quickly, and longevity will be decreased.

Soil Drainage

Soil drainage is simply the ease with which water can move through the soil profile. A lack of good drainage reduces oxygen movement in soils and can interfere with root function. An abundance of micropores, at any depth, can restrict water movement. If any portion of the soil does not transmit water freely, problems can arise. For example, restricted water movement at the surface can lead to erosion and stormwater runoff and water deficits in lower layers. Restricted movement in lower layers can result in flooded root zones, anaerobic soils, and plant death.

Soil drainage affects:

▶ Water-holding capacity

▶ Biological activity

▶ Aeration level

▶ What plants will grow

▶ Likelihood of compaction

▶ Air exchange

TESTING DRAINAGE

A simple percolation test, or "perc" test, will determine drainage for the area of interest for plantings (Figure 5-21). The percolation rate is the speed at which water moves through the soil measured in cm or in. per hr. It is dependent on the soil texture, structure, and compaction level. Percolation results are essential to know when choosing plants that will thrive in wet (poor-draining) or dry (fast-draining) soil conditions. It is common to find variation in drainage between test spots on an urban site (Table 5-12).

FIGURE 5-21: A simple perc test provides a rapid estimation of internal soil drainage.

(Photo from Nina Bassuk)

TABLE 5-12: Testing Soil Drainage—Percolation Test

Materials Needed	Water (at least 8 gal, or access to a water source)
	Shovel
	Yardstick/ruler
	Watch/timer
Procedure	It is ideal to perform this test when the soil has been previously saturated or is very wet.
	Remove the surface vegetation.
	Dig a hole 12 to 18 in. deep and 12 in. wide. The depth of this hole is really dependent upon what soil depth is being assessed. This depth is typically the most useful for plantings.
	If it is not wet already, fill the hole with water and wet the soil all around the hole until it is saturated.
	When water is drained from the hole, fill the hole with water and measure the height with a yardstick or ruler.
	After 15 minutes, measure the water level again.
	Determine the distance the water level has dropped by subtracting the second reading from the first. Multiply that number by 4 to get the distance drained in an hour.
	Repeat the test again to make sure the results are the same in case the soil wasn't adequately wet beforehand.
Pros	Relatively quick and easy and requires no specialized equipment. Gives a very good assessment of drainage when multiple tests are performed.
Cons	In some situations water may find alternative exit paths, leading to an overestimation of percolation rate. This can be avoided by taking care to saturate soil around the test hole.
Use Recommendations	Can be performed at various depths if impermeable layers are present, but generally most useful as an overall assessment of infiltration. Often repeated at each phase of the site assessment.

INTERPRETING SOIL DRAINAGE

If the percolation test indicates:

- ► < 1 in./hr = extremely poor drainage
- ► < 1 to 4 in./hr = poor drainage
- ► 4 to 8 in./hr = good drainage
- ► 8+ in./hr = excessive drainage

Excessive drainage can be caused by granular subsurfaces such as gravel, fill, or utility pipes, which are often found on urban sites. Always consider variability in soil. If one pathway for water exit is available, water may move through that path. That may not reflect the water-holding capacity of other soil areas or layers; however, it does indicate that water may be unlikely to pond if that path is accessible.

DRAINAGE AND SOIL WATER

Soil structure and texture together largely determine soil water-holding capacity and how water moves through a soil (Figures 5-22 and 5-23). A sponge is a good analogy for soil when demonstrating the principles of water storage and movement. When completely saturated, all the sponge's pores, both large and small, are filled with water. Excess water will drop away in response to gravity. The large pores that allow this water to drain out are analogous to the macropores in the soil. When the sponge stops dripping, almost all of the water retained is analogous to water available for plant uptake. The amount of water retained by the sponge/soil at this point is called field capacity. This is the most water that a soil can hold after gravity has moved excess water away.

After water is used by the roots, there is still a little water left that clings tightly to the sponge/soil so that roots cannot take it up. That is plant-unavailable water and when only that water remains, the sponge/soil is considered to have reached the permanent wilting point. Soil texture and structure determine the arrangement of pores in a soil (its porosity and pore size distribution). These, in turn, determine how much water drains away, how much is plant available, and how much is plant unavailable. Another indicator of poor drainage is gleying, a bluish-gray color in the soil indicating prolonged periods of anoxic conditions.

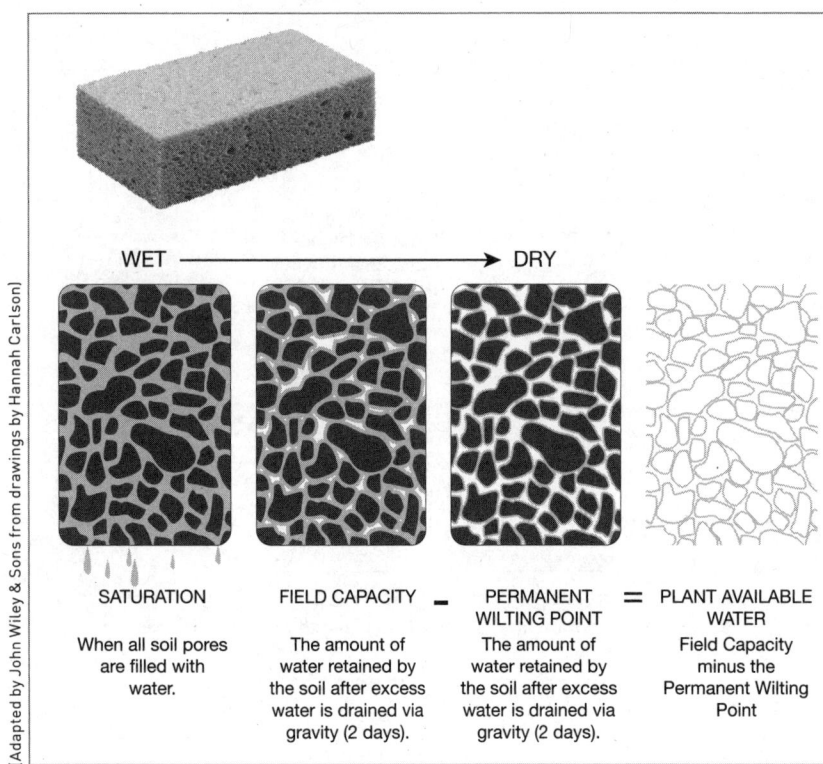

[Adapted by John Wiley & Sons from drawings by Hannah Carlson]

WET ⟶ DRY

SATURATION	FIELD CAPACITY	—	PERMANENT WILTING POINT	=	PLANT AVAILABLE WATER
When all soil pores are filled with water.	The amount of water retained by the soil after excess water is drained via gravity (2 days).		The amount of water retained by the soil after excess water is drained via gravity (2 days).		Field Capacity minus the Permanent Wilting Point

FIGURE 5-22: The principles of soil water movement and storage. Note how the water adheres to the soil surfaces.

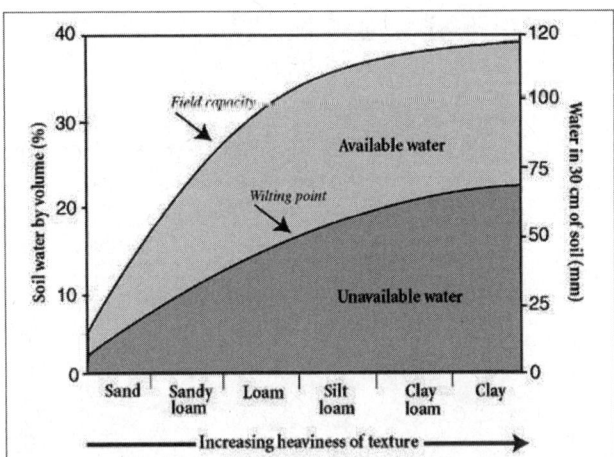

FIGURE 5-23: A generalized representation of the effects of soil texture on water storage in soil. Note that changes in soil structure also affect water storage and availability. (Adapted from Brady and Weil 1996)

PLANT-AVAILABLE WATER-HOLDING CAPACITY

The available water-holding capacity (AWHC) is the amount of water plants can take up in a given volume of soil. In a sandy soil only 6 to 10 percent of the volume of soil is available water. In a clayey soil there may be as much as 15 to 20 percent of available water. In any soil it is rare to have over 20 percent of available water. Available water and usable soil volume are an important part of determining plant selection.

Soil Chemical Status and Nutrient Availability

Soil chemical properties include pH, cation exchange capacity (CEC), salt content, and chemical contaminants such as heavy metals. Chemically contaminated soils, such as are found in brownfields, or soils where chemical processes are radically altered, such as mine spoils, are not discussed here. However, more minor disruptions in soil chemistry are very common and need to be understood and addressed. The chemical properties of soil affect one another and are, in turn, affected by soil physical and biological properties. The pH of the soil determines nutrient availability. The ability of soil to retain those nutrients, which is related to soil texture, is the cation exchange capacity.

The pH and texture of a soil are usually derived from the natural history of the site (the weathering parent materials); but in an urban setting, the chemical properties can be altered significantly by human use of the site. Limestone gravel, concrete, and other calcareous building materials increase the pH, and imported soil, the use of de-icing salts, and other soil contaminants also affect soil chemical status.

Chemical properties can affect:

▶ Soil pH

▶ Nutrient availability

▶ Biological activity

▶ Root growth

▶ What plants will grow

SOIL pH

It is essential to determine soil pH on all sites where plants will grow. Soil pH is the measure of activity of hydrogen ions (H+) in a solution, often known as the acidity or alkalinity of soil. It not only determines nutrient availability but toxicity of other elements. Specifically, pH is the negative logarithm of the hydrogen ion concentration (H+) in the soil solution: pH = –log[H+]. The possible range of pH is from 0 to 14. pH is often talked about in terms of the acidity and alkalinity of the soil, alkaline being levels above 7, and acid being below. Because the pH scale is logarithmic, soil with a value of 8.0 is 10 times more alkaline than soil with a value of 7.0, and 100 times more alkaline than one with a pH of 6.0. Typical soil pH levels are between 4 and 9, with many urban and disturbed soils having pHs above 7. Soil chemistry is complex, and occasionally soils may have extremely low or high pHs due to disturbance or contamination. In developed areas, pavement, building foundations, and other materials can raise the pH of soil. There are also areas where the pH may be extremely low, such as areas previously used for coal mining.

The pH of the soil determines the availability of plant nutrients. For example, iron (Fe) becomes tightly bound to soil solids as the pH rises. For some plant species, this is sufficient to cause severe (and eventually fatal) nutrient deficiencies at even moderate pH levels. Within the values of 6.0 and 7.5, most plant nutrients are sufficiently available for most species (Figure 5-24).

Plants are adapted to growing in soils with particular pH levels; therefore, knowing the pH of soil onsite at a very fine scale is essential for plant selection. Some plants are adapted to a wide range of pH while others require a narrow range. Plants adapted to higher soil pHs may have developed specialized mechanisms for altering the chemistry of micronutrients that are typically unavailable at high pH (iron, for example) such that the root can take them up. Some species can also be used as indicator plants when evaluating pH. *Hydrangea macrophylla* (hydrangea) cultivars can indicate the pH of the soil by the color of their flowers. The color is due to the amount of aluminum taken up by the plant. In soils with a low pH, aluminum becomes more available. The more blue the flower, the lower the pH; the more pink, the higher the pH. In neutral-pH soil, the flowers are usually purple. Other species, such as *Quercus palustris* (pin oak) and *Q. phellos* (willow oak), can exhibit interveinal chlorosis if the soil is at or above neutral (pH 7). It is essential to know what the plant requirements are before choosing them for the site. Although soil pH can be modified slightly, it generally returns to its original pH over time (Table 5-13).

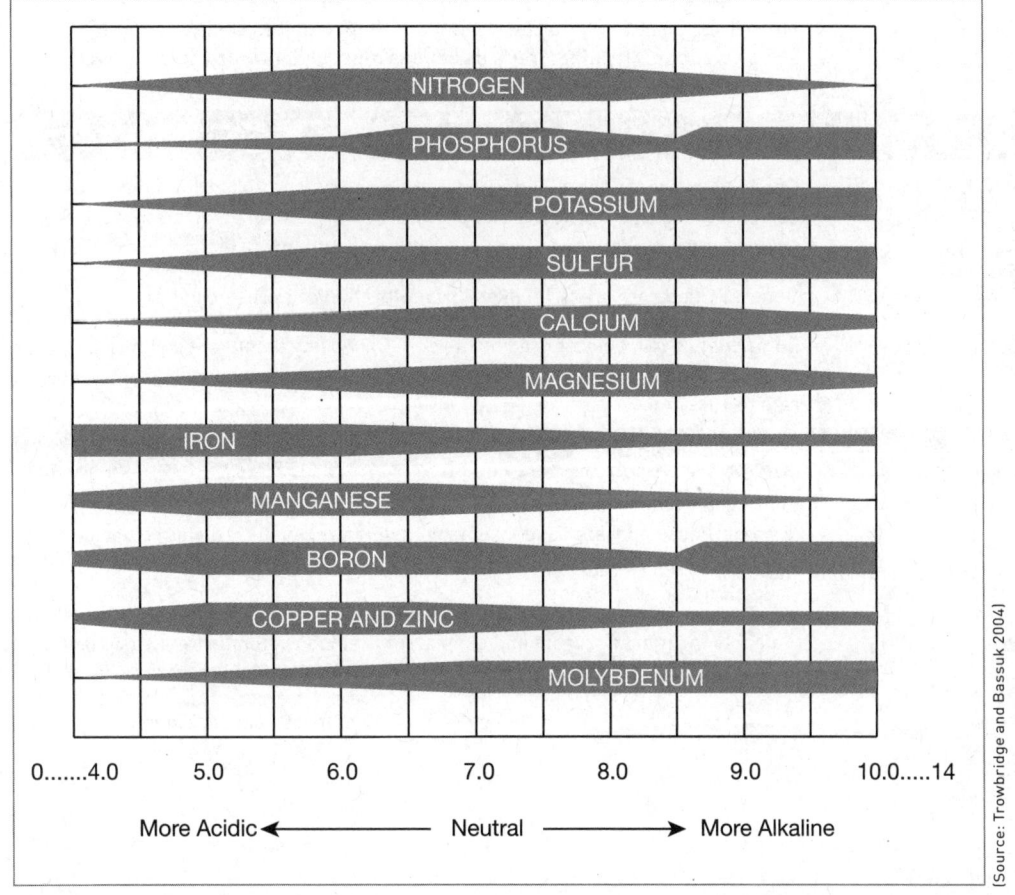

(Source: Trowbridge and Bassuk 2004)

FIGURE 5-24: Availability of plant nutrients at varying soil pHs. Widening of bars indicates greater availability, while tapering bars indicate nutrients will become less available. Common micronutrient deficiencies in alkaline (high-pH) soils are iron (Fe) and manganese (Mn), as can be seen by the narrowing of the bar on the right.

TABLE 5-13: **Comparison of Methods for Testing Soil pH**

METHOD: SOIL pH METER	
How It's Done	A slurry of soil and water (approximately 50/50) is mixed in a container. The electrode(s) of a handheld, battery-operated pH meter is inserted until the reading stabilizes. Letting the mixture stand first may provide a more accurate reading.
Pros	A straightforward, quick field test. Meters are reasonably priced. It is sufficiently accurate for site assessment ($\pm$ 0.1).
Cons	Meters, especially older ones, are not durable. Requires calibration with buffering solutions. Manufacturer's directions must be followed carefully; typically the electrodes must not be allowed to dry out.
METHOD: SOIL pH COLOROMETRIC TEST KIT	
How It's Done	Chemical reagents are added to very small samples of soil. Color change is compared to a chart to determine pH. Test kits should be obtained that are designed for a wide range of pH measurements, from low to high.
Pros	Generally does not break (unlike a pH meter) and requires no batteries.
Cons	Color change can be obscured by the soil. Only a tiny amount of soil may be tested, increasing variability. May take more time to conduct tests. Only accurate to ±0.3 or 0.4.
METHOD: LABORATORY ANALYSIS	
How It's Done	Soil is dried and ground. A sample is extracted and made into a saturated paste or sometimes separate suspensions with deionized water, calcium chloride, and sometimes also potassium chloride. Electrodes are then used to determine pH in the suspensions.
Pros	Probably the most accurate and consistent method available. Reduces interference of carbon dioxide levels and salts that might alter field readings slightly.
Cons	Not instantaneous. Expensive for the number of tests needed. Time consuming.

STANDARDS

▶ ASTM D4972 - 01(2007), Standard Test Method for pH of Soils

SOIL BIOLOGICAL ACTIVITY

Soil biological activity is an essential part of a healthy soil. However, direct assays of soil biological activity are typically not useful without extensive tests and interpretation. Biological activity relates to both soil structure and nutrient availability. Organisms are beneficial to sustain soil health, but they also require particular living conditions. Various organisms in the soil contribute to aggregate formation and help to break down nutrients into simple forms that plants can take up. Most organisms need oxygen for survival and cannot live in poorly drained soil or at extreme levels of pH. It is generally more useful to assess if the conditions that permit healthy biological activity are present, namely the presence of a food source (organic carbon) and adequate air and moisture.

Soil biological activity affects:

▶ Nutrient cycling, retention, and availability

▶ Soil carbon storage

▶ Soil carbon release

▶ Persistence of organic amendments

▶ Development of soil structure

Plant-Available Nutrients

Soils contain nutrients necessary for plant growth. Macronutrients are required in significant quantities while the micronutrients are required in very small or trace amounts (Table 5-14).

TABLE 5-14: Plant-Available Nutrients

PLANT MACRONUTRIENTS	PLANT MICRONUTRIENTS (REQUIRED IN TRACE AMOUNTS ONLY)
Nitrogen (N)	Iron (Fe)
Phosphorus (P)	Manganese (Mn)
Potassium (K)	Copper (Cu)
Sulfur (S)	Zinc (Zn)
Calcium (Ca)	Molybdenum (Mo)
Magnesium (Mg)	Boron (B)
	Chlorine (Cl)

Imbalances in plant-available nutrients can affect:

▶ All aspects of plant growth

▶ Plant vigor

▶ Leaf color and shape

▶ Disease and insect resistance

▶ Nutrient cycling

▶ Viability of employing an organic maintenance program

These are all essential nutrients, whether macro or micro. The availability of all nutrients is affected by soil pH (see Figure 5-24), and there are a variety of interactions that occur among soil minerals and the various nutrients. Therefore, interpretation of nutrient deficiencies determined by soil tests requires careful consideration. State extension service soil testing labs will often have experience with the soils in the region and may be a good source of advice. In general, a healthy soil with sufficient organic matter will have adequate nutrients for most landscape plants. The addition of stable composts, for example, will provide a slow-release supply of nitrogen. Nutrient deficiencies may often be a result of soil pH rather than a lack of a nutrient in the soil. Management of soils for intensive agricultural systems may require more intense scrutiny of plant nutrients available in the soil.

TESTING PLANT-AVAILABLE NUTRIENTS

Soil samples should be sent to a soil testing lab for nutrient analysis. Generally tests will provide plant-available nutrient measures rather than absolute measures of nutrients present. Thus it is important to request information from the testing laboratory concerning how test results should be interpreted. Though plants need a certain amount of nutrients for optimal growth, an excess of nutrients can be detrimental. Excess nutrients can create toxic conditions for plants and microbes, and can leach into stormwater runoff or groundwater, impacting ecosystems on a large scale. If a nutrient deficiency is affecting plant health, then the cause of the deficiency should be determined before any action is taken.

CATION EXCHANGE CAPACITY

The cation exchange capacity (CEC) is a measure of soil fertility. It represents the capacity of the soil to retain positively charged ions (cations), which include many plant nutrients. Organic matter and clay have a high CEC, while sandy and silty soils do not. A high CEC can also attract heavy metals such as lead. This characteristic can be exploited to decrease the leaching of heavy metals into the groundwater. However, in the case of soil contaminated with heavy metals or other toxicants, a specialist in this area should be consulted.

STANDARDS

- ▸ ASTM WK20984, New Test Method for Measuring Soluble Cations (SC), Bound Cations (BC) and Cation Exchange Capacity (CEC) of Inorganic Fine-Grained Soils

SOLUBLE SALTS

Excess soluble salts in the soil can negatively affect plant health. De-icing salts (NaCl or CaCl), or excess fertilizer can create a high concentration of salts in the soil that can cause water deficits and plant desiccation. Irrigation water high in salt content (e.g., recycled water) can also contribute to soluble salts in the soil. High soluble salt levels may also be indicated by trees with abnormal twig growth patterns called witch's broom.

Excess soluble salts can cause:

- ▸ Leaf scorch
- ▸ Plant desiccation
- ▸ Witch's broom

MEASURING SOLUBLE SALTS

Soluble salts are measured via electrical conductivity (EC), SI preferred unit: dS/m (deci-Siemens per meter). It can be measured relatively easily with an EC meter; however, this is often done as part of a typical suite of soil tests by testing laboratories, and additional field samples may not be necessary.

INTERPRETING ELECTRICAL CONDUCTIVITY MEASUREMENTS

Two possible situations for concern emerge: either soluble salts are very low, indicating low fertility, or they are very high, indicating that salt damage to plants will be likely unless this is addressed or very salt-tolerant species are used. In addition, consider sources of salt and the time of year of the measurement. Salt levels can be seasonal especially if they are related to de-icing salts, fertilizer applications, or if rainfall intensity varies during the year (salts may have leached through the soil during periods of heavy rain) (Table 5-15). A few other notes to consider:

- ▸ Units vary, so conversion may be needed.
- ▸ Unit Conversions: 1 dS/m = 1 mS/cm = 1000 QS/cm = 1 mmhos/cm = 1000 Qmhos/cm

TABLE 5-15: Interpretation of EC Measurements from the 1:2 Dilution Method

INTERPRETATION	ECE DS/M
Low EC (fertility)	< 0.38
Ideal	0.38 – 0.75
Acceptable	0.75 – 1.5
Unacceptable (salt injury common)	> 1.5

Soil Contamination

If there is a history of soil contamination on the site due to activity or use, or it is observed that there are areas of soil where nothing is growing, the soil can be sent to labs that perform soil contamination tests. The tests are not necessarily the same as tests for heavy metals. Contaminants on urban sites may include lead, cadmium (from paint), nickel, arsenic, and copper sulfate from herbicides.

Soil contamination may affect:

▶ Root growth

▶ Plant growth

▶ Species composition if site is colonized by plants rather than planted

▶ Human health (especially children)

INTERPRETING SOIL CONTAMINATION TESTS

How and when soil contamination needs to be addressed will depend on the levels of contamination, the nature of the contaminants, and the intended use. There are a variety of strategies for remediating soils or, alternatively for preventing access to these soils via capping or other tools. Each situation will have specific characteristics that will determine appropriate approaches, and new techniques and strategies continue to emerge. An environmental specialist should be consulted in cases of soil contamination. It is desirable to work hand in hand with this specialist to determine how horticultural needs can be satisfied within the remediation program. Phytoremediation and bioremediation techniques that rely on the physiology of plants to provide pollutant treatment or capture are introduced in the "Phytoremediation and Bioremediation" section of Chapter 4.

STANDARDS

► ASTM E1903 - 97(2002), Standard Guide for Environmental Site Assessments: Phase II Environmental

MANAGING SOILS FOR A SUSTAINABLE SITE

Soil characteristics determined during the site assessment will delineate where soil problems need to be addressed to create the healthy soils essential to a sustainable site. The general site assessment and soils assessment can be overlaid for a more dynamic interpretation of existing conditions. This section provides information on methods to address specific soil problems. However, it is important not to lose sight of the larger context. Soils information should be analyzed with respect to other site assessment information, the project goals, program requirements, and design considerations.

Questions to consider at this point may include:

► Can the existing site conditions support thriving ecological systems?

► Does the design accommodate/reflect existing conditions?

► Should the design be modified to accommodate existing conditions?

► Should the site be modified to accommodate program goals?

► Should the site or design be modified to reduce existing environmental stress/ enhance ecological conditions?

► How can the site or design be modified to support sustainable ecosystem conditions and services?

For most projects, soil modifications or specifications will be necessary and the long-term health of the soil conditions will need consideration. The next sections address modification of existing soil conditions, soil protection during site construction, and long-term soil health management.

Remediation of Existing Soils

Soil remediation techniques can be selected in response to both soil assessment and testing results and the design program. Each set of strategies has a different level of cost, complication, and sustainability. Table 5-16 summarizes various strategies for the main groups and reasons for their use.

TABLE 5-16: Classification of Soil Management and Remediation Strategies

MANAGEMENT GOAL	STRATEGY
Preserve	If healthy, desirable soils exist, preservation can be less costly and can also protect existing ecological services onsite. Preserve healthy, functional soils. Preserve desirable vegetation. Protect from construction impact (see "Soil Management Plan" section). Consider long-term management plan (see "Soil Management Plan" section).
Rehabilitate or Amend Onsite	If soils have slightly poor test results or are previously disturbed or disturbed during construction, restoring the soil by amending can be less intrusive and less costly. Amend soil as necessary to restore its health (function). Inform the contractors (see "Soil Management Plan"). Consider long-term management plan (see "Soil Management Plan").
Modify Drainage	If soils are compacted or have low percolation rates that cannot be addressed by soil rehabilitation, adding or modifying drainage systems can help to direct water offsite. Drainage systems need to be developed in concert with other hydrologic systems onsite. Consider how areas need to be modified to meet design goals. Create drainage by modifying the grade or updating/building a drainage system.
Bury	For extremely poor soil conditions, to increase the soil volume, or as part of a strategy for sealing off contaminated soils, new soil can be placed on top of the old soil. Cover entire planting area or create berms with the new soil. Make sure the drainage system will be adequate. Burying poorly draining soils will not improve drainage, only cover it up. If this is a component of remediating contaminated soils, work with a specialist to seal old soils first. Specify new soil.
Replace	Replacing existing poor soils with new soil or having to bring new soil to a site where no soil existed can be a costly choice, and strategies for disposing of old soil sustainably must be considered. However, it can also be a fast and effective way to create the conditions needed for a healthy landscape, especially in confined and difficult sites. Research reasons for adverse test results of existing soils to find out whether there will continue to be problems or if the soil can be amended. Decide to either replace the soil or use the space for hardscaping, structures, and the like. Write specifications for removal (make sure it all goes where it should). Specify new soil.
Increase Soil Volume	For inadequate soil volumes, new soil or other media can be added to meet plant soil requirements according to the design goals and horticultural requirements. Alter designs to create larger soil volumes. Increase ability for plant roots to grow in urban conditions such as under sidewalks (for example, by specifying specialized load-bearing growing media such as structural soils, or creating vaulted sidewalks). Use structural soils strategically to provide trees access to larger soil volumes (on the other side of a paved area, for example).

Preservation of Soils

The value of undisturbed, healthy soil for a variety of ecosystem services—from plant growth, to stormwater mitigation, to carbon storage—is considerable, and such soil and the plant and microbial life within it should be protected from compaction, relocation, and contamination throughout the entire project.

Preservation of soils utilizes healthy soil in place for planting areas and avoids any other modifications such as grading, topsoil stockpiling, excavation, or construction of structures. Soil preservation implies complete protection of soil horizons and their properties by protecting the soil from all disturbances. To preserve the integrity of the soil, it should not be stockpiled and reused as this can negatively affect soil conditions, especially soil structure. Stockpiling and reusing soil can be a valuable option when amending soil or when soil needs to be moved for excavation (see the section "Rehabilitate or Amend Onsite" later in the chapter), but it is not the same as soil preservation.

Soil preservation goes hand in hand with the protection of vegetation, especially trees. If trees are present within the zone of soil protection, the protected area should be enlarged to encompass the majority of the root system. The distance out from the trunk of the tree that protection should extend is 1 to 2 ft per in. of trunk diameter, depending on the health, vigor, and species of tree. Thus a mature white oak (*Quercus alba*) 44 inches in diameter would require a zone of protection of 196 ft in diameter (44 × 2 = 88 ft in radius; 88 × 2 = 196 ft in diameter). A vigorous zelkova (*Zelkova serrata*) of 10 in. trunk diameter would require a 20-ft-diameter protection area. Note that tree protection is considerably more involved than simply calculating protection zones, and a certified arborist, consulting arborist, or other specialist should be consulted.

STRATEGIES FOR SOIL PROTECTION (SEE ALSO "SOIL MANAGEMENT PLAN")

- ▶ Erect sturdy permanent fencing around the perimeter to prevent access during construction.
- ▶ Prohibit all traffic, except incidental pedestrian traffic, within the protected area.
- ▶ Prohibit all stockpiling of materials, parking of vehicles, and so forth within the protected area.
- ▶ Ensure compliance through a well-conceived inspection, education, and penalty program.

Rehabilitating Soils Onsite

Amending the soil can be the most sustainable way of improving soil conditions onsite. Amendments vary in results, cost, and frequency of application.

Soil amendments can be used to modify:

▶ Compaction

▶ pH

▶ Drainage

▶ Texture and structure

▶ Nutrient availability

▶ Biological activity

There are many different materials used for amending soils, and test results of the existing soil can reveal the best ones to use. It may also be useful to get a lab test of the amendment to verify pH, soluble salts, nutrient availability, and organic matter content. Amendments may change the existing soil conditions enough that it will affect plant choice. Involvement of a qualified horticulturalist or soils professional to create an amendment plan can ensure that amendments will enhance soils but not harm healthy soils.

In general, it is not a good practice to only amend the soil around each plant. Improving soil health and planting conditions includes amending the entire planting area, not just the immediate area around the plant roots. Amending soil immediately around new plants or just in planting holes can cause uneven drainage across the site with planting holes acting as surface drains collecting water. In addition, long-term root growth is most important for creating sustainable landscapes.

REHABILITATING COMPACTED SOILS

Compacted soils are one of the most common challenges on new building sites or redeveloped areas. In order to plan a successful decompaction strategy, it should be determined whether the soil is compacted at the surface or in the subsoil (Table 5-17). There are three steps for decompacting soils:

▶ Physically break apart compacted soils.

▶ Prevent immediate recompaction by limiting traffic and introducing something to keep soil broken apart (organic matter is ideal for this).

▶ Create the conditions for long-term soil structure development (aeration, organic matter, and clays).

TABLE 5-17: Rehabilitating Soils Compacted During Building Construction

When to Do It	Appropriate when restoring soils compacted by grading and building construction (or other causes).
How It Works	Organic matter is introduced into compacted lower horizons via subsoiling and topsoil reapplied.
Procedure	Apply 10 cm (4 in.) of compost to surface of compacted subsoil before topsoil is returned to the disturbed area. (Note: If topsoil is already in place, this procedure can still be used, but more topsoil will be required.) If there is no topsoil stockpiled, this technique also works well without adding topsoil. In this case, more organic matter should be applied—approximately 8 in. (20 cm).
	Use a "scoop and dump" backhoe subsoiling technique to create veins of compost 60 cm (2 ft) into the subsoil. Scoop a backhoe bucket of soil and compost, lift, and let drop. Break apart large clods with bucket or by hand.
	If available, apply 10 to 20 cm (4 to 8 in.) of topsoil from a sustainable source.
	Rototill to 20 cm (8 in.) after topsoil is added to create the reconstructed profile (Figure 5-25).
Pros	Backhoe subsoiling technique is ideal for confined spaces. Decompacting soil can dramatically improve tree growth and water infiltration as well as reduce drought stress.
Cons	Backhoe is time consuming for large expanses. Tractor-mounted rippers may be more appropriate in such cases. Soil may not support foot traffic initially.

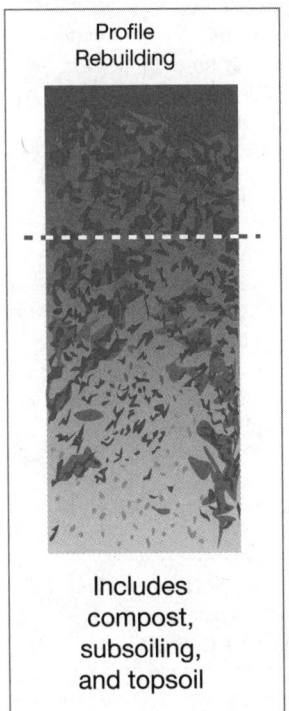

Profile Rebuilding

Includes compost, subsoiling, and topsoil

(Source: Sarah Gugercin)

FIGURE 5-25: Schematic of reconstructed soil profile. Note that the incorporation of organic matter at depth creates veins of compost that prevents soil from recompacting and allows root penetration.

Using Organic Matter to Amend Soils

Using organic matter to amend soil is a sustainable way of maintaining soil health. Though adding organic matter will not change soil texture, in the long run it can increase the water-holding capacity, the drainage, the number of microorganisms, and available nutrients in the soil. Organic matter can help decrease compaction and bulk density. In recent years, commercial availability of high-quality composts that are stable, have known feedstocks (the organic materials used to create the compost), and provide consistent and testable characteristics has dramatically increased. Finer-textured composts can be used as soil top dressings, even over existing plants such as turf grass. When incorporating compost into the soil as an amendment, particle size is less important. For a soil amendment, organic matter may be incorporated into the soil at a rate of about 25 percent by volume for sandier soils and 50 percent by volume for clayey soils (Table 5-18).

TABLE 5-18: Types of Organic Matter

TYPE	IMPACT ON SOIL
Paper or Yard Clippings	Useful source of organic matter if composted correctly.
Shredded Leaves	Useful source of organic matter if composted correctly.
Municipal Wastes (Yard Waste, Biosolids)	Levels of heavy metals should be listed for biosolids. Depending on where it is collected, high lead and cadmium may be a problem. Biosolids should meet state DEP standards. They should also meet the U.S. EPA Part 503 rule that discusses requirements/pathogen vectors for land-applied biosolids.
Food Waste Compost (Post-consumer, Home, Restaurant, Institutional)	Very stable, not always readily available. Increases available water-holding capacity. Less effective at building soil aggregation.
Animal Manure	Animal manure increases NPK. Depending on the animal, it is liquid or solid. Manure analysis may be beneficial. It may be composted or uncomposted. Uncomposted can increase soil aggregation, increase CEC, soil pH, and total pore space, but excess or untimely application can burn plants and increase nutrient loads in stormwater runoff.
Green Manure (Cover Crops)	Increases soil fertility with microbial diversity, aggregate stability, and water infiltration.
Composted Brewer's Waste	Good source of organic matter where consistent composting. Process and nutrient levels, soluble salts, and percentage organic matter should be listed for each source.

TYPE	IMPACT ON SOIL
Sphagnum Peat Moss	Although practices for harvesting peat have improved, peat builds only slowly over time and is typically not available from a local source. Thus it is generally not considered a sustainable material.
Peat Humus	Stable, small particle size. Often difficult to find.
Waste from Paper Mills, Timber Processing	Requires composting before it can be used as an amendment. Uncomposted wood waste can reduce nitrogen availability in the soil.

STRATEGIES FOR USING ORGANIC MATTER

▸ Try to find local materials to use as organic matter.

▸ Select the kinds with the least amount of environmental impact; use only renewable materials.

▸ Using a more stable organic matter such as compost will improve water infiltration and retention.

▸ Apply to entire area of soil to be remediated instead of in planting holes that roots will quickly grow out of.

▸ Mix in to a minimum of 18 in. for woody plants, 12 in. for herbaceous plants.

▸ To minimize disturbance, mix in before planting occurs.

▸ Mix thoroughly to avoid large chunks (>1 in.) that can create pockets of wet soil.

▸ If possible, use machines already onsite to mix organic matter into existing soil.

▸ The total amount of organic matter can equal 4 to 8 percent of the total soil volume by dry weight.

▸ Organic matter should be well composted or it can immobilize nitrogen while it decomposes or releases toxic compounds. Compost maturity can be easily tested onsite with test kits that measure carbon dioxide and ammonia evolution, such as the Solvita test kits (Woods End Laboratories, Inc., Mt. Vernon, Maine).

▸ If the pH of the organic matter is different from that of the soil, it may alter the soil pH.

▸ Make sure the organic matter is not too high in soluble salts.

USING MULCH TO AMEND SOILS

Although considered a maintenance strategy, mulch can also be used in the context of long-term soil rehabilitation. Organic mulches can maintain soil organic matter levels, especially where structures and hardscape interrupt a portion of the natural nutrient cycling. Organic mulches can be created from landscape debris such as fallen leaves and pruned branches, creating an opportunity for onsite management of these items (Figure 5-26). Mulch should be used for almost every project because it can benefit soil health in many ways including:

► Water retention

► Temperature regulation

► Weed growth reduction

► Erosion reduction

► Mechanical damage limitation

Organic mulch can be more beneficial than an inorganic mulch. Organic mulch:

► Provides nutrients

► Improves soil structure

► Creates more biotic activity

► Adds organic matter to the soil

► Eventually increases soil volume

FIGURE 5-26: Existing soil at Centennial Garden on the Cornell Campus, Ithaca, NY, was compacted clay and construction debris. Heavy soil was removed and amended 1:1 (by volume) with organic matter. The remaining soil was graded so that water would drain downhill. The amended soil was brought back and made into planting berms with walkways in between. Three inches of mulch is added once a year to replenish the organic matter that is lost.

(Photo from Nina Bassuk)

Modifying Soil Compaction and Drainage Around Existing Plants

When soil rehabilitation must occur around existing plants, strategies can be employed that allow some soil improvement while minimizing root disturbance. This can be achieved by remediating portions of the soil around trees or shrubs in a radial arrangement, maximizing benefits to the roots.

RADIAL TRENCHING

In areas with poor soil conditions, radial trenching is a strategy used to provide tree roots canals of healthier soil and unrestricted growth and improve drainage around existing trees (Figure 5-27). See the "Modifying Drainage" section of this chapter.

FIGURE 5-27: Radial trenches were excavated to provide a European hornbeam with better drainage. Four years later the tree is thriving.

SAND AMENDMENTS FOR SOIL

Sandy soils generally are less susceptible to compaction and are better drained than clayey soils. Thus sand amendments seem to be an intuitive solution to poor drainage and heavy clays. However, it is difficult to amend soil with sand. It usually requires a large amount of sand, generally between 50 and 75 percent, in a narrow range of sizes (between medium to coarse sand) in order to achieve any improvement in drainage. When insufficient or well-graded sand is added, the small particles of clay can fill the pores between big particles of sand and increase the bulk density, exacerbating drainage problems. Well-graded sand includes all sand particle sizes from very fine to very coarse sands. Furthermore, if a large amount of sand is introduced to improve drainage, it may be at a high cost in terms of nutrient- and water-holding capacity. Thus the amended soil may require irrigation or fertilization to adequately support vegetation. Any extra irrigation or fertility requirements will depend on the amount of sand added and organic matter content of the soil. Consequently, sand amendment may not be a sustainable practice for improving soil characteristics (Figure 5-28).

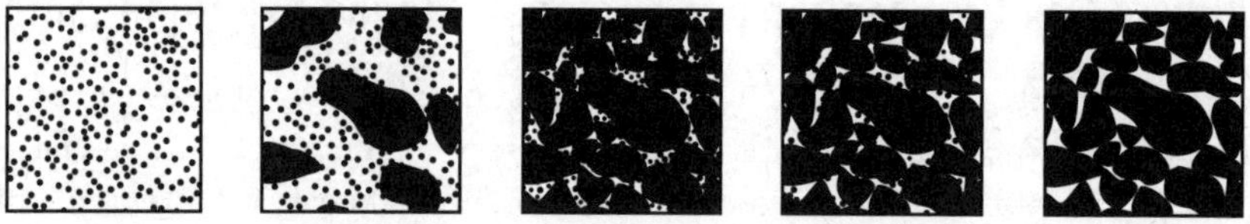

Percent Volume					
Clay	100	75	50	25	0
Sand	0	25	50	75	100
Small Pores	50	37.5	25	12.5	0
Large Pores	0	0	0	25	50

FIGURE 5-28: Adding sand to a clayey, poor-draining soil would require adding a minimum of 50 to 75 percent of the volume of the existing soil to have any effect.

Addressing Soluble Salt Content

High levels of soluble salts in soils can be caused by de-icing compounds, proximity to the sea or other bodies of salt water, high salinity of groundwater/surface water, irrigation water, site locations in arid regions where salt buildup in the soil does not get leached out with rain or overfertilization, or organic matter with too much soluble salt. In addition to testing salt levels in existing soils, organic matter and soils being brought to the site should be tested as well. If the soluble salt content of soils or amendments is high, and seems likely to remain high, due to the use of de-icing salts or fertilizer, it is important to use salt-tolerant plants. Lists of salt-tolerant and salt-sensitive plants can be found in the Morton Arboretum's plant database.

Reducing salt content:

► If the soil has an abnormally high soluble salt level, then it may be possible to leach the soil with water. Repeatedly oversaturate the site with irrigation, if possible, while it is raining. This will only work well if the soils drain well.

► The risk of high salt content in the future can be reduced by altering maintenance strategies. It is possible to keep soluble salt levels down with a thoughtful de-icing, fertilizing, and irrigation management plan.

Adjusting Soil pH

Modification of soil pH is difficult and may not be sustainable, especially in fine-textured soils or in the case where the parent material is calcareous. It is always best to choose plants that tolerate the existing pH instead of trying to change it. If modifying the pH is deemed of paramount importance, consider amending a small or containerized area several months before planting to see if the existing pH can be altered. Amending the soil to maintain a particular pH often requires repeated treatment and is thus a long-term commitment. It is not practical to consider in a perennial landscape. Because of the logarithmic scale and the buffering capacity of soils, slight changes in pH are *much* easier to achieve than large shifts. In the case of soils heavily contaminated with building rubble, limestone gravel, or other calcareous materials, lowering pH may be impossible unless those materials are first removed. If the cause of the existing pH is still present, then adjusting pH will require repeated application of amendments and cannot be considered sustainable. The best time to amend the soil is many months before plant installation, allowing amendments to be thoroughly mixed in, take effect, and be retested before installation.

It is possible to replace soils with ones of a different pH; however, even then the soil pH may change over time from its environment. Materials onsite can have a strong influence on pH levels, including the existing bedrock, history of industrial use, and building materials. Limestone foundations or gravel can increase the pH over time, as can some nitrate fertilizers. The addition of compost tends to have a neutralizing effect on pH, raising the pH of more acid soils and lowering that of extremely alkaline soils. If a very different pH is needed than what exists or a large area needs to be modified, then soil burying or replacement may be necessary.

LOWERING SOIL pH

Soil pH is best lowered by applying elemental sulfur. Granular or pelleted forms are the easiest to handle. Other compounds, such as aluminum sulfate, iron sulfate, and ammonium sulfate, are also frequently marketed for lowering pH. Some of these may be more readily available not because of superior qualities for lowering pH, but because they are by-products of another industry. Except for aluminum sulfate, microbial activity is required for the chemical reaction to reach completion in the soil. Therefore, adequate warmth, moisture, and time are needed for the pH to be lowered. If large adjustments to pH are needed, elemental sulfur is probably the only reasonable choice. Other compounds contain less sulfur by weight and therefore more must be applied. In addition, they include other materials, such as nitrogen in the case of ammonium sulfate, that will not be desirable to add in large quantities. In most cases, the sustainable option is to choose plants that are adapted to the existing soil pH. Changing pH on a large scale is often costly and unsuccessful.

RAISING SOIL pH

Ground limestone is applied to soil to raise pH. Ideally it is worked into the soil, but this may not be possible if established plants are present. Just as for lowering soil pH, knowing the soil texture is essential to accurately determine the correct rate to apply.

Adding Plant-Available Nutrients and Fertilizing

Unless soil tests find the soil to be nutrient deficient, there is no need to add nutrients to it through fertilization. If there are poor results from nutrient-availability tests, the soil pH and organic matter content should be considered. Depending on the soil pH, certain nutrients may not be as available, and the best solution is to choose plants that can handle the existing pH. If the organic matter content is low, adding organic matter can help boost the cation exchange capacity and the nutrient levels. Adding organic matter can be the most sustainable way of adding necessary nutrients to the soil. Stable compost, for example, will provide a slow-release form of nitrogen to the soil. For particular nutrient deficiencies, fertilizers can be used to add those nutrients, but the origin of the nutrient deficiency and whether chemical interactions (such as pH) are playing a role in its low availability should be determined. If fertilizer is required to increase nutrient levels:

- Try to choose fertilizers that only include the necessary nutrients.
- Compare choices of fertilizers, including slow release or those with high percentages of water-insoluble nitrogen and organic fertilizers.
- Consider the timing of nutrient release and the periods of root activity such that they are in sync.
- Check on the best time of year to apply in the region. The timing and amount of fertilizer applied is essential. Poor timing or excessive amounts can be detrimental to the health of plants as well as the ecosystem both at the site and downstream.
- Do not apply fertilizer before rain, to minimize nutrient loading stormwater runoff or groundwater.
- Do not use fertilizer near surface water such as a stream or lake.
- Do not permit any fertilizer overbroadcast onto pavement or other hardscape to remain (sweep it up).
- Try to minimize the need to use fertilizer by creating healthy soil conditions that can support the nutrient cycling system.
- Avoid overfertilizing, which can be toxic to plants or result in leaf scorch from desiccation.

There are organic and/or natural sources for most nutrient amendments. These typically have the advantage of a slower release time, sustainable interactions with soil biological activity, and lower embodied energy in their production. Disadvantages are primarily related to the variety of sources from which such nutrients can be derived, their lower nutrient analysis, and greater cost. Therefore it is essential to ascertain that they are sustainably extracted or harvested and that they do not contain contaminants such as heavy metals (Table 5-19).

TABLE 5-19: **Some Examples of Natural/Organic Nutrient Sources and the Primary Nutrients They Supply**

PLANT NUTRIENT	SOURCES
Nitrogen (N)	Alfalfa, dried blood, cottonseed, feathers, fish, guano, seafood, urine, manure
Phosphorus (P)	Bone meal, bird manure, rock phosphate, vetch
Potassium (K)	Kelp, wood ash, seaweed
Calcium (Ca)	Egg shells, oyster shells
Magnesium (Mg)	Epsom salt (magnesium sulfate)

MICRONUTRIENTS

Very occasionally it may make sense to address specific micronutrient deficiencies in plants via micronutrient applications, even though the initial deficiency is a result of soil pH. For example, if something has occurred to raise pH and resulted in an iron deficiency in a valuable tree, this nutrient deficiency can be addressed immediately while simultaneously addressing soil pH. In such cases, chelated micronutrients must usually be applied to the soils. The chemical structure of chelated iron prevents it from binding to the soil, allowing plant roots to take it up. However, not all chelates will work in high pH soil. Iron (Fe) EDDHA is a chelated form that will be effective.

Modifying Drainage

Water drainage relies first on soil texture and structure, regardless of drainage systems underneath. When soils of different textures are layered, water may not drain unless a zone of soil is completely saturated, just like a sponge, and water will actually move horizontally instead of draining down. Strategies for addressing drainage problems include plant choice, drainage system choice, radial trenching, or amending with sand.

PLANT CHOICE

Even with soil amendment, it may not be possible to achieve a perfectly draining soil unless the soil is replaced and underdrainage installed. If the soil still has occasional poor drainage after amending, choosing plants that can withstand this makes sense. This is especially important if the subgrade under the amended soil doesn't drain well.

DRAINAGE SYSTEM CHOICE

Grading: The idea of subsurface grading or sculpting has been around for several decades. In this instance, before stockpiled topsoil is relaid, the subsoil is graded to collect water at the interface of the topsoil and subsoil and move it to a lower point. This might look like an underground swale. Topsoil or amended soil is then replaced.

Sump drains: On a flat site it is possible to collect excess water at the bottom of a planting hole by creating a gravel-filled perforated pipe sump drain. These work best if the perforated pipe runs from the soil surface to a level well below the root ball—at least 3 ft. It is not a perfect solution in that in heavy rain, excess water may still back up and affect the root system. At best, this system buys time before water may saturate the soil around the root system.

Underdrainage: Underdrainage at the interface between well-draining soil (topsoil, amended or replaced soil) and poorly draining soil (subsoil or compacted fill) that connects to a storm drain or rain garden is the best way to move excess water away from a plant's root system. Perforated pipes are laid with the perforated side down and placed on a sloping grade that moves excess water to another pipe and eventually to connect in a storm sewer or a rain garden. Perforated plastic pipe is often surrounded by gravel, with geotextile to keep the soil out of the gravel. The pipe is laid underneath the rooting zone (18 in.) and is connected to an outlet or connected to the site's closed drainage system/piping. The slope of these underdrains need not be great (perhaps 0.5 to 1.0 percent), but they always prevent soil saturation around the roots. If the topsoil does not drain well, water will not reach the underdrainage system until the soil is saturated. A French drain is basically the same as the underdrainage discussed here, but without the pipe. A French drain collects water under the surface, as well as surface runoff.

RADIAL TRENCHING

Radial trenching is a technique that is most often used around existing trees recently planted in compacted soil to provide "break-out" areas for root growth. Using a backhoe bucket, the intersection of the original planting hole and the surrounding compacted soil is located. This is where root growth is stopped by dense soil. A trench is dug using the bucket from the existing root growth away from the tree beginning at a depth of 12 in. and ending at a depth of 24 in. to help create positive drainage away from the root zone. The trench can be 8 to 10 ft long. The trench soil is removed, amended, and replaced into the trench and then mulched. Several trenches can be dug in this way. Root growth is tremendously increased in the uncompacted trench, and drainage and tree growth is improved.

AMENDING WITH SAND

Soil may be amended with sand to reduce compaction and increase drainage, but some cautions must be taken (refer to "Sand Amendments for Soil" section in the chapter). This is generally not a sustainable choice because of the large quantity of sand required and circumstances of sand harvest and transport. Blended replacement soils may contain high proportions of sand because natural soil structure is limited or absent in blended soils. See the section "Specifying Replacement Soils" later in the chapter. Consider regional climatic factors such as average rainfall before making decisions about a site's drainage. If there are drainage problems onsite, it is possible to choose plants that thrive in wet conditions.

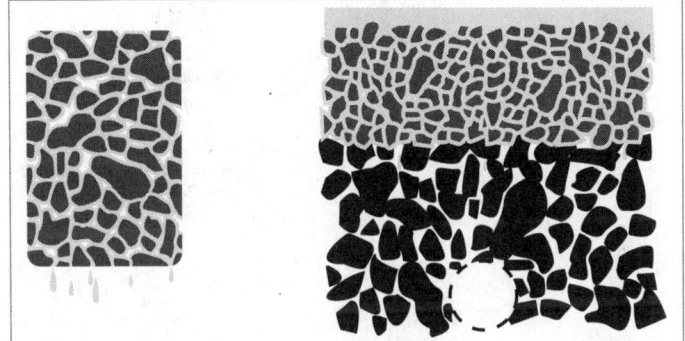

(Hannah Carlson)

FIGURE 5-29: Water drainage relies first on soil texture and structure, regardless of drainage systems underneath. Depending on the soil, water will not drain unless the soil is completely saturated, just like a sponge. Water will actually move horizontally instead of draining down if the soil has more adhesive properties than what lies beneath.

If the drainage problems need to be changed for ecological, programmatic, or design goals, look through the following drainage solutions to find one that is appropriate for the specific site conditions. Even with amended or new soil, drainage systems are important to include in the design. Soil layers may be well draining on top; however, on urban sites there are often compacted layers below the topsoil where water will collect (Figures 5-29 to 5-32). By using a cone penetrometer (see Table 5-9), subsurface compacted layers can be located.

(Photo from Nina Bassuk)

FIGURE 5-30: The effect of a nondraining, compacted subgrade underneath soil that drains well. At the interface of these layers, water does not drain and backs up into the growing medium, severely limiting its usefulness.

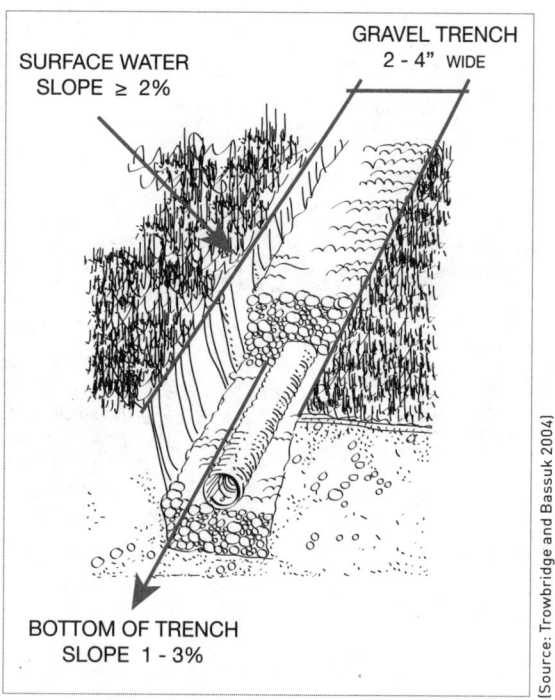

FIGURE 5-31: To drain a soil on top of a nondraining subgrade, a perforated pipe is placed at the interface and graded to empty into a storm drain or "daylight" onto a slope.

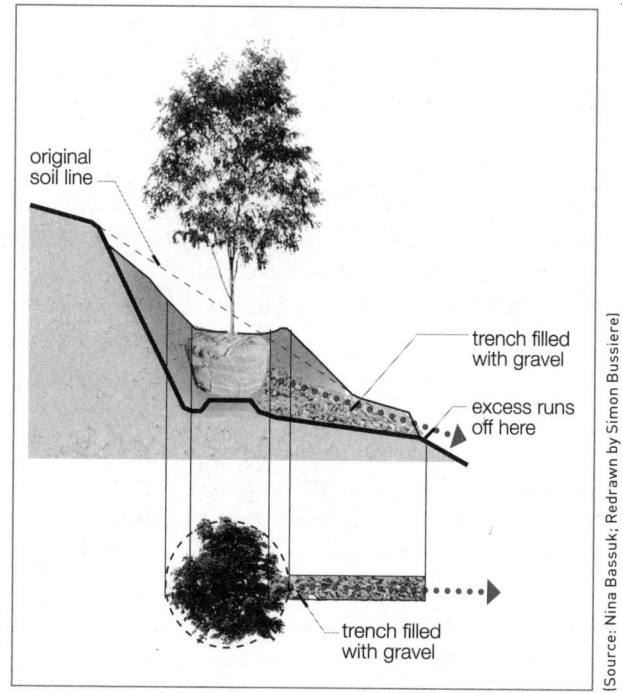

FIGURE 5-32: When a tree is planted near a slope, a gravel-filled trench (French drain) can be placed at the lower end to drain excess water down the slope.

SOIL REPLACEMENT AND SPECIALIZED SOILS

There are times when soil must be replaced or buried. Brownfields, for example, may need to be capped. Or soil can be absent or of such poor quality that it cannot be remediated effectively. In addition, in some built environments, soils with special characteristics, such as the ability to be load bearing, may be required.

Burying Nonfunctional Soil Beneath Good Soil

Burying existing soil is an alternative strategy to amending soil or replacing soil. This may be an appropriate action when:

▶ Existing soils are very poorly drained

▶ Existing soils are compacted and cannot be decompacted

▶ The high water table approaches rooting depth

- ► The volume of soil needs to be increased
- ► Soils are contaminated

The total soil volume should be considered when burying soil. If the existing soil is too compacted or poorly drained, the volume of the new soil has to be enough for all of the plants to use. At least 2 ft^3 of soil per square foot of expected crown diameter of newly planted trees should be allowed when placing the soil.

DRAINAGE CONSIDERATIONS WHEN BURYING SOILS

The drainage of buried soil should be considered before bringing in new soil. Subsurface sculpting or underdrainage must be used to prevent excess water at the interface of the old and new soils from accumulating into the root zone of the new plants.

BUILDING BERMS

Other ways to bury existing soil and add new soil include transforming the topography by building berms or hills, raising the grade of flat areas while still keeping them at a shallow gradient, or creating retaining walls. Instead of adding the same amount of new soil across the site or planting areas, design areas where new soil can be mounded up. Creating a mound, or berm, of organic matter, amended soil, topsoil, or blended sand soil over an unusable site can be a sound strategy. Berms should be considered when:

- ► There are particular areas onsite where larger woody vegetation requires more soil volume,
- ► There are areas of different soil conditions—some to be protected and other areas of poor soil that need to be modified for planting.
- ► Areas cannot be completely buried due to structural obstacles or contamination areas.
- ► There is limited money for purchasing new soil.

Issues to keep in mind when changing the topography of the site include:

- ► The connection between new landforms or elevated areas and existing grades should be smooth and not visually apparent.
- ► If the slope of a berm exceeds 1:3, it will require special technologies to prevent erosion. A slope of 1:3 is much easier to maintain than a steeper slope.
- ► Drainage should be addressed to limit runoff down the sides of the berm
- ► Berms can be used to increase infiltration and decrease runoff
- ► Although berms can improve soil characteristics in some situations, grading to create berms can damage existing soil structure and stimulate carbon release to the atmosphere.

Specifying Replacement Soils

Often, urban soils consist of a blend of imported topsoil, "fill," and compacted soil. When it is not possible to modify existing soils onsite due to financial limitations, time limitations, or poor existing soil conditions replacing the soil may be necessary to design a healthy landscape. Using topsoils from other sites raises a host of red flags in terms of sustainability. It is essential that topsoil not be harvested from greenfields. In addition, transporting topsoil is environmentally costly, so transport distance should be minimized. In many areas, natural topsoils are simply unavailable. Thus using soils existing onsite is preferable. However, very urban sites may have no existing soil and replacement soil may be required. See Table 5-16, "Classification of Soil Management and Remediation Strategies," for situations when soil importation is appropriate.

Instead of just bringing in any soil, or "topsoil," soil needs to be designed by a qualified professional, with a written specification and a quality control program to ensure compliance is established. The contractor submits representative samples of the new blended soil and any soil stockpiled onsite for soil testing. Deficiencies should be corrected after review of the testing report. Soil should be tested, reviewed, and possibly corrected and retested, before used onsite. When the soil is delivered onsite, grab samples should be taken to do a final verification that the placed soils match all of the previous test results, criteria, and expectations. Determining what type of soil to specify depends, of course, on the intended use for the site and what types of soils exist in the region. At a minimum soil specifications should be written and tested for:

- Particle size distribution and texture class
- Source of soil constituents
- Organic amendments, their type and stability and percentage by weight
- Soluble salts
- Chemical analysis including pH

Specifications may require that offsite soil be:

- Natural, fertile friable loam or sandy loam
- Four to 8 percent organic matter by weight (ASTM F-1647)
- A pH between 6.5 and 7.5 (change this depending on plant palette to be used)
- Specific levels of available nutrients (AOAC standards)
- A minimum CEC

Other things to consider for soil specifications are:

▸ The soil should be free of stones 1 in. (25 mm) or larger, and other material harmful to plant growth.

▸ The soil should not be delivered or used for planting while frozen or muddy.

▸ Try to use local materials, and ones that use recycled mineral subsoil and compost. A site is not sustainable if it contributes to the degradation of another site by harvesting healthy topsoil.

A soil scientist who has experience designing soil specifications for different landscapes would be an essential member of the design team should blended soils be required.

Increasing Soil Volume

More soil may be needed onsite based on the soil volume calculations and the planting plan. If there is not enough space for an adequate volume of usable soil in the planting areas, mostly due to the need for hardscaped areas including parking lots or sidewalks, it may be possible to use structural soil. Structural soil can be used under pavement (or turf) which increases the available space for soil volume. For more information on calculating soil volumes, see *Trees in the Urban Landscape* (Trowbridge and Bassuk 2004).

Structural Soils

Soils under pavement need to be compacted to meet load-bearing requirements so that sidewalks and other pavement won't subside and fail. Soils are often compacted to 95 percent peak (Proctor or modified Proctor–ASTM D-698) density before pavements are laid. When trees are planted into these soils, root growth is severely reduced or eliminated beyond the tree-planting hole. When root growth is restricted, tree growth suffers as water, nutrients, and oxygen are limited.

The need for a load-bearing soil under pavement gave rise to the development of structural soil, a blended soil that can be compacted to 100 percent peak density to bear the load of a pavement while allowing tree roots to grow through it.

Structural soil is a mixture of crushed gravel and soil, which may or may not have a small amount of hydrogel to prevent the soil and stone from separating during the mixing and installation process. The keys to its success are the following: the gravel should consist of crushed stone of a very narrow gradation, typically, 0.75 to 1.5 in. diameter, with no fine particles, to provide the largest void space. Soil should be added to the gravel so that the ratio of stone to soil is approximately 80 percent stone to 20 percent soil by dry weight. The soil should have enough nutrient-holding capacity to support plant growth. This proportion ensures that each stone touches another stone, creating a rigid lattice or skeleton, while the soil almost fills the large pore spaces that are created by the stone. This way, when compacted, any compactive load would be borne from stone to stone, and the soil in between the stones would remain uncompacted.

Structural soil requires a large volume of soil under pavement, approximately 2 ft^3 of soil for every square foot of envisioned crown diameter. A 36-in. soil depth is recommended, although several projects have been successful using depths as shallow as 24 in. Structural soils have an available water-holding capacity between 7 and 12 percent depending on the level of compaction. This is equivalent to a loamy sand or sandy loam. Based on water-holding capacity, about 1.5 times the amount of structural soil would be needed for an equivalent sized tree growing in sandy loam. Because of its well-drained nature, trees that prefer well-drained soils do best in structural soil. Depending on the stone type used to make structural soil, the pH of the soil may be affected (e.g., limestone versus granite). Good tree selection practices and establishment procedures should be used with structural soil, as would be done with any tree installation.

As with any soil, it is important to maximize the water infiltration through the pavement to replenish structural soil. A porous opening around the tree of approximately 50 square ft is recommended to allow for water infiltration (Figure 5-33).

STRUCTURAL SOIL FOR STORMWATER CAPTURE

Structural soil has a rapid infiltration rate (>24 in. per hour) and has a large water-holding capcity after it has been compacted. Ordinary loam soil compacted to 100 percent peak density has an infiltration rate of 0.5 in./hr. This allows structural soil to be used for stormwater capture under porous pavements. Eliminating underdrainage can maximize stormwater retention and infiltration into the subgrade. However, overflow drainage is recommended and reservoirs should be designed to empty within approximately 48 hours.

SAND-BASED SOILS FOR UNDER PAVEMENT

A sand-based load-bearing planting medium is a blend of uniform sand (in the medium- to large-size fraction), mature compost, and loam. The uniform gradation of the sand allows for a high degree of compaction yet bulk densities remain low and particles cannot pack into a hard mass. Typical weight ratios are 80 percent uniformly graded sand and 20 percent silt and clay. Compaction of this type of soil to approximately 90 percent proctor density has been successful.

FIGURE 5-33: Cross section of typical tree installation into structural soil under a concrete sidewalk. Note where the tree pit is open, topsoil should be placed around the tree ball, but structural soil can be placed under the ball to prevent tree ball subsidence.

SUSPENDED PAVEMENTS

Still another way of designing soils under hardscape uses suspended pavement over normal mineral soils. A variety of approaches have been used, but all allow uncompacted soils to be placed under pavement since the pavement load is supported structurally, rather than by the soil. Suspended pavements typically require a substantial investment in structural infrastructure that supports the pavement.

THE SOIL MANAGEMENT PLAN

The soil management plan should be developed in conjunction with construction plans. The plan will protect soils during construction; include postconstruction restoration and future management and maintenance, including monitoring soil nutrients and replenishing mulch. A soil scientist, horticulturist, arborist, or forester (if trees are present), and the site engineer should be involved in forming the soil management plan. Because soils are typically present throughout the site, communication and input from contractors, designers, architects, and others are vital. Construction plans are integral to retaining soil health. The plans provide clear communication with contractors as to what is expected across the job site, and contractors should confirm that they have read the details and the plans are clear. Soil health is retained during construction by providing details on the following topics:

▶ Protecting site assets and limiting disturbance

▶ Storing and reusing materials

▶ Restoring soils after construction

Protect Site Assets

Healthy or restored soils are valuable assets for a sustainable site, yet they are easily damaged. The first pass of heavy equipment over moist soil can do considerable damage. Where plants are present, especially mature trees, protecting soil also protects plants. Thus protection zones for plants and soils are typically considered together.

CREATE ZONES TO PROTECT SOILS AND VEGETATION

▶ Clearly mark for protection existing vegetation and soil on demolition and construction documents.

▶ Clearly show the construction boundaries, the areas to protect, and the areas to stockpile materials on the plan. Add enough details to explain what is expected in each zone.

▶ When creating protection zones, check to see if zones could be detrimentally affected by adjacent construction by disturbed hydrology or erosion. Make zones as big as necessary to truly protect the soil or vegetation inside.

▶ Be aware of the contractor's needs in terms of space for machinery, maneuverability, and materials. Try to protect the site assets while accommodating the needs of the people working onsite.

- If possible, it is better to protect a group of trees and the shared root zone than to protect individual trees.

- Protect trees around their roots, which will likely extend farther than the drip line (see the section "Soil Protection" earlier in the chapter) (Figure 5-34).

- The radius of protection zones around shrubs should be twice the diameter of the shrub itself.

FENCING

Strong fencing protects soils and vegetation from traffic and other forms of trespass during construction. Chain link fence, which can be "used and in good shape" to save money, is preferable to wooden fencing in that it is reusable and sturdy (Figures 5-35 and 5-36).

On the demolition and construction plans:

- Add protective fences around the root protection zone of trees—or beyond—not around the trunk.

- Note the type of protection, the size, and the construction of the protection. The size and strength of the fencing depends on the job, but for good protection, fencing should be about 6 ft high.

- Be clear that the areas to be protected should not be used for storage of machinery, vehicles, or materials.

- Include the requirement that fences be regularly inspected and maintained.

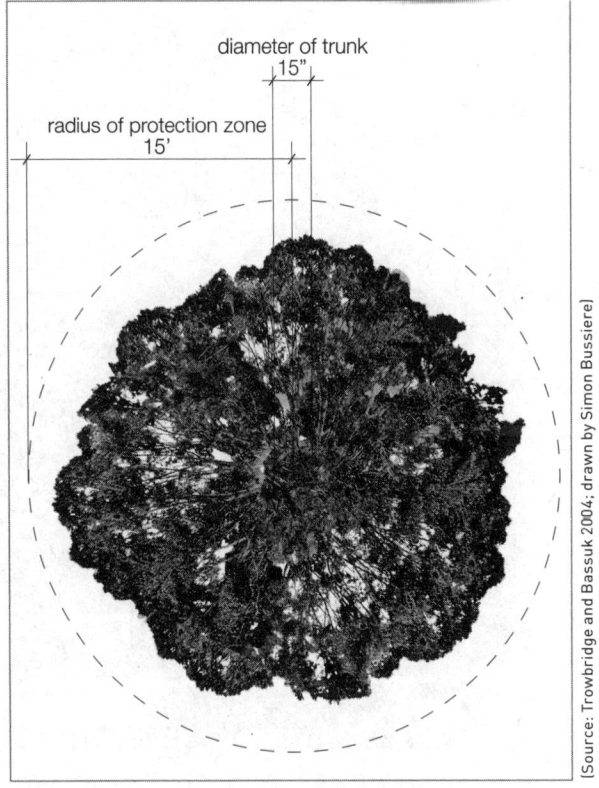

diameter of trunk
15"

radius of protection zone
15'

(Source: Trowbridge and Bassuk 2004; drawn by Simon Bussiere)

FIGURE 5-34: It is important to protect the soil structure and roots of a tree during construction. A general rule is to provide 1.0 to 1.5 ft radius protection per inch of tree diameter breast height, measured at 4.5 ft from the ground.

AVOID SOIL COMPACTION

Grading with heavy machinery and moving desirable existing soil around can destroy soil structure. Together with the design plan, the construction plan should have minimal grading changes. If grading is necessary:

- Do not work on wet or frozen soils with heavy equipment.

- Limit cut and fill to previously disturbed areas.

- Protect the soil from machinery by adding at least 10 in. of mulch or woodchips and putting plywood on top.

FIGURE 5-35: This construction site offers no protection for the existing tree. Consequently equipment is operated and materials storage is occurring within the root zone of the tree.

(Photo from Nina Bassuk)

FIGURE 5-36: This site has provided a good construction fence, but it is not large enough to protect the entire root zone of the tree.

(Photo from Hannah Carlson)

EROSION CONTROL

On the demolition and construction plans:

▶ Protect catch basins and other drainage areas from erosion runoff with hay bales or compost berms in addition to silt fences.

▶ Specify compost berms or other sediment traps in addition to silt fences downhill from any construction areas.

Various erosion control strategies should be employed based on the site-specific problems. Some ways to control erosion include:

- ▶ Seeding
- ▶ Mulching
- ▶ Sediment traps or basins
- ▶ Berms
- ▶ Woody debris

PRECONSTRUCTION MEETING AND SITE VISITS

The best assurance that a soil plan will be followed is to meet with the contractor and owner before construction starts to convey the soil protection, management, and remediation program that has been developed for the site. This can avoid mistakes, establish expectations, and be a positive step to making the contractor part of the soil management team. During construction, landscape architects should be onsite as often as possible and try to be there before or as construction occurs during stages that might require documentation or observation (grading, soil, or plant arrival). There is no substitute for making a regular appearance onsite to enforce the soil management plan.

- ▶ As part of a Q/A, Q/C program, make sure to see documentation and lab tests of the soil specifications, plant arrival and planting, structural soil construction, and so forth.
- ▶ Continuously communicate with the contractors and people working onsite about the soil protection plan, and make sure details on the construction documents are clear.

STORE AND REUSE MATERIALS ONSITE

- ▶ If good soil has to be disturbed during construction, stockpile the soil before construction begins, onsite if possible. Cover stockpiled soil so that it doesn't blow away or erode.
- ▶ Try to limit the amount of time soil is stockpiled and try to keep mound height to a minimum. If it has to wait more than a few months, anaerobic conditions can occur and soil biota can be adversely affected.

RESTORE SOILS

- ▶ Soils compacted during site construction should be modified according to the site design and design goals.

- ▶ After construction, retake soil samples in areas that were affected and complete the soil tests.

- ▶ Based on the results, follow the suggested strategies in the remediation section of this chapter.

- ▶ If soil contamination should occur (from gas/concrete spills), see the "Soil Replacement and Specialized Soils" section for soil replacement strategies.

Soil Management: Maintenance and Monitoring

The best practice for the long-term health of the soil is to create a long-term management plan. The plan should include a preliminary maintenance plan as well as an outline for a monitoring regime. Monitoring provides information and understanding of how successful the design is and how modifications in design and maintenance could benefit the health of the soil. In the first stages of the project, when deciding what the project goals should be, long-term monitoring and maintenance should be included.

MONITORING

Soil tests should be conducted on an annual or semi-annual basis to determine deficiencies and evaluate soil health. The documented changes over time can inform the adjustable maintenance plan. Amending and fertilizing regimes may change, and drainage systems, plantings, or snow and ice management may need adjusting. Likely causes of soil degradation over time include pedestrian or vehicular traffic patterns that compact or re-compact soils, and changes in water management that result in runoff and sealing of the soil surface. Soil improvement should also occur if soils were remediated. A soil remediation plan will have a specific outcome as its goal, and attainment of this outcome should be maintained and monitored. When organic matter is incorporated in a disturbed site to reduce soil compaction, for example, it is necessary to replenish organic matter or in time it will diminish. Adding two inches of composted bark or other organic matter as a mulch onto the soil surface every year will ensure that the soil organic matter content is maintained.

The soils assessment conducted during the preliminary project design, including the observational assessment, can be repeated so that any changes in soil health can be documented. Refer to "Soils in the Site Assessment" section to start creating a monitoring checklist. Keep preliminary plans for reference later on.

Knowledge and communication of the results of monitoring will continue to inform the project and other projects to come. Maintaining and restoring healthy soils can affect every other component of the sustainable site.

References

Craul, P.J. 1985. "A Description of Urban Soils and Their Desired Characteristics." *Journal of Arboriculture,* 11:330–339.

Gugino, B.K., O.J. Idowu, R.R. Schindelbeck, H.M. van Es, D.W. Wolfe, J.E. Moebius-Clune, J.E. Thies, and G.S. Abawi. 2009. *Cornell Soil Health Assessment Training Manual* (2.0 ed.). Ithaca, NY: Cornell University, College of Agriculture and Life Sciences.

Lichter, J.M., and L.R. Costello 1994. "An Evaluation of Volume Excavation and Core Sampling Techniques for Measuring Soil Bulk Density." *Journal of Arboriculture.* 20:160–164.

Thien, S.J. 1979. "A Flow Diagram for Teaching Texture by Feel Analysis." *Journal of Agronomic Education,* 8:54–55.

Trowbridge, P., and N. Bassuk. 2004. *Trees in the Urban Landscape: Site Assessment, Design and Installation.* Hoboken, NJ: John Wiley & Sons.

CHAPTER 6

SITE DESIGN: MATERIALS AND RESOURCES

▶ Meg Calkins

OVER THE LAST 100 YEARS, the construction materials industry has undergone major changes. There has been a shift away from localized use of materials to centralized large-scale production and global distribution; from minimally processed materials to highly processed ones; and from simple materials to engineered composites, mixed materials assemblies, and liberal use of chemical additives to impart a wide array of properties to materials and products. Sometimes this shift can run counter to environmental and human health concerns. World leaders at the 1992 Earth Summit declared: "A principal cause of the continued deterioration of the global environment is the steady increase in materials production, consumption and disposal" (UNCED 1992). Processes of materials extraction, processing, and distribution directly impact ecosystems and their ability to provide life-sustaining ecosystem services. And materials for construction account for a majority of the raw materials harvested and mined each year. In 2006, minerals and metals mined for construction in the United States accounted for 77 percent of all raw materials for manufacturing products (excluding food and fuel) (Matos 2009).

Materials for site construction have evolved in response to many twentieth-century trends: the shift from skilled craftsman to cheap labor in construction, increasingly nationalized standards that do not specifically address regional materials or conditions, centralized production of building materials and products, cheap and abundant resources where "real" costs of ecosystem destruction and pollution are not factored in, increasing use of composite materials, and huge growth in the global materials industry.

The result has been a resource-intensive and sometimes toxic materials industry with use of a limited palette of nationally standardized site construction materials (e.g., concrete, asphalt, pressure-treated lumber, powder-coated steel). Local, low-embodied energy structures such as earthen construction in the Southwest or dry stone construction in New England have decreased in use as labor costs are high, workers skilled in these techniques are increasingly scarce, and national building codes hamper their use.

Abundant resources, inexpensive labor, and minimal environmental regulations in developing countries have shifted production of many building materials overseas. This has further reduced designers' capacity to understand the impacts of construction material production, or even to know where they come from. Aggregate may come by train from a quarry 200 miles from the site, while the aluminum for the handrails may have visited three continents before it arrived at the site. This means that today, a far greater portion of the impacts of building materials are those related to energy consumption incurred in trucking, shipping, and train transport. These are not insignificant given the weight of many site construction materials.

Site construction materials of the twenty-first century must respond to an entirely different set of forces—global climate change, air pollution, rising fuel costs, ecological destruction, and loss of biodiversity. These forces are shaping the site and building construction industry through the rapidly growing sustainable development movement.

And they will necessitate significant changes in the materials industry. These changes may involve closed-loop material manufacturing systems that eliminate waste; use of renewable energy sources for manufacturing, processing, finishing, and transport activities; "mining" of construction demolition sites for "raw materials"; substantial reductions of toxic chemicals and resultant human and environmental exposures from material manufacture, use, and disposal; an emphasis on minimally processed, local or regional materials; and greater reuse of site structures in place or onsite.

Yet while progress is being made, selection of materials and products with minimized environmental and human health impacts remains a challenging, confusing, and sometimes even contentious issue. The appropriate materials for construction of a sustainable site will vary by impact priorities, regional issues, project budgets, and performance requirements. Some will emphasize materials that conserve resources by being reused without remanufacturing, by being extremely durable, or by closing material loops with high recycled content and manufacturer take-back programs. Others place great emphasis on low toxicity of products and emissions throughout their lifecycle, while others may regard low ecological impacts or conservation of water as the highest priority. With this wide variety of priorities comes an even wider variety of "right answers." Portland cement concrete may appear to be a "green" material for those with durability, or regionally produced materials, as a priority, whereas it might be rejected by those who are concerned about the global warming impacts of material manufacture or high-embodied-energy materials. Composite lumber (a mix of recycled plastic and wood fibers) seems like a good alternative to wood lumber for those concerned with the ecological impacts of clear-cutting forestry practices, but it may be rejected for its mixed material composition by those concerned with the closed-loop recyclability of materials.

In addition to varying priorities and goals in green material selection, there are shades of green. For instance, the ideal green material might be a natural, renewable, local and indigenous, nontoxic, low-embodied energy material such as willow cuttings for slope stabilization or rammed earth for a retaining wall; however, these materials are not appropriate in all situations. They may not be able to perform to current construction standards, construction workers may not be skilled in techniques to build structures with these materials, or they may not be appropriate for the scale of construction or performance requirements.

And claims of green abound as product manufacturers capitalize on the rapidly growing "green" segment of the construction materials industry. Yet it can be difficult for designers to cut through the hype and determine just how green the product is, let alone compare it with six or seven alternatives. Evaluating multiple products for a given use can be like comparing apples and oranges. One product may pose global warming impacts while another may involve a known human carcinogen, and a third product may require large amounts of fossil fuel–powered energy to produce, but it may be more durable with the potential to last twice as long as the first two alternatives. Techniques of sustainability assessment and life-cycle assessment are discussed later in the chapter along with resources and databases for information on green materials.

It is important to note that all of the strategies discussed in this chapter are not equal. Just diverting a waste material from the landfill is not always enough. While it is a step in the right direction, what is actually done with the diverted material will determine whether it is a large or small step. In resource conservation, as in other aspects of designing for sustainable sites, there are shades of green from light to dark. For example, chipping a reclaimed old-growth oak beam into mulch is not the highest and best use of the material. Instead, reusing it in whole form is the best use. Better yet, if the beam came from an old barn that is no longer needed, keeping the beam in place and adapting the barn structure to another use will maintain the resource in place, incurring no transportation costs and maintaining the integrity of the beam—and the old structure.

Materials and products for sustainable sites are those that minimize resource use, have low ecological impacts, pose no or low human and environmental health risks, and assist with sustainable site strategies. Within this definition, specific characteristics of materials for sustainable sites are listed in Table 6-1 and are detailed in this chapter.

TABLE 6-1: Materials for Sustainable Sites Defined*

MATERIALS OR PRODUCTS THAT MINIMIZE RESOURCE USE:
Products that use less material
Structures reused *in situ*
Reclaimed materials and products
Reprocessed materials
Postconsumer recycled-content materials
Preconsumer recycled-content materials
Products made from agricultural waste
Materials or products with reuse potential
Materials or products with recycling potential
Structures designed for deconstruction
Renewable materials
Rapidly renewable materials
Durable materials and products
Materials or products from manufacturers with product take-back programs

continues

TABLE 6-1: **Materials for Sustainable Sites Defined*** *(continued)*

MATERIALS OR PRODUCTS WITH LOW ENVIRONMENTAL IMPACTS:
Sustainably harvested or mined materials
Minimally processed materials
Low-polluting materials in extraction, manufacture, use, or disposal
Low-water-use materials in extraction, manufacture, use, or disposal
Low-energy-use materials in extraction, manufacture, use, or disposal
Low-carbon-footprint materials in extraction, manufacture, use, or disposal
Materials made with energy from renewable sources (e.g., wind, solar)
Local materials

MATERIALS OR PRODUCTS POSING LOW HUMAN AND ENVIRONMENTAL HEALTH RISKS:
Low-emitting materials and products
Materials or products that avoid toxic chemicals or by-products in their entire lifecycle
Materials and products that can be maintained without toxic products

MATERIALS OR PRODUCTS THAT ASSIST WITH SUSTAINABLE SITE DESIGN STRATEGIES:
Products that promote a site's hydrological health by reducing stormwater runoff quantities and improving hydrologic qualities
Products that reduce the urban heat island effect
Products that reduce energy consumption of site operation
Products that reduce water consumption of site operation

MATERIALS OR PRODUCTS FROM COMPANIES WITH SUSTAINABLE SOCIAL, ENVIRONMENTAL, AND CORPORATE PRACTICES
Manufacturer has developed an environmental management system
Manufacturer has inventoried and publicly disclosed all intentionally added chemical constituents
Manufacturer engages in environmentally responsible practices such as reduced hazardous air pollutants, toxic water pollutants, and generation of hazardous and nonhazardous waste
Manufacturer or representative has conducted a peer-reviewed full lifecycle assessment (LCA) or an environmental product declaration (EPD)
Manufacturer has reduced energy or water consumption and/or carbon emissions and uses renewable energy sources
Manufacturer engages in occupational safety by protecting the safety, health, and well-being of the workers who produce the products (Pharos)
Manufacturer provides fair compensation and nonexploitive conditions with equal and equitable opportunities for all workers (Pharos)
Manufacturer provides transparency and leadership in reporting and improving corporate impact on environmental, health, and social justice

* Not listed in any order of priority or importance.

SITES AND MATERIALS

Like other topics, the *SITES Guidelines and Performance Benchmarks* related to materials focus on protection and generation of ecosystem services; however, there is one major difference. The ecosystem services being protected by the materials credits are largely remote from the site being designed as most construction materials are mined, harvested, or reclaimed and then manufactured far from the project area.

SITES credits encourage resource conservation through reuse of structures in place, use of both on- and offsite reclaimed materials, reuse and recycling of land-clearing materials, use of recycled content materials, design for deconstruction, and use of regional materials. Protection of resources and sensitive ecosystems is also addressed with a prerequisite requiring projects to avoid lumber from threatened tree species and a credit rewarding use of certified lumber.

Two credits are aimed at the industries that produce site construction materials. One credit targets the plant production industry, asking that growers engage in practices such as water efficiency, recycling, and responsible propagation techniques. The other credit supports products from manufacturers who are improving their operations and production through energy efficiency, carbon reduction, water efficiency, resource reuse, lifecycle assessment activities, and corporate environmental policy measures. Other materials credits focus on reducing health and pollution impacts from volatile organic compound (VOC) release by construction materials and on using materials in a way that it reduces their contribution to the urban heat island effect.

THE LIFECYCLE OF CONSTRUCTION MATERIALS AND PRODUCTS

The typical lifecycle of materials and products begins with the extraction of raw materials from the earth and ends with the disposal of waste products back to the earth or recycled into other materials. Most material lifecycle flows are relatively linear, where materials move through the cycle once and are then disposed of; however, some are circular with product reuse, component remanufacturing, and material recycling. As our economy has globalized, more product lifecycles are becoming increasingly complex with inputs from the environment and outputs to the environment spanning many companies across many miles. The ideal material lifecycle would be a closed-loop circular flow where waste from one process or product is "food" or feedstock for another, and waste released to the environment does not exist (Figure 6-1).

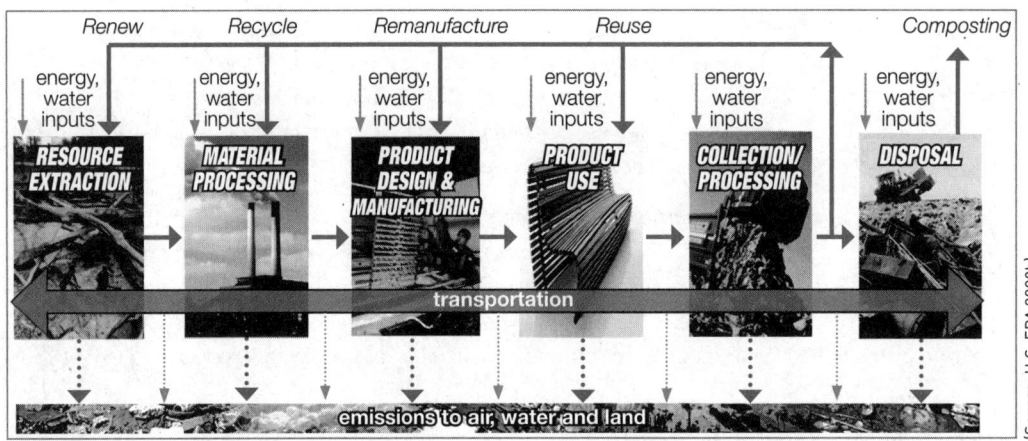

FIGURE 6-1: Typical phases of a material or product's lifecycle are illustrated, along with energy inputs and waste outputs at each phase. The disposal phase can involve reuse, reprocessing, or recycling.

RAW MATERIALS ACQUISITION

Many environmental impacts associated with materials occur very early in their lifecycle as large amounts of material are harvested or mined to obtain the actual material. Habitats are often destroyed at the point of extraction, and surrounding ecosystems are impacted through dispersion of emissions and wastes released to air, land, and water. This can be particularly serious if the wastes are toxic, such as the mineral ore waste extracted along with metals that can oxidize upon exposure to air, resulting in acid mine drainage.

Soil erosion from forest clear-cutting or mining can result in sedimentation of waterways and loss of topsoil. Gravel mining and stone quarrying can destroy habitats directly and indirectly through dust settling on vegetation and blocking photosynthesis processes. Increasingly raw materials are "mined" from both industrial (also called preconsumer) and postconsumer wastes.

PRIMARY PROCESSING AND REFINING OF MATERIALS

This phase can be very waste intensive as large amounts of material are handled and a good portion of it is discarded prior to reaching the manufacturing stage. For example, metal mining produces ore waste to metals ratios of 3:1 for iron and aluminum and far greater for copper.

Emissions, effluents, and solid wastes, some of which are toxic, are generated, and fugitive emissions, those not contained, are released to air, water, and soil. Emissions and waste that are contained are disposed of in controlled releases or recycled. Toxic waste types and quantities vary widely by industry, with the metals sector producing relatively large amounts. The stone industry produces large amounts of waste in the form of overburden, but with minimal toxicity.

Primary materials processing and refining can be very energy intensive, resulting in additional energy-related emissions. For example, the production of 1 kg of aluminum uses 12 kg of input materials and 290 MJ of energy. This leads to the release of about 15 kg of carbon dioxide (CO_2) equivalents per kilogram of aluminum produced (Gutowski 2004).

The substitution of recycled materials for primary materials can greatly reduce virgin material and energy requirements. Substitution of recycled aluminum for virgin will use only about 5 percent of the energy and resources and produces less than 5 percent of greenhouse gas emissions (Aluminum Association 2003).

MANUFACTURING

The manufacturing phase includes secondary processing, fabrication, assembly, and finishing. Compared with primary processing, manufacturing processes pose fewer impacts, partly because the volume of materials processed is smaller; however, it is the design of manufacturing processes that sets many of the requirements for primary process outputs. Manufacturing processes that can use large amounts of recycled materials will have greatly reduced energy and resource impacts in primary processing.

A large environmental and human health concern in the manufacturing phase is the use of cleaning fluids and coatings. Solvents are used for cleaning and preparation of surfaces and as carriers for coatings. Many oil-based solvents can contain toxic constituents and release VOCs, impacting human health and air quality.

Some manufacturers take steps toward minimizing the environmental and human health impacts of their materials/products by incorporating recycled materials and by-products into their products; minimizing energy and water use in manufacturing processes; using mechanical cleaning methods; and using alternative energy sources.

PRODUCT DELIVERY

The product delivery phase involves packaging and transportation. Materials and products are transported from the extraction point to the manufacturer, then to the distributor and site, and after use, to the disposal point. Transport fuel uses nonrenewable resources and releases by-products (VOCs, CO_2, carbon monoxide, particulates, and sulfur and nitrogen compounds) from internal combustion engines, substantially contributing to air pollution, human respiratory problems, and global climate change.

All transportation activities accounted for 28 percent of all greenhouse gas emissions in 2005, having risen 32 percent since 1990 (U.S. EPA 2007b). Transport emissions of trucks, ships and boats, and trains accounted for 53 percent of the total. Most fuels used in transport were petroleum-based products such as gasoline for cars and light trucks, diesel fuel for heavy trucks, or jet fuel for airplanes.

Our materials economy is increasingly global, where natural resources are sometimes extracted in one country, processed in another, and consumed in a third. In general, however, materials production often takes place near where the resources exist. For example, lumber is processed in the regions where it is harvested (Wagner 2002). Transport distances may be among the most important considerations for site designers because materials/products used in site construction are often heavy and bulky. Energy used in transport, especially by less efficient trucks and airplanes, can be greater than energy used in production if the manufacturer is located too far from the site. For example, energy used to transport a truckload of bricks 350 miles is roughly equal to the energy used to produce and fire them (Thompson and Sorvig 2000).

Use of local materials can significantly reduce nonrenewable fossil fuel use for transportation and related air pollution and greenhouse gases. Whenever possible, materials and products should be mined, processed, and manufactured within the following distances: heavy materials such as aggregate, concrete, and brick within 100 miles; medium-weight materials within 500 miles; and lightweight materials within 1,000 miles of the project site.

Packaging of products can use a large amount of materials with only a short use life. Packaging is manufactured, used, and discarded in a very short time period, and the majority of packaging is disposed of rather than reused or recycled. Some site construction materials such as aggregates are not packaged; instead they are transported directly to the site in trucks.

CONSTRUCTION, USE, AND MAINTENANCE

The use and maintenance phase can be important when considering the environmental and human health impacts of building materials and products, as they tend to be in use for very long periods of time. Durability of the product is therefore one of the most important concerns because the longer the installation lasts, the less need for replacements that use more resources and produce more waste. It is important to match the expected life of the product with the expected life of the site or structure, and to ensure that the product is reusable or recyclable after it's useful life.

Plastics, preservative-treated wood, adhesives, finishes, sealants, and cleaners used in construction and maintenance can contain hazardous chemicals. Steps should be taken to specify materials and products that require few chemicals to maintain, or low-VOC and low-toxicity cleaners and sealers should be used.

Products including lights, pumps, and controllers that use electricity can pose large environmental impacts in the use phase as they are generally in use for a long time. Therefore, energy efficiency may be the most important concern in their selection.

FINAL DISPOSITION

The final disposition phase may include "backflows" such as reuse, reprocessing, or material recycling, but it more often includes disposal directly to landfills or incinerators. Landfill access in the United States is diminishing in some regions, particularly in the well-populated Northeast. Some states have moratoriums on new landfill development or waste-reduction mandates that make recycling efforts more economical than landfill disposal. Lined landfills for the disposition of hazardous waste are limited, resulting in increased costs of disposal and transport of hazardous waste long distances.

Waste incineration is not a popular option in the United States due to pollution concerns. Incineration can be combined with an electrical generation facility or even a material-processing facility to produce power. This is called energy recovery. Emissions can be captured or "scrubbed," but pollution control equipment is an expensive capital investment and it is difficult to control the incoming waste stream, so a variety of unanticipated emissions can occur. In the United States, municipal incinerators are one of the largest sources of dioxin—a hazardous chemical and carcinogen that is expensive to scrub (U.S. EPA 2003).

Some construction materials can outlast the life of a site or structure, so planning for their reuse is an important consideration. "Deconstruction" is the term used to refer to the disassembly and salvage of materials from a building or site, as opposed to "demolition," where materials and products are destroyed and hauled to a landfill. While deconstruction takes more time and incurs higher labor costs than demolition, it may ultimately be less expensive than paying landfill costs. Resale of the materials, either whole or ground, can generate additional income.

The lifecycle impact of materials depends strongly on how they are handled after the use phase. Extending the life of materials through reuse or recycling can go a long way toward offsetting the environmental and human health impacts of their initial extraction, processing, and manufacture.

ENVIRONMENTAL IMPACTS OF MATERIALS AND PRODUCTS

The typical site construction product is comprised of a variety of constituents, each with its own complex web of inputs, outputs, and impacts that lead to its existence. This broad web can extend hundreds of miles, across the country, or even around the world—and is largely invisible to those who specify the products. Impacts—both to the environment and to human health—begin during the raw material extraction phase with destruction of ecosystems and habitats to extract mostly nonrenewable materials from the earth. They continue in processing, manufacturing, and fabricating phases, using energy and producing

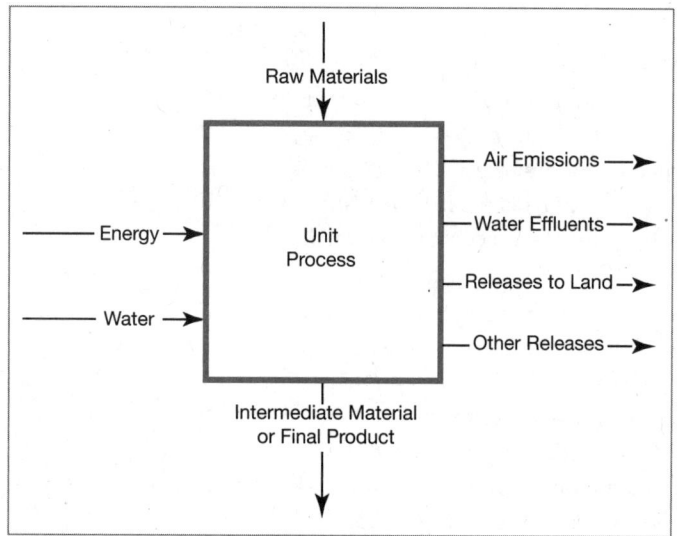

Adapted from Lippiatt 2007.

FIGURE 6-2: This diagram illustrates the flow items of a given unit process within the lifecycle of a material or product. There will likely be several unit processes for a given material or product.

emissions, effluents, and waste. Transport impacts of materials between all phases are often significant because many site construction materials are bulky and heavy. Compared with the average consumer product, the use phase of site materials is relatively long, yet practices to maintain materials and products can pose risks to the environment and to human health as well. After the useful life of the material, disposal will pose another set of impacts, yet recent increases in recycling and reuse of construction materials has substantially reduced disposal to landfills.

The inputs (resources, energy, and water) and outputs (emissions, effluents, and solid waste) that occur during the phases of a product's lifecycle result in a variety of impacts that affect the health of our ecosystems, our planet, and ourselves (Figure 6-2; Table 6-2).

TABLE 6-2: Environmental Concerns and Connections to Construction Materials

ENVIRONMENTAL CONCERNS DEFINED	CONNECTIONS TO CONSTRUCTION MATERIALS
Global climate change Global climate change is defined as long-term fluctuations in temperature, precipitation, wind, and all other aspects of the earth's climate. Climate change holds potential to impact many aspects of life on the planet with rising sea levels, melting glaciers, more violent storms, loss of biodiversity, reduced food supplies, and displaced populations.	Greenhouse gas (GHG) emissions from energy use, non–fossil fuel emissions from material manufacture (e.g., cement production, iron and steel processing), transportation of materials, and landfill gases
Fossil fuel depletion Fossil fuels, the primary source of energy for the industrialized world, are being extracted at a rate thousands of times faster than the time taken for them to renew. They are considered to be nonrenewable resources because they take millions of years to renew. As fuel reserves decrease, it is expected that extraction and refinement costs will increase.	Electricity and direct fossil fuel usage (e.g., power and heating requirements, vehicular power), feedstock for plastics, asphalt cement, and sealants, solvents, adhesives
Stratospheric ozone depletion The naturally occurring ozone layer of the stratosphere is a critical barrier that prevents harmful shortwave ultraviolet radiation from reaching the earth. Human-caused emissions of ozone-depleting substances, such as chlorofluorocarbons (CFCs; used as a propellant in manufacturing and a refrigerant) and halons (used in fire suppression systems), can cause a thinning of the ozone layer, resulting in more shortwave radiation on Earth-impacting plants, agriculture, and human health.	Emissions of CFCs, hydrochlorofluorocarbons (HCFCs), halons, nitrous oxides (e.g., cooling requirements, cleaning methods, use of fluorine compounds, aluminum production, steel production)

ENVIRONMENTAL CONCERNS DEFINED	CONNECTIONS TO CONSTRUCTION MATERIALS
Air pollution Air pollutants are airborne solid and liquid particles and gases that can pose risks to the environment and human health. Amendments to the Clean Air Act were passed in 1990 giving the U.S. EPA rights to restrict levels of criteria air pollutants (CAPS) and emissions of hazardous air pollutants (HAPs) from sources such as power plants and manufacturing facilities.	Fossil fuel combustion, mining, material processing, manufacturing processes, transport, construction and demolition
Smog Smog is a type of air pollution, resulting when industrial and fuel emissions become trapped at ground level and are transformed after reacting with sunlight. For example, ozone is one component of smog and occurs when VOCs react with oxides of nitrogen (NO_x).	Fossil fuel combustion, mining, material processing, manufacturing processes, transport, construction and demolition
Acidification Acidification occurs in surface waters and soils as acidifying gases, primarily sulfur and nitrogen compounds, either dissolve in water or adhere to solid particles. These compounds reach ecosystems primarily in the form of acid rain, through either a dry or wet deposition process.	Sulfur and NO_x emissions from fossil fuel combustion, smelting, acid leaching, acid mine drainage and cleaning
Eutrophication Eutrophication is the addition of nutrients, such as nitrogen and phosphorous, to soil or water, resulting in overstimulation of plant growth. Eutrophication is a natural process; however, it is accelerated by human activities, causing species composition alterations and reducing ecological diversity.	Manufacturing effluents, nutrients from nonpoint source runoff, fertilizers, waste disposal
Deforestation, desertification, and soil erosion Deforestation, the large-scale removal of forests, contributes to negative environmental impacts such as loss of biodiversity, global warming, soil erosion, and desertification.	Commercial forestry and agriculture, resource extraction, mining, dredging
Habitat alteration Habitats are altered or destroyed when human activity results in a change in the species composition of plant and animal communities. This can occur through practices that change environmental conditions and reduce habitat, as well as through differential removal or introduction of species.	Mining, excavating, and harvesting materials. Growing of biomaterials, waste disposal, air, water, and land releases from industrial processes
Loss of biodiversity Global climate change, the destruction of forests and habitats, and air, water, and soil pollution have all contributed to a loss of biodiversity over the past few centuries. Biodiversity is critical to the health of the ecosystems that provide many services keeping humans and the environment in relative balance. The biodiversity of ecosystems plays a role in regulating the chemistry of the atmosphere and water supply, recycling nutrients, and providing fertile soils.	Resource extraction, water usage, acid deposition, thermal pollution, air, water, and land releases from industrial processes

continues

TABLE 6-2: **Environmental Concerns and Connections to Construction Materials** *(continued)*

ENVIRONMENTAL CONCERNS DEFINED	CONNECTIONS TO CONSTRUCTION MATERIALS
Water resource depletion Human activities and land uses can deplete water resources, through use rates that exceed groundwater reserves and through practices that prevent aquifer recharge. Water resource depletion has serious consequences, by disrupting hydrological cycles, reducing the water available to dilute pollutants, and decreasing water for human consumption and for plant and animal communities that require more abundant and constant water supplies.	Water usage and effluent discharges of processing and manufacturing
Ecological toxicity Like substances that have negative effects on human health; air-, water-, or land-borne toxins can harm animals and plants, with potential negative impacts on ecosystem function and health.	Solid waste and emissions from mining and manufacturing use, maintenance, and disposal of construction materials

Sources: Ayers 2002; Azapagic et al. 2004; Graedel 1996; Gutowski 2004; UNEP 1999.

Criteria Air Pollutants

Criteria air pollutants (CAPs) are considered by the EPA to be widespread human and environmental health threats. CAPs are particulate matter (both PM10 and PM2.5), ground-level ozone, carbon monoxide (CO), sulfur oxides (S_2O), nitrogen oxides (NO_x), and lead. VOCs and ammonia are also monitored along with CAPs, as they contribute to human and environmental health risks. CAPs primarily result from fossil fuel combustion to power machinery for mining, material processing, manufacturing, transport, construction, and demolition. CAPs such as NO_x, S_2O, and particulate matter (both PM10 and PM2.5) contribute to smog which impacts respiratory function and can lead to lung damage (U.S. EPA Air and Radiation). These negative health effects have huge economic consequences for healthcare.

Hazardous Air Pollutants

Releases of hazardous air pollutants (HAPs) and other air emissions accounted for 29.5 percent of toxics release inventory (TRI)–reported chemical releases in 2008 (www.epa.gov/triexplorer/). While these air releases are of great concern, improvements in pollution control equipment, fuels, equipment, and manufacturing processes have reduced them bwy 30 percent, or 489,791,442 million pounds, beyond 2001 levels. Table 6-3 lists total on- and offsite disposal or other releases of persistent bioaccumulative toxins (PBTs), carcinogens, HAPs, and metal compounds for select manufacturing sectors for 2008 (Figure 6-3).

TABLE 6-3: Total Releases from Sectors Involved in Construction Material Manufacture from the 2009 Toxics Release Inventory

SECTOR	TOTAL RELEASES (POUNDS/YEAR)			
	PBTs	CARCINOGENS	HAPs	METALS/METAL COMPOUNDS
Metal Mining	343,291,410	431,355,787	477,827,311	1,122,128,731
Wood Products	61,680	2,086,350	6,904,342	592,068
Plastics and Rubber	88,130	12,763,059	26,578,939	3,728,054
Stone, Glass, Clay	661,095	2,179,146	7,658,525	2,802,761
Primary Metals	24,282,674	42,174,282	91,522,334	254,953,653
Fabricated Metals	863,108	6,907,150	18,427,193	21,376,209

Figures based on "Total On- and Off-Site Disposal or Other Releases."

Source: U.S. EPA 2010.

(Photo from the National Asphalt Pavement Association)

FIGURE 6-3: Reducing the temperature at which asphalt pavement is placed can reduce emissions and energy use. A side-by-side comparison of two trucks shows reduced emissions from cooler mix temperatures.

Toxic Releases to Water

Water quality is impacted by all phases of a material's lifecycle. Emissions to water are primarily through wastewater release, and while the contaminant loading is minor in quantity as compared with air emissions, it may have some important large-scale environmental impacts given the critical role that water plays in the health of living things. Direct releases to water are less than 1 percent of all toxic releases, but toxic releases to air can drift, sometimes for substantial distances, to settle on water bodies. And releases to land can find their way into ground- and surface waters.

While quantities are still small, the resulting impacts to water quality and aquatic health can be large. Raw material extraction can affect water quality through habitat alteration, which increases runoff, contributing sediment and pollutants to streams, rivers, lakes, and wetlands. Processing and manufacturing of materials/products use water and create wastewater, which can pollute water bodies. Installation of materials and products can affect water quality around the site (e.g., onsite cleanup from concrete or mortar), and disposal of materials/products can affect groundwater and surface water quality.

Hazardous Waste

Industrial waste releases to land, totaling about 15 percent of total TRI releases, amounted to 643 million pounds in 2005. These releases were disposed of in waste piles, spills, or leaks, some of which worked their way into ground- or surface waters, or into the soil. Another 18 percent, 787 million pounds, were disposed of in surface impoundments or landfills, and 972 million pounds were disposed of in Class I underground injection wells or hazardous waste landfills either on- or offsite. Seventy-three million pounds of TRI-reported chemicals were metals sent for solidification or stabilization. Surface water releases increased by 24 percent from 1990 to 2005 and land releases other than to landfills or underground injection increased 350 percent (U.S. EPA 2007a).

Energy Consumption and Renewable Energy

The industrial sector is the largest end user of energy, greater even than the transportation sector or building operations. Nonrenewable fossil fuels are the primary fuel source for industrial processes in the United States, including manufacture of construction materials (U.S. EPA 2007c). U.S. industry produces much of its power through direct fuel inputs and cogeneration as opposed to purchasing electricity. While use of direct fuel inputs can mean greater energy efficiency as there is less energy loss from power plant to industrial facility, it can result in greater air pollution as some industrial facilities are not equipped with the state-of-the-art pollution control equipment that many power plants are. The recent rise in fuel prices may make the business case for more fuel-efficient practices or use of alternative fuel sources within industry. This is particularly important for the energy-intensive cement and metal processing sectors.

Carbon Impacts

The extraction and use of fossil fuel resources dominate materials output flows with release of carbon dioxide (CO_2) accounting for 80 percent by weight of all industrial waste. This makes the atmosphere the largest dumping ground for industrial wastes (WRI 2000).

In the industrial sector, greenhouse gas emissions result directly from the combustion of fossil fuels and indirectly from the generation of electricity that is consumed by industry. Combined, these accounted for 27 percent of all CO_2 emissions in 2005. Emissions vary widely by industry due to the volume of material produced, the energy requirements to produce the material, and the type of fuel used.

Greenhouse gases and precursors are also released as by-products of non-energy-related industrial processes. These accounted for 5 percent of all U.S. GHG emissions in 2005 (U.S. EPA 2007b). Some industrial processes chemically transform materials, releasing waste gases such as CO_2, CH_4 and N_2O. Manufacturing processes related to construction material production that release significant amounts of non-energy-related GHGs are iron and steel production, cement manufacture, lime manufacture, limestone and dolomite use (in flux stone and glass), titanium dioxide production (for paint and plastic pigments), ferroalloy production (for stainless steels and other steel alloys), aluminum production, and zinc production (for galvanizing coatings and alloys).

Fossil fuels, primarily petroleum, are used as raw materials in the manufacture of asphalt, plastics, synthetic rubber, adhesives, joint compounds, and solvents. GWP emissions can occur during the manufacture of a product, such as occurs in plastics, or emissions can occur during the product's lifetime, as in the off-gassing during solvent use. Nonfuel use of fossil fuels can also sequester carbon. In 2005, nonfuel use of fossil fuels resulted in sequestration equal to 300.9 MMT CO_2 equivalents (U.S. EPA 2007b). Asphalt, road oils, and lumber are a major source of carbon sequestration in the use phase.

FIGURE 6-4: Stone, if quarried and worked locally, is a relatively low-embodied energy construction material. At Teardrop Park in New York, Michael Van Valkenburgh Associates used blue stone for the ice-water wall and other structures in the park that was all quarried within a few hundred miles of the site.

(Design: Michael Van Valkenburgh Associates; Photo credit: Paul Warchol)

Embodied Energy of Materials and Products

The energy used during all stages of a material or product's life is known as *embodied energy* (EE). Embodied energy refers to the total energy consumed in raw material acquisition, manufacture, transport, use, and disposal of a building material/product. Minimally processed materials generally have a lower EE than those with extensive or multiple manufacturing processes (Figures 6-4 and 6-5).

And if a product has high energy requirements in primary processing (e.g., stainless steel and aluminum), then it is likely that recycled-content percentages will be maximized to reduce the energy required to produce the material.

(Design: Michael Van Valkenburgh Associates; Photo credit: Elizabeth Felicella)

FIGURE 6-5: At the Alumnae Valley Restoration for Wellesley College, Michael Van Valkenburgh Associates designed a system of mown and woodland paths for meandering strolls along the marsh edge. These walkways are vegetated, making them a very low embodied energy path surfacing choice.

It is challenging to quantify all the energy used to manufacture a product. EE analyses can set different parameters of study. For example, EE is commonly performed for either cradle to gate (raw material extraction to leaving the manufacturing facility) or cradle to cradle (raw material extraction to disposal, recycling, or reuse), but it may also be performed just to evaluate one segment of the manufacturing process. If the product is complex (made from more than one material, such as a steel and wood bench), then the EE of the bench includes all of the energy inputs from both the wood and steel components and the energy inputs to assemble them. EE figures for common site construction materials are provided in Table 6-4.

Embodied Carbon of Materials and Products

Embodied carbon (EC) refers to the CO_2 released during a material or product's lifecycle. Because fossil fuels are a primary source of energy during most phases of the material or product's lifecycle, EC figures generally correspond to EE figures—if a product has a high EE, it will probably have a high EC. There are some exceptions to this. For example, aluminum has the highest EE of almost any construction material, yet EC is not correspondingly high because the primary power source for aluminum manufacture is relatively clean hydroelectric energy. Parameters of analyses will vary, but common ones are cradle to gate and cradle to cradle.

TABLE 6-4: Embodied Energy and Embodied Carbon of Site Construction Materials

MATERIAL (1 METRIC TON)	EMBODIED ENERGY (MJ/METRIC TON)	EMBODIED CARBON (KG CO_2/METRIC TON)	NOTES*
Hot-mix asphalt pavement, 0% recycled asphalt pavement (RAP)	10,583[b]	185[b]	Includes feedstock energy value Figures based on Canadian average application System boundary is cradle to asphalt plant gate
Hot-mix asphalt pavement, 20% RAP	8,890[b]	177[b]	Includes feedstock energy value Figures based on Canadian average application System boundary is cradle to asphalt plant gate
Portland cement	5,232[b]	908[b]	Canadian average figures
Portland cement, 21–35% fly ash	4,450 to 3,680[f]	740 to 610[f]	
Portland cement, 36–65% GGBFS	4,170 to 3,000[f]	630 to 380[f]	
Concrete	750[f]	100[f]	Use of a specific concrete specification is preferred to gain greater accuracy Assumed use of 12% cement
Concrete pavement	790[b]	116[b]	Canadian average figures for 30 MPa with 13% fly ash and 18% blast furnace slag System boundary is cradle to concrete plant gate Excludes reinforcing steel
Concrete, steel reinforced	1,790[f]	172[f]	100 Kg of steel per m³
Precast concrete	1,200[f]	127[f]	General mix
Concrete masonry units (CMU)	1,855[c]	180[c]	Figures based on Toronto average CMU System boundary is CMU plant gate

continues

TABLE 6-4: Embodied Energy and Embodied Carbon of Site Construction Materials *(continued)*

MATERIAL (1 METRIC TON)	EMBODIED ENERGY (MJ/METRIC TON)	EMBODIED CARBON (KG CO_2/METRIC TON)	NOTES*
Clay brick, general	4,584[c]	232[c]	Figures based on Canadian average clay brick System boundary is brick plant gate
Common Bricks	3,000[f]	230[f]	
Mortar (1:3 cement-sand mix)	1,330[f]	208[f]	Values estimated from the ICE Cement, Mortar & Concrete Model
Mortar (1:4 cement-lime-sand mix)	1,340[f]	200[f]	Values estimated from the ICE Cement, Mortar & Concrete Model
Mortar (1:2:9 cement-lime-sand mix)	1,030[f]	145[f]	Values estimated from the ICE Cement, Mortar & Concrete Model
Tile (ceramic)	12,000[f]	740[f]	Very large data range & limited data
Soil cement	680[f]	60[e]	5% cement content
Rammed earth	450[f]	23[f]	Quantity of cement not specified
Aggregate	83[f]	4.8[f]	Estimated from measured UK industrial fuel consumption data
Granular base	90[b]	7[b]	System boundary is Canadian average from cradle to road building site 50/50 fine and coarse aggregate
Granular subbase	75[b]	6[b]	System boundary is Canadian average from cradle to road building site
Stone/gravel chippings	300[e]	17[e]	
Granite	1,100[f]	640[f]	
Imported granite	13,900[a]	747[a]	To UK from Australia
Limestone	1,500[f]	87[f]	
Sand	81[f]	4.8[f]	
Lime (hydrated)	5,300[f]	760[f]	Embodied carbon was difficult to estimate
Aluminum, cast products	159,000[f]	8,280[f]	14.3 MJ/Kg feedstock; worldwide recycled content of 33%

MATERIAL (1 METRIC TON)	EMBODIED ENERGY (MJ/METRIC TON)	EMBODIED CARBON (KG CO$_2$/METRIC TON)	NOTES*
Aluminum, extruded	154,000[f]	8,160[f]	13.6 MJ/Kg feedstock; worldwide recycled content of 33%
Aluminum, rolled	155,000[f]	8,260[f]	13.8 MJ/Kg feedstock; worldwide recycled content of 33%
Brass	44,000[f]	2,460[f]	Poor data availability; largely dependent upon ore grade
Copper	42,000[f]	2,600[f]	Assumed recycled content is 37% Large data range, dependent on ore grade
Lead	25,210[f]	1,570[f]	Assumed recycled content is 61%
Steel, bar and rod	17,400[f]	1,310[f]	Assumed recycled content is 59%
Steel, galvanized sheet	22,600[f]	1,450[f]	Recycled content: 59%
Steel, pipe	19,800[f]	1,370[f]	Recycled content: 59%
Steel, plate	25,100[f]	1,550[f]	Recycled content: 59%
Steel, section	21,500[f]	1,420[f]	Recycled content not stated
Steel, sheet	18,800[f]	1,300[f]	Recycled content: 59%
Steel, wire	36,000[f]	2,830[f]	
Stainless steel	56,700[f]	6,150[f]	Assumed recycled content is 42.3% World average data from Institute of Stainless Steel Forum (ISSF) for grade 304
Titanium	361,000 to 745,000[f]	19,200 to 39,600	Figures for primary product Lack of modern data, large data range, small sample size
Zinc	53,100[f]	2,880[f]	Uncertain carbon estimates—currently estimated from typical fuel mix; assumed recycled content of 30%
Polyvinyl chloride (PVC), general	77,200[f]	2,610[f]	28.1 MJ/Kg feedstock energy (included); assumed market average use of types of PVC in the European construction industry

continues

TABLE 6-4: Embodied Energy and Embodied Carbon of Site Construction Materials *(continued)*

MATERIAL (1 METRIC TON)	EMBODIED ENERGY (MJ/METRIC TON)	EMBODIED CARBON (KG CO$_2$/METRIC TON)	NOTES*
PVC pipe	67,500[f]	2,560[f]	24.4 MJ/Kg feedstock energy (included)
PVC injection molding	95,100[f]	2,690[f]	35.1 MJ/kg feedstock energy (included). If biomass benefits are included, the CO$_2$ may reduce to 2.23 kgCO$_2$/kg, and GWP down to 2.84 kg CO$_2$e/kg
General polyethylene (PE)	83,100[f]	2,040[f]	Based on average use of types of PE in European construction 54.4 MJ/kg feedstock energy (included). Based on average consumption of types of in European construction
High-density polyethylene (HDPE)	76,700[f]	1,570[f]	54.3 MJ/kg feedstock energy (included). Doesn't include the final fabrication
HDPE pipe	84,400[f]	2,020[f]	55.1 MJ/kg feedstock energy (included)
Low-density polyethylene (LDPE)	78,100[f]	1,690[f]	51.6 MJ/kg feedstock energy (included). Doesn't include the final fabrication
Acrylonitrile butadiene styrene (ABS)	95,300[f]	3,050[f]	48.6 MJ/kg feedstock energy (included)
Nylon 6	120,500[f]	5,470[f]	38.6 MJ/kg feedstock energy (included). Doesn't include final fabrication. Plastics Europe states that two-thirds of nylon is used as fibers (textiles, carpets,…etc.) in Europe and that most of the remainder as injection moldings. Dinitrogen monoxide and methane emissions are very significant contributors to GWP.
Polycarbonate	112,900[f]	6,030[f]	36.7 MJ/kg feedstock energy (included). Doesn't include final fabrication
Polypropylene, injection molding	115,100[f]	3,930[f]	55.7 MJ/kg feedstock energy (included).
Expanded polystyrene	88,600[f]	2,550[f]	46.2 MJ/kg feedstock energy (included)
Polyurethane Flexible Foam	102,100[f]	4,060[f]	33.47 MJ/kg feedstock energy (included). Poor data availability for feedstock energy

MATERIAL (1 METRIC TON)	EMBODIED ENERGY (MJ/METRIC TON)	EMBODIED CARBON (KG CO$_2$/METRIC TON)	NOTES*
Softwood lumber (small dimension, green)	2,226[d]	132[d]	2×6 and smaller products. System boundary is cradle to average US site
Softwood lumber (small dimension, kiln dried)	9,193[d]	174[d]	2×6 and smaller products. System boundary is cradle to average U.S. site
Softwood lumber (large dimension, green)	1,971[d]	101[d]	2×8 and larger products. System boundary is cradle to average U.S. site
Softwood lumber (large dimension, kiln dried)	9,436[d]	179[d]	2×8 and larger products. System boundary is cradle to average U.S. site
Glulam beams	20,440[d]	505[d]	System boundary is cradle to average U.S. site
Parallel strand lumber	17,956[d]	529[d]	System boundary is cradle to average U.S. site
Laminated veneer lumber	10,431[d]	262[d]	System boundary is cradle to average U.S. site
Plywood	15,000[f]	1,070[f]	Carbon data split between fossil fuels and biomass (0.42 fos + 0.65 bio).

* Note: System boundaries are cradle to plant gate unless otherwise noted.

[a] Hammond, G. and C. Jones. 2006.. All data is for materials used in the UK. Data was collected from UK and EU sources and worldwide averages. Values may vary from U.S. figures but are useful for comparisons among materials.

[b] Athena Sustainable Materials Institute. 2006. (Figures converted from cubic meters, assumed density of asphalt pavement is 721 kg/m^3, assumed density of concrete is 2,354 kg/m^3. Figures for CO$_2$ are total CO$_2$ equivalents.)

[c] Athena Sustainable Materials Institute. 1998.

[d] ATHENA® Impact Estimator for Buildings, version 2.0. Athena Sustainable Materals Institute, Merrickville, Ontario, Canada. (Figures converted from cubic meters, assumed density of softwood lumber is 550 kg/m^3, assumed density of parallel strand lumber is 630 kg/m^3, assumed density of laminated veneer lumber is 600 kg/m^3. Figures for CO$_2$ are "Global Warming Potential" total CO$_2$ equivalents.)

[e] Hammond, G., and C. Jones. 2008. All data is for materials used in the UK. Data was collected from UK and EU sources and worldwide averages. Values may vary from U.S. figures but are useful for comparisons among materials.

[f] Hammond, G., and C. Jones. 2011. "Inventory of Carbon and Energy." Version 2.0. Bath, UK: University of Bath Department of Mechanical Engineering.

LIMITATIONS OF EE AND EC ANALYSES FOR CONSTRUCTION MATERIALS

Embodied energy and embodied carbon analyses as a means of evaluating materials or products can be a useful step; however, they should not be the only factor in evaluating or comparing materials and products. Some limitations of EE and EC are as follows:

▶ Unlike lifecycle assessment (LCA), these methods do not directly consider emissions, habitat impacts and waste from materials manufacture and processing.

▶ EE does not differentiate between sources of energy, and some sources, such as coal, pose greater environmental impacts than others, such as natural gas. Use of renewable sources of energy will be reflected in lower EC figures but not in lower EE figures.

▶ EE and EC figures can vary widely, sometimes by as much as 100 percent, for a variety of reasons, such as parameters and techniques of analysis, country, distances of transport, manufacturing processes, fuel inputs, and recycled content.

▶ EE and EC figures are often stated by weight or volume of a material, yet as material densities vary, comparisons can be skewed. For example, EE figures for a ton of aluminum might be compared to a ton of steel. However, the weight of actual structures made from these materials, such as handrails, would differ substantially. By most estimates, the aluminum handrail would weigh one-third of the steel one.

▶ Some embodied carbon analyses don't take into account other greenhouse gases released from the material's production. For instance, pig iron production and thermal processes used to create sinter and metallurgical coke release methane (CH_4), which is a far more powerful greenhouse gas than CO_2. More thorough EC analyses will bring carbon equivalents into the equation.

HUMAN HEALTH IMPACTS OF MATERIALS

Negative human health effects can result from exposure to toxic materials, either human-made or naturally occurring. Toxic chemicals and substances can be encountered in all phases of the lifecycle of construction materials. Many of these substances result from manufacturing, using, or disposing of plastics (e.g., Polyvinyl chloride [PVC], polystyrene, Acrylonitrile butadiene styrene [ABS], metals, metal finishes, solvents, and adhesives.) The effects of these substances vary from momentary irritation (acute) to prolonged illness and disease (chronic) to death. Some compounds are carcinogens, PBTs, mutagens, endocrine disruptors, reproductive toxicants, teratogens, or acute or chronic toxicants (Table 6-5).

Humans are exposed through numerous pathways to toxic substances during the life cycle of construction materials, and because the effects are not always noticeable, they are often overlooked. Some mine tailings left from extraction of raw materials can pollute habitats and watersheds, concentrating in fish and working their way up the food chain. Harmful chemicals can be released into water from processing and manufacture sometimes finding their way into the drinking water supply. Some manufacturing processes can pose a risk to worker health through respiratory and/or dermal exposure. And during use, materials such as asphalt sealants and CCA-treated lumber pose toxic risks to people who come in contact with the materials. Commonly used adhesives, finishes, sealants, and maintenance products can contain toxic chemicals and offgas VOCs. During landfill disposal, materials can threaten drinking water supplies, while incineration of materials such as PVC can release dioxins into the air and eventually the food supply. Material safety data sheets are mandated by the Occupational Safety and Health Administration's (OSHA) hazard communication standard and are available for all materials/products that may pose risks to worker health.

TABLE 6-5: Human Health Concerns and Agencies Tracking Them

HUMAN HEALTH EFFECT AND COMMON CHEMICAL HAZARD	AGENCIES TRACKING THE EFFECT
Carcinogens Carcinogens are defined as substances that cause or increase the risk of cancer. Some chemicals in construction materials, or released during their processing, manufacture, or disposal, are known or suspected carcinogens. Vinyl chloride (used to produce PVC) can cause liver cancer, formaldehyde is linked to cancers of the sinuses and brain, and heavy metal fumes from chromium, nickel, and cadmium can cause lung cancer (Healthy Building Network 2007).	International Agency for Research on Cancer (IARC), World Health Organization U.S. EPA Integrated Risk Information System (IRIS) Carcinogens List National Institute for Occupational Safety and Health (NIOSH), Carcinogen List Lists rank carcinogens by levels of concern such as known, probable, suspected, and so forth.
Persistent bioaccumulative toxins (PBTs) PBT pollutants are chemicals that are toxic, persist in the environment and bioaccumulate in food chains, and thus pose risks to human health and ecosystems. The biggest concerns about PBTs are that they transfer rather easily among air, water, and land, and span boundaries of programs, geography, and generations. They are associated with a range of adverse human health effects, including effects on the nervous system, reproductive and developmental problems, cancer, and genetic impacts (EPA www.epa.gov/pbt/pubs/aboutpbt.htm). Some PBTs of concern for site construction materials include dioxin emissions from manufacture of PVC and cement, from PVC disposal, and heavy metals such as lead, mercury, chromium, and cadmium from metal production and finishing.	Convention on Persistent Organic Pollutants United Nations Environment Programme (UNEP), Stockholm Convention Secretariat Stockholm Chemical Substances Information System, European Commission, Joint Research Centre, Institute for Health & Consumer Protection U.S. EPA Priority PBT List

continues

TABLE 6-5: Human Health Concerns and Agencies Tracking Them *(continued)*

HUMAN HEALTH EFFECT AND COMMON CHEMICAL HAZARD	AGENCIES TRACKING THE EFFECT
Reproductive or Developmental Toxins Reproductive toxins can disrupt both male and female reproductive systems. A teratogen is a substance that causes defects in development between conception and birth or a substance that causes a structural or functional birth defect (Agency for Toxic Substances and Disease Registry [ATSDR]). Lead and mercury, released from fossil fuel combustion and the processing of metals and metal finishes, are some reproductive toxins.	Reproductive Toxicants List, European Commission. See consolidated version of Annex I of Directive 76/769 U.S. National Institute of Health (NIH) National Toxicology Program (NTP) State of California, EPA, Office of Environmental Health Hazard Assessment (OEHHA), Safe Drinking Water and Toxic Enforcement Act of 1986
Highly Acute Toxins OSHA defines substances that are considered to have a high degree of acute toxicity as those substances which are highly toxic or toxic and may be fatal or cause damage to target organs as a result of a single exposure or exposures of short duration. OSHA has set thresholds by dose and weight of receiving body. Some listings rank substances based on a combination of their threat to public health and their presence in the environment and potential for human exposure (CERCLA 2005).	CERCLA Priority List of Hazardous Substances, Agency for Toxic Substances and Disease Registry, Department of Health and Human Services
Endocrine Disruptors Endocrine disruptors are synthetic chemicals that can interfere with hormones and disrupt development.	U.S. EPA, Office of Chemical Safety and Pollution Prevention, Endocrine Disruptor Screening Program (EDSP) European Commission for the Environment Priority List National Institute of Environmental Health Sciences (NIEHS)
Neurotoxin A neurotoxin is a poisonous protein complex that acts on the nervous system.	Neurotoxin Institute (NTI)
Mutagen A mutagen is a substance or agent that causes an increase in the rate of change in genes. These mutations (changes) can be passed along as the cell reproduces, sometimes leading to defective cells or cancer. Examples of mutagens include certain biological and chemical agents as well as exposure to ultraviolet light or ionizing radiation.	Environmental Mutagen Society (EMS) University of Maryland Partial List of Mutagens

THE LIVING BUILDING CHALLENGE MATERIALS RED LIST

The Living Building Challenge (LBC), a program of the International Living Building Institute, contains a prerequisite benchmark called the "Materials Red List." LBC requires projects that are attempting to achieve certification to avoid construction materials with the constituents listed below because of their potential impact on human and environmental health.

The project cannot contain any of the following Red List materials or chemicals.[*]

- ► Asbestos
- ► Cadmium
- ► Chlorinated polyethylene and chlorosulfonated polyethlene[†]
- ► Chlorofluorocarbons (CFCs)
- ► Chloroprene (neoprene)
- ► Formaldehyde (added)
- ► Halogenated flame retardants[‡]
- ► Hydrochlorofluorocarbons (HCFCs)
- ► Lead (added)
- ► Mercury
- ► Petrochemical fertilizers and pesticides[‡‡]
- ► Phthalates
- ► Polyvinyl chloride (PVC)
- ► Wood treatments containing creosote, arsenic, or pentachlorophenol

There are temporary exceptions for numerous Red List items due to current limitations in the materials economy.

[*] Due to manifold manufacturing processes, there is a small component exception for complex products made from more than ten constituent parts. A small component is discrete and contained in its form as introduced into the product's assembly, and must be less than 10 percent of a product by both weight and volume. It is acceptable to jump one zone, as defined in Imperative 14: Appropriate Sourcing, if compliant materials or products are not procurable within apportioned zones. Once a compliant product is available within the zone as originally designated in this standard, the exception will be removed.

Each exception request must be submitted in writing with explanation. Final documentation for granted exceptions must be accompanied by a copy of a letter sent to the manufacturer stipulating that the product purchase does not constitute an endorsement, together with a statement that requests that the company stops using the Red List material/chemical. Letters to the manufacturer are required for all exceptions, including those listed in the Standard and User's Guide. Sample letter templates are posted online in the Living Building Community. Refer to the User's Guide for more information.

[†] HDPE and LDPE are excluded.

[‡] Halogenated flame retardants include PBDE, TBBPA, HBCD, Deca-BDE, TCPP, TCEP, Dechlorane Plus, and other retardants with bromine or chlorine.

[‡‡] To attain Living Building status, petrochemical fertilizers and pesticides may not be used for the duration of the certification period or be needed for subsequent operations and maintenance.

(Source: Living Building Institute 2010)

EVALUATING ENVIRONMENTAL AND HUMAN HEALTH IMPACTS OF MATERIALS

Environmental and human health impacts associated with building material/product use can be minimized with careful attention to environmental and human health costs throughout their lifecycle. Yet materials evaluation and selection may be one of the most confusing and controversial areas of sustainable site design, with multiple variables and many right and wrong answers. Other aspects of sustainable site design may be more easily quantified. For example, hydrological analysis can disclose the necessary dimensions and type of a bioswale along a street to infiltrate and cleanse stormwater, but it is difficult to know if the path along the bioswale should be constructed from asphalt pavement made 20 miles away that may release polycyclic aromatic hydrocarbons (PAHs) over time into the water in the swale, or decomposed granite with stone fragments from a quarry adjacent to a wetland 300 miles away stabilized with renewable plant-based binder produced 1,500 miles from the site.

"What are the impacts?" is the first question that must be asked in evaluating the environmental and human health impacts of a material or product. Taking a complete inventory of all environmental and human health impacts resulting from *all* inputs and outputs at *all* phases of a material's lifecycle is a huge undertaking—some would call it endless. This practice, called a lifecycle inventory (LCI), is a complex process best undertaken by material scientists and lifecycle analysts. And an inventory of impacts takes a certain expertise to interpret and will not provide answers in comparing materials without some idea of their relative importance and the assumptions used in collecting and calculating the data.

"What is the relative importance of the magnitude and risks of the impact compared to the other materials/products impacts?" is the second question and is most critical in successful evaluation of materials. Determining how much importance to assign to a given environmental or human health impact is challenging, and different weightings can produce highly variable results. Some emphasize that using resources efficiently, reusing them in closed-loop cycles, and eliminating waste is of paramount importance (McDonough and Braungart 2002). Others claim that global climate change and reduction of carbon footprint is the most critical issue (www.architecture2030.org), and still others place greatest emphasis on reducing human health impacts of construction materials (www.healthybuilding.net).

Lifecycle Assessment

Lifecycle assessment (LCA), also called lifecycle analysis, is a qualitative technique for the evaluation of environmental impacts of construction materials and products, services, and processes. It is the most comprehensive tool for evaluating the environmental and human health impacts of materials and products. However, it is also the most challenging to understand, and clear answers are often elusive. LCA identifies and quantifies environmental impacts of a product for a given scope, usually cradle to gate (manufacturer's gate) or cradle to grave (use then disposal or reuse). All inputs (e.g., energy, water, and material resources) and outputs (e.g., emissions, effluents, and waste to air, water, and land) are quantified. The International Organization for Standardization (ISO) defines LCA as a compilation and evaluation of inputs, outputs, and the potential environmental impacts of a product throughout its lifecycle (ISO 1996). An LCA is comprised of four phases: goal and scope definition, inventory and analysis, impact assessment, and interpretation (ASTM 2005) (Table 6-7).

Environmental Product Declarations

An environmental product declaration (EPD) is a disclosure of a product's environmental impact for its full lifecycle. An EPD uses comprehensive lifecycle assessment data and is based on categories and criteria in the International Organization for Standardization's 14025 series of standards. It is then verified by a third-party audit. Theoretically, this allows for comparison of products with consistent criteria for evaluation. Currently, EPDs are used primarily among manufacturers and while they could be useful for designers' comparison of products, the challenge will be finding site construction products that have EPDs.

Sustainability Assessment

Where LCA information does not exist for a given material or product, some evaluation of the impacts can still be made using the less formal and quantitative method of sustainability assessment. The sustainability assessment (SA) method involves a set of questions and instructions for the collection of pertinent data on environmental and human health impacts of a building material or product from cradle to gate or cradle to grave. Information is gathered in categories of product feedstock materials acquisition, manufacturing, installation and operational performance, end-of-life recovery or disposal, and corporate policy. Information gathered is then evaluated based on the priorities and goals of the particular project or owner (ASTM International 2003).

Table 6-6 lists questions to consider when performing an SA for a construction material or product. It has been adapted with permission from ASTM's Committee E60 on Sustainability for use with site construction materials. The questions are not intended to produce one right answer for which product is best—that is nearly impossible given the potential complexity of information garnered. Also, different projects and owners will have differing priorities. Rather, the questions are designed to bring the major environmental impacts, hazards, and opportunities to light and to assist with material/product selection. Information and answers to the questions can be obtained from a variety of sources, including manufacturers and distributors, government resources and standards, health risk fact sheets from government agencies (U.S. or international), material safety data sheets (MSDSs), and an ever-evolving group of print and Web-based resources. Each question is written so that "yes" answers are preferred. Not all of the questions will be applicable to all materials/ products, and some may require additional questions not listed.

TABLE 6-6: Sustainability Assessment Questions

SUSTAINABILITY ASSESSMENT QUESTIONS (ASTM E 2129-10)	CONSIDERATIONS FOR EVALUATION AND COMMENTS
1. PRODUCT FEEDSTOCK MATERIALS AND ACQUISITION	
1.1 Have efforts (such as mining management, site restoration, etc.) been made to minimize and/or avoid negative environmental impacts (such as impact to rare or endangered resources or species, releases of toxic chemicals or hazardous air pollutants, and so forth) in obtaining raw materials for this product? If yes, describe these efforts.	Acquisition of feedstock materials should not involve clear-cutting, strip mining, or dredging. Refer to the IUCN Red List; the Convention on International Trade in Endangered Species (CITES); and the U.S. Fish and Wildlife Service.
1.2 Is the product a recycled content product? If YES, indicate what percentage of the product is recycled contents and differentiate between preconsumer and postconsumer recycled content.	Refer to the U.S. EPA's Comprehensive Procurement Guidelines for recommended percentage of recovered materials byproducts. Where possible, recycled content should be recovered in the same region as the recycled product manufacturing facility.
1.3 If applicable, does the recycled content product contain the percentage of recovered materials recommended by the U.S. EPA's Comprehensive Procurement Guidelines?	Where not specified in the guidelines, products with recycled content should have a minimum 25 percent postconsumer and 50 percent preconsumer content.
1.4 Is the product 100 percent recyclable? If NO, please indicate what percentage of the product is recyclable.	Composite materials and mixed material assemblies that are not easily dismantled may not have recycling potential.
1.5 Is the product a bio-based product (i.e., agricultural or forestry material)? If YES, please indicate the source and bio-based content percentage. If percentage refers to a component rather than the entire product, please specify.	Organic agriculture practices are preferred. Is the product designated under the USDA's Bio-based Affirmative Procurement Program? If YES, does it meet or exceed the program's bio-based content recommendations?
1.6 Is the product made from a renewable resource? If YES, indicate the renewable cycle time and what percentage of the product that resource represents.	A product can be considered renewable if its use life is longer than the time it takes to renew the material. For instance, a redwood lumber 2×10 can be considered a renewable product if it is in use for over 25 years.
1.7 Does the product, in the specified condition of use, meet EPA's National Volatile Organic Compound (VOC) Standards?	
1.8 Does the product, in the specified condition of use, meet the requirements of South Coast Air Quality Management District for content of VOCs?	
1.9 Are raw materials for 80 percent of the mass of the product mined/harvested /extracted and/or reclaimed within 150 miles of the site for a heavy product, 500 miles for a medium-weight product, or 1,000 miles for a lightweight product?	Environmental impacts vary by transport method. Shipping by rail and boat is more fuel efficient than by truck or plane. Full loads and direct delivery methods are more fuel efficient.

SUSTAINABILITY ASSESSMENT QUESTIONS (ASTM E 2129-10)	CONSIDERATIONS FOR EVALUATION AND COMMENTS
2. MANUFACTURING	
2.1 Has the manufacturer taken steps to minimize the use of nonrenewable energy from the point at which raw materials are gathered to the point at which the final product is transported to the building site? If yes, describe these measures.	Manufacturers should be able to provide energy use information. Does the manufacturer engage in any voluntary industrial sector energy reduction programs with the U.S. EPA, U.S. DOE, or others? Does the manufacturer purchase Green-E certified energy?
2.2 Is any of the waste produced in making this product reclaimed onsite? If YES, what percentage of the waste is reclaimed? Of the waste that is not reclaimed onsite, how is that waste handled?	Does the manufacturer recycle waste offsite into other manufacturing processes? Does the manufacturer engage in any supply chain or industrial ecology practices such as waste reuse or exchange with other manufacturers?
2.3 Does the process for manufacturing this product avoid the use of listed substances above the levels that would require reporting under the U.S. EPA's Toxics Release Inventory (TRI)? If NO, indicate how much of each substance is released per unit of product.	Refer to health impact tracking agencies listed in Table 6-5 for potential impacts.
2.4a Does the process for manufacturing the product avoid the addition of substances listed in the National Toxicology Program's Report on Carcinogens?	2.4b If substances listed in the National Toxicology Program's Report on Carcinogens are added directly in the manufacturing process or are reported by suppliers on (MSDS) do the concentrations fall below levels required to be reported under federal regulations on the products' MSDS? If NO, indicate the substance, classification, and concentration per unit of product. 2.4c Does the process for manufacturing the product avoid the addition or byproduct production of substances listed in the EPA's Persistent Bioaccumulative Toxin (PBT) list or the Stockholm Convention list of Persistent Organic Pollutants (POP)?
2.5 Have any recent improvements been made to limit negative environmental impacts relating to the manufacturing process? If YES, describe the benchmark against which the improvements are measured and the degree of improvement.	
2.6 If water is used during the production process, have water conservation or recycling measures or both been initiated? If YES, describe the measures and what percentage of the total water usage they address.	When process water is released has it been cleansed, filtered, or treated to remove pollutants?

continues

TABLE 6-6: Sustainability Assessment Questions *(continued)*

SUSTAINABILITY ASSESSMENT QUESTIONS (ASTM E 2129-10)	CONSIDERATIONS FOR EVALUATION AND COMMENTS
2.7 Has the manufacturer undertaken any of the following actions? If YES, indicate when the action(s) was (were) taken and describe the benchmark against which the improvements are measured and the degree of improvement.	2.7a Redesigned a production process to decrease greenhouse gas emissions? 2.7b Redesigned a production process to decrease liquid effluents? 2.7c Redesigned a production process to utilize less toxic materials? 2.7d Substituted safer solvents in a production process? 2.7e Instituted more stringent dust controls? 2.7f Installed smokestack particulate collectors or gas scrubbers? 2.7g Installed or improved in-plant solid and toxic waste reduction programs?
2.8 Does the manufacturing facility comply with or exceed applicable occupational, health, and safety requirements?	Are MSDSs required for manufacturing or fabrication workers? Does the manufacturing facility comply with OSHA requirements?

3. INSTALLATION AND OPERATIONAL PERFORMANCE

3.1 If applicable, does the product qualify for an EPA Energy Star Program rating or meet the energy efficiency recommendations of the DOE's Federal Energy Management Program?	
3.2 Describe the product's energy efficiency impacts.	
3.3 Describe routine maintenance procedures for the product.	Can the product be maintained without use of toxic cleaners, sealers, or coatings?
3.4 How long will the product last in the site construction if maintained properly with routine maintenance procedures?	Does the expected life of the product (or the warranty) meet or exceed the expected life of the built site? Does the manufacturer provide information on the service life of the product or encourage the use of professional guidelines to determine the service life of the product?
3.5 Does the manufacturer provide detailed instructions with the product upon delivery to the job site for the proper use and maintenance required in order to ensure that this product will last this long?	
3.6 Is any component of the product an installation hazard for construction workers? If YES, describe steps that are taken to minimize these impacts.	Refer to MSDSs for information.
3.7 If applicable, does the product qualify for an EPA WaterSense® rating?	

SUSTAINABILITY ASSESSMENT QUESTIONS (ASTM E 2129-10)	CONSIDERATIONS FOR EVALUATION AND COMMENTS
4. END-OF-LIFE RECOVERY OR DISPOSAL	
4.1 Can the product be easily removed from the installation and reused/recycled after its use?	Does the manufacturer facilitate ultimate deconstruction of the site (in which components are taken apart for reuse) by, for example, designing products for disassembly DfD? If YES, describe. Refer to DfD strategies later in this chapter.
4.2 Is the product recyclable?	Do recycling facilities for the material or product exist within reasonable transport distances of the site? Some finishes or adhesives may render the product unrecyclable.
4.3 Is the product biodegradable or compostable?	Will the product break down into benign, organic components within a reasonable period?
4.4 If not recyclable, is the product hazardous to dispose of?	Does the material or product pose hazards in disposal either in landfills or incinerators? If landfilled, will chemicals from the material/product affect soil or groundwater? If incinerated, will harmful chemicals or particulates be released? Is it difficult to "scrub" any constituents (e.g., dioxins)? Has the EPA targeted any chemicals released during disposal for reduction?
5. CORPORATE ENVIRONMENTAL POLICY	
5.1 Does the manufacturer have a written environmental policy?	Has the manufacturer implemented an Environmental Management System (EMS) plan?
5.2 Does the manufacturer have a reclamation program or any other program in place to facilitate the recycling or reuse of its product by accepting return of the product at the end of its useful life?	If NO, comment on the environmental impact of the product as a waste material. If YES, comment on how much of the product is actually reused or recycled at the end of the product's useful life.
5.3 Does the manufacturer have a program in place to reduce the amount of the product's packaging? If YES, describe.	
5.4 Does the manufacturer have a program in place to facilitate the return, reuse, recycling, or composting of the product's packaging? If YES, describe.	
5.5 Does the manufacturer provide information on the service life of the product or encourage the use of professional guidelines to determine the service life of the product?	

continues

TABLE 6-6: Sustainability Assessment Questions *(continued)*

SUSTAINABILITY ASSESSMENT QUESTIONS (ASTM E 2129-10)	CONSIDERATIONS FOR EVALUATION AND COMMENTS
5.6 Does the manufacturer provide information regarding natural disaster mitigation, such as performance of the product during a natural disaster or appropriate response after a natural disaster?	
5.7 Is documentation available to support the product's environmental claims?	Has the manufacturer engaged with credible third-party product certification or evaluation systems?
5.8 Is there other information about the environmental quality of the building product that should be taken into consideration?	Has the manufacturer conducted a full LCA or Environmental Product Declaration (EPD)?

Sources: Adapted from ASTM E2129-10 2010; HBN Pharos Project (www.pharosproject.net/wiki/); Mendler, Odell, and Lazarus 2006; Center for Sustainable Building Research 2007.

Lifecycle assessment (LCA) and sustainability assessment (SA) differ from lifecycle costing (LCC) in that an LCA and SA deal with environmental and human health costs over the life of a material and LCC deals with the economic costs. They all consider the length of time that the product will be in use and what maintenance it will need during that time. While LCA is of primary importance to sustainable design, performing an LCC may also be helpful as it could demonstrate that higher first costs of a material will be recovered over the material's life.

TABLE 6-7: Tools for LCA Data for Construction Materials

TOOL	SPONSORING ORGANIZATION
Athena Environmental Impact Estimator (EIE)	ATHENA
Building for Environmental and Economic Sustainability (BEES)	National Institute of Standards and Technology
EcoScan	TNO Built Environment & Geosciences
EIME	Bureau Veritas CODDE
GaBi	PE International GmbH
Green-E	Ecointesys—Life Cycle Systems
LCA-Evaluator	GreenDeltaTC
LEGEP	LEGEP Software GmbH
OpenLCA Framework	GreenDeltaTC
REGIS	Sinum AG
SimaPro	PRe Consultants B.V.
WISARD	Ecobilan—PricewaterhouseCoopers

Source: European Commission, Joint Research Centre (n.d.).

Standards, Labels, and Certification Systems

As more attention is paid to environmental and human health impacts of construction materials, a wide variety of standards, rating systems, regulations, labels, guidelines, and certification programs have been developed to guide specifiers in material and product selection. They have been created by nonprofit organizations, government agencies, for-profit organizations, manufacturers, and trade associations. Self-declarations are created by the product manufacturer as marketing claims, specifications, or MSDS sheets. They are not often verified by an outside source. Second-party declarations may be generated by a trade group or an outside consulting firm; however, as the manufacturer is likely contributing partial or full funding for the generation of information, there is potential for conflicts of interest. Certifications by neutral third-party organizations are generally preferable for this reason.

Criteria of standards and labels vary widely from addressing a single issue, such as recycled content or indoor air quality, to inclusion of a broad range of evaluation criteria. Tables 6-8, 6-9, and 6-10 list summaries of some major green product certification programs, standards, and databases that include site construction materials.

TABLE 6-8: Product Certification Systems

EcoLogo, Environmental Choice EcoLogo Program Third-party certification	EcoLogo is a third-party certification system established in 1998 by the Canadian government with over 250 products. Site construction products include: paints, wood preservatives, adhesives, release agents, sealants, and steel. The development of EcoLogo certification criteria is a multistep process involving purchasers, environmental groups, industry, consumers and consumer groups, academia, government, and other interested groups. As a "Type I ecolabel" (as defined by the International Organization for Standardization in the Standard ISO 14024), criteria are developed and evaluated using a lifecycle approach.
Greenseal	Greenseal is a nonprofit organization that utilizes a science-based lifecycle approach to establish standards for a variety of materials and coatings. Greenseal Standards related to site construction materials address paints, degreasers, adhesives, cleaners, and maintenance practices. Greenseal also lists products that achieve their standards.
Cradle to Cradle (C2C) Certification McDonough Braungart Design Chemistry (MBDC) Second-party certification	C2C is a certification program for building products. Products can be certified as Silver, Gold, or Platinum products with a focus on chemical hazards, material reuse, recycled content and recyclability, energy use, water use, and social responsibility. Homogeneous materials or less complex products can be labeled as Technical/Biological Nutrients with Cradle to Cradle Certification. Certified products are listed by product type, company name, and certification ratings are listed on the MBDC website. C2C certified site construction products include: wood treatments, concrete additives, athletic surfaces, coatings, and cleaners.

continues

TABLE 6-8: Product Certification Systems *(continued)*

Energy Star U.S. EPA and U.S. DOE Third-party certification	Energy Star is a voluntary labeling system for energy efficient appliances, lighting, and heating and cooling equipment that is a joint program of the Department of Energy and the EPA. Thresholds are set to capture about one-quarter of the market for a given product or appliance. Manufacturers must follow a set of third-party procedures to verify their information.
WaterSense U.S. EPA Third-party certification	This EPA program recognizes water-efficient products that are independently tested and third-party certified. Site construction products that are certified include irrigation systems and irrigation control technologies.
Forest Certification Systems	*See section on Certified Wood*
Green-e Energy	The Green-e Energy certification assures consumers and businesses in the United States and Canada that they are reducing the environmental impact of their electricity use. Green-e Energy was established in 1997 in order to provide consumer protection in the emerging and unregulated voluntary renewable energy market through clear guidelines, disclosures, and standards. Green-e Energy is a rigorous consumer protection program for renewable energy with a transparent standard and hundreds of stakeholders participating in setting and revising that standard.
SMaRT (Sustainable Materials Rating Technology) Third-party certification	SMaRT is a multi-attribute standard that uses a point system to evaluate products on a wide range of impacts. Developed by the Institute for Market Transformation to Sustainability (MTS), the aim of SMaRT is to *"Provide Substantial Global Benefits for Building Products, Fabric, Apparel, Textile & Flooring covering over 80% of the world's products with Environmental, Social, & Economic criteria."*
EU Ecolabel	The European Union Ecolabel is a third-party certification program that awards its label to a wide variety of products and services that meet its environmental criteria. Products from non-European countries can be certified if those products are placed on the European market.

TABLE 6-9: Standards for Green Materials and Products

Comprehensive Procurement Guidelines U.S. EPA Environmentally Preferable Purchasing Program	The Comprehensive Procurement Guideline (CPG) program is part of the EPA's continuing effort to promote the use of materials recovered from solid waste. Buying recycled-content products ensures that the materials collected in recycling programs will be used again in the manufacture of new products. The CPG sets recycled-content guidelines for many site construction materials.

South Coast Air Quality Management District **Rule 1113 Architectural Coatings** **Rule 1168 Adhesives and Sealants**	VOC limits per liter for hundreds of architectural coating and adhesive and sealant types. Threshold limits are revised every few years. Commonly used coating limits for site construction materials are as follows: Flat paints: 50 g VOC/liter Nonflat coatings: 50 g VOC/liter Wood preservatives: 350 g VOC/liter Waterproofing sealers: 100 g VOC/liter Traffic coatings: 100 g VOC/liter Concrete-curing compounds: 100 g VOC/liter

TABLE 6-10: Green Product Directories, Databases, and Information

EPA Environmentally Preferable Purchasing Program U.S. EPA	The U.S. EPA's Environmentally Preferable Purchasing (EPP) program is designed to assist the federal government with green purchasing but it also provides useful information for finding and evaluating information about green products and services.
GreenSpec **Pharos Project** Building Green Healthy Building Network	Initially established as two separate entities, GreenSpec and Pharos have recently partnered to offer both services from one location. GreenSpec is a subscription online and print directory of environmentally preferable product manufacturers by BuildingGreen, the publishers of *Environmental Building News*. The directory lists over 2,100 listings from more than 1,500 companies organized by the CSI MasterFormat structure. Pharos is a materials evaluation system, database, and building product information site with a focus on environment and resources, health and pollution, and social and community sustainability of construction materials and products. Joint membership offers access to both systems.
California Integrated Waste Management Board (CIWMB)	The CIWMB's Recycled Content Product (RCP) Directory lists thousands of products containing recycled materials as well as information about the manufacturers, distributors, and reprocessors of these products. Some products are certified under the state's State Agency Buy Recycled Campaign (SABRC).
Whole Building Design Guide National Institute of Building Sciences	The Whole Building Design Guide offers the Federal Green Construction Guide for Specifiers. The guide contains model green guide spec sections for many site construction materials and technologies.
Material Safety Data Sheets (MSDS)	OSHA-required documents supplied by manufacturers of products containing hazardous constituents. MSDSs contain information regarding potentially significant levels of airborne contaminants, storage and handling precautions, health effects, odor description, volatility, expected products of combustion, reactivity, and procedures for spill cleanup.

SITE AND REGIONAL ASSESSMENT FOR MATERIALS

Several inventory, analysis, and research activities should be undertaken in the predesign and assessment phase of a site design project to identify opportunities for resource conservation, material reuse, priorities of the client, and environmental issues related to materials and products. Table 6-11 offers a checklist for site and regional assessment activities related to site construction materials and products.

TABLE 6-11: Site and Regional Assessment for Site Construction Materials and Products

ASSESSMENT ITEMS	CONSIDERATIONS
RESOURCE CONSERVATION ASSESSMENT	
In situ structure reuse	Identify and inventory structures, including subgrade ones, on the site that can be refurbished and reused in place.
	Structure reuse can influence the design of the site so a detailed inventory of all structures must be undertaken prior to preliminary design.
On-site reclaimed materials	Identify and inventory structures, including subgrade ones, that can be deconstructed and the members reused in whole form (Figures 6-6 and 6-7).
	Including a deconstruction contractor can help identify materials for reuse.
On-site reclaimed land clearing materials	Identify and inventory plants, soil, or rocks that can be reclaimed during site preparation and reused in new construction.
On-site reprocessed materials	Identify and inventory structures onsite that can be removed and the materials reprocessed for reuse in new site construction.
On-site reprocessed land clearing materials	Identify land-clearing materials that can be reprocessed for use onsite.
Deconstruction material outlets	Identify local deconstruction material outlets that will take materials for either whole reuse or recycling.
	These facilities should be in close proximity to the project site. Facilities that will take heavy materials should be within 50 miles of the site. A deconstruction contractor can help identify material outlets during the site assessment phase.
Off-site sources of materials	Identify sources of locally manufactured, reclaimed, recycled content, bio-based, FSC-certified, and/or other appropriate construction materials and products.
	Sources for appropriate materials and products should be identified prior to the design phase of a project, so that the material and products can inform the design.
	Soils and aggregates should be extracted within 50 miles of the site, plants within 250 miles, and other materials within 500 miles.

ASSESSMENT ITEMS	CONSIDERATIONS
OWNER AND STAKEHOLDER PRIORITY ASSESSMENT	
Assess owner and stakeholder priorites	Assess priorities of owners and project stakeholders with respect to environmental and human health impacts of materials and products. Some will want to minimize toxicity of materials while resource use will not be as big a concern. Others will want to use as many local materials as possible to support the local economy. Given that there are few materials and products that minimize all impacts, priorities by which potential materials can be evaluated should be established early in the design process.
Understand the expected life of the project	Materials and products should be specified to match their expected durability with the anticipated life of the site. Appropriate detailing and connections can maximize durability of materials. More durable materials may have fewer maintenance requirements.
Understand the expected maintenance intensity of the site during operation	Maintenance priorities of owners will vary widely and can impact choices of materials and products specified for the site construction. For instance, if an owner does not want to maintain pavements, porous pavements should not be used.
ENVIRONMENTAL CONCERNS ASSESSMENT	
Identify sensitive ecosystems on or around the site that may be impacted by construction materials or maintenance products and processes	Care should be taken to reduce pollution impacts from materials installation and maintenance activities, and even the materials themselves. Polycyclic aromatic hydrocarbons from asphalt pavement sealants can impact adjacent waterways. Wood with copper-based preservatives can impact adjacent aquatic ecosystems as the copper leaches out of the wood over time.
Identify local issues and priorities related to pollution and urban heat islands around the site.	Construction materials for sites located in urban or densely developed suburban areas should be selected to minimize pollution and urban heat island impacts. Pavement areas should be minimized, and/or high-albedo or porous materials specified. Care should be taken to reduce pollution impacts from materials installation and maintenance activities, and even the materials themselves. Asphalt pavement can pose pollution impacts during installation, use, and maintenance, and concrete containing fly ash with high levels of mercury may impact air quality and adjacent receiving waters (EPA 2000; Golightly et al. 2005; Lawrence Berkeley National Laboratory 1999).
Identify climate or pollution conditions that might impact materials or products on the site.	Climate and pollution conditions can impact the longevity of construction materials. Some metals will corrode in environments with acid rain, high pH levels, or salt air. Wood use in extremely damp environments will need to be decay resistant or preservative treated. Areas of extreme temperatures will impact specification of pavement materials and deck/fence materials. Understanding potential climate impacts such as depth of frostline and freeze/thaw extremes can allow for adequate sizing for durability, but not oversizing of structures resulting in inefficient resource use.

FIGURE 6-6: Miller Company Landscape Architects "mined" steel canopy structures from a nearby defunct train station and repurposed them for reuse at the 14th Street Pocket Park in Oakland California.

FIGURE 6-7: The repurposed canopy structure in the 14th Street Pocket Park.

(Source: Miller Company Landscape Architects)

RESOURCE EFFICIENCY

Efficient use of resources may be the single most important strategy when specifying construction materials and products for sustainable sites. Using fewer resources can reduce environmental and human health impacts, including habitat alteration from excavation and harvesting, and waste, air pollution, and energy use from manufacturing. It can also reduce the volume of waste sent to a landfill. Proponents of closed-loop systems advocate the elimination of waste either by not producing it or using it as "food" for new products and processes. Early efforts at recycling focused on what could be done with the mountain of waste that exists. While this can minimize the amount of waste that is landfilled and incinerated, it will not significantly address the problem of excessive use of limited resources. Instead, a shift in the construction material production, design, and specification strategies can move the industry toward closed-loop design.

Many of the principles discussed in this chapter advocate some form of closed-loop material systems, yet closing loops is challenging in our current manufacturing culture, particularly in the manufacture of construction materials. Recycling outlets can be scarce, products and structures are not designed for disassembly, demolition is still more common than deconstruction, and in the United States there are no requirements for manufacturers to take back products after their use life, or even to take back packaging.

A culture of market response, minimal government intervention, inexpensive virgin resources, and low waste disposal costs all contribute to these challenges to closing material loops. It can be challenging for recycled-content or remanufactured products to compete economically with products made from virgin resources. Table 6-12 lists a hierarchy of waste reduction strategies that can work toward the ideal of a closed-loop lifecycle of materials.

TABLE 6-12: Resource Efficiency Hierarchy in Generally Decreasing Order of Preferability

	REDUCE
Prevent building and rebuilding— use no new material	Don't build or rebuild, and design sites for adaptability with open plans and multi-use spaces so the site and its structures do not require adaptation in a short period of time. Engage in scenario planning during the programming phase to envision multiple scenarios of site use.
	Design long-lasting structures with durable materials and details.
	Detail long-lasting connections.
Reuse site structures in place, in whole form	Don't tear down and rebuild structures (Figures 6-10 and 6-11).
	Adapt and modify sites and site structures to new uses.
Use less material	Use durable materials that will last the life of the landscape and are reusable multiple times in other structures.
	Design to minimize construction waste such as "cutoffs," excessive finish waste, and so forth.
	Design smaller structures (e.g., smaller decks, thinner slabs and walls, flexible footings, cable ballustrades rather than hollow steel tube rails) (Figures 6-8 and 6-9).
	Use fewer elements.
	Specify smaller members (e.g., use 4×4 posts, not 6×6, unless structurally necessary).
	Expose structures as the finish (e.g., leave concrete walls exposed, don't coat with stucco or face with stone or brick).
Design for disassembly (DfD)	Designing sites with deconstruction and reuse of materials after their useful life in the current application can extend the lives of materials, save resources, and limit associated impacts of new material production. See below for principles of DfD.
	RENEW
Use materials from renewable resources	Use living materials (e.g., slope stabilization with plants, willow wattles, willow fences, and domes).
	Use bio-based materials (e.g., jute, hemp, bamboo, strawbale, plant-based stabilizers, and form-release agents).
	Use renewable materials (e.g., wood if it is certified as sustainably grown and harvested).
	Look for renewable materials that can be reused, recycled, or composted.

continues

TABLE 6-12: Resource Efficiency Hierarchy in Generally Decreasing Order of Preferability *(continued)*

	RECLAIM AND REUSE
Reuse components whole and onsite	Structures such as buildings, pavements, retaining walls, fences, and decks that exist onsite can be dismantled and the members can be reused onsite in whole form.
	Care should be taken to not compromise the materials during dismantling.
	Can save material procurement expenses; however, preparing the materials for reuse may incur labor costs.
	Storage facilities onsite should maintain the integrity of the material (e.g., recovered wood should be protected from moisture).
	Survey all potentially reusable materials prior to the design phase.
	Budget for additional labor required to make the components reusable.
	Use of reclaimed materials from the site can save money and add meaning and richness to a site design.
	Trees, plants, rocks, and soil can be salvaged, stored, and reused onsite preserving vegetation, existing biomass, and soil resources. Care should be taken to store vegetation and stockpile soil to preserve their integrity.
Reclaim components whole for use on other sites	Employ deconstruction rather than demolition techniques to reclaim materials for reuse first or recycling if not reusable in whole form.
	Store for use on other projects, distribute to salvage facilities, or place in online material exchanges.
	Budget for additional labor required to make the components reusable.
Use reclaimed materials from other sites	Use of reclaimed materials from other sites can save money and add meaning and richness to a site design.
	Source materials prior to the design phase to let the materials inspire the design and ensure type and quantity.
	Budget for additional labor required to make the components reusable.
	REPROCESS AND RECYCLE
Reprocess existing structures and materials for use onsite	Structures such as concrete paving and walls and asphalt pavement can be removed during site demolition, crushed, graded, and reused as fill and base material onsite.
	Noise and dust may be a concern; however, bringing reprocessing equipment to the site can save haul costs and transport energy use.
	Reprocessing materials downcycles them from their original form. Materials should only be reprocessed onsite if there is room to store them during construction without damage to site ecosystems.
	Although downcycled, reprocessing materials uses less energy and produces fewer emissions than remanufacturing for recycling.
	Demolished vegetation and trimmings can be reprocessed and reused onsite. Felled trees can be cut into cordwood and reused in structures. Branches and brush can be reused whole or composted.
	Excavated soil can be used for earth construction in the form of rammed earth, soil cement, compressed earthblock or adobe brick.

Reclaim onsite structures and distribute to off-site reprocessing facilities	Demolished concrete, asphalt, aggregate, wood, asphalt shingles, and glass can be taken to local reprocessing facilities where they will be stockpiled for use on other sites. Care should be taken to minimize haul distances.
Use reprocessed materials from other sites	Crushed concrete, tires, asphalt, glass, and other materials can be obtained from reprocessing facilities for use as aggregates in base and backfill applications as well as in new asphalt, concrete, and other pavements. Care should be taken to minimize haul distances.
Specify recyclable materials	By specifying materials with recycling potential, the chances that they will be recycled after the useful life of the site or structure are increased. Commonly recycled materials are clean wood (not pressure treated or coated with lead-based paint), metals (unless coatings prohibit), polyethylene-based plastics, concrete, asphalt, precast concrete products, and bricks. Avoid mixed material assemblies or products where materials are not easily separated.
Use recycled-content materials	With the exception of metals and some plastics, most recycled-content products are down-cycled. Refer to U.S. EPA Comprehensive Procurement Guidelines for recycled-content thresholds for site products.
Reclaim onsite materials and distribute to offsite recycling facilities	While reuse of reclaimed, deconstructed materials in whole form is preferable, there will be some materials that are not reusable, so sending the materials offsite to recycling facilities and secondary production processes can save resources for new products. Recycling can be challenging because the material composition is diverse or the assembly is comprised of mixed materials.
Facilitate onsite recycling with area for storage and collection of recyclables	Facilitate recycling over the life of the site with facilities for storage and collection of both organic and inorganic recyclables. Plan for these facilities in the site design process.

RECOVER

Divert nonusable materials for energy recovery	Where materials can't be reclaimed or recycled, recovering their calorific value in waste-to-energy facilities with adequate pollution controls is preferable to disposal in a landfill. Energy recovery can be accomplished by either direct incineration in municipal waste incinerators to generate heat and electricity or directly in industrial production processes to replace other fuels. An example of this is waste tires burned to power cement kilns. Energy recovery is controversial because while it recovers energy from waste, pollution impacts can be substantial if not well controlled. High-efficiency pollution control equipment is a large capital investment that many facilities are not willing or able to make unless mandated by regulations.

DISPOSE

Disposal of materials in controlled landfills	The least preferable option for waste is disposal to landfills. If the waste can't be reclaimed, recycled, or energy recovered, it should be disposed of in an appropriately controlled landfill.

FIGURE 6-8: A parking arbor in Asperg, Germany, uses smaller wood members to provide enclosure. Small lumber sizes and built-up members can be derived from younger trees, shortening the renewability period for wood products.

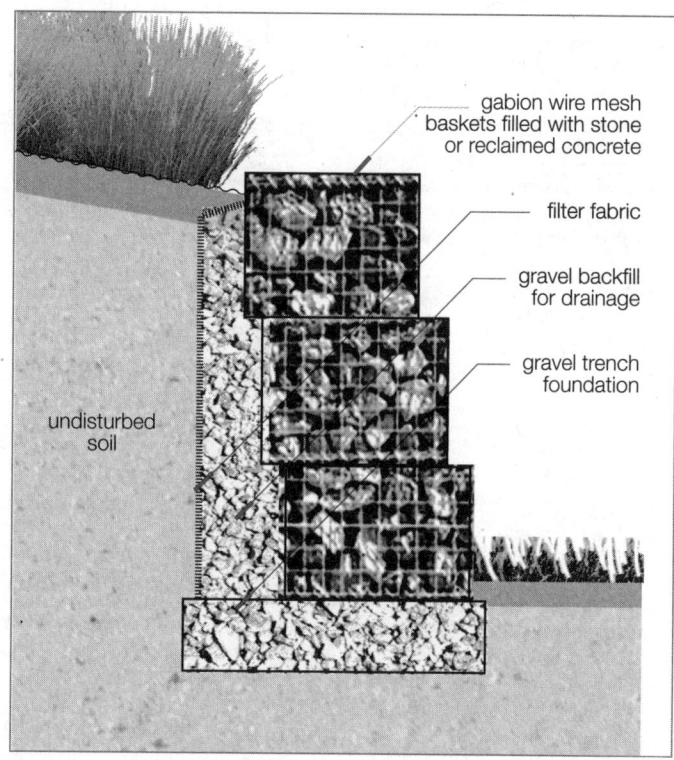

gabion wire mesh
baskets filled with stone
or reclaimed concrete

filter fabric

gravel backfill
for drainage

gravel trench
foundation

undisturbed
soil

FIGURE 6-9: Low gabion retaining walls can be set on a gravel trench footing that is 6 to 12 in. deep, avoiding the extensive material use of a poured-in-place concrete footing that must extend 6 in. below the frost line. Gabion walls are particularly resource efficient if the gabions are filled with reclaimed broken concrete or rubble from on or nearby the site.

FIGURE 6-10: In section one of The Highline, James Corner Field Operations with Diller Scofidio Architects collaborated to transform 2,640 linear feet of an abandoned elevated New York City rail line into a neighborhood park and promenade.

[Design: James Corner Field Operations (project lead) and Diller Scofidio + Renfro; Photo by Iwan Baan © 2009 courtesy of Friends of the High Line]

FIGURE 6-11: The existing rail structure of the High Line was retrofitted to make it safe, accessible, and usable, yet the majority of the structure was reused. The design retains elements of the historic railroad.

EU PRINCIPLES FOR WASTE MANAGEMENT

As part of the EU waste management directive from 2003, the following principles guide individual countries' efforts at waste management and reduction (European Commission 2003):

Waste Management Hierarchy   Waste management strategies must aim primarily to prevent the generation of waste and to reduce its harmfulness. Where this is not possible, waste materials should be reused, recycled, recovered, or used as a source of energy. As a final resort, waste should be disposed of safely (e.g., by incineration or in landfill sites).

Self-sufficiency at community and, if possible, at member state level. Member states need to establish, in cooperation with other member states, an integrated and adequate network of waste disposal facilities.

Proximity Principle   Wastes should be disposed of as close to the source as possible.

Precautionary Principle   The lack of full scientific certainty should not be used as an excuse for failing to act. Where there is a credible risk to the environment or human health of acting or not acting with regard to waste, that which serves to provide a cost-effective response to the risk identified should be pursued.

Producer Responsibility   Economic operators, and particularly manufacturers of products, have to be involved in the objective to close the lifecycle of substances, components, and products from their production throughout their useful life until they become waste.

Polluter Pays   Those responsible for the generation of waste, and consequent adverse effects on the environment, should be required to pay the costs of avoiding or alleviating those adverse consequences.

Best Available Technique Not Entailing Excessive Cost (BATNEEC)   Emissions from installations to the environment should be reduced as much as possible and in the most economically efficient way.

Design and Detailing for Durability

Designing and detailing a site and its structures to last a long time is the best way to mini-mize use of resources. Structures that double their use life essentially halve the environmen-tal impacts of their construction. Designing for durability is twofold. The first aim is to detail structures with *physical* durability in mind (Table 6-13). The structure should be designed and maintained to last at least for the intended life of the site, and ideally beyond either in place or reclaimed and reused elsewhere. The second aim should be to design a *functionally* durable site for flexible use and with adaptive reuse in mind. Designing sites for adaptability with open plans and multiuse spaces, so the site and its structures do not require adaptation in a short period of time, can help minimize future use of resources. This can allow a second life for a site without total reconstruction should the current use of the site change.

TABLE 6-13: Environmental Factors That Can Impact the Durability of Site Structures

Sunlight and UV rays can fade or degrade the surfaces of some materials including most plastics, wood, fabrics, and paints.
Thermal stress from weather extremes can cause expansion and contraction, disfiguring materials and joints.
Insects can damage wood structures and bio-based materials.
Various atmospheric pollutants, especially ozone and acid rain, can degrade building materials such as metals, limestone, rubber, and paints.
Salts can degrade materials such as metals, plastics, and paints.
Prolonged exposure to moisture can damage metal, wood, and masonry structures and their joints.

Strategies for design and detailing of durable structures include:

▸ Use materials and products that are UV-resistant or contain UV inhibitors, although some UV inhibitors can be toxic.

▸ Avoid use of bright-colored materials that might fade.

▸ Seal materials with appropriate sealants to slow UV degradation.

▸ Protect structures from excessive heat and sun by planting trees, vines, and other vegetation.

▸ Size members and spans to avoid warping and sagging due to thermal expansion.

▸ Detail joints to avoid failure from expansion and contraction of materials. Use fasten-ers such as bolts and screws that can withstand these forces.

▸ Treat wood to protect from insects. Use low-toxicity treatments.

▶ Specify a higher grade of stainless steel in areas with high pollution and salt exposure.

▶ Use flashing under wall caps and employ overhangs on wall caps, decks, and other structures vulnerable to moisture.

▶ Seal all joints.

▶ Drain water from behind walls.

▶ Grade surfaces away from structures.

▶ Connections between structural members should be designed to shift forces away from the connectors and onto the structural members themselves. For example, setting a deck beam directly on a post offers the most stability without relying on fasteners, which can corrode or wear out over time (Figure 6-12).

▶ Transitions between materials should be detailed with durability in mind, making use of dowels, reinforcing, adhesives, and connectors that are appropriate to the type of materials used.

▶ Structural integrity of aggregate bases and foundations are key to longevity of structures. However, a thicker base or slab will not always lead to a longer-lived structure; instead care in the specification of appropriate pavement mixes and adequate grading and compaction of the subsurface may prolong the life of structures.

▶ Detail metal connections and mechanical finishes to shed water, not trap it (Figures 6-13 and 6-14).

▶ Provide site operators with specific information on the maintenance of materials and products to ensure long life.

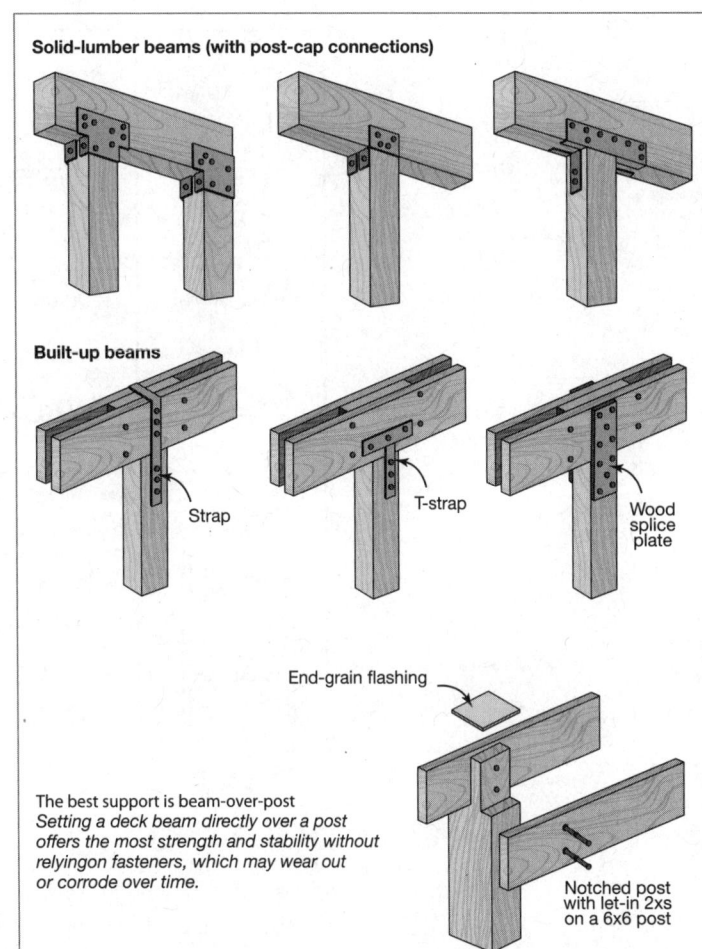

Solid-lumber beams (with post-cap connections)

Built-up beams

Strap

T-strap

Wood splice plate

End-grain flashing

The best support is beam-over-post
Setting a deck beam directly over a post offers the most strength and stability without relying on fasteners, which may wear out or corrode over time.

Notched post with let-in 2xs on a 6x6 post

[Source: Drawings by Vince Babak, *Fine Homebuilding Magazine* © 1996, The Taunton Press, Inc.; Redrawn by John Wiley & Sons]

FIGURE 6-12: Durable connections can ensure that a wood structure lasts long enough for new wood to be grown, making the wood a renewable choice. Setting a deck beam directly on a post offers the most stability without relying on fasteners, which can corrode or wear out over time.

left

FIGURE 6-13: These figures from the Nickel Institute's Stainless Steel in Architecture, Building, and Construction publication illustrate problematic metal connection details that may encourage standing water and accumulation of chemicals that can lead to corrosion of metal and a reduced life of the structure. Typical solutions to the problems are also offered.

right

FIGURE 6-14: More connection details to avoid trapping water, which can lead to corrosion.

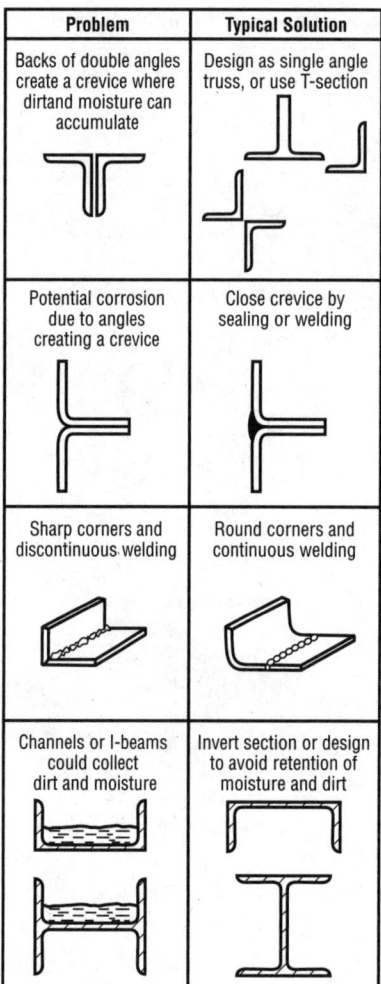

(Source: Nickel Institute, n.d.; Figures redrawn by John Wiley & Sons)

Problem	Typical Solution
Backs of double angles create a crevice where dirt and moisture can accumulate	Design as single angle truss, or use T-section
Potential corrosion due to angles creating a crevice	Close crevice by sealing or welding
Sharp corners and discontinuous welding	Round corners and continuous welding
Channels or I-beams could collect dirt and moisture	Invert section or design to avoid retention of moisture and dirt

Problem	Typical Solution
Dirt accumulates and moisture penetrates into crevices created by bolted joints	Consider using welded or butt-welded joints or sealing with mastic
Lapped joint creates ledge exposed to weather	Arrange joint so that ledge is not on the weather side
Gussets create pockets for dirt and moisture	Design without gussets or allow drainage

Deconstruction

Construction and demolition (C&D) debris is waste material that is produced in the process of construction, renovation, or demolition of the built environment. This includes buildings of all types (both residential and nonresidential) as well as roads and bridges and other structures. Common components of C&D debris include concrete, asphalt pavement, wood, metals, gypsum wallboard, floor tile, and roofing materials. Land-clearing debris, such as stumps, rocks, and soil, are also included in some state definitions of C&D debris.

In 2003, the most recent year for which data is available, an estimated 170 million tons of debris was created from building- (and site-) related construction and demolition activities in the United States. Of this, 39 percent came from residential sources and 61 percent from nonresidential sources. Building demolitions generated 49 percent of the debris, renovations generated 42 percent, and 9 percent was from new construction (U.S. EPA 2009a). Waste managed onsite is not included in these figures. This is a 25 percent increase from the C&D debris amount estimated to have been generated in 1996.

Landfilling is still the most common management practice for C&D debris, with an estimated 52 percent discarded in C&D landfills, municipal solid waste (MSW) landfills, or at nonpermitted landfills. In 2003, it was estimated that 48 percent of C&D debris was recovered for processing and recycling. Unfortunately, only eight states collect recovery and disposal amounts that could be used to estimate this figure. Therefore, this number represents a weighted average of these states, and provides only an approximation of total C&D materials recovery in the United States (U.S. EPA 2009a). This figure has rapidly grown over the last two decades as landfill tipping fees have increased, the number of landfills has decreased, and reuse and recycling markets have developed.

Research by the EPA's Office of Resource Conservation and Recovery C&D Recycling group in 2003 estimated the material composition of building- (and site-) related C&D debris as shown in Table 6-14.

TABLE 6-14: Building-Related C&D Debris Generation: Estimated Percentages by Material

MATERIAL AND COMPONENT CONTENT EXAMPLES	ESTIMATED PERCENTAGE OF BUILDING-RELATED C&D DEBRIS GENERATED ANNUALLY (%)
Concrete and mixed rubble: concrete, asphalt, cinder blocks, rock, earth	40–50
Wood: forming and framing lumber, stumps, plywood, laminates, scraps	20–30
Drywall: Sheetrock, gypsum, plaster	5–15
Asphalt roofing	1–10
Metals: pipes, rebar, flashing, steel, aluminum, copper, brass, stainless steel	1–5
Bricks: bricks and decorative block	1–5
Plastics: vinyl siding, doors, windows, floor tile, pipes	1–5

Source: Sandler 2003

Growing concerns for resource and energy use in material production coupled with waste reduction mandates have led to an increase in recycling of construction and demolition debris in recent years. To facilitate the practices of recycling and reuse, the processes of dismantling an existing site or building have shifted from demolition to deconstruction. *Deconstruction* involves the dismantling of a building or site in such a way that materials and components can be reclaimed and reused or recycled. In contrast, *demolition* reduces the building or site to debris without preserving the integrity of its components. Materials are commingled and usually landfilled. A good deconstruction contractor should be able to reclaim/recycle 75 to 95 percent of the site and building if salvage or recycling facilities are available nearby.

While deconstruction takes more time and incurs higher labor costs than demolition, recent studies indicate that it may be less expensive than paying landfill costs; and resale of the materials, either whole or ground, can generate additional income. Where the demo contractor is also responsible for the new construction, it may make economic sense to stockpile materials onsite. It is common for materials like concrete to be removed, crushed onsite, and stockpiled for backfill on the new construction. Table 6-15 summarizes both benefits and challenges of deconstruction.

TABLE 6-15: Benefits and Challenges of Deconstruction

BENEFITS OF DECONSTRUCTION	COMMENTS
Reduced environmental and health impacts from raw material use, acquisition, manufacture, and processing of new materials	Use of reclaimed or recycled materials will reduce virgin resource use, habitat destruction, energy use, and emissions from acquiring and manufacturing new materials.
Reduced landfill debris	Reductions in material that must be landfilled can save costs of landfill tipping fees, which are substantial in some areas. In some cases the savings will pay for the increased labor costs of deconstruction.
Management of hazardous resources	Deconstruction allows for management of hazardous materials, such as pressure-treated lumber, as they can be segregated and disposed of appropriately rather than commingled and landfilled, where they hold the potential to leach hazardous substances.
Strengthens the salvage and recycling industry	Growth in markets for reclaimed and recycled materials is directly related to the increase in deconstruction activities. The more deconstruction taking place, the stronger the markets for reused and recycled materials.
Design opportunities with use of reclaimed materials (e.g., aesthetic, historic, symbolic)	Reclaimed materials can add a layer of meaning to a project, revealing the cultural history of a place that is often difficult to achieve with mass-produced, internationally distributed, new materials. Reclaimed materials are sometimes unique and one of a kind.
Can achieve SITES and LEED credits	Both SITES and LEED offer multiple points for construction waste management and material reuse. Deconstruction can also contribute points for use of regionally sourced materials.
Can save costs of new materials	Using reclaimed and reprocessed materials can often be cost effective, saving material acquisition expenses. Hauling and landfill expenses can be saved if materials are reused onsite.

CHALLENGES OF DECONSTRUCTION	
More time required for deconstructing	As deconstruction involves careful dismantling of a structure, often by hand, versus knocking a structure down with heavy machinery, it takes more time. This can be problematic if construction schedules are tight. If possible, begin deconstruction activities during the design and documentation processes. An added benefit may be the discovery of potentially reusable unknown structures in time to incorporate them into the design.
May cost more than demolition	The additional time for dismantling a building or site translates to higher labor costs. Cost is the single most prevalent reason that buildings and structures are not typically deconstructed.
Time required for cleaning, processing, and refurbishing materials	Cleaning, processing, and refurbishing materials can take time, which translates to added costs. Removal of connectors such as nails, screws, and joist hangers, as well as cleaning paints, mortar, sealants, and adhesives from materials, is necessary to prepare them for reuse.
Increased worker safety/health risks	Deconstructing structures such as retaining walls or buildings can pose hazards to workers, as structures can be weakened and fail during the deconstruction process. Also, materials for stripping paint, sealers, and adhesives can be hazardous to worker health.
Lack of well-established supply-demand chains	Lack of salvage or recycling markets is the second most prevalent reason that project planners choose to demolish and not to deconstruct. In many regions markets for reclaimed or recycled materials are weak. This almost always corresponds to the cost of landfill tipping fees as there is a point at which it becomes more cost effective to deconstruct than to pay the landfill fees. Many states run online databases listing salvage outlets, salvage dealers, recycling centers, and materials exchanges.
Inexperienced contractors	In some areas, there are few contractors who are experienced with techniques of deconstruction. Demolition contractors are typically used to very different methods of removing buildings and may inflate the price due to the unknown aspects of the job. Look for contractors with deconstruction experience or put them in touch with remote deconstruction contractors to learn techniques.
Lack of standards for use of some recovered materials	Lack of standards and established track records for some recovered materials will inhibit their use, decreasing the market for them. Recycled aggregates such as concrete rubble and waste tire chips are a good example of this. An increasing number of states have incorporated standards for their use in the past few years, and as a result, the market for natural aggregate substitutes has expanded quickly. Other recovered materials are relatively untested and not widely collected or reused.
Buildings and sites are not designed to be deconstructed	There is a high variability in assembly techniques. Connections such as pneumatically driven nails, welding, and adhesives make disassembly challenging, and materials can be ruined during efforts at removal.

(Sources: Guy and Shell n.d.; National Association of Home Builders; U.S. EPA 2009a)

DECONSTRUCTION STRATEGIES AND SITE INVENTORY

The following activities can maximize the harvest and reuse of onsite resources:

▸ Conduct an inventory to identify all site and building components that can be removed and reused or recycled (Table 6-16) (Figures 6-15 and 6-16).

▸ Obtain as-built plans of the building and site to be deconstructed. Bring the contractor onto the project as soon as possible.

▸ Set the goal of deconstruction early in the design process and acquaint all consultants, contractors, and subs with the goal, techniques, and strategies.

▸ Write specifications for deconstruction and job-site waste management and include them in construction documents. Refer to these resources for model specifications and techniques of designing for disassembly: The Federal Green Construction Guide for Specifiers provides specification language intended to be inserted into project specifications. Section 01 74 19 (01351) provides such guidance for construction waste management.

TABLE 6-16: Sample Deconstruction Inventory

STRUCTURE TO BE REMOVED	MATERIAL OR PRODUCT DESCRIPTION	QTY	DIMENSIONS	EXISTING FINISH	REMOVAL NOTES	REFURBISHING ACTION REQUIRED
Building A structural bay	I beam column	16	8x8	None	Bolted to slab and welded to beams	None
Building A wall	16 light steel casement window	8	34 x 50 outside frame, lights are 8-in. x 12-in.	Painted	Bolted to structure	Strip and repaint, reglaze
Parking lot B	Concrete slab, no reinforcing	3,000 sf	6-in. deep	None	Jackhammer in roughly 18 in. squares	Powerwash prior to removal
Parking lot C	Asphalt pavement	2,250 ft²	4-in. thick asphalt, 6-in. aggregate base	Asphalt-based sealant	Mill up with aggregate base	Crush, grade, and stockpile onsite for reuse
Trees A, C and D	Silver maple trees	3	12-, 14-, and 15- in. caliper	N/A	Remove and cut trunk into roughly 11 ft lengths	Use portable sawmill to process into standard lumber sizes

(Source: Andrea Cochran Landscape Architecture)

FIGURE 6-15: At the Nueva School in Hillsborough, California, Andrea Cochran Landscape Architecture collaborated with project architects Leddy Maytum Stacy Architects to reclaim wood from diseased cypress trees that needed to be removed from the project site. Reclaimed cypress wood serves as decay-resistant shade screens, decking, and outdoor furniture, engaging the site's history, keeping material sourcing local, and reusing construction and demolition debris.

(Source: Ten Eyck Landscape Architects)

FIGURE 6-16: The design for the Underwood Family Sonoran Landscape Laboratory incorporates onsite recycling of demolition materials. Rubble consisting of bricks and concrete from a portion of the older architecture building demolished early in the project was used by Ten Eyck Landscape Architects, Inc. within the desert arroyo "microbasins" as a substitute for imported natural stones.

DESIGN FOR DISASSEMBLY AND DECONSTRUCTION

Design for disassembly (DfD), also called design for deconstruction, involves design of sites, built structures, or products to facilitate future modifications or dismantling with the intent that components or materials can be reused. In this way, the site or building being deconstructed is the resource for the next structure either on or off the site. This can help to ensure multiple-use phases for a material and promote closed-loop material lifecycles. This process includes assemblies, connections, materials, construction techniques, and information and management systems to accomplish the goal of DfD (Table 6-17). DfD in construction has borrowed design for disassembly concepts developed in the consumer product design industry.

TABLE 6-17: Principles and Strategies of Design for Disassembly and Deconstruction

DfD PRINCIPLES	STRATEGIES FOR SITE DfD
Design the site and structure for maximum flexibility and plan for adaptation of the site over time. Planning for change and differing occupancy patterns can ensure that a site or structure, as built, will last a long time.	Design a flexible spatial configuration. Design multiuse spaces to allow for flexible programming. Order extra materials or spare parts in small amounts so repairs/replacements can be made without removal of the entire structure.
Document materials and methods to facilitate deconstruction and disassembly after the useful life of the structure or site.	Documenting materials and methods of construction and developing a deconstruction plan either during construction documentation or shortly after construction can facilitate deconstruction efforts several decades later at the end of the structure's/site's life. The deconstruction plan can include the following: • As-built drawings labeling connections and materials • List of all components and materials in project, including all manufacturer contacts and warranties. • Specifics on finishes and materials chemistries • Specifics on connections and how to deconstruct them • Information on hidden or subgrade materials • Three-dimensional drawings showing disassembly of key connections Copies of the deconstruction plan should be given to the owner, designers, builders, and/or other stakeholders who may be involved with the project for its use life.
Specify materials and products with good reuse or recycling potential. When specifying materials for DfD, plan for reuse of materials before recycling of materials.	Refer to Table 6-18 for easily removed, reused, and recycled materials. Avoid composite materials unless they are reusable in whole form. Specify simple products, not complicated assemblies that can reduce the likelihood of reuse or recycling. Specify materials and products from manufacturers with take-back programs in place. (Note: These are few and far between but are expected to increase.)
Specify materials that are durable, modular, and/or standardized to facilitate reuse many times. Materials that are standard sizes are more likely to be useful to another structure. If they are durable and carefully deconstructed, they can be reused many times.	Interface with manufacturers to better understand the expected life of the product/material/finish and how the life can be extended. Research standard sizes of materials, structural bays, parking spaces, etc., and design with these in mind. Design structures and modules of structures based on standard sizes to help ensure their viability in reuse. Where a component is not easily reusable, it should be recyclable.

DfD PRINCIPLES	STRATEGIES FOR SITE DfD
Design connections that are accessible. Visually, physically, and ergonomically accessible connections will increase efficiency and avoid requirements for expensive equipment or extensive environmental health and safety precautions for workers.	Components should be readily accessible for disassembly and easily dismantled for repair and replacement of parts.
Detail connections that facilitate disassembly. Chemical connections can make materials difficult to separate and recycle. Too many types of connections can lengthen deconstruction time and require many different tools.	Chemical connections such as mortar, adhesives, and welds can make materials difficult to separate and recycle. And it can increase the likelihood that the material will be destroyed during attempts at deconstruction. Use of bolted, screwed, or hand-nailed connections can ease disassembly (Figure 6-17). Use of lime mortar can facilitate disassembly of brick walls. Using standard and limited connector palettes can also simplify deconstruction. Design joints to withstand repeated assembly and disassembly Refer to Table 6-19 for an evaluation of connection alternatives for deconstruction.
Avoid finishes that can compromise the reuse or recyclability of the material. Some coatings and finishes are difficult to remove and can compromise the reusability or recyclability of a material.	Coatings such as paint or sealers can make it difficult to reuse deconstructed materials. While technically they can be reused, the chances of reuse are low due to the costs of cleaning the material. Some plastic-coated or electroplated metals are not recyclable.
Support the DfD process in the design process. Designing for deconstruction or disassembly can necessitate modifications to the traditional design process. If a design process that supports general principles of sustainable design is used, such as early goal-setting and inclusion of all team members at the project inception, it may accommodate DfD design activities.	Design process techniques that can facilitate DfD are: • Allow extra time in the design process for full incorporation of DfD principles. Involve the whole team and client with the idea of DfD in project goal-setting and throughout the design process. • Establish deconstruction targets and benchmarks to design for both the percentage of structure/site reused, and also the number of times a component can be reused. • Brief and train contractors in DfD principles to ensure compliance with strategies. • Budget for extra time spent on as-builts and deconstruction plan during C&D phase. • Balance aesthetic concerns with disassembly goals. • Provide an operating manual for the site and structure to ensure longevity. • Maintain a formal connection with the project to periodically monitor the site and structure. The owner will need to be convinced of this as this is very nontraditional.

Adapted from sources: Hamer Center for Community Design 2006; SEDA 2005; NAHB n.d.; Addis 2006

TABLE 6-18: Components and Materials for DfD

RELATIVELY EASY DISASSEMBLY
Nonmortared unit pavers: concrete, brick, stone
Interlocking block retaining wall systems: no mortar
Low-impact foundation technology (LIFT)
Gravel trench foundations
Aggregates
Precast concrete elements
DISASSEMBLY REQUIRES SOME ADDITIONAL LABOR
Unit walls (e.g., brick, stone, CMU) with lime mortar
Unit paving (e.g., brick, stone, concrete units) with lime mortar
Untreated lumber connected with bolts and screws
Plastic lumber
Metal structures with mechanical connections
POTENTIALLY REPROCESSED MATERIALS
Concrete slabs and walls
Asphalt pavement
Soil cement
Rammed earth
Aggregates
RECYCLABLE CONSTRUCTION MATERIALS
Metals: steel, aluminum, stainless steel, copper, iron
Wood (not pressure treated)
Some plastics: HDPE, LDPE, PE, PP, PS
Glass
NONRECYCLABLE CONSTRUCTION MATERIALS AND PRODUCTS
PVC products
Treated lumber
Some coated metals
Composite products (e.g., fiberglass, composite lumber)
Mixed-material assemblies that are not easily separated

TABLE 6-19: Evaluation of Connection Alternatives for Deconstruction

TYPE OF CONNECTION	ADVANTAGES	DISADVANTAGES
Screw fixing	Easily removable	Limted reuse of screws Cost
Bolt fixing	Strong Can be reused a number of times	Can seize up, making removal difficult Cost
Nail fixing	Speed of construction Cost	Difficult to remove Removal usually destroys a key area of element
Friction	Keeps construction element whole during removal	Relatively undeveloped area Structurally weaker
Mortar	Can be made to variety of strengths	Strength of mix often overspecified, making it difficult to separate bonded layers
Resin bonding	Strong and efficient Deal with awkward joints	Virtually impossible to separate bonded layers Resin cannot be easily recycled or reused
Adhesives	Variety of strengths available to suit task	Adhesives cannot be easily recycled or reused; many are also impossible to separate
Riveted fixing	Speed of construction	Difficult to remove without destroying a key area or element

Source: SEDA 2005

[Design by: William McDonough + Partners; Barnette Bagley Architects]

FIGURE 6-17: The mechanical connections and reconfigurable modules at the Bernheim Arboretum Visitor Center in Clermont, Kentucky, allow for ease of disassembly and deconstruction for building alterations.

Walklet | 2010

(Source: REBAR Group)

FIGURE 6-18: "Walklet," a project by REBAR Group in San Francisco, is a modular, flexible sidewalk extension system designed to create new public spaces for people by extending the pedestrian realm into the parking lane.

(Source: REBAR Group)

FIGURE 6-19: Each 3-ft-wide prefabricated Walklet module provides a single, specific program (e.g., benches, planters, bike parking, and tables) that can be mixed and matched with other Walklet modules. Modules, constructed of bamboo and redwood, are easily disassembled and removed. They can be recombined and reused in other locations.

Material Reuse

A major resource conservation strategy is to reuse materials in new site constructions. Common materials that can be reused are metals, lumber, concrete units, bricks, stone, and organic land-clearing materials such as plants and soils. Using reclaimed materials, also called salvaged materials, in new site construction has many potential benefits. Materials are diverted from landfills, and virgin resources and energy that would have gone into manufacture of new materials are conserved. From a design standpoint, reusing materials can add a layer of meaning to a project, revealing the cultural history of a place that is often difficult to achieve with mass-produced, internationally distributed, new materials. Reclaimed materials are sometimes unique and one of a kind. Last, using reclaimed materials can sometimes be cost effective, saving material acquisition expenses and demolition hauling and landfill expenses if obtained on or near the site.

Yet use of reclaimed materials is not without challenges. Perhaps the greatest challenge for designers is locating appropriate type, size, and quantity of materials for a given application. Issues of storage, inventory, and limited markets are challenges facing the rapidly expanding salvage industry. Sometimes it is easier for salvage companies to grind up the materials and sell them immediately to manufacturers in reduced form for recycling rather than house the materials while waiting a few months for a buyer or find a salvaged material outlet that will purchase the material whole. Other challenges stem from refurbishing activities, such as paint stripping and nail pulling, that are required before the reclaimed material can be reused.

LOCATING RECLAIMED MATERIALS

Reclaimed materials can be sourced from onsite, other construction sites, online materials exchanges, or local salvage stores. Sourcing materials from on-site can be cost effective from both an economic and environmental point of view, as both landfill fees and material acquisition and transportation costs are saved.

Many salvaged materials are located by word of mouth between designers, with contractors, and even with owners, especially municipalities and developers. If the contractor is included in the project during schematic design, he or she may be able to procure reclaimed materials from other projects they are involved in.

As the salvage industry grows due to waste reduction mandates, many nonprofit and for-profit *salvage material stores and dealers* are springing up around North America. Salvage stores, both nonprofit and for-profit, are more commonly found in areas of the country with a lot of deconstruction activity. The drawback to obtaining reclaimed materials from salvage stores is that the inventory is constantly changing, so one will need to spend time going to see what they have, sometimes multiple times.

The Internet offers an abundance of *materials exchanges and salvage distributors* with extensive listings for commonly used landscape materials. Exchanges vary by the scale of the inventory and the quantities of any given material available. Exchanges geared to residential projects will advertise one pallet of salvaged bricks, for example, while those geared to larger projects and broader areas might advertise 100 pallets of salvaged bricks. The term *exchange* is slightly misleading. While some are advertising free materials, many materials must be purchased. Larger quantities of materials can be found on industrial materials exchanges. These exchanges deal not only with salvaged materials but also reprocessed/recycled materials and industrial byproducts.

When locating reclaimed materials online, it is important to keep in mind that sourcing the materials needed on the other side of the country may not make environmental (or economic) sense as shipping energy and cost will be high. Designers must use their judgment as to an appropriate limit on the shipping distance with respect to the weight and volume of the material being purchased. Also, inventory of these exchanges is always changing, so some communication with the party listing the material should occur immediately.

DESIGN PROCESSES WITH RECLAIMED MATERIALS

The techniques of finding and using salvaged materials can cause a typical design and specification process to vary from the traditional sequence. As finding appropriate types and quantities of materials can be challenging, often additional design time is required resulting in more fee usage for material procurement. Designers must often leave their office to go look at reclaimed materials in salvage stores or on job sites.

Use of reclaimed materials may be easiest if the materials are sourced early in the design process while they can still influence the design of structures on the site. Some designers generate a design idea and then look for the reclaimed materials to support the idea, while others find materials first and let them inspire the design. In either case, it is best if the design remains as flexible as possible until materials are found.

Specifications may also be more time consuming as there is no standard specification language or details for most reclaimed materials. While it takes extra effort, it is very important to clearly document the performance and environmental requirements of reclaimed materials in clear specification language to avoid miscommunication, as reclaimed materials can contain irregularities not found in new materials.

Another issue when using reclaimed materials can be difficulty in finding the correct amount and size of the materials needed. Sometimes the lengths or sizes vary, and that can cause each piece to be unique. The lack of uniformity—each piece being different—makes it more time consuming for the contractor who will refurbish the materials. Figure 6-20 presents a typical design process when using new products and materials. Figure 6-21 presents a design process that can facilitate use of reclaimed materials and products.

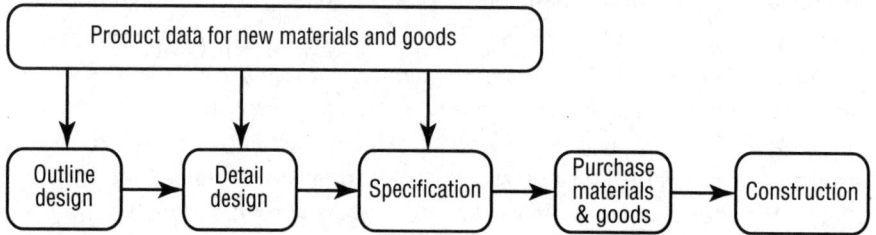

FIGURE 6-20: This and the next figure illustrate the difference in material and product specification techniques between use of reclaimed materials and new materials. This figure illustrates the typical specification sequence for new products or materials. .

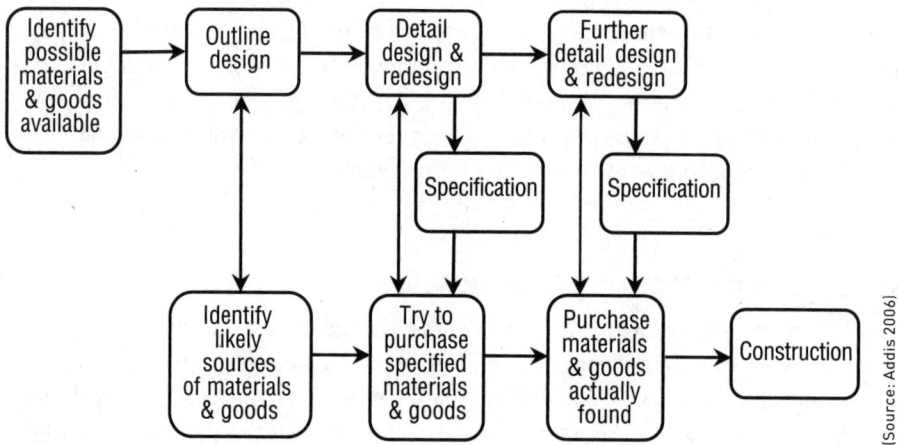

(Source: Addis 2006)

FIGURE 6-21: Use of reclaimed materials necessitates identification and purchase of potential materials and products prior to and during the design process rather than just prior to the construction phase.

IMPLEMENTATION CONSIDERATIONS FOR USE OF RECLAIMED MATERIALS

While there are clear financial advantages to salvaging construction and demolition materials onsite, there can be hidden costs in reusing certain types of these reclaimed materials. The cost of obtaining salvaged materials is often substantially less than if one purchased similar new materials, but the cost of refurbishing and installing the reclaimed materials may be higher. Reclaimed materials can have irregularities that make working with them more challenging, resulting in higher labor costs. They may need to be obtained from many different sources, not easily delivered to the job site like new materials. Contractors may be nervous about these "unknown" factors, so they may price the job higher to accommodate any extra labor, extra transport, or timing delays.

Another hidden cost of using salvage can be the required testing of reclaimed materials that are being used in structural or high-performance situations. When using salvaged wood in certain structural applications, inspectors will require that the wood be regraded. An existing grade mark on a piece of wood is usually not acceptable. Some mills or distributors will have wood regraded, but the price will increase. For large amounts of wood, independent graders can be hired.

USING RECLAIMED MATERIALS IN THE LANDSCAPE

- ▸ Let the materials inspire the design (Figures 6-22, 6-23 and 6-24).
- ▸ Locate and procure materials early in the design process to avoid major design revisions when materials are found.
- ▸ Maintain flexibility in the design until materials are found.
- ▸ Use materials with interesting "stories" or cultural significance to the project.
- ▸ At the start of the project, evaluate project sites and old buildings for materials to reuse.
- ▸ Budget for extra labor to prepare the materials for reuse.
- ▸ Hire demo contractors with experience in deconstruction and salvage.
- ▸ Require contractors to provide a plan for construction and demolition salvage and recycling.
- ▸ Use materials for their highest use—avoid "down-cycling," if possible.
- ▸ Include appearance and environmental performance standards in the specifications.
- ▸ Get the contractor on board with using salvage early in the process.
- ▸ Avoid reuse of materials that are considered hazardous (e.g., CCA-treated lumber) or remove hazardous finishes (e.g., lead paint) in a controlled manner, according to regulations.
- ▸ Storage facilities should maintain the integrity of the material. For example, salvaged plants should be stored in similar light, temperature, and moisture conditions as their in-ground habitat. Recovered wood should be protected from moisture.
- ▸ Look beyond conventional uses of wood, stone, and soil. Stones that lack the shape, size, or quality for traditional wall construction can be used in gabion cages. Irregularly shaped felled trees can be cut into cordwood and stacked to form structures. Excavated subsoil can be used in earthbag, adobe, or rammed earth constructions.

FIGURE 6-22: The Panhandle Bandshell is a modular performance stage structure constructed entirely from reclaimed materials that occupied a place in San Francisco's Panhandle Park for a three-month period in 2007.

FIGURE 6-23: The project was a collaboration between The Finch Mob, The REBAR Group, and Christopher Guillard of CMG Landscape Architecture. Inside the bandshell, computer circuitboards were a facia for the reclaimed steel structural members.

(Source: CMG Landscape Architecture and REBAR Group)

FIGURE 6-24: Sixty-five reclaimed auto hoods clad the structure with a back wall constructed from 3,000 plastic water bottles.

Reprocessed Materials

Reprocessed materials are broken down or size-reduced from their original size. Common materials that are reprocessed are concrete, asphalt, tires, glass, asphalt shingles, and cleared vegetation (Table 6-20). Although they are down-cycled, reprocessing materials use less energy and produce fewer emissions than remanufacturing for recycled products. Some demolition and site clearing materials can be reprocessed onsite with portable crushing or chipping equipment. A common challenge to this practice on space-constrained sites is storage of the crushed material during the construction process.

TABLE 6-20: Common Reprocessed Materials

MATERIAL	CONSIDERATIONS FOR USE IN REPROCESSED FORM
Concrete, sometimes called reclaimed concrete aggregate (RCA)	Portable crushing, grinding, and grading equipment can be brought to a demolition site to crush concrete slabs for reuse as aggregate base material in new site structures, saving cost and energy use of transport offsite. Dust and noise from crushing can be a negative aspect of this process.
	The angularity of RCA can increase structural stability of the base, resulting in improved load-carrying capacity.
	RCA aggregates generally have a lower fines content, so they are more permeable and drainage through the base is better than with conventional gravel.
	RCA is not always available in standard graded mixes, so if it is to be used in an application, such as porous pavements, where gradation is critical, some additional grading may be required.
	The compressive strength of recycled concrete aggregate is related to the compressive strength of the original concrete and the water–cement ratio of the new concrete.
	Alkaline leachate can occur if free lime or unhydrated cement is present in the RCA. This could affect the pH of surrounding soil and water, potentially harming plants or aquatic organisms.
	Use of RCA with fly ash content can pose a risk to groundwater as it may contain high levels of mercury or other heavy metals from the fly ash. Material should be tested prior to use.
	When used as aggregate in concrete, RCA absorbs more water and absorption increases as particle size decreases, modulus of elasticity may be lower, and drying shrinkage can increase with use of RCA fine aggregates.

continues

TABLE 6-20: Common Reprocessed Materials *(continued)*

MATERIAL	CONSIDERATIONS FOR USE IN REPROCESSED FORM
Asphalt	Recyled asphalt pavement (RAP) bases can allow use of less paving surface course material. For new asphalt pavements, bases constructed from RAP can sometimes require only a very thin layer of hot-mix, chip seal, or slurry seal for a surface course if they are stabilized with asphalt binders or are well compacted mechanically.
	When properly crushed and screened, recycled asphalt pavement makes a very stable base or subbase, as the asphalt residue binds the aggregate together, resulting in a better bearing capacity over time. RAP aggregates generally have a lower fines content, so they are more permeable and drainage through the base is better than conventional dense-graded gravel.
	Properties of RAP can vary widely according to properties of the reclaimed asphalt pavement and the re-pairs, patching, crack sealing, or surface layers that were applied. Testing of RAP should be performed in critical base applications.
	Milling up, grinding, or pulverizing reclaimed asphalt may generate undesirable fines.
	The adhesive qualities of the asphalt binder that make for a stable base may make placement and grading of the base challenging.
	Asphalt cement can contain small amounts of polycyclic hydrocarbons that may leach into soil or water near the pavement application.
Wood and cleared vegetation	Cleared vegetation can be used for mulch, compost, erosion control measures, retaining walls, brush barriers, and site furnishings.
	Strive for the least amount of reprocessing and size reduction. For example, consider using felled tree logs in fencing structures rather than chipping for use as mulch. This will extend the useful life of the wood.
	Avoid reprocessing and reuse of diseased, invasive, or pest-laden vegetation.
Glass, also called cullet	Supply consistency varies by region.
	Glass aggregate used in surface applications can impart a variety of color qualities and some reflectance (Figure 6-25).
	The quality of crushed glass can vary widely, with some possibly containing dirt, paper, and plastics. Gradations and sizes available vary widely by recycling facility. Some glass may need additional crushing and screening. When waste glass is crushed to the size of sand, it exhibits properties of natural sand. Recycled glass is angular, compacts well, and yet still forms quite permeable bases. It has almost no water absorption and is very hard. It is easily flowable and placed.
	When used as an aggregate in new concrete, alkali silica reaction (ASR) can occur with coarse glass aggregate and to a much lesser degree with fine glass. Green and amber glass cause little or no reaction.
Tires	Can be reprocessed for use in a wide variety of applications: low-cost gravel, aggregate and stone substitutes, lightweight fill, embankment material, base material, drainage layers for landfills, septic tank leach fields, rubberized asphalt pavement, playground surfacing, and mulch.
	They are lighter weight than soil and other aggregates.
	Consolidation over time can be a concern with use of tire shreds and chips. They can typically compact between 10 and 15 percent of the height of the layer. Leaching of metals and other constituents from tires may be a concern.
Brick	Crushed brick is more angular so it will not pack as efficiently and may produce larger voids than typical virgin aggregates.
	Where possible, reuse bricks in whole form rather than crushing them for use in aggregate applications.

Source: PATH (n.d.); Brown et al. (2005); TFHRC 2011.

FIGURE 6-25: At the Pacific Cannery Lofts in Oakland, California, Miller Company Landscape Architects mined elements from the cannery structure to reference the West Oakland's labor history and the historic use of the site. The stormwater channel is a reprocessed glass "riverbed" while other elements in the courtyards are abandoned equipment found on the site.

Recycled–Content Materials

Recycled-content materials and products are manufactured using reclaimed materials, scrap, or waste as a portion of the feedstock. Recycled-content building products may be the most commonly used "green" building materials as the market for them has rapidly grown, spurred by increased waste recycling efforts by consumers and industry and supported by "buy-recycled" programs at federal, state, and local agencies aimed at reducing solid waste disposal.

Recycling waste and specifying recycled-content products and materials can reduce use of virgin resources and divert materials from landfills. In many cases, use of waste material as a feedstock for new products can also reduce energy use, waste, and emissions that would have resulted from the primary processing of new raw materials for the new product. For example, use of recycled aluminum can reduce energy use and air pollution by up to 95 percent and water pollution by up to 97 percent from primary processing of virgin materials.

However, waste product recycling, collection, and remanufacturing still do pose environmental impacts—often greater than recovered material that is reused in whole form without remanufacturing. Collection and transportation of recovered materials uses fuel resources and produces emissions, and distances that recovered materials travel to recycling plants can be substantial.

In many cases, recycling results in a down-cycled material that is used for a lesser purpose and can never be reused for as high a value as the original product. Exceptions to this are metals and some plastics. Steel, aluminum, copper, iron, and others can be recycled many times into products with as high a quality as those made with virgin materials. Plastic products made from HDPE can also be recycled several times.

TYPES OF RECYCLED CONTENT

There are two types of recycled content that are distinguished by the source of the recovered material. The EPA defines *postconsumer* recycled content as "a material or finished product that has served its intended use and has been diverted or recovered from waste destined for disposal, having completed its life as a consumer item." *Preconsumer* recycled content is "materials generated in manufacturing and converting processes, such as manufacturing scrap and trimmings/cuttings." (www.epa.gov/epawaste/conserve/tools/cpg/glossary.htm). Postconsumer recycled content is preferable to preconsumer as it is more likely to have been diverted from landfills. Preconsumer recycled content often can be reused in other industrial processes.

Some materials and products are comprised of multiple comingled recycled content that renders the finished product not easily recyclable. For instance, mixed resin plastic lumber or composite lumber (wood fiber and plastic) can't be recycled as the different materials are permanently mixed and inseparable.

Most recycled materials contain some percentage of virgin materials and are usually defined by percentage and type of recycled content. In product advertising, recycled-content percentages are not always clearly stated, or if they are stated, distinctions are not always drawn between percentages of postconsumer and preconsumer content. Careful review of the product literature or questioning of the manufacturer to determine content percentages is recommended. If clear answers are not forthcoming, or the manufacturer is not willing to certify the percentages, the recycled-content claims may be exaggerated. Third-party certification of recycled content by independent agents can verify recycled content percentage and types of materials and products.

EPA COMPREHENSIVE PROCUREMENT GUIDELINES

As a result of amendments to the Resource Conservation and Recovery Act (RCRA) of 1976, the EPA developed the Comprehensive Procurement Guidelines (CPGs) and issued Recovered Materials Advisory Notices (RMANs) to encourage federal purchasing agencies to buy recycled-content products. The CPGs and RMANs designate products that can be made with recovered materials, and they recommend minimum postconsumer and total recycled-content percentages. Site construction products covered are listed in Table 6-21. The CPG program also offers a database of vendors who sell or distribute designated products. The database is searchable by product, material, or location (www.epa.gov/epawaste/conserve/tools/cpg/index.htm).

TABLE 6-21: EPA Comprehensive Procurement Guidelines for Site Construction Materials and Products

RECYCLED-CONTENT SITE CONSTRUCTION PRODUCT	RECYCLED/RECOVERED MATERIAL	PERCENT POSTCONSUMER RECYCLED CONTENT	PERCENT TOTAL RECYCLED CONTENT
Parking stops	Plastic and/or rubber	100	100
	Concrete containing fly ash	-	20–40
	Concrete containing GGBF slag	-	25–70
Park benches and picnic tables	Plastics	90–100	100
	Plastic composites	50–100	100
	Aluminum	25	25
	Concrete	-	15–40
	Steel[a]	16 67	25–30 100
Bike racks	Steel[a]	16 67	25–30 100
	HDPE	100	100
Playground equipment	Plastic	90–100	100
	Plastic composites	50–75	95–100
	Steel[a]	16 67	25–30 100
	Aluminum	25	25
Playground surfaces and running tracks	Rubber or plastic	90–100	90–100
Water hoses—garden	Rubber and/or plastic	60–65	60–65
Soaker hoses	Rubber and/or plastic	60–70	60–70

continues

TABLE 6-21: **EPA Comprehensive Procurement Guidelines for Site Construction Materials and Products** *(continued)*

RECYCLED-CONTENT SITE CONSTRUCTION PRODUCT	RECYCLED/RECOVERED MATERIAL	PERCENT POSTCONSUMER RECYCLED CONTENT	PERCENT TOTAL RECYCLED CONTENT
Plastic fencing	Plastic	60–100	90–100
Hydraulic mulch, paper based	Paper	100	100
Hydraulic mulch, wood based	Wood and paper	–	100
Lawn and garden edging	Plastic and/or rubber	30–100	30–100
Plastic landscaping timbers and posts	HDPE	25–100	75–100
	Mixed plastics/sawdust	50	100
	HDPE/fiberglass	75	95
	Other mixed resins	50–100	95–100
Patio blocks	Plastic or rubber blends	90–100	90–100
Nonpressure pipe	Steel[a]	16 67	25–30 100
	HDPE	100	100
	PVC	5–15	25–100
Modular threshold ramps	Steel[a]	16 67	25 100
	Aluminum	–	10
	Rubber	100	100
Cement/concrete with coal fly ash	Fly ash	–	20–30[b] (blended cement) 15 (replacement admixture)
Cement/concrete with ground granulated blast furnace slag	Slag	–	70[c] (replacement % of portland cement)
Cement/concrete with cenospheres	Cenospheres	–	10

RECYCLED-CONTENT SITE CONSTRUCTION PRODUCT	RECYCLED/RECOVERED MATERIAL	PERCENT POSTCONSUMER RECYCLED CONTENT	PERCENT TOTAL RECYCLED CONTENT
Cement/concrete with silica fume	Silica fume	–	5–10
Flowable fill	Coal fly ash or ferrous foundry sands	–	Varies by state
Reprocessed latex paint[d]	Latex paint: white, off-white, and pastel colors	20	20
	Latex paint: gray, brown, earth tones, and other dark colors	50–99	50–99
Consolidated latex paint	Latex paint	100	100

[a] The recommended recovered materials content levels for steel in this table reflect the fact that the designated item is generally made from steel manufactured in a basic oxygen furnace (BOF). Steel from the BOF process contains 25 to 30 percent total recovered steel, of which 16 percent is postconsumer steel. Steel from the EAF process contains a total of 100 percent recovered steel, of which 67 percent is postconsumer.

[b] Replacement rates of coal fly ash for cement in the production of blended cement generally do not exceed 20 to 30 percent, although coal fly ash blended cements may range from 0 to 40 percent coal fly ash by weight, according to ASTM C595, for cement Types IP and I(PM). Fifteen percent is a more accepted rate when coal fly ash is used as a partial cement replacement as an admixture in concrete.

[c] According to ASTM C595, GGBF slag may replace up to 70 percent of the portland cement in some concrete mixtures. Most GGBF slag concrete mixtures contain between 25 and 50 percent GGBF slag by weight. The EPA recommends that procuring agencies refer, at a minimum, to ASTM C595 for the GGBF slag content appropriate for the intended use of the cement and concrete.

[d] The EPA's recommendations apply to reprocessed latex paints used for interior and exterior architectural applications such as wallboard, ceilings, and trim; gutter boards; and concrete, stucco, masonry, wood, and metal surfaces; and to consolidated latex paints used for covering graffiti, where color and consistency of performance are not primary concerns

Source: U.S. EPA CPG, accessed 5/2011

IMPLEMENTATION CONSIDERATIONS

Some recycled content products may require specialized connections, finishes, or details. For instance, some plastic lumber structures can't be joined in the same way as a wood structure due to differing material properties such as density and coefficient of expansion. Some composite lumber products have proprietary fastening systems. Other materials with recycled content will perform differently during installation and in use. For instance, concrete with fly ash or ground granulated blast furnace slag will be slower to cure and reach full strength impacting finishing times and standard performance specs.

There are a number of online databases and resources for locating materials and products with recycled content. While the listings in the resource section at the end of the book include national and a few state sources, it is important to note that using locally or regionally produced recycled-content products is preferable to using a heavy or bulky recycled-content product that has been trucked across the country. Many of these databases offer vendors by state; however, this does not mean that the product was manufactured in the region.

LOW-VOC MATERIALS AND PRODUCTS

Volatile organic compounds (VOCs) are a variety of organic compounds that vaporize at room temperature. They are the principal component in atmospheric reactions that form ground-level ozone and other photochemical oxidants, causing a variety of negative health effects from dizziness, eye and respiratory tract irritation, nervous system damage, developmental effects, and cancer. In construction materials, VOCs originate from solvents, adhesives, cleaners, finishes, paint, stains, engineered wood products, wood preservatives, metal coatings, and many other products. Common VOCs in construction products are formaldehyde, acetaldehyde, toluene, benzene, and polycyclic aromatic hydrocarbons.

Strategies for minimizing VOC levels in site construction products are:

▶ Review production information for items that will be specified on a project. Choose products that conform to low-VOC standards.

▶ Write specifications that require low-VOC materials and communicate the benefits of this strategy to the client.

▶ Choose products that have VOC levels at or below the South Coast Air Quality Management District (SCAQMD) standards. SCAQMD Rule 1168 sets acceptable VOC levels for adhesive and sealant applications, and Rule 1113 sets acceptable VOC levels for paints and coatings.

▶ Look for formaldehyde-free wood products.

▶ Specify asphalt from companies who take extra steps to limit emissions of PAHs and other air pollutants during heating and placement.

▶ Specify warm-mix asphalt instead of hot-mix asphalt pavement.

MATERIALS TO MINIMIZE HEAT ISLAND IMPACTS

Twelve of the hottest years on record have been in the last sixteen years. Numerous cities in the West set all-time high temperature records in the summer of 2005 (Gore 2006). Scientists attribute this phenomenon to a combination of global climate change and the urban heat island (UHI) effect (Intergovernmental Panel on Climate Change 2007). Contributors to the UHI effect include dark roofing and paving materials and lack of vegetative cover in urban areas to shade paving and buildings and cool the air. The EPA Heat Island Reduction Initiative defines the UHI effect as "a measurable increase in ambient air temperatures resulting primarily from the replacement of vegetation with buildings, roads, and other heat absorbing infrastructure" (www.epa.gov/heatisland/). Pavement and roofing materials often have very low reflectivity, or albedo (the measure of a surface's ability to reflect solar radiation) so they absorb much of the solar radiation contacting them, which heats up the materials, and then reradiates the heat, elevating surrounding ambient air temperatures.

Design of the urban landscape, including choices of pavement materials, can have a tremendous impact on the intensification or mitigation of the UHI effect. LBNL studies of four urban areas (Sacramento, Chicago, Salt Lake City, and Houston) estimate that pavement (roads, parking lots, and sidewalks) comprises between 29 and 45 percent of land cover, while roofs make up 20 to 25 percent. Vegetation covers just 20 to 37 percent (Pomerantz et al 2000). Clearly, pavement and planting design play a major role in causing (or mitigating) the urban heat island effect.

Asphalt pavement, along with other dark surfaces in the urban environment, is a primary contributor to the UHI. Conventional black asphalt pavement absorbs rather than reflects the sun's radiation, resulting in increased temperature of pavement surfaces and ambient air. The surface temperature of asphalt pavement can be up to 50 degrees higher than a reflective white surface (Pomerantz et al. 2000), making the pavement uncomfortable to occupy.

While use of reflective materials may be the best-known approach to mitigating pavements' contribution the UHI effect, multiple strategies can be employed to work together, and it is important to remember that not all strategies will be appropriate for every situation and location. Porous paving or composite pavement structures can also minimize heat storage. One must examine all aspects of thermal diffusivity, including heat storage capacity, thermal conductivity, and so forth, based on the function of the material and diurnal impacts from urban morphology and meteorology (Table 6-22).

Use High-Albedo Paving Materials

Increased surface reflectance of pavement materials may be the most straightforward heat island reduction strategy, reducing absorption and reradiation of solar heat. Solar reflectance, or albedo, refers to a material's ability to reflect the visible, infrared, and ultraviolet wavelengths of sunlight. An albedo of 0.0 indicates total absorption of solar radiation, and a 1.0 value represents total reflectivity. Generally, albedo is associated with color, with lighter colors being more reflective. Emittance, a material's ability to release absorbed heat, is indicated on a scale of 0 to 1 or 0 to 100 percent.

The Solar Reflectance Index (SRI) combines albedo and emittance into a single value expressed as a fraction (0.0 to 1.0) or percentage. Weathering of pavements can substantially alter albedo and SRI values. The albedo of new asphalt pavement is 0.04 because of the black asphalt binder coating the aggregate. Over the years, black asphalt oxidizes and lightens in color, and aggregate is exposed as traffic wears away the surface coat of black binder. The albedo increases to an average of 0.12 or even higher (Lawrence Berkeley National Laboratory 1999). This value varies with the color of the aggregate, with lighter aggregates increasing the albedo of the pavement (see Figure 6-27).

While lighter pavement colors may help mitigate UHI effects, they may not be desirable from an aesthetic or functional standpoint. Appearance of asphalt pavement is important to property owners, and they may want to seal or coat the asphalt to maintain darker hues for clear striping and a well-maintained image. White concrete and high-albedo surfaces reflect UV radiation that can cause glare, which may be uncomfortable to pedestrians (including increasing ground-level UV radiation), and even potentially limiting to visibility.

In addition, dark-colored paving is useful for melting ice and snow in cold climates. And if light-colored pavement is used, ecologically toxic de-icing chemicals may be required to melt ice. White concrete can also result in increased light pollution if fixtures are aimed directly at the paving, although it can also result in reduced site lighting requirements, reducing energy use.

Alter the Pavement Composition

Thickness and conductivity of pavement will affect its contributions to the UHI effect. Thinner pavements will heat faster during the day but cool quickly at night. Pavements that conduct heat quickly from the surface to the cooler base will retain less heat (Figure 6-26).

Make Paving Permeable

Porous pavement is a porous paving surface that allows water to infiltrate and collect until it can infiltrate the subsoil. As an alternative to conventional pavement, porous pavement promotes the onsite infiltration of

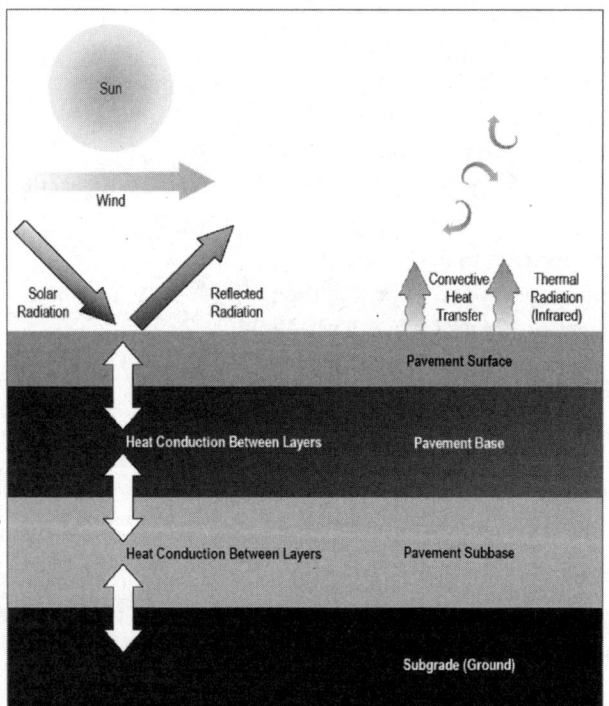

(Illustration from Cambridge Systematics 2005)

FIGURE 6-26: This schematic pavement section demonstrates heat-related processes of reflectivity, conductivity, and emissivity that can contribute to the urban heat island effect.

stormwater, reducing pollutants and recharging groundwater. Porous paving systems can be constructed with a variety of materials including porous asphalt, pervious concrete, and paver systems with infiltration voids between paving units.

Permeable or porous paving cools pavement through evaporation and percolation of water and, in some instances, convective airflow through the voids, cooling base layers and soil under paving. Turf-based porous paving can also cool air through evapotranspiration. Permeable paving systems used to mitigate the UHI effect can assist with Clean Water Act compliance by infiltrating and cleansing stormwater, and reducing thermal pollution from runoff heating as it moves across paving. Infiltration also allows for the recharge of ground-water, up to 70 to 80 percent of annual rainfall by some estimates. These stormwater performance benefits may also result in reduced costs for pipes and other infrastructure. Porous pavement should be sited at least 2 to 5 ft above the high water level in the water table and at least 100 ft from sources of drinking water (NIBS 2010).

While porous paving is not appropriate in all conditions, research has shown that some cooling benefits can be achieved with an open-graded asphalt friction course on a standard asphalt or concrete base (Cambridge Systematics 2005). Additional benefits of this include reduced tire noise and increased traction during rain, as standing surface water is virtually eliminated.

Shade Pavement

Like porous paving, shading pavement with trees has many benefits beyond mitigation of the UHI effect. Vegetation cools the air, absorbing carbon dioxide and producing oxygen; offers habitat; and improves the aesthetic qualities of a place. Decidu-ous shade trees will cool pavement in the summer and allow solar access in the winter. And shading asphalt will retard oxidation of the binder, prolong-ing the pavement life, possibly recouping some of the costs of the trees.

(Photo from Blastrac)

FIGURE 6-27: Asphalt pavement can be abraded with shot blasting to remove the black asphalt from the surface. This process exposes the aggregate in the asphalt pavement. If it is a light-colored aggregate, the surface will be lightened and reflect more solar radiation, reduc-ing the pavement's contribution to the urban heat island effect.

Shading pavement to mitigate the UHI effect may be most effective in parking lots, as new street trees tend not to shade road pavement for several years, if at all. Urban geom-etry has an effect on the shading of pavement, as careful placement of buildings can shade paved surfaces at critical sun times. However, if buildings are too close together, as in a downtown area, they can produce an "urban canyon" that reduces nighttime radiational cooling as release of long-wave radiation requires access to the sky.

TABLE 6-22: Cool Pavement Alternatives

PAVING TYPE	UHI ISSUES	OTHER BENEFITS/DRAWBACKS
Gray portland cement concrete (PCC) loosing	SRI 35;[a] surface reflectivity is affected by color of cement and color of aggregate.[b]	Durable, long life Can incorporate a wide variety of recycled materials Fly ash varies widely in color, so look for sources of lighter ash. More expensive than asphalt paving[c]
Concrete (mix of slag cement and portland cement)	Lighter color than standard gray Portland Cement Concrete (PCC)[c] Lighter-colored aggregate will further lighten.	Durable, long life Incorporates recycled materials Improves workability and performance (e.g., strength, chemical resistance)[c]
Exposed aggregate PCC	SRI depends on color of aggregate	Can incorporate a wide variety of recycled materials Not suitable in all applications[c]
White PCC	SRI new 86, weathered 45[a]	More expensive than gray PCC May cause glare; less suitable for high-pedestrian spaces Can show dirt and oil more than gray PCC[c]
Porous concrete	Surface reflectivity is affected by color of cement and color of aggregate. Water and, in some cases, air filtering through pavement cools it.	Reduces stormwater runoff Reduces thermal pollution of stormwater Not appropriate in all applications (e.g., track traffic, high speeds) Snow removal can't use sand or it will clog the pores. Needs some ongoing maintenance[c]
Asphalt	SRI new 0, weathered 6[a] Does not meet SITES or LEED heat island reduction credits Ongoing research at ASU on nano-coatings and engineered feedstocks may increase surface reflectance.[d]	Less expensive than concrete Long installation life with resurfacing periodically required Can incorporate recycled materials[c]
Whitetopping (4 to 6 in.), ultra-thin whitetopping (UTW); 2 to 4 in. (concrete applied over milled asphalt pavement)	Provides SRI of concrete on an asphalt base	UTW gaining widespread use, but relatively new techniques still being refined[c] Can incorporate recycled materials
Synthetic binder concrete pavement (graded aggregate mixed with clear, amber-colored hot-mixed polymer modified synthetic binder)	Clear binder allows for lighter colors. Color is determined primarily by the aggregate.[c]	More expensive than standard asphalt Relatively new product Can incorporate recycled materials Requires clean asphalt mixing and placing equipment[c]

PAVING TYPE	UHI ISSUES	OTHER BENEFITS/DRAWBACKS
Resin-modified pavement (open-graded asphalt with voids filled with latex rubber–modified cement grout)		Lower cost than PCC Limited to less-than-40-mph roads and 5 percent slopes[c] Relatively new in United States (common in France), so experienced contractors may be hard to find. Can incorporate recycled materials
Light aggregate in asphalt (e.g., limestone)	Will start as very low SRI like traditional asphalt, but as binder wears away, aggregate color will dominate surface color[b]	Light aggregates are not always locally available, and economic and environmental costs to transport light aggregate long distances are high.
Chip seal with light aggregate	Aggregate color will determine surface color.	Light aggregates are not always locally available, and economic and environmental costs to transport light aggregate long distances are high. For applications with light traffic volumes[c]
Traditional asphalt pavement with surface "shot-blasting" abrasion		Removes asphalt binder from surface and exposes aggregate. Can be used for decorative purposes as well.
Microsurfacing (slurry seal surface treatment that is a polymer-modified emulsified asphalt with dense graded fines)	Can be tinted with light colors to increase reflectance of pavement surface[c]	Experienced contractors may be hard to find. Cold-mix results in lower energy requirements than other asphalt products.
Porous asphalt	Water and, in some cases, air filtering through pavement cools it.[d]	Reduces stormwater runoff Reduces thermal pollution of stormwater Not appropriate in all applications (e.g., track traffic, high speeds) Snow removal can't use sand or it will clog the pores. Needs some ongoing maintenance[c]
Rubberized asphalt friction course on asphalt or concrete base	ASU research has found cooler night surface temperatures than adjacent PCC concrete; further studies in progress.[d]	Reduces tire noise Reduces splash and skid potential during rain events
Plastic or masonry modular porous pavement systems		Suitable for parking lots, driveways, and pedestrian paving, but not most roadways.[c]

[a] USGBC 2005

[b] Cambridge Systematics 2005

[c] Maher et al. 2005

[d] Jay Golden, personal communication, November 2006.

CONCRETE

Concrete is the most commonly used material in construction of the built environment. It is produced from a mix of coarse and fine aggregates, cement—usually portland—water, air, and often admixtures. Concrete's popularity is due to its versatility, strength, durability, and other advantages listed below. Yet concrete is not without environmental impacts—impacts that stem primarily from production of portland cement, the binding constituent in concrete. However, improved methods in the manufacturing, material use, and placement of concrete are available to reduce these impacts (Table 6-23). In 2009, the concrete industry produced 3 billion metric tons of cement worldwide—78 million metric tons of which were produced in the United States.

Potential benefits of concrete use in site construction:

▶ It can be durable and high strength with the proper mix of cementitious and pozzolanic materials, admixtures, aggregates, and water.

▶ A high reflectance value can be achieved to aid in heat island reduction.

▶ It is generally locally available.

▶ It can be used without finishes and, with the right mix, is resistant to weathering.

▶ It can be made porous to aid in stormwater infiltration and groundwater recharge.

▶ Recycled materials can be incorporated into the mix, reducing consumption of raw materials and disposal of waste products.

▶ It can be low maintenance.

Potential impacts of concrete use in site construction:

▶ High energy consumption and CO_2 release during the production of portland cement. Production of portland cement accounts for about 5 percent of worldwide anthropogenic CO_2 emissions both through energy use in processing and from the chemical conversion in the calcination of limestone. About one ton of CO_2 is released for every ton of cement produced.

▶ Cement kilns release hazardous substances including chromium and mercury—both bioaccumulative neurotoxins. Kilns also release arsenic.

▶ The resources for aggregate and cement are considered abundant but they are limited in some areas, and more important, mining and extraction of the raw materials result in habitat destruction and air and water pollution.

▶ Many concrete structures today are not constructed to be durable, causing overuse of resources resulting from their premature replacement.

▶ Concrete pavement is an impervious surface that concentrates stormwater runoff and inhibits infiltration and groundwater recharge.

TABLE 6-23: Strategies to Minimize the Environmental Impacts of Concrete Use

STRATEGY	CONSIDERATIONS FOR STRATEGY USE
Specify a lower percentage of cement in concrete mix.	Less cement can be used by specifying a 56-day full-strength requirement instead of the traditional 28-day full-strength requirement. Research has shown that this also results in a more durable structure.
	Strengthening the subbase may allow reduced cement use in concrete slabs as well.
Specify concrete with cement substitutes.	Supplementary cementitious materials (SCMs) can be used to replace a portion of the portland cement (PC) in concrete without compromising strength. Common SCMs include fly ash, blast furnace slag, and silica fume. The amount of their PC replacement value varies. Some will even increase the strength and durability of concrete by reducing its porosity. Workability of uncured concrete with SCMs varies from portland cement concrete so placement activities will need to vary accordingly. Refer to EPA's Comprehensive Procurement Guidelines for recommended percentage ranges of SCMs.
	Fly ash should be tested to make sure that mercury levels are below 2 ppb prior to using it in concrete. How much if any mercury leaches from concrete structures is unknown. There is some initial evidence of increased leaching from porous concrete with flyash (Bernot et al. 2010).
Specify concrete with recycled materials substituted for natural aggregates.	Concrete can be easily recycled by crushing the old product and using it as aggregate in new concrete.
	Other recycled products that can be used for coarse or fine aggregates in concrete are crushed blast furnace slag, brick, glass, foundry sand, granulated plastics, waste fiberglass, and many others. Use of recycled aggregates may alter concrete mix proportions of water, cement, and admixtures.
Avoid oversizing concrete structures.	Design smaller structures and size concrete sections only as large as needed for the application. However, thinner sections of walls and paving may increase the reinforcing needed, potentially negating any resource savings. Use of pier foundation systems may use less concrete than spread footing foundation systems.
Design durable concrete structures.	Extending the life of a structure and preventing premature failure reduces the need for resources. Mixes tailored to specific installations, use of 56-day full-strength requirement concrete, or use of high-performance concrete (HPC) can extend the life of concrete structures.
Specify porous concrete pavement.	Porous concrete is concrete with uniformly graded coarse aggregate with no fines. The uniformly sized aggregate creates pore spaces between 11 and 21 percent of the mix for water to flow through the pavement.
	Requires more portland cement than standard concrete.
	If porous paving is an integral part of a site's stormwater management system, the added cost of porous paving can be offset by reduced stormwater infrastructure costs.
	In areas where organic debris or sand is washed onto the pavement, porous pavements may require periodic vacuuming or pressure washing.
	Using fly ash as a cement substitute in porous concrete will slow set times and also has the potential to leach heavy metals from the fly ash into the soil.
Reduce impacts from concrete formwork.	Reuse of formwork can save resources and reduce material sent to landfills. Steel or plastic forms can be reused many times. Wood forms can be reused if form-release agents that don't damage the wood are used, such as those made from plant oils. Wood formwork from a reclaimed source will also save resources.
	Use form-release agents that allow reuse of formwork. Plant-based form-release agents using rapeseed oil, soybean oil, or vegetable oil are usually VOC free and allow reuse of forms.
	Use earth cuts for subgrade formwork where possible.
Specify concrete containing cement produced in kilns from burning hazardous waste as fuel.	Waste fluids, such as solvents, inks, and cleaning agents, are often designated as hazardous because they are flammable and have high fuel values. These wastes can be burned to destruction in a cement kiln, while reducing the use of fossil fuels. This is a controversial practice as there can be pollution control issues.

AGGREGATES AND STONE

By weight, aggregates such as crushed stone, sand, gravel, and recycled materials are the most used building material in construction. They are the largest component of concrete and asphalt, and they are used for base or fill material for structures, as setting beds for paving units, as the key structural component in porous pavements and structural soil, and in gravel pavements. Aggregates, natural or recycled, are an integral component of many sustainable site structures, such as porous pavements, other stormwater structures, gravel pavement surfacing, and structural soil. They are both a structural and drainage medium in porous pavements. Crushed stone, or even recycled aggregates, can be used as a lower-impact alternative surfacing material to concrete or asphalt pavement for paths, parking areas, driveways, and even low-traffic roads (Table 6-24).

Local stone, or even broken concrete, can be used to construct dry stack walls, gabions, and sand-set stone or broken concrete can be used in paving. Without the use of mortar these materials could be reused multiple times in new structures or new applications after the useful life of the structure (Figures 6-28 and 6-29).

Potential benefits of aggregate and stone use in site construction:

▶ High strength and durability

▶ One of the most accessible and abundant natural resources on earth

▶ Can be relatively low-impact building materials when they are quarried locally, selected carefully, minimally processed

▶ Waste products from both postconsumer and postindustrial processes can be substituted for natural aggregates

▶ An integral component of many sustainable site structures such as porous pavements, other stormwater structures, gravel pavement surfacing, and structural soil

▶ Can provide a strong aesthetic relationship with natural site conditions

Potential impacts of aggregate and stone use in site construction:

▶ Extraction process can cause significant harm to habitat, water quality, and other ecological systems

▶ Mining generates large quantities of waste from overburden removal

▶ Processing of stone can produce large amounts of waste and water contaminates

▶ Natural aggregates are transported from increasingly greater distances, incurring substantial energy and economic costs

TABLE 6-24: Strategies to Minimize the Environmental Impacts of Aggregate and Stone Use

STRATEGY	CONSIDERATIONS FOR STRATEGY USE
Specify durable and appropriate stone and aggregate materials.	Consider the environmental and use conditions to which the installation will be subjected and choose a stone that will ensure durability. Some stone, such as soft sandstone, may wear easily and will not be durable in high-traffic paving applications. Other stone, such as some limestone or marble, can be affected by water, causing them to crush or deteriorate. Limestone is also absorbent and will stain easily, so it may not be appropriate for cut stone pavements. Slate is subject to spalling from water penetration, which can freeze, expand, and loosen the stone layers.
Use less material.	Avoid using dimensions that are larger than structurally necessary. For instance, most dimension stone veneer for walls and stairs need not be more than 3/4 to 2 in. thick. Thicker veneer is often used on stair treads to impart a solid look to the stairs, but in parts of the structure where stone thicknesses are not visible, thickness of stone should be minimized.
Design for disassembly and reuse of stone.	Structures such as dry stack walls or sand-set paving can theoretically be reused over and over again. Avoid mortar to ensure ease of reuse. Stone or recycled concrete "stones," called urbanite, used in dry stack walls with minimal mortar may be reusable whole if mortar is held back from the face of the wall and used sparingly. Sand-set stone or urbanite paving on sand can be easily releveled during use and reclaimed for reuse after the useful life of the structure. Gabions offer ease of disassembly, as steel cages are easily cut to remove and reclaim stones.
Use recycled materials.	In urban areas or regions of heavy manufacturing, construction, and demolition or postindustrial waste can make good aggregate and stone substitutes. Potential aggregate substitutions include reclaimed concrete, reclaimed asphalt, iron and steel slag, waste glass, and waste tires. Quarry byproducts can also be used as coarse and fine aggregates in construction.
Source stone and aggregate materials locally.	As some of the largest impacts of stone use are the energy used and emissions released in transportation, use of locally quarried and worked stone can minimize these impacts. If local stones or rubble-size waste materials are available, but are not suitable for constructing walls, consider using the material in gabion cages.
Use plant-based stabilizers and avoid stabilizers with toxic constituents for gravel pavements.	Use of stabilizers can increase pavement life spans and decrease gravel loss, displacement, and maintenance. Yet some stabilizers such as lignosulfates, chlorides, and petroleum-based emulsions can negatively impact ecosystems adjacent to the pavement. Consider use of plant-based stabilizers from tree resins or plant byproducts.

FIGURE 6-28: Working in partnership with the New York City Department of Parks & Recreation, Michael Van Valkenburgh Associates reclaimed and reused over 300 pieces of granite salvaged from the reconstructed Roosevelt Island Bridge.

FIGURE 6-29: The reclaimed stone was used for the "granite Prospect" at Brooklyn Bridge Park in New York. Structures in future phases of the park will be constructed of 3,200 cubic yards of granite salvaged from the demolished Willis Avenue Bridge.

ASPHALT

Asphalt pavement, formally called asphalt concrete pavement, is a mix of coarse and fine aggregates bound with asphalt cement. Asphalt cement is a coproduct of petroleum production, composed of heavy hydrocarbons after lighter fractions of crude oil have been extracted. It is a good adhesive, waterproofing agent, and preservative. Asphalt pavement is the most commonly used site and road construction material, used on 90 percent of new roads. Hot-mix asphalt pavement (HMA) is the most common type, with all aggregates and asphalt cement heated at the asphalt plant to temperatures ranging from 250°F to 350°F and then delivered and placed onsite immediately. Two types of asphalt pavement are placed at ambient temperatures. They are cold-mix (also called emulsified asphalt) and cutback asphalt. Warm-mix asphalt, with reductions of 50 to 100 degrees in mix temperatures, is achieved through use of asphalt emulsions, foam processes, or additives that increase the workability of the asphalt at lower temperatures (Table 6-25).

Potential benefits of asphalt pavement use in site construction:

▶ It is inexpensive to install and maintain.

▶ The pavement is somewhat flexible.

▶ A wide range of surface finishes or overlays can be applied to fit almost any design setting.

▶ Resurfacing can extend the pavement's lifecycle without removal of the full paving section.

Potential impacts of asphalt pavement use in site construction:

▶ Production of hot-mix asphalt requires energy to heat the aggregate and binder to temperatures ranging from 250°F to 350°F while mixing at the plant, and to keep it heated as it is transported to the site, and during placement.

▶ Heating, mixing, and placement of asphalt concrete releases emissions and fumes, affecting air quality and posing human health risks.

▶ It uses nonrenewable petroleum (as feedstock) and aggregate resources.

▶ Petroleum processing and distillation releases hydrocarbons, VOCs, and mercaptans, affecting air quality, and wastewater containing emulsified and free oils, sulfides, ammonia, phenols, heavy metals, and suspended and dissolved solids.

▶ In use, the imperviousness of asphalt paving can contribute to increased stormwater runoff and concentrations of NPS pollution.

▶ Black or dark gray surfaces retain solar radiation and then release that energy as heat contributing to the urban heat island effect and associated air pollution.

TABLE 6-25: **Strategies to Minimize the Environmental Impacts of Asphalt Pavement**

STRATEGY	CONSIDERATIONS FOR STRATEGY USE
Lower the mix temperature. Specify warm-mix or cold-mix instead of hot-mix asphalt.	Asphalt mixed at a lower temperature requires less energy and releases fewer emissions. It may also produce more durable asphalt pavement with reduced aging of the binder. While warm-mix asphalt can be used for primary paving surfaces, it is still in experimental stages in North America. Cold-mix asphalt is primarily applicable for road patching, cold in-place asphalt recycling, and chip and slurry seals.
Use less asphaltic cement binder.	Using less asphalt binder will reduce hot-mix asphalt emissions and fumes. Thickening the aggregate base course can allow for a thinner asphalt course, resulting in the use of less binder. Care should be taken to not thin the asphalt section to the point that it does not last the full expected life.
Use recycled aggregates.	Many pre- and postconsumer waste materials can be used for aggregate, mineral filler, and granular base in an asphalt installation. Potential aggregates include reclaimed asphalt, tires, glass, roofing shingles, slag, and concrete.
Specify reclaimed or recycled asphalt.	Cold in-place recycling (CIR), the least energy-intensive method, involves milling up an existing asphalt installation and mixing the reclaimed material with an emulsified asphalt and recycling agent to restore the properties of the asphalt binder. Other options include hot in-place recycling (HIPR), recycled asphalt pavement (RAP), and full-depth reclamation.
Specify lighter-colored asphalt pavement surfaces to reduce urban heat island impacts.	Lighter pavement colors help mitigate the urban heat island effect. Using lighter-colored aggregates, internal pigments, white topping, or chip seals with light aggregate will increase the solar reflectance of the asphalt pavement, thus reducing the urban heat island effect.
Specify permeable asphalt.	In addition to reducing stormwater runoff, porous paving cools pavement through evaporation and percolation of water. Permeable asphalt, however, can require more maintenance to ensure porosity
Shade pavement.	Shading asphalt pavement with trees or buildings will reduce the urban heat island effect and prolong the life of the pavement.
Avoid sealants.	The volatile organic compounds (VOC) and polycyclic aromatic hydrocarbons contained in asphalt sealants, particularly coal tar–based ones, negatively impact soil, sediments, and living organisms. The best strategy may be to not seal asphalt, but to let it fade and then resurface it every seven to ten years.
Extend the life of asphalt surfaces.	"Perpetual pavements" or long-life pavements are engineered such that any distress that occurs is confined to the upper surface layer. Surface damage can be repaired during regular periodic maintenance. When specifying long-life asphalt pavement, it is important to communicate the importance of periodic maintenance.
Specify less pavement.	Strategies include reducing road widths, parking space sizes, and width of drive aisles. The number of parking spaces can be reduced by using shared parking strategies.

BRICK MASONRY

Clay bricks are known for their durability, and when used in a well-built structure, they can last for hundreds of years with little maintenance. While bricks have a relatively high embodied energy as compared with other alternatives, this can be offset by their durability. And bricks can be used over and over again in many different structures, often outlasting the life of a landscape and giving new life to another (Table 6-26).

Potential benefits of brick masonry use in site construction:

► High durability.
► Bricks are made primarily from clay and shale, abundant nontoxic natural resources found in many locations around the world.
► Potential for many design forms.
► Less waste and fewer emissions are generated in brick manufacture than in the production of portland cement for concrete "bricks."
► Some solid wastes are incorporated into brick as well, as high firing temperatures neutralize and encapsulate wastes.

Potential impacts of brick masonry use in site construction:

► Clay bricks require from 150 to 400 percent more energy to produce than concrete paving bricks or CMUs, but the primary fuel source for bricks is cleaner-burning natural gas while the primary fuel source for production of portland cement for use in concrete products is coal.
► Substantial energy and costs are required for transportation if a manufacturer is not located near the site.
► Mortar can limit the potential for brick reuse.
► The firing of clay bricks produces fluorine and chlorine emissions.

TABLE 6-26: Strategies to Minimize the Environmental Impacts of Brick Masonry

STRATEGY	CONSIDERATIONS FOR STRATEGY USE
Design for reuse.	If properly detailed, bricks can be reclaimed and reused multiple times. Avoiding use of mortar is the simplest way to ensure that the bricks can be reused. This is relatively easy for paving applications. It is more challenging to avoid mortar in brick wall applications; however, new interlocking clay masonry wall products are entering the market. Where mortar is used, specifying lime mortar will make reuse of bricks easier.
Use less material in brick structures.	Avoid over-designing brick structures. Single-wythe walls use fewer bricks and materials than double-wythe or brick veneer walls. Adding curves or angles to a single-wythe wall can produce a structurally sound freestanding wall. Other strategies include pier and panel walls, perforated walls, cavity walls, and using thinner brick veneer units.

continues

TABLE 6-26: **Strategies to Minimize the Environmental Impacts of Brick Masonry** *(continued)*

STRATEGY	CONSIDERATIONS FOR STRATEGY USE
Design and detail the brick structure to last.	Walls: The durability of a brick wall is largely determined by its ability to resist moisture penetration. Careful detailing of joints and mortar can help ensure this. Proper use of control and expansion joints is also critical. Pavement: Contrary to popular belief, rigid, mortar-set pavements are more likely to fail and require replacement sooner than flexible brick pavements that are easily repaired and reset.
Minimize the impacts of mortar.	Specify mortar with less portland cement. Fly ash, blast furnace slag, portland-pozzolan cement, and slag cement can be substituted for a portion of the cement in mortar mixes. Lime mortars also offer an alternative to cement mortar.
Design brick pavements for stormwater infiltration.	Bricks can be laid in a variety of patterns with the use of plastic spacers that can encourage water to flow through gravel-filled joints.

EARTHEN MATERIALS

Earth construction building methods have been in use worldwide, both in buildings and site structures, for thousands of years. The adobe walls of Jericho, dating to 8300 BC; parts of the Great Wall of China over 2,000 years ago; and some of the oldest historic structures in the western United States are of earth construction, having survived for hundreds of years (McHenry 1984). And while earth structures are currently not widely used in the United States particularly outside the Southwest, it is estimated that 40 percent of the world population lives in earth structures (Houben and Guillard 1994).

The materials for earth construction vary slightly by construction type, but all incorporate soil, with some percentage of clay, and water (Table 6-27). The soil is minimally processed, and is used efficiently, as any waste can be returned to the earth or used in other structures. For instance, any leftover soil from a rammed earth wall or building can be used to make soil cement paving for paths onsite, or if it does not contain cement, it can be used as soil in other site applications. Soil used in earth construction is locally obtained, often from the site, and the type of earth construction used is often determined by the suitability of local soils (Figures 6-30 and 6-31).

Potential benefits of earth construction materials:

▶ The raw materials for earth construction, primarily soil and sand, are inexpensive, and often can be found on or near the project site, saving transport energy costs as well.

▶ The materials are minimally processed and, coupled with minimal transport, result in relatively low embodied energy.

- Most earth materials are nontoxic and nonpolluting.

- Earth buildings perform very well thermally, with the thick walls moderating temperature extremes and acting as thermal mass for storing heat gain from sunlight.

- After a structure's useful life, the materials can either be returned to the earth or reused easily in a new earth structure.

- Earthen materials can provide a strong aesthetic relationship to natural site conditions.

Potential challenges of earth construction materials:

- Many challenges stem from the lack of its use in modern construction.

- Codes only minimally address earth construction methods, if at all—structural performance of some methods is not well documented, structural engineers are not trained to design earth structures, and contractors skilled in earth construction are not easily found in many parts of the United States.

- Public perception of earth construction limits its viability to the southwestern United States, although many methods are appropriate for areas of temperature extremes and even heavy rainfall.

- There is a perception that earth structures are not as structurally sound as concrete or wood frame construction, although many adobe structures have survived earthquakes in California that other buildings have not.

- There is less consistency in materials.

- Potentially higher maintenance. The surface of earth structures is vulnerable to weather extremes such as rain, wind, and freeze-thaw cycles. In arid climates, waterproofing or wall finishes may not be necessary, but in temperate climates, earth structures will almost always need additional protection.

FIGURE 6-30: Rammed earth walls enclose an amphitheater at the University of British Columbia Botanical Garden. Constructed by Cliffton Schooley & Associates, the circular wall is 55 ft long and fades into the grade.

(Photo by Clifton Schooley www.rammedearth.info)

FIGURE 6-31: Constructed and rammed in lifts, rammed earth walls have variations in color among the lifts due to variations in soil color.

TABLE 6-27: Earth Construction Methods

METHOD	CONSIDERATIONS FOR USE
Adobe bricks are formed and air-dried bricks from clay and sand, and sometimes straw or stabilizing additives.	The bricks must cure in sun for 10 to 14 days before use. Many building sites contain soil that is suitable for adobe bricks, and portable brick-making equipment is available to travel to sites. There is a misconception that adobe structures are only suitable in dry climates; however, adobe is used in locations such as England, France, Central America, and China. The incorporation of stabilizers such as asphalt and/or plastering and roof overhangs will allow an adobe structure to resist the erosional forces of rain.
Compressed earth blocks are soil, water, and sometimes cement, pressed into block molds with a high-pressure or hydraulic press.	They are quite similar to adobe block but stronger, more dense, and uniform. They can be manufactured onsite with a portable block-making machine. Although the blocks will take days to fully cure, they can be laid immediately after being formed.
Rammed earth construction consists of moist, sandy soil lifts in formwork tamped solid to form walls.	It offers an advantage over adobe as rammed earth is produced simultaneously as it is built and does not require at least ten consecutive dry days to cure as do adobe bricks. Also, the monolithic properties of rammed earth differ from adobe bricks and mortar, which can be susceptible to water penetration in wet climates. Rammed earth is more labor-intensive and time consuming than other earth construction methods.
Cob construction uses a mix of clay, sand, and straw to hand-form monolithic walls, requiring no formwork, ramming, or machinery.	Because it is hand formed, cob structures are often appropriate where sculptural, irregular, or curved forms are desired. Cob has lower embodied energy than other earth systems because it does not require machinery or stabilizing additives.
Earthbags are plastic or textile bags filled with earth or other local material, laid in courses and tamped solid.	Because the bags act as formwork, earthbags are very versatile, as many types of soil or local material can be used. Excellent in retaining walls. Curvilinear forms are easily achieved. Earthbag structures will require an applied finish as bags are susceptible to weathering.
Earth tires are reclaimed tires filled with a damp soil mix and tightly packed using sledgehammers or a pneumatic tamper.	Because the tires act as formwork, soil composition is not critical. Tires should be stacked with a batter for retaining walls. Stability depends on dead weight of filled tires, which is about 300 to 400 pounds per tire. Rammed earth tires make good foundation systems for other types of earth construction.
Earth plaster, also called mud plaster, is a breathable plaster that is one part clay (often native soil) to three parts sand with straw chopped into short lengths. Clay coats the particles of sand, silt, and straw and binds them together.	Can be applied in single or multiple layers; finish layer can be made without straw. Adheres very well to earth walls. Cracks and chips in mud plasters will have to be repaired annually. Clay offers a variety of colors specific to a particular place. No uniformity of material—some experimentation is usually needed to obtain a suitable texture. In rainy climates, mud plaster should be stabilized with cement, asphalt, lime, or pozzolans or sealed with a protective but breathable coating. Manure can be used, with one part manure to five parts soil.

PLASTICS

Over the past 60 years, plastics have become one of the more common materials in site construction. Numerous products are made from plastics or have plastic components or coatings. This rapid growth is part of the trend in building products toward use of more sophisticated materials involving more complex manufacturing processes. The most common plastic-based products in site construction are pipes, drainage and irrigation systems, plastic and composite lumber, and modular fence and rail panels. Some metal products, such as chain link, bike racks, and playground equipment, are coated with plastics for protection, and many paints, coatings, adhesives, and joint compounds contain polymers as well. Despite the drawbacks discussed here, plastics are a viable alternative for some site construction products, and it is important to emphasize that not all plastics pose equal environmental and human health risks (Tables 6-28 and 6-29).

Potential benefits of plastics use in site construction:
- Plastics can be waterproof, decay resistant, flexible, integrally colored, inexpensive, and low maintenance.
- They can incorporate substantial recycled content and can be recycled themselves.
- They are relatively lightweight, conserving transportation energy use.
- Plastic lumber can reduce pressure on forests by replacing use of old-growth and pressure-treated lumber.
- Plastic pipes can replace use of energy- and pollution-intensive metal pipe.
- Plastics can be low maintenance.

Potential impacts of plastics use in site construction:
- Plastics are made from nonrenewable fossil fuel feedstocks and additional fuels are consumed in their production.
- Waste and emissions from some plastics (e.g., PVC, ABS, polystyrene), plastic by-products, and chemical additives can release toxins, such as dioxins, furans, and heavy metals, during both production and disposal.
- Among the most serious of impacts is the 28.9 million tons of plastics that are disposed of in the U.S. municipal solid waste stream each year—11.8 percent of all municipal solid waste (U.S. EPA 2006).
- With the exception of some HDPE products, most plastics are disposed of in landfills where they break down very slowly, sometimes leaching toxins into the soil.
- The recycling infrastructure for plastics used in construction is limited, and recycling markets for PVC, the most commonly used plastic in construction, are almost nonexistent.
- Plastic lumber may not perform well in spans greater than 6 ft or where deflection or creep is a serious consideration. In these cases, plastic mixed with a fiber, such as wood, cellulose or glass, will provide better structural performance but inhibit recyclability.

TABLE 6-28: Common Plastics Used in Site Construction

TYPE OF PLASTIC	CHARACTERISTICS	STRATEGIES FOR USE
High-density polyethylene (HDPE) Resin code #2	Polyethylene is one of the most recycled and recyclable plastics and can be recycled numerous times without significant change to its properties. HDPE has higher tensile strength and density than LDPE.	Common site products made from HDPE include plastic lumber, sewer pipes, flexible irrigation lines, and stormwater structures. Offers a good substitute for PVC in many applications.
Low-density polyethylene (LDPE) Resin code #4	Like HDPE, LDPE is very recyclable. It has lower tensile strength and density than HDPE, and will soften at lower temperatures.	Common site uses are geomembranes and geotextiles.
Polyvinyl chloride (PVC) Resin code #3	PVC, also called vinyl, is lightweight, durable, and highly adaptable to many uses. Because of these attributes, it is the most common plastic used in the construction industry. Although it has a lower embodied energy than other plastics, the production and disposal of PVC poses significant risk to environmental and human health.	PVC should be avoided. Look for similar products using HDPE. Site applications include pipe, decking, fencing, and many others.
Polypropylene (PP) Resin code #5	Polypropylene is resistant to many chemical solvents and acids. It is less tough than HDPE and less flexible than LDPE. However, it has good resistance to fatigue.	Site applications include geotextiles, geomembranes, pipe, and synthetic reinforcing fiber in concrete.

TABLE 6-29: Strategies to Minimize the Environmental Impacts of Plastics in Site Construction

STRATEGY	CONSIDERATIONS FOR STRATEGY USE
Specify recycled or reclaimed plastic products.	Recycled content quantities of plastic products vary widely from zero recycled content to 100 percent recycled content. Products with high recycled content, particularly postconsumer recycled content, should be favored to minimize the use of virgin resources and reduce plastic waste (Figure 6-32).
Specify products that can be easily recycled or reused.	Specify plastic products that can be easily disassembled from their current installation. Specifying products made from a single plastic resin (with the exception of PVC) will maximize the recyclability of the product. Composite products made with fiberglass, PVC, or wood fibers are not recyclable because they are comprised of mixed materials.
Specify types of plastics with less environmental impact.	Polyethylene and polypropylene, while still posing some risks, are comparatively benign. Avoid PVC, ABS, and polystyrene. Only specify plastic products that number each component.

[Source: Hoerr Schaudt Landscape Architects]

FIGURE 6-32: At the Rooftop Haven for Urban Agriculture at the Gary Comer Youth Center in Chicago, Hoerr Schaudt Landscape Architects used plastic lumber pavers made from recycled milk containers to form pathways within the garden that align with the courtyard garden's window frames.

METALS

Metals in site construction offer many advantages (Table 6-30). Used appropriately, metal can be an enduring material with a longer life span than wood, concrete, or plastics. Many have a high strength-to-size ratio. A vast array of metal shapes, sheets, and prefabricated products are available, and metals can be cast or shaped into custom forms. The variety of metal finishes and alloys available offer a wide range of aesthetic possibilities.

Longevity of metal products and installations is a key strategy in sustainable use of metals. A long use life can offset the substantial resource use and emissions and waste resulting from a metal's manufacture. If a metal product or structure remains for many years in the use phase, the negative impacts from its production can be "amortized" over a longer period, reducing their intensity. Specification of an inappropriate metal or metal finish can lead to rapid corrosion, yet in another site or application, the same specification may perform well for 50 years (Table 6-31).

Potential benefits of metals in site construction:

▶ There is potential for nearly endless recycling of metals.

▶ Use of both pre- and postconsumer scrap conserves substantial energy and reduces waste and pollution in the manufacture of new metals.

▶ The metals recycling industry is generally well established and economically strong.

Potential impacts of metals in site construction:

▶ There are serious environmental and human health impacts from mining, production, finishing, and use of metals. Impacts vary widely by metal type, product, and finish, yet they are among the most significant of any construction material.

▶ Metal production uses large amounts of resources—often three to eight times the amount of metal actually produced, resulting in a huge amount of waste. This waste, some of which is toxic, is released to air, water, and soil where it can affect ecosystems and lead to negative human health effects.

▶ Mining of the vast quantity of resources required for metal production impacts habitats, air, and water around mining sites. Extraction of the mineral bauxite for aluminum production is a significant factor in the clear-cutting of tropical rain forests.

▶ While not all metal pollution is in a bio-available form, metal fumes, particulates, and liquids can find their way into the bodies of humans and living organisms through drinking water, food, and breathable air.

▶ Energy consumption for the production of metals varies by metal type, product, and manufacturing facility, but it is generally high compared with alternative building materials.

▶ Metals used in exterior environments can be affected by corrosive conditions resulting from seawater contact, deicing salts, and industrial or urban pollution. Areas of particularly acidic rain, those with high airborne particulate levels and high sulfur/nitrous oxides and ozone amounts, require more corrosion-resistant metals (Table 6-32).

▶ Specification of an inappropriate metal, metal finish, or connection can lead to rapid corrosion and a short use life for the metal structure.

▶ The metal finishing industry is one of the largest users of toxic chemicals and is responsible for managing large amounts of hazardous materials and wastes.

TABLE 6-30: Common Metals Used in Site Construction

TYPE OF METAL AND CHARACTERISTICS	STRATEGIES FOR USE
Carbon Steel The most common metal used in the construction industry, carbon steel is used primarily for structural applications. With exposure to exterior conditions or moisture, it is extremely vulnerable to corrosion. It should therefore be protected or coated. Energy use for steel manufacturing accounts for 2.3 percent of total U.S. energy consumption. Electric arc furnace (EAF) steelmaking is less than half as energy intensive as the basic oxygen furnace (BOF) process. Ore-to-metal ratio = 3:1.	Specify less toxic protective coatings such as powder coating, thermal spray, and vapor deposition. Design joints and surfaces to shed water. Specify high-recycled-content steel.
Stainless Steel One of the most important properties of stainless steel is its resistance to corrosion, which is provided by a passive surface layer formed by the chromium and sometimes nickel and molybdenum contents upon exposure to oxygen. Production of stainless steel uses approximately 60 percent more energy than that used to produce carbon steel.	Use appropriate grade (304 or 316) for location and expected chemical exposure. Clean structure regularly to remove corrosive chemical deposits. Design joints and surfaces to shed water. Avoid mechanical finishes that can trap chemical pollutants.
Aluminum It is a corrosion-resistant, lightweight, yet relatively structurally strong material that offers many opportunities for use in site construction. One of the most severe environmental impacts resulting from the production of aluminum is the tremendous amount of electricity required to process it. However, 55 percent of energy used to produce aluminum is from relatively clean hydroelectric sources. Ore-to-metal ratio = 4:1.	Specify high-recycled-content aluminum where possible. Avoid use of aluminum in coastal environments where the structure may be quickly compromised due to the saline environment. The energy needed to produce aluminum from recycled content is 5 percent the amount needed to produce it from bauxite ore, and every 1 ton of aluminum recycled saves 4 tons of bauxite.
Copper Copper is used in landscape applications, primarily in sheet form, for flashing, caps, and panels. Brass and bronze are copper alloys. Copper is mined in open pits, with approximately 2 tons of overburden removed for every ton of copper ore mined; then just 0.7 percent of copper is in the ore. Water runoff from copper mining and processing wastes can carry significant quantities of heavy metals, potentially contaminating groundwater and surface supplies. Ore-to-metal ratio: 400:1.	Avoid use of copper structures and copper wood preservatives in aquatic applications as copper is toxic to aquatic organisms.

TABLE 6-31: **Strategies to Minimize the Environmental Impacts of Metals in Site Construction**

STRATEGY	CONSIDERATIONS FOR STRATEGY USE
Design for deconstruction to encourage reuse.	Specifying standard sections and grades will ensure that the members can be reused. Mechanical connections such as bolts allow for easier reuse than welded connections.
Salvage and reuse metal members.	Salvaging and reusing metal members whole will save energy use and reduce emissions that occur from secondary smelting, forming, and finishing of recycled metals (Figure 6-33). Structural steel, stainless steel, and, to a lesser extent, aluminum are made in standard sections and grades (strengths). This means that structural metal members can be easily reused in whole form without the regrading that must occur with use of salvaged wood. Use of some salvaged metals may require field finishing techniques to prevent corrosion.
Specify recycled metal.	Recycled metals can be evaluated by the percentage of their recycled content but also by the recycling potential. Stainless steel, for example, is 100 percent recyclable with no down-cycling.
Avoid toxic coatings and finishes.	Specify factory finishing rather than field finishing. Specify powder coating rather than solvent-based coatings. Where possible, specify mechanical finishes rather than chemical.
Design the metal structure to reduce corrosion potential.	Rough surfaces accumulate more contaminants and will make rain washing or manual cleaning more challenging. Smooth finishes reduce the risk of corrosion staining. Vertical finish grain orientations make it easier for rain to wash the surface and drain contaminants away. Dirt and contaminants will accumulate more on sheltered components or horizontal surfaces. Corrosive contaminants that are left on the surface of metals can result in corrosion staining. Crevices resulting from joined members or prefabricated meshes can trap water and corrosive contaminants. Exposed fasteners and rivets are more likely to provide places for water and pollutants to pond and corrode.

TABLE 6-32: **Chemical Agents Found in the Environment and Their Effect on Metals**

CHEMICAL AGENT	MAJOR SOURCE	METAL AFFECTED	RESULT OF EXPOSURE
Sulfur	Combustion	Copper Monel Lead Silver	Green patina Green/brown patina Dark patina Dark tarnish
Carbon	Carbon dioxide	Lead Zinc	Whitish oxide Dark blue-gray patina
Chlorine	Sea De-icing salts	Aluminum Copper Stainless steel	Pitting Green-blue patina Red spots
Silicon	Airborne blast particles and sealers	Stainless steel Titanium	Discoloration Discoloration

Source: Zahner 2005.

FIGURE 6-33: A reclaimed steel duct is used as a runnel and scupper at the Underwood Family Sonoran Landscape Laboratory in Tucson.

BIO-BASED MATERIALS

The United States Department of Agriculture defines bio-based products as commercial or industrial products (other than food or feed) that are composed, in whole or in significant part, of biological products. Bio-based products include renewable domestic agricultural materials, forestry materials, marine and animal materials, or an intermediate ingredient or feedstock (USDA 2002). According to this definition, wood and wood products are bio-based; however, this section addresses rapidly renewable bio-based materials as defined by their feedstock's harvest within a ten-year growing cycle. These feedstocks include fiber crops, bamboo, agricultural residues, and plant seed oils (Table 6-33).

In the bio-based manufacturing industry, a product is generally considered bio-based if it contains 90 percent or more biomaterial content (by mass or volume, depending on whether the product is a solid or liquid; the percentage excludes inorganic materials in the product, including water). Products with less than 90 percent biomaterial composition still can be considered as having "bio-based content." The number of species of plants and animals on which the construction industry depends is exceptionally small compared to the number available to meet its needs. By promoting the use of alternative bio-based materials, designers can decrease dependence on toxic, scarce, and less renewable resources, while revitalizing market interest in preserving biodiversity (Table 6-34).

Potential benefits of bio-based materials:

▶ Many are biodegradable, nontoxic, and do not create hazardous waste byproducts.

▶ Can utilize agricultural waste that would otherwise be burned.

▶ Reduce emissions of pollutants and energy use by displacing use of petroleum-based products.

▶ Some products have comparatively low embodied energy because they are not petroleum based.

▶ Costs vary widely, but may be less expensive than conventional materials.

Potential drawbacks of bio-based materials:

▶ If not derived from waste or recycled material, bio-based products can generate many of the harmful impacts of modern agriculture practices (e.g., soil erosion, habitat alteration, eutrophication, acidification, water consumption, and so forth).

▶ Production can be petroleum-intensive and cause polluting due to chemical inputs to grow the feedstocks.

▶ Potential to divert arable lands away from food production.

▶ Performance and environmental impact data is limited.

▶ Can be susceptible to weathering, moisture, and UV degradation.

TABLE 6-33: Major Categories of Bio-Based Product Inputs

INPUT CATEGORY	EXAMPLE OF BIO-BASED MATERIAL OR PRODUCT USED FOR SITE CONSTRUCTION
Recycled and reprocessed bio-based waste	Cellulose fiber mulch (e.g., newsprint) Compost for soil amendment and erosion control
Agriculture and timber industry waste byproducts	Coir erosion control products Straw mulch and erosion control products Straw bale Cellulose fiber mulch Compost for soil amendment and erosion control
Cultivated or harvested materials	Jute erosion control products Rope or twine Tackifiers Soil stabilizers and aggregate binders Concrete and asphalt release agents Concrete curing agents Bamboo products

TABLE 6-34: Applications for Bio-Based Materials in Site Construction

APPLICATIONS	CONSIDERATIONS FOR USE
Jute, coir, straw, and recycled fiber for erosion control, revegetation, and mulching	Natural-fiber geotextiles and mulches can replace synthetic plastic products used for erosion control. These products can be left to decompose in place and amend the soil. Consider, however, if simply amending the soil with organic matter could eliminate the need for supplemental erosion control measures. Keep in mind that straw mulches can be a source of unwanted seeds and could potentially spread invasive plants. They can also inhibit sufficient sunlight from reaching seeds and seedlings. While natural mulches are adequate as a temporary measure on low slopes, natural-fiber rolled erosion control products (RECPs), such as jute and coir, should be used in more demanding applications such as (Kansas City Metropolitan Chapter APWA 2003): • In an area needing protection for longer than eight months • In windy areas • In areas that will experience concentrated flow of runoff • For slopes steeper than 3:1
Bio-based products in concrete and pavement applications	Bio-based materials are available as form release and curing agents for cast concrete and as binding agents for aggregate. These products have lower environmental impacts than petroleum-based products. Bio-based form release and concrete curing agents appear to perform comparably to their petroleum-based counterparts. However, bio-based aggregate binders made with psyllium are not as durable as asphalt-based binders for higher-traffic applications.
Bamboo products	For many uses in the landscape, bamboo can provide an alternative to wood, concrete, steel, and plastic. One application being studied is bamboo's potential to be used as reinforcement in concrete (Farrelly 1984). Bamboo is highly renewable, nonpolluting, and biodegradable. Bamboo's high growth rate allows it to have up to 25 times greater yield than timber. Joining bamboo poles is a critical issue—it is labor intensive, and the joints can be a major limitation on the load-bearing capacity of bamboo structures. As a plant-based material, bamboo is susceptible to attack by insects and microbes. However, additional curing after harvest lowers carbohydrate content in culms, making them less susceptible to attack. Also, harvesting older culms results in lower carbohydrate levels.
Straw bales	The performance of a straw bale structure depends on the condition of the bales as well as proper installation and plaster finishing. Bale considerations (U.S. Department of Energy 1995): • Should have a maximum moisture content of 14 percent. • Bales should be virtually free of residual seed heads, which will attract pests and microbes. • Choose bales tied with bailing wire or polypropylene fiber to ensure they are well-compressed. • Straw bale length should be about twice its width. Design considerations: • Site the structure above grade on a well-drained foundation, being sure that water cannot be wicked up into the straw from the ground. • Apply several coats of plaster, allowing adequate curing time between coats. • The plaster on horizontal surfaces may need to be capped with an impervious material (e.g., tile) or treated with a water-repellent coating to ensure that water doesn't infiltrate the structure. • Use an overhead structure or incorporate roofing material in the design to shed water away from the structure.

WOOD

Wood has been used for centuries as a building material in forested regions. It is easily worked, structurally strong, and warm and inviting to touch. A renewable resource, grown primarily with solar energy inputs, wood sequesters carbon, even after harvest and processing into lumber products. But until recently, modern use of wood in construction has been dominated by largely unsustainable practices. Standard softwood harvesting techniques clear-cut large expanses of forests, destroying habitats and soil quality. Many southeastern and Pacific Northwest tree plantations are monoculture forests with little habitat value and liberal use of pesticides and fertilizers. Sensitive rain forests are cleared and indigenous people displaced for valuable decay-resistant species that are shipped around the world. These issues have resulted in wood's being viewed as a somewhat unsustainable material, yet along with the general shift in the building industry toward environmental awareness and "greener" practices, opportunities are increasing to specify sustainable wood in construction (Table 6-35):

Potential benefits of wood use in site construction:

▶ Lower embodied energy structural material than steel and concrete; milling primarily uses biofuels.

▶ Wood is a renewable resource as long as the lumber lasts longer in use than it takes to grow a comparable replacement.

▶ Lumber continues to sequester carbon until it decays or is burned.

▶ Very durable if properly preserved

▶ Versatile—can be customized to many applications

▶ Local resource in Pacific Northwest, northern California, the Midwest, and the Southeast

▶ Salvageable, reusable, and recyclable

Potential impacts of wood use in site construction:

▶ Harvesting impacts often involve extensive environmental degradation including deforestation, habitat alteration, soil erosion, pollution, and even loss of biodiversity.

▶ Production results in a large amount of waste.

▶ Chemical constituents used in pressure treating can be toxic, and energy use from processing is high.

TABLE 6-35: Strategies to Minimize the Environmental Impacts of Wood Use

STRATEGY	CONSIDERATIONS FOR STRATEGY USE
Detail wood structures for durability.	Connections between structural members should be designed to shift forces away from the connectors and onto the structural members themselves. For example, setting a deck beam directly on a post offers the most stability without relying on fasteners, which can corrode or wear out over time (see Figure 6-12). Use fasteners such as bolts and screws that can withstand these forces. Treat wood to protect from insects. Use low-toxicity treatments.
Build small.	An important way to conserve forest resources is to design structures that require less wood. Designers are in a position to utilize creative and innovative solutions that minimize the size of structures, while satisfying the usage needs of the space.
Design to reduce waste.	Wood structures should be designed with standard lumber dimensions in mind to minimize trimming waste.
Specify engineered wood products.	Many engineered wood products are made from recycled or scrap wood. An increasing number of engineered wood products are available with Forest Stewardship Council (FSC) certification. Avoid engineered wood products that use formaldehyde binders. Alternative binders include paraffin wax, rosin, starch, and methyl diisocyanate.
Specify lumber from less common species to reduce pressure on forests.	Use of less popular wood varieties can reduce pressure on overharvested species and encourage biodiversity in plantations.
Use the lowest quality of wood for an application.	There is tremendous pressure on forest resources for the top-grade lumber, as forests produce a limited quantity of it. By specifying less desirable grades of lumber, the forest will be utilized more efficiently. Lower-appearance grades should be used especially where the wood is not visible, as long as the structural quality is not compromised.
Balance wood preservation needs with the toxicity of preservatives.	With the exception of decay-resistant species, wood used in exterior applications must be treated or preserved to inhibit decay. But while extending the life of wood structures will save habitats and resources, the often-toxic chemicals of wood preservatives can place a different burden on the environment and human health. Generally, the more toxic the preservative, the more effective it is. Therefore, preservative and finishing strategies should be carefully chosen for the conditions in which the wood will be used. Copper-based wood treatments should be avoided where possible.
Design for deconstruction.	Screws and bolt connections as opposed to glued or pneumatically nailed connections will facilitate disassembly. Specify standard dimensions to maximize future reuse needs.
Specify reclaimed wood.	Use of reclaimed wood prevents new wood from being harvested and keeps good material out of landfills. Very often, reclaimed lumber is of higher quality and larger dimensions than lumber from virgin wood. It is important to locate reclaimed wood sources near the site to avoid the environmental and financial cost of transportation.
Specify certified wood.	Use of certified lumber can ensure that the wood comes from companies practicing sustainable forest management and harvesting. The Forest Stewardship Council (FSC) has the support of the U.S. Green Building Council and ensures rigorous environmental and social standards for the wood that it certifies.
Specify decay-resistant woods.	Lumber from tree species that are naturally resistant to decay should be specified for use in exterior applications. This will increase the longevity of the structure and reduce the need for toxic preservatives. However, tropical hardwoods should be used only if they are from certified sustainable sources (Figure 6-34).

(Source: Miller Company Landscape Architects|credit: Paul Warchol)

FIGURE 6-34: Wood for the benches in the Dining Arbor at the Pacific Cannery Lofts in Oakland, California, is FSC-certified Ipe, a very decay-resistant Brazilian hardwood.

Wood Certification Systems

Use of certified lumber and wood products can ensure that the wood comes from companies practicing sustainable forest management and harvesting. Some certification systems also require sustainable social and economic practices as well. Globally, there are multiple forest certification systems with varying priorities and standards. The five systems in use in the United States and Canada are summarized in Table 6-36.

TABLE 6-36: Forest Certification Systems

Forest Stewardship Council www.fscus.org	The Forest Stewardship Council (FSC), an international organization created in 1993, certifies environmentally and socially responsible forestry management practices and tracks forest products resulting from the operations. It has established principles and criteria for responsible management of forests that focus on ecological function, restoration, old-growth forests, plantations, native habitats, indigenous people rights, and management practices. The FSC accredits and monitors independent third-party auditors who certify forest managers and forest product producers to FSC standards. The two types of certification are: **Forest Management (FM) Certification** applies to actual forests. Parcels can receive certification if their forest management practices meet the FSC's principles and any regional criteria that may exist. This certification is performed by an FSC-accredited independent third-party auditor. Audits of forest parcels are performed annually. **Chain-of-Custody (COC) Certification** applies to the supply chain through which the FSC-harvested wood travels until it reaches the consumer. COC certification is awarded to manufacturers, distributors, and suppliers through audits that verify the tracking of all FSC materials back to the certified forest source. FSC COC certification can be applied to any product from lumber to paper to furniture. Certified products will have the FSC logo printed on them or on their packaging. The FSC currently has the support of the U.S. Green Building Council, the World Wildlife Fund, Greenpeace, and the Rainforest Action Network.
Sustainable Forestry Initiative www.sfiprogram.org	The Sustainable Forestry Initiative (SFI), a certification system created by the American Forest and Paper Association, developed polices to which all member organizations adhere. The SFI is currently managed by an independent nonprofit so it is a third-party certification system and trained auditors carry out the process of certification. SFI addresses many of the same issues as the FSC standard, but it is less prescriptive than FSC. This has led to criticism that the standards could be interpreted differently by individual companies with the risk of compromised practices. Proponents of SFI argue that it allows a company to adjust to local conditions, which could actually improve environmental and social practices. SFI forests are primarily located in North America. It currently does not certify forests in Asia, South America, or Africa, so tropical hardwoods are not addressed by SFI.
American Tree Farm Systems www.treefarmsystem.org	The American Tree Farm Systems (ATFS) was founded in 1941 and is a program of the American Forest Foundation. The program offers standards for environmental and silvicultural issues related to forestry practices. The standards are not as prescriptive as FSC or SFI. Certification of forests is performed by independent foresters.
Canadian Standards Association, Sustainable Forest Management: Requirements and Guidance www.csa.org	Standard Z809, Sustainable Forest Management: Requirements and Guidance, sets similar standards for forestry practices to the SFI. The standard addresses environmental, silvicultural, social, and economic issues. The standard requires a chain of custody that tracks products from forests through manufacturing and distribution.
Program for the Endorsement of Forest Certification www.pefc.org/	The Program for the Endorsement of Forest Certification schemes (PEFC) is an international, non-profit, nongovernmental organization, founded in 1999, which promotes sustainably managed forests through independent third-party certification. PEFC is an umbrella organization for the assessment of forest certification systems in various countries around the world. Forest certification systems must go through an assessment process involving public consultation and the use of independent assessors to be considered for endorsement.

Designing With and Specifying FSC-Certified Wood

► Work with FSC-US or the FSC chapter for the country in which the project is located early in the project to determine appropriate and available types of wood for the project.

► During the design phase, contact suppliers to determine availability of wood species, products, sizes, and quantities needed for the project.

► Provide bidders with a list of certified vendors. "FSC Certified Bid Assurance Form" and "FSC Qualified Vendor List" are forms that can be used to assist contractors in finding FSC suppliers and ensure provision of certified wood. These forms can be located in the publication *Designing and Building with FSC* (FSC 2005)

► Availability of wood may change over the life of the project. Consider having the owner prepurchase and store wood. The items can then be supplied to the contractor as "furnished by owner, installed by contractor (FOIC)." Be sure that wood is stored in a moisture condition similar to the one in which it will be installed.

► If possible, specify FSC-certified wood from local sources.

► In contract documents, specify that wood should come from FSC-certified sources and require chain-of-custody documentation. If possible, employ a line-item strategy that is based on research for availability of lumber rather than a blanket spec requiring FSC certification. This may ensure better success with contractors being able to find the required wood.

► If appropriate, use detailed specification language from the FSC publication *Designing and Building with FSC*.

(Souce: Adapted from FSC 2005)

Avoid Specifying Endangered Species of Lumber

Many tropical hardwoods from Central America, Asia, and Africa are highly resistant to decay and insects, making them valuable site construction materials. These woods (e.g., Ipe, teak, mahogany spp., and many others) are used primarily in exterior furniture and decking, although their use is growing in fencing and other site structures. While they are very durable in exterior applications, many are unsustainably harvested from rain forests and other sensitive habitats. Overharvesting for the lumber industry has threatened some species and even brought some near to extinction.

Two sources list the threatened status of tree species by region. The Convention on International Trade in Endangered Species (CITES) Appendix I lists species that are threatened with extinction, and CITES' Appendix II lists species that require trade controls to avoid use or harvesting that may threaten their survival. An example of a trade control for lumber would be certification of sustainable practices by the Forest Stewardship Council. The International Union for the Conservation of Nature (IUCN) provides a Red List of Threatened Species searchable by species and region. Their classifications for threatened species fall into the following categories:

▶ Extinct (EX)—reasonable doubt that the last individual has died

▶ Extinct in the wild (EW)—known only to survive in cultivation, in captivity or as a naturalized population (or populations) well outside the past range

▶ Critically endangered (CR)—facing an extremely high risk of extinction in the wild

▶ Endangered (EN)—facing a very high risk of extinction in the wild

▶ Vulnerable (VU)—facing a high risk of extinction in the wild

▶ Near threatened (NT)—close to qualifying for or is likely to qualify for a threatened category in the near future

▶ Least concern (LC)—widespread and abundant

Lumber species that are on the extinct in the wild, critically endangered, or endangered lists should not be specified unless they are certified by a third-party sustainable forestry management certification program.

SITE LIGHTING

Appropriate lighting is a critical component of a sustainable site to ensure human safety, healthy wildlife habitat, and energy efficiency. With good lighting design, it is possible to develop and maintain site lighting to meet all of these criteria. Studies show that most people only see about 3 percent of the night sky in an urban or suburban setting due to light pollution. Light pollution occurs when outdoor lighting is misdirected, misplaced, unshielded, excessive, or unnecessary. As a result, light spills unnecessarily upward and outward, causing glare, light trespass, and a nighttime urban "sky glow" overhead, indicating wasted energy and obscuring the stars overhead (Dark Sky Society 2009) (Figure 6-35).

Too much skyglow can disrupt human sleep patterns and circadian rhythms. Studies have shown reductions in the production of melatonin, a beneficial hormone, and increases in the risk of breast and other cancers (Davis, Scott, and Mirick 2001; Navara and Nelson 2007). Unsafe glare from too much lighting can contribute to accidents and hinder visibility as lighting that is too bright interferes with the eyes' ability to adapt to darker areas. The psychological impacts of disconnection from the stars as a source of inspiration, information, and contemplation may be less easy to quantify, but are important losses that affect many people.

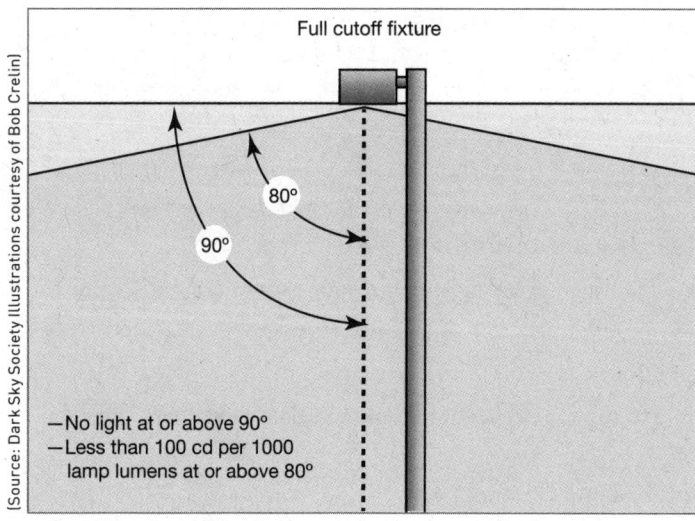

Full cutoff fixture

80°

90°

—No light at or above 90°
—Less than 100 cd per 1000
  lamp lumens at or above 80°

(Source: Dark Sky Society Illustrations courtesy of Bob Crelin)

FIGURE 6-35: This diagram shows a full cutoff fixture. These fixtures are independently certified by manufacturers, and do not allow light to be emitted above the fixture. The fixture reduces glare by limiting the light output to less than 10 percent at and below 10 degrees below the horizontal.

Light pollution has economic consequences as well. It is estimated that over $4.5 billion is wasted every year in the United States on light pollution, light trespass, and unnecessary lighting (Dark Sky Society 2009). This has tremendous energy consumption impacts as well.

The ecological consequences of excessive night lighting are numerous, affecting both plant and animal physiology. Light pollution can confuse animal migration, altering their interactions and predator-prey relations. It can disrupt feeding and pollination, which in turn impacts other species. Breeding habits are also impacted. Growth patterns of trees and blooming of night flowers are disrupted.

Exterior lighting is necessary, yet it should be carefully designed with consideration of placement, intensity, timing, duration, and color. The Dark Sky Society offers the following goals for good exterior lighting plans:

▶ Promote safety

▶ Save money

▶ Conserve natural resources

▶ Be better neighbors

▶ Retain communities' character and reduce sky glow

▶ Protect ecology of flora and fauna

▶ Reduce heath risks

Table 6-37 offers a framework for development of lighting plans that can meet the above goals. SITES and LEED credits related to exterior lighting are both generally in line with this framework.

TABLE 6-37: Objectives of Exterior Lighting Plans

OBJECTIVE	CONSIDERATIONS
Identify where as well as when lighting is needed. Confine and minimize lighting to the extent necessary to meet safety purposes.	Plans should define the areas for which illumination is planned. Itemize each area (e.g., parking lot, doorways, walkways, signage, foliage) with the anticipated hours of use. Commercial outdoor lighting should be used for safe pedestrian passage and property identification, and lit during active business hours and shut off afterward.
Direct light downward by choosing the correct type of light fixtures. Refer to Figure 6-36.	Specify IES (Illuminating Engineering Society) "full cutoff" designated or "fully shielded" fixtures, so that no light is emitted above the lowest light-emitting part of the fixture. Top-mounted sign lighting is recommended with "RLM" (dish) type shields, and aimed so that the light falls entirely on the sign and is positioned so that the light source (bulb) is not visible from any point off the property or into the roadway to reduce glare. For each one square foot of sign, usually no more than 200 lumens is necessary for good visibility.
Select the correct light source (bulb type).	Compact fluorescent (2300 K) or high-pressure sodium is recommended unless the light is motion sensor activated, in which case incandescent or the instant-start compact fluorescent bulbs can be used. Metal halide (due to its higher costs, energy use, impact on the environment, and greater contribution to sky glow) is discouraged, as well as light sources rated over 3000 Kelvin, and outdated mercury vapor bulbs are prohibited.
Utilize "shut off" controls such as sensors, timers, motion detectors, and so forth.	Automatic controls turn off lights when not needed. All lights should be extinguished no later than one half hour after the close of business. Additional motion sensor activated lighting can be used for emergency access. Avoid dusk-to-dawn sensors without a middle-of-the-night shut-off control. Lights alone will not serve to protect property and are a poor security device. Examine other means of protecting property and to discourage criminal activity. Let your local police know that you have a lights-out policy so that they can investigate if they see lights or activity after hours.
Limit the height of fixtures.	Locate fixtures no closer to the property line than four times the mounting height of the fixture, and not to exceed the height of adjacent structures. (Exceptions may be made for larger parking areas, commercial zones adjacent to highways, or for fixtures with greater cut-off shielding behind the pole mount in commercial zones.)
Limit light crossing property lines (i.e., "light trespass").	Limit light to spill across the property lines. Light levels at the property line should not exceed 0.1 footcandles (fc) adjacent to business properties and 0.05 fc at residential property boundaries. Utility-leased floodlight fixtures mounted on public utility poles in the public right-of-way should not be used.
Use the correct amount of light.	Light levels and uniformity ratios should not exceed recommended values, per IESNA RP-33 or 20. (See IESNA Appendix 5, Recommended Illumination Levels, for various tasks.) "Lumen cap" recommendations for areas to be illuminated are as follows: commercial properties in nonurban commercial zones = 25,000 lumens per acre; for projects in residential and LBO zones = 10,000 lumens per acre. For residential properties: for suburban: 50,000 lumens per acre cap, and in urban areas: 100,000 (Table 6-38).

continues

TABLE 6-37: Objectives of Exterior Lighting Plans
(continued)

OBJECTIVE	CONSIDERATIONS
Ask for assistance.	Your planning department and local lighting sales representatives can assist you in obtaining the necessary information for good lighting. For large projects over 15,000 lumens: Greater energy conservation and control of light pollution, light trespass, and glare may be achieved with the help of a professional lighting designer with "dark sky" lighting plan experience.
A postinstallation inspection should be conducted to check for compliance.	Substitutions by electricians and contractors are common and should not be accepted if they do not fit specifications. Final approved site plans will not allow additional exterior fixtures or substitutes without reviews.
Design interior lighting so that it does not illuminate the outdoors.	Provide interior lighting photometrics for the building's perimeter areas, demonstrating that the interior lighting falls substantially within the building and not through the windows. After closing, interior lighting that extends outdoors needs to be extinguished by the use of shut-off timers.

Source: The Dark Sky Society 2009

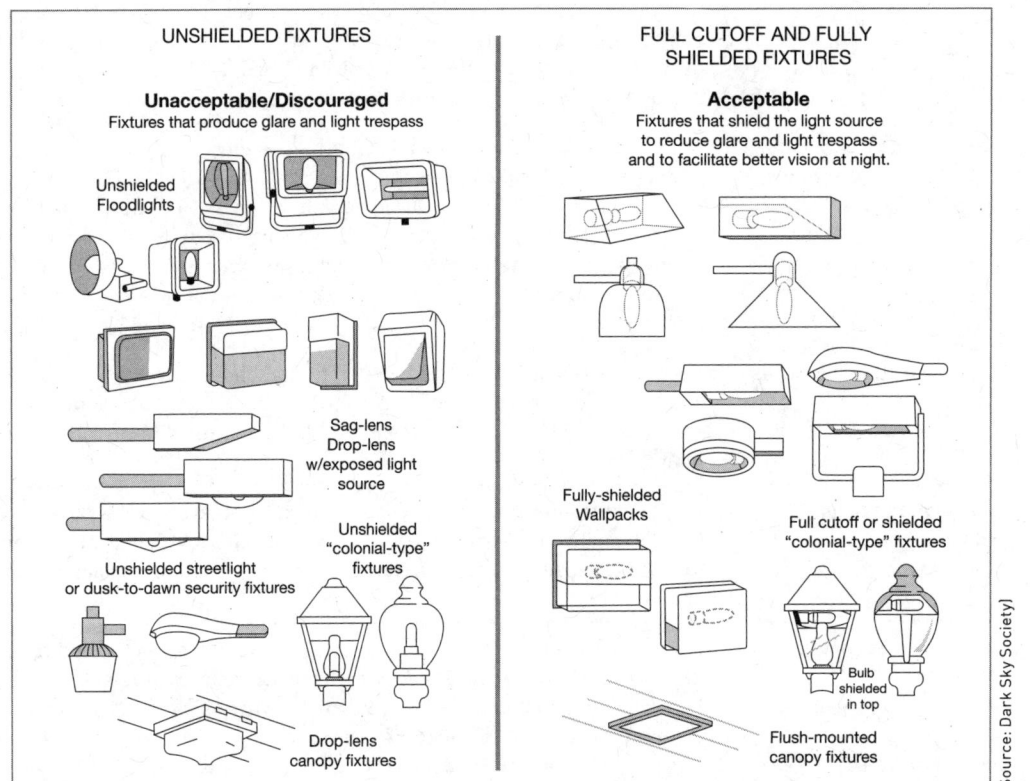

FIGURE 6-36: This image illustrates a range of light fixtures on the left that are discouraged as they produce glare and light trespass. Fixtures on the right are acceptable as they reduce glare and light trespass while facilitating better vision at night.

TABLE 6-38: **Illuminating Engineering Society of North America Lighting Zones**

LZ1	Dark (park and rural settings)
LZ2	Low (residential areas)
LZ3	Medium (commercial/industrial, high-density residential)
LZ4	High (major city centers, entertainment districts)

Source: IESNA.

References

Addis, B. 2006. *Building with Reclaimed Components and Materials: A Design Handbook for Reuse and Recycling.* London: Earthscan.

The Aluminum Association, Inc. 2003. *Aluminum: Industry Technology Roadmap.* Washington, DC: The Aluminum Association.

ASTM International. 2003. ASTM Standard E2129-03, "Standard Practice for Data Collection for Sustainability Assessment of Building Products." West Conshohocken, PA: ASTM International (www.astm.org).

_____. 2005. ASTM Standard E1991, "Standard Guide for Environmental Life-Cycle Assessment of Building Materials/Products." West Conshohocken, PA: ASTM International, (www.astm.org).

_____. 2010. ASTM Standard E2129-10, "Standard Practice for Data Collection for Sustainability Assessment of Building Products." West Conshohocken, PA: ASTM International (www.astm.org).

Athena Sustainable Materials Institute. 1998. *Life Cycle Analysis of Brick and Mortar Products.* (Prepared by Venta, Glaser & Associates). Athena Sustainable Materials Institute: Ottawa, ON.

_____. 2006. *A Life Cycle Perspective on Concrete and Asphalt Roadways: Embodied Primary Energy and Global Warming Potential.* Ottawa, ON: Athena Sustainable Materials Institute.

Ayers, Robert. 2002. "Minimizing Waste Emissions from the Built Environment." In *Construction Ecology: Nature As the Basis for Green Building*, ed. C.J. Kibert. London: Routledge.

Azapagic, A., S. Perdan, and R. Clift (eds.). 2004. *Theory and Practice of Sustainable Development in Practice: Case Studies for Engineers and Scientists.* Chichester, U.K.: John Wiley & Sons.

Brown, Hillary, Steven A. Caputo, Kerry Carnahan, and Signe Nielsen. 2005. *High Performance Infrastructure Guidelines: Best Practices for the Public Right-of-Way.* New York: Design Trust for Public Space. A copublication with the New York City Department of Design and Construction.

Cambridge Systematics. 2005. *Cool Pavement Report. EPA Cool Pavements Study Task 5, Draft Report.* Prepared for U.S. EPA Heat Island Reduction Initiative by Cambridge Systematics, June 2005. Chevy Chase, MD: Cambridge Systematics. www.epa.gov/heatisld/resources/pdf/CoolPavementReport_Former%20Guide_complete.pdf.

Center for Sustainable Building Research. 2007. *The State of Minnesota Sustainable Building Guidelines*. Center for Sustainable Building Research, College of Design. Minneapolis: University of Minnesota.

Cervarich, Margaret B. 2007. National Asphalt Pavement Association. Personal communication with the author, November 8.

Comprehensive Environmental Response, Compensation, and Liability Act (CERCLA). 2005. *CERCLA Priority List of Hazardous Substances. 2005*. Agency for Toxic Substances and Disease Registry, Department of Health and Human Services, www.atsdr.cdc.gov/cercla/.

Dark Sky Society. 2009. *Guidelines for Good Exterior Lighting Plans*, www.darkskysociety.org.

Davis, Scott, Dana K. Mirick, and Richard G. Stevens. 2001. "Night Shift Work, Light at Night, and Risk of Breast Cancer." *Journal of the National Cancer Institute,* 93 (20):1557–1562.

Demkin, J., ed. 1998. "Application Report 10: Metal and Plastic Plumbing Pipe." In American Institute of Architects, *Environmental Resource Guide*. New York: John Wiley & Sons.

European Commission. 2003. "Waste Management."In *Handbook for the Implementation of EU Environmental Legislation*. Brussels: European Commission, Europa, December 2003.

European Commission, Joint Research Centre, Institute for Environment and Sustainability. n.d. "LCA Tools, Services and Data." http://lca.jrc.ec.europa.eu/lcainfohub/toolList.vm, accessed January 2011.

Farrelly, David. 1984. *The Book of Bamboo*. San Francisco: Sierra Club Books.

Forest Stewardship Council (FSC). 2005. *Designing and Building with FSC*. Developed by Forest Products Solutions. Washington, DC: Forest Stewardship Council.

Golden, Jay. 2006. National Center of Excellence, SMART Innovations for Urban Climate and Energy, Arizona State University. Personel communication with the author, November.

Golightly, D., P. Sun, C. Cheng, P. Taerakul, H. Walker, L. Weavers, W. Wolfe, and D. Golden. 2005. "Mercury Emissions from Concrete Containing Fly Ash and Mercury-Loaded Powdered Activated Carbon." 2005 World of Coal Ash, Lexington, KY.

Gore, Al. 2006. *An Inconvenient Truth: The Planetary Emergency of Global Warming and What We Can Do about It*. New York: Rodale Press.

Graedel, T. E., and B. R. Allenby. 1996. *Design for Environment*. Upper Saddle River, NJ : Prentice-Hall.

Gutowski, Timothy G. 2004. "Design and Manufacturing for the Environment." In *Springer Handbook of Mechanical Engineering*. K.H. Grote and E.K. Antonsson, eds. New York: Springer-Verlag.

Guy, B., and S. Shell. *Design for Deconstruction and Materials Reuse*. www.deconstructioninstitute.com/.

Hamer Center for Community Design, The Pennsylvania State University. 2006. *DfD Design for Disassembly in the Built Environment*. Prepared for City of Seattle, King County, WA, by B. Guy and N. Ciarimboli.

Hammond, G., and C. Jones. 2006. "Inventory of Carbon and Energy," Version 1.5 Beta. Bath, UK: University of Bath, Department of Mechanical Engineering.

———. 2008. "Inventory of Carbon and Energy," Version 1.6a Beta. Bath, UK: University of Bath, Department of Mechanical Engineering.

———. 2011. "Inventory of Carbon and Energy." Version 2.0. Bath, UK: University of Bath, Department of Mechanical Engineering.

Houben, H., and H. Guillard. 1994. *Earth Construction: A Comprehensive Guide*. London: Intermediate Technology Publications.

Intergovernmental Panel on Climate Change. 2007. *Climate Change 2007: Impacts, Adaptation and Vulnerability.* Contribution of Working Group II to the Fourth Assessment Report of the Intergovernmental Panel on Climate Change, ed. M.L. Parry, O.F. Canzlani, J. P. Palutikof, P. J. van der Linden, and C. E. Hanson. Cambridge: Cambridge University Press.

International Standards Organization (ISO). 1996. Environmental Management—Life-Cycle Assessment: Principles and Framework. Draft International Standard 14040. Geneva, Switzerland: International Standards Organization.

Kansas City Metropolitan Chapter, American Public Works Association. 2003. "Division II Construction and Material Specifications: Section 2150 Erosion and Sediment Control," www.kcmo.org/pubworks/stds/spec/Temp/APWA2100.pdf.

Lawrence Berkeley National Laboratory. 1999. Lawrence Berkeley National Laboratory Heat Island Group, http://eetd.lbl.gov/HeatIsland/Pavements/Overview/Pavements99-03.html.

Lippiatt, Barbara C. 2007. *BEES 4.0 Building for Environmental and Economic Sustainability Technical Manual and User Guide.* Gaithersburg, MD: National Institute of Standards and Technology.

Living Building Institute. 2010. "Living Building Challenge 2.0." http://ilbi.org/lbc/Standard-Documents/LBC2-0.pdf.

Matos, Grecia R. 2009. *Use of Minerals and Materials in the United States from 1900 through 2006.* Reston, VA: U.S. Geological Survey Minerals Information Team.

McDonough, William, and Michael Braungart. 2002. *Cradle to Cradle: Remaking the Way We Make Things.* New York: North Point Press.

McHenry, P. G. 1984. *Adobe and Rammed Earth Buildings.* Tucson: University of Arizona Press.

Mendler, Sandra, William Odell, and Mary Ann Lazarus. 2006. *The HOK Guidebook to Sustainable Design.* Hoboken, NJ: John Wiley & Sons.

National Association of Home Builders (NAHB) Research Center. n.d. "Deconstruction: Building Disassembly and Material Salvage." www.nahbrc.org/.

National Institute of Building Science (NIBS). 2010. "Federal Green Construction Guide for Specifiers, Section 32 12 43 (02795)." www.wbdg.org/ccb/FEDGREEN/fgs_321243.pdf.

Navara, K.J., and R.J. Nelson. 2007. "The Dark Side of Light at Night: Physiological, Epidemiological, and Ecological Consequences." *Journal of Pineal Research,* 43 (3):215–224.

Partnership for Advancing Technology in Housing (PATH). n.d. "Concrete Aggregate Substitutes: Alternative Aggregate Materials." PATH: Toolbase Resources, www.toolbase.org/Construction-Methods/Concrete-Construction/concrete-aggregate-substitutes.

Pomerantz, M., B. Pon, H. Akbari, and S. Change. 2000. "The Effect of Pavements' Temperatures on Air Temperatures in Large Cities. Report No. LBNL-43442." Berkeley, CA: Lawrence Berkeley National Labratory. http://eetd.lbl.gov/HeatIsland/PUBS/2000/43442rep.pdf.

Sandler, Ken. 2003, November. "Analyzing What's Recyclable in C&D Debris." *Biocycle*, 51–54.

Scotland Environmental Design Association (SEDA). 2005. *Design and Detailing for Deconstruction.* Prepared by C. Morgan and F. Stevenson for SEDA Design Guides for Scotland: No. 1.

Thompson, J.W., and K. Sorvig. 2000. *Sustainable Landscape Construction: A Guide to Green Building Outdoors.* Washington, DC: Island Press.

Turner-Fairbank Highway Research Center (TFHRC). 2011. *User Guidelines for Waste and By-product Materials in Pavement Construction.* Federal Highway Administration, Turner-Fairbank Highway Research Center, Available at www.fhwa.dot.gov/publications/research/infrastructure/pavements/97148/index.cfm (accessed May 2011).

United Nations Environment Programme. (UNEP). 1999. *Global Environment Outlook 2000.* London: Earthscan Publications Ltd.

United Nations Conference on Environment and Development (UNCED). 1992. *Agenda 21: United Nations, Report of the Conference on Environment and Development.* Rio de Janerio: United Nations Conference on Environment and Development.

U.S. Department of Agriculture (USDA). 2002. Farm Security and Rural Investment Act of 2002, Pub. L. No. 107-171 116 Stat. 475, §9001 ¶ 2.

U.S. Department of Energy. 1995. *House of Straw: Straw Bale Construction Comes of Age.* Washington, DC: USDOE Office of Energy Efficiency and Renewable Energy, Washington, DC: U.S. Department of Energy. www.kcmo.org/pubworks/stds/spec/Temp/APWA2100.pdf.

U.S. Environmental Protection Agency (U.S. EPA). 2000. "Hot Mix Asphalt Plants Emission Assessment Report." Report EPA-454/R-00-019, www.epa.gov/ttn/chief/ap42/ch11/related/ea-report.pdf.

———. 2003. "Exposure and Human Health Reassessment of 2,3,7,8-Tetrachlorodibenzo-p-Dioxin (TCDD) and Related Compounds." Washington, DC: National Center for Environmental Assessment: Research and Development.

———. 2006. *2005 Municipal Solid Waste in the United States: Facts and Figures.* EPA530-R-06-011, October 2006. Washington, DC: U.S. EPA Office of Solid Waste.

———. 2007a. *2005 Toxics Release Inventory (TRI) Public Data Release Report.* EPA 260-R-07-001. Public data release March 2007. Washington, DC: U.S. Environmental Protection Agency.

———. 2007b. *Inventory of U.S. Greenhouse Gas Emissions and Sinks, 1990–2005.* Report EPA 430-R-07-002. Washington, DC: U.S. Environmental Protection Agency.

———. 2007c. *Energy Trends in Selected Manufacturing Sectors: Opportunities and Challenges for Environmentally Preferable Energy Outcomes.* Prepared by ICF International, March. Washington, DC: U.S. Environmental Protection Agency.

———. 2009a. *Estimating 2003 Building-Related Construction and Demolition Materials Amounts,* EPA-530-R-09-002, Office of Resource Conservation and Recovery. Washington, DC: U.S. Environmental Protection Agency. Available at www.epa.gov/wastes/conserve/rrr/imr/cdm/pubs/cd-meas.pdf (accesssed May 2011).

———. 2009b. *Sustainable Materials Management: The Road Ahead.* EPA-530-R-09-009. The 2020 Vision Workgroup, June. Washington, DC: U.S. Environmental Protection Agency.

———. 2010. Toxics Release Inventory (TRI). *2009 TRI National Analysis,* available at www.epa.gov/tri/tridata/tri09/nationalanalysis/index.htm.

———. n.d. Air and Radiation. "What Are the Six Common Air Pollutants?" www.epa.gov/oaqps001/urbanair/. Accessed December 2010.

U.S. Green Building Council (USGBC). 2005. *LEED-NC for New Construction Reference Guide, Version 2.2.* Washington, DC: USGBC.

Wagner, L. A. 2002. *Materials in the Economy: Material Flows, Scarcity, and the Environment.* U.S. Geological Survey Circular 1221. Denver, CO: U.S. Geological Survey.

World Resources Institute (WRI). 2000. "Weight of Nations: Material Outflows from Industrial Economies." Washington, DC: WRI.

Zahner, William L. 2005. *Architectural Metal Surfaces.* Hoboken, NJ: John Wiley and Sons.

CHAPTER 7

HUMAN HEALTH AND WELL-BEING FOR SUSTAINABLE SITES

▶ Robert Ryan

TRADITIONAL DEFINITIONS OF SUSTAINABILITY, such as that of the Brundlandt Commission (World Commission on Environment and Development et al. 1987), have encompassed the three Es—ecology, equity, and economy. The first E, ecology, has received focused attention within the fields of landscape design and planning. In fact, one could not imagine a sustainable site that did not address ecological health and the impacts of site design on hydrological, terrestrial, and biological systems. However, the ability of a site to sustain social equity or promote local economies in a sustainable manner has received much less attention in landscape architecture and related disciplines. The reasons for this oversight have to do with the challenge of measuring these concepts, as well as the lack of expertise that designers may feel in addressing these subjects in a rigorous manner. One would have to ask the question: What characteristics would a site need in order to promote social equity and sustain an economy that benefitted local people while not depleting resources for future generations? How does a site impact the human health and well-being of those who use it?

Environmental psychologists Rachel and Stephen Kaplan (1989, 2008) have worked extensively on understanding the ways in which landscapes can provide psychological, emotional, and cognitive benefits for people in a wide range of settings from urban neighborhoods to wilderness areas. They describe the need to design environments that "bring out the best in people." People are at their best when they can explore the world around them and gather new information that is useful for understanding our complex world. Some environments foster this exploration by the ways in which they are designed, while others are needlessly complex and frustrating, challenging one to find such basic information as the entrance to a building, the park restroom, or the trail to the scenic overlook.

Feeling frustrated in an environment is not without costs. People tend to avoid places that are confusing and get angry when they can't find their way. Vandalism is rampant in those sites where no one feels a sense of ownership to the place. Feeling frustrated that the site doesn't support the type of activities one would like to pursue may also manifest itself in vandalism. At the extreme level, road rage and similar antisocial behavior can be linked to frustration and mental stress caused by such environmental stressors as traffic. In fact, research has shown the psychological toll that the fast-paced modern world can have on people's physical, psychological, and emotional health (Richtel 2010).

Fortunately, landscapes can provide the antidote for many of the stresses of modern life. The restorative benefits of trees and other vegetation has been found in a wide range of settings from schools, to offices, public housing, and even prisons. In an often-cited study, Roger Ulrich (1984) found that hospital patients recovered more quickly when their rooms viewed trees versus other buildings or parking areas. Rachel Kaplan (1993) and others found that office workers were more productive, had less absenteeism, and were more satisfied when their offices had views of nature.

In another groundbreaking study, psychologist Francis (Ming) Kuo and landscape architect William Sullivan (2001) at the University of Illinois, Champaign Urbana, found that trees made a huge difference in one of Chicago's poorest public housing complexes. Those people who lived in buildings with trees and other landscape surrounding their buildings indicated lower levels of crime, domestic abuse, and other negative indicators. In addition, these residents described a stronger sense of community. These landscapes provided a place for people to meet their neighbors and work out their problems. One might argue that social equity is about providing humane environments for all people. As this research shows, trees and other vegetation are essential elements of humane environments.

The ability of well-designed landscapes to foster social interaction and potentially build community has been a goal of designers, beginning with Frederick Law Olmsted's goals for New York's Central Park. However, if one can think of parks and plazas that are devoid of people, the potential envisioned by their designers may never be realized. Understanding the features and configurations that create vibrant public places is critical to the success of a sustainable site that promotes social equity. Landscape architect Marc Francis (1987) describes successful urban open space as having a range of characteristics, including being democratic and open to all. The importance of civic spaces that promote social interaction and dialogue between various groups should not be underestimated. In his book *Bowling Alone*, author Robert Putnam (2000) describes the withdrawal of modern society from public places and the potential for alienation, as well as diminished psychological and physical health associated with fewer close social ties. The long-term impacts of a society that has limited ties to one another are unknown, but a diminishment in the social capital needed to address the challenges of environmental issues, such as climate change, could have a cumulative effect.

Sites can also have an impact on the physical health of those who use them. Other chapters in this book look at avoiding the use of toxic materials in landscape features and

maintenance programs, including limiting noise and air pollution from landscape maintenance equipment. The idea of "doing no harm" in site development is a critical beginning
point for any sustainable site. However, from a more proactive stance, one must ask: How
can a site actually benefit the physical health of those who use it?

Research in the medical field has shown that one of the greatest threats to physical
health is a sedentary lifestyle. Poor dietary habits combined with lack of an active lifestyle
have led to epidemic obesity levels in the United States and other developed countries
worldwide (World Health Organization 2009). Obesity in turn is linked to a variety of chronic
health problems including diabetes and heart disease (U.S. Department of Health and
Human Services 2001). The increase in childhood obesity is especially troubling when one
considers the health of future generations. In addition to the diminished quality of life associated with poor health, the economic costs in healthcare are staggering at over $100 billion
in the United States (Finkelstein et al. 2005). Active living by design research, funded by the
National Institutes of Health and Robert Wood Johnson Foundation, advocates for increased
physical activity levels and built environments that can support an active lifestyle. Sites that
can encourage alternative modes of transportation, such as walking and biking, as well as
recreational opportunities for site users, can help increase physical activity levels with the
associated health benefits.

Thus, promoting greenspaces in the built environment can provide multiple benefits for
both people and the natural environment. The challenge is to plan and design sites that can
accomplish both. This chapter describes strategies to promote human health and well-being
while acknowledging the synergy between many of these strategies and those in other chapters to promote ecological benefits. For example, the same tree that provides a place for
children to play or shaded areas for people to socialize has the potential to promote native
vegetation, provide habitat, ameliorate climate, and store carbon.

Fortunately, people love to solve problems and can develop creative solutions to many
environmental issues. However, oftentimes the environment or design process does not
capitalize on the combined human capital that people possess. One can think of many parks
and sites that are used in ways that the designers never imagined, as people adapt them to
their needs. A truly sustainable site would expand site users' knowledge about environmental issues and at the same time engage them in addressing these issues in a creative manner. The goal behind sustainable certification for a site is providing a model for other places
to emulate, as well as to expand awareness about larger, more global issues. For example,
a rainwater garden at a local park or school can encourage local residents to consider the
environmental benefits or to consider one for their own yard.

Environmental issues, such as climate change and loss of biodiversity, are unique in
that they can appear so daunting as to create a feeling of helplessness in people. Sites that
can demonstrate tangible benefits for the environment in ways that are understood by site
users have the potential to engage people in meaningful action on a range of environmental

issues. Previous research has shown that ecological restoration projects in which volunteers remove invasive exotic species, clean trash out of neighborhood streams and rivers, and plant trees all have the opportunity to build local knowledge about the environment and engender the feeling of helping the environment in a tangible manner (Ryan et al. 2001). Equally important are the multiplier benefits that engaging in meaningful action can have on other aspects of people's lives. The same study found that engaging in ecological restoration projects led to durable change in volunteers' environmental actions at their own homes, such as using more native plants in their residential landscape. When creatively designed and managed, sustainable sites have the power to increase the public's awareness of environmental issues and potentially create lifestyle changes in the larger populace beyond the borders of the site itself.

The "evidence-based design" approach, which has its roots in the healthcare design field, can be used to address the multiple benefits of a sustainable site, including the social aspects. However, it has to be acknowledged that the same metrics that make calculating site stormwater runoff rather straightforward, for example, are not at the same level of accuracy for many of the human health and well-being areas. In other words, people are complex in the way in which they respond to various environments. Nonetheless, there are over four decades of environment and behavior research that informs many of the strategies recommended in this chapter. This body of knowledge continues to grow as designers and researchers team together to create sites that provide a range of benefits for people.

ASSESSING THE SITE'S SOCIAL SETTING

Identifying Neighbors, Users, and Other Stakeholders

A key component of designing for human health and well-being is understanding more about the people who will use the site. In some instances, such as the renovation of an existing park or school, the site has existing site users from which the designer can learn. However, in other instances, the site users are future homeowners, employees, and others who have not yet moved to the site or have not even been identified specifically. Designers do not always have the chance to interact directly with the specific people who will use the site. While designers can extrapolate the expected user population using marketing studies, demographics, and other predictive devices, there is no substitute for talking to site users and stakeholders directly. Ideally, the project planning process would include stakeholder and user involvement with an inclusive process, reaching as many potential users and stakeholders as possible. The first step is to identify potential users and stakeholders. In the same way as one identifies the watershed in which a site is located, so should designers identify the "human-shed" or community context that this site will attract. For example, neighbors can be defined as simply people living adjacent or within some preconceived distance, such as the typical one-quarter-mile walking distance of a site. However, for more regional facilities, the quarter- or half-mile radius may vastly underestimate the people who will come to use the site or travel by it on a daily basis. For particular facilities, such as neighborhood parks, there is a vast amount of literature on the "service" area (Mertes and Hall 1996; other NRPA standards). The "human" catchment area for many facilities and sites is not a uniform area, but will vary by transportation mode, geographic and political boundaries, and other competing destinations (see Figure 7-1).

Project stakeholders could include:

▶ Those who physically use, work, play, or otherwise inhabit the site

▶ Walkers, joggers, bike riders, and others who move through a site

▶ Those who stop and rest to eat lunch, picnic, bird watch, and so forth

▶ People who may view a site from their home, office window, or walk or drive by as part of their daily routine

▶ Those who are actively engaged in physically restoring the habitat on a site, or engaged in other ongoing gardening or maintenance activities

▶ Government officials, and others who may have jurisdiction or planning power over a site

▶ Land owners

▶ Environmental and other interest groups

▶ Environmental education and interpretive experts

▶ Industry and business interests

▶ Neighborhood leaders and organizations

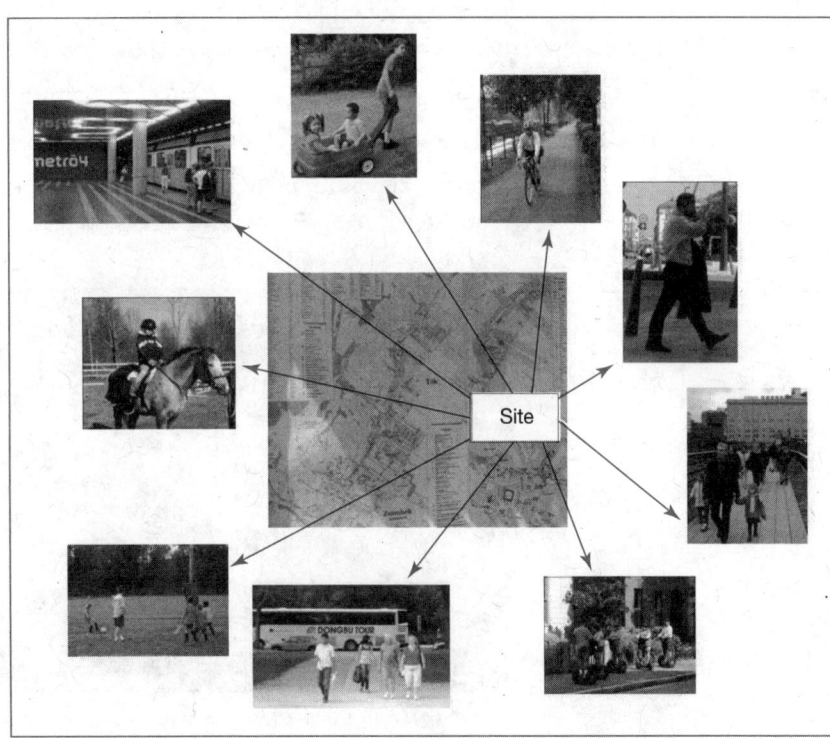

FIGURE 7-1: A human-shed should draw from a diverse set of project users and stakeholders.

Strategies for Understanding Human Needs and Perceptions

The following are some strategies to enhance participation in the design process. These strategies are organized around information gathering, promoting a common knowledge or beginning point (i.e., cognitive map building), and fostering innovation in design.

- ▶ Engage in other methods of information gathering beyond the public meeting as this may only represent a narrow slice of the population.

- ▶ Use mail-out surveys to engage a broader range of opinions.

- ▶ Create Web-based surveys for communities with wide ownership of this technology.

- ▶ Set up displays at popular public places, such as town squares, libraries, and malls (Figure 7-2).

- ▶ Partner with planners and others trained in social science techniques to increase the rigor and validity of survey work.

- ▶ Conduct charettes and workshops with stakeholders. Ask site users and other stakeholders to describe the qualities that they would like for a site rather than having them illustrate them if they are uncomfortable with a drawing. Or ask stakeholders to generate collages of images to show qualities of what they would like in a space.

- ▶ Educate stakeholders about sustainable design strategies and technologies.

- ▶ Take stakeholders on field trips to see real sustainable design project examples.

- ▶ Other resources for public participation techniques are: Cooper-Marcus and Francis 1998; Kaplan et al. 1998; Hester 1990; Project for Public Spaces 1998; and Sanoff 2000.

(Graduate landscape planning studio team members, Department of Landscape Architecture and Regional Planning, University of Massachusetts, Amherst: Yaser Abunnasr and Benneth Phelps [pictured]; Israel J. Monsanto, Frank Varro, Amy Verel [not pictured]; Photo: Israel J. Monsanto)

FIGURE 7-2: Use a range of strategies to engage the public including setting up displays at local community gatherings, such as this fall festival in Ashfield, Massachusetts.

HUMAN HEALTH AND WELL-BEING APPROACH FOR SUSTAINABLE SITES

In this chapter, we take the approach that sustainability requires understanding and responding to human needs. The ecological health of a site is interconnected to the human health and well-being of the people who will use, inhabit, or otherwise be part of it. This interconnection between people and sites requires giving equal value to the human condition as part of sustainable site design, planning, and management as is given to biophysical factors. A sustainable site has the ability to improve and address the stresses and challenges of modern life by providing restorative environments, improving the physical and mental health of site users, fostering community, and creating more equitable economic opportunities.

Beginning the sustainable design process from the human perspective requires understanding and assessing the existing site users, neighbors, and other stakeholders. There may be existing social ties, patterns of use, and other benefits that a site provides to local residents that need to be respected as part of predesign assessment. We take the approach that a sustainable design process needs to be inclusive, transparent, and democratic where public participation makes a meaningful impact on the final site design. Local people have a wealth of knowledge that can inform and improve sustainable sites from both an ecological and human perspective, helping to create solutions that merge both professional and local expertise.

Economic sustainability: Sustainable sites need to provide economic opportunities for local residents, especially those from underserved communities, by creating jobs, as well as providing new services and access to greenspace.

Educational opportunities: Sites can expand knowledge about sustainability and promote sustainable behavior/attitudes both onsite and offsite by interpreting and revealing sustainable practices.

Community building and social ties: Sustainable sites can be a mechanism to promote stronger communities and social connections, which are a vital part of human health and well-being. Local culture and connection to place can also be protected by preserving and enhancing the site's cultural and historic features.

Mental health: People also need quiet respites from the hectic modern world. Providing physical and/or visual access to such greenspaces can help restore stress, promote mental health, and have other cognitive and physical benefits.

Physical health: Providing equitable access for all is a key aspect of promoting physical health for a wide range of users. Likewise, sustainable sites need to address concerns about public safety, which is a precursor to encouraging site use.

Connections to place: Sustainable sites need to be transformative places for people and nature alike, where long-term stewardship of a site is sustained by healthy connections to place.

SUSTAINABILITY AWARENESS AND EDUCATION

One goal behind many sustainable site designs is to create demonstration projects that illustrate the latest innovations in ecologically beneficial technologies and practices. In doing so, designers and advocates can show the public, as well as policy makers, how they can adapt these strategies in other settings—spreading sustainability practices beyond the borders of the individual site.

It can be challenging to change people's existing knowledge, attitudes, and behaviors. Therefore, a sustainability message must be relevant, timely, and related to people's existing knowledge. Fortunately for sustainable landscape designers, people are fascinated by the natural world, its palette of materials, and its experiences.

The design of a sustainable landscape itself can convey environmental information by revealing ecological processes, patterns, and forms. Termed "eco-revelatory" design by landscape architects over a decade ago, sustainable sites can become a microcosm of the hydrological, biological, and geologic systems (Helphand and Melnick, 1998). Using the design to educate people about the site's ecosystem context is at the heart of promoting sustainability awareness.

The following are some strategies for promoting sustainability awareness:

Know your audience: The first step in planning strategies to convey sustainable information is to identify the audience for this message as part of the predesign assessment, including the age range of users, learning challenges, literacy level, and languages spoken or written (Figure 7-3). Since the goal is to reach the broadest range of people, it is important to not only consider site users who currently use or are planning to use the site, but plan for future audiences as well.

Understand existing knowledge: While everyone comes with different levels of knowledge about a topic, it is useful to understand people's general areas of knowledge, attitudes, and frame of reference for a topic. Surveys, interviews, and other strategies for evaluating knowledge are useful here (Babbie, 2008). It is also important to know people's current practices in a particular area (for example, plant choices in landscaping), including concerns about sustainable design or practices and their motivations for their current choices.

(Photo: Robert L. Ryan)

FIGURE 7-3: This model allows the visually impaired to understand the skyline and landscape of Castle Hill and the Danube River in Budapest, Hungary.

Address different learning styles: People learn through a variety of methods and styles—visual, auditory, reading/writing, and experiential (Fleming 2001; c.f. Hawk and Shah 2007). Since people will vary in the style or experience that bests suits them, it is important to address a range of learning approaches. Combining visual material with written material is much more effective than using words alone (Kaplan et al. 1998). Experiential or hands-on learning about the environment, particularly with a mentor, is the most durable strategy for producing dedicated environmentalists (Louv 2005; Tanner 1980).

Keep it simple: The message should be kept simple, while at the same time conveying the complex reality of sustainable practices. In most cases, using less information and fewer words is the best approach to avoid overwhelming the public with too much information. Visual material (photographs, graphics, and diagrams), however, can be particularly useful to convey complex information in an easy-to-understand manner. Research suggests that having one clear message with a few (three to seven) subpoints is the right amount of information to convey per image (Kaplan et al. 1998).

Tell a story: Creating a compelling argument for sustainability can be enhanced by using a story format that provides concrete imagery as well as the uncertainty (suspense) of not knowing what will happen next. Stories are more memorable than simple facts, providing a structure for conveying more complex information (Kaplan et al. 1998). Stories can be told in a variety of formats, from the oral recordings of "sustainability" testimonials from those who have engaged in sustainable practices to well-illustrated storyboards in brochures or other visual material.

Go beyond signage: Use multiple strategies to convey information. Since people learn in a variety of ways, it is important to provide multiple methods to convey sustainable practices and elements. While creative signage with simple graphics is one strategy, the intention here is to provide multiple creative formats, including:

1. **Models**. Using models that show how the sustainable features and processes operate will allow more interaction.

2. **Brochures.** As with signage, these are standard practices but have the benefit of not disrupting the visual environment of a setting.

3. **Interactive displays.** Displays that allow site users to manipulate and interact with the environment are great learning devices. For example, allowing site users to manipulate the amount of water flowing through a stormwater runnel would help them to see different effects of water flow and infiltration (Figure 7-5a and b; Figure 7-6a and b; Figure 7-7).

4. **Electronic kiosks.** Kiosks allow Web-based and other interactive programs to be used by site users. These same applications can be also made accessible for cellphones and other hand-held electronic devices (Figure 7-4).

(Photo: Robert L. Ryan)

FIGURE 7-4: Interactive kiosks such as this one in Chicago allow the public to learn more about sustainable practices.

(Photo: Robert L. Ryan)

FIGURE 7-5: This display at the Herbert H. Bateman Educational and Administrative Center for the Chincoteague National Wildlife Refuge, Virginia, tells the story of using wetlands to decompose onsite waste in a creative, engaging manner.

(Photo: Robert L. Ryan)

FIGURE 7-6: Interactive displays at Chicago's Brookfield Zoo show visitors about the hydrologic cycle and their role in affecting water quality.

5. **Portable audio/visual devices.** MP3 players, cellphones, and audio players allow visitors to learn at their own pace and can allow for oral storytelling opportunities, especially if onsite programming is not possible. Combined with newer technologies and cellphone applications, these devices could allow visual material to be incorporated as well.

6. **Format.** Provide written and audio information in a variety of languages.

(Photo: Robert L. Ryan)

FIGURE 7-7: This Plexiglas panel at Millenaris Park in Budapest, Hungary, allows visitors to see the soil profile of these mounds which symbolizes surrounding landscape of the Buda Hills.

Creating Programming for the Site

Some of the most engaging environmental education requires some sort of hands-on or experiential learning. Developing onsite programs where possible can be a critical aspect to enhancing sustainability awareness at public and private sites. Inviting the public to learn about sustainability through onsite programming can also build social capital and encourage site use. The challenge is to sustain onsite programming over the long term. Here are some strategies to make this possible:

1. Partner with nearby schools, nature centers, and other educational facilities to develop programming as well as other educational information.

2. Draw on local knowledge. Many communities are filled with local experts on nature, ecology, and sustainable practices who may want to share their knowledge with others.

3. Fund ongoing programming; creating a separate endowment or other self-funding mechanism to ensure the sustainability of ongoing programming can be critical.

4. Encourage volunteering and learning. Research has shown that people who volunteer doing ecological restoration and monitoring are motivated by opportunities for environmental learning. Onsite maintenance that engages local residents and other volunteers can provide valuable learning opportunities, while providing other practical benefits for maintaining the site (Ryan et al. 2001).

SOCIAL EQUALITY IN SITE DEVELOPMENT, CONSTRUCTION, AND USE

The goal is to ensure that a site provides social and economic benefits to the surrounding community including expanding site use to populations who traditionally would not have access to a site, especially those from disadvantaged communities. In many instances, local communities, especially disadvantaged communities, bear the burden of new development—including increased traffic, air pollution, noise, and other potential environmental consequences—without sharing in the social or economic benefits, such as construction and permanent jobs in which profits are given to nonlocal workers and companies. Research has shown that locally based companies invest about 80 percent back into the community in the form of local wages, purchases, and other investments, compared to only 20 to 40 percent for national or international firms (Wyant 2006). Moreover, despite continued globalization of the world's economy, communities that have a greater diversity and number of locally based jobs and companies have greater resilience to deal with economic and social challenges.

Sustainable construction projects can provide the opportunity for valuable job training and skill development for local residents, opening up careers in the green industry. In addition to construction-related jobs, sustainable site design projects can provide job training and internship opportunities for local residents with the consulting firms that are part of the interdisciplinary project team. For example, some offices have internships for local high school or community college students to introduce them to design professions, as they develop their technical skills.

A sustainable site has the opportunity to become an "environmental commons" that provides the social and economic means that sustain local populations, as well as environmental value. Long-term sustainability of any site depends upon the stewardship provided by local residents. Private corporations and institutions (e.g., Yale University, New Haven; General Motors, Detroit) have realized that being a good neighbor to local communities is "good business" in the benefits it provides for neighborhood reinvestment, education, workforce training, and even reduced vandalism.

Identify the community: As part of the predesign assessment (see Chapter 2), designers should identify the neighborhood or larger community that has a stake in the project, including the relevant community organizations. For projects in higher-income, less-diverse communities, this requires partnering with organizations in the greater region that represent low-income and/or minority populations, including those who work on or near the site, but cannot afford to live in the community due to the high cost of living.

Identify community economic and social needs: After identifying the community organizations and other stakeholders, as part of predesign planning, work with the community to identify the most pressing economic and social issues that could be addressed on the site, such as lack of park and recreation facilities, community centers, jobs for youth, or educational opportunities (Figures 7-8, 7-9, and 7-10). Research has shown that many inner-city neighborhoods lack adequate open space, particularly in low-income, disadvantaged communities (Trust for Public Land 2009).

Engage community and other stakeholders in site design: This step is already part of the predesign process (see Chapter 2). The key here for equitable site development is to make sure to include the larger group of stakeholders beyond the primary site users.

Consider sharing public and private facilities: For a privately owned site (e.g., commercial, industrial, office, or institutional), allowing the public access to amenities that are part of the existing program can address community needs. For example, the hotel or private university pool could allow community use. Sharing parking facilities is another strategy for assisting local communities who may lack parking for nearby community buildings or events. Another example might be the use of restroom facilities in an adjacent private building as part of an urban plaza design. These limited or temporal uses should be formalized within a community benefits agreement or other agreement.

Develop community-centered space with local control: Another longer-term strategy would be to develop community facilities that are under the direct control and management of local residents. For example, community gardens could be developed on a large corporate campus with a long-term lease or even deeded to a local nonprofit group.

(Photo: Robert L. Ryan)

FIGURE 7-8: Lafayette Square Park, designed by Hood Design, in downtown Oakland, California, was designed using an inclusive process to accommodate a wide range of users, from immigrants, children, the elderly, office workers, and even the homeless. This landform helps create different zones that allow these disparate groups to share this small park.

FIGURE 7-9: Restroom facilities at Lafayette Square Park, which are a rarity in many downtown parks, were designed in a creative manner that allows for human needs while responding to concerns about public safety.

(Design by: Hood Design, Inc.; Photo: Robert L. Ryan)

FIGURE 7-10: Large mature trees were retained in the redesign of this historic square. A new play area, buffered from the surrounding busy streets, was designed to provide a safer environment for younger children and allows comfortable seating areas for their parents and other caregivers.

Create volunteer opportunities within public spaces and gardens: Site use can foster opportunities for local residents to volunteer in environmental stewardship or gardening activities in both public and /or private facilities. For example, volunteer groups can help maintain edible landscapes in schoolyards, therapeutic gardens in hospitals, or help restore habitat while learning valuable skills and knowledge.

Develop community benefits agreement: A community benefits agreement is a legally binding contract between a local community organization(s) and a developer or in some instances a government authority, that outlines the specific benefits that the proposed site development will provide to a community (Gross et al. 2005). These benefits can include providing a percentage of living-wage jobs, community services, child-care facilities, park developments, and public access to private onsite facilities. Community benefit agreements differ from the typical development agreements between a city and private developer in that they create a more specific, legally enforceable document that is shaped by the local community and its specific needs. In addition, these agreements help ensure that the public investment required in many large-scale projects, especially public-private partnerships, create benefits for the local community as well as the region. Maintaining programs can be challenging; thus an endowment or percentage of revenue can be set up to fund local programs, as one way to sustain these events over time.

Implementation and Maintenance Considerations for Social Equality

Implementing an equitable project has many challenges, including making the project profitable or economically feasible, while providing public benefits. The following are some strategies to address these challenges:

Determine living wage: Promoting equality in site development is not just about providing minimum-wage jobs but providing jobs that pay a living wage. Living wages vary by region and can be determined by using the Living Wage Calculator (www.livingwage. geog.psu.edu/) or working with local economic development agencies.

Plan construction to include local employment: As part of the preconstruction planning, developers, contractors, and designers can determine the number of potential jobs/employees, and subcontractors. Develop a plan to include local businesses and low-income workers as a percentage of the total labor force and budget.

Develop skilled labor: In spite of the current high rates of unemployment (2010), labor statistics point to a shortage of skilled workers, especially with technical or community college–level education. Advertising campaigns and partnerships with local employment agencies and community organizations can help reach local skilled workers. Develop an ongoing partnership with local job-training organizations for employing students/youth who are learning skills in the green industry. In many instances, these training programs subsidize the labor costs to lower the economic burden to businesses of providing on-the-job training.

FIGURE 7-11: Community gardens, such as this one in Boston's Dorchester area, provide much-needed locally grown produce and can generate small-scale local economic opportunities, such as areas for social interaction.

FIGURE 7-12: Farmers' markets provide local business opportunities, as well as fresh produce. This market is in the plaza in front of the U.S. Department of Agriculture in Washington, DC.

Create ongoing economic opportunities: Allow local residents to use private sites for farming, fishing, or other natural resource-based employment to sustain traditional local economies. In more urban settings, allowing local business owners to conduct business in a private setting, such as food vendor in a corporate plaza or a farmer's market in a government building, is another example of providing equitable site use after construction (Figures 7-11 and 7-12). Use local businesses and employees for ongoing site maintenance.

Provide programming for community events: These onsite programs should address community needs, such as providing educational events or places for outdoor concerts.

Employ program and educational coordinators: For larger, more popular sites, educational and events coordination staff are needed to plan, schedule, advertise, and potentially lead programs for the public. These coordinators can work with the local community to evaluate the success and effectiveness of programs and events.

Create discounts for local residents to events/facilities: Some local residents may be excluded from using a nearby site and events, due to economic circumstances. Providing free or discounted access for local residents, along with extended hours and/or transportation, can create more equitable access.

Use easements and other access agreements: Public-use easements for trails and walkways across private land are another formal mechanism to ensure community access to high-value amenity areas, such as urban waterfronts (for example, Boston's Harborwalk).

SITE ACCESSIBILITY

The more accessible a site is to a wide range of users, the more they are able to benefit from the ecological, social, or economic opportunities that it provides. In fact, equal access is at the heart of social equity aspects of sustainability. The Americans with Disabilities Act (ADA), along with other required accessibility standards at the local, state, and federal levels, already clearly outlines the legal responsibility of site designers to provide a minimum level of access to a site, especially with regard to physical mobility. The challenge for sustainable design is to go beyond the minimum requirements and enhance equitable use for all people.

"Universal design" is the term used for a people-centered approach to design that is not simply about meeting accessibility standards, but taking a holistic approach in which a range of people's abilities and life stage is considered at the beginning of the design process rather than as an afterthought (Ostroff 2001). In other words, instead of considering designing for people with disabilities, universal design has at its core the notion of designing for all people, acknowledging that everyone at some stage in their life will have access challenges, whether it be physical mobility, visual or auditory impairment, verbal ability (i.e., language under-standing and comprehension), or mental/psychological challenges. The Center for Universal Design outlines seven principles of universal design (see Table 7-1).

TABLE 7-1: The Principles of Universal Design

PRINCIPLE ONE: Equitable Use	The design is useful and marketable to people with diverse abilities.
PRINCIPLE TWO: Flexibility in Use	The design accommodates a wide range of individual preferences and abilities.
PRINCIPLE THREE: Simple and Intuitive Use	Use of the design is easy to understand, regardless of the user's experience, knowledge, language skills, or current concentration level.
PRINCIPLE FOUR: Perceptible Information	The design communicates necessary information effectively to the user, regardless of ambient conditions or the user's sensory abilities.
PRINCIPLE FIVE: Tolerance for Error	The design minimizes hazards and the adverse consequences of accidental or unintended actions.
PRINCIPLE SIX: Low Physical Effort	The design can be used efficiently and comfortably and with a minimum of fatigue.
PRINCIPLE SEVEN: Size and Space for Approach and Use	Appropriate size and space is provided for approach, reach, manipulation, and use regardless of user's body size, posture, or mobility.

Design Considerations for Site Accessibility

As with many sustainable site strategies, promoting site accessibility necessitates a detailed predesign site assessment to determine the best location for high-use areas and buildings to minimize site disturbance while maximizing access opportunities and microclimate amelioration, especially in areas with steep topographic change and harsh climatic conditions.

Plan for equitable site access early: Equitable use is about ensuring that the majority of site amenities are accessible and centrally located to serve the widest range of site users and that those with disabling conditions are not relegated to peripheral or secondary entrances or use areas.

Go beyond the handicap ramp: Designers should consider eliminating the ramp, when possible, in favor of site designs where the entire plaza or entrance is barrier free (i.e., lacks steps and meets maximum slope requirements under 5 percent). In other words, make the ramp the main route for all pedestrian traffic and stairs, if necessary, the secondary route.

Design for the five senses: In many ways, the strategy of designing gardens for the five senses of sight, sound, hearing, scent, and touch is one proactive approach to universal design. To consider each of these senses in turn allows one to maximize the experience for those who may rely on particular senses more than others (i.e., visually impaired reliance on touch or sound) while creating an experience for all to share.

Provide options based upon ability: Providing flexibility and options are important for site accessibility to allow for a range of abilities. In the field of recreation, the term "graduated difficulty of access" is used to describe "a wide variety of trail types with a range of opportunities and experiences to accommodate or challenge all abilities" (Fishbeck 1998, p. 240.2). This same concept from hiking trail design can be applied to any type of site accessibility situation where the idea is not to segregate users, but to allow for exploration and challenge.

Choose materials with mobility in mind: Surface paving materials strongly influence accessibility. The challenge for sustainability is overcoming the tension between provided paved surfaces for accessibility, while still allowing for the permeability that is beneficial for stormwater infiltration and heat island reduction. In certain situations, soft surface material, such as decomposed granite, if properly graded and compacted, can be used in lieu of hard pavement and still allow for universal access. In other instances, a combination of hard surface materials for the main path of travel can be augmented with adjacent soft surface materials paving or other porous paving.

Communicate accessibility information in a simple format: International graphic symbols are useful to communicate site information for foreign visitors, young children, and

others who may not read or have learning imp[...]
graphic symbols with signage in multiple
languages is also helpful, as not all symbols
may be readily understood. For the visually
impaired, tactile materials for warning strips,
Braille letters, and other devices should be
used (see ADAAG 2005; Fishbeck 1998).

Design for human comfort: Seating. The
importance of comfortable seating as part
of site access should not be underestimated. For those with mobility challenges,
as well as the general public, seating
should be designed ergonomically for the
human body with back support at a comfortable angle, armrests to assist in standing and seating, and comfortable material
(i.e., smooth, minimizes surface temperature extremes) (see ADAAG 2005; Harris
et al. 1998). Flexibility in seating height is

FIGURE 7-13: This free-standing restroom facility in Budapest, Hungary, is designed for human comfort, unlike the adjacent bollards, which serve as makeshift seating areas.

another strategy to expand site access. Movable seating also
provides benefits, because users can move chairs to their preferred microclimate (i.e., sun or shade), as well as rearrange
seating configuration for the number of people in a group,
and comfortable social distance. In addition, seating needs to
be placed at regular intervals and especially near entries to a
site to allow people to experience the entire site without fear
of having no place to rest, which is critical for the elderly and
those with physical mobility and endurance challenges.

Design for human comfort: Drinking water and restrooms.
Providing drinking fountains within a sustainable site along
with restroom facilities is another obvious, but overlooked,
aspect of human comfort that is often eliminated due to
budget or maintenance concerns. Connections to facilities in
adjacent buildings are not always possible, suggesting creative solutions, such as these well-designed restroom facilities
first piloted in Paris and now found in many cities worldwide
(see Figures 7-13 and 7-14).

FIGURE 7-14: Providing drinking water is another key aspect of designing for human comfort, as shown in this foot-activated drinking fountain in Budapest, Hungary.

Design for human comfort: Microclimate designs. Microclimate design includes the provision of shaded areas during summer months and can extend the usability of outdoor spaces beyond the usual season by providing sun pockets, sheltered from the wind in winter. Water features including recirculating fountains can cool a space through evaporation without using excessive amounts of water. Misters and fans in outdoor seating areas have been used successfully in hot-climate areas as well. Prevailing winds can be channeled to cool outdoor areas. Microclimate design also includes providing windbreaks in heavy wind areas and to improve human comfort, as well as to reduce wind chill in cold climate areas (Brown and Gillespie 1995). See Table 4-5, "Summary of Regional Bioclimatic Strategies," in Chapter 4, for examples of regionally specific approaches to microclimate design (Figure 7-15).

(Photo: Robert L. Ryan)

FIGURE 7-15: Water features can cool the nearby environment. However, this example from the Native American Museum in Washington, DC, does not allow people to use it.

Implementation and Maintenance Considerations for Site Accessibility

Adapt site accessibility as site changes: A postoccupancy evaluation and adaptive management plan will allow site managers to adapt to user needs and longer-term changes. Additional populations may use the site or find that their access is limited by certain site conditions. Likewise, new buildings may shade previously sunny site areas or cut off existing access points to a site.

Site maintenance and access: Walkways need to be kept free of snow, leaf litter, seedpods, and other natural and human-created litter to provide safe access to a site (Figure 7-16). Pruning of plant material is also essential to keep pathways clear and avoid hazardous conditions, especially for those with mobility or visual challenges. In addition, maintenance of paving and other site features is important to avoid future hazards for users, as paving can deteriorate, crack, and change over time.

(Photo: Robert L. Ryan)

FIGURE 7-16: Barrier-free design includes providing access to hard-to-reach places for all people, such as this bridge at the National Botanic Garden in Washington, DC.

SITE WAYFINDING

People need to find their way around a site to access the resources and amenities that it provides. If people cannot find a sustainable site or its features, they will not be able to benefit from it or learn about it. Moreover, people become extremely frustrated if they can't find the entrance to a park or nearby building, or if they can't find the features that they expect to find when visiting a site. Being lost not only discourages site exploration and use, it can be a fearful experience for most people, especially in a setting where safety concerns are heightened by unfamiliarity or fear for personal safety. For example, being lost in the overgrown area of an urban park or natural area in most U.S. cities at dusk would unnerve urban residents and visitors alike.

The term "wayfinding" is used to describe the site design and other cues, including signage and devices used to help people orient themselves to new surroundings. While signage is the traditional way to address wayfinding, designers should strive to create a legible design in which signage can be minimized. Urban planner Kevin Lynch (1960) pioneered some of the early research and theories about wayfinding in the urban environment and found that people often conceptualize cities as a series of districts, paths, nodes, edges, and landmarks. This "classic" urban design vocabulary is useful for planning at the landscape site level as well.

An overall plan is needed to address wayfinding beginning with the initial design decisions about entrances into the site, spatial organization, and circulation. Often, for larger and more complex sites, wayfinding experts should be consulted as part of the process.

Emphasize site entrances and gateways: The entrance to a site should be clearly visible, discernible, and memorable to communicate to the public that it provides access to the site. In many cases, sites have multiple entry points; therefore, a hierarchy of entry points may be necessary to differentiate major and minor entrances.

The term "gateway" can also be used to describe entrances that provide access through some type of edge or barrier, such as wall, hedge, or other natural or built enclosure. Gateways are also important to announce the transition from one space to another within the site itself (Figure 7-17).

[Photo: Robert L. Ryan]

FIGURE 7-17: Gateways should focus on landmarks, such as this flowering tree at the entrance to a college arboretum, which has both distinctive flowers as well as a weeping form.

Provide clear site lines, vantage points, and overlooks: Humans orient themselves primarily through sight, as opposed to the other senses. Wayfinding is facilitated by providing viewpoints to key areas in a site from major pathways and gateways. Vantage points and other overlooks that provide an overview of the site are particularly useful to help orient visitors, which is why people are naturally attracted to such places that provide a "prospect" of the surrounding environment (Appleton 1975).

Create a small number of discernible regions: Regions are a part of the landscape that is unique or discernible from other areas, such as grassland (Figure 7-18), evergreen forest, or pavement. Subdividing larger areas into smaller, memorable regions helps wayfinding. In particular, research suggests that smaller numbers of regions (approximately three to seven) will not overwhelm the memory of most people (Kaplan et al. 1998). In smaller sites, regions may consist of distinct paving patterns, enclosed spaces, or different use areas (Figure 7-19).

Use site landmarks: A landmark is a unique element that is memorable and distinguished from its surroundings by size, form, material, or other unique characteristics. Research suggests that humans distinguish form by silhouette or outline, which is why some of the most memorable objects often take the classic vertical form, such as an obelisk or specimen evergreen tree (Figure 7-20). Gateways, bridges, and other unique built or natural forms are

(Photo: Robert L. Ryan)

FIGURE 7-18: This wide-open prairie landscape makes wayfinding difficult.

(Photo: Robert L. Ryan)

FIGURE 7-19: Dividing the landscape into discernible regions and providing a landmark such as this native tree helps wayfinding and increases the ease with which people are able to explore this natural area in the University of Michigan's Nichols Arboretum.

also good landmarks. Landmarks need to be visible from different vantage points, particularly from gateways, entrances, and other choice locations.

Provide information at decision points: In Kevin Lynch's terms (1960), the node is often the point of activity, but can also act as the point where visitors can choose between different paths or destinations. Nodes are important locations for orientation information, including views to other areas and their respective landmarks.

Develop a hierarchy for paths and other circulation systems: Major pathways should lead to main entrances, gateways, and other destinations, and should be distinguished from minor or secondary paths by size and material. Hard surface paving, when used, should be reserved for major paths, while soft surfaces can be used for more secondary pathways. Paving materials can also be used to distinguish paths that lead to or are associated with different regions—for example, boardwalks in wetland areas, mulched trails in woodland areas, and so forth. Separating vehicular and pedestrian paths by material type and width can also help with wayfinding and pedestrian safety.

Employ orientation devices: The standard approach to facilitate wayfinding is to put a "you-are-here" map at entrances and other choice points. While these maps certainly have their merits, in many instances, plan-view maps can create even more confusion, since many people find such maps difficult to read. However, there are other more innovative approaches to facilitate wayfinding, including providing physical models of the site (Figure 7-21), or interactive display kiosks with computer models, as well as audio tours. Computer applications for cellphones and other hand-held electronic devices also provide many creative means to assist in wayfinding, but in some instances, they may actually distance users from the cognitive experience of exploring the site or developing a mental map for further exploration (Richtel 2010).

(Photo: Robert L. Ryan)

FIGURE 7-20: Focusing trails on landmarks, such as this existing tree, helps visitors orient themselves in unfamiliar natural areas. In addition, this barrier-free boardwalk allows visitors to experience an ecosystem that would otherwise be difficult to access, as well as provides a clear pathway and travel route.

Use color coding carefully: Many wayfinding strategies include color-coding pathways, signs, and other markers to aid in distinguishing particular areas or paths. Color should be used judiciously, as it is difficult for many people to distinguish different shades of the same color, some people are color-blind, and color does not necessarily communicate hierarchy. In addition, colors used on maps, such as a blue-blazed trail, need to be used on path signage or marking in the field to avoid further confusion.

FIGURE 7-21: Providing wayfinding information at decision points is critical to help in wayfinding. Models that show an overview of a site are particularly useful.

Implementation and Maintenance Considerations for Site Wayfinding

Take a site walk-about during and after implementation: While in theory many wayfinding issues should be addressed during the design phase of the project, conducting a site walk-through with potential users and first-time visitors can help identify potential confusing areas or those where further orientation information is required.

Provide maps and brochures: Physical onsite maps should be located at decision points, entrances, and nodes. While it is standard to orient maps with north upward, cognitive research suggests that maps should be oriented toward the view. In addition, as noted before, many people find plan views difficult to read, so bird's-eye-view maps and axonometric views are much better for communicating spatial and wayfinding information. Labels should be placed directly on important areas rather than relying on numbered keys or other approaches.

Keep views clear: Ongoing maintenance of vegetation is necessary to keep sight-lines open at gateways and entrances, to ensure that landmarks are visible, as well as to maintain views from overlooks and alongside trails. It is important that the initial planting design take these views into consideration, so that future maintenance for wayfinding (and safety) does not conflict with other site goals related to reestablishing native plantings and ecosystem health.

SITE SAFETY

The public's perception of the safety of a site has a profound influence on its use. This section discusses perceptions of crime and personal safety rather than the risk associated with rock climbing or other types of adventure recreation that people choose to do on a voluntary basis. Perceptions of safety may not relate to actual likelihood of a crime occurring, but can still be a strong deterrent to people using a landscape, particularly urban parks.

The fear that people experience in the landscape is not only related to fear of others, but to the fears posed by "nature" itself. Fears of beestings, snakes, and getting lost in the woods are all often-unstated reasons that people may be deterred from using the sustainable landscapes that promote native ecosystems (Kaplan et al. 1998). In fact, researchers have found that urban dwellers in particular, who have little familiarity with natural landscapes, including many inner-city children, consider urban natural areas to be dangerous, overgrown, messy, and uncomfortable (Bixler and Floyd 1997). The challenge for designers promoting native landscapes, as part of sustainable sites, is to increase familiarity with these places by encouraging site use, so that all people can share in their social and ecological benefits. In addition, increased site use can raise awareness and understanding about natural systems.

Site safety is directly related to the social equity aspects of sustainability. Fear for safety can preclude certain groups from using a space, including the elderly, children, or women who may feel vulnerable to crime. Thus, those groups that may benefit the most from a sustainable site or park are excluded for reasons of fear creating an inequitable situation. Temporal use of spaces is also often limited, such as use of parks or other spaces after dark.

Early researchers and observers of urban open space from the 1960s and 1970s, including William Whyte and Jane Jacobs, found that increased use of an urban open space was associated with increased perceptions of safety. In other words, it is those spaces that are heavily used by a wide range of people in which people feel the safest. Conversely, the isolated place with few people is often perceived as lonely and dangerous.

At the same time, architect Oscar Newman in his analysis of failed public housing projects developed the term "defensible space" to address what he determined to be necessary principles to create safer, more humane housing and urban neighborhoods (Newman 1996). These principles, which influenced the more recent Crime Prevention through Environmental Design (CPTED) movement, are relevant for the built as well as the natural environment. From a theoretical perspective, Newman's work focuses more on having residents policing their local environments while CPTED focuses more on deterring criminals by changing the environment (S. Michaels 2010).

Design Considerations for Site Safety

Define perceived ownership of space: Spaces for different types of perceived owner-ship: public, semipublic, semiprivate, and private—should be delineated. Spatial cues, such as fences, hedges, and other types of boundaries including changes in paving pat-terns, can be used to show that particular spaces, for example a play area for children, are under the "ownership" or oversight of a particular group of people, whether it be the nearby apartment dwellers or particular group of park users. Separating public areas, such as parking lots, entrances, and public walkways from private areas, allows local resi-dents better control over who accesses the more private areas of a site. By subdividing larger areas into smaller areas, this strategy overcomes the "no-man's land" situation that can occur in undifferentiated landscapes where no one appears to own or care for them, and it can achieve the smaller "regions" that help with local identity and wayfinding.

Design for natural surveillance: The term "eyes on the street" is shorthand for the con-cept of natural surveillance where site users and inhabitants can easily see the coming and going of visitors. This can be accomplished by siting entrances, walkways, and other points of site access so they are visible from adjacent building windows or, in the case of sites without buildings, within sight of heavily used areas and centers of activity.

Improve visibility/sight lines: A concept related to natural surveillance is the provision of visibility from walkways, so that users can survey the surrounding landscape. This is not a license to clear-cut all vegetation or to promote planting of wide-open lawn areas, which unfortunately has been the result of some cases of overzealous community polic-ing efforts, but designing to minimize vegetation that blocks views at eye level from key points. Using lower ground cover (under 2 to 3 ft, or 75 cm, in height) as well as overstory canopy (above 6½ ft or 2 m) will allow for improved visibility while still accomplishing other sustainability goals, such as increasing biodiversity and landscape structure. Sight lines are also important to maintain with regard to walls, fences, and other landscape elements.

Promote a positive image: The design quality, materials, and style conveys a message to the public about the image of a particular site, the type of potential users or inhabitants, and level of safety. Newman's research found that public housing developments that con-veyed an institutional image, such as unpainted concrete or block, instead of a residential image, were stigmatized as not fitting into their setting and were less cared for by resi-dents as well. For designers, this suggests that the industrial materials of chain-link and metal that are sometimes used in parks or residential settings to convey a postindustrial landscape may be perceived negatively by site users or residents as not compatible with their setting.

Understand the influence of context or milieu on perceptions of safety: An important aspect of predesign assessment is understanding the surrounding context of the site. Defensible space principles suggest that sites that appear different or isolated are more vulnerable to crime and less likely to be defended by local residents. For example, a public housing complex in an otherwise industrial or commercial setting is marginalized from other residential areas and may be targeted by criminals. In the same manner, urban open spaces which are in isolated areas, such as derelict and abandoned warehouse districts, may appear less safe until redevelopment changes the characteristics of the surrounding area into a vibrant, mixed-use district. Thus, designers intent on increasing perceptions of site safety need to be involved in and consider future plans for the area, as well as the original site context. Extending sustainable design to neighboring properties, such as street tree plantings or other improvements, in addition to improving ecological connectivity, can improve the image or context.

Provide multiple-options for egress: Research studies show the importance of providing site users with alternative access points to a site (Luymes and Tamminga 1995). Avoid designs that create long dead-end or cul-de-sac circulation patterns in which site users may be isolated and feel trapped. The idea is to allow users to "choose different routes" through the landscape—give them the freedom to explore while having a sense of control and predictability (SSI 2009, p. 153). The importance of designing a legible landscape with clear wayfinding patterns and cues, as discussed in the previous strategy, is critical so that users can quickly and intuitively become aware of the circulation system and the implications of different routes.

Consider site lighting and safety: The typical reaction to site safety concerns is to overdesign site lighting, which can contribute to light pollution and increase energy use. The key is to "place lighting in such a way that it allows people to be recognized from 25 feet away" and to avoid creating harsh shadows and contrasts between lit areas and unlit areas (SITES 2009). Brightly lighting paths with a sharp drop-off to darkness in the adjacent planting areas should be avoided. From a safety perspective, using lighting that allows faces to be recognized and not in shadow is important, for this is how people recognize others and make judgments, right or wrong, about others, their potential behavior, and level of threat. Site lighting is further discussed in Chapter 6.

Implementation and Maintenance Considerations for Site Safety

Maintain site to provide cues to care: Site safety is judged by how well maintained a site appears. Termed the "broken windows" syndrome, a neglected site appearance can actually be a self-fulfilling prophecy that leads to more vandalism and crime. Thus, using site materials that are long-lasting, durable, and low maintenance is not just important from an embodied energy perspective; it can help in overcoming this stigma. The challenge for sustainable sites that use native plants and ecosystem patterns is that they can often appear messy and unmanaged to the lay public and can contribute to the sense that a place is less safe (Ryan 2005). Landscape architect Joan Nassauer (1995) talks about the importance of using cultural "cues to care," such as mowing the edge of native grasslands, using larger masses of heavily flowering plants, and other design strategies to show that native plantings are intentionally managed and designed (Figures 7-22 and 7-23).

Prune to maintain visibility: Over time, landscapes can become more overgrown than originally intended. In this era of declining maintenance budgets, plants need to be selected and spaced to minimize the need for frequent pruning and trimming. Maintaining site safety requires that sight lines and visibility be kept clear through routine thinning and even plant removal if necessary.

Program sites for increased use, and safety: Ongoing strategies to improve site safety include increasing site use, as described in other sections, through programming and activities. In addition, community policing efforts may be part of some community benefits agreements and other efforts. Volunteer programs that promote stewardship of native landscapes and other open spaces can also increase community oversight and safety of many places, such as community gardens, restored habitat areas, and parks.

(Photo: Robert L. Ryan)

FIGURE 7-22: Dense vegetation along trails, especially in urban areas, increases concerns for safety.

(Photo: Robert L. Ryan)

Crime Prevention through Environmental Design (CPTED) is defined as a multidisciplinary approach to deterring criminal behavior through environmental design. CPTED strategies rely upon the ability to influence offender decisions that precede criminal acts by affecting the built, social, and administrative environment (International CPTED Association, www.cpted.net/default.html).

FIGURE 7-23: Improving visibility by routine pruning along trails along with mowing the trails' edge conveys the message that this native landscape is being intentionally maintained.

DESIGN FOR PHYSICAL ACTIVITY

Human health and well-being is linked to people being physically healthy, and one of the key predictors of being healthy is being physically active. Unfortunately, the vast majority of U.S. residents (75 percent) are not engaged in the minimum recommended 30 minutes daily amount of physical activity (CDC 2010). This lack of physical activity has been linked to soaring obesity levels in both adults and children and associated chronic conditions, such as heart disease and diabetes. In addition to the personal costs of being unhealthy, the associated medical costs of obesity are staggering with national estimates of upwards of $139 billion (in 2004 dollars); approximately 5 to 7 percent the nation's entire medical costs are attributed to obesity (Finkelstein et al. 2005).

Obesity levels of children are particularly troubling as they predict the early onset of chronic illness and are strong predictors of adult obesity. Furthermore, "results from the 2007–2008 National Health and Nutrition Examination Survey (NHANES), using measured heights and weights, indicate that an estimated 17 percent of children and adolescents ages 2–19 years are obese" (CDC 2010). Children in the United States and other developed countries are less physically active than previous generations (World Health Organization 2009). Decreases in physical activity are influenced by many environmental and behavioral factors, including less physical education in schools, more sedentary and indoor lifestyles, parents' concerns for children's safety, decreased access to open space, and a less pedestrian- and bike-friendly environment (CDC 2010).

Research has shown that children who spend more time outdoors are more likely to be physically active (Cleland et al. 2008). Unfortunately, children are spending less time outdoors than in the past, which not only has consequences for their health and well-being, it has also resulted in a decrease in knowledge about the natural world. In his book *Last Child in the Woods*, writer Richard Louv coined the term "nature deficit disorder" to refer to this increasing childhood disconnect with nature. Reconnecting children to the natural world can provide a range of benefits, cognitively, physically, and psychologically, which are shared by adults as well.

Sustainable sites have a significant role to play in providing opportunities to increase the public's physical activity levels and, in turn, improve public health. The design of the built environment can have a profound influence on whether people have access to safe, convenient, and comfortable places to walk, bike ride, or engage in other physical activities. Moreover, research has also shown that people are more likely to walk when there are destinations along the way. In the case of urban neighborhoods, these destinations can be places to shop, work, or conduct other errands; while on greenway trails, these destinations can be places like scenic overlooks, parks, and other types of nodes (Lusk 2002 ; Moudon 2007). Likewise, providing convenient places for physical activity at work, where people spend a majority of their time, can improve their health, reduce absenteeism, and manage healthcare costs.

Design Considerations to Promote Physical Activity

Understanding the potential user groups and the surrounding community is critical to determining their physical health issues, lifestyles, and preferred type of physical and recreation activities.

Plan an environment that makes physical activity seamless: The built environment can be designed to encourage or even require physical activity to be part of the routine of daily life, rather than as a "special" time or place. Walking and biking to work should be given priority, and driving should be made more inconvenient, for example, by providing more direct access to site entrances for those on foot or bicycles. Providing less parking can also motivate alternative transportation.

Create a more pedestrian-friendly environment: People are encouraged to walk when there are street trees and shade, safe sidewalks, places to rest along the way, including benches and other landscape features, and things to see along the way, such as views, vistas, or other destinations. Therefore, walkway systems should meet these criteria from other sections: providing universal access, designing for human comfort, and creating safe environments. In addition, providing physical or visual access to nearby vegetation is also important to creating more humane walking areas, as well as promoting the benefits that connections to nature provide.

The walkway or trail design is also important. Walkways should be wide enough to accommodate the intended number of users without conflicts, but narrow enough to avoid feeling like a road. Separating hard surface trails for biking and roller-skating from soft surface trails for hiking and walking is also desirable to avoid user conflicts. People are encouraged to explore a site if the walkways have a sense of "mystery," such as the curving pathway that gives a hint of what's coming next (Kaplan et al. 1998). Narrower pathways that allow nature to be at "arm's length" create a more intimate experience and allow people to better understand and remember their surroundings.

For an existing site, conduct a walkability audit to determine the current conditions of the existing circulation system (CDC 2010). These audits can also be undertaken after construction.

Seek partnerships with public health professionals: The public health fields have taken a major lead in working to improve physical activity levels and are key partners on a sustainable design team. For example, the Robert Wood Johnson Foundation's "Active Living by Design" initiative provides key resources and models for partnerships between designers, planners, and public health officials.

Provide connections to a larger open space network: Greenway and trail research has shown the importance of connectivity to promote trail use, as well as ecological function. Likewise, connectivity of the urban fabric by sidewalks is critical to promote walkability and use. Thus, a small site can promote physical activity by connecting local and regional networks of walkways, trails, bikeways, and other nonmotorized circulation systems. For example, onsite walkways can link disconnected sections of offsite trails or be a spur trail to a destination (Figure 7-24). The individual site is critical to build these regional trail systems that often rely on incremental implementation to complete the entire network.

Plan for an appropriate length of onsite walkways and bikeways: For larger sites, providing onsite trail networks for physical activity can encourage physical activity if they are sufficient in length to create 30 minutes of activity. Trail networks as short as a quarter mile or 400 meters, the length of the average athletic track, can be long enough if the experience is varied by the other factors of good trail design, such as providing a sense of mystery, landmarks, destinations, and other natural and built amenities or places of interest along the way (Kaplan et al. 1998). As mentioned before, instead of making separate athletic or exercise tracks, they can be integrated in the overall circulation and design system. Creating interconnected systems of trail or pathway loops that follow the wayfinding principles described earlier give users more choices about the distance, degree of difficulty, and experience. Minimizing the amount of road crossings is critical from both a safety perspective, but also in making a more efficient network where people do not need to make frequent stops for cars.

(Photo: Robert L. Ryan)

FIGURE 7-24: Pathways and trails that connect to larger regional networks allow for more extensive physical activity options, including biking and walking.

Design playgrounds for all ages: Playgrounds should foster exploration, creativity, and even environmental learning, and be designed for the particular age group in mind in order to promote cognitive, physical, and mental development (Brett et al. 1993 ; Herrington 1997). It may be appropriate to design for adult play and even the elderly. Climbing over a boulder-strewn river or balancing on a log in the woods are all experiences that engage young and old alike. Research has shown that walking on more natural surfaces and environments, as opposed to paved walkways and sidewalks, helps develop a better sense of balance and coordination, especially if this nature experience occurs in childhood. At the other extreme, one can consider elegant workout stations that double as environmental art or other design features. The efficient use of materials and space suggests a multiplicity of uses for physical design elements rather than a single static use.

Plan for sports facilities and recreation fields: Incorporating features such as basketball courts, swimming pools, and sports fields can encourage physical activity (Figure 7-25).

The challenge is to determine the usefulness and interest of potential site users (and community members) for particular types of recreation. From the sustainability perspective, minimizing turf grass is important, but field sports play a large role in providing areas for active recreation, so using sustainable principles for turf management is critical.

(Photo: Robert L. Ryan)

Provide support facilities: Sometimes the biggest barrier to physical activity is lack of the support facilities that make activity both possible and convenient. This includes providing drinking fountains at key intervals, restrooms, locker rooms, and shower facilities, as well as the equipment support for the respective activities, such as bike racks and lockers.

FIGURE 7-25: Recreation areas should be designed to include a wide range of ages from adults to children as a means to promote physical activity more broadly.

Encourage gardening as physical activity: The act of gardening and other manual landscape maintenance can provide both physical and psychological health benefits (R. Kaplan 1973). Furthermore, gardening is one of those activities that many people do not consider in the same way as going to the gym or jogging. Providing community gardens and other opportunities for residents, employees, and other users to garden not only benefits the individuals by providing fresh produce or flowers. It also has important benefits for the environment in the form of sustainable agriculture, ecological restoration, and other benefits.

Program for physical activity: One of the best strategies to encourage physical activity is to implement programs and activities, both onsite and offsite. Examples include organizing coworkers who like to walk, run, or otherwise exercise together at lunchtime, team sports leagues, or tai chi classes.

Maintain recreation facilities and structures: Poorly maintained facilities are likely to discourage use, as well as create unsafe conditions for site users. Recreation equipment needs to be properly inspected, maintained, and replaced as needed. Pathways and sidewalks need to be kept clear of snow, ice, leaves, litter, and debris to allow for year-round use. Follow Sustainable Sites Guidelines for maintaining turf with integrated pest management, minimal fertilization, and irrigation with nonpotable water supplies.

RESTORATIVE SETTINGS

Contact with nature can help relieve the mental fatigue and stress of modern living. It can restore people's cognitive function, relieve stress, and improve physical health. The restorative power of nature has been shown in a variety of populations, conditions, and settings, including improving hospital patients' recovery from surgery, children's ability to focus and do well in school, and office workers' health and job satisfaction (R. Kaplan 1993; Kuo and Taylor 2010; Taylor et al. 2002; Ulrich 1984). The mechanism for this restoration has to do with humans' innate fascination with nature, which allows us to restore our mental reserves, reflect on decisions we need to make, and connect us to a world which is much larger and timeless than our individual selves or even the built environments we have created. In addition, humans have a biological connection to nature, such as the circadian rhythm of our sleep patterns and other biologic functions. People are also connected to and find solace in the seasonal cycles of nature. Therefore, it is important to develop a site that is both a place for mental restoration as well as a place in which users can actively garden or otherwise nurture the natural environment.

Design Considerations for Restorative Settings

While in general natural settings are restorative, it is not necessarily true that all designed or even natural landscapes create the restorative benefits described earlier. The following are some characteristics of restorative settings to consider in the design process:

Consider the view from the window: Much of the research on restorative settings has looked at the importance of views of nature from building windows. People need not be within the landscape to receive some restorative benefits; simply seeing trees or other plants from nearby windows can have positive impacts on human health and well-being, which is critical since people spend much of their time indoors at home, work, and school.

While much of the sustainable building literature and standards have focused on the importance of natural light, which has its own health benefits, sustainable site designers should work with architects on the predesign team to maximize views from building windows to the landscape. Digital technology as well as site plans can be used to determine the viewshed/angle from building windows during the design phase to analyze how much of the onsite planted areas can be seen from each room. It is particularly important to maximize landscape views from rooms that will be occupied by the most people for the longest period of time (Figure 7-26).

Borrow offsite views: In addition to providing nature views of the site itself, framing or "borrowing" views of the surrounding landscape, trees, or other natural areas is another strategy to provide a restorative setting, especially in the case where there are fewer opportunities for onsite window views. The Japanese use the term "shakkei" to refer to borrowed views and have mastered the art of screening unsightly views in the foreground or middle ground with hedges and other devices to help frame views to more distant landscapes, such as mountains, waterscapes, or simply a beautiful grove of trees (Itoh 1984).

(Photo: Robert L. Ryan)

FIGURE 7-26: Views of gardens and nature from building windows have been shown to have tremendous health benefits. Designers need to strive to maximize landscape views from the majority of interior spaces, especially those rooms that are heavily used.

Provide small-scale and intimate spaces: Neither the amount of vegetation nor size of an outdoor space needs to be large to have a restorative benefit. In fact, smaller, more intimate spaces are better for smaller groups of people or individuals who want a quiet area for reflection. This suggests that in some cases, subdividing larger areas into smaller ones may facilitate these types of spaces and experiences.

Provide enclosures: An important characteristic of restorative spaces is that they have a sense of "being away" from everyday life, which requires being "separated from distractions" of noise, traffic, unsightly views, and even surrounding buildings (Kaplan et al. 1998). The use of hedges, fences, walls, berms, and other screening devices can enclose a space to achieve a smaller, more intimate scale as well as buffer it from both aesthetic and sensory impacts (Figures 7-27 and 7-28). However, there is also a security factor to be considered, which requires visual connection to others while achieving this sense of enclosure.

FIGURE 7-27: Separation from distractions means screening out unwanted views, such as this adjacent parking area from this small connector park in Washington, DC.

FIGURE 7-28: A lattice fence and low plantings screen unwanted views.

Reduce noise pollution: High levels of noise can have significant negative impacts on public health and the quiet needed for a restorative experience. A noise level study should be conducted during the predesign assessment to determine existing onsite noise levels that exceed acceptable noise level standards of a maximum 55 dba. If the site includes structures, buildings, major roadways, or major mechanical equipment, conduct a postconstruction assessment to determine new noise impacts prior to final site design. While sound barriers of walls and earthen berms are the most effective, where space permits, dense evergreen plant material can also help minimize sound. The use of water features to "mask" noise pollution is another strategy employed successfully at places like Seattle's Freeway Park; however, these features can require large volumes of water and energy.

Provide seating: While restorative benefits can occur by experiencing nature in a variety of activities, including physically moving through the landscape (i.e., walking, jogging activities) or engaging in nature-related activities like bird-watching, or even hunting and fishing, designers should provide comfortable seating, preferably with a variety of seating options. One strategy, movable seating, allows users to create seating arrangements that respond to the need for quieter, more private areas, as well as the desire for sun or shade. Seating along pathways is important as well.

Focus on beauty: The importance of aesthetics. The beauty of nature inspires restoration. Focusing the design on specimen trees or other vegetation, along with other natural features and elements, can be important. Contact with plants, in particular, has been found to foster mental and physical restoration, which suggests designing to maximize opportunities for close interaction with a variety of plant material.

Design for multisensory experiences: Designing for all five senses can also be a good framework to achieve a restorative setting. Scented flowers or foliage, the sound of the wind through the trees, the tactile experience of moss, or the taste of fresh fruit are all aspects of creating a multisensory restorative experience (Figure 7-29). Mental restoration can often be achieved by letting the environment fill one's mind with the positive sensory experience that comes from nature, which is a contrast to the negative sensory distraction of the built environment, such as adjacent traffic or mechanical noise.

(Photo: Robert L. Ryan)

FIGURE 7-29: Providing quiet landscaped spaces with the sound of water can create a restorative setting, even in the heart of a large institutional building, such as this courtyard at the Boston Public Library.

Provide water for sensory experience: Use of water features, as well as providing access to natural bodies of water, can be important strategies for creating a restorative environment (Kaplan et al. 1998). Small fountains that use minimal water yet provide the sound of water can provide great benefits (Kaplan et al. 1998). Open water rather than marshy or overgrown wetlands; clear, moving water rather than stagnant, algae-filled, muddy water; natural edges rather than built edges; and easy access to the water's edge with lawn, sand, or other walkable, natural surface rather than paving are preferred (Kaplan et al. 1998).

Keep the site quiet: Routine landscape maintenance, building maintenance, and deliveries can greatly increase the noise level on the site and disturb the quiet, restorative experience for site users. These activities should be scheduled at times when the fewest people will be using a site. Manual equipment, such as push mowers and leaf rakes, should be used where possible. Electric landscape equipment is usually quieter than their gas engine counterparts and does not increase localized air pollution for site users. The site maintenance manual should detail strategies to minimize noise disturbance, including specifying equipment, expected noise levels, and maintenance schedule.

DESIGN FOR SOCIAL INTERACTION AND COMMUNITY BUILDING

Sustainable sites can play an important role in fostering social interaction and building community. Research has shown that residential settings with more trees were associated with stronger social connections and a better sense of community, and were perceived to be safer by local residents than those settings with few or no trees (Kuo et al. 1998). Furthermore, strong social ties at the individual level as well as the neighborhood level have significant human health and well-being benefits.

At the community level, stronger social connections result in communities with a stronger sense of community and social capital that are better able to handle economic, social, and environmental challenges. Tighter-knit groups are able to use this social capital in the political arena, defend themselves against crime, and work together to solve the community's problems (SITES 2009).

Successful greenspaces are the setting for community activities in places as diverse as the traditional town green or park, schoolyard, courtyard of an office building, or simply the front yards of a tree-lined residential street. These outdoor spaces are where people can get to know one another, share opinions, learn about common concerns, and help work out their differences. These "democratic" spaces are the public arena where community members of diverse backgrounds can come together to create a better civil society. Additionally, outdoor open spaces are places to celebrate community life as venues for concerts, festivals, and other events, as well as places for formal and informal social gatherings of families, friends, and other groups.

Design Considerations for Social Interaction and Community Building

Locate social spaces near activity generators: William Whyte (1980) made the observation that, in urban plazas, people seem to attract more people. Thus, locating open space areas for social interaction near where many people are already going or congregating makes the most sense. For sites with buildings or adjacent to buildings, the activities within the building may be the initial activity or destination for people, which suggests locating outdoor open space near major pedestrian circulation areas, building entrances, and other focal points. For existing buildings and sites, a predesign assessment of pedestrian movement is critical to determine existing high-use areas. Improving the indoor-outdoor connection between social spaces within a building and outdoor spaces can also foster a synergy and movement of people and activities into the landscape.

Plan for onsite activities: Onsite activities and amenities can help attract people to a site and foster social interaction. Amenities can involve outdoor restaurants and food vendors (see the following discussion); outdoor amphitheaters and other entertainment venues; skating rinks and other recreational features, playgrounds, game areas; or a myriad of other amenities. The key aspect here, as described in the "Social Equality" section, is that these features respond to the needs/desires of the community and other potential users (Francis 2003).

Of course, the landscape itself is an amenity and in many cases may be the "attraction." For example, people are attracted to water, so providing beaches, piers, boardwalks, or other access to the water's edge can act as an attractor. Further amenities might be facilities for picnicking, outdoor cooking, bonfires, or other features.

The newest site amenities are technological innovations. Public spaces now provide free wireless service, large screens for performances or sporting events, or digital artwork to attract the public (Figure 7-30 and 7-31).

Provide for movement and rest: Places for social interaction should be near major pedestrian pathways; however, the space should not be bisected by too much pedestrian and bicycle traffic, as it won't function as well for social interaction. Creating bays and eddies, seating nooks and subspaces adjacent to or bounded by circulation routes that allow good access and people-watching will provide groups smaller subspaces.

(Photo: Robert L. Ryan)

FIGURE 7-30: By providing amenities such as free outdoor wireless services, sustainable sites can foster more activity.

(Photo: Robert L. Ryan)

FIGURE 7-31: Water features can generate lots of activity during the hot summer months.

FIGURE 7-32: Bryant Park in New York City, which was redesigned using the principles of William Whyte, includes a variety of seating options including movable chairs that allow people to customize their seating arrangements.

FIGURE 7-33: Creating a comfortable microclimate with shade during the summer is essential for promoting use.

FIGURE 7-34: The Dutch *woonerf* or living street incorporates trees and park space to slow down vehicular traffic and create a shared street for bikes and people.

Provide a variety of seating options: A variety of seating options with some movable seating or chairs that allow people to configure their own spaces will provide a sense of control of one's environment and encourage site use (Figure 7-32). Comfortable seating, as described in the "Accessibility" section, is also key so that people can use the space for longer periods of time. The most comfortable seating has back support and/or armrests. Small movable tables are also useful so people can eat, read, or otherwise make themselves at home.

Permanent or nonmovable seating and benches should be designed to allow groups of various sizes rather than follow one static pattern or configuration. Having various heights and types of seating, including seating stairs, benches, and seat walls, can also maximize seating options. Inward-facing seating arrangements versus outward-facing ones have very different implications for social interaction (for example, Jacob Javits Plaza in Manhattan).

Create opportunities for people-watching from seating: Locating seating alongside major pedestrian circulation routes allows for people-watching—a major attraction or activity in open spaces. It also allows places of rest for those passing by.

Provide access to trees and shade: Trees are an essential part of gathering areas and other social spaces (Figure 7-33). In addition to the multiple environmental benefits of trees, they provide shade with an overhead canopy that creates a more comfortable microclimate and provides a buffer from surrounding buildings. Other plant materials, especially flowering plants, are another attraction that brings people to an outdoor space.

Provide separation from vehicular traffic: While separating social spaces from busy, high-volume roads makes sense in general, depending upon the speed of traffic, less separation may be needed or even desired along quieter streets. The livable streets movement has many strategies for creating people-friendly streets, such as the Dutch *woonerf*, which mixes people and cars in a way that slows traffic, improves safety, and creates more activity at street level (Figure 7-34).

Implementation and Maintenance Considerations for Social Interaction and Community Building

Program for social interaction: Many of the factors that affect the success of open space from the perspective of site users occur after construction, including programming events, recreation, and other activities (Francis 2003; Project for Public Spaces 1998). Thus, the type and format of programs may vary widely, but the key is having personnel and strategies for site programming, and working with the local community and site users to determine their ongoing needs and desires.

Plan for food vendors and farmers' markets: According to William Whyte and others, food is one critical ingredient for a successful urban open space. Providing food not only meets our basic human needs, it attracts people to use an open space and fosters social interaction.

Farmers' markets that sell locally produced food create vibrant social settings and also provide multiplicative benefits for sustainable agriculture, promoting healthy diets, and local economies. They can also provide an economic outlet for local community gardens in the inner city and other areas. Markets can be temporal, setting up in parking lots or streets on the weekend or at night, or be housed under more permanent shelters (Figure 7-35).

(Photo: Robert L. Ryan)

Plan for adaptability and flexibility: Another strategy for promoting social interaction and extending site use is to change the type of programs by season, time of day, and day of the week (Gehl and Gemzøe 1996 c.f. Francis 2003). For example, in many European cities, restaurants are set up on major pedestrian areas for the summer season and taken down in winter. Likewise, creating ice skating

FIGURE 7-35: Food vendors, such as this innovative eco-friendly snack truck, generate activity and provide essential services for outdoor spaces. Promoting locally grown food and businesses also helps sustain the local economy.

rinks on plazas or ponds during the winter can allow for seasonal variation. Street fairs can use underutilized downtown plazas and streets during the weekends or at night. In fact, spaces for social interaction complete with street furniture, planters, and other features can create temporary people-friendly areas for the summer or simply for the weekends in underutilized areas, such as international Park(ing) day, where people temporarily transform parking spots into parks and other open space (www.my.parkingday.org). In some cases, these "small experiments" at creating people-friendly spaces have led to permanent changes.

Adaptability allows people to create their own spaces or redesign areas as user needs change. From an implementation and maintenance perspective, this suggests using materials, furniture, forms, and plant material that can be modified, shaped, and changed by site users. For example, many offices and institutions now have planters that workers can "adopt" for the season and plant as they like with flowers and vegetables.

PRESERVING HISTORIC AND CULTURAL FEATURES

Sustainability is about using resources wisely, and one of the first tenets is to reuse what is already on the site before considering recycling or other strategies. Historic preservation is central to adaptive reuse of sites. In addition to energy and materials savings, preserving historic and cultural landscape patterns and features is essential for maintaining a "sense of place" and cultural meaning. Preserving local or indigenous culture also requires preserving the cultural landscape in which it is embedded.

According to landscape architect Charles A. Birnbaum (1994) in his seminal report for the U.S. National Park Service, A *cultural landscape* is defined as "a geographic area, including both cultural and natural resources and the wildlife or domestic animals therein, associated with a historic event, activity, or person or exhibiting other cultural or aesthetic values." He goes on to describe four overlapping types of cultural landscapes: historic designed landscapes, historic vernacular landscapes, historic sites, and ethnographic landscapes that are useful to consider for design, planning, and management. While the designed landscapes, such as Olmsted's Central Park and the Biltmore Estate, come readily to mind as cultural landscapes, as do historic sites, such as battlefields, it is often the everyday or vernacular landscapes that are most often overlooked in cultural resource planning (Meinig 1979). Features of local significance or cultural meaning may be known within a community, ethnic group, or neighborhood, but go unrecognized or unappreciated by outsiders with different values, including developers, government officials, or even design consultants. Sustainability practices based on social equity, celebrating local culture, and sustaining local communities require preserving and interpreting cultural and historic landscapes. From the sustainability perspective, local people often have a strong attachment to cultural landscapes that can manifest itself in a sense of ownership, stewardship, ethic, and willingness to mobilize to protect these landscapes from potential threats (Walker and Ryan 2008). By preserving and even enhancing historic and cultural landscapes, designers and planners can maintain a site's "sense of place," strengthen or preserve people's connection to the site, and help ensure the cultural and environmental sustainability of the site over time.

Design Considerations for Preserving Historic and Cultural Features

Conduct a predesign inventory of historic and cultural features: As part of the pre-design assessment of the site, inventory the onsite cultural and historic features, patterns, and artifacts. The National Park Service's Historic American Landscapes Survey (HALS): Guidelines for Historical Reports provides one format for such an inventory (see Table 7-2), but there are many others as well. The key is to not only inventory the elements that would occur under a typical site analysis, such as natural features, including topography and vegetation, circulation patterns, buildings, and so forth, but to assess how these elements and their spatial organization contribute to the landscape character of the site.

TABLE 7-2: Outline for Historical Assessment

PART I. HISTORICAL INFORMATION

A. Physical History
   1. Date(s) of establishment
   2. Landscape architect, designer, shaper, creator
   3. Builder, contractor, laborers, suppliers
   4. Original and subsequent owners, occupants
   5. Periods of development

B. Historical Context

PART II. PHYSICAL INFORMATION

A. Landscape Character and Description Summary (also include an evaluation of the integrity of the feature)

B. Character-Defining Features:
   1. Natural features
   2. Spatial organization
   3. Sources of information including site plan(s), photographs, and maps. Other sources of information may include interviews and drawings.

Source: Adapted from National Park Service's Historic American Landscapes Survey (HALS): Guidelines for Historical Reports provides one format for such an inventory (SSI, 2009, p. 150)

Partner with historic resource experts: Cultural landscape planning requires that archaeologists, historians, anthropologists, and other experts be part of the interdisciplinary design team. In many cases, local historic societies also have lay experts who are extremely knowledgeable about local site history.

Determine eligibility or historic status: Review local, state, national, and international historic and heritage designations to determine if a site is currently on a particular register or list, or may be eligible. Also, review and adhere to any cultural and historic regulations.

[Photo: Robert L. Ryan]

FIGURE 7-36: Interpreting the relationship between a site's historical, cultural, and ecological history can help reveal the layers of history for site users, as shown here in Guelph, Ontario.

Conduct archival research into previous site history: Much of a site's physical and cultural history may not be evident on the site in its current condition. Archival research of historic photographs, plans, reports, letters, diaries, and other information can reveal how a site developed, was used over time, and reached its current state. Historical research may also reveal the ecological history of the site (Figure 7-36).

Work with the local community to identify resources with local history and cultural meaning: Engaging the community in predesign assessment has been discussed previously in this chapter, but a particularly relevant strategy for identifying cultural and historic resources is to conduct interviews with local residents. Ethnographies can elicit rich social and cultural information from the perspective of local people that are hard to find with other techniques, because they are often not part of the "official" history books or sources (Figures 7-37 and 7-38).

Historic and cultural resources as an inspiration for sustainable practices: In addition to simply documenting site and local history, cultural practices, patterns, and materials can be an inspiration for "new" sustainable design. The rediscovery of culturally based sustainable strategies can inform the response to all aspects of site design and maintenance including managing water, planting design, and handling microclimate.

Use onsite materials and local construction techniques: Another aspect of maintaining historic and cultural history is to use materials that are available onsite or nearby as well as construction techniques, designs, and practices that are historic and culturally derived (Figure 7-37).

Determine approach to manage/plan for cultural resources: There are many different approaches that can be taken to plan and manage cultural landscapes. See Table 7-3.

(Photo: Robert L. Ryan)

FIGURE 7-37: Highlighting historical building materials and practices, such as brick-making at Colonial Williamsburg, not only educates visitors, but also provides valuable landscape construction materials for a restoration and rehabilitation project.

(Design by Thomas Balsley Associates; Photo: Robert L. Ryan)

FIGURE 7-38: Maintaining the historic train signs at Gantry State Park, Queens, New York City, connects this waterfront park to its history.

TABLE 7-3: Treatments for Cultural Landscapes

SECRETARY OF THE INTERIOR'S STANDARDS FOR THE TREATMENT OF HISTORIC PROPERTIES	
Preservation	Preservation is defined as the act or process of applying measures necessary to sustain the existing form, integrity, and materials of an historic property. Work, including preliminary measures to protect and stabilize the property, generally focuses on the ongoing maintenance and repair of historic materials and features rather than extensive replacement and new construction.
Rehabilitation	Rehabilitation is defined as the act or process of making possible a compatible use for a property through repair, alterations, and additions while preserving those portions or features which convey its historical or cultural values.
Restoration	Restoration is defined as the act or process of accurately depicting the form, features, and character of a property as it appeared at a particular period of time by means of the removal of features from other periods in its history and reconstruction of missing features from the restoration period.
Reconstruction	Reconstruction is defined as the act or process of depicting, by means of new construction, the form, features, and detailing of a nonsurviving site, landscape, building, structure, or object for the purpose of replicating its appearance at a specific period of time and in its historic location.

Source: Birnbaum, National Park Service, 1994, www.nps.gov/hps/tps/briefs/brief36.htm.

Implementation and Maintenance Considerations for Preserving Historic and Cultural Features

Maintain historic trees, plantings, or other cultural patterns: Preserving large historic trees or other plants is important to local residents. However, the challenge for sustainability is that those plants that have cultural meaning may not be native to the region, such as the flowering cherry trees in Washington, DC.

Find historic materials for restoration: It may be extremely difficult to find materials that were used historically if the local sources, such as quarries, or factories have ceased operation.

Find skilled labor to maintain cultural landscapes: Another equal challenge is finding local tradespeople who know historic building methods or are skilled in maintaining a cultural landscape. However, this challenge can provide an opportunity for job training and resurrecting cultural traditions and craftsmanship, while providing jobs for local residents (see the section "Social Equality in Site Development, Construction, and Use," earlier in this chapter.)

Preserve historic resources versus the patina of decay: Cultural historian and writer J.B. Jackson (1980) talks about the "necessity for ruins" to inform a society about its past. The maintenance challenge is that the natural decay and patina of age that reveals the history and age of a place may be detrimental to the long-term structural stability of landscape features, such as retaining walls. One preservation approach is to use new bricks and mortar that do not exactly match the original material so that visitors can tell the difference between original and new areas of a wall, as opposed to trying to mimic or match the patina of age. Ongoing maintenance must keep landscape features intact and usable over time while remaining true to their history. This latter issue has been the subject of lengthy debates among historic preservation experts and is dependent upon the type of treatment.

(Photo: Robert L. Ryan)

FIGURE 7-39: The Highline Park in New York City interweaves the historic train line with a sustainable park design using native plants.

References

Americans with Disabilities Accessibility Guidelines and Standards (ADAAG). 2005. Washington, DC: United States Access Board. Available at www.acess-board.gov/adaag/about.

Appleton, Jay. 1975. *The Experience of Landscape*. New York: John Wiley and Sons.

Babbie, Earl R. 2008. *The Basics of Social Research*. (4th ed.). Belmont, CA:Thomson/Wadsworth.

Birnbaum, Charles A. 1994. *National Park Service's Historic Landscape InitiativeProtecting Cultural Landscapes Planning, Treatment and Management of Historic Landscapes*, www.nps.gov/history/hps/TPS/briefs/brief36.htm.

Bixler, R.D. and M.F. Floyd. 1997. "Nature Is Scary, Disgusting and Uncomfortable." *Environment and Behavior*, 29 (4): 443–467.

Brett, A., R.C. Moore, and E.F. Provenzo, Jr. 1993. *The Complete Playground Book*. Syracuse, NY: Syracuse University Press.

Brown, R. and T. Gillespie. 1995. *Microclimatic Landscape Design: Creating Thermal Comfort and Energy Efficiency*. New York: John Wiley and Sons.

Carstens, Diane Y. 1985. *Site Planning and Design for the Elderly: Issues, Guidelines, and Alternatives*. New York: Van Nostrand Reinhold.

Carr, Stephen, Marc Francis, Leeanne G. Rivlin, and Andrew M. Stone 1992. *Public Space*. New York: Cambridge University Press.

Center for Universal Design. 1997. The Principles of Universal Design, Version 2.0. Raleigh, NC: North Carolina State University. Available at www.ncsu.edu/project/design-projects/udi/center-for-universal-design/the-principles-of-universal-design/ (accessed August 11, 2010).

Centers for Disease Control and Prevention (CDC). 2010. www.cdc.gov/obesity/childhood/index.html.

Cooper-Marcus, C., and Marni Barnes (eds.) 1999. *Healing Gardens: Therapeutic Benefits and Design Recommendations*. New York: John Wiley and Sons.

Cooper-Marcus, C., and C. Francis. 1998. *People Places: Design Guidelines for Urban Open Space.* 2nd ed. New York: John Wiley and Sons.

Cullen, Gordon. 1971. *The Concise Townscape.* New York: Van Nostrand Reinhold Co.

Dines, Nicholas T. 1998. "Section 220 Energy and Resource Conservation." In Harris, Charles W., Nicholas T. Dines, and Kyle D. Brown (eds.). *Timesaver Standards for Landscape Architecture,* 2nd ed. New York: McGraw-Hill. pp. 220.1–220.13.

Finkelstein E.A., C.J. Ruhm, and K.M. Kosa. 2005. "Economic Causes and Consequences of Obesity." *Annual Review of Public Health*, 26: 239–257.

Fishbeck, Gary M. 1998. "Section 240, Outdoor Accessibility." In *Timesaver Standards for Landscape* , Charles W. Harris, Nicholas T. Dines, and Kyle D. Brown (eds.). *Architecture* (2nd ed.). New York: McGraw-Hill, pp. 240.1–240.24.

Fleming, N. D. 2001. *Teaching and Learning Styles: VARK Strategies.* Christchurch, New Zealand: N.D. Fleming.

Francis, M. 1987. "Urban Open Spaces." In E. H. Zube and G. T. Moore (eds.) *Advances in Environment, Behavior, and Design,* Vol. 1. New York: Plenum Press, pp. 71–105.

_____. 2003. *Urban Open Space: Designing for User Needs.* Washington, DC: Island Press, Landscape Architecture Foundation.

Gehl, Jan, and Lars Gemzøe. 1996. *Public Spaces, Public Life.* Copenhagen: Danish Architectural Press.

Gerlach-Spriggs, Nancy, Richard Enoch Kaufman, and Sam Bass Warner, Jr. 1998. *Restorative Gardens: The Healing Landscape.* New Haven, CT: Yale University Press.

Golledge, Reginald G. (ed.) 1999. *Wayfinding Behavior: Cognitive Mapping and Other Spatial Processes.* Baltimore: Johns Hopkins University Press.

Gross, Julian, Greg LeRoy, and Madeleine Janis-Aparicio. 2005. "Community Benefits Agreements: Making Development Projects Accountable." Washington, DC: Good Jobs First and the California Partnership for Working Families. Available online at www.goodjobsfirst.org/sites/default/files/docs/pdf/cba2005final.pdf.

Hawk, Thomas F., and Amit J. Shah. 2007. "Using Learning Style Instruments to Enhance Student Kearning." *Decision Sciences Journal of Innovative Education*, 5 (1): 1–19.

Helphand, K.I., and R.Z. Melnick. 1998. Editor's introduction"Eco-Revelatory Design: Nature Constructed/Nature Revealed" *Landscape Journal*, 17: i–xv.

Herrington, S. 1997. "The Received View of Play and the Subculture of Infants." *Landscape Journal*, 16 (2): 149–160.

Hester, R. T., Jr. 1990. *Community Design Primer.* Mendocino, CA: Ridge Times Press.

Institute of Medicine. 2005. *Preventing Childhood Obesity—Health in the Balance.* Washington, DC: The National Academies Press.

Itoh, T. 1984. *The Gardens of Japan.* New York: Harper & Row.

Jackson, J.B. 1980. *The Necessity for Ruins.* Amherst: University of Massachusetts Press.

Kaplan, R. 1993. "The Role of Nature in the Context of the Workplace." *Landscape and Urban Planning*, 26 (1–40): 193–201.

Kaplan, R., and S. Kaplan. 1989. *The Experience of Nature: A Psychological Perspective.* New York: Cambridge University Press.

_____. 2008. "Bringing Out the Best in People. A Psychological Perspective." *Conservation Biology*, 22(4): 826–829.

Kaplan, R., S. Kaplan, and R.L. Ryan. 1998. *With People in Mind: Design and Management of Everyday Nature.* Washington, DC: Island Press.

Kaplan, S., and R. Kaplan. 2009. "Creating a Larger Role for Environmental Psychology: The Reasonable Person Model as an Integrative Framework." *Journal of Environmental Psychology*, 29(3): 329–339.

Kuo, F.E., and W.C. Sullivan. 2001. Aggression and Violence in the Inner City: Impacts of Environment via Mental Fatigue." *Environment and Behavior*, 33(4): 543–571.

Kuo, F.E., W.C. Sullivan, R.L. Coley, and L. Brunson. 1998. "Fertile Ground for Community: Inner-City Neighborhood Common Spaces." *American Journal of Community Psychology* 26 (6): 823–851.

Kuo, F.E., and A.F. Taylor. 2005. "A Potential Natural Treatment for Attention-Deficit/Hyperactivity Disorder: Evidence from a National Study." *American Journal of Public Health,* 94 (9):1580–1586.

Lewis, Charles A. 1990. "Garden as Healing Process. In M. Francis and R. T. Hester, Jr. (eds.) *The Meaning of Gardens.* Cambridge, MA: MIT Press. pp. 244–251.

_____. 1996. *Green Nature, Human Nature: The Meaning of Plants in Our Lives.* Champaign-Urbana: University of Illinois Press.

Louv, Richard. 2005. *Last Child in the Woods: Saving Our Children from Nature-Deficit Disorder.* Chapel Hill, NC: Algonquin Books.

Lusk, A.C. 2002. "Guidelines for Greenways: Determining the Distance to, Features of, and Human Needs Met by Destinations on Multi-Use Corridors." Doctoral dissertation. University of Michigan, Ann Arbor, MI.

Luymes, D.T. and K. Tamminga. 1995. "Integrating Public Safety and Use into Planning Urban Greenways." In Julius G. Fabos and Jack Ahern (eds.) *Greenways: The Beginning of an International Movement.* Amsterdam: Elsevier. pp. 391–400.

Lynch, Kevin. 1960. *The Image of the City.* Cambridge, MA: Technology Press.

Meinig, D.W. (ed.). 1979. *The Interpretation of Ordinary Landscapes: Geographical Essays.* New York: Oxford University Press.

Mertes, J., and J. Hall. 1996. *Parks, Recreation and Open Space and Greenway Guidelines.* Ashburn, VA: National Recreation and Park Association.

Moudon, A.V., C. Lee, A.D. Cheadle, C. Garvin, D.B. Johnson, T.L. Schmid, and R.D. Weathers. 2007. "Attributes of Environments Supporting Walking." *American Journal of Health Promotion*, 21 (5): 448–459.

Nassauer, J.I. 1995. "Messy Ecosystems, Orderly Frames." *Landscape Journal,* 14(2): 161–170.

National Historic Landmarks (n.d.), www.nps.gov/history/nhl/QA.htm#2.

National Register of Historic Places (n.d.), National Register of Historic Places Fundamentals, www.nps.gov/nr/national_register_fundamentals.htm.

Ostroff, Elaine. 2001. "Universal Design: The New Paradigm." In Wolfgang Preiser and Elaine Ostroff (eds.), *Universal Design Handbook.* New York: McGraw-Hill, pp. 1.3–1.12.

Project for Public Spaces. 1998. "Transit-Friendly Streets: Design and Traffic Management Strategies to Support Livable Communities." Washington, DC: National Academy Press.

Putnam, Robert D. 2000. *Bowling Alone: The Collapse and Revival of American Community*. New York: Simon & Schuster.

Relf, D. (ed). 1992. *The Role of Horticulture in Human Well-Being and Social Development*, Portland, OR: Timber Press.

Richtel, Matt. 2010. "Hooked on Gadgets, and Paying a Mental Price." *New York Times*, June 7, 2010. p. A1.

Ryan, R.L. 2005. "Exploring the Effects of Environmental Experience on Attachment to Urban Natural Areas." *Environment and Behavior*, 37:3–42.

Ryan, R.L., R. Kaplan, and R.E. Grese. 2001. "Predicting Volunteer Commitment in Environmental Stewardship Programmes." *Journal of Environmental Planning and Management*, 44 (5): 629–648.

Sanoff, H. 2000. *Community Participation Methods in Design and Planning*. New York: Wiley.

Sustainable Sites Initiative (SITES). 2009. The Sustainable Sites Initiative: Guidelines and Performance Benchmarks 2009. Available at www.sustainablesites.org/report/Guidelines%20 and%20Performance%20Benchmarks_2009.pdf, accessed Aug. 10, 2010.

Tanner, R. T. 1980. "Significant Life Experiences: A New Research Area in Environmental Education." *Journal of Environmental Education*, 11(4): 20–24.

Taylor, A.F., F.E. Kuo, and W.C. Sullivan. 2002. "Views of Nature and Self-Discipline: Evidence from Inner City Children". *Journal of Environmental Psychology* 22 (1–2): 49–63.

Trust for Public Land. 2009. *City Parks Facts Report*. San Francisco: Trust for Public Land.

Ulrich, R.S. 1984. "View through a Window May Influence Recovery from Surgery." *Science*, 224: 420–421.

Unger, D.G., and A. Wandersman. 1985. "The Importance of Neighbors: The Social, Cognitive, and Affective Components of Neighboring." *American Journal of Community Psychology*, 13, 139–169.

U.S. Department of Health and Human Services. 2001. "The Surgeon General's Call to Action to Prevent and Decrease Overweight and Obesity." Rockville, MD: U.S. Department of Health and Human Services, Public Health Service, Office of the Surgeon General.

Walker, A., and R.L. Ryan. 2008. "Place Attachment and Landscape Preservation in Rural New England: A Maine Case Study." *Landscape and Urban Planning*, 86: 141–152.

Whyte, William H. 1980. *The Social Life of Small Urban Spaces*. Washington, DC: Conservation Foundation.

World Commission on Environment and Development, G.H. Brundtland, and M. Khalid. 1987. *Our Common Future*. Oxford, UK: Oxford University Press.

World Health Organization. 2009. *Global Strategy on Diet, Physical Activity and Health*. www.who.int/dietphysicalactivity/pa/en/index.html, accessed August 11, 2010.

Wyant, Sylvia. 2006. "Why Shop Local?" *Elephant Journal*. Spring. www.elephantjournal.com/2008/09/why-shop-local-local-businesses-return-80-of-each-dollar-to-the-community, accessed August 30, 2010.

Zervas, Deborah. 2010. "Communicating Design Intent to the Non-Expert: Small Experiments Using Collage." Master's thesis. Amherst, MA: University of Massachusetts.

CHAPTER 8

OPERATIONS, MAINTENANCE, MONITORING, AND STEWARDSHIP

▶ Amy Belaire and David Yocca

AFTER A SITE HAS BEEN PLANNED, DESIGNED, and built, the occupancy phase begins. This is the critical transition from one set of activities (and often funding and other resources) to another. This transition will be successful with a carefully planned maintenance, management, and stewardship plan developed in concert with the site design. The basis of this plan is to anticipate, describe, and secure all of the activities and resources necessary to retain or evolve the desired characteristics, function, and beauty of every element of the site.

In addition to all of the traditional maintenance requirements one would anticipate for site elements, it is especially important to maintain elements of the site that are intended to function in a certain way—such as porous pavements, rain gardens, and cisterns that supply makeup water for water features—so that the site will perform sustainably over the life of the landscape. It is also important to employ sustainable practices to meet the traditional operations and maintenance needs, like controlling pests with integrated pest management methods instead of relying on chemical pesticides or nourishing soil and plant health with compost instead of synthetic fertilizers.

This chapter is devoted to strategies for operating and maintaining a sustainable site. At the heart of sustainable operations and maintenance is the written maintenance plan that guides the site toward long-term sustainability goals. The written plan outlines the activities, timelines, equipment, and personnel necessary over the short term to achieve the ultimate desired outcomes in the long term.

The strategies discussed in this chapter provide examples of sustainable practices that can be included in the written maintenance plan to help achieve sustainable outcomes during operations and maintenance. The concept of active and adaptive management is integral to sustainable operations and maintenance and is discussed in many strategies and again at the end of the chapter. Active and adaptive management involves closely monitoring the site and adapting maintenance activities over time to provide the most effective stewardship for the site.

ENVIRONMENTAL AND HUMAN HEALTH IMPACTS OF SUSTAINABLE SITE OPERATIONS, MAINTENANCE, AND MONITORING

Traditional site operations and maintenance practices, such as widespread use of pesticides, fertilizers, and emission-generating equipment, can impact environmental quality and human health. For example, conventional lawn mowers generate carbon monoxide and other pollutants that contribute to the formation of ground-level ozone. Widespread application of chemical pesticides can harm nontarget plants and organisms. Organic materials like landscape trimmings and food waste comprise the largest component of the municipal waste stream in the United States but are often disposed of in a landfill, where their decomposition generates greenhouse gases. Table 8-1 outlines environmental concerns and sustainable site operations and maintenance practices that can help abate those concerns. Many of the practices listed in the table are discussed in detail in the following sections.

TABLE 8-1: Environmental Concerns Related to Site Operations and Maintenance

ENVIRONMENTAL CONCERNS	CONNECTIONS TO SUSTAINABLE SITE OPERATIONS AND MAINTENANCE
Impaired water quality	Maintain bioretention features, green roofs, and porous pavements to capture and treat water onsite instead of conveying it to traditional stormwater management systems
	Nourish soil with sustainable amendments like compost instead of synthetic fertilizers that could be transported by runoff and cause eutrophication of receiving waters
	Use integrated pest management methods to minimize use of pesticides, herbicides, and the like that could leach into stormwater
Water resource depletion	Capture and reuse surplus water onsite instead of using potable water for created water features, irrigation or other water needs.
Air pollution	Use low- or zero-emission equipment for landscape maintenance instead of traditional gas-powered engines that contribute to air pollution like ground-level ozone and particulate matter
Waste generation	Recycle waste and organic matter like landscape trimmings and food scraps instead of sending them to a landfill

continues

ENVIRONMENTAL CONCERNS	CONNECTIONS TO SUSTAINABLE SITE OPERATIONS AND MAINTENANCE
Habitat degradation and biodiversity loss	Treat water in onsite water features with biologically based methods instead of chemicals that may harm aquatic life
	Use integrated pest management methods instead of widespread application of pesticides to reduce impacts to nontarget organisms
	Control and manage invasive species to protect native species and prevent ecosystem alteration
Catastrophic wildfire	Manage landscapes around structures and in surrounding natural areas to reduce fuel loads and minimize risk of catastrophic wildfire
Soil degradation and erosion	Build new soil by onsite composting and other activities
	Establish and maintain healthy, deep-rooted native landscape systems wherever feasible
	Employ and maintain soil erosion control measures during site construction and establishment

SITES AND OPERATIONS, MAINTENANCE, MONITORING, AND STEWARDSHIP

The SITES Guidelines and Performance Benchmarks related to occupancy, maintenance, monitoring, and stewardship are focused on protecting and restoring ecosystem services throughout the life of a site. The Operation and Monitoring credits, as well as one Monitoring and Innovation credit, are meant to ensure that the site continues to function as it was originally intended.

At the heart of the Operation and Maintenance SITES credits is the prerequisite requiring a project to develop a comprehensive maintenance plan to achieve sustainable maintenance goals. This prerequisite helps protect and maintain over the long term all the ecosystem services the site was originally designed to provide, ranging from conserving potable water to reducing air emissions. A second prerequisite is aimed specifically at conserving resources and reducing waste sent to a landfill through collection of recyclable materials, such as paper, glass, plastics, and metals. One credit extends recyclable materials to include organic matter such as landscape trimmings and food scraps.

Four SITES credits related to Operations and Maintenance encourage energy efficiency and renewable fuel sources to reduce greenhouse gas emissions associated with fossil fuels. One credit focuses on air quality for users at a more local level by restricting outdoor tobacco smoke.

The SITES credits addressing the occupancy phase are complemented by a Monitoring and Innovations credit for monitoring performance of sustainable design practices. This credit is meant to provide detailed information on the long-term sustainability of features or programs that were implemented onsite to meet various SITES credits or prerequisites.

INCORPORATING OPERATIONS, MAINTENANCE, AND MONITORING CONSIDERATIONS INTO SITE DESIGN

As discussed in previous chapters, a predesign site assessment will reveal important site conditions (e.g., soil characteristics, hydrology, and climate) that should be considered during the site design process. The design process should also take into account how the site will eventually be used, including consideration of the full spectrum of operations and maintenance practices to support the site design. To ensure these aspects are considered during the design phase, the design team should include professionals who are knowledgeable in sustainable operations and maintenance.

During site design and plant selection, an important factor to consider is the anticipated maintenance practices on each portion of the site. It is critical to plan for the intended plant habitat (combination of site conditions and cultural landscape maintenance and management practices) in concert with the selection of appropriate plant species. Then, within that paradigm, other plant composition considerations follow—form, color, texture, variety, and so forth. Appropriate plant species are those that are genetically adapted to both biophysical site conditions (e.g., soil moisture, soil pH, sun/shade levels) *and* anticipated maintenance regime (e.g., prescribed burning versus pruning/clipping of dormant perennial material).

Additionally, the design form will greatly affect the maintenance regime (Figure 8-1). For example, a garden landscape with formal, geometric shapes, defined edges, and a complex plant arrangement may require more attentive and more frequent maintenance to keep it in design than a garden with more organic shapes and simpler plant groupings, which can be more forgiving and can look as intended even if plants move a bit over time. However, garden forms that are more naturalistic may require a higher level of skilled care and knowledge about different plant species' growth patterns and appropriate maintenance practices. The important point is that all factors affecting long-term care and maintenance should be considered during the design stage.

Other questions about operations and maintenance must be considered during design in order to allocate appropriate space for anticipated practices and processes. For instance, if onsite composting of landscape trimmings and food scraps is planned, an appropriately sized and conveniently located spot for composting must be designated during site design. The only way to ensure that operations and maintenance needs are considered during the design process is to use an integrated site development process in which a knowledgeable maintenance professional is part of the integrated design team from early on.

Native landscape system
(e.g., restored or re-created native landscape that relies on stewardship practices that mimic ancient cultural relationships such as prescribed burning, selective harvesting, etc., to maintain a healthy system.)

Naturalized plantings
(e.g., informal groupings of plants, with native species, native cultivars, and other noninvasive plants well adapted to local conditions and climate/rainfall that will require minimal weeding, pruning, etc.)

Planted bed/garden
(e.g., formally structured plantings with well-adapted, appropriate noninvasive plant species that will require regular weeding, pruning, dividing, and other horticultural practices, in addition to supplemental watering, ideally from nonpotable sources.)

(Photos by Conservation Design Forum and OWP/P I Cannor Design)

Less intensive maintenance ——————————————————————▶ **More intensive maintenance**

FIGURE 8-1: Maintenance intensity depends on the design form. LEFT: A native landscape system requires knowledge of the ecosystem processes that shape it, but it does not require the attentive and frequent maintenance typical in more formal garden designs. CENTER: Naturalized plantings favor more organic shapes and simpler designs that are relatively forgiving and can look as intended even if plants move a bit over time. RIGHT: A garden landscape with formal, geometric shapes, defined edges, and a complex plant arrangement will likely require more attention and more frequent maintenance to keep it in design.

Developing Maintenance and Management Plans

An important component of sustainable maintenance is having a written plan describing the anticipated steps required to achieve long-term sustainable outcomes for the site. A written record can provide guidance for future management efforts as time goes on and site personnel change.

The first step in the development of a maintenance plan is to define the long-term (e.g., ten or twenty years) desired outcomes for the site. Desired outcomes will depend on the type of site and the functions it is intended to perform, in addition to programmatic, aesthetic, and cost considerations. A discussion with the integrated design team, including site owner and/or client, will be helpful to identify the long-term expectations for the site, such as providing specific ecological functions and supporting site uses as described in the program plan. Examples of desired outcomes include achieving a net zero waste site, maintaining a water balance with no net export or import of water, or providing habitat for native wildlife (see earlier section, "Environmental and Human Health Impacts of Sustainable Site Operations, Maintenance, and Monitoring," for additional examples of long-term sustainability goals). Record the long-term desired outcomes for the site in the maintenance plan. In defining these goals, consider questions such as:

- ▸ What resources are available to maintain and steward the site and landscape over time (e.g., budget, staff members, volunteers, local master gardeners group, and the like)?

- ▸ What are the long-term aesthetic and appearance objectives and expectations? Do these match the design, or do interpretive materials and elements need to be incorporated into the site maintenance activities?

- ▸ Who will be using the site (e.g., children, elderly, those suffering from various illnesses, pets, and so forth), and will they affect the timing or delivery of any intended maintenance activities (e.g., controlled fire, compost applications)?

- ▸ What goals does the site have in terms of long-term energy use and potable water use?

- ▸ When materials or plants must be replaced? How and from which sources will replacements be selected?

- ▸ What treatment methods are preferred for problems with pests, weeds, or invasive species?

- ▸ How will organic matter, recyclable materials, and waste be dealt with?

- ▸ Which features are expected to function in a certain way (e.g., highly reflective surfaces, rain gardens, water features) and will require routine upkeep to maintain their performance over the life of the site?

- ▸ How can the site design be adapted over time to meet the changing needs of the users/stakeholders/owners?

After long-term desired outcomes have been defined, operations, practices, materials and schedules can be defined to achieve the outcomes and ensure that long-term goals for the site are met. The written maintenance plan should include details on the short-term steps—including specific activities, timelines, personnel requirements, and any potential coordination issues—that will allow the long-term goals to be realized.

In addition to documenting the long-term desired outcomes and short-term activities that will help achieve them, keeping a written log of maintenance activities throughout the life of the site can provide an organized resource for site managers over the life of the site. It should include specific activities, timelines, findings of inspections, the effectiveness of various methods, and other details to serve as a guide for future management actions.

Recycling Waste from Operations and Maintenance

Much of the "waste" material generated on a site, such as plastic containers, tires, wooden pallets, aluminum cans, and paper, isn't waste at all. Many materials used during site operations and maintenance can be reused or recycled rather than being sent to the landfill. Reusing and recycling conserves natural resources and reduces pollution associated with manufacturing of new materials. In 2008, 250 million tons of municipal solid waste were generated in the United States—an average of 4.5 pounds per person per day. Over half of the United States' municipal waste stream in 2008 was disposed of in a landfill and almost 24 percent was recycled (U.S. EPA 2009).

Sustainable waste management starts with a waste assessment or waste audit to characterize the waste generated at a site. A waste audit involves a systematic review of a site and its operations (including purchasing practices) to identify the quantities and types of waste materials that are generated. This audit can take a variety of forms, from physically sorting through a day's worth of waste, to examining records such as purchasing logs, to conducting a thorough walk-through of the site to observe and identify waste-generating activities that regularly occur. Each waste audit approach will provide different types of information (Table 8-2), so a combination of these approaches will provide the most robust characterization of the site's waste stream.

TABLE 8-2: Three Approaches to Waste Audits

WASTE AUDIT APPROACH	EXAMPLE ACTIVITIES	TYPES OF DATA PROVIDED
Physical sort of the waste	Collect representative sample of waste generated, sort by material type, and weigh total waste in each type	Types of waste generated onsite Quantities of specific waste types
Review records	Review purchasing, maintenance, and operating logs; review invoices or contracts with waste hauling, disposal, and recycling services	Overall quantity of waste generated Potential major sources of waste
Conduct walk-through	Tour site; observe typical activities that may generate waste; talk with site personnel about waste-generating practices	Qualitative information on how or why wastes are generated Types of waste generated (might not capture all types) Estimated quantities of specific waste types

Source: U.S. EPA WasteWise Waste Assessment Approaches.

The waste audit will determine the amounts and types of waste generated by all types of activity on the site, including that generated by users during typical onsite activities and by site personnel during routine operations and maintenance procedures. Areas that consistently generate the most waste should be the primary focus (e.g., outdoor eating spaces and grounds maintenance storage locations). Results of the waste audit can be recorded in a spreadsheet (see U.S. EPA Waste Assessment Approaches for spreadsheet templates), including details regarding material types, estimated amounts generated, and source of waste.

At the conclusion of the waste audit, the spreadsheet should be examined for opportunities to reduce the amount of waste generated and reuse materials where possible. These two options should be the first explored because they require less energy and resources than recycling. An example of reducing waste could be as simple as replacing disposable plates, cups, and utensils for food services with reusable items, or returning shipping materials (e.g., crates, pallets, and the like) to the supplier when possible. Reusing materials rather than sending them directly to a landfill should also be explored whenever possible. For instance, save and reuse objects such as wooden pallets onsite or break them down and use them for a new purpose, such as wood chips for mulch. Alternatively, if the objects can't be reused onsite, local "waste exchanges" or other local sites or businesses may be interested in reusing them.

After reduction and reuse options have been investigated, recycling opportunities should be indentified. For instance, many containers associated with site maintenance, including bedding trays, plant containers, and plastic commercial containers, can be recycled, as well as tires and oil from vehicles and equipment. Site users may also generate waste that can be recycled, such as aluminum cans, newspapers, and plastic bottles. Organic materials, including yard trimmings and food waste, can also be recycled.

Appropriate space should be allocated during the design phase for collection of all recyclable items generated onsite. The information collected in the waste audit can be used as a guide for calculations and container placement. Collection containers should be sized appropriately to handle the volume of recyclable materials typically generated onsite and placed near the locations of waste-generating activities. Locate recycling containers immediately adjacent to trash cans, along with appropriate signage, to encourage users to separate their waste into appropriate containers (see Figure 8-2).

The last step is to identify a recycling service for the materials collected onsite. The service should be contacted to determine the schedule of collections, how materials should be prepared (e.g., baled, compacted, loose), and other details.

Over the life of the site, types and amounts of materials generated onsite should be reassessed to be certain that collection units and placement are still appropriate for site use patterns. For instance, if the number of site users increases during certain seasons or increases steadily over the years, it may be helpful to add more collection units or schedule pickup service more often to prevent containers from filling up. It may be helpful to conduct waste audits periodically (e.g., every three to four years) to determine if the types and amounts of recyclable materials generated on a site have changed.

[Designed by Ignacio Ciocchini for the Bryant Park Corporation; Photo by Meg Calkins.]

FIGURE 8-2: Recycling containers should be located adjacent to trash containers adjacent to separate recyclable materials before disposal. Recycling containers should be clearly marked with appropriate symbols, colors, or signage to help users distinguish appropriate bins for waste materials.

Recycling Site Organic Waste from Operations and Maintenance

Landscape trimmings and food waste can be reused and recycled to imitate natural nutrient cycling processes and prevent organic materials from being disposed in landfills. Of the 250 million tons of waste generated in the United States in 2008, organic materials—yard trimmings and food waste—represented the largest component (25.9 percent) of the waste stream, with almost 65 tons (U.S. EPA 2009). A substantial portion of yard trimmings (over 64 percent) were recovered for composting (U.S. EPA 2009), which helps to keep these materials out of landfills and reduces the greenhouse gas emissions associated with their decomposition in landfills.

Managing organic wastes generated during operations and maintenance starts with a waste audit (as described in detail in the previous section) to estimate the amount and types of waste produced. Two types of organic wastes could be produced onsite: (1) landscape-based waste such as grass clippings, leaves, and woody debris like twigs and branches, and (2) food scraps, if applicable. As with other waste and recyclable materials, it is important to allocate appropriate space for collection and storage of organic wastes generated during operations and maintenance, if required. Space requirements for organic materials will vary based on the management strategy selected for the site (e.g., onsite versus offsite composting).

LANDSCAPE TRIMMINGS

Landscape trimmings are generated in all types of vegetated systems on a site, including rain gardens, bioswales, and green roofs, in addition to typical horticultural landscapes and restored sites.

The first option to explore for landscape-based waste is leaving the trimmings in place to decompose and return nutrients directly to the soil. For lawn areas, this involves grass-cycling, or letting grass clippings drop back onto the lawn instead of collecting them in a mower bag. Studies in California indicate that grass-cycling reduces mowing time by about 50 percent by eliminating time spent on bagging and disposing clippings (California Department of Resources Recycling and Recovery 2003). Grass-cycling requires a relatively diligent mowing schedule so that clippings are short and do not cover the grass surface. Almost any mower can be used for grass-cycling, but mulching or recycling mowers (mowers fitted with mulching blades and discharge covers) may help with this process, as they shred grass blades up into small pieces before dropping them. For trees and shrubs, woody trimmings can be chipped or shredded and used for mulch underneath the plant. For sites with large amounts of woody waste, another option to explore is burning it onsite. When possible, use low- or zero-emission mowers and equipment to reduce emissions from maintenance equipment).

A second option is to collect trimmings for composting either onsite or at an offsite composting facility. The most sustainable option is to compost materials onsite, but if space or other constraints do not support onsite composting, look for an offsite composting facility as an alternative. Compost generated onsite can be used to build and maintain soil health. Onsite composting will require consideration during the design phase of the site to ensure that areas allocated for organic matter collection are easily accessible and of sufficient size to accommodate the estimated volume produced (Figure 8-3).

(Photo from Nick Normal)

FIGURE 8-3: A large rooftop garden in Queens, New York, allocates an easily accessible area for the organic matter composting facility.

Generally, onsite composting is a simple process that requires compiling your trimmings into a bin or pile, monitoring the pile, and turning it occasionally. Different sites will have different requirements for their composting techniques depending on climate, available composting materials, space constraints, and other factors, but a few general guidelines will be helpful to keep in mind:

- ▶ Keep the pile relatively moist (think of a slightly damp wrung-out sponge).
- ▶ Chop up large woody debris into smaller pieces before adding to the pile.
- ▶ Mix "green" materials like fresh grass clippings with "brown" carbon-heavy items like dry leaves to keep the appropriate carbon:nitrogen ratio.
- ▶ Keep diseased and invasive plant trimmings out of the compost.

A third option to explore is the potential for harvesting dead plant material for reuse for other purposes, such as fiber for paper, art, cardboard, chipboard, or biofuel.

FOOD SCRAPS

Some sites may generate excess food in the form of leftovers from events or surplus inventories that can be donated to feed people instead of being sent to a landfill. Opportunities to donate food should be explored whenever possible by contacting local food banks or rescue programs.

Foods that cannot be donated, like scraps from individual plates, can be collected and composted rather than being sent to a landfill as trash. The final compost can be used to build and maintain soil health. As with other recyclable materials, information gathered in the waste audit can guide the size and placement of collection containers for food scraps. Containers should be sized appropriately to contain the anticipated volume of food scraps generated, and they should be placed near locations where food preparation and eating occur. Food scrap collection containers should be located adjacent to trash and other recycling containers, along with clear signage instructing users on what can and cannot be composted (Figure 8-4). Generally, nonmeat and nondairy foods like fruits, vegetables, and bread, plus food-soaked paper or cardboard (or compostable plates, cups, and utensils), can be composted. Meat, fish, poultry, oil, bone, or other animal byproducts require a different process (rendering) and should be excluded from small-scale food composting operations. If food scraps will be sent offsite for composting, the composting facility should be contacted to determine what can be included with food scraps because some services may not be equipped to deal with meat and animal byproducts.

FIGURE 8-4: Explicit signage is helpful for guiding users about what can be composted. Note that this example signage allows all food scraps in compost, including meat, bone, and dairy, which is not typical for small-scale composting operations.

[Source: Eco-Cycle redrawn by Simon Bussiere]

Daily collection of food scraps can quickly accumulate into a high volume of material. In addition, food waste is often heavier and quicker to rot than landscape trimmings, so collection of food waste must occur at regular and frequent intervals. If food scraps will be composted onsite, adequate space must be available to contain the volume of material generated and sufficient personnel available to collect and manage the composting process.

Nourishing Soil with Sustainable Amendments

Organic matter in soil is carbon-containing material from partially decomposed plant and animal matter. Organic matter improves soil health in several ways—it can reduce compaction and erosion, increase the nutrient content of the soil, improve water retention, and reduce the need for additional supplements such as fertilizers and pesticides.

The overarching concept behind this strategy is to use organic matter generated onsite as a resource, so that a loop of onsite generation and reuse is maintained (instead of importing from or exporting to offsite locations). The first step is to recognize sources of organic matter onsite as resources instead of waste products. Sources such as landscape trimmings and food scraps can be recovered from the waste stream and recycled for compost (Figure 8-5). Another less obvious source of organic material is partially filtered wastewater, which can be retained and used onsite instead of being transported offsite as a waste product.

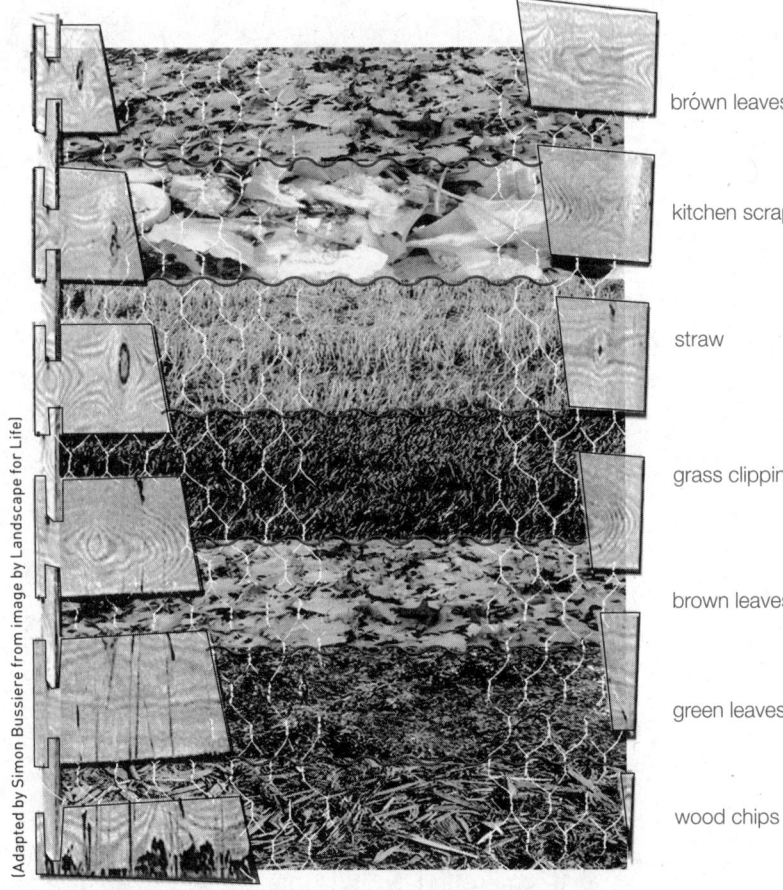

(Adapted by Simon Bussiere from image by Landscape for Life)

brown leaves

kitchen scraps

straw

grass clippings

brown leaves

green leaves

wood chips

FIGURE 8-5: Healthy compost contains a mixture of "greens" and "browns," like grass clippings and green leaves mixed with dry leaves and wood chips.

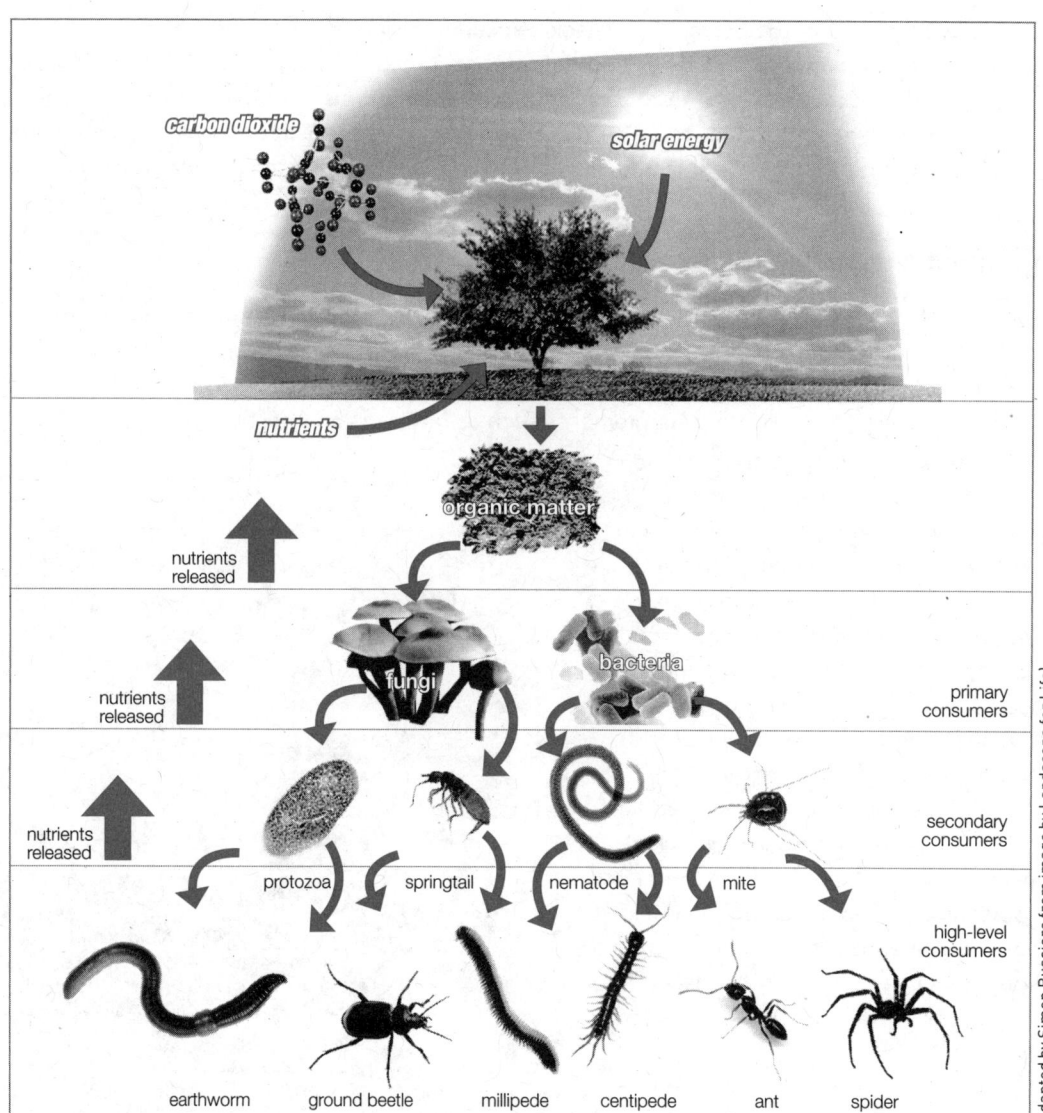

FIGURE 8-6: Organic matter in compost supports a soil food web that builds healthy, nutrient-rich soil.

[Adapted by Simon Bussiere from image by Landscape for Life]

Compost provides an excellent source of organic matter for soils, because it builds soil structure, supports biological activity in the soil (Figure 8-6), and provides slow-release nutrients for plant uptake. While the ideal scenario is an ongoing cycle of generation and reuse onsite, compost can also be obtained from offsite suppliers if the site does not have a composting facility onsite. Refer to Chapter 5, Site Design: Soils, for more information on compost specifications, volume, and methods of incorporation. Larger woody debris like dead branches can be chipped onsite and applied as a mulch to protect soil moisture and keep weeds at bay. Nutrient-rich effluent derived from wastewater treated in a living system such as a constructed wetland, aerated lagoon, or ecological engine can be used for landscape irrigation (Table 8-3).

TABLE 8-3: Maintain a Cycle of Organic Material with No Net Import or Export: Potential Sources and Methods of Reuse Onsite

POTENTIAL SOURCES OF ORGANIC MATERIAL	POTENTIAL REUSES FOR ORGANIC MATERIAL
Landscape trimmings, food scraps	Compost for soil amendment
Large woody debris	Chip and use as mulch
Lawn cuttings	Use grass-cycler to leave clippings *in situ*
Wastewater treated onsite with a living system	Nutrient-rich effluent applied to landscape

If fertilizers must be applied to soils, organic options should be used in lieu of synthetic chemical fertilizers. Generally, organic fertilizers contain nutrients derived from plant or animal products and often include organic matter that acts as an amendment to improve soil structure. Synthetic fertilizers, on the other hand, are chemically manufactured to provide certain nutrients. Any fertilizer, whether organic or synthetic, should be applied in minimal quantities to and only to specific areas in need (i.e., spot-fertilize) to reduce fertilizer contribution to runoff and greenhouse gas emissions. Both organic and synthetic fertilizers can cause environmental problems if they are not properly used. Apply nitrogen fertilizer only during times of active plant uptake (from late spring to early fall), and do not apply if soil is currently flooded or if rain is expected.

During design and plant selection, only plants that are *appropriate* for site conditions—including soil conditions—should be selected. Appropriate plant species are those that are genetically adapted to both biophysical site conditions (e.g., soil moisture, soil pH, sun/shade levels) and the anticipated maintenance regime (e.g., prescribed burning versus pruning/clipping of dormant perennial material) and are noninvasive. In other words, site vegetation should not require consistent supplements to survive during operations and maintenance.

Integrated Pest Management

Integrated pest management (IPM) is a sustainable approach to managing landscape pests (e.g., unwanted vegetation, insects, or diseases). IPM combines a suite of biological, cultural, physical, and chemical tools in a way that minimizes economic, health, and environmental risks. IPM emphasizes reduced use of pesticides in favor of preventive measures and alternative control techniques. A key element of the IPM approach is informed decision making—gathering information about pest problems and identifying effective, low-risk potential solutions before taking any action. IPM focuses on managing pests with targeted actions specific to the problem rather than relying on a broad, "one-pesticide-fits-all" approach.

IPM can be thought of as a step-wise process in which pest management solutions with the least environmental, economic, and health risks are used first. During the operations and maintenance phase of a site, integrated pest management will include the following components: (1) preventive measures to reduce the attractiveness of the site to pests, (2) establishing an "action threshold," or the level at which pest density or conditions would necessitate treatment, (3) monitoring to identify pest presence, (4) an array of potential treatment options that minimize risks, and (5) post-treatment evaluation. An IPM plan should be developed that addresses all of these elements in writing, and maintains records of treatment types, schedules, and results, to provide guidance for future management efforts as time goes on and site personnel change.

PREVENTIVE MEASURES

The first element of the IPM approach—prevention—should be considered during the design and plant selection phases of the site. This component of IPM focuses on identifying possible or likely pest problems that could occur on the site and eliminating conditions that attract those pests. Prevention should initially be considered during the design phase of the site, with selection of a diverse plant palette that includes species with natural resistance to pests and disease. Plant spacing, another issue to consider during design, is also very important for minimizing pest problems.

Prevention continues during operations and maintenance. Maintaining a healthy vegetative cover over all soil areas is critical to preventing establishment of invasive plant species and sustaining soil health. The maintenance plan should identify the long-term intent for plant spacing and specify if additional plants are to be added over time, or if plants should be divided, allowed to germinate from seed, and so forth. Healthy soils, with diverse and active soil biota, play an important role in supporting plant health and reducing the effects of plant pathogens and diseases. Other preventive measures include mulching to prevent unwanted vegetation species, pruning and removing vegetative trimmings to allow light penetration, and removal of annual weeds before they go to seed.

ESTABLISHING AN "ACTION THRESHOLD" AND MONITORING THE SITE

The second and third elements of IPM are linked: determining the threshold of pest density (e.g., number of pests per acre) or conditions that require action to be taken, and monitoring the site to identify the presence and type of pests. The threshold conditions will differ depending on the pest, plant, and site type. For example, the action threshold could be set at zero for a species whose presence in any number would be considered a threat (such as invasive plant species listed on federal, state, or regional noxious weed lists). Or, at the other end of the spectrum, some pests (e.g., certain annual weeds) may not be considered a threat until they reach a certain density, so the action threshold could be set relatively high. Action thresholds should be determined early in maintenance of a site, with regular follow-up monitoring to identify pest species accurately and assess their extent and density. To be most effective, monitoring should be scheduled according to the natural life cycle or growing cycle of the pest—for example, elimination of certain weeds before going to seed to avoid a profusion of the same weed the following year—so that actions can be taken before the problem becomes a more serious threat. It is important that the maintenance plan be explicit about the intended character and condition of the landscape, as minor changes may not be noticeable in the short term, but can have a large impact if left unchecked. An example of this would be the germination of unintended woody trees and shrubs in an open prairie landscape that could shade out native grasses and forbs, and have an established root system that could become more difficult and expensive to remove over time.

TREATMENT OPTIONS

The fourth element involves determining an array of effective potential treatment methods to implement if pest density exceeds the predetermined threshold. Treatment can include a variety of biological, cultural, physical, and chemical control methods listed in Table 8-4. Integrated pest management will often involve a combination of different methods to maximize effectiveness and minimize risks. When selecting possible treatment options, consider the possible impacts of each method (Table 8-4). Questions to consider may include the following:

- What is the reason (or reasons) for the presence of the pest species?
- Is there an onsite or offsite factor that is allowing the pest and precluding the health of desired species?
- If the site is stable, with appropriate hydrology, and free from other impacts, is there a recommended treatment to eradicate the pest?
- Is the treatment appropriate for the site conditions, including soil types, drainage patterns, and the intended use(s) of the site?
- Is the treatment appropriate for the target pest species?
- What are the possible human health effects of the treatment, including both short-term and long-term impacts?

▶ What are the possible environmental effects of the treatment, including impacts to nontarget organisms and nontarget plants?

▶ Is the treatment cost-effective and feasible for both short-term and long-term pest management?

▶ Are there any special characteristics of the product that should be considered prior to use, such as combination effects with other products, weather conditions that influence its effectiveness, or residual effects?

TABLE 8-4: **Categories of Integrated Pest Management and Example Methods**

TYPES OF PEST MANAGEMENT METHODS (OFTEN USED IN COMBINATION)	EXAMPLES
Biological	Using naturally occurring competitors or predators to control populations
	Using biologically based, nontoxic materials, such as pheromones to disrupt pest mating
Cultural	Removing pest sources by raking, removing dead wood, and so forth
	Providing conditions that optimize plant health, such as appropriate watering regimen and soil amendments where necessary
Physical	Manual clearing of unwanted vegetation
	Physical traps targeted for animal pests
Chemical	Targeted spraying (not broadcast spraying) of reduced-risk pesticides to unwanted vegetation species prior to seed formation
	Using reduced-risk pesticides that affect only the target pest species, taking care to apply no more than the recommended dose

POST-TREATMENT EVALUATION

The fifth and final element of IPM is to evaluate the effectiveness of control measures and adjust management strategies accordingly. For example, the presence of certain indicator plant species can be tracked to inform the site steward or manager about soil conditions, moisture, and so forth.

Throughout the IPM process, records should be kept documenting treatment types, schedules, and results. It is helpful to have a written plan that addresses all elements of IPM to guide future management efforts through landscape and personnel changes over time.

Training courses and certification in IPM are available for site managers and stewards from many state extension services and other local organizations (Figure 8-7).

(Photo by Conservation Design Forum)

FIGURE 8-7: Monitoring for pest species is critical for early detection and should be scheduled regularly according to the natural life cycle of the pest.

Controlling and Managing Invasive Plants

Invasive plant species are an especially aggressive subset of the "pests" addressed in the "Integrated Pest Management" section. The official federal definition (Executive Order 13112) of an invasive species is a species that is: (1) nonnative (or alien) to the ecosystem under consideration and (2) whose introduction causes or is likely to cause economic or environmental harm or harm to human health.* While the term "invasive species" includes plants, animals, and other organism (e.g., microbes), this section is focused specifically on the control and management of invasive plants.

Invasive species compete with and harm native plant and animal communities and can be costly to control and manage. One example is the purple loosestrife (*Lythrum salicaria*), which was introduced as an ornamental plant in the United States in the early nineteenth century and has since aggressively spread to 48 states, often changing the structure of the wetland habitats it invades and threatening native plants and wildlife (Pimentel, Zuniga, and Morrison 2005). Controlling the purple loosestrife is estimated to cost almost $45 million annually (Pimentel, Zuniga, and Morrison 2005).

An invasive species management plan is similar to an IPM plan but with more specific details on controlling and managing existing and potential invasive plant species onsite. This section will discuss each of the five IPM elements with specific considerations for invasive plant species control and management.

PREVENTIVE MEASURES

The first element of the invasive plant species management plan begins during the design phase of the site and focuses on preventive measures that reduce the probability of invasive species colonizing the site. The first step is to identify the invasive plants that already exist or could exist on the site in the future (using the same lists referred to earlier). The site assessment that occurs prior to site design should document the locations and species of invasive plants that exist on the site, if any. It will also be helpful to identify nearby areas with invasive species that could spread to the site, such as adjacent or upstream sites.

In many instances, invasive species are a symptom of an underlying problem, such as disturbance in hydrologic regime, suppressed fire, or other instability in the natural system. The most effective management for controlling invasive species, then, is to design and maintain a healthy, stable landscape system, which includes all of the characteristics and activities necessary for plant vigor. Only noninvasive plant species should be specified. Check regional, state, and federal lists and noxious weeds laws to ensure that all plants maintained onsite or added to the site are not considered invasive (see Figures 8-8 and 8-9).

In addition to the species known to occur onsite, it is important to be aware of other invasive species in the region that could potentially colonize the site. Extensive lists that designate certain plants as invasive are maintained at the federal, state, and sometimes

---

*Note that the Federal Invasive Species Advisory Committee recommends extending this definition to also include species whose introduction is likely to cause "harm to human, animal, or plant health." Beck, K.G. et al. 2008. "Invasive Species Defined in a Policy Context: Recommendations from the Federal Invasive Species Advisory Committee." Invasive Plant Science and Management 1:414–421.

regional level (federal and state noxious weeds lists are maintained at the USDA Natural Resources Conservation Service's online plants database). The lists should be revisited periodically (e.g., once per year) to be aware of newly listed species as they are recognized by authorities.

(Photo of purple loosestrife by Robert H. Mohlenbrock @ USDA-NRCS Plants Database / USDA SCS. 1989. *Midwest Wetland Flora. Field Office Illustrated Guide to Plant Species*. Midwest National Technical Center, Lincoln.)

(Photo of blue lobelia by Jennifer Anderson @ USDA-NRCS Plants Database)

FIGURE 8-8: Invasive species, such as purple loosestrife shown here, can be replaced with native alternatives that attract native wildlife species.

FIGURE 8-9: Blue lobelia is a beautiful native species that could be selected as an alternative to an invasive like purple loosestrife.

After identifying invasive species that are or could be a problem for the site, the next step is to implement preventive measures to minimize the likelihood of colonization. For the most part, this will involve maintaining the components of a healthy, stable landscape system (e.g., stable hydrologic regime or controlled burns).

ESTABLISHING AN "ACTION THRESHOLD"

The second element of the plan involves an "action threshold" which necessitates action for invasive plant species that exist or could exist on the site. Generally, the action threshold is set at a very low density or even at zero for invasive plant species.

MONITORING THE SITE

The third element of an invasive plant species plan focuses on monitoring for early detection of new populations that may have colonized the site. The goal is to identify problem species when they first appear to implement treatment immediately and minimize control costs. The plan should clearly outline field sampling methods and anticipated schedule for monitoring. Scheduling can be based on a predetermined interval (e.g., every two years), or it can be based on the timing of events that are known to provide a pathway for a new species (e.g., after disturbance from vehicles). Prior to annual monitoring, federal, state, and regional noxious weeds lists should be revisited so that monitoring personnel will be aware of any newly added species during the survey.

TREATMENT OPTIONS

The fourth element of the plan addresses appropriate initial treatment, follow-up treatment, and long-term treatment for invasive plant species that exist on the site in quantities beyond the "action threshold" for that species. The same categories of management methods discussed in the "Integrated Pest Management" section above—biological, cultural, physical, and chemical—are applicable for invasive species. In many instances, techniques that bring stability back to the system (e.g., controlled burns or prescribed grazing) should also be considered. Because each invasive species may require a unique combination of treatment types, local invasive species management experts and/or your local USDA cooperative extension system offices should be contacted for specific guidance. In some cases, treatment may be focused on containment of the invasive species, especially in situations where control methods are too costly or impractical on the site. Appropriate methods for collection and disposal of invasive plant material should be specified to prevent spread.

POST-TREATMENT EVALUATION

Finally, the plan must address monitoring to assess the success of management actions. The plan should be specific about the field sampling methods that will be used and the expected timeline for monitoring. To evaluate the effects of treatments or management actions, schedule monitoring before and after treatment events to quantify the impacts of the treatment. This type of monitoring can also simultaneously assess the effect of management on nontarget species such as adjacent plants.

Throughout the invasive species management process, written records should be kept to supplement the invasive species management plan documenting treatment types, schedules, and results. These written documents will provide guidance for future management efforts as time goes on and site personnel change.

Maintaining Landscapes to Reduce Risk of Wildfire

This section addresses management of fuels to reduce risks of catastrophic wildfire both onsite and in adjacent landscapes to protect local ecosystems, property, and lives. The activities described in this section pertain to sites with and without buildings in wildfire-prone areas. The best fire management approach in general is the proactive removal of fuel—dead or dormant vegetative material—and the maintenance of a generally open, fire-resistant landscape. This does not mean avoiding the use of woody trees and shrubs; rather, it involves the establishment of a drought-tolerant landscape that keeps moisture in the upper levels of soil through the use of native plant systems, and keeping vegetation low around structures and buildings. Recommended vegetation maintenance practices will vary depending on the distance from structures, and this section contains recommendations in three primary zones: (1) building protection zone (within 30 ft of all sides of structures), (2) building buffer zone (extending at least 100 ft from structures), and (3) natural area fuel reduction zone (existing or restored native landscapes beyond 100 ft from structures) (Figure 8-10) (Table 8-5).

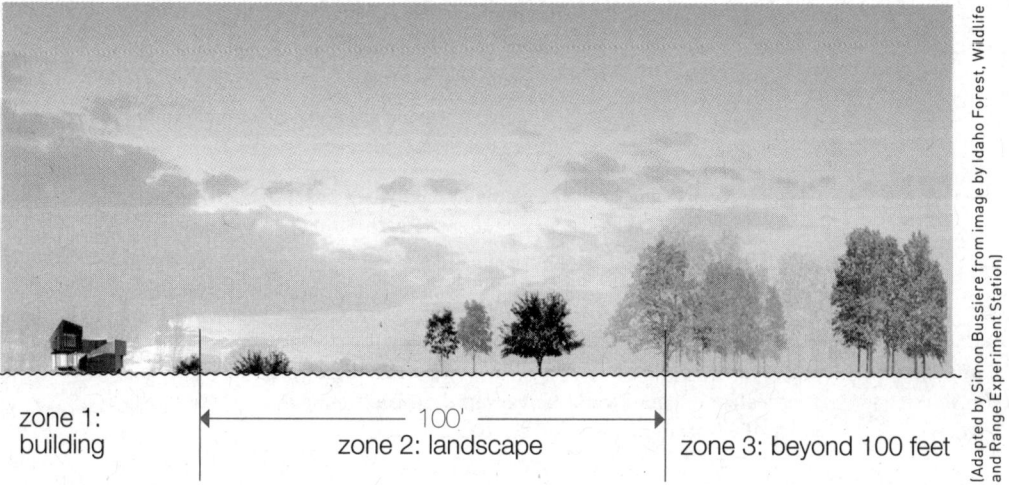

zone 1: building   ← 100' →   zone 2: landscape   zone 3: beyond 100 feet

(Adapted by Simon Bussiere from image by Idaho Forest, Wildlife and Range Experiment Station)

FIGURE 8-10: Vegetation maintenance to reduce fire risk varies with distance from structure.

During design and plant selection, the focus should be primarily within the *building protection zone*. The goal of maintenance in the building protection zone is to reduce the structure's vulnerability to ignition and to allow easy access for fire suppression equipment if an emergency arises. This zone should encompass at least 30 ft in all directions from structures.

In the building protection zone, only low-flammability, low-stature plant species should be included in the designed landscape. Highly flammable existing species (e.g., ornamental junipers) should be removed and replaced with less flammable species. Local or state fire management agencies in fire-prone regions may offer a list of suggested plants.

Site furnishings and other features should be made of nonflammable material such as metal, brick, or stone. Structures made of wood should be avoided in fire-prone sites. Likewise, use of wood-based mulches should be avoided in this zone, and gravel, recycled glass, or other nonflammable material should be used instead.

TABLE 8-5: Summary of Maintenance Practices to Reduce Landscape Vulnerability to Catastrophic Wildfire

ZONE	LOCATION RELATIVE TO STRUCTURE	RECOMMENDED MAINTENANCE PRACTICES
Building Protection Zone	Extends from walls of structure outward at least 30 ft	Maintain low-flammability species Use nonflammable material for mulch, furniture, and the like, and do not store flammable items near building Mow, rake, and prune to maintain vegetation height and spacing Collect and remove trimmings and other debris promptly Consider using gasoline-powered equipment only in cool, nonwindy conditions
Building Buffer Zone	Extends from edge of building protection zone to at least 100 ft from structure walls	Same maintenance practices as suggested for building protection zone Prune (and remove plants if necessary) to achieve islands of vegetation and eliminate "ladder fuels"
Natural Area Fuel Reduction Zone	Existing or restored natural landscapes more than 100 ft from nearest structures	Prevent fuel buildup with selective thinning and harvesting, brush removal, and regular prescribed burning Prune and thin vegetation to eliminate "ladder fuels"

BUILDING PROTECTION ZONE

Maintaining this zone appropriately during site operations is critical to reducing the structure's ignition vulnerability. Flammable materials (e.g., wood piles, gasoline) should not be stored in the building protection zone. Mowing, raking, and pruning should be scheduled as often as necessary to maintain the short stature and wide spacing of the vegetation in this zone. Consider limiting use of gasoline-powered equipment to early mornings and in still conditions to reduce the possibility of ignition. Trimmings, debris from gutters and other areas, and dead shrubs, branches, and leaves should be removed promptly in the building protection zone. It is also recommended to keep this zone well irrigated to provide additional protection for the structure(s) onsite.

BUILDING BUFFER ZONE

The vegetation maintenance goal in the building buffer zone is to provide a fire-resistant buffer surrounding the structure(s) for at least 100 ft from all sides. Unlike the building protection zone, taller-stature plants, such as well-spaced and pruned trees, may exist in the building buffer zone.

All of the maintenance practices used in the building protection zone should be extended to the building buffer zone, with the addition of several additional practices for tree maintenance and reduction of "ladder fuels." Ladder fuels transmit fire from the grass layer to neighboring trees via a vegetation pathway that reaches from low to high. To prevent ladder fuels, low tree branches should be removed and well-spaced "islands" of vegetation should be maintained. Ideally, individual trees and shrubs will be spaced at least 10 ft from other trees or shrubs, as measured from the crown. Tree and shrub branches can be pruned to achieve desired spacing, or plants should be removed if density is too high. In addition, trees should be pruned to remove low tree limbs that could allow fire to jump from ground to tree. Branches that are within 6 ft or one-third of live crown height (whichever is greater) from the ground should be removed. Pruning should be scheduled as often as necessary to maintain spacing and branch structure that limits ladder fuels.

NATURAL AREA FUEL REDUCTION ZONE

Fuel management activities should also occur in existing, native, or restored landscapes beyond the building protection and building buffer zones. The goal in this zone is to remove accumulated organic matter (e.g., dead branches, brush, and debris) that causes fuel buildup in the landscape, but fuel reduction activities may be less aggressive in this zone than those in the areas immediately surrounding the building. Selective thinning and harvesting, brush removal, and regular prescribed burning are the best, most cost-effective ways to keep a naturalized area free of fuel buildup (and are also beneficial from an ecological standpoint). As in the building buffer zone, trees in the natural area fuel reduction zone should be thinned and lower branches should be removed to prevent "ladder fuel" formation, and excess organic material and debris should be collected and removed. Preventing the overgrowth of woody trees and shrubs will reduce fire risk, and also allow an appropriate sunlight level on the ground surface to foster the growth of ground plane vegetation—grasses and forbs.

Prescribed burns are an option for managing fuel loads in the natural area fuel reduction zone. Prescribed burns help recycle biomass, promote nutrient cycling, and maintain robust and self-sustaining landscapes. Most sites can be safely burned. If the context or local codes preclude the use of prescribed fire, other methods of regular removal of dead and dormant vegetative matter must be employed. Each situation must be carefully assessed by experts in ecological landscape management, and a plan to stabilize the site and get it down to a safe level of fuel before conducting a prescribed burn is essential. Once suitable for controlled fire, annual burning is typically the best way to steward a healthy, stable native landscape system. Most landscape fires were human-set annually by native populations, and a part of their cultural relationship with the land. A burn plan should mimic the season, intensity, and frequency of the natural/cultural fire regime in the ecosystem. The plan should include a map of fire management zones and fire breaks; identify nearby structures, such as fences, pavilions, and shelters, and/or trees to be protected with mow lines or wet lines; and the approach for working with prevailing winds. Both the fire plan and the actual burning should be conducted by professionals trained in controlled landscape burn practice.

Prior to prescribed burning, obtain a proper burn permit and ensure compliance with local ordinances regarding burning. Coordinate with local fire department, and make sure neighbors are aware of the controlled burn before it is conducted. Make sure to address any concerns neighbors might have with burning, and cast a positive light on this essential ecological landscape management practice (Figure 8-11).

(Photo by Conservation Design Forum)

FIGURE 8-11: Many sites can be safely burned. Burning prevents fuel buildup and is also beneficial from an ecological standpoint. Coordinate with local fire agencies and neighbors prior to prescribed burning. Communicate the ecological benefits and reduced wildfire risk associated with prescribed burns.

Reducing Environmental and Human Health Impacts from Maintenance Equipment

Power equipment used for landscape maintenance, such as lawn mowers and leaf blowers, can generate excessive noise and release air pollutants that impact the site user experience and public health. Notably, conventional small engines generate carbon monoxide and other pollutants that contribute to the formation of ground-level ozone. Carbon monoxide and ozone are both "criteria" pollutants, subject to the U.S. Environmental Protection Agency's National Ambient Air Quality Standards (NAAQS) due to their impacts on public health and the environment. Carbon monoxide can negatively affect the cardiovascular and nervous systems, and ozone can impair lung function and is a key ingredient in smog.

The first step to reduce the impacts of power maintenance equipment is the identification of strategies to reduce mowing time and/or mowing frequency. These should first be considered during the design phase of a site. Some strategies that can reduce mowing are minimizing the size of turf areas, selecting low-maintenance adapted plants, or designing a site with informal plant groupings that do not rely on a rigid aesthetic structure (Figure 8-12).

During the maintenance phase of a site, a flexible mowing regimen should be implemented that meets the needs of site users while extending the interval between mowing for as long as possible.

Equipment with zero- or low-emission engines can further reduce emissions. Electric equipment or engines powered by alternative fuels, such as solar energy, compressed natural gas, propane, or hybrid sources, release fewer emissions than gas-powered equipment. Newer equipment that meets or exceeds U.S. EPA exhaust emissions standards and evaporative emissions standards (fully implemented in the 2012 model year) will also pro-

FIGURE 8-12: Minimized turf area reduces the maintenance time required and thus reduces emissions associated with landscape equipment. This site incorporates vegetated areas that require minimal maintenance adjacent to traditional lawn.

(Photo by Conservation Design Forum)

vide lower-emission options for vegetation maintenance equipments. Zero-emission manual tools, like push reel mowers, shears, and edgers, may be especially practical for smaller sites. Grazing animals can also help maintain vegetation without fossil fuel emissions (Figure 8-13).

If zero- or low-emission equipment is not feasible for site maintenance, site managers can still schedule routine maintenance to minimize the impacts of noise and localized air pollutants to site users. Maintenance can be scheduled when the site is closed for use or when site occupancy is at a minimum (i.e., days or times not during operation). Scheduling emissions-generating maintenance activities later in the day will reduce smog formation.

(Photo by Havi Hoffman)

FIGURE 8-13: Grazing animals, like the goats pictured here, can maintain vegetation without the noise and emissions of traditional landscape maintenance equipment.

Maintaining Bioretention Features

Bioretention features, such as rain gardens and bioswales, use soil and vegetation to capture, slow, and treat stormwater runoff. These structured landscape elements are designed to remove pollutants from runoff using mechanisms that occur in natural vegetated ecosystems—infiltration, evapotranspiration, and microbial soil processes. Design and construction considerations of bioretention structures are addressed in Chapter 3, Site Design: Water.

Maintenance of bioretention features can be divided into three categories: (1) typical horticultural maintenance activities, (2) monthly monitoring and repair as necessary to maintain bioretention performance, and (3) long-term management.

TYPICAL HORTICULTURAL MAINTENANCE FOR BIORETENTION FEATURES

Typical bioretention maintenance involves activities that accompany any landscaped area, such as weeding, pruning, and supplementing with additional plantings as necessary. Initial vegetation establishment should get the plantings established, lush, healthy, well rooted in, and weed-free. Rain gardens and bioswales are typically very dry, except immediately following a rain event. Plant species should be chosen for the soil and hydrology conditions created with the feature. Immediately following installation, plantings in the feature should be kept well watered (e.g., twice per week for the first six weeks, and periodically when rainfall is insufficient throughout the first two years of establishment of perennial grasses and forbs, potentially longer for trees and shrubs) and spot-fertilized (if necessary) to ensure successful vegetation establishment. After establishment, pruning, mulching, and weeding should be performed as necessary to maintain plant health. The plantings should be monitored monthly for pest problems and diseased plants, and integrated pest management methods should be employed to address any problems.

MONTHLY INSPECTIONS AND REPAIR

Monthly visual inspections of the components of bioretention features should be performed in addition to regular vegetation maintenance. The timing of these inspections can be scheduled around rain events—generally, bioretention features are designed with a specific drain time (e.g., 48 hours after the last rain event), so any standing water observed beyond the designed drain time is an indicator that the feature needs special attention to identify potential problems (see Figure 8-14).

[Photo by Conservation Design Forum]

FIGURE 8-14: A bioretention feature, such as this one at the Northwest Community Hospital in Arlington Heights, Illinois, should be monitored after storm events to evaluate for signs of clogging or erosion.

Monthly inspections can identify issues that may be affecting the performance of the bioretention feature, such as eroded areas, litter, debris, cracks or clogs at the inflow point, or clogging in the outflow device. Potential sources of sedimentation (including offsite sources, such as adjacent development) that may contribute excessive sediment to the feature should be identified (Table 8-6).

TABLE 8-6: **Inspection Checklist for Bioretention Features. (Inspect monthly or after major storms for problems that may affect bioretention performance; conduct repairs as soon as possible.)**

CHECK FOR THE FOLLOWING POTENTIAL ISSUES:	POSSIBLE SOLUTIONS:
Eroded areas	Regrade soil if necessary; add elements to control future erosion (e.g., ground cover, riprap, reinforced turf matting)
Litter or debris	Remove litter or debris by hand
Cracks or clogs at inflow or outflow points	Repair or replace cracked device; remove debris that is causing clog and clean as necessary
Clogged soil or mulch	Remove and replace the clogged media; locate the source of the excess sedimentation and look for ways to stop future sediment transport
Mulch absent in spots	Add mulch in void areas as necessary
Pests or diseased vegetation	Integrated pest management methods as used in other landscaped areas

LONG-TERM SCHEDULED MAINTENANCE

Long-term maintenance activities for bioretention facilities should occur over the life of the structure. The two primary functions of the soil and underdrainage elements of the bioretention feature are to absorb rainwater and to provide a suitable growing condition for the vegetation. Because these systems are designed to receive surface water runoff, they will need to be monitored and maintained to ensure proper function long term. If areas become filled with silt or sediment, they may need to be periodically cleaned out to remove this material. If infiltration capabilities decline over time due to siltation, the porous underlayment may need to be removed and washed or replaced to maintain proper infiltration. Also, the growing media may be affected by the constituents of the runoff. The vegetation should be specified to address the runoff water quality, but if it isn't thriving, certain plants may need to be replaced or augmented (see Chapter 4 for more information on plant characteristics and identifying replacement options) (Table 8-7).

TABLE 8-7: Long-Term Maintenance Checklist for Bioretention Features and Suggested Intervals for Scheduling

ACTIVITY	SCHEDULING INTERVAL
Add new mulch	1 to 2 times per year
Remove and replace dead vegetation	1 to 2 times per year
Conduct soil tests	1 to 2 times per year
Remove entire mulch layer and replace with fresh mulch	Once every 2 to 3 years, in spring
Restrict compacting activities (e.g., heavy vehicles or snowpiling)	Ongoing

In cold weather climates, de-icing salt is the most problematic issue, as most plants cannot thrive when exposed to salt. Plants may need to be replaced and/or augmented each spring depending upon the impact of salt, and salt may need to be flushed through the system in the spring, although the salt will impact downstream conditions. If possible, the initial design should address salt by using other green infrastructure practices, such as porous pavement and snow-melt systems heated with renewable energy, to negate the need for de-icing salt, and/or salt alternatives used that are compatible with the landscape and downstream ecology.

The addition of new mulch, removal and replacement of dead vegetation, and soil testing should be performed one to two times per year. Maintenance practices should be customized, and adjusted over time if necessary, to reflect the deficiencies or issues revealed by soil tests; however, if no soil issues are identified, amendments are not necessary. Soil may grow acidic over time due to acidity in precipitation and runoff, so if soil tests indicate a problem, lime or other alkaline substance should be added to regulate pH. If soil tests reveal that heavy metals have accumulated in the feature, extra care should be taken to ensure these soils do not present a human health risk to those who work and play on the site. Every two to three years, during spring, the entire mulch layer should be removed and replaced. Snow removal is not recommended within bioretention features. Any activities that compact the soil (e.g., use of heavy equipment, piling of snow) should be restricted from occurring within the feature if they have not been designed into the system. If conditions change and the system reduces function significantly over time, the soil and/or underlayment may need to be replaced or amended occasionally.

Finally, a maintenance log for the bioretention feature should be kept to record the results of monthly inspections, the solutions employed to remedy any problems, and the schedule for long-term activities required to maintain the feature's performance.

Maintaining Green Roofs and Green Walls

Vegetated roofs are classified into two basic categories: *intensive* and *extensive*. Extensive green roofs are the lighter and thinner (e.g., soil media is 2 to 6 in. deep) of the two, generally planted with shorter-stature vegetation (typically 6 in. or less) such as mosses, smaller shrubs, and sedums. Intensive roofs are heavier and thicker, with a deeper layer of soil media that can support larger and more elaborate vegetation, including shrubs and trees. All green roof and green wall systems, from extensive to intensive, will require structural and horticultural maintenance. Generally, intensive roofs require more maintenance, which can mimic maintenance activities on ground-based landscapes. The green roof/wall system, including soil media and vegetation selected for a green roof during the design phase, will ultimately determine the maintenance required over the life of the system, so it is critical to carefully select plants that will match maintenance expectations. For more information on design and construction of green roofs, refer to Chapters 3 and 4.

TYPICAL HORTICULTURAL MAINTENANCE FOR GREEN ROOFS AND GREEN WALLS

Typical green roof and green wall maintenance involves activities that accompany typical horticultural sites, such as weeding, watering, and supplementing with additional plantings as necessary. Following initial planting, the vegetation should be watered, fertilized, and weeded intensively for approximately six months to two years from installation to get the initial vegetation matrix well established and thriving, and on an as-needed basis after the plants are established.

After establishment, the green roof/green wall should be monitored monthly for pest problems, soil problems, and diseased plants. Integrated pest management methods should be used to address any invasive species and pest problems. The vegetation should be monitored to ensure it is thriving with available moisture.

MONTHLY INSPECTIONS AND REPAIR

In addition to regular vegetation maintenance, monthly visual inspections of the components of the green roof/wall are suggested to identify any problems that may be affecting the roof/wall's performance. As green roofs become more popular and widespread, typical issues become more apparent. For example, use of green roofs as a dog-walking area can impact vegetation not tolerant of pets, and may need to be adjusted, or rules instituted, to ensure compatibility and a healthy system. The best indicator of problems with the green roof or green wall system is the health and vitality of the vegetation. If areas are not getting established, or if plants are dying, the local conditions (soil, moisture, presence of competitive weeds, sun/shade) must be evaluated and corrective measures taken to replace the plants with more suitable species and/or modify the conditions. Depending upon the type of system and the visibility of the green roof or wall, regular inspections must be made. The maintenance plan will specify the inspection schedule, typically once per growing season for lower-maintenance, less complex systems to weekly and after major storm events for more elaborate systems. In addition to vegetation evaluation and care (primarily weed removal), drainage layer flow paths and the waterproof roof membrane should be inspected, along with any other potential areas for leaks. Problem areas should be repaired immediately to restore the function of the feature (Table 8.8). If an irrigation system is included, it must be checked regularly as well.

TABLE 8-8: Inspection Checklist for Green Roofs.

CHECK FOR THE FOLLOWING POTENTIAL ISSUES:	POSSIBLE SOLUTIONS:
Vegetation decline	Weed removal, replanting, replacing with better-suited species; address use, e.g., dog-walking, intense public use, etc.; soil conditions; watering
Litter or debris	Remove litter or debris by hand
Backups in drainage layer flow paths	Remove obstructions, address source of obstructions if possible
Root puncture	Replace root barrier, replace plant(s) with other species with less aggressive root growth
Leaks in vulnerable areas such as at perimeter, adjacent vertical walls, outlets, etc.	Remove portion of green roof system and repair structure and waterproofing, flashing, etc.

LONG-TERM SCHEDULED MAINTENANCE

There are several additional maintenance activities that will be required over the life of the green roof. Low-input sedum-based systems will require very little input, whereas systems that include perennial grasses and forbs, trees and shrubs, and/or annuals may need more care and soil amendments. The green roof system and maintenance plan will include testing protocols and recommendations for soil amendments to support the intended vegetation. For example, to prevent acidification of soil, small doses of lime, slow-release fertilizer, or other alkaline substances may be needed, perhaps twice yearly, to regulate the pH as necessary (Figure 8-15).

For all maintenance activities on the green roof or green wall, a maintenance log should be kept to record the results of monthly inspections, the solutions employed to remedy any problems, and the schedule for long-term preventive or maintenance activities that will maintain the green roof's performance over time.

(Photo by Conservation Design Forum)

FIGURE 8-15: Site users can be engaged in green roof maintenance and replanting activities. Vegetation on green roofs, such as that shown here on the Chicago City Hall green roof, requires maintenance similar to that of typical horticultural sites.

Conserving Potable Water and Treating Makeup Water in Created Water Features

This section is dedicated to the sustainable water use and treatment of water in *created water features*—landscape elements in which water is made visible for aesthetic purposes—such as ponds, streams, pools, water gardens, and fountains. This section addresses two aspects of maintenance for created water features: (1) maintaining a sustainable water source (i.e., nonpotable) for the feature, and (2) treating makeup water without chemicals that are likely to harm aquatic life (e.g., chlorine and bromine). Maintaining a sustainable water source for created water features reduces water waste and conserves potable water for more important purposes, such as drinking water. Integrating rainwater into visually accessible and aesthetically pleasing features also strengthens the connection of people to water and their local climate while also providing a restorative landscape setting.

MAINTAINING A SUSTAINABLE WATER SOURCE FOR THE FEATURE

Eliminating or limiting use of potable water is a major goal of a sustainable water feature. Sustainable sources of makeup water include harvested rainwater or surplus water from building or site operations, such as graywater collected from buildings. Other water sources, such as natural surface water or subsurface water, are not sustainable over the long run and should be avoided, especially in large quantities, and in arid climates where aquifers can be drawn down with unsustainable water removal over time. Capturing surplus water onsite and conveying it to a created water feature onsite must be considered initially during the design phase of a site.

During the maintenance phase, monthly inspections and/or inspections after rain events are recommended to ensure that collection and conveyance elements (e.g., rainwater collectors to harvest rainwater from rooftops or pipes to convey graywater from buildings) are functioning as intended to supply a sustainable water source to the created water feature. Water quality is typically the most pervasive issue with these types of systems. Poor water quality due to surface water runoff, temperature, and other inputs such as sediment, latent phosphorous in the soil, and so forth can lead to algae and other aesthetic problems in water features. Water quality may need to be addressed temporarily while the living system gets established and settles in. Close monitoring and corrective measures are essential to match expectations with water features both during initial establishment and long term. Other problems to look for include leaking fittings and valves, mosquito larvae, and signs of clogging in the collection and conveyance elements (Table 8-9).

TABLE 8-9: Inspection Checklist for Rain Collectors and Conveyance Elements.

CHECK FOR THE FOLLOWING POTENTIAL ISSUES:	POSSIBLE SOLUTIONS:
Leaking fittings and valves	Replace parts as necessary to create watertight seal
Inspect for mosquito larvae	Seal the feature during warm seasons to prevent mosquito breeding
Inspect conveyance elements (e.g., screens, gutters, downspouts, and overflow devices) for signs of clogging	Remove debris by hand; clean or flush to remove sediment; replace devices if damaged
Algae or other indicators of water quality	Look for surface water inputs that may have water quality impacts; test water for phosphorous and nutrient levels; address as needed

In addition to monthly inspections, occasional draining and cleaning of rain collectors and cisterns may be necessary to remove debris, such as leaves, that may fall into the vessel. Draining and cleaning will also prevent stagnation and buildup of algae. Once a year, the collector should be disconnected, drained, and cleaned thoroughly; debris should be removed from the bottom and sides of the tank by hand, and then the tank should be brushed or power-washed to scrub the surfaces. In cold winter climates, above-ground systems should be drained and cleaned during late autumn (Table 8-10).

A maintenance log should be kept to record the results of monthly inspections, the solutions employed to remedy any problems, and the schedule for long-term activities required to maintain a sustainable water source and avoid potable water use in created water features onsite (Figure 8-16).

(Photo by Conservation Design Forum)

FIGURE 8-16: Water storage facilities, such as the cistern pictured here, should be inspected regularly to ensure a sustainable water source will be maintained over the long term.

TABLE 8-10: Long-Term Maintenance Checklist for Rain Collectors and Suggested Intervals for Scheduling

ACTIVITY	SCHEDULING INTERVAL
Remove debris, leaves, etc., that fall into the collector	1 to 2 times per year
Disconnect, drain, and thoroughly clean the inside surfaces of the collector	1 time per year (just prior to winter)

MAINTAINING WATER QUALITY WITHOUT TOXIC CHEMICALS

Water features should be designed in such a way that water quality can be maintained without the use of chemicals (e.g., chlorine and bromine) that may harm aquatic life. Water features can be designed to incorporate movement or recirculation and interface with vegetation and/or gravel with living systems. Living systems include constructed treatment wetlands, pond restorers, and biofilters designed to remove nutrients, decompose bacteria, and improve water quality. During the site occupancy and use phase, it is important to keep those elements in good working order. Monthly inspections of water for quality, the presence of algae, and weedy aquatic plant species will inform any activities necessary to maintain water quality (Figures 8-17 and 8-18).

FIGURE 8-17: The water in this water feature at the Queens Botanical Garden is from rainwater that is cleansed via filtration through plant root systems.

Water quality can be enhanced with biologically based water treatment including certain beneficial bacteria, enzymes, minerals, and oxygen-based additives, especially during initial establishment. Ozonation or thermal treatment may be used for features designed for human contact.

If the water feature is intended for public access, other water treatment measures may be required to meet local health regulations, such as UV (ultraviolet) disinfection, or other filtering methods. Energy use and long-term maintenance of these systems are also a consideration.

FIGURE 8-18: The wastewater at the Omega Center for Sustainable Living is treated using a natural water reclamation process without chemicals and with net zero energy.

Maintaining Pavements

This section will focus on two aspects of sustainable pavement maintenance: (1) regular maintenance activities required for porous pavement, and (2) methods to remove snow/ice on roads and walkways. Design and construction issues of pavements are addressed in Chapters 3 and 6. Porous pavement options, primarily porous interlocking unit pavers, but also including porous asphalt, pervious concrete, and grass pavers, are primarily considered in the design phase of a site but can also be added later during site occupancy as a retrofit.

POROUS PAVEMENTS MAINTENANCE

Regular maintenance of porous pavements is critical to ensure their effectiveness over the long-term use of a site. Without routine maintenance, porous pavements can clog with sediment and become ineffective. Studies indicate that maintenance activities that remove sediment from voids can improve surface infiltration rates in pervious pavements by over 60 percent (Bean et al. 2007). With proper maintenance and inspections, these pavements can last for 50 years or even longer (using interlocking unit paver systems), even in cold-weather climates, as an effective method for infiltrating and treating surface runoff, and providing other benefits as well.

It is essential to maintain the porous pavement system properly to maintain the effectiveness of the site's infiltration, as well as other pavement functions. Use and access to the pavement must be matched to the design. For example, if the porous pavement is located in a passive setting and a lighter pavement system such as open-graded gravel or gravel-grass is used, heavy vehicles that could cause compaction and limit the infiltration capacity of underlying soils might need to be restricted. It is useful to install signs to identify areas of pervious paving to ensure that site personnel are aware of the pervious pavement and that specific maintenance activities are required, especially if the material is not obviously porous, such as porous asphalt or concrete. It must be made clear that there are differences between the porous pavement and traditional pavement so that they are properly maintained (e.g., never seal or repave pervious pavements with nonporous materials; do not store soil/mulch on pavement surface).

As with all stormwater best management practices, regular inspections are recommended to ensure the porous pavement is functioning as intended, especially in the first few months after installation. The pavement should be checked to make sure that water is infiltrating between storms, and areas of clogging should be noted. Potential sources of sedimentation (including offsite sources, such as adjacent development) that may be contributing excessive sediment to the pervious pavement should be identified. Leaves and other organic material should be removed from the pavement surface once a month. For grass pavers, regular mowing and watering may be required (similar to typical turf grass maintenance). Porous asphalt and porous concrete paving will have higher maintenance requirements, and less overall durability, than permeable interlocking unit pavers (Table 8-11).

TABLE 8-11: Inspection Checklist for Pervious Pavement.

CHECK FOR THE FOLLOWING POTENTIAL ISSUES:	POSSIBLE SOLUTIONS:
Litter or debris on pavement surface	Sweep or remove litter or debris by hand
Turf in grass pavers needs maintenance	Water and mow (similar to typical turf grass maintenance)
Damaged interlocking pavement blocks	Remove and replace damaged pavement blocks
Potholes or cracks in porous asphalt or porous concrete	Repair using porous patch mixes
Clogged pavement	Regularly remove sediment with street sweeping at least 3 to 4 times per year (see below); if clogging is occurring in a specific spot, drill ½-in. holes every 2 to 3 ft; locate any sources of excess sedimentation and look for ways to stop future sediment transport

In addition to regular inspections of the pervious pavement, a long-term plan for sediment removal should be developed to prevent clogging (Table 8.12). It is important to remove sediment that builds up from the pavement surface to avoid particles sinking into voids and getting compacted into the deeper pockets of the pavement drainage profile where they are more difficult to remove. The long-term plan for sediment removal should include a schedule for removing sediment from the surface with appropriate street vacuum sweeping equipment three to four times per year (see Figure 8-19). Walk-behind push vacuum sweepers may be used for smaller areas like sidewalks. Pavement surfaces may need to be power-washed after sweeping to remove remaining sediments. In areas with exceptional clogging, other measures may be necessary. If

FIGURE 8-19: Vacuum sweepers should be used several times a year to clear debris and clogging from porous pavements.

(Photo by Charles R. Taylor)

it is not possible to address the source of clogging—for example, sediment-laden runoff—it may be helpful to use a low-pressure washer first to soak into voids and then follow with vacuum sweeping. If clogging is occurring in a specific spot, ½-in. holes can be drilled every 2 to 3 ft in the pavement surface.

TABLE 8-12: Long-Term Maintenance Checklist for Porous Pavements and Suggested Intervals for Scheduling

ACTIVITY	SCHEDULING INTERVAL
Vacuum sweeping (followed by power-washing, if necessary)	Up to 3 to 4 times per year; for sites in cold winter climates, at least 2 times per year (following last snowfall)
For exceptionally high clogging, soak first and follow with vacuum sweeping	As needed
For clogging in specific small spots, drill ½-in. holes every 2 to 3 ft in the pavement surface	As needed

Nylon-tipped snow-plow blades or brushes are recommended for snow removal on porous pavements due to the slightly uneven surface of the pavement and to avoid visible scratching on the surface of unit pavers if it is this type of system. Blade height should be set similar to that used for unpaved roads, keeping the blade lifted enough to clear the surface of the pervious pavement. Sand, ash, and other abrasive materials should not be used on pervious pavements, although de-icing treatments are acceptable. All maintenance activities and timelines should be recorded in a written log to ensure pavements are maintained adequately over the life of the site.

SNOW AND ICE TREATMENT FOR PAVEMENTS

Nonchemical treatments such as shoveling, plowing, and other manual removal techniques should be the first options explored for snow and ice removal on roads and walkways. De-icing agents that cause minimal damage to vegetation, metals, and hardscapes are a second option. Various forms of de-icing salt, most commonly used, contributes pollution to downstream aquatic habitats and can harm plants, animals, and soil health. Instead, nontoxic, environmentally friendly alternatives should be explored. Examples include calcium magnesium acetate (CMA), de-icers made from liquid residues from corn and grain processing, or rock salt treated with liquid agricultural byproducts.

Although abrasives such as sand can be used to provide traction, these substances are not recommended for use on porous pavements or near other infiltration features like rain gardens due to potential clogging problems.

Of course, the best option is to negate the need for de-icing to begin with, through the use of integrated green pavement systems that foster an ice-free surface. Porous pavement, especially porous interlocking unit paver systems, minimize the need for de-icing due to its ability to infiltrate meltwater that can otherwise refreeze, and the air void space that keeps the ground temperature more moderate. Also, snow-melt systems using renewable energy, such as ground-source heat, or waste heat will keep the pavement ice-free without any de-icing agents, and greatly extend the life of the pavement. Communities such as Holland and Grand Rapids, Michigan, have snow-melt systems in public streets and sidewalks of their downtown districts, and have experienced numerous economic and environmental benefits (Figure 8-20).

(Photo by Conservation Design Forum)

FIGURE 8-20: Snow and ice melting systems, such as the one shown here in Holland, Michigan, can use renewable energy sources to keep pavement surfaces ice-free and eliminate the need for de-icing agents.

MONITORING TO INFORM ACTIVE AND ADAPTIVE STEWARDSHIP

A recurring theme in sustainable site operations and maintenance is active, regular monitoring of the site for indicators that the systems and/or elements are performing as intended. In short, effective site management depends on a thorough understanding of the site conditions and dynamics over time.

In many of the sustainable strategies discussed in this chapter, regular inspections and monitoring are critical to ensure that the site is functioning in ways that are in line with long-term desired outcomes. The written maintenance plan for a site should incorporate timelines for monitoring, and the findings from all routine monitoring should also be kept in a written log. While various sustainable site practices have been tested to ensure proper function before widespread application or use in public spaces, the benefits of many of these practices have not been fully quantified in different applications, contexts, geographic locations, and climates. More data and research over many growing seasons in varying conditions will provide the opportunity to optimize the performance and value of these systems over time. Publishing the results of monitoring in a discipline-wide professional magazine or peer-reviewed journal or sharing the results via presentations at professional national or international conferences can contribute to the body of knowledge on long-term sustainability.

Over the life of a site, reevaluation and revisions to maintenance practices will likely be needed to adapt to changing conditions and unforeseen events. Continually learning (and relearning) about the site—and the effects of various maintenance and stewardship practices—should be a high priority. The written maintenance plan should be revisited on a yearly basis to consider if the site performance is maintaining or improving over time with respect to the sustainability goals initially established for the site. And the effectiveness of previous and current maintenance activities in guiding the site toward the long-term desired outcomes should be evaluated. During the reevaluation and revision process, it may be helpful to revisit the original program plan to ensure the functions and uses intended for the site are still being supported by current maintenance practices.

The maintenance plan (activities, timelines, personnel, etc.) should also be updated and adapted to reflect new findings (e.g., current research on maintenance practices) and new knowledge of the site's conditions. For example, if new research indicates that innovative management techniques for a pest species have proven to be effective in your region, consider revising the written maintenance plan to incorporate these updates. Likewise, if a new plant species is added to invasive species lists relevant to your site, incorporate monitoring and preventive measures for early detection and control of the newly listed invasive plant. An adaptive approach continuously informed by the health, vitality, and performance of the site systems is essential for long-term site sustainability.

Sustainable sites are living, breathing, evolving systems, and can be optimized to achieve the wide range of intended ecosystem services only through proper maintenance and stewardship that is continuously modified and adjusted based upon the needs of the system as determined through regular inspection and monitoring. When planned and managed as part of the integrated design and implementation process, these activities ensure sustainable sites are functional, cost-effective, and increasingly beautiful over time.

References

Bean, E.Z., W.F. Hunt, and D.A. Bidelspach. 2007. "Field Survey of Permeable Pavement Surface Infiltration Rates." *Journal of Irrigation and Drainage Engineering*, 133(3): 249–255.

California Department of Resources Recycling and Recovery (CalRecycle). 2003. "Managing a Waste-Efficient Landscape: Landscapers Guide." Available at www.calrecycle.ca.gov/Organics/Landscaping/KeepGreen/Manage.htm (accessed July 2010).

Pimentel, D., R. Zuniga, and D. Morrison. 2005. "Update on the Environmental and Economic Costs Associated with Alien-invasive Species in the United States." *Ecological Economics*, 52:273–288.

U.S. Environmental Protection Agency (U.S. EPA). 2009. "Municipal Solid Waste Generation, Recycling, and Disposal in the United States: Facts and Figures for 2008" (EPA-530-F-009-021). Available at www.epa.gov/osw/nonhaz/municipal/pubs/msw2008rpt.pdf.

RESORCES

CHAPTER 1 INTRODUCTION

Sustainable Sites Initiative. www.sustainablesitesinitiative.org.

U.S. Green Building Council. www.usgbc.org.

Building Green. www.buildinggreen.com.

Whole Building Design Guide, National Institute of Building Sciences, www.wbdg.org/.

Living Building Institute. Living Building Challenge, www.ilbi.org/.

Benyus, J. M. 2002. Biomimicry. New York: Harper Collins.

Dramstad, Wesche, J.D. Olsen, R.T.T. Forman, *Landscape Ecology Principles in Landscape Architecture and Land-Use Planning.* Washington, DC: Island Press, 1996.

Kellert, S., *Building for Life: Designing and Understanding the Human Nature Connection.* Washington, DC: Island Press, 2005.

Kibert, Charles J., *Sustainable Construction: Green Building Design and Delivery* (2nd ed.). Hoboken, NJ: John Wiley and Sons, 2007.

Kibert, C.J., J. Sendzimir, and B. Guy (eds.), *Construction Ecology: Nature as the Basis for Green Buildings.* London: Spon Press, 2002.

Johnson, Bart R. and Kristina Hill, *Ecology and Design: Frameworks for Learning.* Washington, DC: Island Press, 2002.

Lyle, John Tillman, *Design for Human Ecosystems: Landscape, Land-use and Natural Resources.* New York: Van Nostrand Reinhold, 1985.

Margolis, Liat and A. Robinson, *Living Systems.* Basel: Birkhauser Verlag, 2007.

Marsh, William, *Landscape Planning: Environmental Applications.* Hoboken, NJ: John Wiley and Sons, 2005.

McDonough, William, and Michael Braungart, *Cradle to Cradle: Remaking the Way We Make Things.* New York: North Point Press, 2002.

McHarg, Ian, *Design with Nature.* Garden City, NY: Doubleday/Natural History Press, 1969.

Mendler, Sandra, William Odell, and Mary Ann Lazarus, *The HOK Guidebook to Sustainable Design.* Hoboken, NJ: John Wiley and Sons, 2006.

Sarte, S. Bry, *Sustainable Infrastructure: The Guide to Green Engineering and Design.* Hoboken, NJ: John Wiley and Sons, 2010.

Thompson, George F. and Fredrick R. Steiner (eds.), *Ecological Design and Planning.* New York: John Wiley and Sons, 1997.

Thompson, J. William and Kim Sorvig. *Sustainable Landscape Construction: A Guide to Green Building Outdoors.* Washington, DC: Island Press, 2007.

Van der Ryn, Sim and Stuart Cowan, *Ecological Design.* Washington, DC: Island Press, 1996.

Windhager, S., F. Steiner, M.T. Simmons, and D. Heymann. 2010. "Towards Ecosystem Services as a Basis for Design." *Landscape Journal* 29(2):107–123.

CHAPTER 2 PREDESIGN: SITE SELECTION, ASSESSMENT, AND PLANNING

General

LaGro, J. A., *Site Analysis: A Contextual Approach to Sustainable Land Planning and Site Design.* Hoboken, NJ: John Wiley and Sons, 2008.

Russ, T., *Site Planning and Design Handbook.* New York: McGraw-Hill, 2009.

Site Assessment

National Park Service Rivers, Trails and Conservation Assistance, Community Toolbox, www.nps.gov/nero/rtcatoolbox/.

Federal Emergency Management Center, Map Service Center, Flood Insurance Rate Maps, (FIRMs), www.msc.fema.gov/.

Natural Resource Conservation Service Maps, Imagery, Data and Analysis www.nrcs.usda.gov/technical/maps.html.

U.S. Army Corps of Engineers, National Wetlands Inventory, www.usace.army.mil/CECW/Documents/cecwo/reg/ . . ./list96.pdf.

U.S. Census Bureau: Topologically Integrated Geographic Encoding and Referencing System Database www.census.gov/geo/www/.

U.S. Fish and Wildlife Service Species Reports by State, Environmental Conservation Online System http://ecos.fws.gov/tess_public/StateListing.do?state=all.

U.S. Geological Survey: Maps and GIS Data Library www.usgs.gov/pubprod/.

Site Selection and Planning

Center for Transit-Oriented Development, www.ctod.org/.

Congress for New Urbanism, www.cnu.org/.

Project for Public Spaces, Building Community through Transportation www.pps.org/building-communities-through-transportation/.

Urban Land Institute www.uli.org/.

Team Development and Process

National Charrette Institute, www.charretteinstitute.org/.

Lennertz, B., and A. Lutzenhiser, *The Charrette Handbook: The Essential Guide for Accelerated, Collaborative Community Planning.* Chicago, IL: American Planning Association, 2006.

Macaulay, D.R., and F. McLennan, *Integrated Design.* Bainbridge Island, WA: Ecotone Publishing, 2008.

Sanoff, H., *Community Participation Methods in Design and Planning.* New York: John Wiley and Sons, 1999.

Yudelson, J., *Green Building through Integrated Design.* New York: McGraw-Hill, 2009.

7 group and B. Reed, *The Integrative Design Guide to Green Building.* Hoboken, NJ: John Wiley and Sons, 2009.

CHAPTER 3 SITE DESIGN: WATER SYSTEMS

Water Systems, General

Center for Watershed Protection, www.cwp.org/.

Low Impact Development Center, www.lowimpactdevelopment.org.

U.S. Environmental Protection Agency, Water: Wastewater Technology, Fact Sheets, http://water.epa.gov/scitech/wastetech/mtbfact.cfm.

U.S. Environmental Protection Agency, Water: Sustainable Infrastructure, http://water.epa.gov/infrastructure/sustain/index.cfm.

The Conservation Fund, Green Infrastructure, www.greeninfrastructure.net/.

Campbell, C.S., and M. Ogden, *Constructed Wetlands in the Sustainable Landscape.* New York, John Wiley and Sons, 1999.

Dreiseitl, H., and D. Grau (eds.), *New Waterscapes: Planning, Building, and Designing with Water.* Basel: Birkhauser, 2005.

Federal Interagency Workgroup on Wetland Restoration, "An Introduction and User's Guide to Wetland Restoration, Creation, and Enhancement." www.epa.gov/owow/wetlands/restore/finalinfo.html, 2003.

France, Robert L., *Handbook of Water Sensitive Planning and Design* (Integrative Studies in Water Management & Land Development). Boca Raton, FL: CRC Press, 2002.

France, Robert L. 2003. *Wetland Design: Principles and Practices for Landscape Architects and Land Use Planners.* New York: W.W. Norton & Company, 2003.

Kincade Levario, Heather, *Design for Water: Rainwater Harvesting, Stormwater Catchment, and Alternate Water Reuse.* Gabriola Island, BC: New Society Publishers, 2007.

Palmer, M.A., E. S. Bernhardt, et al., "Standards for Ecologically Successful River Restoration." *Journal of Applied Ecology* 42(2):208–217.

Perrin, C., L.-A. Milburn, and L. Szpir, *Low Impact Development: A Guidebook for North Carolina.* Raleigh: North Carolina State University, 2009.

Schueler, T., "The Architecture of Urban Stream Buffers," *Watershed Protection Techniques* 1(1995): 159–163.

Todd, Nancy Jack and John Todd, *From Eco-Cities to Living Machines: Principles of Ecological Design.* Berkeley, CA: North Atlantic Books, 1994.

Stream Corridor Restoration: Principles, Processes, and Practices, Federal Interagency Stream Restoration Working Group, 08/2001 revision of 10/1998 version.

Walsh, C.J., A.H. Roy, et al., "The Urban Stream Syndrome: Current Knowledge and the Search for a Cure." *Journal of the North American Benthological Society* 24(3):706–723.

Weiler, Susan and K. Sholz-Barth, *Green Roof Systems: A Guide to the Planning, Design and Construction of Building over Structure.* Hoboken, NJ: John Wiley and Sons, 2009.

Winter, T.C., "The Role of Ground Water in Generating Streamflow in Headwater Areas and in Maintaining Base Flow." *Journal of the American Water Resources Association* 43(1):15–25.

Stormwater Management Resources

U.S. Environmental Protection Agency, "National Pollutant Discharge Elimination System (NPDES), Stormwater Program, http://cfpub.epa.gov/npdes/home.cfm?program_id=6.

U.S. Environmental Protection Agency, "National Management Measures to Control Non-point Source Pollution from Urban Areas" (EPA 841-B-05-004), http://water.epa.gov/.polwaste/nps/urban/index.cfm.

Washington State Department of Ecology, *Stormwater Management Manual*, www.ecy.wa.gov/programs/wq/stormwater/manual.html.

King County, Washington, *Surface Water Design Manual*. www.kingcounty.gov/environment/waterandland/stormwater/documents/surface-water-design-manual.aspx, 2009.

Portland Bureau of Environmental Services, Sustainable Stormwater Management Program, www.portlandonline.com/bes/index.cfm?c=34598.

Portland Bureau of Environmental Services, *Stormwater Management Manual*. www.portlandonline.com/bes/index.cfm?c=47952&.

Seattle Public Utilities, Green Stormwater Infrastructure Program www.seattle.gov/util/About_SPU/Drainage_&_Sewer_System/GreenStormwaterInfrastructure/index.htm.

State of Maryland. *Maryland Stormwater Design Manual*, Volumes I and II, www.mde.state.md.us/programs/Water/StormwaterManagementProgram/MarylandStormwaterDesignManual/Pages/programs/waterprograms/sedimentandstormwater/stormwater_design/index.aspx, 2009.

New York Department of Environmental Conservation, *New York Stormwater Management Manual*. www.dec.ny.gov/chemical/29072.html, 2010.

North Carolina Sedimentation Control Commission, *North Carolina Erosion and Sediment Control Planning and Design Manual*, 2009.

City of Santa Barbara, *Storm Water BMP Guidance Manual*, www.santabarbaraca.gov/Resident/Community/Creeks/Storm_Water_Management_Program.htm.

State of Delaware, Division of Soil and Water Conservation, Sediment and Stormwater Control Program, www.swc.dnrec.delaware.gov/Pages/SedimentStormwater.aspx.

Green Roofs for Healthy Cities, www.greenroofs.org/.

International Green Roof Association, www.igra-world.com/.

American Society of Civil Engineers, Urban Drainage Standards Committee et al., *Standard Guidelines for the Design of Urban Stormwater Systems* (ASCE/EWRI 45-05); *Standard Guidelines for the Installation of Urban Stormwater Systems* (ASCE/EWRI 46-05); *Standard Guidelines for the Operation and Maintenance of Urban Stormwater Systems* (ASCE/EWRI 47-05). Reston, VA, American Society of Civil Engineers, 2006.

Bernhardt, E.S., and M.A. Palmer, "Restoring Streams in an Urbanizing World." *Freshwater Biology* 52(4):738-751.

Booth, D.B., J. R. Karr, S. Schauman, C.P. Konrad, S.A. Morley, M.G. Larson, and S.J. Burges, "Reviving Urban Streams: Land Use, Hydrology, Biology, and Human Behavior." *Journal of the American Water Resources Association* 40(5):1351-1364.

Coffman L., *Low-impact Development Manual*, Prince Georges County, Maryland Department of Environmental Resource, 2000.

Doll, B.A., G. L. Grabow, K.R. Hall, J.H. Halley, W.A. Harman, G.D. Jennings, and D.E. Wise, *Stream Restoration: A Natural Channel Design Handbook*. Raleigh: North Carolina State University, 2003.

Dunnett, Nigel and A. Clayden, *Rain Gardens: Managing Water Sustainably in the Garden and Designed Landscape.* Portland, OR: Timber Press, 2007.

Ferguson, B., *Porous Pavements.* Boca Raton, FL: CRC Press, 2005.

Ferguson, B. and Debo, T., *On-site Stormwater Management* (2nd ed.). New York: Van Nostrand Reinhold, 1990.

Ferguson, B.K. *Introduction to Stormwater: Concept, Purpose, Design.* New York: John Wiley and Sons, 1998.

Graham, P., L. Maclean, D. Medina, A. Patwardhan and G. Vasarhelyi, "The Role of Water Balance Modeling in the Transition to Low Impact Development." *Water Quality Research Journal of Canada* 39(4):331–342.

Smart, P. HydroCAD Stormwater Modeling System. Tamworth, NH: HydroCAD Software Solutions LLC, 2010.

Onsite Wastewater Treatment Resources

Kadlec, Robert and Wallace, Scott, *Treatment Wetlands* (2nd ed.). Boca Raton, FL: CRC Press, 2008.

Steinfeld, Carol and David Del Porto. 2007. *Reusing the Resource: Adventures in Ecological Wastewater Recycling.* New Bedford, MA: Ecowaters, 2007.

U.S. Environmental Protection Agency. *Onsite Wastewater Treatment Systems Manual.* www.epa.gov/nrmrl/pubs/625r00008/html/625R00008.htm, 2002.

Wallace, S.D. and R.L. Knight, *Small Scale Constructed Wetland Treatment Systems: Feasibility, Design Criteria and O&M Requirements.* Alexandria, VA: Water Environment Research Foundation, 2006.

Water Conservation Resources

U.S. Environmental Protection Agency, "Water Sense," www.epa.gov/WaterSense/.

U.S. Environmental Protection Agency, "WaterSense Landscape Water Budget Tool," http://water.epa.gov/action/waterefficiency/watersense/spaces/water_budget_tool.cfm, 2009.

American Rainwater Catchment Systems Association, www.arcsa.org/.

On-line Rainwater Harvesting Community, www.harvesth2o.com/.

Water Budgeting Technical Paper, www.greenco.org/downloadables/Water%20Budgeting.pdf.

Water Reuse Association, .www.watereuse.org/association.

Rainwater Harvesting Books, www.harvestingrainwater.com/.

Graywater Harvesting Books, http://oasisdesign.net/.

American Society of Irrigation Consultants, www.asic.org/.

Irrigation Association, www.irrigation.org/.

U.S. Department of the Interior, Bureau of Reclamation, Lower Colorado Region, Southern California Area Office. 2007. "Weather and Soil Moisture-Based Landscape Irrigation Scheduling Devices" Technical Review Report (2nd ed.).

The Irrigation Water Management Society, www.iwms.org/.

CHAPTER 4 SITE DESIGN: VEGETATION SYSTEMS

Vegetation and Ecosystem Services

Natural Resources Conservation Service, "Windbreaks," www.nrcs.usda.gov/TECHNICAL/ECS/forest/wind/windbreaks.html.

National Renewable Energy Laboratory "Landscaping for Energy Efficiency" www.nrel.gov/docs/legosti/old/16632.pdf.

USDA Forest Service, Pacific Southwest Research Station, Community Tree Guides and Tree Carbon Calculator, www.fs.fed.us/psw/programs/uesd/uep/.

U.S. Department of Energy, "Landscaping," www.energysavers.gov/your_home/landscaping/index.cfm/mytopic=11910.

U.S. Environmental Protection Agency, "Heat Island: Heat Island Mitigation Strategies," www.epa.gov/heatisld/mitigation/index.htm.

Lawrence Berkeley National Laboratory, Heat Island Group, http://heatisland.lbl.gov/.

Reed, Sue, *Energy-Wise Landscape Design: A New Approach for Your Home and Garden.* Gabriola Island, BC: New Society Publishers, 2010.

Sustainable Plant Production

National Sustainable Agriculture Information Service, National Center for Appropriate Technology, Sustainable Small-Scale Nursery Production, https://attra.ncat.org/attra-pub/nursery.html.

Sustainable Planting Design and Management

USDA Natural Resources Conservation Service Plants Database, Invasive and Noxious Weeds Lists, http://plants.usda.gov/java/.

Nature Conservancy, Global Invasive Species Team, http://tncinvasives.ucdavis.edu/.

University of Connecticut: Plant Database, www.hort.uconn.edu/plants/.

Lady Bird Johnson Wildflower Center, Native Plant Database, www.wildflower.org/plants/.

North American Native Plant Society (NANPS), Plant Database, www.nanps.org/plant/plantlist.aspx.

NatureServe website, U.S. Invasive Species www.natureserve.org/consIssues/invasivespecies.jsp.

The National Invasive Species Council (NISC) www.invasivespeciesinfo.gov/council/main.shtml.

Center for Plant Conservation, www.centerforplantconservation.org/.

Center for Invasive Plant Management, www.weedcenter.org/.

Urban Horticulture Institute, Cornell University, www.hort.cornell.edu/uhi/.

American Forests, www.americanforests.org/.

Trowbridge, P.J., and N.L. Bassuk, *Trees in the Urban Landscape: Site Assessment, Design, and Installation.* Hoboken, NJ: John Wiley and Sons, 2004.

Urban, James. 2008. *Up by Roots: Healthy Soils and Trees in the Built Environment.* Champaign, IL: International Society of Arboriculture.

Vegetation for Green Roofs and Living Walls

Green Roofs for Healthy Cities, www.greenroofs.org/.

International Green Roof Association,www.igra-world.com/.

Greenroofs.com, Greenroof and Greenwall Projects Database, www.greenroofs.com/projects.

Dunnett, Nigel and Noel Kingsbury, *Planting Green Roofs and Living Walls.* Portland, OR: Timber Press, 2008.

Vegetation and Urban Agriculture

American Community Gardening Association, www.communitygarden.org/.

U.S. Department of Agriculture, National Agricultural Library, Urban Agriculture, http://afsic.nal.usda.gov/.

National Sustainable Agriculture Information Service, National Center for Appropriate Technology, https://attra.ncat.org/.

Wildlife Habitat

National Wildlife Federation, Wildlife Habitat Program www.nwf.org/.

Natural Resources Conservation Service, U.S. Department of Agriculture, Wildlife Habitat,www.nrcs.usda.gov/programs/whip/.

Wildlife Habitat Resources, Natural Resources Conservation Service, U.S. Department of Agriculture www.nrcs.usda.gov/FEATURE/backyard/wildhab.html.

Conservation Buffers: Design Guidelines for Buffers, Corridors, and Greenways, U.S. Department of Agriculture, National Agroforestry Center www.unl.edu/nac/bufferguidelines/.

Firewise Landscapes

National Fire Protection Association, Firewise Communities resources, www.firewise.org/.

The Fire Safe Council. www.firesafecouncil.org/.

Barkley, Y., C. Schnepf, and J. Cohen, *Protecting and Landscaping Homes in the Wildland/ Urban Interface.* Moscow, ID: Idaho Forest, Wildlife and Range Experiment Station, 2004.

Brzuszek, R.F., and J.B. Walker. "Trends in Community Fire Ordinances and Their Effects on Landscape Architecture Practice" *Landscape Journal* 27, no.1 (2008): pp. 142–153.

Safer from the Start: A Guide to Firewise Friendly Developments. Quincy, MA: National Fire Protection Association and the USDA Forest Service, 2009.

Ecological Restoration

The Society for Ecological Restoration, www.ser.org.

Clewell, Andre F. and James Aronson, *Ecological Restoration: Principles, Values, and Structure of an Emerging Profession.* Washington, DC: Island Press, 2008.

Egan, Dave, Evan E. Hjerpe, Jesse Abrams and Eric Higgs, *Human Dimensions of Ecological Restoration: Integrating Science, Nature, and Culture* Washington, DC: Island Press, 2011.

Tongway, David J. and John A. Ludwig, *Restoring Disturbed Landscapes: Putting Principles into Practice.* Washington, DC: Island Press, 2010.

CHAPTER 5 SITE DESIGN: SOILS

General

Trowbridge, P., and N. Bassuk, *Trees in the Urban Landscape: Site Assessment, Design and Installation.* Hoboken, NJ: John Wiley and Sons, 2004.

Gugino, B.K., O.J. Idowu, R.R. Schindelbeck, H.M. van Es, D.W. Wolfe, J.E. Moebius-Clune, J.E. Thies, and G.S. Abawi, "Cornell Soil Health Assessment Training Manual," Edition 2.0. Cornell University, College of Agriculture and Life Sciences, 2009.

Brady, N.C., *The Nature and Properties of Soils* (10th ed.). New York: Macmillan, 1990.

Craul, Timothy A. and Phillip J. Craul, *Soil Design Protocols for Landscape Architects and Contractors.* Hoboken, NJ: John Wiley and Sons, 2006.

Urban, James, *Up by Roots.* Champaign, IL: International Society for Arboriculture, 2008.

Soil and Site Assessment

U.S. Geological Survey, Earth Resources Observation and Science Center (EROS), http://eros.usgs.gov/.

Environmental Systems Research Institute (ESRI,) www.esri.com/.

Geospatial One Stop, www.geodata.gov.

U.S. Fish and Wildlife Geospatial Services, www.fws.gov/GIS/index.htm.

U.S. Environmental Protection Agency, Regional Environmental Information, http://water.epa.gov/type/location/regions/.

U.S. Environmental Protection Agency, *Surf Your Watershed,* http://cfpub.epa.gov/surf/locate/index.cfm.

U.S. Department of Agriculture, The Cooperative Extension System, www.csrees.usda.gov/Extension/.

National Center for Appropriate Technology (NCAT), National Sustainable Agriculture Information Service, https://attra.ncat.org/.

Cornell University pH test kit http://cnal.cals.cornell.edu/.

University of Massachusetts, Soil and Plant Tissue Testing Laboratory, www.umass.edu/soiltest/.

Primal Seeds, Nutrient Chart, www.primalseeds.org/nutrients.htm.

University of Minnesota, Sustainable Urban Landscape Information Series, www.sustland.umn.edu/.

CHAPTER 6 SITE DESIGN: MATERIALS AND RESOURCES

General

Building Green, GreenSpec® Product Guide, www.buildinggreen.com.

Healthy Building Network, www.healthybuilding.net/.

Pharos Project, www.pharosproject.net/.

The Athena Institute, www.athenasmi.org/about/index.html.

National Renewable Energy Laboratory (NREL), U.S. Lifecycle Inventory Database www.nrel.gov/lci/.

U.S. Environmental Protection Agency, Air Toxics Website, Hazardous Air Pollutants per Clean Air Act, Code of Federal Regulations at 40 CFR 61.01, www.epa.gov/ttn/atw/orig189.html.

U.S. Environmental Protection Agency,Water: Clean Water Act, Toxic and Priority Pollutants, http://water.epa.gov/scitech/methods/cwa/pollutants-background.cfm.

U.S. Environmental Protection Agency,Wastes: Resource Conservation and Recovery Act (RCRA) Information Resources, www.epa.gov/epawaste/inforesources/online/index.htm.

Center for Resource Solutions (CRS), Green-e products certification www.green-e.org/.

Whole Building Design Guide, National Institute of Building Sciences, Construction Waste Management, www.wbdg.org/.

Calkins, Meg, *Materials for Sustainable Sites.* Hoboken, NJ: John Wiley and Sons, 2008.

Hammond, G., and C. Jones, "Inventory of Carbon and Energy," Version 2.0, Bath, UK: University of Bath, Department of Mechanical Engineering, 2011.

Lippiatt, Barbara C., *BEES 4.0: Building for Environmental and Economic Sustainability Technical Manual and User Guide.* Gaithersburg, MD: National Institute of Standards and Technology, 2007.

Resource Conservation

Addis, B., *Building with Reclaimed Components and Materials: A Design Handbook for Reuse and Recycling.* London: Earthscan, 2006.

Guy, B., and N. Ciamrimboli, *Design for Disassembly in the Built Environment: A Guide to Closed-Loop Design and Building.* University Park, PA: Hamer Center for Community Design, The Pennsylvania State University, 2007.

Building Materials Reuse Association (BMRA), www.bmra.org/.

Habitat for Humanity ReStores, www.habitat.org/restores/.

California Integrated Waste Management Board (CIWMB), www.calrecycle.ca.gov/.

Recycler's World, www.recycle.net/.

U.S. Environmental Protection Agency, Resource Conservation, Construction & Demolition Materials www.epa.gov/osw/conserve/rrr/imr/cdm/reuse.htm.

Construction Waste Management Database. Whole Building Design Guide. National Institute of Building Sciences, www.wbdg.org/tools/cwm.php?s=PA.

Construction Materials Recycling Association www.cdrecycling.org/

U.S. Environmental Protection Agency, Comprehensive Procurement Guidelines (CPG) www.epa.gov/osw/conserve/tools/cpg/index.htm.

California Integrated Waste Management Board (CIWMB) Recycled Content Product Directory.

Earth Construction Resources

Elizabeth, Lynne and Cassandra Adams, *Alternative Construction: Contemporary Natural Building Methods.* New York: John Wiley and Sons, 2005.

Houben, H., and H. Guillard, *Earth Construction: A Comprehensive Guide.* London: Intermediate Technology Publications, 1994.

McHenry, P. G., *Adobe and Rammed Earth Buildings.* Tucson: University of Arizona Press, 1984.

Heat Island Resources

U.S. Environmental Protection Agency, Heat Island: Heat Island Mitigation Strategies, www.epa.gov/heatisld/mitigation/index.htm.

Lawrence Berkeley National Laboratory, Heat Island Group, http://heatisland.lbl.gov/.

Wood Resources

Forest Stewardship Council www.fsc.org/.

IUCN Red List of Threatened Species, searchable by species, www.iucnredlist.org/.

CITES, online searchable species database, www.cites.org/eng/resources/species.html.

Site Lighting Resources

International Dark Sky Association (IDA) www.darksky.org/

Dark Sky Society www.darkskysociety.org.

CHAPTER 7 HUMAN HEALTH AND WELL-BEING FOR SUSTAINABLE SITES

Sustainability Awareness

National Association for Interpretation. www.interpnet.com/.

North American Association for Environmental Education, www.naaee.org/.

Beck, L., and T. Cable. *Interpretation for the 21st Century: Fifteen Guiding Principles for Interpreting Nature and Culture.* Champaign, IL: Sagamore Publishing, 2002.

Gross, M., R. Zimmerman, and J. Bucholz, *Signs, Trails, and Way-side Exhibits: Connecting People to Places.* 3rd ed. Interpreter's Handbook Series. University of Wisconsin- Stevens Point Foundation Press, 2006, www.uwsp.edu/cnr/Schmeeckle/Handbooks/.

Social Equality

Community Benefits Agreements, The Partnership for Working Families, http://communitybenefits.org/search.php.

Land Trust Alliance, www.landtrustalliance.org/.

Living wage calculator, www.livingwage.geog.psu.edu/.

Green collar jobs, www.greenforall.org/green-collar-jobs.

National Charrette Institute, Project for Public Spaces, www.charretteinstitute.org/.

Hester, R. T., Jr., *Community Design Primer.* Mendocino, CA: Ridge Times Press, 1990.

Kaplan, R., S. Kaplan, and R.L. Ryan, *With People in Mind: Design and Management of Everyday Nature.* Washington, DC: Island Press, 1998.

Lennertz, B., and A. Lutzenhiser. *The Charrette Handbook: The Essential Guide for Accelerated, Collaborative Community Planning.* Chicago: American Planning Association, 2006.

Sanoff, H., *Community Participation Methods in Design and Planning.* New York: John Wiley and Sons, 1999.

Site Accessibility

Americans with Disabilities Accessibility Guidelines (ADAAG), www.acess-board.gov/adaag/about.

The Center for Universal Design, www.design.ncsu.edu/cud.

Universal Design Symbols: www.aiga.org/content.cfm/symbol-signs.

Preiser, Wolfgang F.E., and Elaine Ostroff (eds.), *Universal Design Handbook.* New York: McGraw-Hill, 2001.

Site Wayfinding

Arthur, P., and R. Passini, *Wayfinding: People Signs and Architecture.* New York: McGraw-Hill, 1992.

Gibson, David, *The Wayfinding Handbook: Information Design for Public Places.* Princeton, NJ: Princeton Architectural Press, 2009.

Golledge, Reginald G. (ed.), *Wayfinding Behavior: Cognitive Mapping and Other Spatial Processes.* Baltimore: Johns Hopkins University Press, 1999.

Kaplan, R., S. Kaplan, and R.L. Ryan, *With People in Mind: Design and Management of Everyday Nature.* Washington, DC: Island Press, 1998.

Monmonier, Mark. 1996. *How to Lie with Maps.* Chicago: University of Chicago Press.

Site Safety

International Crime Prevention through Environmental Design (CPTED) Association www.cpted.net/.

Illuminating Engineering Society (IES), www.iesna.org/.

Newman, O., *Creating Defensible Space.* Washington, DC: U.S. Department of Housing and Urban Development, Office of Policy Development and Research, 1996.

Michael, S.E., and R.B. Hull, IV, "Effects of Vegetation on Crime in Urban Parks Blacksburg, VA," Virginia Polytechnic Institute & State University, Department of Forestry, 1994.

Design for Physical Activity

Active Living by Design www.activelivingbydesign.org/.

Centers for Disease Control and Prevention, Healthier Worksite Initiative, Walkability Audit Tool www.cdc.gov/nccdphp/dnpao/hwi/toolkits/walkability/audit_tool.htm.

National Center for Bicycling and Walking, *Increasing Physical Activity through Community DesignA Guide for Public Health Practitioners.* Washington, DC: National Center for Bicycling and Walking, 2010.

American Association of State Highway and Transportation Officials (AASHTO). Design GuidanceAccommodating Bicycle and Pedestrian Travel: A Recommended Approach *www.fhwa.dot.gov/environment/bikeped/design.htm.*

Restorative Settings

Cooper-Marcus, C., and Marni Barnes (eds.), *Healing Gardens: Therapeutic Benefits and Design Recommendations.* New York: John Wiley and Sons, 1999.

Gerlach-Spriggs, Nancy, Richard Enoch Kaufman, and Sam Bass Warner, Jr., *Restorative Gardens: The Healing Landscape.* New Haven, CT:Yale University Press. 1998.

Kaplan, R., S. Kaplan, and R.L. Ryan, *With People in Mind: Design and Management of Everyday Nature.* Washington, DC: Island Press, 1998.

American Horticultural Therapy Association, www.ahta.org/.

Therapeutic Landscapes Network, www.healinglandscapes.org/.

Wiesen, Anne, and Lindsay Campbell, *Restorative Commons: Creating Health and Well-Being through Urban Landscapes.* Newtown Square, PA: USDA Forest Service, 2009.

Design for Social Interaction and Community Building

Project for Public Spaces www.pps.org/.

Cooper-Marcus, C., and C. Francis, *People Places: Design Guidelines for Urban Open Space* (2nd ed.). New York: John Wiley and Sons, 1998.

Gehl, Jan, and Lars Gemzøe, *Public Spaces, Public Life.* Copenhagen: Danish Architectural Press, 1996.

Whyte, William H., *The Social Life of Small Urban Spaces.* Washington, DC: Conservation Foundation, 1980.

Preserving Historic and Cultural Features

Cultural Landscape Foundation, http://tclf.org/.

National Park Service, Historical American Landscapes Survey (HALS), www.nps.gov/hdp/hals/index.htm.

National Trust for Historic Preservation, www.preservationnation.org/.

Secretary of the Interior's Standards for Treatment of Historic Properties www.cr.nps.gov/hps/tps/standguide/.

National Historic Landmarks, www.nps.gov/history/nhl/QA.htm#2.

Birnbaum, Charles A., *National Park Service's Historic Landscape InitiativeProtecting Cultural Landscapes Planning, Treatment and Management of Historic Landscapes,* www.nps.gov/history/hps/TPS/briefs/brief36.htm, 1994.

CHAPTER 8 OPERATIONS, MAINTENANCE, MONITORING, AND STEWARDSHIP

General

VanDerZanden, Ann-Marie and Thomas W. Cook, *Sustainable Landscape Management: Design, Construction, and Maintenance.* Hoboken, NJ: John Wiley and Sons, 2010.

Site Waste Recycling

U.S. Environmental Protection Agency, WastesWastewiseWaste Assessments Approaches, www.epa.gov/osw/partnerships/wastewise/approach.htm.

U.S. Environmental Protection Agency, WastesResource ConservationReduce, Reuse, RecycleGreenScapes Program, www.epa.gov/epawaste/conserve/rrr/greenscapes/index.htm.

California Department of Resources Recycling and Recovery (CalRecycle) www.calrecycle .ca.gov/.

Biocycle Magazine, www.jgpress.com/biocycle.htm.

Cornell Waste Management Institute, http://cwmi.css.cornell.edu/.

Nourishing Soil

U.S. Composting Council, http://compostingcouncil.org/; *Field Guide to Compost Use,* http://compostingcouncil.org/admin/wp-content/plugins/wp-pdfupload/pdf/1330/Field_ Guide_to_Compost_Use.pdf.

Washington Department of the Environment, *Building Soil: Guidelines and Resources for Implementing Soil Quality and Depth BMPT5.13 in WDOE Stormwater Management Manual for Western Washington,* www.buildingsoil.org/tools/Soil_BMP_Manual.pdf.

Integrated Pest Management

U.S. Department of Agriculture, State Extension Services, www.csrees.usda.gov/.

IPM World Textbook, University of Minnesota, http://ipmworld.umn.edu/.

U.S. Environmental Protection Agency fact sheets: PestWise and Landscaping Initiative, www.epa.gov/pesp/htmlpublications/landscaping_brochure.html.

Controlling and Managing Invasive Plants

USDA Natural Resources Conservation Service Plants Database, Invasive and Noxious Weeds http://plants.usda.gov/java/noxiousDriver.

Center for Invasive Plant Management, www.weedcenter.org/.

Maintenance Equipment

U.S. Environmental Protection Agency Office of Mobile Sources resources, including "Your Yard and Clean Air" (EPA-420-F-94-002), www.epa.gov/oms/consumer/19-yard.pdf.

U.S. Environmental Protection Agency Office of Transportation and Air Quality, "Proposed Emission Standards for New Nonroad Spark-Ignition Engines, Equipment, and Vessels" (EPA420-F-07-032), April 2007, www.epa.gov/nonroad/marinesi-equipld/420f07032.pdf.

U.S. Department of Energy Alternative Fuels and Advanced Vehicles Data Center www.afdc. energy.gov/afdc/.

Maintaining Bioretention Facilities

U.S. Environmental Protection Agency, "Storm Water Technology Fact Sheet: Bioretention" (EPA 832-F-99–012). Washington, DC: U.S. EPA Office of Water, 1999.

Hunt, W.F., and W.G. Lord, *Bioretention Performance, Design, Construction, and Maintenance.* North Carolina Cooperative Extension Service, 2006.

Bitter, S.D., and J.K. Bowers, "Bioretention as a Water Quality Best Management Practice." Article 110, Technical Note #29 from *Watershed Protection Techniques* 1(3) (1994): 114–116.

Bioretention Manual. Prince George's County, MD: Environmental Services Division, Department of Environmental Resources, 2007, www.princegeorgescountymd.gov/der/esg/bioretention/bioretention.asp.

"Low Impact Development Urban Design ToolsBioretention Maintenance," www.lid-stormwater.net/bio_maintain.htm.

Anderson, James L. and John S. Gulliver (eds.), *Assessment of Stormwater Best Management Practices.* Minneapolis: University of Minnesota, 2008, http://wrc.umn.edu/randpe/sandw/bmpassessment/index.htm.

Maintaining Green Roofs and Green Walls

"Green Roofs for Healthy Cities," www.greenroofs.org/.

Dunnett, Nigel and Noel Kingsbury, *Planting Green Roofs and Living Walls.* Portland, OR: Timber Press, 2008.

ASTM E240006, "Standard Guide for Selection, Installation, and Maintenance of Plants for Green Roof Systems." West Conshohocken, PA: ASTM International.

Maintaining Pavements

U.S. Environmental Protection Agency. 1999. *Storm Water Technology Fact Sheet: Porous Pavement* (EPA 832-F-99–023). Washington, DC: U.S. EPA Office of Water, 1999, www.epa.gov/npdes/pubs/porouspa.pdf.

Bean, E.Z., and W.F. Hunt. "NC State University Permeable Pavement Research: Water Quality, Water Quantity, and Clogging." *North Carolina State University Water Quality Group Newsletter*, No. 119 (November 2005).

Low Impact Development Urban Design ToolsPermeable Pavers Maintenance, www.lid-stormwater.net/permpavers_benefits.htm.

Stormwater Manager's Resource Center fact sheets, www.stormwatercenter.net; "Stormwater Management Fact Sheet: Porous Pavement," www.stormwatercenter.net/Assorted%20Fact%20Sheets/Tool6_Stormwater_Practices/Infiltration%20Practice/Porous%20Pavement.htm.

INDEX

NOTE: Page references in *italics* refer to illustrations.

A

accessibility, of site, *445*, 445–448, *447, 448, 449*

action threshold, establishing, 494–495

aesthetics, designing for, 15, *15, 16*, 102–103, *103*, 464–465. *See also* human health impact

aggregates (construction material), 398, *399, 400*

aggregate stability (soil), *275*

air quality
impact of materials and resources on, 331–334, *332–334*
National Ambient Air Quality Standards (EPA), 505
vegetation and, 206
VOCs, 390

albedo, 391–392

American Society of Landscape Architects, 2, 23–24, *25*, 62

aquatard, 90

asphalt, *335*, 401, *402*

ASTM. *See* standards

awareness. *See* education

B

bag filters, *183*

base flow, 71

berms, 311

Best Available Technique Not Entailing Excessive Cost (BATNEEC), 365

bikeways, 460, *460*

bio-based materials, 413, *414, 415*

Biomass Density Index (BDI), 204

biomimicry, 11–12, 165

bioremediation, *212*, 212–213

bioretention systems
design approaches, 123–127, *125, 126*
maintenance, 506–509, *507, 508, 509*
sizing, 92–93

bioswales, *132*, 132–136, *133, 134, 135*

Birnbaum, Charles A., 470

"borrowing" views, 463

Bowling Alone (Putnam), 430

brick masonry, 403, *403–404*

"broken windows" syndrome, 456–457

brownfields
site selection, 34, 35–36
soil replacement, 310
vegetation, 199

Brundtland Report, Our Common Future (U.N.W.C.E.D.), 2, 17, 429

building protection zone, 501–504, *502, 504*

bulk density (dry density), 276, 277–278, *278*

C

Calkins, Meg, 27–30

carbon
air quality and vegetation, 206
carbonaceous biological oxygen demand (CBOD), *170*
carbon sequestration, 206
embodied carbon (EC), 338–344, *339–343*
impact, 337
inputs to organic carbon in soil, *274*
understanding carbon cycle in soil, *273*

cartridge filters, *184*

cation exchange capacity (CEC), *252*, 287, 292–293

certification systems, materials and resources, 355, *355–357*, 418–421, *419*

chlorides, 89

cisterns
aboveground, *112, 113*
belowground, *113*, 165, *165*
maintenance of, 514
water conservation, *153*, 154
See also stormwater

clays. *See* soil

Clean Water Act (CWA), 40, 46, 48, 67, 393

closed-loop systems
defined, 17
materials and resources, 324, 327, 348, 360–361, 374

color coding, 452

combined sewer overflow (CSO) event, 166

comfort, designing for, *447*, 447–448

community involvement
designing for, 55, 466–470, *467, 468, 469*
human health impact and, 432–433, *433*, 440–442, *441, 442*
stakeholder engagement, 20
vegetation for food, 233–236, *234, 235*

compaction, soil, 276, *276, 277*, 278–279, *303*, 303–304, *304*, 317

compost
compost blankets, 106–107, *107, 108*
maintenance and, 487, 488–493, *489, 490, 491, 492, 493*
See also reuse

Comprehensive Procurement Guidelines (EPA), 386–387, *387–389*

concrete, 396, *397*

concrete tanks, *173*

conservation (water), 148–166
efficient irrigation, 157–162, *158, 160, 161*
feature efficiency, 162–166, *164, 165*
reuse and recycling, *149*, 149–157, *151, 153, 154, 155, 156*
See also water systems

constructed wetlands, for wastewater treatment, 174–175, *175*, 176, *177*, 177–178

construction and demolition (C&D) debris. *See* deconstruction

Construction Ecology, 11–12

construction materials. *See* materials and resources

contaminants, in soil, 287–288, 294–295

Convention on International Trade in Endangered Species (CITES), 420

core samplers (soil), *279*

crime, site safety and, 454–457, *457*

Crime Prevention through Environmental Design (CPTED), 454, 457

criteria air pollutants (CAPs), 334

cultural issues
ecosystem services, 3–5, 15
human health impact, 470–475, *472, 473, 475*
site inventory, 52–53
sustainable site design and operation, 23

culverts, 144–145, *145*

D

data collection (soil)
designing sampling and data-collection scheme, *261*, 261–265, *263*
mapping and planning, 258–260, *260*

Decision Tree, *220*

deconstruction, 368–377
benefits and challenges, *370–371*
construction and demolition (C&D) debris, 368–369, *369*
design for, *373*, 373–374, *374–375, 376, 377*
strategies and site inventory, 372, *372*

"defensible space," 454, 456

de-icing salt, 509, 518–519

Denver Water Utility, on xeriscaping, 217

design and management processes
developing maintenance and management plans, 483–484 (*See also* maintenance)
economic services as basis for design, 1–2, 7–8
integrating soil into, 249–251
for sustainable sites, 18–20, *19*
team development and planning strategies, 54–57, *57* (*See also* predesign)
See also human health impact

design landscape water requirements (DLWR), 159–160, *160, 161*

dry combustion (soil), *272*

durability, of sites/structures, *366*, 366–368, *367*

Dutch elm disease (DED), 226

E

earthen materials, 404–405, *405, 406*

ecological restoration, 240–243

eco-revelatory design, 436

ecosystem services, 1–32

  attributes of sustainable sites, *13,* 13–17, *14, 15, 16, 18*

  as basis for design, 1–2, 7–8

  defined, 3–5

  design and management processes for, 18–20, *19*

  economic value of, 6–7

  ecosystems in nature, 12

  function of, *5*

  goals for, 20–22, *22–23*

  by landscape type, *4*

  Leadership in Energy and Environmental Design (LEED), 14, 26–27

  learning from natural systems, 11–12

  sustainable design, defined, 2–3

  The Sustainable Sites Handbook (Calkins) on, 27–30

  triple bottom line and, 3, *3*

  in urban settings, *8, 9,* 9–10, *11*

  vegetation and, 202–213, *203, 205, 207, 208, 209, 210, 211, 212*

  See also human health impact; materials and resources; soil; Sustainable Sites Initiative™ (SITES™); vegetation; water systems

education

  human health and awareness, *436,* 436–440, *438, 439*

  learning from natural systems, 11–12

  stormwater design and, 97–98, *98*

efficient irrigation systems, 157–162, *158, 160, 161*

egress, options for, 456

electrical conductivity (EC) measurements, 293, *294*

embodied carbon (EC), 338–339, *339–343*

enclosures, planning, 463

Endangered Species Act (ESA), 41

energy

  embodied energy (EE) of materials and products, *337,* 337–344, *338, 339–343*

  energy value of onsite wastewater treatment, 189–190

  renewable, 336

  site inventory, 44

  sustainable site design and operation, *23*

  vegetation for energy conservation, *209,* 209–210, *210, 211*

  See also materials and resources

erosion control

  soil management, 318–319

  stormwater design approaches, 145–147, *146, 147*

evaporation, defined, 71

evapotranspiration, 76

  defined, 71

  mitigating runoff by, 119–129, *120, 121, 122, 125, 126, 128*

evidence-based design approach, 432

excess runoff, 71

Exotic Pest Plant Councils (EPPCs), 219

"eyes on the street," 455

F

farmland, 38–39

fencing, 317

fertilizing (soil), 306–307, *307*

fiberglass tanks, *173*

filtration (water), *155,* 155–157, *156. See also* onsite wastewater treatment

fine mesh screens, *184*

fire prevention, 238–240, *239, 501,* 501–504, *502, 504*

first flush, 71

Flood Control Act (1960), 39

floodplains

  site selection, 39

  stormwater design, 142–144, *143*

flow models, stormwater, *77, 78*

flow rates, 81–82

food

  composting food scrap, 487, *490,* 490–491, *491, 492, 493 (See also* reuse)

  designing for vendors and markets, 469, *469*

  sustainable planting for, 233–236, *234, 235, 236*

Forest Stewardship Council (FSC)-certified wood, 420

Francis, Marc, 430

"full cut off" lighting fixtures, *424*

G

gabion retaining walls, *364*

gardening, 461

gateways, *450,* 450–451

genotype, restoration and, 241–242

geographic information systems (GIS), 54

grayfields
  site selection, 34, 37
  vegetation and, 199

greenfields, site selection, 37–38

green rating certification programs. *See* Leadership in Energy and Environmental Design (LEED); Sustainable Sites Initiative™ (SITES™)

green roofs. *See* roof systems

green walls, 232–233, 510–511, *511, 512*

groundwater
  contamination, 87–90, *88–89*
  recharge, 71
  Guidelines and Performance Benchmarks (Sustainable Sites Initiative), 2, 24, *25*
  soil, 249

H

Habitat Suitability Index (HIS) (U.S. Fish and Wildlife Services), 237

hazardous air pollutants (HAPs), 334

hazardous waste, 336. *See also* waste management

heat island reduction, 207, *207–208,* 390–393, *392, 393, 394–395*

Historic American Landscapes Survey (National Park Service), 471

historic features, 470–475, *472, 473, 475*

horizons, soil, *253,* 253–254

human health impact, 429–478
  assessing site's social setting, 432–435, *433, 434*
  community building, 466–470, *467, 468, 469*
  education, *436,* 436–440, *438, 439*
  historic and cultural features, 470–475, *472, 473, 475*
  maintenance and, 480, *480–481,* 504–505, *505, 506*
  material safety data sheets, 345
  materials and resources, 344–355, *345–346, 350–354, 355–357*
  physical activity, 458–462, *460, 461*
  research, 429–432
  restorative settings, 462–464, *463, 464*

safety, 454–457, *457*

site accessibility, *445,* 445–448, *447, 448, 449*

site lighting, 421–422, *422, 423, 424, 425,* 456

site safety, 454–457, *457*

site wayfinding, 449–453, *450, 451, 452, 453*

social equality in site development/construction/ use, 440–444, *441, 442, 444*

stormwater design amenities, 100, *100*

stormwater management, 81–82

The Sustainable Sites Initiative: Guidelines and Performance Benchmarks 2009, 481

vegetation and, *197,* 197–198, 461

See also materials and resources

"human-shed" context, 433, *433*

hydrology, site inventory, 45–48

I

impervious surfaces, reducing, 105–106

infiltration, 71, 76
  enhanced infiltration basins/trenches, *128,* 128–129
  mitigating runoff by, 119–129, *120, 121, 122, 125, 126, 128*
  sizing infiltration systems, 93–94
  See also stormwater

initial filtration, 155

integrated pest management, 221, 493–497, *496, 497*

intermittent sand filters (ISF), 178

International Union for the Conservation of Nature (IUCN), 421

interveinal chicrosis (trees), *256*

invasive plant species, 218–223, *219, 220, 221, 222, 223,* 497–500, *499*

inventory. *See* site assessment

irrigation
  efficient, 157–162, *158, 160, 161*
  onsite wastewater treatment, 188

J

Jackson, J. B., 474

Jacobs, Jane, 454

K

Kaplan, Rachel, 429

Kaplan, Stephen, 429

Kibert, Charles, 11–12

Kuo, Francis, 430

L

labels, materials and resources, 355, *355–357*

Lady Bird Johnson Wildflower Center, University of Texas at Austin, 2, 23–24, *25, 154*

LaGro, J. A., 34

landmarks, site, *451,* 451–452, *452*

landscape trimmings, 487, 488–493, *489, 490, 491, 492, 493*

land-use history
  soil assessment, 254, *255*
  stormwater and natural water cycle, *72*

Last Child in the Woods (Louv), 458

Leadership in Energy and Environmental Design (LEED), 14, 26–27

level spreaders, 136–138, *137, 138*

lifecycle, of construction materials/products, 327–331

lifecycle assessment (LCA), 348–349, *354*

lighting, 421–422, *422, 423, 424, 425,* 456

Living Building Challenge (LBC), 347

living machine (LM) waster treatment systems, *193,* 193–194, *194, 195*

location. *See* site selection

Loss on Ignition (LOI), *271*

Louv, Richard, 458

Lynch, Kevin, 452

M

maintenance, 479–520
  anticipating, 482
  bioretention features, 506–509, *507, 508, 509*
  developing plans for, 483–484
  environmental and human health impact of, 480, *480–481*
  equipment used for, 504–505, *505, 506*
  fire prevention, *501,* 501–504, *502, 504*
  of green roofs and green walls, 510–511, *511, 512*
  human health impact and, 443–444, *444,* 448, 453, 461–462, 465, 469–470, 474–475
  integrated pest management, 493–497, *496, 497*
  intensity, *483*
  invasive plant control, 497–500, *499*
  monitoring and stewardship, 519–520
  nourishing soil with sustainable amendments, *491,* 491–493, *492, 493*
  of pavement, 516–519, *517, 518, 519*

postoccupancy management/monitoring, 20
  recycling waste from operations and, *485,* 485–491, *487, 489, 490*
  of water features, 512–515, *513, 514, 515*

maps. *See* data collection (soil)

material safety data sheets, 345

materials and resources, 323–428
  aggregates and stone, *337,* 398, *399, 400*
  asphalt, *335,* 401, *402*
  bio-based, 413, *414, 415*
  brick masonry, 403, *403–404*
  concrete, 396, *397*
  earthen materials, 404–405, *405, 406*
  efficiency, *360,* 360–364, *361–363, 364,* 365
  efficiency, deconstruction, 368–377, *369, 370–371, 372, 373, 374–375, 376, 377*
  efficiency, durability, *366,* 366–368, *367, 368*
  efficiency, recycled content, 385–390, *387–389*
  efficiency, reprocessed materials, 383, *383–384, 385*
  efficiency, reuse, *378,* 378–382, *380, 382*
  efficiency, waste management, 365
  environmental impact, 331–344, *332–334, 335, 337, 338, 339–343,* 348–355, *350–354, 355–357*
  heat island impact minimization, 390–393, *392, 393, 394–395*
  human health impact, 344–355, *345–346,* 350–354, *355–357*
  inventory and analysis, 358, *358–359*
  lifecycle of construction materials and products, 327–331, *328*
  metals, *368,* 409–410, *411, 412, 413*
  plastics, 407, *408, 409*
  production, 323–325, *325–326*
  site inventory, 51–52
  site lighting, 421–422, *422, 423, 424, 425,* 456
  sustainable site design and operation, *23*
  The Sustainable Sites Initiative: Guidelines and Performance Benchmarks 2009, 327
  volatile organic compounds (VOCs), 390
  wood, *364, 367,* 416–421, *417, 418, 419*

"Materials Red List" (Living Building Challenge), 347

Maximum Allowable Bulk Densities (MABDs), *252,* 280, *280, 281*

metals, *368,* 409–410, *411, 412, 413*

Meyer, Elizabeth, 15

microclimate
  human health and, 448
  site inventory, 44–45
  vegetation for microclimate modification, *209*,
    209–210, *210, 211*
micronutrients (soil), 307
micropools, *132*, 132–136, *133, 134, 135*
Millennium Ecosystem Assessment (U.N.), 1, 3, 6
moisture sensors, 162
monitoring, of sustainable design, 519–520. *See also*
    maintenance
mulch, 302
multifunctional sites, 16

N

National Ambient Air Quality Standards (EPA), 505
National Fire Protection Association (NFPA) Firewise
    Communities, 238
National Park Service, 471
National Resource Conservation Service (NRCS), 38
native plants, for sustainable design, 216, *216*
Natural Resource Conservation Service, 48–49
Newman, Oscar, 454, 455
nitrification trickling filters, *182*
nodes, 452
noise pollution, 464, 465
nonpoint source pollution, 71, 84, *85*, 86, *86*
"novel" landscape substitution, ecological
    restoration and, 241–243
Nowak, D. J., 6

O

obesity, health and, 431, 458–462
Occupational Safety and Health Administration
    (OSHA), 345
Olmsted, Frederick Law, 430
onsite wastewater treatment, 166–195
  energy value, 189–190
  permit requirements, 189
  primary treatment, 171–173, *172–173, 186–187*
  quality parameters, 170, *170–171*
  reuse options, 187–188, *189*
  secondary treatment, 174–182, *175, 177, 186–187*
  tertiary treatment, 182, *182–185, 186–187*
  types of systems, *190*, 190–194, *191, 192, 193, 194, 195*
  See also water systems

operations. *See* maintenance
organic matter, soil, 270–274, *271, 272, 273, 274,*
    300–302, *301–302*
orientation devices, 452, *453*
oversized culverts, stormwater design approaches,
    144–145, *145*
oxygen production, vegetation and, 206
ozone disinfection, *185*

P

package treatment systems, 193
panel walls, 233
pathways, hierarchy of, 452
pavement
  asphalt, 401, *402*
  heat island reduction, 207, *207–208*, 390–393,
    392, 393, 394–395
  maintenance of, 516–519, *517, 518, 519*
  soil under, 315, *315*
  See also materials and resources
pedestrian-friendly design, 459–460, *460*
Peggy Notebaert Nature Museum, 165, *165*
percolation ("perc") test, *284*, 284–285, *285*
permit requirements, onsite wastewater
    treatment, 189
photosynthesis, 204
pH (soil), *256*, 288–290, *289, 290*
physical activity, design for, 458–462, *460, 461*
physiology, plant, 203–206. *See also* vegetation
phytoremediation, *212*, 212–213
planting design/management
  fire prevention, 238–240, *239*
  for food, 233–236, *234, 235, 236*
  for green roofs and walls, 230–233, *231*
  invasive plants, 218–223, *219, 220, 221, 222, 223,*
    497–500, *499*
  native plants, 216, *216*
  plant production, 223–224
  reusing vegetation, 224–225
  for stormwater structures, 228–230, *229*
  in urban setting, 225–228
  visibility, 457, *457*
  for wildlife habitat, 236–238
  xeriscaping, 217, *218*
  See also vegetation
plastics, 407, *408, 409*

playground design, 460–461

pocket walls, 233

polluter pays principle, 365

porous pavement, 117–119, *118*, 392–393, 516–519, *517, 518*

precautionary principle, 21, 365

precipitation, defined, 71. *See also* water systems

predesign, 33–63

  developing project direction, 58–62

  site assessment, 41–54

  site selection, 33–41

  soil management, 319

  team development and planning strategies, 54–57, *57*

pressure-dosed sand mounds, 178–179

pressure-dosed soil absorption fields, 179–180

primary clarifiers, *172*

prime farmland, 38–39

producer responsibility, 365

project direction development, 58–62

proprietary systems, for wastewater, 193

protection techniques, for vegetation, 213–215

provisioning, ecosystem services and, 3–5

proximity principle, 365

Putnam, Robert, 430

R

radial trenching, 303, *303*, 308

rain barrels, *153*

rain gardens/rain pockets, *121*, 121–123, *122*

rainwater, harvesting, 94–95, *95. See also* stormwater

raw materials. *See* materials and resources

receiving water bodies, protecting, 136–145, *137, 138, 139, 140, 143, 145*

recirculating sand filters (RSF), *183*

Recovered Materials Advisory Notices (EPA), 386–387, *387–389*

recovery, ecological restoration and, 240–243

recreation

  community building and, 467

  planning for, 461

  stormwater design amenities and, 98–99, *99*

recycled content materials, 385–390, *387–389*

recycled water. *See* reuse

Red List of Threatened Species (IUCN), 421

regenerative balanced systems, 17, 21–22

regulation. *See* predesign

remediation (soil), 285, *286*

replacement

  ecological restoration and, 240–243

  soil, 310–315, *315*, 319–320

reprocessed materials, 383–384, *385. See also* reuse

resource efficiency, *360*, 360–364, *361–363, 364, 365*

  deconstruction, 368–377, *369, 370–371, 372, 373, 374–375, 376, 377*

  durability, *366*, 366–368, *367, 368*

  material reuse, *378*, 378–382, *380, 382*

  recycled content, 385–390, *387–389*

  reprocessed materials, 383, *383–384, 385*

  waste management, 365

  See also materials and resources

restorative settings, health impact and, 462–464, *463, 464, 467*

reuse

  calculating rainwater reuse volumes, 94–95, *95*

  maintenance and operations, *485*, 485–491, *487, 489, 490*

  material and resource efficiency, *378*, 378–382, *380, 382*, 383, *383–384, 385*, 385–390, *387–389*

  of onsite wastewater treatment, 187–188, *188, 189* (*See also* onsite wastewater treatment)

  soil management, 319

  of vegetation, in sustainable design, 224–225

  water conservation, *149*, 149–162, *151, 153, 154, 155, 156, 158, 160, 161*

riparian enhancement, stormwater design approaches, 142–144, *143*

roof systems

  maintenance, 510–511, *511, 512*

  stormwater design approaches, 114–117, *115, 116*

  vegetation for, 230–232, *231*

runoff

  conveying, from larger storm events, 129–136, *130, 131, 132, 133, 134, 135*

  mitigating, by evapotranspiration and infiltration, 119–129, *120, 121, 122, 125, 126, 128*

  reducing, 105–119, *107, 108, 109, 110, 112, 113, 115, 116, 118*

  See also stormwater

S

safety. *See* human health impact

salt
  de-icing, 509, 518–519
  in soil, 287–288, 293, 304

samples. *See* data collection (soil)

sand
  amending soil with, 303, *304*, 309, *309*
  sand-based soil for under pavement, 314
  See also soil

Science and Environment Health Network, 21

screens, *172, 184,* 206

seating, 447, *447,* 464, 468

sediment control, stormwater design approaches, 145–147, *146*

Sedum, for roof designs, 231

sensory experience, designing for, 465

shakkei, 463

silt. *See* soil

site assessment, 41–54
  analysis, 41–42, 53–54
  human health and site's social setting, 432–435, *433, 434*
  inventory, 41–53, 358, *358–359*
  soil, 251–257, *252, 253, 255, 256, 257,* 320
  soil, data collection, 258–260, *260, 261,* 261–265, *263*
  for stormwater systems, 90, *90–91*

site design. *See* materials and resources; soil; vegetation; water systems

site selection, 33–41
  brownfields, 34, 35–36
  endangered or threatened species, 40–41
  farmland, 38–39
  floodplains, 39
  grayfields, 34, 37
  greenfields, 37–38
  urban infill, 36–37
  wetlands, 40

snow removal, 509, 518–519

social equality, in site development/construction/ use, 440–444, *441, 442, 444*

social interaction. *See* community involvement

sodium hypochlorite, *185*

soil, 247–321
  absorption fields, 180–181
  amending, with organic matter, *300–301,* 300–302, *302*
  contamination, 294–295
  drainage, 283–287, *284, 285, 286, 287,* 307–309, *309, 310,* 311
  integrating, in design process, 249–251
  maintenance and, *491,* 491–493, *492, 493*
  management, 247–249, *248,* 316–320, *317, 318*
  nutrients, 287–294, *289, 290, 291, 294,* 306–307, *307*
  organic matter, 270–274, *271, 272, 273, 274*
  pH, *256,* 288–290, *289, 290,* 304–305
  preservation, 297–299, *299*
  remediation, 295–296, *296*
  replacement and specialized soil, 310–315, *315*
  site assessment, 251–257, *252, 253, 255, 256, 257*
  site assessment, data collection, 258–260, *260, 261,* 261–265, *263*
  site inventory, 48–49
  soil compaction, 276, *277, 278–279, 303,* 303–304, *304,* 317
  soil cone penetrometer, *276,* 280
  soil slide hammer, *279*
  structure, 275, 275–281, *276, 277, 278, 279, 280, 281*
  sustainable design and operation, range of approaches, *22*
  The Sustainable Sites Initiative: Guidelines and Performance Benchmarks 2009, 249
  texture, 205, *205,* 265–270, *266, 267, 268, 269*
  urban, *247*
  volume, 281–283, *282,* 313

solar aquatic systems (SAS), *193,* 193–194, *194, 195*

Solar Reflectance Index (SRI), 392

sports facilities, planning for, 461

Stahre, Peter, 97

stakeholders. *See* community involvement

standards
  materials and resources, 349, *350–354,* 355, *355–357,* 390
  soil, 269, 281, 295

step pools, 129–131, *130, 131, 133*

stewardship, of sustainable design, 519–520. *See also* maintenance

stone, *337, 398, 399, 400*

storage (water), 152-154, *153, 154*

stormwater, 72-103

  accelerating development and, 67

  amenity opportunities, 96-103, *98, 99, 100, 101, 103*

  calculations, 92-96, *95*

  conveying runoff from larger storm events, 129-136, *130, 131, 132, 133, 134, 135*

  design example, *15, 16*

  general installation guidance, 104

  mitigating runoff by evapotranspiration and infiltration, 119-129, *120, 121, 122, 125, 126, 128*

  natural water cycle and, *72,* 72-73

  protecting/restoring receiving water bodies, 136-145, *137, 138, 139, 140, 143, 145*

  reducing runoff, 105-119, *107, 108, 109, 110, 112, 113, 115, 116, 118*

  sediment and erosion control, 145-147, *146, 147*

  site and regional assessment, 90, *90-91*

  stormwater quality, 13

  structural soil for, 314

  sustainable design practices, *75-76,* 75-90, *77, 78, 79, 82, 85, 86, 88-89*

  traditional management practices, 73-74, *74*

  vegetation for stormwater structures, 228-230, *229*

  See also water systems

Stormwater Control Measures (SCMs), 121

stream flow, defined, 71

streams, stormwater design approaches, 142-144, *143*

structural soil, 313-314, *315*

structure, of soil, *275,* 275-281, *276, 277, 278, 279, 280, 281*

substitution, ecological restoration and, 241-243

subsurface flow (SSF) constructed wetlands, 174-175, *175*

Sullivan, William, 430

surface flow (SF) constructed wetlands, 176, *177*

suspended pavement, 315

sustainability assessment (SA) method, 349, *350-354*

sustainable design

  attributes of, *13,* 13-17, *14, 15, 16, 18*

  defined, 2-3

  goals of sustainable sites, 20-22, *22-23*

  sustainability, defined, 429-432

  See also ecosystem services; human health impact; maintenance; materials and resources; predesign; soil; Sustainable Sites Initiative™ (SITES™); vegetation; water systems

Sustainable Sites Handbook, The (Calkins), 27-30

Sustainable Sites Initiative™ (SITES™)

  Biomass Density Index (BDI), 204

  defined, 2, 23-24, *25*

  landscape water requirements, 159-160, *160, 161*

  stormwater flow model, 77-78, *78* (*See also* stormwater)

  The Sustainable Sites Initiative: Guidelines and Performance Benchmarks 2009, 2, 19, 24, 27, 198-199, 249, 327

  vegetation, site assessment, 199-200, *200*

  Vegetation Soil and Protection Zones (VSPZ), 215

Sustainable Urban Drainage Systems (SUDS), 97

"Sustaining Beauty: The performance of appearance" (Meyer), 15

T

tank and treat systems, 193

team development and planning, 54-57, *57*

texture, soil, 265-270, *266, 267, 268, 269*

thermal pollution, sustainable stormwater management, 84

Todd, John, 193

topography, soil assessment, 257, *257*

total suspended solids (TSS), *170*

trail use, designing for, 459-460, *460*

transpiration, defined, 71

transportation, site inventory, 43

treatment elements and associated ecologies (wastewater), *190*

trees

  air quality and, 206

  designing social spaces with, 468, *468*

  Dutch elm disease (DED), 226

  economic value of economic services, 6-7

  for energy conservation, 210, *210, 211*

  interveinal chicrosis, *256*

  multifunctional sites, 16, *16*

  shading pavement, 393

  soil management, *317, 318*

  See also vegetation; wood

trellis walls, 233

trickling filters, 181–182

triple bottom line, 3, *3*

TRM channels, 129–131, *130, 131*

turf, 228

U

undisturbed core method (soil), *278*

unique farmland, 38–39

United Nations

  Brundtland Report, 2, 429

  Millennium Ecosystem Assessment, 1

  World Commission on Environment and
    Development, 2, 17, 429

United States Botanical Garden, 2, 23–24, *25*

universal design, *445,* 445–448, *447, 448, 449*

University of Texas at Austin, 2, 23–24, *25, 154*

U.S. Army Corps of Engineers, 39, 237

U.S. Department of Agriculture, *266*

U.S. Department of Interior, *474*

U.S. Environmental Protection Agency (EPA)

  Comprehensive Procurement Guidelines (CPGs),
    386–387, *387–389*

  on materials and resources, 334

  National Ambient Air Quality Standards, 505

  Recovered Materials Advisory Notices (RMANs),
    386–387, *387–389*

  site inventory, 42

  site selection criteria, 35–36

  on water systems, 87, 107, 119, 145, 159

  See also predesign

U.S. Fish and Wildlife Services, 237

U.S. Green Building Council (USGBC), 26

  See also Leadership in Energy and
    Environmental Design (LEED)

V

vegetation, 197–246

  ecological restoration, 240–243

  ecosystem services and, 202–213, *203, 205, 207,
    208, 209, 210, 211, 212*

  Firewise landscape design, 238–240, *239*

  food, 233–236, *234, 235, 236*

  green walls, 232–233

  human health impact, *197,* 197–198, 461

invasive plants, 218–223, *219, 220, 221, 222,
    223,* 497–500, *499*

native plants, 216, *216*

observational soil assessment and, 255, *256*

plant production, 223–224

plant selection, 201–202, *202*

protection techniques, 213–215

pruning for visibility, 457, *457*

reusing vegetation, 224–225

roof systems, 114–117, *115, 116,* 230–232, *231,
    510–511, *511, 512*

site assessment for, 199–200, *200*

site inventory, 49–51

soil drainage and plant choice, 307

for stormwater structures, 228–230, *229*

sustainable site design and operation, *22*

*The Sustainable Sites Initiative: Guidelines and
    Performance Benchmarks 2009,* 198–199

in urban setting, 225–228

vegetated swales, 129–131, *130, 131*

Vegetation Soil and Protection Zones (VSPZ)
    (SITES), 215

for wildlife habitat, 236–238

xeriscaping, 217, *218*

See also planting design/management; soil; water
    systems

vehicles, separating social spaces from, 468, *468*

vertical flow constructed wetlands, 177–178

visibility

  lighting, 421–422, *422, 423, 424, 425,* 456

  planting design/management, 457, *457*

volatile organic compounds (VOCs), 390

volume, soil, 281–283, *282,* 313

volume, water, 92, 94–95, *95*

W

Walkley-Black procedure (soil), *272*

walkways, human health and, 459–460, *460*

waste management, 365

  hierarchy, 365

  maintenance and operations, *485,* 485–491, *487,
    489, 490*

  See also materials and resources

wastewater treatment. *See* onsite wastewater
    treatment

water balance concept
  sizing water balance systems, 96
  sustainable stormwater management, 83–84
Water Reuse Association, 149
water systems, 65–196
  accelerating development and deteriorating
      stormwater, 67
  conservation, 148–166 (*See also* conservation
      (water))
  goals for water systems, 65–68, *67*
  holistic design, *69*
  human impact on, and mitigation, *66*
  maintenance of water features, 512–515, *513,
      514, 515*
  onsite wastewater treatment, 166–195 (*See also*
      onsite wastewater treatment)
  quality parameters for wastewater, 170, *170–171*
  soil assessment, 257, *257*
  soil drainage, 283–287, *284, 285, 286, 287, 303,
      303–304, 304, 307–309, 309, 310,* 314
  sustainable site design and operation, *22*
  toxic releases from materials to, 335–336
  vegetation and plant physiology, 204–205, *205*
  volumes, calculating, 92, 94–95, *95*

water cycle, 69–73, *70, 72*
water features and human health, 465, *465, 467*
  See also stormwater
wayfinding, 449–453, *450, 451, 452, 453*
wetlands
  site selection, 40
  stormwater wetlands with emergent aquatic
      vegetation, 138–142, *139, 140*
whole systems design, *13,* 13–14, *14*
Whyte, William, 454, 466, 469
wildlife, vegetation for, 236–238
Windhager, S., 8
windows, views from, 462–463, *463*
Wingspread Conference, Science and Environment
    Health Network, 21
wood, *364, 367,* 416–421, *417, 418, 419. See also*
    materials and resources
World Commission on Environment and
    Development (U.N.), 2, 17, 429

X– Z

xeriscaping, 217, *218*
zero runoff, 74